O'S BIG BOOK OF HAPPINESS

O'S BIG BOOK OF HAPPINESS

THE BEST OF O, THE OPRAH MAGAZINE

WISDOM, WIT, ADVICE, INTERVIEWS, AND INSPIRATION

Oxmoor House®

CONTENTS

HERE WE GO

It's almost more joy than one volume can hold: *O's Big Book of Happiness* features more than 100 of the richest, juiciest, and most enthralling articles, all rounded up from the pages of *O, The Oprah Magazine*. As we set out to select this year's compendium of delights, we've focused on you—your pleasure and personal fulfillment. That's why this best-of-the-bunch edition teems with the deeply inspiring ("Only Connect," page 149), the encouraging ("Your Great Idea Whose Time Has Come," page 250), the irresistible ("A Little Mouse Music," page 184), and, by all means, the let's-dance-a-jig celebratory ("Baby Steps, Olé!" page 135).

With trademark *O* candor, we've taken on some challenges as well. We've covered everything from the sags, the droops, and the wrinkles ("Uncrumpling My Face," page 118, and "The Gray Is Coming!" page 112), to confidence woes ("The Cure for Self-Consciousness," page 131), to relational missteps ("Love Traps 101," page 174). In fact, here in our eighth year of stories there isn't a single topic we've shied away from—right down to the super-duper personal ("Don't Do It in the Dark!" page 186). Your sex dilemmas, family dramas, spiritual Saharas, health hang-ups, age anxieties—think of this book not only as a shot of color for your coffee table or bookcase, but also as a gathering of sage voices on every imaginable subject.

Among the wisest people in these pages are the new friends I've had the privilege of interviewing. I've borrowed strength and inspiration from the resilient Christine McFadden, who crawled her way back to emotional equilibrium after the murder of her four children (page 90); the charismatic Bobby Kennedy Jr., an environmental lawyer who couldn't be more passionate and articulate on the subject of what we need to do to rescue our planet (page 306); and, finally, the unconventional British entrepreneur Richard Branson, whose latest brainchild is an assembly of 12 "elders" who just might be able to intervene in long-standing global conflicts and finally usher in a worldwide détente (page 316).

We weren't kidding when we called this the Big Book—a comprehensive guide to the great adventure that is your life. Wherever your quest takes you, I hope this collection will be your companion.

Oprah

YOUR MIND/
YOUR BODY

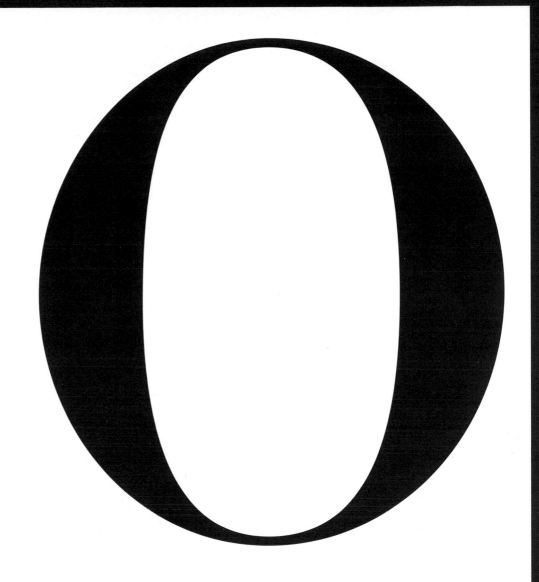

DIET AND EXERCISE

WHY IS IT SO DAMN HARD TO CHANGE?

She wanted to exercise more. But rain, fatigue, looming deadlines, and bad sneakers (that's right—blame the sneakers) got in her way. What was *really* going on? Rebecca Skloot explores why dieters falter and armchair athletes remain seated. Turns out it's not about "weakness." (We can all stop beating up on ourselves right now!) And what we're learning about the brain points to new strategies that will really—finally!—make all the difference.

Nora Volkow wants my chocolate. I'm sitting at a round conference table in her large-windowed office at the National Institute on Drug Abuse, where she's the director. Volkow is telling me about her research into the neurology of eating and how, for some people, quitting foods—like, say, chocolate—can be as hard as kicking heroin is for a junkie. Food, she says, hooks people by triggering the exact chemical reactions triggered in the brain by hard drugs. Or nicotine. Or alcohol. Or shopping. Or sex.

"I can't stop looking at your chocolate," Volkow says, her eyes darting from me to the chocolate and back. It's a Hershey's Kiss Volkow's secretary gave me moments earlier. I took it with a smile and a thank-you, but I'm one of the few women in the world who actually don't like chocolate. So I bit off the tip to be polite, put the rest back in its metallic wrapper, and slid it onto the table next to my notebook. This makes Volkow uncomfortable, which isn't what I expected.

Most articles about Volkow focus on her childhood in Mexico City. They say, Isn't it amazing she was raised in the same house where Stalin had her great-grandfather—Leon Trotsky, the exiled Russian revolutionary—murdered with an ice ax? They talk about how Volkow started medical school at 18, then went to the United States and became one of the nation's leading research psychiatrists. But to me, the most fascinating thing about Volkow is the fact that she—the head of the country's national drug abuse agency—is not just a chocolate junkie. She's also a chocolate pusher. Volkow paces back and forth in her Bethesda, Maryland, office—frizzy hair bouncing, black knee-high boots clacking—then stops, narrows her eyes, and grins. "I have some good stuff," she says, reaching into her desk drawer. "Seventy-seven percent pure cocoa." She throws a quarter-eaten bar on the table next to me. "Go ahead," she says, "have some." I tell her no thanks, and she raises her eyebrows.

"I do experiments with people," she says. "I put the chocolate there and see how long it takes them to pick it up." She shakes her head. "I am very bad with chocolate. I take it immediately. I fail my own test. But you," she says, pointing at my Kiss, "you have very good inhibitory control!" This makes me laugh, because if she'd offered cheesecake or Swedish Fish, I wouldn't have lasted five seconds.

But my problem isn't food; it's exercise and the fact that I seem incapable of doing it. No matter how many times I join a gym or buy new workout clothes or make workout dates with friends, I simply don't exercise. I've always got good reasons: I'm too busy, it's raining, I need better shoes, there's no gym in my neighborhood. I have a deadline, a headache, or cramps; it's too hot or too cold, running hurts my feet, weights are heavy...I could go on. The rational part of my brain knows I should exercise: I've read articles saying it prevents nearly every human disease, fights depression, and strengthens the immune system. I hear it reduces stress and anxiety, that it helps you focus and sleep and have better sex. I want all that—who doesn't? But apparently, another part of my brain—which happens to be the dominant part—wants everything to stay exactly as it is.

And clearly, I'm not alone. At this point, it's common knowledge that the leading causes of death in the United States—heart disease, diabetes, and some cancers—are largely preventable through behavior change. Hundreds of thousands of people wake

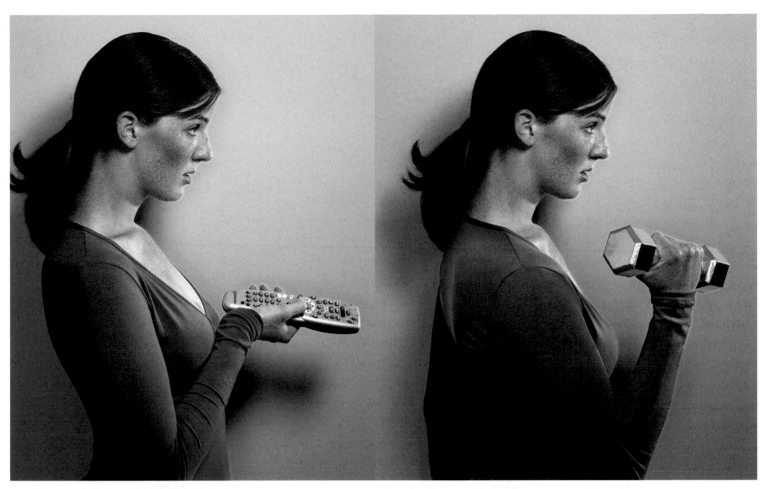

How to trick your brain into breaking a bad habit? The secret is in thinking up rewards for the new healthy behavior.

up each January 1 and say, "Starting today, I'm going to diet/exercise/quit smoking/taking drugs/gambling/whatever." They try, often very hard, but most fail.

I want to know why. And I'm not talking about external factors, like too much work and not enough time. I'm looking for what happens in our brains when we try to change, and how we can use that knowledge to actually succeed.

This is how I ended up in Nora Volkow's office listening to her obsess about my chocolate. Volkow and colleagues have spent the past 15 years researching the link between drug abuse and obesity by studying one thing that makes it so freakin' hard to change a habit: dopamine, a chemical in the brain that transmits signals from cell to cell and gets us hooked on everything from food to cigarettes to shopping to sex.

Dopamine teaches your brain what you want, then drives you to get it, regardless of what's good for you. It does this in two steps. First you experience something that gives you pleasure (say,

do it again. This is precisely how habits form. Eventually, if the fries become salient enough, your brain will release dopamine and push you to get fries anytime you see the colors yellow and red, even if you're nowhere near McDonald's.

And this is true for any behavior that results in a reward: Orgasms cause dopamine surges. So does hitting the jackpot when you gamble, winning a race, acing a test, doing cocaine or methamphetamines, smoking, drinking. "Dopamine is motivation," Volkow tells me. "If you create animals in the lab that don't have dopamine, they have no drive. They can eat food and it tastes good, but they have no motivation to actually do anything, so they won't eat, and they'll die."

As she's talking, I nod and take notes until, suddenly, her computer dings: She's got an e-mail. I am not compulsive when it comes to food, but e-mail? Forget it. Volkow doesn't share my obsession. She keeps talking about dopamine, I go back to taking notes, then there's that ding again, and I think, *She has two new e-mails.* Volkow is unfazed. We go on like this until she must have ten messages and I can barely resist getting up and reading them myself. Then it hits

Science's new promise: You can learn to crave a carrot.

McDonald's French fries), which causes a dopamine surge. Some of that dopamine travels to the area of your brain where memories are formed and creates a memory connecting those fries with getting a reward. At that point, in sciencespeak, the fries have become "salient." And when you're exposed to something that's salient, you may think, *That's bad for me, I shouldn't,* but your brain registers, *Dopamine jackpot!*

Which is where step two comes in: On top of creating memories, dopamine controls the areas of the brain responsible for desire, decision making, and motivation. So once fries become salient, the next time you see or smell them, your brain releases a surge of dopamine that drives you to get more fries. When you succeed, your brain produces more dopamine, which reinforces the memory that made fries salient in the first place, etching it further into your brain. It's a never-ending cycle: The more you do something that's rewarding, the more dopamine makes sure you

me: E-mail is as salient for me as chocolate is for Volkow. I often work months, sometimes years before seeing my books or articles in print, but e-mail gives me the reward of instant gratification. I tell Volkow this and she laughs. "You're right," she says. "I bet if I put you in an MRI machine and played that e-mail noise, you'd get the same dopamine surges I see in cocaine addicts when they think someone else is getting high."

This is why it's so hard to change. Doing so means fighting one of the most fundamental neurological systems in the brain. "Think about it," Volkow says. "If you're designing a species and you want to make sure it does things that are crucial for survival—like eating and reproducing—you create a system that's all about pleasure so they want to repeat those things. Then you have dopamine make those behaviors become automatic. It's brilliant, really."

Although she hasn't proved it yet, Volkow has a theory about why diets often fail: Based on animal studies, she thinks people may experience withdrawal when they try to kick certain foods their brains have become dependent on. "This makes it hard for them to eliminate those foods," she tells me, "because they may feel depressed or sluggish or generally horrible." If this turns out to be the case, she says, perhaps changing your diet more slowly will help.

But my big question for Volkow is this: How do you get yourself hooked on something that's not inherently pleasurable to you—like living on salads and broccoli or, in my case, exercising? Many people get a natural high from working out. I, however, am not one of them. "Isn't there some way to trick the dopamine sytem?" I ask her. "Some way to fool my brain into craving execise?"

Sure, she says: The secret is thinking up rewards. My payoff for working out could be a pedicure or a new pair of shoes. For someone trying to diet: Maybe you get a massage after a week of good eating, or have a friend dole out gift certificates if you stay on track (you pay, but she controls the vouchers). "Giving yourself rewards for a behavior engages the dopamine system so your brain will associate the positive outcome with it, which will help you form the habit."

When I get home, I try it. I make a deal with myself: If I exercise every day for a week, I get a new mini MP3 player. I wake up in the morning and it's raining. I remind myself about the MP3 player. After several confused minutes of figuring out what a person wears to exercise in the rain (a poncho? an umbrella?), I end up in waterproof hiking boots and my boyfriend's hooded sweatshirt, which is three times my size. I leash the dog and we start running, but my boots are too heavy and my lungs burn, plus I can't see because the hood keeps falling over my eyes. And, of course, there's the rain. So we drop to a speed walk. An hour later we get home looking like we've been dunked in a river. I strip off my wet clothes and tell myself, *Do that six more times and you get an MP3 player.* Then I think, *Yeah, right, you can't possibly exercise again without music.* So I buy an MP3 player and tell myself I really need exercise clothes before I try something like running again.

The next day, I find myself in a very green and blue cafeteria at the Kennedy Krieger Institute in Baltimore, the renowned center for children and adolescents with developmental disabilities. I'm sitting across from Michael Schlund, PhD, a research psychologist who divides his time among several scientific institutions where he explores areas of the brain involved in learning and behavior change. For Schlund, this work is part of a larger project aimed at helping people with developmental disabilities, such as autism, learn. But what I'm interested in is a study he recently finished at the University of North Texas, where he spent months observing the brains of healthy adults as they learned new behaviors based on rewards.

Here's what happened: After sliding the volunteers into an MRI machine, he gave them two buttons—one for the right hand, one for the left—then said, "You'll have to make some decisions. If you're correct, you earn money. If you're wrong, no money." Then he fired up the machine, which rattled and clanged as it began scanning their brains. Inside the machine, on a computer screen above the volunteers' heads, a circle appeared and vanished. Next, the word CHOOSE flashed, which meant they had to pick a button, right or left. The game made no sense. There was no correct response: All they could do was click a button randomly, then the computer said WRONG and the circle appeared again. So they picked the other button and the computer flashed, CORRECT. YOU'VE EARNED 50 CENTS.

Once the volunteers knew which button to press in response to the circle, they repeated the process over and over. Circle. Correct button. Reward. Circle. Correct button. Reward. This is where it got interesting for Schlund, because he wants to know what happens in the brain when you learn a new behavior based on rewards, which parts light up, how big that activation is, and how it changes over time as the behavior becomes habitual.

On the first click, when they were guessing, the volunteers' brains lit up a little in the frontal lobe—an area associated with self-control, decision making, and behavior change. After the second click, when they got the reward for answering correctly, suddenly their brains kicked into high gear, and with each repetition, their frontal lobes lit up more and more, which meant their brain activity continued to increase as they learned the new behavior. But—and this is the good news—within about 50 repetitions, Schlund says, the reverse will start happening—the frontal lobe lights up less and less until the brain is exerting minimum effort, which means the new task has officially become a habit.

When Schlund tells me this, I ask if it means I only have to force myself to exercise 50 times and then it will be a habit. "I wish I could say yes," he answers. "But we really have no idea. What I can tell you is, there are many variables." The biggest one is stress. It turns out that the hormones released by the body in response to stress are our worst enemy when it comes to changing: They actually inhibit the frontal lobe, which makes the brain revert to behaviors that don't require conscious decisions (eating our familiar foods, drinking, smoking). Not only do stress hormones impair the areas of our brains that need to be active to change, they also stimulate our emotional centers, which send out signals telling us to decrease the stress. And what decreases stress? Food (because it triggers the release of natural opiates), alcohol, and cigarettes.

So successful change depends in part on stress management. But, Schlund says, it also depends on finding the right rewards. "If people got paid to exercise," he tells me, "everyone would do it. And this country would be much better off."

I ask if he'll pay me to exercise. He folds his hands on the Formica table between us, looks me in the eye, and says, "If you want to convince your brain you should exercise, you have to treat yourself the way you'd treat your dog." It's hardly the answer I'm looking for, but at this point, I'm open to anything.

"Imagine she's wetting on the floor every day," he says. "Are you going to say, 'Hey dog, if you don't wet on the floor for a week, I'll buy you a rawhide bone'? That would be like your boss saying, 'If you work five years, then you'll get your check.' It's too far off."

Obviously, this is why my MP3 player failed: A week was too long to wait. If I'm going to associate exercise with a positive payoff, the reward has to be immediate. But beyond that, Schlund tells me, I have to unlearn the rewards I've already associated with not exercising (no pain, more time for other things). Doing this actually requires changing my neural circuitry. And rewiring an adult brain, I am about to discover, is very tricky.

A few days after my meeting with Schlund, I'm sitting at a small desk in a psychiatric ward at Yale, staring at a computer screen with two clickable buttons: CHE and SHE. The computer says "che" (or is it "she"?), and I'm supposed to press the appropriate button. I click CHE. The computer buzzes and tells me to try again. "Che" or "she"? I click SHE. Buzz. Over and over, I get the buzz. I'm thinking this must be a joke, but then I squint, listen hard, and finally hear it. I hit CHE. The computer dings, then two pink kissing fish appear on the screen and do a funky dance with a hermit crab. That's my reward, which clearly gets my dopamine going: I start playing compulsively, completely hooked on picking the right answer so I can see what my next goofy reward will be. After a while, my attention starts wandering.... *Buzz.* So I squint, listen hard, and hear it again: "che." A spaghetti-thin man suddenly appears on the computer screen playing a xylophone, until a musical note hits him on the head. Then Bruce Wexler, MD, walks in the room.

Wexler, a leading neuroscientist and the author of *Brain and Culture*, studies brain plasticity and how it affects our ability to change. I've come to try out this program, which he uses to help patients with schizophrenia improve their audio processing and memory. "You're very good at that," Wexler tells me. Not really, I say, pointing out how many errors I made before figuring it out. But actually, that's the whole idea of the program: Successful change requires abnormally intense, uninterrupted concentration and repetition. Why? Because we're working against evolution:

When you're a kid, it's a different story: Young brains are constantly forming new connections between neurons, changing the way children process information based on their experiences. That's plasticity, and it's why children soak up language and adapt to new cultures at rates that put adults to shame. "By the time we hit our 20s," Wexler says, "our brains have lost most of their plasticity." But fortunately, they haven't lost all of it.

Imagine you've got one strong eye and one weak eye, he tells me. If you cover the good eye with a patch, so it gets no stimulus, the weak eye will get stronger. But the second you remove the patch, the strong eye kicks in again and the weak one gets weaker. The same is true of all pathways in the brain. Once established, they stick around and remain strong as long as they're being used. So the first step toward change, Wexler says, is putting a "patch" over the pathway you want to lose (like, say, a chocolate obsession), which means eliminating anything that activates it (having chocolate in the house, going places where you usually buy chocolate). This is why, for many people who try to quit drinking or smoking, it's impossible to have just one glass of wine or cigarette. It's why

Try again. The more times you make the switch (cigarette, no; rose, yes), the easier it becomes.

Our brains are designed to conserve energy for really important things, like breathing and coordinated motion, even though sometimes, altering behavior is just as important as breathing. Our brains revert to habits when given the chance because they require less energy than change. That silly exercise with "che" and "she" actually changes the way adults hear because it doesn't let that happen. It forces intense concentration resulting in instant rewards that make you want to repeat the exercise over and over again.

"You want to know why it's hard to change?" Wexler asked when I first walked into his office. "There are a hundred billion neurons in your brain. Each one is connected to thousands of others. Everything you're talking about—behaviors and learning and memory—involves the integrated actions of hundreds of thousands of cells in intricate systems throughout the brain." In adults those systems are essentially hardwired.

heroin and coke addicts must avoid places and people connected to their drug days.

For dieters, just walking into your regular grocery store can activate an old familiar food pathway and keep it alive. So successful weight loss is as much about lifestyle change as it is about what you eat: Shop at a new store; buy new brands of food; use a new set of plates; eat in another room, at a different time of day. All these things will help starve an old, unhealthy pathway so you can develop a new, healthy one. "The more drastically you restructure your habits," Wexler says, "the more the established pathway that you're trying to change is weakened."

But disabling the old pathway isn't everything. Searching your brain for an existing healthy pathway—even a tiny weak one—and then strengthening it can make things much easier. So Wexler tells me to find an "I like exercise" pathway. I tell him I don't think I have one. He doesn't buy it. "Wasn't there some activity you loved as a kid?" he asks. I don't think so.

On the train ride home, however, as I stare out the window listening to my new MP3 player, David Bowie's "Changes" comes on and I start laughing. Appropriate, yes. But it was also the song my next-door neighbor and I skated to in my backyard when I was a girl. For my entire young life, I was obsessed with roller-skating. My first kiss was on skates; I roller-skated to high school every day, then rolled down the hall from class to class. I actually convinced my high school to waive my PE requirement and give me credit for my constant skating. Sitting on the train remembering all this, I smile and think, *I just hit my dopamine jackpot.*

When I get home, I strap on my ten-year-old Rollerblades and give it a try. I turn on some disco and start rolling. It's sunny; my dog is running next to me. I can practically feel the dopamine coursing through my veins. My exercise problem is solved. Life couldn't be better.

The next day I wake up, walk into my living room, then sit down at my computer thinking, *Oh my God, I have so much to do.* A few hours later I think, *I should go Rollerblade now.* But I'm busy.

I've got a deadline, I exercised yesterday, and besides, it looks like it's going to rain. I'll do it later. But when later comes, I'm tired from working all day, and now it's getting dark. Then I think, *Wait a minute. Why isn't all that dopamine from yesterday driving me to get up and Rollerblade again? Did my brain forget?*

A week later, I call Monika Fleshner, PhD, a neuroimmunophysiologist at the University of Colorado at Boulder who has done extensive research into the physiology of exercise. I explain my situation. I say I found an exercise I like, and I think I've got the dopamine thing solved, but funny thing is: I'm still not doing it.

You know what her bottom line is? Suck it up—just make yourself exercise.

Fleshner is very clear: It's not like you find your dopamine jackpot and your brain immediately says, *Now we exercise every day.* For

a while, you still have to force yourself to do it. But, I tell her, I have a very good reason not to: I know her research found that in animals, forced exercise doesn't lead to the same physiologic benefits that voluntary exercise does. In fact, it actually weakens the animals' immune systems by causing an increase in stress hormones in the body. I ask her about this, and she says it's true, but I don't have to worry about that. Why? Because I won't have to make myself exercise long enough to cause problems. To which I say, "Excuse me?"

Then she tells me something wonderful: All I have to do is force myself to exercise regularly for about two weeks, maybe three, and my brain will start producing a protein called brain-derived neurotrophic factor (BDNF), which she calls Miracle-Gro for the brain. It increases brain plasticity, so you can think clearly and focus for longer periods of time. It also increases dopamine neurotransmission, which means the more I exercise, the more reward I get, and the more my dopamine system is activated to make exercising a habit I'll soon crave.

"Just put on your Rollerblades," Fleshner tells me. "Strap on some headphones, leash up your dog, go outside, and start exercising right now."

Long, silent pause.

"I'm serious," she says.

I sit there holding the phone for a second before thinking, *Oh, what the hell. Three weeks isn't that bad.* So I head out for day one. And yes, it's day one again, because I didn't go out for day two last time, which means I'm starting from scratch.

When I began this quest to find out why it's so hard to change unhealthy behaviors, I talked with more than a dozen scientists. Each one laughed and said some version of this: "If I could answer that question, I'd win a Nobel Prize and have drug companies lining up at my door for miles."

But the truth is, scientists *have* uncovered some very important things. To begin with, change is monumentally difficult. Some people can just wake up one morning, decide to change, and stick with it. But many, perhaps most, can't. The reason may be genetic; it may be the way you were raised; perhaps some people have stronger frontal lobes than others. Scientists still aren't sure. What they do know is, if you're one of those people who struggle, that's nothing to beat yourself up over—it's just the way your brain works. But it's also not an excuse to toss in the towel and say, *Well, I don't have enough dopamine* or *My bad pathways are too strong.* As Bruce Wexler told me, "The more we understand what we're up against, the more we can develop strategies that will help us work with our brains to change successfully."

So instead of waking up New Year's morning and saying, "I'm going to do X now," then berating yourself a month later when that resolution didn't work, remember: You're doing nothing less than rewiring your brain. Approach change as if you're learning a new language or a new instrument. Obviously, you're not going to be fluent or play symphonies instantly; you'll need constant focus and practice. Overcoming an unhealthy habit involves changing the behaviors associated with it and managing stress, because stressing about change (or anything else) will knock you off the wagon faster than you realize. Above all, get that dopamine system going: Find rewards—make them instant, and don't be stingy. Your brain needs them. And I promise (well, Volkow, Schlund, Wexler, and Fleshner promise) it gets easier. That's not a bunch of self-help nonsense. It's biology. ⬛

Give yourself credit for resisting forbidden foods.

THINK LIKE A THIN PERSON

Can you resist cravings? No problem. Set realistic weight goals? Piece of cake. But what if your diet coach challenged you to go eight hours without eating a single bite? Barbara Graham reports on getting over her deep, dark, self-sabotaging fear of hunger.

My favorite fat joke is that I'm still trying to lose my pregnancy weight—only my son just turned 35. Needless to say, I'm no stranger to dieting: I've been to South Beach, Scarsdale, and Beverly Hills, with too-many-to-count excursions to Weight Watchers. It's not that these diets don't work—they do. But each time I shed some weight, sooner or later I get blindsided by stress and start to eat wantonly again. Like most chronic dieters, I've felt helpless, out of control, demoralized by my inability to keep weight off. So when an advance copy of Dr. Judith Beck's *The Beck Diet Solution: Train Your Brain to Think Like a Thin Person* landed on my doorstep last fall, I took it as a sign. Judy is the psychologist daughter of Aaron Beck, the famed psychiatrist who pioneered cognitive therapy, which helps people overcome self-defeating thoughts and is now a gold standard of treatment for depression, anxiety, and other psychological disorders. I knew about the approach from a friend whose depression was cured by working with Beck père at the Beck Institute for Cognitive Therapy and Research—now run by Judy—near Philadelphia. If cognitive therapy could change Natalie's life, maybe it could be my ticket out of yo-yo hell. I rang up Judy and arranged to get together.

The day before we met, I boned up on the book. Instead of presenting a specific diet (any reasonable eating plan—I chose Weight Watchers again—will do), Beck guides the reader through a six-week, step-by-step process designed to eliminate every self-sabotaging thought that makes dieters throw up their hands and open their mouths. (Thoughts such as *I can't diet when I'm stressed* or *I know I shouldn't eat this, but it's my birthday/Thanksgiving/Groundhog Day/fill-in-the-blank day* hit me squarely in my size 12 gut.) Along the way, she outlines a comprehensive regimen based on her own experience and 20 years of counseling dieters. Some of the strategies—eat slowly, while seated; give yourself credit for resisting cravings or dropping even half a pound; set realistic weight loss goals—seemed manageable, but others provoked anxiety. Would I really be required to plan every meal in advance? Account for every last morsel to my diet coach—Judy herself!—and allow myself "no choice" about sticking to my plan? Scariest of all was the "hunger experiment," during which I was to go eight hours without eating in order to learn that "hunger is not an emergency." *Moi,* I thought, *hypoglycemic moi?* My blood sugar is prone to plummeting, leaving me feeling as if I'm on the brink of starvation at least three times a day! And the kicker: As I read on, I realized that the program isn't just a six-week commitment—*it's for life!*

"Almost everybody has the idea that once they stop dieting, they'll be able to eat whatever they want, but that is absolutely false," Judy told me when we met over lunch. Slim, energetic, and incredibly empathetic even when making tough-love pronouncements, she was a veteran yo-yo dieter who lost 15 pounds ten years ago and has kept it off ever since. "I had to accept that for the rest of my life, I would have to eat differently from how I used to eat," she said. "When I work with people, I stress this from the first day. It's not a popular message, especially with so many fad diets around, but I don't see any point in losing weight if you're just going to gain it back." What's more, she added, "I've discovered that to some degree almost every thin person restricts what she eats. We all need to learn to do that. When the going gets tough, we have to keep reminding ourselves of the advantages of maintaining a healthy weight."

In fact, the very first exercise in *The Beck Diet Solution* asks readers to pinpoint the reasons they want to lose weight. To the predictable examples listed—"I'll look better. I'll be able to wear a smaller size. I'll live longer"—I added, "So I can put on a little black dress." Judy urges dieters to review their reasons at least twice daily. On the flip side, she asks them to unearth the sabotaging thoughts that keep them from dieting success—and then create written response cards that will act as a reality check to each thought. As my coach, she planned to use our lunch to help me hand-craft such cards.

"What are some of the self-defeating ideas that stop you from losing weight?" she asked me, cutting to the chase as we waited for our grilled salmon.

"Uh," I stammered, "I blame my metabolism. It's really hard for me to lose weight."

"Those are just thoughts," she replied brightly. "We'll find out if they're true. I'm guessing you *can* lose weight—you just haven't learned the skills to keep it off."

"Maybe, but I don't think I overeat. Basically, I believe I'd have to starve myself in order to be thin," I said, feeling suddenly sheepish. There was something humbling, even humiliating, about voicing the machinations of my weight-obsessed mind out loud.

"You probably do overeat, so we have to figure out how we can get you to eat less and still feel satisfied."

"But mostly I eat only when I'm hungry, which is fairly often, because of my hypoglycemia."

Judy wasn't buying it. "If you're trying to lose weight, you can't go by hunger; you have to go by a plan. I can't tell you how wonderful it was to figure out that I can stand being hungry no matter what," she said, beaming. "Before I was able to keep weight off, I always worried about being hungry."

Maybe I'm dense, but I was having trouble connecting the dots here. Doesn't Judy herself advise dieters to choose an eating plan that works for them—the operative word being *eating*? "What's so great about going hungry?" I asked.

"Almost every dieter has difficulty distinguishing between true hunger, a desire to eat, and cravings," she explained. "And most people who struggle with weight loss tend to feel hunger pangs intensely and often eat to avoid those feelings. But the point is, hunger comes and goes. Thin people know this and don't worry about being hungry."

Uh-oh, I thought. *Here it comes.*

"Purposely skipping a meal is the only way to prove to yourself that you can withstand hunger," she said, leaning closer. "We have to get you over the fear of being hungry if you want to keep weight off for the rest of your life."

"I'll do anything," I pleaded. "I'll go on Weight Watchers and stick to it. I'll keep a record of every microbite. Just please, not *that*. I'm sure I'd drop dead."

I could tell that Judy harbored serious doubts about the severity of my hypoglycemia, the existence of which, I was forced to admit, had never been clinically proved. But she graciously turned her attention to writing the response cards—such as "If I want to lose weight, I have to do things I don't want to do"—that were supposed to counter my negative thoughts. My homework was to read the cards before each meal, as well as commit to a food plan every night for the following day, then fax it to her. We agreed to touch base by phone in one week.

When I called at the appointed time, I was feeling proud of myself—"giving myself credit" in Judyspeak. I'd dropped a pound and a half and had been fanatical about staying within the points allotted me by Weight Watchers. But I didn't get the *You go, girl* reaction I was expecting.

"Eventually, it will be fine to substitute foods as long as they're the same number of points or calories," Judy told me, referring to the fact that I'd eaten broccoli instead of the artichoke I'd committed

MY INNER REBEL PUT DOWN HER DUKES, AND I GREW TO ENJOY PLANNING MY MEALS.

to in writing. "But for now I'd like you to follow your plan exactly."

I felt deflated. What was the big deal? Wasn't one green vegetable as good as the next?

"You won't have to plan every meal for the rest of your life, but for now I'd like you to master the skill of 'no choice,' so that in the future when you start to slide, you'll know how to get back on track."

"I get it," I said, "but I don't like it."

"I know I'm being a hard-ass," Judy conceded. "But 90 percent of people who lose weight gain it back, which is what happened to you." Then she instructed me to write out a new response card: "Unless I get really good at following my plan, I'll be at risk for regaining the weight I lose. Rigidity is essential right now, but it's only temporary."

Though I felt like a chastened schoolgirl when I hung up the phone, in subsequent weeks something strange occurred: My inner rebel put down her dukes, and I grew to enjoy planning my meals. It made me feel safe and in control—and saved me on my birthday, Thanksgiving, and at several holiday parties. The proof showed up on the scale. By the time I went to see Judy a month after our initial meeting, I had dropped seven pounds.

Judy warmly congratulated me on my progress and my shift in attitude. She even told me I could be more flexible in my eating and stop planning every meal—something *I* was not yet ready to do. She also issued a sober warning. "It's a fallacy to think you'll continue losing weight at this rate. There'll be weeks when you won't lose anything and other weeks when the scale will go up a pound or two. That's normal. You have to take the long view; otherwise you could become demoralized and abandon your diet the way you did in the past." Then she leaned back in her chair and smiled. "It would be good—in fact it's 100 percent necessary—for you not to be afraid of hunger so you can maintain your weight loss your whole life."

The dread hunger experiment was back on the table. Even though it still terrified me, I buckled and agreed to eat nothing between breakfast and dinner—unless I started shaking uncontrollably, a true symptom of hypoglycemia—the very next day. Judy promised to be available by phone every hour after noon.

For insurance that morning, I ate a super-high-protein breakfast; when I telephoned Judy at 1 P.M., I was able to say I wasn't dead yet. "Still here," I reported at 2. By then I was feeling light-headed and cranky as well as famished, but the feelings were more or less tolerable and I agreed to press on. The real shock came at 3, when not only was I still alive but my hunger had diminished significantly. And at 4, though I was starving again, I was able to distract myself by combing the Internet for cheap flights to visit my baby granddaughter in Paris.

When Judy picked up the phone at 4:15 and heard that the experiment was still in full swing, she was elated. "Now that you've experienced for yourself that hunger comes and goes, you never have to worry about feeling hungry again."

"You mean I can stop? Now? And *eat*?" I couldn't believe I'd passed the test.

"Absolutely. You've proved yourself."

"Wow," I said, "that's amazing. But if it's all the same to you, I think I'm going to try to hold out until 5." ◖

"BUT I DON'T EAT THAT MUCH!"

You may think you're eating less and working out lots. So why can't you lose any weight? Emily Yoffe finds out what's really going on. Before you blame your metabolism—or yourself—read this.

In one study, people were eating twice the number of calories they'd estimated.

There's your friend in size 6 jeans who always seems to be attacking a cookie-dough ice cream cone; there's the stick-figure colleague who lunches on burritos the size of her head. And then there's you. Day after day, you toss the bread from your turkey sandwich, nibble on a Baggie of carrots, and refuse desserts—yet you can't get the scale to budge downward. How is it that you're still heavy when you'd swear on a stack of pancakes, "But I don't eat that much!"

Of course, many will acknowledge there's no mystery as to why they struggle with their weight: They eat more than they should. But a persistent minority of people recount tales of heroic food deprivation followed by a humiliating inability to lose a single pound. What's going on with them? Here are three possible explanations.

SECOND-HELPING AMNESIA

Most people underestimate the amount they eat, studies show, and it's more likely to be true the heavier a person is. "Scientists have searched for people who eat very little yet weigh a lot," says James O. Hill, PhD, director of the Center for Human Nutrition at the University of Colorado and cofounder of the National Weight Control Registry (NWCR), which tracks people who have maintained a loss of at least 30 pounds for at least a year. "What they have found instead are people who say they eat very little but

turn out to eat quite a bit when their food intake is monitored. Rigorous studies show that it's impossible to be a really large person and not eat that much."

Obesity researchers say this gap between perception and reality is not due to conscious lying; these people truly believe they're living on very little. For a study published in 1992 in the *New England Journal of Medicine,* Steven Heymsfield, MD, and colleagues used a sophisticated technique to monitor nine women and one man who weighed, on average, nearly 190 pounds, even though they insisted they ate only about 1,000 calories a day. The results were startling, especially to the subjects. It turns out they were actually consuming about 2,000 calories a day—twice what they'd estimated. And though they guessed they were active enough to burn about 1,000 calories a day, the number was closer to 770.

Mary Schreiner, 61, a retired weight management counselor for the University of Colorado's Health Sciences Center, understands how this could happen. Barely more than five feet tall and 160 pounds as a young woman, she tried counting calories and eliminating fattening foods, but the weight just wouldn't come off. The problem, she realized later, was that "while there were 75 calories in the cookie I wasn't having, I didn't know how many calories there were in the orange juice I was guzzling." Many of her clients were like her—drinking a lot of lattes because "coffee has no calories, right?" But they never registered the fact that each latte can have 200 calories. Or those who said that sure, they walked 10,000 steps a day but, when given pedometers, clocked in at only 1,500.

Another reason people may feel they're starving themselves, says Hill, has to do with the metabolic drop caused by dieting: The lower your body weight, the fewer calories you need to maintain that weight. (Exercise, especially weight training, helps mitigate this unfair truth.) "Let's say you weigh 250 pounds and eat 3,000 calories a day," explains Hill. "Then you lose 50 pounds. To keep that off, you're going to have to eat only 2,300 calories a day—and it is very difficult to eat 700 fewer calories than you're used to."

As for simply being born with a slow metabolism, that may be another common misperception among the overweight. When Heymsfield carefully tested his subjects—several of whom claimed to have this problem—all ten had metabolisms within the normal range. But instead of being relieved to discover that there was nothing medically wrong with them—they just needed to readjust their intake and output—"they were angry," recalls Heymsfield. "They said, 'No, you can't be right.' Some said, 'My metabolism really is slow; you just don't know how to find it.'"

STEALTH SPUD SYNDROME

Heymsfield's subjects might be onto something, according to new research by James A. Levine, MD, a professor of medicine at the Mayo Clinic College of Medicine in Rochester, Minnesota—but not in the sense that their bodies don't burn food efficiently. Levine says some people have a biological drive to beach themselves in a Barcalounger while others constantly flit around like humming-birds. He calls this nearly unconscious physical activity NEAT, for "nonexercise activity thermogenesis." NEAT encompasses everything from sitting up straight to tapping your foot to gesturing with your hands when you talk. A hundred or so years ago, he says, people typically burned 1,500 more calories a day than they do now. Even those who would rather be relaxing, thank you, had to plow the fields or walk to town or take the laundry to the creek and slap it on rocks. But in our age, people born with the urge to sit find that the world is one big, comfy couch—an inert way of life that, Levine believes, is enough to explain the obesity epidemic.

For a study published in 2005 in *Science,* Levine took 20 self-described couch potatoes—ten lean and ten mildly obese—and dressed them in high-tech underwear that recorded their bodily movements every half second for ten days. He discovered that his leaner spuds burned about 350 more calories a day through NEAT—or 33 pounds a year.

In an earlier NEAT study, Levine recruited 16 volunteers and for two months had them eat 1,000 calories a day over what they needed to maintain their weight. You would expect they'd all put on weight—1,000 extra calories a day is a lot. But at the end of the study, the gain per individual ranged from less than a pound to more than nine pounds. And all the variation, says Levine, could be explained by the amount of NEAT.

The good news is that if you're not a natural-born fidgeter, you can consciously work at over-riding your biology. When Levine noticed his body starting to thicken as he hit middle age, he put a treadmill in the living room, and every night when he came home and watched *The Simpsons* (some have their wine, others de-stress with Homer), he did it while walking. He lost 15 pounds over a period of nine months without changing anything he ate.

FIDGETERS BURNED ABOUT 350 MORE CALORIES A DAY THAN THE SEDENTARY—OR 33 POUNDS A YEAR.

A WEIGHT VACCINE?

It may sound far-fetched, but the theory that a virus can make you fat is gaining credibility. In 1986 Nikhil Dhurandhar was treating obese patients in Bombay, India, while working on a PhD in bio-chemistry, when he had a conversation with a fellow scientist about an avian virus that was killing poultry. The scientist mentioned an odd effect the virus had on the infected chickens: Their abdominal cavities were full of fat, and the dead birds were far heavier than their healthy counterparts. *A sick chicken should be a skinny chicken,* Dhurandhar thought. He wondered what would happen if he exposed normal chickens to the virus. Sure enough, the ones that got infected developed significantly more body fat than the healthy birds and, paradoxically, lower cholesterol and triglycerides.

The findings were so compelling that he decided to test his patients for antibodies to the virus—and he discovered nearly 20 percent of them had been infected. Not only that, these were among the heaviest people in his practice, and they had lower cholesterol and triglycerides than most of his other patients.

Today Dhurandhar is a scientist at the Pennington Biomedical Research Center in Louisiana, studying a field he has named infec-tobesity. He and others have found nine viruses that cause obesity in animals, four of which also infect humans. He may have discovered part of the mechanism as well: After animals are infected with one particular human virus, their prefat cells mature and proliferate, increasing the number of fat cells in the body.

Dhurandhar says we are a long way from being able to tell some overweight people that their problem is a virus, or better yet, offering an obesity vaccine. But he points out that there is exploding research in the area of germs causing other chronic illnesses such as heart disease, autoimmune diseases, even depression. And he cites the experience of the two Australian researchers who suggested that a bacterium was responsible for stomach ulcers and were scoffed at for years—until they won the Nobel Prize for Medicine in 2005. Famously, one of those researchers swallowed a Petri dish of the bacteria to prove his case. Is the slender Dhurandhar willing to infect himself with one of his viruses to prove his thesis? He laughs and says if he did it and gained weight, "people would just say I ate too much."

Chicken viruses, NEAT factor—maybe these culprits explain why we're fat. Or maybe we get too little sleep. Or have too much stress. Or modern indoor temperature control protects us from the hot, sweaty, appetite-dulling days and shivering cold that used to keep people trim. Every few months, there seems to be a new theory. But whatever pans out among these ideas, science knows right now what works to lose weight and keep it off: Move more and eat less. That means making active choices whenever possible—getting up and changing the TV channel, taking the stairs, and being more conscious when it comes to diet (keep a food diary; look up calories at nal.usda.gov/fnic/foodcomp/search, and check out nwcr.ws). As for those people who holler that they eat like birds but complain they look like butterballs, whatever the cause of this dilemma, if you're mindful about what you put in your mouth, it feels as if you're eating a lot more. **O**

TAKING THE WEIGHT OFF... AGAIN

They're tired, anxious, food obsessed: It's just another day in the dieting lives of two Lisas who've lost about 40 pounds each—and *gained it right back*. (In the case of one Lisa, more than once.) Now what? Martha Beck has a simple explanation for why most dieters fail—and a new way to achieve lasting Thinner Peace.

The most important weight management skill in the history of the universe begins with imagining the wild child and the dictator in yourself.

The Lisas do not have the time or energy to stay thin. They agree on that point from minute one of our mutual project. Lisa Romeo, a 47-year-old part-time freelance writer and former public relations executive, now a candidate for an MFA degree, and Lisa Kogan, *O*'s 45-year-old writer at large, have each lost, then regained, more than 40 pounds. They say they're excited to get in shape again. They sound as if they'd be as excited if I beat them with a crowbar.

"I've yo-yoed more times than I want to remember," says Lisa Romeo. "I'm always positive I won't rebound, but then life gets busy and the weight comes back." For her part, Lisa Kogan says: "Staying thin is just another source of stress for me."

I empathize completely. These women are combining motherhood and professional life, caring for elderly relatives, juggling infinite responsibilities. Adding a fitness program to such a schedule is like packing a piano on a mountain-climbing expedition. On the other hand...

Not having time or energy for weight loss makes no sense. Does it take more time or energy to eat fish than prime rib? No. Do either of the Lisas lack access to healthy food? No. Are they short on information? Lord, no—like most dieters, they're walking weight loss encyclopedias. The problem they and the rest of us weight watchers have isn't that we don't know what to do; it's that we don't *do* what we know. Why not? The most fundamental answer isn't in our fast food restaurants or overstocked refrigerators. It's in our heads.

FATTENING THOUGHTS

The way we eat reflects the way we think, and the way the Lisas think keeps making them fat. The same is true for other failed dieters. Every time we drop weight without changing our psychology, we may be changing our brains so that we become more prone to overeating. The only way to beat the relapse syndrome is to both eat and think differently.

I've been studying this topic for years, doing endless reading and consuming entire cheesecakes to...um...subjectively observe the dynamics of binge eating. The thing about research is that it often leads you to a solution. That's why I'm now coaching the Lisas, and why, after spending years in the diet trenches, I'm confident I can teach them to lose weight permanently. As I talk to both Lisas about their struggle with weight relapse, I recognize two thought patterns typical of dieters, which are two sides of the same coin: the "I Need More Nurturing" syndrome and the mind-set that says, "I Need No Nurturing."

DOOR NUMBER ONE: "I NEED MORE NURTURING"

During our first conversation, it's clear that Lisa Romeo wants a lot of help and guidance in many areas. Her previous diet counselor, she tells me, gave her a few suggestions about diet and exercise but didn't provide the kind of structure she needed. Her academic adviser has provided less attention than she promised. Lisa's father is ill, and doctors have been appallingly uninterested in arranging his care. Lisa is also worried that she's not providing enough high-quality mothering to her two children.

These complaints include an implicit core assumption: People's lives depend on nurturing guidance from authority figures, and if those advisers don't measure up, their underlings are out of luck. This is true—for infants. But Lisa is an adult. In fact she's more competent and intelligent than several of the authority figures in her life. That's why she's so frustrated when they don't perform adequately. I'm a little worried that I'll end up on Lisa's list of failed advisers. I also realize that she doesn't exempt herself from judgment: She's trying to be the ideal mother who protects her own children from all suffering—and she's not meeting her own expectations.

DOOR NUMBER TWO: "I NEED NO NURTURING"

Lisa Kogan, on the other hand, seems averse to accepting nurturing from anyone. In the past year, she's had two beloved friends die back-to-back of cancer, but when I ask if she's been able to grieve, she brushes off the question with a joke. She's hilarious, kind, sensitive, engaging, and her life is as busy as Lisa Romeo's. She's a caretaker for her young daughter, long-distance boyfriend, coworkers, and friends. Her energy pours into every life she touches—except her own. As a result, she's starving for everything but food.

We spend a little time talking about the role food has played in her life, the times she's used it for comfort or distraction, and how she remembers her father coming home from his high-stress job and nibbling compulsively all night. Eating is the one way Lisa K. takes in nourishment, so it isn't surprising that she often goes overboard. Weight loss will be permanent for her only if she can acknowledge her own vulnerability, take some of the effort she puts into helping others and direct it toward herself, and allow

other people to reciprocate.

Like many dieters, both Lisas have extreme mind-sets when it comes to nourishment. The blunt way to put it is that the Lisas need to mind their own business—that is, pay close attention to their own needs. It's the old serenity prayer solution: The Lisas must find the serenity to accept what they can't change (other people and their problems), the courage to change what they can (their own lives), and the wisdom to know the difference.

That wisdom comes from "clear seeing," achieving the viewpoint of wisemen and wisewomen, sages, mystics. Amazingly, science is showing that this mental perspective changes our brains and bodies in precisely the ways necessary to stop unsuccessful dieting and become permanently slender.

THE RELAPSE DIETER'S BROKEN BRAIN

Can you imagine the circumstances in which a hungry wild animal would increase physical activity? Not good scenarios, right? Famine, predator attacks, natural disasters—basically, extreme stress. For most of history, most people's biggest challenge wasn't losing fat but avoiding starvation. Our bodies are designed to keep weight on, not take it off, especially when we're stressed. In times of danger or shortage, our brains drive certain physiological reactions: We become more driven to seek and consume rich food, while stress hormones cause us to bank "emergency" fat supplies.

> A DIET MAY TEMPORARILY CHANGE YOU FROM A CATERPILLAR INTO A THINNER CATERPILLAR. BUT THIS EXERCISE CAN TURN YOU INTO A BUTTERFLY.

Rebound dieting—to the body, repeated famines—changes what Harvard-trained Ronald Ruden, MD, PhD, calls the landscape of the brain. With every diet, we develop a worse case of what Ruden describes as the craving brain. It feels so much harder to try to lose weight on the second or 72nd time (Oh God, again?) because it is, both psychologically and physically. This is why, before starting our project, Lisa Kogan begins dodging my calls and goes on a junk food bender. It's why Lisa Romeo becomes silent and tense when I suggest she stop eating by 9 P.M. Do the Lisas lack willpower? Absolutely not. They have enormous control—that's how they imposed starvation on their bodies long enough to create the craving brain. Now they're hyperresponsive to hunger impulses and desperately (though unconsciously) afraid of another "famine." Conscious logic is telling these women to diet. Unconscious bio-logic is screaming at them to resist at all costs. The situation would be hopeless, except that scientists are showing we can actually repair the craving brain. How?

By minding our own business.

THE CHANGEABLE BRAIN

Weirdly enough, devoting gentle attention to one's own thoughts—the mind-set Lisa R. and Lisa K. both need—may literally restructure our neuroanatomy, changing a craving brain to a serene one.

For instance, Jeffrey Schwartz, MD, is a psychiatrist who treats those with obsessive-compulsive disorder (OCD). These patients feel compelled to repeat behaviors like hand washing, becoming terribly anxious if they can't. Schwartz knew that his OCD sufferers' brains showed excessive activity in a region associated with fear. So he gave them PET scan images of their brains, showing synapses in this area firing away like tiny power plants. When a hand-washing urge arose, Schwartz had them look at the pictures and tell themselves, "It feels like I should wash my hands, but it's really a short circuit in my brain." Then they'd do something else (gardening, waltzing, whatever) for 15 minutes.

The more they did this exercise, the more these people's urges and anxiety dropped. Amazingly, follow-up scans showed that the structure of their OCD brains had changed. Schwartz is just one of many scientists who are using new technology to demonstrate that we can alter the physical configuration of our brains by observing their impulses closely and calmly without obeying them. The way to heal a wounded brain is to have it observe itself.

ZEN AND THE ART OF WEIGHT LOSS

I challenge both Lisas to make this weight loss effort different by focusing first on self-observation. I want them to pay as much attention to themselves as they do to their children—especially the way they react to all forms of physical and emotional nurturing, from food to kisses.

I tell Lisa Romeo that we will have daily contact—but instead of me checking on her, she has to e-mail me. I'm not the authority on her life: She is. So I ask her to send daily reports of her own eating, feelings, and thoughts. That pushes her into the role of self-observer, while making her the leader in our interactions.

Lisa Kogan's job is quite different. I want her to ask less of herself, and view me as a soft place to land, not someone who wants more from her. Though she's wary, she eventually allows me to cajole her into observing herself as she would a friend. For example, to help Lisa K. forgive herself for rebound weight gain, I describe a 1940s diet in which healthy young men volunteered to participate. Many of the subjects became binge eaters. Their self-esteem plummeted, they became hostile and angry, and a couple of them began to steal things. When the study ended, the bingeing got worse, not better. That's what starvation—even a voluntary diet—does to the human psyche. When Lisa K. finally agrees that she deserves the same forgiveness, her energy changes. It's like ice melting.

After both Lisas promise to observe themselves in general terms, I teach them a specific self-observation technique, one I've humbly named the Most Important Weight Management Skill in the History of the Universe.

THE MASTER TOOL

I call this mental exercise Becoming the Watcher. When I first learned it, I never suspected that one unprepossessing visualization would free me, and many of my clients, from the hellish roller coaster of rebound dieting. Going on the fad diet du jour may—temporarily—change you from a caterpillar into a thinner caterpillar. This exercise can turn you into a butterfly: a different body, no going back.

BECOMING THE WATCHER

Hold out your right hand, palm up. Imagine that standing there is an inch-tall version of yourself—the part that insists on losing weight. We'll call her (or him) the Dictator. The Dictator wears a uniform, carries a whip, screams insults and orders—the things you tell yourself when you're feeling fat: "You'd better stop eating *now,* you disgusting blob of &*%$!" Let these words, and the Dictator's hostile energy, fill your consciousness.

Now notice: Do you want to eat more, or less?

Both Lisas, along with everyone else I've ever guided through this exercise, respond, "More."

Interesting.

Now hold up your left palm. Standing on it is another tiny version of you; the animal part that isn't verbal or logical, and doesn't understand what the Dictator wants. I call this the Wild Child, because it's like a kid who's continually assaulted by the Dictator's attacks and privations. The Wild Child is tired, afraid, and frightened. Notice: Is she planning to obey the Dictator in its effort to starve her? No?

Interesting.

Now hold out both hands (you may have to set down this book). See the Dictator in your right, Wild Child in your left. This next part's tricky: Notice that both mini-yous are essentially good. The Dictator gets frantic when you gain weight just as you would if you saw a toddler wandering into traffic. It screams and yells, pushes and forces, because it's trying to save you from a terrible, fat fate. And your Wild Child isn't remotely malicious, just devastated, confused, and afraid. Consider both perspectives until you can empathize with them.

At this point, it's time to realize that the Wild Child and the Dictator deserve compassion. Offer it to them. Say this: "May you be well. May you be happy. May you be free from suffering." Repeat it to both Dictator and Wild Child, until you mean it. Take your time.

All right, now answer the following question: Where are you in this picture?

The only reason you can "see" both the Dictator and the Wild Child is that you're not either of them. You've moved into a third realm of consciousness, in a different part of your brain. I call it the Watcher.

The wisdom traditions of every culture teach techniques (meditation, prayer) for aligning with this compassionate, observing self. Monks who do this regularly have unusually abundant neural activity in brain regions associated with happiness. The OCD patients Schwartz treated used similar techniques to change their brains. In short, the unassuming visualization you've just done is a portal leading away from futile conflict—including the diet wars—to a place of peace.

Notice: When you feel genuine kindness toward your Wild Child and Dictator selves, do you feel more compulsive about eating, or less?

Interesting.

Lisas K. and R. struggle with this exercise, partly because it's unfamiliar and touchy-feely, partly because they're rarely compassionate toward themselves. I push them to persist until they connect, however fleetingly, with their nonjudgmental Watcher sides. Both report that their compulsiveness about food recedes a little. The metamorphosis has begun.

I ask the Lisas to repeat this exercise at the times they'd usually attack or hate themselves. They can't sustain the Watcher perspective continuously; no one can. The point is to return—over and over. If they do, their brains will lose that famine-stricken edge. Food compulsions will fade, so they'll eat only when physically hungry. Contrary to what they've always thought, the antidote to obesity is not starvation; it's compassion. The opposite of being out of control isn't being in control, but being in love—not

> "IT'S GOING SO WELL, I'M SCARED—I'M WAITING FOR THE OTHER SHOE TO DROP," LISA ROMEO CONFESSES. "BECOME THE WATCHER," SAYS MARTHA.

as in romance, but as in that particular consciousness that abides in compassion.

After learning this exercise, both Lisas spontaneously mention horses. Lisa Romeo recalls riding a balky horse toward a jump. "Something clicked," she says. "I felt myself connect, and I knew it'd clear the fence." Lisa Kogan remembers learning to calm herself so that a horse, sensing her peaceful energy, would let her raise its foot.

These stories tell me that both Lisas have experienced the mental balance that allows weight loss, because this mind state elicits trust from animals. Treated compassionately, consistently, Dictators and Wild Children react like horses; they eventually follow the Watcher's lead. I ask the Lisas to repeat the Watcher visualization, observing their inner state without fighting it, at least once a day for four days.

Which takes us to our other essential tool: the Second Most Important Weight Management Skill in the History of the Universe.

THE FOUR-DAY WIN

When I asked successful weight losers what finally enabled them to slim down, I kept hearing the phrase "four days." Something—illness, travel, business—put many of these folks off their feed for about four days. At that point, they noticed a slight but highly motivating weight loss. After that, continuing to lose was much easier.

I wasn't expecting this, but it made sense. Adult development theorists know that significant change requires an "early win," evidence that our efforts are yielding success. It takes about four days of virtuous living to create a little weight loss. That also happens to be the time required to get used to eating less. In other words, if you can get past day three of a fitness regimen, things improve. I began to think about weight loss as a series of four-day wins.

Once you've started healing your brain with gentle, kind self-observation, you can lose weight by "sneaking up" your exercise and "sneaking down" your food intake in four-day increments. Sneaking is another way to prevent famine responses. If you're totally sedentary and eat 2,500 calories a day, don't instantly go to 1,200 calories and hours of aerobics—your weight loss will be sudden and violent, but also fleeting. Try dropping your intake by 100 to 300 calories and taking 500 more steps each day for four days. Then cut out another 100 to 300 calories, and add another 500 steps. Sustain for four days. Repeat until you see a weight loss. It will feel strangely easy to stay the course.

Because this takes patience at first (it soon becomes highly motivating), it's essential to reward yourself for meeting the four-day goals. I suggest Substituting Inedible Nurturance, or SIN. Don't replace overeating with virtuous work or exercise; instead, make a list of things you love, from watching TV to hanging out with favorite people. Nurturing touch (a pedicure, a massage, sex) is especially

IT TAKES ABOUT FOUR DAYS OF VIRTUOUS LIVING TO CREATE A LITTLE WEIGHT LOSS. THAT'S ALSO THE TIME REQUIRED TO GET USED TO EATING LESS.

effective, since it triggers production of the same opioid hormones as eating. SIN isn't sinful, but it should feel wickedly good.

THE RESULT

Lisa Romeo follows the instructions, albeit with low hopes. I half-expect her to bail on the program. But she blows me away with her persistence, constancy, and courage. In her daily e-mails from the front, Lisa articulates that in many relationships where she's been longing for nourishment, she actually needs to assume leadership. She ultimately gets a new faculty mentor more in sync with her goals. She stops taking undue responsibility for her children's feelings and becomes a calmer mother.

"It's going so well, I'm scared," she confesses. "I'm waiting for the other shoe to drop."

"So become the Watcher," I say. "Be kind toward your anxious self. Remember riding that horse toward that fence? Balance."

Several weeks into our program, Lisa's ailing father passes away. Under this massive stress, any dieter could be forgiven for falling off the wagon. Instead, after her father's funeral, she writes, "I've discovered it's impossible to overeat while you're having a good cry." She's able to observe herself so kindly that hurricanes can blow through her life without driving her to compulsive eating. I'm awestruck.

Lisa Kogan, funny, brave, and tough, writes me an e-mail saying she has new empathy for members of the cannibalistic Donner party, and another confessing, "I have just eaten my own arm." As much fun as she is, I'm worried: There's a germ of truth in every joke, and Lisa K. is still trying to live on energy she alone produces. I'm concerned that she's too hungry and almost cruelly indifferent to her own needs.

Then something good happens: Lisa K. contracts a virus that usually affects only children. Why is that good? I'm not glad she's ill, but I suspect being physically sick enough to absolutely need rest and TLC could be a great gift, teaching Lisa to receive more nurturing. When she gets that right, her craving brain can heal, and she'll be able to lead her innocent animal self in dropping excess weight—forever. The body is a persistent teacher, and though many of us greet its lessons with anger and resistance, the thing it's always trying to teach us is acceptance: of our bodies, our emotions, our situations.

Getting past rebound dieting means choosing kind perceptiveness when our reflexive responses—and those taught by most diet advisers—are to resist and control. Paradoxically, effective change begins with acceptance of everything that makes up our lives at any present moment. It's really true: Love, in the form of kindness to ourselves, is what never fails. It's working for the Lisas—to the extent that they're allowing it—and it will work for you. Persist in compassionately observing any scared, crazy, over-eating vestige of yourself, and the miserable feeding frenzies that may have dominated your life, as they did the Lisas, really will give way to peace.

Thinner peace. O

LISA K.'S DIET DIARY

"I was always a skinny kid, yet now I can't imagine turning down a treat. How did I lose my natural instincts?" By Lisa Kogan

SEPTEMBER 5: It's D-day. My diet-and-exercise program starts this morning. Two weeks earlier, in anticipation of the big event, I began my Farewell to Food 2006 tour. And as a result, I've gained an additional six and a half pounds. Weight is so blessed easy to put on and so goddamned miserable to take off.

When I tell Martha Beck—my new life coach, courtesy of *O*—and Jim Karas and Don Scott—my trainers (I also have a psychiatrist, a hairdresser, parents, and a cadre of concerned citizens throughout the tristate area)—that in 2003 I lost 50 pounds and then spent the next three and a half years gaining close to 40 of them back, they all have the exact same reaction: "Great! That means we know you're capable of losing it." But the truth is, I don't feel capable of anything. I'm afraid I don't have the self-control. I'm afraid I'll be cranky(er) than anyone can tolerate. I'm afraid I'll let myself (and everybody else) down. I'm afraid my 45-year-old metabolism has slowed to a crawl. I'm afraid of feeling hungry and deprived. Fortunately for my thighs, and at least two of my chins, the only thing I'm more afraid of is having a stroke or massive coronary.

I was so proud of myself for losing the weight (granted, it took a diabetes diagnosis and the birth of my daughter, Julia, to galvanize me), and I promised I'd never allow myself to go back to that place—but here I am. My endocrinologist (I have one of those, too) has tried to make me feel a little less awful by explaining the role genetics plays in weight loss, and Martha is trying to get me to give myself a break by explaining the neurobiology of weight. They make perfect sense…and I'm still mad at myself.

SEPTEMBER 9: I always feel as if I'm just keeping my head above water as I attempt to be clever, focused, insightful, all day long at work and patient, interested, fun, all night long at home. And now instead of dialing for dinner, I'm trying to plan meals, organize snacks, and work out three times a week.

Why do I have the world's only 3-year-old who refuses to go to bed before the 11 o'clock news? I feel guilty that I'm gone till 7 every night, so I don't blame her for not wanting to go to bed at 8:30, but it makes for a very long day.

For the record, I also feel guilty about being a single mother, the Beatles breakup, and the war in Iraq. As a single mother and a diabetic, I have an obligation to be as healthy as possible for my daughter. It's kind of a no-brainer: Eat less, move more, buy cute clothes. But this simple concept feels like the hardest thing in the world. I'm hungry. REALLY HUNGRY.

SEPTEMBER 10: Passed woman eating a cheeseburger at a sidewalk café on Columbus Avenue. I thought very seriously about how simple it would be to grab it and run. The thought of running is probably what kept me from committing a felony, but I can still smell the grilled onion. I'm completely serious. It was within reach, and she didn't appear to have any communicable diseases.

SEPTEMBER 14: I offer Jules an oatmeal raisin cookie after dinner. "No

thanks," she says and returns to forming my vintage Hermès scarf into a tutu for her stuffed penguin. She loves those cookies, but she's busy or full or not in the mood. It's an extremely natural response.

I used to be the same way. I was always a skinny kid, yet now I can't imagine turning down a treat. So how and when did I lose my natural instincts?

SEPTEMBER 15: I tell Martha about the time a few years ago when I went to lunch at Le Cirque with the editor in chief of *Food & Wine*. She was lovely and skinny, and I couldn't imagine how she stayed so thin—until dessert came. They brought us something called a white lacquered peach. It was exquisite. She took a bite and proclaimed it "heaven." She wasn't kidding. It was the kind of dessert that makes you stop and close your eyes for a second. The earth

moved, the angels sang; it was light and creamy and cakey and sticky and gooey and exotic and everything a girl could want in a white lacquered peach. I felt I demonstrated remarkable restraint by not shouting to the waiter, "Keep 'em coming." But the editor in chief, who was clearly as enthralled as I was, didn't take another bite. I couldn't get over it.

"Well," Martha says, "the editor in chief of *Food & Wine* can probably get incredible food 24/7." She then has me try an experiment. "Imagine I have magical powers and can guarantee you a white lacquered peach any time of day or night. You are lousy with desserts. A guy follows you around with one in his briefcase—the way the president always has somebody three feet away with the nuclear launch codes. Now we go back to the restaurant and you get this white lacquered peach again. Here's the question: Do you finish it?" My first reaction is to say, "Martha, if I'm hit by a cab on the way to Le Cirque, and I fall into a coma, I want it pureed and fed to me intravenously." She laughs (Martha has a warm, easy laugh) and says, "Fair enough, if that's really how you feel." I think a little more and realize it isn't. The truth is, if I really, really, really knew I could have another one in, say, 20 minutes, there's a decent chance I might not finish it. "Well, my friend, you're in luck," says Martha, "because you earn a good living and live in New York City, and you can get anything you feel like eating practically anytime you want." This is shockingly comforting in the same way the knowledge that I have Ambien in my medicine chest just in case I can't fall asleep allows me to relax and fall asleep.

She then gives me a homework assignment: When you're tempted to eat, take a second to jot down (1) exactly what you're thinking at that moment and (2) exactly what you're feeling. She wants me to start paying attention, to be aware of *specifically* why I'm eating, and to separate my intellect from my gut.

SEPTEMBER 19: Don starts every workout by recording my weight and blood sugar. He then asks what I had for breakfast and lunch. He usually suggests modifications along the lines of: "Now, when you say a poached egg, do you mean with the yolk? Because you should limit yourself to one yolk a week." Or "Grilled salmon is a great dinner, and that fillet looks to be about six inches, so you can get two meals out of it!" He is matter-of-fact in his approach. Low-key, benevolent. "Wait, you're saying I'm allowed only *half* a fillet?" I can't believe it. He gently points out that my protein shouldn't be bigger than my palm. I gently point out that I hate him. He puts a ten-pound weight in each of my hands and the session begins.

SEPTEMBER 20: I'm honoring Julia's macaroni and cheese dinner order. And it's killing me. I can live without chocolate, but pasta, bread, potatoes, risotto, that's my weakness. My "dessert at Le Cirque" mantra kicks in. I tell myself, *If you still want the mac and cheese in three hours, it's yours for the taking.* I'd like to report that the urge passed. It did not, but I resisted nonetheless.

SEPTEMBER 23: My boyfriend and I stop for lunch in Soho. I order mixed greens with vinegar. He orders a burger with fries. I take seven of his French fries and try to stab him in the face with my salad fork. How come he never gains weight?

OCTOBER 10: The needle on my scale is going down, and, as a bonus, there's a spot on my bathroom floor that makes it register two pounds lighter than I actually am. Progress is slower than I'd imagined (and I wasn't exactly thinking I'd be a size 4 in a year). Still, Jim tells me, "Every pound is a victory." I cling to this. The great news is that just by losing 11 and a half pounds and exercising (cardio and strength training), my blood sugar is back under control. That feels like a fairly major accomplishment.

OCTOBER 13: I'm astonished by what lousy shape I'm in. Don shows me the movement he wants me to perform. He's fluid, graceful, flawless. He makes it look easy. I try to copy him and fall on my face. Don is responsible for my new least favorite phrase: "And five more." As in, "seven, eight, nine, ten…and five more." I eye the clock, waiting for each session to be over.

OCTOBER 14: If this undertaking were only about aesthetics, I'd bake a lasagna and buy something with dolman sleeves.

OCTOBER 15: Martha tells me about a startling experiment that I can't get out of my head. Back in the seventies, psychologist Bruce Alexander noticed something a bit odd: Most people who try drugs don't get hooked, yet lab rats almost always become addicts. He wondered if lab rats had such miserable lives that when offered sugar water laced with morphine, they leaped at it. To test his theory, he created Rat Park, a 200-square-foot stretch of rodent paradise…greenery, balls, cans, rat porn videos, whatever. He put another group of rats in conventional cages. When offered the morphine solution, the caged rats became little rat junkies; the residents of Rat Park just said no.

Martha asks me, "If you could live any way you wanted, what would that involve? What's your idea of Rat Park?"

I draw a blank. Most people would say I already have Rat Park, so I feel ridiculous and ungrateful wanting anything more. "I mean, I have a big New York City apartment," I say, and then tentatively add, "but I just hate it. I have a job that people envy, but it stresses me out and keeps me from the kind of writing I'd like to be doing." Now I'm on a roll. "I have a very good man, but 13 years of a long-distance relationship takes its toll. I have a healthy, happy child, but my social life is virtually nonexistent…. I spent Saturday night watching a documentary on dwarves at Auschwitz. My Rat Park would be in a lovely downtown neighborhood in a family-friendly building; I'd write a book, maybe try my hand at a TV series; I'd see my friends on a regular basis; my boyfriend and I would raise our daughter together full-time. I'd have a tiara and a driver. And dammit, that driver would have a car and…" Martha laughs. She thinks it's time to start gradually tunneling my way to Rat Park and that entertaining a few big dreams will go a long way toward stopping the food cravings. I guess maybe spaghetti Bolognese is only part of what I hunger for.

OCTOBER 17: I'm sick. The kind of sick where you lie around thinking about how lucky dead people are. Now that Julia is in preschool, it's like living with a petri dish. I caught a virus that has my hands and throat covered in blisters. I can't eat (What's that line from *The Devil Wears Prada?* "I'm just one stomach flu from my goal weight"?), and I can't work out for three weeks. All the strides I'm making with Don are going down the drain. Very, very depressing.

OCTOBER 20: I'm chatting with my boyfriend while eating my daily slice of low glycemic sprouted wheat Ezekiel bread with mustard and a slice of chicken breast. It is delicious, but I interrupt our conversation with an aha moment: "I believe I've had enough. I love this, and I'm far from full, but I'm not hungry, either." I carefully wrap the three remaining bites and put the sandwich back in the fridge for later. Nobody is more surprised than I am. ◑

LISA R.'S DIET DIARY

"It happened tonight. I got the itch, the wild, raving cravings, the kind that tug at my brain and push me to the pantry." By Lisa Romeo

AUGUST 22: When Martha and I first talk, I tell her how much I know about the forces that drive weight gain. She tells me I need someone who can help me to not only lose weight—hell, I know how to do that, as I have demonstrated so many times in the past—but also drive the overeating binge monster into remission. I think she is onto something. But later that evening, after learning that my father, 2,700 miles away, is quite ill, I consume two giant cookies, handfuls of pretzel sticks, Goldfish crackers, a heaping tablespoon of (low-fat) peanut butter, a bagel with margarine, coffee with (low-fat) vanilla creamer, and two handfuls of M&M's (we, stupidly, have a dispenser).

AUGUST 26: Martha asks me to tell her about myself. I e-mail her about my husband and two sons, and how I recently started a demanding graduate program. The next day, I fly to Las Vegas; my father has had a stroke; my mother is at the end of already frayed nerves. I have school and work deadlines approaching, so I take the laptop. Martha wants to know what makes me eat—the next eight days are a vivid example.

AUGUST 27–SEPTEMBER 1: I spend all day at the hospital, helping my mother to navigate the doctorspeak, arranging for her to see her own doctors to regulate her blood thinning medication; most of the night, I work on my MFA work for grad school. I meet deadlines. I do not binge. I eat according to hunger. I even walk. I do not have time to think about why or how this is so. I talk to Martha by phone and write her long e-mails every night. Once, while talking by cell phone from the ICU lounge with Martha, I begin to cry, and she asks me to visualize three or four scenes from my past that make me happy, offer comfort. I am to keep these in a "box" in my mind for future stressful times. A nice idea, I think, but a bit out there for me, a pragmatic, give-me-the-facts kind of person. But I promise to consider it.

AUGUST 28: Martha says we will not focus on the scale, and I am relieved. I know that watching numbers move down is enticing, but it takes the focus off the issues that make me eat. Still I want the scale to move. How to separate the "success" of weight loss from the tangle of dealing with the things that drive me to the pantry?

SEPTEMBER 4: The scale says I have lost seven pounds. I am worried it is a fluke. Martha wants me to think about all the cruel things I say to myself. I am heartsick at how easy it is for me to make a lengthy mental list. Martha suggests that if I stop saying these things to myself, I may be able to give my kids something I have grieved that they do not have: a mother who is happy.

SEPTEMBER 6: Martha has asked me to move my "brain candy" books—the ones I read for pleasure—from an upstairs bookshelf to a basket next to my couch, closer than the kitchen door when I'm relaxing late at night. She tells me to avoid speaking in the second person when discussing weight and food issues. Suddenly, I cannot generalize and say, "You know when you want to binge..." It is tough at first, but I make the switch to saying, "When *I* overeat..." "Diets make *me* crazy...." I notice an immediate shift in my outlook. This is personal. This is about me.

SEPTEMBER 11: It happened tonight. I got the itch, the wild, raving cravings, the kind that tug at my brain and push my legs toward the pantry and freezer and bread box, the ones that start about an hour or so after the kids are tucked in. We have leftover party food around—miniature Italian and French pastries, bakery-fresh butter cookies, tubs of full-fat ice cream, loaves of baguettes, and sliced deli meats. I consider all the options and decide on a few cookies and coffee, and then I stop. In the moment, I can't tease out why I stop, but later I start to connect the dots between the mindful self-awareness Martha and I have worked to create, and I am able to observe myself and respond with compassion (a tasty snack) instead of contempt (bingeing to the point of distress). Click.

SEPTEMBER 13: I told Martha I would not eat anything after 10:15; this was a compromise; she had said 9:00, figuring I went to bed around 11. Typically, I am up till 12:30. I decide I will choose one snack to have before that time, and one only. This may seem ridiculously obvious, but to me this represents a huge step. As they pile up, those two-hour segments, night after night, filled with not eating, are an accomplishment, not just because I am not overeating but because when I get those desires to use food as a cure-all, I am able to think before acting. This is major. I am thinking about what happens when people—when I—regain weight and how we discuss it: We say it "creeps up." But that is not true, we—no, I mean I—let it creep up. Weight does not "come back." *It is invited back.*

SEPTEMBER 22: I think in circular, familiar, and frustrating patterns: I eat out of emotional stress, reliving childhood eating patterns; choose to allow what others do or say to influence my opinion of

myself; and go to food for comfort. But I get sick of my own thoughts because they don't seem to lead me to a break in the cycle. I tell this to Martha. If I know all this intellectually, why can't I change it? Instead of allowing myself to eat right away in response to stress, Martha wants me to locate the underlying negative thought driving me to eat. And not the superficial thought, such as *I'm mad at Susan because she berated me for something I said at a PTA meeting.* No, it's the larger, more elemental belief Martha wants me to identify. Like this: *I want everyone to like me, and when someone does not, it makes me feel unworthy, unlikable.* Ouch. This hurts, acknowledging and feeling those negative, self-destructive thoughts, but I can see it also helps.

SEPTEMBER 26: Martha said something to me last night that may have been the most important thing I have learned yet. I already was aware, of course, that I eat to avoid negative feelings, but here's what I never knew: that I binge because it actually serves *to keep me in the negative thought patterns, and that is what I actually want.* Huh? The longer I stay in the negative thought patterns, the longer I get to wallow in self-pity, the longer I get to avoid doing anything about the negative situations themselves, the longer I get to *rest,* because, like it or not, negative is where I feel comfortable. This information comes as such a shock that I keep saying to Martha, *Stop, say that again.* I am stunned and appalled and happy all at once—upset to learn that I do this (and I absolutely see, immediately and with utter clarity, that I *do*), and at the same time, I'm glad to know something so important, something that could, possibly, help me to stop this self-abusive behavior.

OCTOBER 3–6: My father is recovering from hip surgery; well, *recovering* might be the wrong word. He needs another transfusion and has contracted pneumonia. This is the kind of emotional trauma that normally ignites an eating frenzy. I do not eat. I am shocked that I do not eat.

OCTOBER 6: I've done it now—agreed to have my photograph appear in a national magazine. After losing, let's see, 18 pounds, I still weigh...yikes, I cannot even write the number. What was I thinking? When the photographer invited me to look at the photos halfway through, on his assistant's laptop, I was horrified by my fat face, wide neck, poor posture, huge thighs...fat is all I see. "You're way too critical of yourself," he says. Martha nailed me on that the first day we talked. He is kind, however, and I think about how this all started, and how far I've come, and I recover enough to continue.

OCTOBER 14: I get the phone call I was dreading. When I get off this airplane, I will fall into the arms of my 80-year-old mother, widowed yesterday. Before takeoff, I wrote in my journal: "Oh no, here goes, this could lead me right back to bingeing." The flight attendant offers three food choices—a heavy breakfast; a snack box filled with chocolate, cookies, and chips; a fruit-and-cheese platter. I choose grapes, pull out my journal, and write. Something, there on the page, satisfies. **O**

> I AM ABLE TO OBSERVE MYSELF AND RESPOND WITH COMPASSION (A TASTY SNACK) INSTEAD OF CONTEMPT (BINGEING TO THE POINT OF DISTRESS).

From thought to action: Being active is easier in short bursts.

EXERCISE: THE LEAST YOU CAN DO
(WOULD YOU BELIEVE TEN MINUTES?)

Imagine if exercising ten minutes a day were enough to improve your health, cheer you up, and help you maintain a steady weight. Well, it *is,* even though most experts stubbornly insist that you need 30 to 60 minutes daily to see results. The case for shorter sessions has been building for some time, but in 2007 results from a watershed study made the point loud and clear. Researchers at Pennington Biomedical Research Center in Baton Rouge, Louisiana, reported findings from a study involving 464 women who weren't exercisers. After six months, a group who walked an average of 72 minutes a week at two to three mph—that's about ten minutes of mall-pace striding a day—had significantly improved heart strength and general fitness, nearly matching the efforts of women exercising almost twice as long. "Your body responds very positively, very quickly to even small amounts of exercise," says lead study author Tim Church, MD, PhD. "If you're sedentary, you'll see a lot of your greatest gains going from zero to ten minutes a day."

More exercise is definitely better, but based on Church's findings and the studies below, there's evidence you can take your time easing into those longer workouts.

BUILD MUSCLE A study of 22 couch potatoes found that those who did just one set of ten repetitions of seven strength-training moves (about ten minutes of lifting) three days a week gained as much strength as those who did a 30-minute, three-set routine.

BOOST YOUR MOOD In a recent study of 48 men and women, spinning on a bike for ten minutes led to a mood lift and drop in depression and fatigue—similar to what they'd get riding three times as long.

PROTECT YOUR JOINTS After tracking nearly 4,000 women in their 70s for three years, researchers found that those who reported often having arthritis pain needed only 75 minutes a week of moderate exercise like brisk walking to reduce the frequency of symptoms by nearly 30 percent.

MANAGE YOUR WEIGHT Both Church's study and a larger study of 13,711 men and women reveal that just 70 to 75 minutes of brisk walking or about 40 minutes of jogging a week is enough to begin shrinking your waistline. And targeting the waist is important because belly fat is directly tied to heart disease, diabetes, and early death.

QUELL STRESS "We've seen significant changes in the autonomic nervous system—fewer incidences of the fight-or-flight stress reflex being triggered—with even 70 to 75 minutes a week of exercise," says Church. "A little exercise can do much more than people think, so there's no excuse for not getting up and just doing something." —Selene Yeager

29

HEALTH

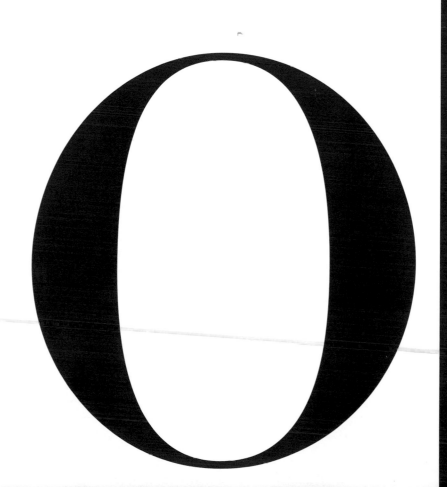

"HI, MY NAME IS AMANDA... AND I *MIGHT* BE AN ALCOHOLIC"

She never threw china, drove under the influence, or sabotaged her marriage. But drinking was taking over her life, one wineglass at a time. Amanda Robb finds a new kind of happy hour.

I remember the exact moment I developed my drinking problem. I was writing a scene for the NBC soap opera *Sunset Beach*. The show's sweet young thing had just been abducted by a Mayan-themed cult, and my boss told me to "up the drama and make it real." I thought, *I can't—not without a glass of wine*. So I got one.

That was seven years ago. Nothing terrible has happened since. Except an occasional glass of wine became a glass of wine every night became two glasses of wine became sometimes three and, if no one was looking, most of a bottle—which once emptied, I would hide. I also became intensely interested in time. To make sure I wasn't becoming an alcoholic, I never allowed myself to drink before 6:00 P.M. But very quickly I knew that our bedroom clock was the fastest in our home, and therefore the authoritative household timepiece every evening.

I never drove drunk. I never endangered my daughter. I never let loose with a single hateful tirade. I never wound up strung out and naked in some skanky guy's pickup.

But I knew that hiding bottles from my husband wasn't a great idea. The problem was I didn't know what to do next. I couldn't imagine showing up at Alcoholics Anonymous...what was I going to say? "One morning I woke up [*dramatic pause*] bloated." Plus, I didn't ache for an alcohol-free life. I pined for the relationship I had with the stuff for the first 18 years of my drinking life—supercasual, occasional one-night stands, a sweet feel-it-and-forget thing.

I'm not shy about asking for help in figuring out ways over the molehills that appear in my path. At first I got two useless pieces of advice from friends—"Check into Betty Ford!" (and pay for it how?) and "Relax, the entire population of France drinks more than you do!" Finally, my friend Lisa, whose husband is a substance-abuse counselor, suggested I call New York City's Center for

"Drinking took the edge off my dirtiest little secret: boredom."

Motivation and Change. "They're flexible," she promised.

"I want to be a normal drinker again," I told Nicole Kosanke, PhD, the psychologist I met at my two-hour "psychosocial/motivational evaluation."

"What's normal?" she asked.

"Not drinking at home."

"How much when you're out?"

"Two glasses to start," I said. "But when I get better, I won't be so rigid."

"That's a good beginning," Dr. Kosanke said.

My snake-oil radar clanged. Sure, I was absolutely desperate to keep Kendall-Jackson Vintner's Reserve in my life, but every recovering alcoholic I'd ever met swore up, down, and sideways, "Half measures avail us nothing!" And seared in my memory was the day Audrey Kishline, the founder of the "responsible drinking" group Moderation Management, killed a 38-year-old man and his 12-year-old daughter while driving drunk.

Still, I answered Dr. Kosanke's questions. I'd started nonsocial drinking because I was anxious (that Mayan-themed scene I had to write), convinced I was a hack and would never be able to finish a script. Then, after I had a baby, drinking took the edge off my most dirty little secret—boredom.

FOR ME, THE BENEFITS OF ALCOHOL CONSUMPTION SLIGHTLY OUTWEIGHED THE COSTS. WINE *WORKED.*

I swear nothing has made me happier than motherhood, but God forgive me, I find parenting after work between 5 and 9 P.M. a Sisyphean hell—picking Play-Doh out of the carpet; putting Polly Pocket clothes in one bin, shoes in another; coaxing my daughter into the tub; apologizing for the soap in her eyes and snagging knots in her hair; making dinner and lunch for the next day; folding laundry; strongly suggesting table manners; cleaning up dinner and more toys; and finally reading stories about lizards and princesses and talking cars. What can I say? It's a lot easier with a little buzz going.

Dr. Kosanke has me do a cost-benefit analysis about my alcohol consumption. I rate how drinking affects my relationships, job, health, and finances. I discover that, for me, the benefits of alcohol consumption slightly outweigh the costs. Wine *worked.* If it hadn't, as Dr. Kosanke pointed out, I would not have kept using it. The list showed me wine makes me a calmer, if hazier parent; and it's not very expensive since I like only cheap Chardonnay. On the downside, my sleep is totally disrupted, and my husband is worried because I've begun drinking every day. (Also, I am *really* bloated.)

"So, um, do you think the fact that it sort of works means I should keep drinking?" I ask.

"I think that you need to find other ways to get the benefits you get from alcohol," says Dr. Kosanke.

The Center for Motivation and Change is a freesia-scented, tastefully decorated place on New York's Fifth Avenue and 30th Street. It is staffed by bizarrely good-looking psychologists who offer a spa-like menu of services, such as a "mindfulness immersion day" (yoga, breathing, and meditation exercises), a two-week "readiness for change" evaluation (to see if you really want to give up your habit), and a "tracking program" (a way to assess how using drugs or alcohol is affecting your life). Inside its East-West/postmodern chicness, though, one of the center's philosophies is the extremely basic 33-year-old community reinforcement approach (CRA).

Taught by psychologist Robert J. Meyers, PhD, research associate professor of psychology at the University of New Mexico, CRA works on the principle that the most effective way to get people to reduce their substance abuse is to make sobriety more rewarding than addiction. "Some people drink because their personal relationships are terrible," says Dr. Meyers, who is the coauthor of *Get Your Loved One Sober: Alternatives to Nagging, Pleading, and Threatening.* "Others drink because their work is meaningless. Some are depressed. Some are anxious. Some are just bored. A few are burdened with a genetic predisposition for alcoholism. Many drink for an amalgam of all those reasons. But if you ask a person what they want out of life and help them start to achieve it, they're more likely to reduce their drinking than if you just tell them to stop drinking."

CRA has been lauded by the *Journal of Studies on Alcohol* as among the most cost-effective alcohol treatment programs and has been shown, in studies funded by the National Institutes of Health, more effective than traditional interventions. For instance, in one 2001 University of New Mexico study, alcoholics were randomly assigned to a CRA program or a 12-step treatment program. Over a six-month follow-up period, the CRA participants averaged 3 percent of drinking days, and those in traditional treatment averaged 19 percent of drinking days. In an earlier in-patient study, the CRA participants averaged only 5 percent of days unemployed, but the hospital's Alcohol Anonymous participants averaged 62 percent.

Still, CRA has never been widely implemented because many substance-abuse counselors think it's dumb (and potentially dangerous) to let people with drug and alcohol problems use at all. They cite the Kishline case. They point to Mel Gibson.

Dr. Meyers acknowledges that "the world would be a better place if no one used drugs or alcohol at all." But he thinks that the reason 21 million drug and alcohol abusers in America are not getting help is that our culture tells them that their only hope of getting better is giving up the thing they can't imagine living without. And giving it up every day for the rest of their natural lives. "If a guy goes from drinking a fifth of Jack Daniels a day to drinking a couple of beers a day," Dr. Meyers says, "and in that process he does better at work and his relationship with his wife and kids improves, I think that's success."

Three weeks later, back at the Center for Motivation and Change, Dr. Kosanke and I barely talk about my drinking. She has me fill out another form—a Happiness Scale—and we strategize how to make my life more joyful. She coaches me to talk back to the "You suck!" voice in my head and to ask my husband and mother-in-law for more help with childcare. (They both say yes.) She wonders if I could buy more prepared food for dinner and asks where it is written that 6-year-olds need to be bathed every night.

I still crave Chardonnay and am drinking about three glasses of it, three or four nights a week. I complain that my therapy isn't working.

"You still haven't found something you like to do more than drink," Dr. Kosanke says.

"I have meaningful work and relationships. You think I need a hobby, too?"

"Yes," she says.

This is not a novel idea in addiction treatment. In fact, many studies have found that lab rats ignore food and water in order to gulp drug-laced solutions.

"I like watching TV," I tell Dr. Kosanke.

"Too passive," she says.

Over the next several weeks, I try furniture refinishing (a puke-green-paint disaster), Shakespeare and American musical theater (too expensive), opera (didn't get it), meditation (dullsville for me but surprisingly useful for my daughter), and sex (my husband began to appear frightened whenever I looked at him).

"I'm not a hobby person," I wail.

"You go to ballet," Dr. Kosanke says.

"So I don't get fat," I say.

"You make dinner," she says.

"Because I have to," I say.

Turns out a lot of people endure lives that are cages of sorts—they have grueling, mind-numbing work; they spend time with selfish relatives; they are lonesome. Me, I put myself in a cage by thinking *task* instead of *pleasure*.

Dr. Kosanke thinks this is a bad habit I can basically cognitive-behavior myself out of. I worry that I don't have whatever synapses you need to anticipate fun. Although I often enjoy parties, I don't look forward to them. Ditto travel, romantic dinners, even shopping. I think the best I can cognitive-behavior myself into is imagining fun as a dear, devoted friend—one always out there, waiting for me to arrive.

By now, my fourth month in treatment, I'm doing what Dr. Kosanke calls reducing the risk—when I drink, which is a few times a week, I pour myself two glasses of wine and dump the rest of the bottle out.

She gives me another worksheet—one that assesses which people, places, times, and feelings are "triggers" for my alcohol consumption. I tell her we already know that I drink because I'm anxious and bored, and that I'm probably one of the few people on the planet who is surrounded by teetotalers.

"How about not keeping any wine at home?" she suggests.

"I'll give in and buy it at the wine store," I say.

"Where's that?"

"On the way home from my daughter's school."

"Arrange to be doing something during your 'witching hour.' Take a ballet class. Go to a movie with a friend. You don't have to tell them they're babysitting."

"Thanks."

"Do something pleasant every single afternoon," she orders.

The next month is much less stressful than previous months: My work anxiety is being argued with by the new voice Dr. Kosanke had me practice (When I think, *I suck*, the new voice says, *You sure get published a lot for someone who sucks*. Or, *I hear Van Gogh sometimes thought he was a lousy painter*. Or just, *That's not a very helpful thing to think*.) My home life is much improved because my husband and mother-in-law are doing much more childcare, and now (big surprise) when I'm with my daughter, I enjoy her more than resent her. And since my family is around more, we have dinners together, which are relaxed and fun because I've recently discovered the joys of heat-and-eat meals.

When weary of being positive and engaged, I indulge myself with a vengeance. I get a massage, a manicure, a stupidly expensive headband, a puppy, Botox. I think I watch every *Law & Order* episode ever made (even though TV isn't on Dr. Kosanke's list of approved hobbies) and take more bubble baths than I have during the previous 40 years of my life. I stop drinking for a whole ten days...the last three of which I spend counting the hours to an Academy Awards party, where I—a newly normal drinker—am going to enjoy two glasses of wine! (Wow, my joyful anticipation synapses roar to sudden life!) I wind up guzzling four filled-to-the-brim glasses and cease and desist only because my hostess stops pouring and I'm too embarrassed to ask her to open a new bottle just for me.

The next day, because I'll be staying in, I plan not to drink at all. But the second my bedroom clock hits 6:00 P.M., I call the liquor store and ask them to deliver me a bottle pronto, which I suck straight down.

"I can't be a normal drinker," I tell Dr. Kosanke.

"So what do you want to do now?" she asks.

Part of CRA is reassessing goals," Dr. Meyers had told me. "When people come in, they are overwhelmed by the idea of never drinking again. So we get them to sample sobriety to see what it's like. Then we talk about how they're doing and how things are changing. We coach them to supplement their drinking with other fun activities."

It dawns on me that Dr. Kosanke probably knew I couldn't be a normal drinker. She admits that she thought it might be difficult. "I was concerned you might not be able to be a controlled drinker," she says. "But if I had told you that in the beginning, you probably wouldn't have believed it. I thought it was more useful to examine the role alcohol was playing in your life, then make a decision that you could feel good about and one that would be sustaining."

"Do some people come here and choose to keep alcohol in their lives?"

"Sometimes," she says, "after a period of abstinence. When they create a new relationship with alcohol."

I want more than anything to be that kind of person. But deep in my soul—a hardy though delicately edged thing I'd come to know far more intimately during the past six months—I feel that even if half of France drinks more than I do with no problem, I was still in the cold, wretched clutch of something that, if I let it, would drop me someplace very, very bad.

I quit drinking completely.

It's hard. Brutally so. I don't go to parties when I'm feeling like being boozy. I meet my favorite drinking buddies only for lunch or breakfast. I spend too much money on flowers, furniture, clothes, and cosmetic procedures. I imagine my daughter finding me dead, drowned in my vomit, which is how a friend of mine's alcoholic mother died.

Dr. Kosanke tells me that she feels our work is pretty much over. (Dr. Meyers says CRA tends to be short-term—its therapists want their clients out mountain biking or writing poetry.) In our last session, I ask Dr. Kosanke if I'll ever be able to return to casual drinking. "That's probably not a question you should ask for a couple of years," she says. "But if you do have a drink, it's not the end of world. You always have everything you learned in here."

Some days I feel it would have been more useful to have been released into the world with an admonishment to stay sober no matter what. I guess it's the little girl in me who's used to being punished, not soothed when she misbehaves. But another part of me is relieved to know I don't have to be perfect to be better. And every day, I'm grateful to no longer be living for the tick, tick, tick of my bedroom clock. ◙

To find a CRA program, call 505-925-2361 or e-mail cra-craft@robertjmeyersphd.com. To find a counselor at the Center for Motivation and Change, call 212-683-3339 or visit centerformotivationandchange.com.

C IS FOR COURAGE

We all know someone who's been diagnosed with cancer. To reporter Geraldine Brooks, who made a living dodging bullets in war zones, the disease was the most terrifying thing she could imagine. But after surviving a bout with breast cancer, she's here to tell you that the "C" word isn't a death sentence—far from it, in fact. Read on for the good news.

The photograph on the big screen was beautiful. Curvaceous, shell-pink clusters of little buds snuggled against one another, forming a sphere that was held afloat by a skein of creamy threads. Sitting in the dim lecture room at the Radcliffe Institute for Advanced Study at Harvard, where I had a fellowship a year ago, I looked around and realized I was the only one in the whole place who was smiling.

The slide on the screen illustrated a lecture about cancer research. It showed a magnified image of metastatic breast cancer cells that had invaded someone's lung tissue. Nothing to smile about. But I had spent so much time being afraid of cells like these that it was a relief to actually see them, to meet up with them in the anonymous dark of a university lecture hall, and to know them for what they were.

I felt a kind of calmness that day, the way I'd felt on a night long ago in 1991, during a battle in the Iraqi city of Kirkuk, when the sky suddenly lit up with a streaking peacock's tail of green and blue tracer fire. The explosions were beautiful and deadly, like the multifoliate metastasis on the medical lecturer's slide. A newspaper reporter at the time, I had been afraid of finding myself in the midst of a firefight. But when it actually happened, the fear dissolved. *So*

it's this, I remember thinking. *But it's only this. I will survive it, or not. And if I do, there will be one less thing in life to be afraid of.*

The day in 2004 when the radiologist told me I had invasive cancer, I walked down the hospital corridor looking for a phone to call my husband, and I could almost see the fear coming toward me like a big, black shadow. I had been so sure the call for more tests following a routine mammogram would turn up nothing that I had gone to the appointment alone. Now I knew if that approaching shadow caught up with me, there was a good chance it would crush me. I would crumple into a sobbing heap.

The fear coming for me was an old adversary. I had been afraid of breast cancer, as I suspect most women are, from the time I hit adolescence. At that age, when our emerging sexuality is our central preoccupation, the idea of disfigurement of a breast is particularly horrifying. There were plenty of things I had more business being afraid of: actual, statistically significant risks such as boyfriends who drove too fast or drank too much, party drugs from sketchy sources, adolescent recklessness in treacherous surf or on too-difficult ski slopes. But somehow my imagination could not compass the very real, proven danger of these behaviors; cancer was the killer that stalked my teenage nightmares.

It is a most commonplace fear. Although a cursory exploration of health statistics reveals that heart disease kills many more of us, cancer remains our most potent metaphor for that which is

Targeted therapies are only one of the advances that are turning cancer into a manageable disease.

deadly and dreaded and out of our control. In the last century, wrote Susan Sontag in her memorable 1978 essay "Illness as Metaphor," it was tuberculosis that provoked fearful fantasy. "Now it is cancer's turn to be the disease that doesn't knock before it enters... treated as an evil, invincible predator."

Why is this? Blame the movies, in part. If screenwriters have to kill off a female character, they love to give her cancer. We've seen so many great actresses go down to the Big C: Ali MacGraw, Meryl Streep, Emma Thompson, Debra Winger, Susan Sarandon.

Hollywood cancer distorts the truth of the disease in two highly significant ways. In a study of American movies from the 1930s to the 1990s, more than half of all cancer patients depicted are under 30, and three-quarters under 40. In the real world, cancer is overwhelmingly a disease of older age.

Hollywood's other big cancer lie is that almost no one survives. You get cancer onscreen, you'll almost certainly be dead, or poignantly celebrating your very last Christmas, by the film's final reel. The much happier truth: In the United States, two-thirds of all treated cancer patients are alive at the five-year mark, and for breast cancer, the number is nearly 90 percent.

So if cancer in general and breast cancer in particular are mostly survivable, why are we still so afraid? Perhaps it is because we are just not that up-to-date; our perception of cancer's lethality is lagging the statistical reality by a decade or more.

Perhaps the fear is also a product of our fortunate First World lives. In countries with good maternity care and without childhood epidemics, most of us are likely to reach adulthood before anyone we personally know dies of anything at all. Unless we live in the inner city, or came of age in the 1980s AIDS explosion, fewer still among us will know someone who dies young. But some of these few will be cancer deaths. And if the young person is a celebrity, we will read all about it over and over again. So that when we come upon a statistic that is truly alarming—say, that one in eight American women will get breast cancer—we subject it to imagination rather than information, failing to note that the incidence increases dramatically as we age (in our 30s, for example, the odds are only about one in 233) and that for many women, breast cancer will be a disease that one dies with, rather than dies of.

Like me, my half sister was among the one in eight. Almost two decades older than I, she received the diagnosis in her 60s, when the incidence of breast cancer begins its marked increase. A feminist, environmental activist, and believer in alternative therapies, she was deeply suspicious of high-tech medicine. She had her lump removed but refused to undergo radiation or chemotherapy. Given the type and early stage of the cancer she had, her decision, at the time, seemed a logically supportable one. She felt that not enough people consider whether it is morally justified to chase after uncertain cures even though the radioactive material used to do so would linger dangerously, polluting the planet, for centuries. She felt, also, that chemotherapy prolonged life at too high a price. Instead, after her surgery, she went traveling to places she had always wanted to see. By the time it became clear, just two years later, that her cancer had

metastasized and soon would kill her, she had visited Europe, Hawaii, and Crete. She died, eight years ago, seemingly at peace with the choices she had made.

But now, having lain under the radiation beams and watched the bright-colored cytotoxins of chemotherapy travel down the drip lines into my own veins, I wish I could counsel her differently. Take your best shot, I would tell her. For most people, chemotherapy is no longer the chamber of horrors we often conceive it to be. Yes, it is an ordeal for some people, but it wasn't for me, nor for most of the patients I got to know during my four months of periodic visits to the chemo suite. Dosage now is so carefully calibrated and buffering drugs so effective that on the days after treatment, I felt no worse than if I had a bout of low-grade flu. Steroids staved off nausea, and white cell boosters took care of other potentially debilitating symptoms. While I certainly would have preferred to go through life without having to learn to self-inject the white cell booster, eventually even jabbing a hypodermic into my own abdomen became routine.

Because of those steroids and white cell boosters, I never took to my bed. I never threw up. I covered my bald head with beautiful scarves and went on as usual, taking my son to school, walking the dog, going to the theater, seeing friends. Life developed its own odd rhythm: I learned to allow for one lousy week immediately following treatment, and then to expect two pretty ordinary ones, when I felt almost normal and forgot about cancer for hours at a time.

There were gifts I would never have received were it not for cancer. Friends and family showed their love in every conceivable way, from casseroles and flowers to handmade necklaces and copies of diverting trash such as the *National Enquirer*. From Denver my atheist friend sent a note saying that as he could not include me in his daily prayers, he was including me in his daily anxieties. I felt buoyed by believing friends who sent Lourdes water or pictures of the Medicine Buddha, stood up to pray for me in synagogues or arranged for a monastery of Tibetan monks to chant on my behalf. One friend trudged into Kurdistan to tie a scarf to a holy rock, another solicited the prayers of a Shiite ayatollah. The very ecumenism of all this reminded me of the many odd corners my life had led me into, and made me more appreciative of the time I'd already had to live so fully, to travel and explore.

Like my Denver friend, I am not a believer, and cancer didn't convert me into one. But although I didn't consciously turn to any higher power, I did experience something for which the only useful term I can find is "grace." It is hard to explain the feeling, but it was a sense of being given just as much strength as the time demanded. I thought of the physicist Niels Bohr, who reportedly kept a horseshoe over his door. Friends would say to him, disparagingly, "You can't possibly believe in that," and Bohr would answer, "Of course not." And then he'd add: "But I hear it brings good luck whether you believe in it or not."

I saw another side of my husband, whom I had always loved for his abundant, productive energy, not knowing that a gentler, patient man lurked within. Setting aside my book deadlines, I had more time to enjoy being with my son, then just 8 years old. The steroids I took gave

IN THE UNITED STATES, TWO-THIRDS OF ALL TREATED CANCER PATIENTS ARE ALIVE AT THE FIVE-YEAR MARK. FOR BREAST CANCER, THE NUMBER IS NEARLY 90 PERCENT.

Over it: The author, postcancer, in 2006 on Martha's Vineyard, where she lives.

me an unnatural, jagged energy and kept me up at night. It wasn't fun, being unpleasantly wired. Sometimes I felt as if I'd been taken over by an incubus on those steroid-addled days and nights. But even this had an upside. When my son would wake from a bad dream, instead of grunting sleepy words of consolation and ordering him back to bed, I'd invite him to join me for hot cocoa and a midnight chat.

What else? The disfigurement that my younger self had dreaded turned out to be nothing very drastic. Spared a mastectomy, I have instead a trio of fading scars, each a couple of inches long: one diagonally across my breast where the cancer had been, another under my arm where they removed the nodes it might (but fortunately hadn't) spread to, a third beneath my clavicle, where a valve was temporarily implanted to ease the administration of chemo. In the locker room after workouts in the hydrotherapy pool, women who had undergone mastectomies unself-consciously displayed bodies that were by no means mutilated. In fact, to me they were beautiful: the bodies of brave Amazons who had done what was required to survive the particular engagement in which they found themselves.

Lest this sound like Pollyanna, I want to acknowledge that my experience was shaped by my good fortune. I had the support of a loving partner and fabulous friends and family. As a writer, I controlled my days. I didn't have to show up in an office or depend on the empathy of an employer. I had an income that could withstand the loss of earnings as I slowed my work pace down. I had health insurance. And at 48, one of the potentially tragic side effects of treatment, infertility, was not an issue for me. I am well aware that had I had a more advanced or more aggressive cancer, treatment would have been harsher and harder to bear. Some people suffer horribly, and for some there is no hope. During radiation, I shared a waiting room every weekday for six weeks with pediatric cases, geriatric cases, and people for whom the treatment was palliative, to ease their pain, without promise of cure.

But I can only speak from my own experience, and my experience tells me that the exaggerated fear we have of this disease and its treatment is unwarranted, and dangerous, because it keeps women from seeking potentially lifesaving care.

Of course, I know all this now. I did not know any of it on the day of my diagnosis. I stood in that hospital corridor, halfway to the phone booth, as the sum of all my years of cancer fear sped toward me. All those years, visiting someone in a maternity ward or an elective surgery department, I'd hurry past the signs pointing to ONCOLOGY, making some kind of modern version of the old medieval sign against the evil eye. I didn't know what went on in there; I didn't want to know. But now I was going to find out.

"Not, I'll not, carrion comfort, Despair, not feast on thee." The line from Gerard Manley Hopkins's poem arrived unbidden. It had somehow unpacked itself from the mental closet of my high school English classes. Then my own more prosaic, slightly querulous inner voice started up: *You've always liked to think you're pretty tough,* it instructed sternly. *Well, here's where you get to prove it.* I turned the stalking shadow of fear back with the force of all my willpower. There would be no tears that day, or any day following. (Unless you count the day of my second surgery, when I made the mistake of watching *Map of the Human Heart* while I waited for my turn in the OR. When the orderlies finally came in to wheel me from the theater, I was boo-hoo-hooing my head off. They wouldn't believe I was crying over the movie's tragic story of unrequited Inuit love, and not my own predicament. After that, I made a new rule: Watch only comedies.)

Now, more than two and a half years since my treatment finished, I have no idea how my own story will end. But that is really no different from anyone else on earth, when you think about it. Of course, I believe I will be in the lucky majority who are still doing well when the doctors stop paying attention. But if not, "oncologist" has ceased to be a synonym for "scary witch doctor." These days, the word evokes a thoughtful, wise, and amiable man who has become a friend. When I was working as a foreign correspondent in the Middle East, I learned many things. One of them is that you embrace your life most fully when you feel the nearness of death. Another lesson came from a journalist colleague, John Hockenberry, who had been in a car crash that had left him paraplegic. As we covered stories in Gaza and Tehran and other difficult, dangerous places, I forgot that he was in a wheelchair, for the simple reason that he seemed to have forgotten it. "You take what you have left," he told me once, "and you go on."

Because of cancer, I have certain things I never wanted: an ID card in my wallet from the Dana-Farber Cancer Institute, a "chemo perm" that has turned my once very manageable straight hair into a toilet brush of coarse, unruly curls, and a slight aversion to the pleasant shade of lilac that hospitals use to denote cytotoxic medical waste. But I also have one less thing to be afraid of. ◘

DEFENDING MY LIFE

Both her mother *and* her father wrestled with breast cancer. She was sick of radiologists and mammograms, tired of watching, waiting, fearing the worst. So former anchorwoman René Syler made one of the most difficult—and strangely exhilarating—decisions of her life.

**M**ost women may forget about their breasts until they put on a bra or have sex. But I think about mine all the time. I look at them, study them, wonder if something heinous is growing inside them— the deformed one, a constant reminder of the trouble they've been to me over the past several years.

Then I think, *In less than a month, after my mastectomy, they won't be with me anymore. What will I look like? What will I feel like?*

Just curious.

DEC. 23 Time: dark. Place: Kiawah Island, South Carolina. We ran out of New York City yesterday, and man, did I need to get out of there. The past month has been hell, because in the midst of preparing for life-changing surgery, I lost my job as an anchor on *The Early Show.* Oh, and did I mention, we're also renovating the house? So, huge surgery looming, getting fired, house torn up—the only thing missing is divorce, and I probably should check with Buff on his intentions!

When I got fired, all the energy I'd been spending on myself had to be transferred to wrapping things up at CBS. I haven't really had much time to absorb all the nuances of what's about to happen to my body. All I know is that I feel very tired, not just physically but emotionally, too, and the number of gray hairs has quadrupled overnight.

I'm on my way, this afternoon, to pick up Mom. She'll spend Christmas with us in Kiawah. You know what that means? Many more gray hairs.

DEC. 24 My kids, Casey, 10, and Cole, 8, are trying to make up for 364 days of bickering. I need to tell them that Santa has a really long memory.

Fortunately, Mom is not making me crazy yet. It's actually very nice to see her because she does know what it's like to deal with breast issues. She was diagnosed with breast cancer at age 64, when I was pregnant with Cole. I remember her calling and asking me if I was sitting down. I said yes, and that's when she dropped the bomb. It stole the wind from my lungs, because if there were ever an unlikely candidate for breast cancer, it would be Anne Syler. She ate well and exercised long before it was fashionable to do so, didn't drink excessively. At the time, she was the picture of health.

Later she confided how much she feared the "legacy" she was leaving my sister and me. I tried to make her understand that she hadn't done anything to get BC; it was just an unlucky draw. But I wonder if she feels responsible for my health problems. I hope she doesn't.

DEC. 26 Not only was my mother a breast cancer patient (nine years later, she is doing well, praise God); my father had it, too. Male breast cancer is rare, only about 1,700 cases are diagnosed each year in the United States. So when you tell a doctor your father had breast cancer, it's a *big* red-flag moment.

I had my first mammogram in 1992. I was 29. It turns out that I don't have the breast cancer gene, and things were all right until my late 30s. Then little white flecks started showing up on the film, like buckshot on my breast—microcalcifications, which can indicate cancer. I used to always schedule my mammograms near my birthday, a gift of health and life to myself. In 2003 my present was a long-faced radiologist who said, "You need a biopsy." I had a fibroid adenoma removed from the right breast. No cancer. The buckshot-looking stuff in my left breast was taken out, too. No cancer. Whew. But I was diagnosed with a condition called atypical ductal hyperplasia, which substantially raises your odds of BC.

A year later, another biopsy. Left breast, same diagnosis: No cancer.

And the next year, you guessed it. Cut open again, same breast, same diagnosis: No cancer.

Then in August 2006, I went in for my mammo. More of those microcalcifications—a lot this time, and in a suspicious constellation. Another biopsy. Three long days of calling the Dr. every few hours. Ultimately, same diagnosis: No cancer.

Not that I wished for cancer; that's plain stupid. But not having it meant going back to square one. Only I didn't want to go back there. I was tired. Tired of the anxiety each year leading up to the mammogram, tired of long-faced radiologists, tired of being cut on...tired, tired, tired.

After the last biopsy, I had to go in once a week to have fluid drained from my left breast. Three weeks later, when the swelling subsided, I stood in the mirror, horrified by what remained: The breast was about a half-cup size smaller than the other with a huge scar running under it. The nipple was misshapen and the area where they had cored out the breast tissue had basically shriveled up and collapsed in on itself. I sat on a stool in the closet and cried.

When I asked my doctor, Virgilio Sacchini, what we could do to fix the breast, he said we would have to use an implant, but then I could never have the less invasive biopsy again; I would be limited to the surgical kind, like the one I just had.

In that moment, the futility of it all hit me: At 43, I had to get off the merry-go-round. Instead of asking, "Is this the year I get breast cancer?" I had to say, "I will not get breast cancer this year. Or ever." That's when I decided to have the bilateral prophylactic mastectomy. It wasn't an easy decision.

DEC. 27 Mom went home today. I love her, but now I can really relax. Been thinking a lot about my breasts and what they mean to me. Will I feel differently when I don't have them? Will the new ones move like real breasts? I hear women talk about having these phantom pains postsurgery, or an itch way down deep that they can't scratch. Ugh, not looking forward to that.

JAN. 2 Seven days until surgery. My 10-year-old daughter asked me for a bra, even though our dining room table has more bumps than she does. How ironic that she's starting to think about breasts and I'm about to lose mine.

JAN. 3 It's down to the short strokes now—that's what Buff likes to say: a golf term for the swing you use when the ball is close to the hole.

I went to see Dr. Sacchini. He took a final look at my breasts, and we had one more detailed conversation about the operation. The next time I see him, we'll both be in surgical gowns and one of us will be getting ready for a four-hour nap.

Dr. Sacchini again promised to take good care of me. And just to make sure I wasn't going to change my mind, he ran over my non-surgical options, including tamoxifen and watchful waiting. Again we came to the conclusion that surgery is the way to go for me.

I then went on to Dr. Joseph Disa, the plastic surgeon. He's a young guy, and terribly good-looking. He went into more depth about what he'll actually do: Dr. S. will remove the breast tissue first. Then Dr. D. will take over, using a temporary implant partially filled with saline. Every couple of weeks after the surgery, I'll come in for a filling (like pumping a tire with air) until I get to the size I want to be. I think I'm going to stay roughly the way I am, even a bit smaller.

The interesting thing about today was how sure I feel about this decision now.

JAN. 3 Nighttime. Just got home. All the positive glow gone because Casey threw a frozen blueberry at Cole. He dodged it, fell, and hit his mouth on a metal table, chipping two teeth. Didn't look serious to me, but the dentist says, "Guess what? It is." He'll need the teeth filed down and bonded.

That's why I'm doing the surgery, so I can be around to break up fights and pick up the pieces for a long, long time.

JAN. 5 I'm baffled. I have not felt this good in years. The other day I was riding on the train, listening to "Optimistic," by Sounds of Blackness, and I just started crying like a big ol' fool, praying no one could see through my sunglasses as the tears streamed down my face. But here's the kicker: I wasn't crying because I was sad. I was crying because I'm so damn happy! How does that work? Here I am, fired from CBS and a job I love, facing major surgery, and yet I awake every morning with a smile and a song?

I have a couple of theories. Maybe I didn't love the job as much as I thought, and looking back on it now, the push may have been just what I needed— because I really wasn't allowed to be true to who I am. The box they had me in was getting smaller by the day. But that's a hard thing to admit to yourself. I think so many of us sleepwalk through life, afraid of the risks it takes to achieve success. Like rats in a science lab, we keep pressing the same lever, satisfied with the one pellet that comes out. Well, not me anymore. I feel the fresh air and am suddenly filled with excitement of where the next day might take me.

The other reason for my good mood, I think, is the way I'm taking control of my health. I see now that the specter of breast cancer has been permeating my life. I couldn't really *live* because I was always playing defense—watching and waiting, wondering if this would be the year I'd be diagnosed.

JAN. 6 Went to dinner with one of my best friends. As is our custom, we shared a bottle of wine and salad, and I had a slice of pizza. (Just an aside here: My diet has completely gone to hell—dessert after every meal, bread, pasta. It takes energy to maintain good eating habits and my energy now is directed into other parts of my life. So I'm cutting myself some slack for a while. And it feels GOOOOOOD!)

I had a chance to talk with both kids about the surgery. When I asked Casey if she knew what I was doing, she said, "Yeah, you're getting plastic boobs." There you go. She wanted to know if she would have to have plastic boobs someday, too, and I said, "No, not necessarily, but you will need to be screened sooner than your friends." Poor Casey will probably start having mammograms in her late 20s. That sucks. I thought about how my mother felt when she told me about her diagnosis.

Cole wanted to know if I could die. I said, "Yeah, some people do if they don't catch their breast cancer early." He was very somber, but then he asked, "No, can you die from having plastic boobs?" I tried not to laugh.

Today I'm going to type up some last-minute instructions for Buff, the babysitter, and the kids to help them get by while I'm gone.

JAN. 8 Well, there's no turning back now, although I must admit the thought crossed my mind today (only half-joking). My plan was to have a stress-free night, a nice dinner, and a little wine, without much whining.

None of the above.

Very busy from sunup to sundown. When Buff got home, we all gobbled prepared food off paper plates. Then the whining began. My daughter was angry because I said she had to read a book instead of watching TV. I explained why I made this decision and Buff started yelling, "This is not a negotiation!" I swear, can't we just have one night chaos-free? How about the night before I get my breasts cut off? Is that too much to ask?

I grabbed Cole's face today and asked him to be a good boy while I am gone. With his big brown eyes staring up at me, he promised he would be. What if tonight is the last time I see him?

JAN. 9 Leaving for the hospital. In the shower, I ran my hands over my breasts for what will be one of the last times ever. I looked at them, these sad, pitiful little things, pitted and scarred from years of being poked and cut open. I'm going to miss them. I prayed a lot. God, please take good care of me.

JAN. 10 Hospital room. I had a moment of panic before surgery. Lying on the table, I started to cry—it was all hitting me, I guess. But then I was out.

When I woke up, I felt like a truck had run over me, backed up, then put itself in drive and run over me again. Later I got up, had a shower (from the waist down), and got a first look at my new girls! They are incredible. They feel like two 500-pound boulders on my chest—completely disconnected from my body—but the plastic surgeon was able to repair the damage from past biopsies, something he wasn't sure was possible. I am thrilled. Both doctors have made me whole again.

The man I really need to thank, though, is my husband. Even though I called him Nurse Ratched, because trust me, he did have his moments, he came through like a champ. I almost forgive him for lying in my bed when they hauled me up from recovery and listening to FOX News Channel and eating potato chips from a crinkly bag when all I wanted was soft music and even softer-sounding food. I do love that man.

JAN. 13 First the good news: My doctor called me yesterday and said that there was no cancer in the tissue they removed. What a relief. Now the sobering news: They did find several areas of atypical ductal hyperplasia—and the frightening thing about that bit of information is that the hyperplasia was in the right breast, not the left one, which had been subjected to all the biopsies.

Clearly, this was the time to take action. ◑

> I HAD TO STOP ASKING, "IS THIS THE YEAR I GET BREAST CANCER?"

THE BREAST CANCER NOBODY IS TALKING ABOUT

The Question: Funmi Olopade, MD (*right*), at the University of Chicago Medical Center, was one of the first to ask why women like Angel Jacobs (*left*) and Lori Booker (*center*) are getting so sick, so young.

The news about breast cancer is good, and better all the time—except for one virulent, fast-acting type that attacks more than twice as many young black women as all other women. Mary A. Fischer delves into a highly charged medical mystery.

I n May 2006, as she was getting dressed for work, Lori Booker felt a small lump in her left breast. Only 32, she was concerned but thought it was probably just a cyst, and made an appointment to see her gynecologist. With a demanding job as a computer teacher at a Chicago public high school, Lori missed a couple of appointments, and two months later, when she finally had her first mammogram, the lump had doubled in size. A biopsy came back with grim results: She had aggressive, advanced-stage breast cancer. Crying, Lori thought the lab must have made a mistake. "I'm too young for this," she sobbed.

Angel Jacobs, 29, figured the same thing. A single mother of a 3-year-old, she was sure what she felt in her right breast was nothing to be anxious about, but an ultrasound found a tumor. It turned out to be the same type as Lori Booker's.

A decade ago, the fact that both of these women were under 35 would have surprised oncologist Olufunmilayo Olopade, MD, director of the Cancer Risk Clinic at the University of Chicago

Medical Center. But not anymore. Lori and Angel are like many of the breast cancer patients Olopade (nicknamed Funmi) has seen, both in her native Nigeria, where she studied medicine, and on Chicago's South Side—women who are black, unusually young, and diagnosed with aggressive "triple negative" tumors that are difficult to treat.

"I had never heard of that type of cancer before," Lori recalls. "I was scared. It made me think I was a triple loser."

THE LAST DECADE has delivered increasingly good news about breast cancer. Although the disease is expected to strike an estimated 240,510 American women this year, the majority are diagnosed after menopause and have tumors that can be treated with a combination of chemo and the latest hormone or targeted therapies. For the most common kind of breast cancer—hormone receptor positive (meaning tumor growth is driven by estrogen or progesterone)—drugs like tamoxifen and Femara have boosted survival rates. Herceptin, a breakthrough targeted drug, improved

43

the outlook for HER2-positive tumors, which have an excess of a protein called human epidermal growth factor receptor 2.

None of the new treatments, however, can touch breast cancers that test negative for estrogen, progesterone, or HER2; the only option for such triple negative cases is chemotherapy, which may or may not work.

Striking the young and spreading rapidly, this type of virulent breast cancer was hardly a blip on the radar of oncology research until about five years ago, when groundbreaking studies by Olopade and others brought it to the attention of the medical community.

The daughter of an Anglican minister, Olopade came to the United States in 1982 hoping to coax her brother back home after he finished graduate school here. During her visit, though, political unrest in Nigeria worsened and she decided to stay put and complete her residency at Chicago's Cook County Hospital. Later she joined the faculty at the University of Chicago as a professor of medicine and human genetics. It was on a trip home to Nigeria for a niece's wedding in 1997 that Olopade visited a cancer clinic and paused when she passed the women in the waiting room—they were all so young. *What is this about?* she wondered. "It was the same thing I was seeing with my patients back in Chicago." Later she decided to initiate a study. A collaborating doctor collected tumor samples from 378 women in Nigeria and Senegal and brought them back to her lab. This was a big step. "In some African languages," says Olopade, "there are no words for 'breast cancer.'"

After her research team analyzed the tissue samples and compared them with those of more than 900 Canadian women primarily of European descent, Olopade was amazed by the results. The tumors in the African women were very different, a whole other form of the disease. They often lacked estrogen receptors and were more likely to originate from the outer basal cells of the breast rather than the more usual inner milk-secreting luminal cells. A landmark study by researchers at the University of North Carolina-Lineberger Comprehensive Cancer Center in 2006 found that, remarkably, this basal-like "triple negative" subtype showed up in 39 percent of the study's premenopausal women who were African-American, compared with only 16 percent in those who weren't. A larger study published this summer in the journal *Cancer* confirmed that in the United States black women overall are twice as likely to have triple negative tumors as white women. In general, this type of breast cancer has one of the worst survival rates. These findings help explain why young black women are more likely to get breast cancer early—ten, 20, 30 years before menopause—and have nearly double the odds of dying from it.

What causes this aggressive cancer, and why would it affect one population more than another? One clue may be the BRCA1 gene. "Women who have mutations of this gene are at higher risk of getting breast cancer," says Ruth O'Regan, MD, associate professor of hematology and oncology at the Emory Winship Cancer Institute in Atlanta. "And that mutant gene also appears to play a role in these triple negative cancers. But exactly how is not clear."

Mary Jo Lund, PhD, research assistant professor at the Rollins School of Public Health at Emory, coauthored two studies of women in Atlanta to see whether economics plays a role in triple negative disease. "Even when we adjusted for socioeconomic status and delayed access to healthcare," she says, "black women were twice as likely as white women to have triple negative tumors. So it is not just about poverty. There appear to be true biological differences."

Still, she and other oncology researchers, including Olopade, who received a $500,000 MacArthur award in 2005 for her work, remain convinced that some interaction between genetics and the environment triggers the disease. As a result, some researchers are now exploring how prolonged stress—from factors like income deprivation, social isolation, and exposure to violence—may be altering the body's biochemistry to produce gene mutations.

Lund goes on to quote a colleague who said, "I can't help but think that if these prevalences had been seen in white women, we'd have already found new targeted treatments for these tumors." Asked if she believes that's true, Carolyn Runowicz, MD, past president of the American Cancer Society, counters, "It's not that researchers are dragging their feet. The technical ability to diagnose cancer subtypes like triple negative tumors has only emerged in the last decade." And many African-Americans may be wary of participating in clinical trials—a suspicion that dates back to the notorious Tuskegee experiment, in which 399 unwitting black men with syphilis were used as guinea pigs in a government-sponsored study. For 40 years beginning in 1932, researchers withheld treatment so they could study the progress of the disease, and many of the men died.

When Karen Neely, 35, an African-American corporate defense lawyer in Atlanta, was diagnosed with triple negative breast cancer in June 2006, she quickly discovered that tamoxifen, Herceptin, and other targeted drugs would not be part of her treatment. Neely's cancer was caught early, and after four cycles of chemotherapy followed by a lumpectomy and radiation, she is cancer-free. But she knows that her disease is more likely to return after two years than hormone-driven cancers. "I do a lot of praying," says Neely, who started Triple Pink, a nonprofit organization devoted to educating and raising research funds for her kind of cancer.

Lori Booker and Angel Jacobs weren't as lucky. Diagnosed with advanced tumors that had spread to their lymph nodes, they both underwent mastectomies. Angel is being treated experimentally with specific chemotherapy drugs that kill off connections between the tumors and their blood vessels. She is also participating in Olopade's $9.7 million study at the University of Chicago, funded by the National Institutes of Health, in which researchers are examining various medical and social factors affecting triple negative women both in Nigeria and Chicago. Other researchers are looking for clues to help doctors recognize the disease long before the tumors develop with the goal of finding an effective treatment.

In the meantime, Olopade wants women to know that a diagnosis of triple negative cancer is "not a death sentence. It's aggressive but can be treated," she says. "The earlier the detection, the better." Most of the current general screening guidelines—including an annual mammogram beginning at age 40—are primarily drawn from data based on Caucasians, according to Olopade. That's clearly too late for some women. "If you're at risk," she says, "you don't want to wait until you're 40 to be screened."

As for Lori and Angel, they have their good days and bad days. In Lori's case, she went through a particularly difficult patch when she and her boyfriend broke up and her beloved cat died. Through her tears, she asks: "Is there something I did to get this type of cancer? Is it the food I ate? Something in the water? Stress from my job? What's really going on here?"

Researchers are racing to find out. The answers, they say, could be just around the corner. ◘

HOW TO TAKE CARE OF YOUR BEAUTIFUL MIND

Do you ever have those moments when you feel you're losing it? You're totally overwhelmed, or you're soaking in sadness, or everyone's driving you nuts. You're having a really bad day...or month...or life. Well, hold on! We've got some important answers for you, starting with a mental health kit of proven techniques to bring you back from the edge, center you, help you breathe again....If you think psychotherapy is only for the seriously batty, a psychiatrist in training takes you behind closed doors to hear how three women learned to untangle the past and live their best lives now. And even for those who have to deal with severe emotional chaos, therapy combined with advances in medication is creating a way out and a way forward—as a highly successful artist who has bipolar disorder tells us with remarkable candor. Here's to clarity, calm, and the joy and power of knowing yourself.

O'S MENTAL HEALTH KIT

For those times when your mind is addled, your heart feels turbulent, your center is shaky—a little black bag full of cures, from experts who are devoted to keeping us all in beautiful balance.

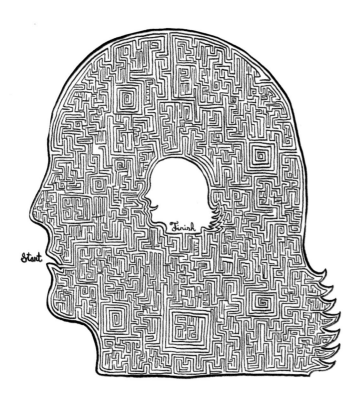

MORNING DREAD 7 WAYS TO RESTART A DAY

You've just woken up, and you're on the wrong side of the bed. Is there any way to switch to the other side? Absolutely.

1 AS SOON AS THE ALARM RINGS: Spend your first 15 seconds awake planning something nice to do for yourself today. "This can really set you up in a good mood—even if it's just going by the farmers' market and getting fresh strawberries," says Alice Domar, PhD, coauthor of *Be Happy Without Being Perfect: How to Break Free from the Perfection Deception*.

2 GET UP. The longer you lie there, the more you ruminate, the darker your outlook is likely to become, says Christine Padesky, PhD, coauthor of *Mind Over Mood*. So get vertical and make a cup of coffee, take a shower, feed the cat…

3 …AND DRINK—make that two glasses of water upon awakening, the time when our bodies are dehydrated, says Susan M. Kleiner, PhD, coauthor of *The Good Mood Diet*.

Dehydration causes fatigue, which affects your mood.

4 MOVE IT. You already know the number one way of chasing away a bad mood: exercise. A workout at the gym sure helps. But even just a few minutes of movement—a fast walk, for example—raises energy and reduces tension, says mood expert Robert Thayer, PhD, professor of psychology at California State University, Long Beach, and author of *Calm Energy*.

5 INVESTIGATE. When you're dogged by anxiety or the dread you woke up with, try to pinpoint what's causing it. Did someone say anything the day before? Do you have a meeting today you wish you didn't? Was it the dream you were having when the alarm went off? "If you can figure out why you're upset, that's halfway to feeling better," says Domar.

6 BE KIND AND THANKFUL. This isn't exactly news, but generosity and gratitude are both big contributors to happiness, according to

Todd B. Kashdan, PhD, who directs the Laboratory for the Study of Social Anxiety, Character Strengths, and Related Phenomena at George Mason University in Fairfax, Virginia. Do something nice for a stranger or friend and see if you don't feel better about yourself. Also jot down three things that you're grateful for. It seems so simple, but counting your blessings just has a way of making you remember the sun is shining.

7 LAUGH AT YOURSELF. The best comedians point out the mundane aspects of life—relationship strife, a boring job, a closet full of too-tight clothes; they exaggerate those circumstances, and give us a perspective we can laugh about, says Mark Ridley, owner of the Comedy Castle in Royal Oak, Michigan. Look at your own life and try to appreciate the absurdity of what doesn't go exactly according to plan (the diets, the men, the buzz cut). Acknowledging how little control we actually have over what happens is sometimes a most freeing gift to yourself. —Kathryn Matthews

ANGER 5 WAYS TO DERAIL RAGE

For the third time now, the hardware store clerk has brought you the wrong lightbulb, maybe because she still hasn't gotten off her [@#*!] cell phone. Bad service isn't a crime, but it sure can make you want to commit one, as can any number of daily irritants (being cut off on the highway, just missing the train). Americans report losing their temper on average three to four times a week, according to Raymond W. Novaco, PhD, the University of California, Irvine, psychology and social behavior professor who coined the term "anger management" in 1975. To cool down fast:

1 CALL IT: The minute you feel your temperature rise, tell yourself, "I'm bothered, and that may blur my judgment," Novaco suggests.

2 DON'T WAIT TO INHALE: Each of us has a unique anger threshold based on chemicals like serotonin, says Emil Coccaro, MD, chair of the department of psychiatry at the University of Chicago, where he runs an aggression research lab. Depending on the kind of day you're having, your arousal varies, and when it's high, it's easier to explode. Regular exercise and relaxation practices can help you lower your arousal level

and, in turn, stay below your breaking point so you're more immune to rude remarks and other daily aggravations. If you do feel yourself getting worked up, just start breathing deeply to calm down: Imagine the breath going in and out through your heart while thinking about something in your life with appreciation, suggests Deborah Rozman, PhD, a California psychologist and coauthor of *Transforming Stress: The HeartMath Solution for Relieving Worry, Fatigue, and Tension,* who has successfully tested this approach in clinical trials. After just five cycles, your system should be back to a more emotionally balanced, even keel.

3 NOTE TO SELF: "I'm great." At the root of anger is self-doubt—a salesperson's incompetence doesn't throw you into a rage unless you're feeling helpless, harried, overextended, or otherwise victimized—says Steven Stosny, PhD, a Maryland anger specialist who has treated more than 6,000 people and written *You Don't Have to Take It Anymore*. So as soon as you start bristling, turn your mind to whatever or whoever makes you feel good about yourself—an achievement, future goals, a pet—as long as it has nothing to do with the

issue at hand. The quick shift in focus can snap you out of a temper flare.

4 THINK OF SOMETHING FUNNY: If you're already in a full-throttle rage, you can startle yourself out of it with humor, says Coccaro. One old trick is to imagine the person who's enraging you standing there buck naked—maybe they even slip on a banana peel or get a pie thrown in their face. Another standby is to remember your favorite comedic moment (*I Love Lucy* in the candy factory? Jerry Seinfeld yada-yada-yada-ing? Chris Rock's last concert? Any 2-year-old eating a cupcake?).

5 CLEAR YOUR MIND: At high levels of arousal, thinking gets fuzzy (attention narrows, and we're operating from our primitive fight-or-flight instinct). To cut through the fog, have questions ready to ask yourself, Stosny suggests: If there's an aggressor, what are at least two reasons this person might be acting out? In a traffic jam, acknowledge the frustration of the situation with a quick mental note—"So here we are"—and then jump to "How am I going to get on with it?"
—Sara Reistad-Long

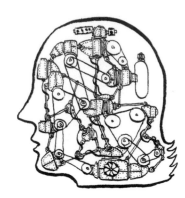

DEPRESSION 5 WAYS TO BREAK A DOWNWARD SPIRAL

Sometimes a funk can equal more than the sum of its parts. For instance, you wake up to discover there's no milk for your coffee, the highway is backed up so you're late for work, and you're sinking into another bad—and worsening—day.

You don't have to go there. It's not the events themselves but the way the mind reacts to them that can cause a minor annoyance to snowball into an all-encompassing black mood—good news because, while you can't control traffic or someone hogging the milk, you can change how you respond when things go wrong.

1 THE FACTS, PLEASE: Downward spirals are often provoked by jumping to the worst-case conclusion. You make a beeline from a boss's critical e-mail right to "I'm going to be fired." Or you take a friend's failure to call as a sure sign she doesn't like you anymore. But the boss's complaint is probably just business as usual; the friend is simply distracted by a problem in her own life that has nothing to do with you. So before taking a flight of bad fancy, reread the boss's e-mail more carefully (you may be surprised to find positive comments you hadn't noticed before), and review all possible explanations. Who knows, maybe she was just stressed out by her boss.

2 LET IT BE: Humans are highly evolved problem solvers. No sooner do we experience a negative emotion than we feel compelled to fix it. Usually that urge goes with the assumption that there's something wrong with us for feeling blue, which only compounds the depression.

Another problem is that by trying to think our way out of sadness, we paradoxically fuel it. "The more you feed these downward cycles with attention, the more you allow them to proliferate," says *The Mindful Way Through Depression* coauthor Zindel Segal, PhD. "The negative ideas and experiences will just multiply, spinning from one thing to two things to four things to eight things." Instead, he suggests accepting your sadness as a natural state, experiencing it in the moment, and allowing it to pass. This doesn't mean letting yourself slide passively into a deeper slump but, rather, engaging with your feelings in a mindful way. The following meditation exercise can help you do this:

Sit comfortably, close your eyes, and take a few full, slow breaths. Bring to mind the difficulty you're struggling with (the boss's e-mail, the incommunicado friend). Now let your attention sink into your body. Take note of any physical sensations that arise—tension, pressure, shakiness, aching—especially in the throat, chest, and stomach. After you identify where the sensations are strongest, focus there in an attitude of acceptance, even embrace. Try breathing as if the air is going in and out of that area, and as you do, observe any changes— are the sensations more intense, for example, or less? If your mind drifts back to your difficulty, simply notice the thoughts (self-flagellating? plotting revenge?) and return your focus to your body.

It's important to realize that this process won't get rid of your feelings, but it should help them pass more quickly. One of the most common mistakes we make when we fall into a funk is to think that the unhappiness will persist, says Matthew McKay, PhD, coauthor of *Thoughts & Feelings: Taking Control of Your Moods & Your Life.* Knowing it's transient will keep you from getting pulled down further.

3 PENCIL IN A GOOD TIME: When you are tugged by depression, not only does the world seem crummy but you don't want to do the very things that could make you feel better, like seeing friends or getting a massage. Research strongly suggests, however, that planning and engaging in an activity you find enjoyable or meaningful can break a negative mood slide. So as soon as you find your spirits sinking, make an appointment for a Swedish rubdown or schedule dinner with a great friend— even if you can't get out and do anything right now, the planning should help distract you from your misery.

4 MOVE: Depression also pushes exercise to the back burner, despite its being one of the most effective stimulants of a good mood. To slip through this Catch-22, forget the idea of jogging for an hour or slogging to the gym. Science has now shown that even ten- to 20-minute bouts of exercise can provide physical benefits as well as mood-boosting effects— and a brisk walk to look at a neighbor's garden or a bike ride to the bookstore both count. "The first few minutes of preparing for activity are the most difficult," says Kristin Vickers Douglas, PhD, a psychologist at the Mayo Clinic in Rochester, Minnesota, who has been studying the benefits of exercise for depression. "Focus just on the five minutes it will take to put your shoes on and get out the door." Once you're outside, your momentum will likely carry you. It can also be helpful to recruit a friend to join you.

5 TAKE ACTION: Escaping the downward spiral is just the first step. Once you've recovered some degree of internal equilibrium, consider what action you might need to take. Perhaps it's relatively minor, along the lines of scheduling a talk with your boss to discuss your report in more detail. Or you may need to think about serious life changes, like looking for a new job or a new husband. Now that you're in a grounded state of mind, you can draw on your inner wisdom to act not reactively, but skillfully.
—Gabrielle Leblanc

RIGIDITY 4 WAYS TO KEEP YOUR BRAIN LIMBER

We are creatures of habit; we love a good routine because doing the same old same old doesn't take much mental effort. But getting stuck in certain ways of thinking can hinder our ability to both enjoy and respond effectively to new situations. Like a body, the mind needs regular stretching to stay agile and resilient.

People, by nature, are more or less receptive to new activities and ideas. "Open" types are typically imaginative, creative, intellectually curious, and hold unconventional beliefs compared with "closed" types, who tend to resist change. Although you don't have to have an "open" personality to be mentally healthy, experts say that anecdotally in cases where close-minded people are forced to become more flexible in their approach to the world—by a shattering event, for example—they report that life is richer and more fulfilling as a result. Fortunately, all it takes to keep your mind limber is…

1 INSIGHT: We each have a book of rules in our head about how we "should" behave—"I've got to be perfect," "Never ask for help," "I always put others ahead of myself." Start trying to pinpoint the rules that drive you, and write them down (we're not saying this is easy, but once you start looking, you may be surprised at what you discover). For each, ask: "Does it serve me and enhance my life? Or is it one I'm following because I'm afraid not to?" If the rule belongs to the latter category, question it. For example, if you "never ask friends for help," why not? Are you afraid that they might reject your request? Or that you'll end up feeling beholden to them? You could be right, so test the rule by asking a good friend for a small favor. You may find that your request is cheerfully granted, and that your friendship deepens rather than becomes tense as a result.

2 BEHAVIOR: If a night out usually means dinner and a movie, buy tickets for a flamenco performance instead. Drive the slow, scenic road to work versus the highway. Take a class in a subject that interests you but has nothing to do with your job. When you follow a routine, your brain can operate in low-energy mode, via relatively primitive structures known as the basal ganglia, says Jeffrey Schwartz, MD, coauthor of *The Mind and the Brain: Neuroplasticity and the Power of Mental Force.* In contrast, new activities engage the prefrontal cortex, an evolutionarily younger area that needs more energy to function. That's why breaking a routine may feel hard—but if you push past that effort, Schwartz says, new experiences can help stimulate fresh states of mind that leave you feeling both more focused and energized.

3 EMOTION: The next time you have a bad day, resist the urge to retreat to the TV or an extra glass of wine. Instead, let yourself sense any anger, disappointment, sadness, whatever is going on in you. Write the feelings down, talk about them to a friend, or simply sit with closed eyes and allow them to be (for a meditation exercise, see "5 Ways to Break a Downward Spiral,"). According to personality researchers, the willingness to experience both positive and negative feelings is another factor that distinguishes extremely open people from closed ones; it's also associated with increased longevity after heart problems, according to a recent study at Duke University. On the flip side, denying emotions is a well-known driver of addictions.

4 FOCUS: The way we pay attention to the world can make a huge difference in the way we experience it. "Many adults in our culture are addicted to a very narrowly focused attentional style in which we beam-in sequentially on the tasks of work, shopping, paying our bills, and so on," says Les Fehmi, PhD, coauthor of *The Open-Focus Brain: Harnessing the Power of Attention to Heal Mind and Body.* This gripping form of attention, which can be identified by a characteristic brain wave pattern on an electroencephalogram (EEG), is the mode we typically use when poring over a written report or staring into a computer monitor at the office. It's tiring to sustain (doing so often requires periodic infusions of caffeine and sugar), and is correlated with physiological reactions such as muscle tension, stress hormone secretion, and increased blood pressure, all of which take a toll on our health. This kind of attention can also wreak havoc on our relationships—what romantic partner wants to be scrutinized with the same intensity that we direct toward an important work assignment? Yet because we're called on to use the narrow focus so much, it's hard to let go of.

Only on vacation do many of us broaden our awareness to include the smell of pine trees, the crunch of pebbles underfoot, the way a color mutes in the rain—a mode of taking in the world that Fehmi calls open-focus attention. This mode is correlated with more synchronous EEG patterns (the famous alpha activity) and physiological relaxation. You can get a small sense of it by trying this exercise: Close your eyes and let your mind respond to the following series of questions, allowing about 15 seconds for each. There are no correct answers. Simply notice whatever sensations or feelings arise.

CAN YOU IMAGINE…
- the space between your eyes?
- the space inside your nose as you inhale and exhale naturally?
- the space occupied by your jaw?
- the space inside your throat, expanding until your entire neck is filled with space?
- the space inside your throat and neck expanding to fill the entire region of your shoulders?
- the space that your whole body occupies expanding out into the room?

Preliminary clinical research suggests that practicing exercises like this can reduce muscular tension, anxiety, and depression, and improve intellectual performance. —G.L.

ANXIETY 5 WAYS TO CALM THE JITTERS

Sweaty palms, jagged nerves, choking insecurity: Level orange. Heart pounding out of your chest: Level red. Most of us know what it is to feel like a walking Homeland Security alert system. In fact, an estimated 40 million Americans suffer from anxiety disorders, and millions more face the everyday panic that comes with job interviews, public speaking, entering a party, and other stressful situations. What's surprising, especially to the highly strung, is that we don't have to live with it.

1 ACCEPT THAT YOU'RE HAVING AN ANXIETY MOMENT:: Allow yourself to be nervous—trying to squelch or deny it will only make it worse—and just focus on what's in front of you, says David Barlow, PhD, founder of the Center for Anxiety and Related Disorders at Boston University. If you're at an interview, meeting, or party, listen intently to what the other person is saying. Make eye contact. When it's your turn to speak, be conscious of every word you say. If you're at your desk, respond to overdue e-mails or tackle the pile in your in-box. Whatever you're doing, take a few deep breaths to help let the anxious thoughts and feelings float on by.

2 STOP TRYING TO BE PERFECT: "Almost by definition, if you're anxious, you're being overly perfectionistic in the goals you're setting for yourself," Barlow says. "You see all the ways you won't meet them, the thought of failure makes you anxious, and anxiety makes you think the worst." Look at the hard evidence from past experiences. Honestly, have you ever been laughed out of a job interview or a work presentation for not getting every word just so? "Most of the time, people will see that things went all right, even if they thought they could have done better," says Barlow. "Tell yourself, 'It's extremely unlikely that anything will ever go as badly as I think.' "

3 AND STOP BEING SO NICE: When you find yourself on edge for no obvious reason, it's your body's way of signaling there's a problem you're avoiding, says David Burns, MD, author of *When Panic Attacks: The New Drug-Free Anxiety Therapy That Can Change Your Life*. Most anxiety-prone people try so hard to be agreeable, he says, that when confronted with an upsetting situation (being denied a promotion though they know they deserve one, for example), they'll sweep their feelings under the rug rather than stand up for themselves. Look back over the last week or so, he suggests, to see if something like this happened, then take steps to express your thoughts and resolve the situation.

4 TAKE A WALK ON THE MINDFUL SIDE: "Whether a threat is from a scary thought or an actual danger, your body tenses up," says Jeffrey Brantley, MD, director of the Mindfulness-Based Stress Reduction Program at Duke Integrative Medicine and author of *Calming Your Anxious Mind*. A walking meditation sends an instant message that it's okay to relax. To begin, turn your attention to your right foot. Slowly start to walk, noting every sensation as your foot lifts up, swings forward, and settles to the floor. Do the same with your left foot, observing and allowing whatever thoughts and feelings arise. Keep moving until you feel the sense of urgency ebb. "Walking like this helps restore balance so you can gain some insight into what's bothering you," says Brantley.

5 FACE YOUR FEAR: If there's a specific activity like public speaking that always makes you break into a cold sweat, try a technique used by cognitive-behavioral therapists: First do something similar but less frightening (making a toast each night at dinner), then gradually move your way through more nerve-racking occasions (giving a toast at a wedding, guest-teaching a class). "Your fear diminishes with each step," says Martin Antony, PhD, professor of psychology at Ryerson University in Ontario, so by the time you get to the original alarming activity, it will feel less overwhelming. It helps to progress quickly through the list and practice as frequently as possible, he adds: Research shows that this is one of the best ways to reduce anxiety. —Naomi Barr

OBSESSION 6 WAYS TO STOP DWELLING ON IT

EXAMPLE A: It's 5 p.m., the deadline for an important work project is at 6, and all you can think about is the fight you had with the next-door neighbor this morning. You're dwelling, says Susan Nolen-Hoeksema, PhD, a professor of psychology at Yale and author of *Women Who Think Too Much*. "It's natural to look inward," she says, "but while most people pull out when they've done it enough, an overthinker will stay in the loop." Ruminating regularly often leads to depression. So if you're prone to obsessing (and you know who you are), try these tactics to head off the next full-tilt mental spin cycle:

1 DISTRACT YOURSELF: Put on music and dance, scrub the bathtub spotless, whatever engrosses you—for at least ten minutes. "That's about the minimum time needed to break a cycle of thoughts," says Nolen-Hoeksema, who's been studying rumination for more than 20 years. Or choose something to focus on. "A friend told me that she once started counting the number of times the speaker at her conference said 'like,' " Nolen-Hoeksema recalls. "By the time he finished, she'd stopped ruminating."

2 MAKE A DATE TO DWELL: Tell yourself you can obsess all you want from 6 p.m. to 7 p.m., but until then, you're banned. "By 6 p.m., you'll probably be able to think things through more clearly," says Nolen-Hoeksema.

3 TAKE A 3-MINUTE DOSE OF MINDFULNESS: For one minute, eyes closed, acknowledge all the thoughts going through your mind. For the next minute, just focus on your breathing. Spend the last minute expanding your awareness from your breath to your entire body. "Paying attention in this way gives you the room to see the questions you're asking yourself with less urgency and to reconsider them from a different perspective," says Zindel Segal, PhD, coauthor of *The Mindful Way Through Depression*.

4 ASK YOURSELF: "What's the worst that could happen?" and "How would I cope?" Visualizing yourself handling the most extreme outcome should alleviate some anxiety, says Judith Beck, PhD, director of the Beck Institute for Cognitive Therapy and Research in Bala Cynwyd, Pennsylvania. Then consider the likelihood that the worst will actually occur. Next, imagine the best possible outcome; by this point, you'll be in a more positive frame of mind and better able to assess the situation more realistically.

5 CALL A BUDDY: Ask a friend or relative to be your point person when your thoughts start to speed out of control.

6 SAY "OH, WELL": Accept that you're human and make mistakes—and then move on, says Beck. Be compassionate. It's harder than it sounds, so keep practicing. —N.B.

HELP!

Whether you've tripped into a black hole of depression or simply feel that your life has become one big rut, psychiatrist-in-training *Christine Montross* explains how going into therapy can get you back on solid ground—then listens in as three women and their therapists talk candidly about how the process works.

In my first year of training as a psychiatric resident, a friend called to ask whether I thought she needed to be on an antidepressant. She'd been dating the same man for several years, and despite the fact that nothing in the relationship had recently changed, she was feeling mounting anxiety about its future. "Some days I have this impulse to just end things with him," she said, "and other times I wonder if I just want out because I'm afraid *he's* going to leave *me*." I could hear the stress and emotion in her voice, which suddenly got uncharacteristically quiet. "I've been pretty miserable lately."

I was quiet for a second, too. Then I asked if she'd thought of talking her problems over with a therapist. And just like that, her voice was back to its full decibel range, and fully indignant. "What, you think I'm crazy?"

I laughed. I assured her I didn't. But it wasn't the first time I'd heard this response to what seemed to me to be a most logical suggestion.

Maybe people genuinely believe that therapy is helpful only to those who are severely mentally ill. In fact, the opposite tends to be true. The decision to go into therapy is often an emblem of sanity, a marker that a person is wise enough to know when she needs some help and support, and responsible enough to get it.

There is no set list of issues that require therapy, but there is a common reason to begin: A problem looms large, and there are no good solutions in sight. For the millions of women who suffer from depression or anxiety, the central issue may be the sometimes-crippling impact of those illnesses. Women with depression may lose interest in activities that once brought them pleasure. They may sleep too much, or not enough. They might feel hopeless or helpless. In the most extreme cases, they may have thoughts of killing themselves. Women with anxiety may be plagued by excessive or unrealistic worry that can cause shortness of breath, diarrhea, sweating, or panic attacks.

For others who seek therapy, the trigger is not the debilitating symptoms of mental illness but rather ordinary life—the quotidian problems that make us feel sad or helpless or interfere with our ability to be happy and productive. We are each, of course, differently equipped to handle challenges. The same woman who confidently navigates a career change might find herself unexpectedly devastated by her mother's death, while a woman whose marriage has always been a solid source of comfort and strength may find her partnership unmoored when she is unable to conceive a child.

By its very nature, the therapy relationship is targeted toward just this individuality. And by this I mean that when you enter into therapy, those sessions are a time and place wholly *for you*. Therapy is focused on helping you understand your feelings and, if need be, changing your behavior. The issues you face may involve others in your life—a difficult boss, an aging parent, a distant spouse—but you and your therapist will focus on how to steady your own life, regardless of the storms that rage around you. In other words, therapy is focused on helping you understand who you are.

At first blush, this kind of goal may seem abstract and ethereal, even flighty and aimless—calling to mind the teenager who drops out of school to "find herself" while hitchhiking to California. And who has the time or money for such self-indulgence?

In reality, it is hard to imagine a more pragmatic and worthy task. With a clear sense of yourself, it becomes easier and easier to grasp why you feel the things you feel, and why you react to your emotions the way you do. Your behaviors and the decisions you have made in your life begin to emerge in comprehensible patterns. And once you can identify the patterns, and the emotions and actions that bring them about, you can begin to steer your life toward those patterns that give you fulfillment and away from those that are stagnant or even harmful.

Which is not to say that therapy isn't work, or that it doesn't require looking at yourself with unflinching honesty, because it is, and it does. And although the therapist is there to guide you, he or she cannot do the work for you. One of my mentors in psychiatric training once told me, "You should never work harder than the patient." Not because a therapist isn't willing to dive with you fully into the struggle but because, in the end, the struggle belongs to the one who must live it.

SO, WHEN THERAPY IS WORKING PROPERLY, there is not a smidge of self-indulgence around. It is sometimes uncomfortable—we are, for the most part, unaccustomed to scrutinizing our deepest selves, let alone sharing the view. And that type of truthful assessment can be scary. Often, when a problem seems thorny enough to merit therapy, the feeling is a bit like being stuck in a foxhole in the middle of a war: The situation becomes more and more miserable, but the thought of leaving it is utterly terrifying. (This may help explain why, according to psychologist and marriage expert John Gottman, PhD, couples are unhappy with their relationships for an average of six years before they seek help.)

Therapy can also be draining—some patients cry the whole session, every session. Others find it exhausting to constantly be asked to identify and articulate their feelings about the situations they describe. But as is true with many things in life, from triathlons to flawless presentations to raising children, great effort can translate into great reward. There is a kind of exhilaration that comes with each new moment of self-knowledge, and an enormous sense of relief and joy when the most impenetrable problems begin to crack open.

From a scientific standpoint, there is researched evidence that therapy is effective; that it can decrease physical pain, nausea, and fatigue; that it improves quality of life for people with cancer; that it actually *restructures the pathways of neurons in the brain* so that cognitive and behavioral patterns that have been deeply entrenched for years are rerouted.

And then there is evidence of the less scientific kind: a friend whose panic attacks stopped when her therapist taught her relaxation techniques; a family on the verge of rupture who learned in counseling how to be happily and deeply involved in one another's lives; an acquaintance who tells me she did not know who she was until she gave herself the gift of therapy to find out.

CASE IN POINT "THE LIGHT HAD JUST SEEMED TO GO OUT OF ME"

Olivia* was a 42-year-old working mother, married with three children, when she entered psychodynamic therapy—a form of traditional talk therapy—with Peggy Edwards, a licensed clinical social worker in Indianapolis. Here, Olivia and Peggy tell O how, for the past five years, therapy has been a safe place for Olivia to address her depression and, in the process, figure out how to trust herself and feel satisfied with the direction she has chosen for her life.

OLIVIA: At first I was a little embarrassed at the thought of going into therapy, because I hadn't suffered any major traumatic life event that seemed to warrant seeing someone. I had a loving husband and three wonderful daughters and a job that I enjoyed, but I just didn't feel content and I couldn't understand why I wasn't happier. There were times when I was depressed. It wasn't so bad that I gained weight or couldn't eat or get out of bed, but certainly I wasn't myself. I'm pretty positive and happy-go-lucky, but the light had just seemed to go out of me.

I had also suffered from postpartum depression, so I was on an antidepressant before I saw Peggy. I think at this point it may be more socially acceptable to be on an antidepressant than to go to therapy. But I felt it was necessary to take a two-pronged approach.
PEGGY: People enter therapy for so many different reasons. They might feel stuck in their career or relationships. They might feel unhappy or anxious. They might find themselves getting mired in the same kinds of conflicts over and over. They might lack the ability to figure out how to do things differently so they don't keep stepping in the same hole. My training has been in psychodynamic therapy, which attributes a person's emotional problems to her unconscious motives and conflicts. Often those motives and conflicts have roots in one's childhood. In therapy we try to develop insight by bringing what was unconscious into consciousness. I help people look at the patterns in their relationships and the ways in which those patterns create glitches in their life. The patient gains insight into her behaviors and can begin to work on changing them.
OLIVIA: One of my problems had always been accepting criticism from my mother, because she can be hypercritical. She'd criticize me, I'd bristle and become confrontational, and we'd both walk away unhappy. I thought our interactions would go on the same way until the day I died or she died. But Peggy helped me see that while I couldn't control her criticism, I could control the way I reacted.
PEGGY: We've worked a lot on that. With a mother who pushed her to be the best and placed great importance on looks and how people perceived her, Olivia was always looking for affirmation from others to feel good about herself. Despite success in many areas of her life, she felt empty and unfulfilled.
OLIVIA: I think I was almost obsessed with what other people thought of me. But Peggy has never been judgmental. Of course, opening up to someone you don't know that well is challenging.

*Names and some identifying details have been changed.

You have to get beyond the fact that you're telling someone the most personal things about your life, and you have to feel confident that they won't be spilling your secrets at a cocktail party. With Peggy I had that trust.

Our sessions have always felt like a place of refuge, and right away I felt accepted by her. I don't have to impress her. Before therapy I always believed that to get people to like me, I had to accomplish things. But she'll say, "Look, you're *relating* to people. They like *who* you are, and it doesn't matter to them what you accomplish."

PEGGY: One of the things Olivia has always been very good at—and it's sometimes very hard for people—is a necessary component of therapy: feeling that you can talk about anything with the therapist. That includes anything about the therapist and the therapy relationship. The whole idea of transference—where patients unconsciously project onto the therapist their ideas and feelings about significant people in their lives—is an important part of what we discuss. In Olivia's case, transference has been especially helpful in dealing with her mother issues. She could see me in something of a maternal role that was very different from what she's used to. And experiencing acceptance from me has allowed her to accept herself more, thereby reducing her depression, which I believe was fueled by a pervasive drive to succeed at all costs.

OLIVIA: I used to think it was the therapist's job to give you answers. But what Peggy does is help me come to my own answers. She asks me what I think. And at first, it was almost like: What does it matter what I think? What does my mom think? What does my boss think? What does my husband think? Therapy has focused on how I need to live my life based on what *I* think is important. Because otherwise I'm just going to be chasing my tail trying to please others—which I may or may not be able to accomplish. I don't want that anymore. I want to try to feel happy with my efforts and not be such a perfectionist. I still struggle with that, but Peggy says, "Olivia, you're too hard on yourself.... Olivia, why isn't that enough?" And when I don't have a good answer, I realize that I've got to let it go.

PEGGY: Without awareness, no behavior change is going to happen. Awareness—being able to think about and struggle with your behavior—is just essential.

OLIVIA: I wonder if women sometimes start therapy because of problems in a relationship with someone else, only to find that the therapy turns into something so much more. For me, it became a relationship with myself, a chance to get to know myself better and

Getting help and support when you need it is a sign of sanity.

figure out what's important to me. As a woman, you're always making sure that the needs of others are being met. You have all these demands placed on you. But in therapy there are no demands other than trying to get to know yourself better.

PEGGY: Olivia has had a growing realization that while her competitiveness has served her well in many areas, it has also prevented her from enjoying a lot about her life. If you're so focused on winning or doing things perfectly, you miss a lot. Now she has less of a drive to do things perfectly, and more of a deep satisfaction at juggling the roles of mother, wife, and career person.

OLIVIA: More than anything, I think I was struggling with the question, Is this all there is to life? And I think what I've found out through therapy is, yes, and that's okay. That's kind of my mantra from Peggy: "That's okay." It's wonderful to be happy with life. And to finally feel like that's enough.

CASE IN POINT "WE'D STARTED TO GROW APART"

Nicki* was a 35-year-old surgical resident when she and her husband began having serious problems in their marriage and started couples counseling with Richard Archambault, a family therapist in Providence, Rhode Island. The couple was in therapy for two and a half years—initially going two to three times a month and eventually tapering down to one monthly session. Here, Nicki and Dr. Archambault discuss why she and her husband entered therapy, and how it transformed their marriage.

NICKI: We started therapy at the end of my first year of residency. We had been together for seven years and married for one. There was a lot of pressure in our lives with my training and my husband

having a new job, and we were beginning to have trouble communicating. Then my husband started showing signs of depression—concentration and memory issues, and a lack of motivation.

At that point, we realized there were deeper issues in the relationship that we weren't addressing. My husband felt that he was "second" to my work. And he was concerned that my focus on advancing my career meant I wouldn't ever have time for children. He also felt that his own career goals were not a priority.

DR. ARCHAMBAULT: Most couples know what their issues are. They know what's going on, but they just can't talk about it, or it's too sensitive or maybe too explosive. When they bring it into therapy, it becomes more manageable, safer. Often the causes of stress are not big, overwhelming concerns but rather relatively small, every-day things that seem hard to change. My job is identifying those issues, getting the couple to articulate them, and finding ways for the couple to work on them.

NICKI: I had no control over my schedule, and there was a lot of anxiety in the relationship because of that. Surgical residents can work more than 100 hours a week, leaving very little time for any-thing other than eating and sleeping. I had no time even to care for myself, and my husband had become very frustrated about how I wasn't contributing to the home and how he was bearing the brunt of the responsibilities. That was a major sore point. And even when I was home, I was a shell of a person. I felt a lot of guilt and blame for not being able to devote everything to the relationship.

My husband resented that I had no time. But I suppose even if we had time, we wouldn't have utilized it to sit down and really talk, because we'd started to grow apart.

DR. ARCHAMBAULT: In any kind of couples therapy, you have an "I" and you have a "we." It's okay to be an "I," an individual, but you also have to be a "we."

I try to get the couple to step back from their individual per-spectives and look at a problem from the perspective of the rela-tionship. This helps them understand that while they may not have control over work or stress or children or many other things, they do have control over their relationship.

As a therapist, I first observe the strengths and problems in the way the couple interacts, and then help them recognize and iden-tify ways they can improve their relationship. To do this, I point out perspectives and behaviors I think are working and not work-ing. Then I try to help the couple reshape those things in order to make their relationship more effective.

NICKI: Dr. Archambault would always start by asking us how we were doing. Often we would try to paint a rosy picture. But as the session progressed, we would uncover stuff—perhaps a comment I made a few days earlier that hurt my husband. Sometimes we would argue and cry because of hurt feelings that we hadn't recog-nized until the session. Dr. Archambault would then redirect the argument into something more constructive, so we could learn something about each other. For example, when my husband would tell me that I wasn't contributing to the home and that he was doing everything, Dr. Archambault helped us see that the real issue wasn't about my cleaning or cooking but rather about show-ing love for my husband, who was trying to tell me he missed me. Once I started to understand that, the arguments at home began

to abate. And my husband became more understanding of me.

We also had to work on the fact that our interpretations of and reactions to each other's comments or actions were often based on events that preceded our relationship. In therapy we discovered that my husband was always worried about being "deceived" by people. I, on the other hand, worried that I was to blame for every-thing and always felt like the "bad child." As we started to under-stand each other's perspective, we were able to avoid pushing buttons that would cause bad feelings. Throughout this process, Dr. Archambault never took sides. He would ask each of us how we felt about what the other person was saying. And he would make sure we were addressing one another, not directing our comments to him.

DR. ARCHAMBAULT: It's important for the couple to decide what changes they're going to make in their relationship, and how they're going to make them. If suggestions come from the thera-pist, the couple does not feel like the plan is theirs.

So I always end each session with, "What did you learn? What can you take home with you? What can you specifically do about the problem? What steps can you take to bring about change?"

The next time I meet with them, I might begin by checking back: "Did you follow through with what you agreed to do? How did it work? What didn't work? How would you want to change things?"

NICKI: It can be very challenging to change the habits in a relation-ship. For example, we were not used to really thinking together as a couple. So Dr. Archambault had us work on a five-year plan for our lives. This turned out to be an excellent exercise. We not only learned more about each other's hopes and dreams—and how we each envisioned the present and future of our relationship—but we also started to grasp the importance of seeing ourselves as a unit.

DR. ARCHAMBAULT: The relationship is what they created. And it's the thing that's going to soothe and heal them—and be their therapist—in the long run. They created it and they can change it.

NICKI: When we first started therapy, there were a lot of tears and accusations. We sat far away from each other and barely made eye contact. As we proceeded, we started to "visit" with each other during the sessions. Most important, we smiled and laughed more often. Dr. Archambault helped us see the qualities that brought us together in the first place. We started to realize that we did still genuinely like—and love—each other.

We ultimately came to see our relationship as a sanctuary. It was us against the world. And the importance of keeping us strong and safe was the lesson we took away.

CASE IN POINT "I FELT AS THOUGH MY LIFE WAS STANDING STILL"

Lauren* was a single 26-year-old lawyer troubled by her lack of roman-tic connections when she entered therapy with Barbara Goldman, PhD, a clinical psychologist in Coral Gables, Florida. Together they discov-ered that the romance issue was connected to broader limitations Lauren had placed on herself. Through a combination of growth-oriented ther-apy and cognitive-behavioral therapy, Goldman helped Lauren start to overcome those limitations. The two met weekly for a year, and then on and off for three more years as Lauren integrated the work she did in therapy into her life.

LAUREN: I tend to be a little introspective, and at some point I started to realize that other people's lives were moving at a rate that mine wasn't. Although on the surface my life was fine, I felt as though it was staying still. And I started wondering if that still-ness was me missing out on things. Everyone I knew was starting to get married and have children, but that inclination was not in me and I wondered why. Romantic relationships were never a big part of my life; they weren't something I was emotionally invested in or dedicated a lot of time to. To me that was just the normal course, what I felt was natural for me. But then I started to realize, maybe it wasn't so normal.

So part of the work we did in therapy was figuring out why I was in that position. My problem was that I was filled with self-doubt about everything. I needed some grounding.

DR. GOLDMAN: The thrust in growth-oriented therapy is in increasing self-awareness and self-acceptance and developing coping strategies to have more choices and a greater sense of power and control. The people I treat may, like Lauren, be high-functioning in a generally well-managed and stable life, but they seek a deeper sense of fulfillment, meaning, and satisfaction.

I spend the first several sessions gathering history and doing an evaluation of personality strengths and challenges. This helps us start to see where the client may be blocking her progress with coping strategies that may have been useful earlier in life but are outdated and unhelpful now.

With Lauren, I also employed a basic principle of cognitive-behavioral therapy—that our thoughts affect our feelings and behavior, and that changing thoughts will change feelings and behaviors, which in turn will impact how we think and feel.

LAUREN: The changes had to do with becoming emotionally independent. Because after I started therapy, that question about romantic relationships turned into an understanding: I was not available. Why? Because I had all these other emotional connections to people that I needed to become somewhat independent of.

In my family, as in most Latin families, family is the most important thing, and every personal decision quickly escalates into a group decision. *Who should I date? Who should I be friends with? Where should I work? What should I do as a career?* There was no independent Lauren thought. It was, *What does the collective family think about this situation? Or think about Lauren in this regard?*

Dr. Goldman helped me look at that dynamic closely to see that sometimes the decisions my family made for me were not decisions I would have made. She also stressed that going against my family's opinions did not make me a bad person.

DR. GOLDMAN: Many of Lauren's strengths were getting in her way. She's a very bright and sensitive and responsible person. But at that stage in her life she was having trouble figuring out how to balance her own needs and wants with other people's.

LAUREN: I always thought I would stay in my hometown, marry someone I knew from high school, and live the exact same life my parents lived. I knew there was a life outside of the pictures I had created in my head; I just didn't know it was a life I could live.

DR. GOLDMAN: When she began therapy, Lauren felt pressure to spend time with family to help them feel happy, but she also wanted to be out with her friends. It took her a while to acknowledge that developing a broader social life was at least as important as keeping her family content. She had to practice speaking up and declining some opportunities with family in favor of socializing.

LAUREN: The idea we discussed that sustained me was that I couldn't keep doing the same things over and over and expecting a different result. I saw that I needed to stand on my own two feet and trust my own reactions. It was time to say to my family, "Okay, you can think that, and I appreciate what you have to say; however, I'm going to do what I think is right."

DR. GOLDMAN: Lauren wanted very much to maintain close relationships with family and friends, and over the years her strategy for feeling close was to avoid conflict. Conflict, in her eyes, was not a potentially constructive way to change relationships but instead something potentially damaging.

LAUREN: I remember telling Dr. Goldman about my relationship

Therapy can help you pick yourself up and get on with life.

with my father. She asked me about him and I gushed, saying all these wonderful things about his personality, who he was and how much he supported and understood me.

Then in subsequent sessions, I told stories about how he hurt my feelings by creating different standards for me compared with my siblings. After a number of sessions, Dr. Goldman just said to me point-blank: "Is it possible that your father is different from the perfect person you wish he was?"

Whoa! It was as if a bell went off: I had set up this dependence on people who weren't who I thought they were—and then I'd get upset when they didn't give me what I expected from them. I needed to align my expectations with actual people and not my ideas of people. Especially since I probably was not who they thought I was, either.

I eventually moved to another city. I left a comfortable job in a law firm and moved into a different field of law. These moves were not things I had necessarily consciously wanted to make. But therapy helped me realize that I had to change my life to become more engaged.

Taking the leap was hard. I felt as though I was being really selfish. I would get resistance from my family and just say, "Thank you. I will think about that." I also had to learn to express what I needed out of my relationships. I would say over and over, "Dad, I have to work this out on my own, and I need you to respect that."

DR. GOLDMAN: Part of the work, from my perspective, involved your hearing your own inner voice more loudly. It involved trusting your feelings and being able to assert yourself.

LAUREN: That is absolutely the thing I feel the most. Sure, there are still issues I need to work on, but I trust my inner voice one hundred percent now, whereas before I didn't at all.

As for romance, I'm still looking, but at least I'm putting myself in situations where I'm more likely to find someone. I'm not perfect at it, but I'm moving in the right direction. Plus, I'm having a lot more fun. **O**

THE BIPOLAR DIARIES

Imagine being on a small boat on a rocky sea. Waves whoosh back and forth. You can't get your bearings. There's no land in sight. Now imagine that this boat is you and that perfect storm is caused by a disorder in your brain's chemistry. Playwright Elizabeth Swados lets you in on what it takes to keep herself afloat.

I hate this politically correct term—*bipolar.* On the surface it can seem sexy, like bicoastal or bisexual. Or it might suggest that I'm into saving the environment, traveling to those places where penguins mate and whales eat seals. *Bipolar.*

I'm too aware of how any clinical psychiatric term brands a person. When the term was *manic-depressive,* the associations were somewhat romantic. Mad, feverish, dancing through the night to no music, buying out the women's department of a clothing store, even buying out the company, sleeping with the population of a whole town, cutting off an ear—in other words, life as loud and erratic as an out-of-time drum solo. Although many still believe an illness of this kind is brought on by what one of my relatives once called "spoiled brattedness," at least now science has shown it to be a serious brain disorder, as chronic as diabetes. And the newer bipolar is a little less hysterical, as in a woman who cooks and cleans all night and then can't get out of bed, or the quintessential diabolical boss, or the party-girl student out every evening, self-medicating with cocaine and alcohol until she drops. But even these images are off. Bipolar behavior isn't always so dramatic or public. Very often the sufferer functions quite well and struggles with the constant whiplash of mood in devastating privacy.

I, for instance, have started no world wars lately. I haven't bought a new wardrobe or physically attacked a singer who was out of tune. Nor have I ever missed a rehearsal or show, or stopped teaching, due to my disorder. Only those closest to me know when I am thinking too fast, coming to drastic conclusions, imagining friendly atmospheres as threatening, or having to censor all the words that ricochet through my brain. Although there are still periods when I am pushed around by my moods, I've learned what I have to do not to succumb to bipolar disorder's more extreme symptoms.

OVER 25 YEARS AGO, I was in my late 20s, weighing in at 93 pounds, talking as fast as an auctioneer, dashing from one activity to another with such intensity that I practically burned rubber. I'd noticed since college that I could go for weeks on high energy, not sleeping, barely eating, and then I'd end up sick and utterly exhausted. But that was the rhythm of university life, right? Still, at 27, 28 years old, my erratic energies weren't evening out. In fact, the dips and highs became more exaggerated. I was composing and writing a show in New York while working on my first novel. Everything, and I mean everything, was vital, essential, and urgent, and my obsession with work and relationships went beyond the outrageous self-absorption created by adolescent hormones. Weeks of frenetic activity, extreme intellectual and sexual passion, would result in a temper that could see me throwing a tape recorder out a window if a song wasn't going right. This razorlike edginess would be followed by the bottom dropping out: I wouldn't understand what all my energy had been for. I didn't know why I had cared so much about what I'd been caring so much about. I felt stupid and clumsy, unworthy, and doomed to a life of meaningless existence. In my shame, any thought that entered my head was aimed at letting myself know I was a failure in every measure of my person. When this happened I would hole up—isolate myself, and go out only for whatever work I knew I had to face. When I did go out, I'd fake interest and try to maintain the project and friendships I'd created as that seemingly completely other person.

After several years, these extreme back-and-forths took such a toll on me and were so confusing, I began to want only silence and the end of unpredictability. There were too many voices screaming and singing and whispering in my head. So noisy. I used to count the layers of tracks going on at the same time. They praised and whipped at me. They mocked me and raised me to heights of unrealistic grandeur. They led me toward even more self-destructive behavior. And finally they exhausted my will.

Luckily, I had several friends who insisted that I see a psychiatrist.

At first when I spoke to the doctor it was as if I were auditioning for the role of a 19th-century poet. I talked about how I felt the power of the gods and the ominous presence of danger at the same time. I thought I was possessed with a heavenly vision, and yet I was unworthy and incapable of keeping up with the greats of history. I needed sex. I hated sex. I was a vampire with no libido. I was a savior of humanity with no friends. I understood the deep symbolisms of shapes, numbers, colors, and letters, but I barely had the energy to spell or add.

After listening to my tirades, the psychiatrist asked me if I had ever considered taking medication. I was stunned and extremely skeptical. I'd watched my mother slowly deteriorate into a woman who lay on the couch for hours. I never could erase her slurred speech from my head. I didn't know what drugs she'd been on, but

myself: Was that a dull observation? Is the melody I wrote less edgy than two years ago? Was that not funny, and if it wasn't funny, is it because I'm drugged? Have I been quiet for too long? Am I becoming a cow?

As it turned out, the medication hardly turned me into a zombie. Instead it cleared some of the noise in my head and helped replace the feeling of relentless inevitable doom with a shaky determination to join the rest of the human race in the basic day-to-day ups and downs of life. As the poet Nazim Hikmet writes, "Living is no laughing matter: / you must live with great seriousness / like a squirrel for example— / I mean without looking for something beyond and above living, / I mean living must be your whole occupation." For me it was definitely quite a job, but at least with medication I had the will to struggle.

I was lucky enough to find a doctor who was part scientist, part

A bipolar person may function quite well, battling the constant whiplash of mood in devastating privacy.

they made her bloated and dull. I knew certain psychiatric conditions could be passed on, and my mother's downward slide, as well as the mental illnesses of several other family members, haunted me. Was there a genetic strain that I could do nothing about? I dreaded being paralyzed as she seemed to be, or labeled. Medication equaled cowardice to me, the height of luxurious narcissism. Didn't drugs wipe out creativity? Didn't medicine take away your sense of humor and neutralize you? I thought of Aldous Huxley's *Brave New World.* I would be one of a nation of lazy do-nothings addicted to the "happy drug" soma. How could I help rectify the problems of the world if I had to take pills? I really went on and on about this. My noisy brain burst with more tracks berating myself for even needing to consider the possibility of medication. Illegal drugs were much cooler. Bob Dylan never wrote a song called "O Lithium" or "Antidepressant Blues."

Because of my opposition to medication, life continued to be agony. I never knew who I was going to be in the morning, and my reactions to everyday events continued to crash, clang, and resonate in my brain like a huge Japanese gong. I came very close to suicide, and since the final chapter of my mother's story had ended exactly that way when I was 23, I felt in danger. Now in my late 20s, I realized that I loved life enough to be terrified of following her actions. I finally decided to take the risk.

For the first two years, I would go on medication, then abandon it. The idea of needing drugs still seemed proof of a kind of failing that I had trouble facing. I wanted to be able to control my inner demons and not be "ill." And I hated the thought of chemicals playing with my brain. So in the beginning I was constantly monitoring

alchemist, and part shaman, while being up on the latest medical discoveries and courageous enough to try continual adjustments in treatment. This was also a doctor who listened to me. I found it unacceptable to be overdrugged, for example—to lose access to the energy that connected me to those I worked with who kept me creative in my pursuits. In order for the doctor to help me, I had to be able to describe with extreme accuracy what I was feeling. I also saw a therapist who showed me how to clarify what was chemical and what was not.

Slowly I was able to teach myself to ignore the bad voices, because they were softer and not so insistent. I could think twice about a reaction to another person or event now that the reaction didn't happen so instantly I couldn't do anything about it. I learned to watch myself going through an impulsive or manic action and stop myself before that one snowballed into another—and another and another. The high court of my brain didn't judge me, or others, quite so severely. Often it was hard to know—and still is—whether my reactions were legitimate or tainted by chemical imbalance. But time and experience continue to teach me to understand my mood changes and how to differentiate an emergency from a simply lousy day.

Most important, therapy has guided me over the years in learning how to "behave well." One of my rules now is that regardless of the situation, there is no reason whatsoever to impose my inner storms on others. It's perfectly okay to let someone know I'm having trouble or to confide fears in a trusted friend, but to act out a misguided interpretation of an event, or to impose a rush of anger on another person, is destructive and has consequences. It reads well to have a madwoman trashing her apartment, getting into a fistfight with a saleslady, and, of course, staring down at the bottom of a whisky glass with cigarette smoke swirling into the neon lights of an all-night bar. It reads well to have the mad lady not eating for months, writing pages of incoherent poetry, or calling friends at 4 in the morning to discuss the meaning of life. Yet in reality, even the most outrageous rock 'n' rollers, poets, and anarchists get bronchitis, lose jobs, alienate friends, and come too close to doing themselves in for very little purpose. So learning to behave may seem prissy, but in the long run, life to me offers much more vibrant, important moments of discovery and light because I've gained some semblance of self-discipline, dignity, and privacy about my problems. While being rather strict with myself, however, I do try to hear those close to me when they remind me that I am one of many who suffer from a real disorder. I am not a freak. I am not "wrong." And I'm certainly not unique.

Let me be honest. Even with medication and therapy, nothing has been "fixed." I am not "cured." Living with this disorder is a continuous virtual sports tournament. There are so many images that come to mind: tightrope walking, bullfighting with powerful snorting moods, or sometimes it's like my mind is still a breathless animal panting through an agility course. It burrows into tunnels, leaps over walls, pushes turnstiles, keeps my endurance up just enough so I can barely make it to a last free, open run in the field. And that run ultimately ends, like a *Road Runner* cartoon, falling off a steep cliff.

One difficult reality of the bipolar condition is that the medicines may need to be changed or adjusted quite often—sometimes even within the same year. Certain drugs can stop working, or they cause side effects when combined with others. For instance, one gave me the shakes. I switched to another and my mind went back to zooming and careening. You find sometimes that without an antidepressant, a mood stabilizer will push you into the muck of depression. An antidepressant without a mood stabilizer can send you flying dangerously. And side effects include severe anxiety and headaches.

It takes a certain kind of patience to put up with this perpetual game of musical meds. At one point, I got incredibly discouraged and angry. I felt like a toxic waste dump. I scolded myself that I was no more than a downtown avant-garde version of Jacqueline Susann's *Valley of the Dolls,* although it wasn't true. And since I never missed a work appointment or deadline, I couldn't help but think: *If there are so many moments when, despite my problems, I can focus, maybe I don't need medication at all.* Like most people burdened with bipolar disorder, too, I was very sensitive to others who think we are addicts taking the easy way out. So, in my frustration, I decided to stop all medication. Clean out.

It was a disaster. After a couple of weeks my mind became a protest march with all the different contingents demanding their rights. There was nonstop commentary from a newscaster telling me that I must do this, I must do that, get to this, get to that, not be like this, start right now, stop it! Pundits gave opinions on the judgments of the newscaster and fights inside my brain broke out that were worse than anything on *The View*. All the mania put me on the brink of total exhaustion, and the whole situation was made worse because I knew I was irrational and had to direct myself moment by moment like a drill sergeant to behave normally, say the right things in conversation, and even just lift a glass of water to my lips without shaking. Inevitably, of course, after the violent waves of energy, I ended up fighting a depression so thick that for weeks it felt like I was moving through a solid bog of grayish Jell-O. Most devastating of all, here was absolute proof I needed medication, and that caused me great shame.

Then came the fear. What if this was it? What if there was no medicine left to calm me down or dig me out? No way to regain a semblance of quiet or of light? Was I going to end up old and crazy pushing a shopping cart filled with Robert Johnson CDs and torn workout clothes?

The answer is no. Once I resumed medication and found even newer combinations, my rapid mood cycling eased, which has given me more time to take in the small gifts life has to offer. I can even experience a quietness now and again. A restfulness, and more and more often, all the tracks in my brain harmonize and there is joy.

I have also discovered other ways to help stave off the mania and its dreaded other side, absolute despair. The list is somewhat boring but extremely essential. First, I must take care of myself physically—eat well, keep hydrated, and exercise. Second, I try to go outside as much as possible and absorb the life around me by watching—anything from dog walkers and young couples to skateboarders and hip-hoppers with iPods dancing out the beats. A crucial part of my survival is to take solace and pride in my work because it reminds me of who I am. It also reminds me of my vital connection to all the actors, singers, and writers who keep me focused. I buy books, go to movies, socialize, stay abreast of the news and culture—in other words, I try to keep myself in the world, away from the captivity of my mind.

Another form of relief is to read about my disorder, including the latest research. And I've learned to write down descriptions of my mind's travels and perceptions when I am in certain moods to help me remember that all of this has happened before, and whatever is torturing me will pass. Finally, I look to the wisdom of those who have seen me through the bad cycles and can tell me that they love me any which way I am.

In the last several years, scientists have made incredible progress in treating bipolar disorder, and today there are many more choices for mood stabilizers and antidepressants. I have been on a fairly consistent combination of drugs for a while now without any overwhelming side effects. And I can cautiously say that, for quite a long time, I've been able to claim my days and haven't had to be a constant mediator between my moods. I'm not about to bring out the bells, strings, and drums just yet, but I do have more good days than bad—and even the bad days aren't lost in hours of battling frantic energies or the dead weight of mania's reciprocal depths.

As I write this, I think about those who are just beginning the treacherous roller-coaster ride and, for anyone who hasn't found methods to help restore evenness and calm, I want to say: Hold on tight. Move slowly and with hope. Even if you are in the most chaotic state of mind or the most deadly despair, trust in time. Help is on the way. ◐

ON MEDICATION I WAS CONSTANTLY MONITORING MYSELF: WAS THAT A DULL OBSERVATION? WAS I NOT FUNNY? AM I BECOMING A COW?

IF YOU'VE EVER THOUGHT ABOUT GOING INTO THERAPY…OR GETTING OUT OF IT

Novelist, short story writer, and psychotherapist Amy Bloom has looked at therapy from both sides of the couch. Here, a few things she wants every patient to know about the sane way to get help.

1 GREAT THERAPISTS ARE WHERE YOU FIND THEM
It does not matter what the person's training is. Intelligent, insightful, empathetic people with a sense of humor and of boundaries appear with anything from a nursing degree to an MD and ten years of psychoanalytic training. On the other hand, a person whose only training is a crazy mother, a weekend of reflexology, and a fondness for dream interpretation is not a great bet. The Internet has made it easy to look up anyone and see if they got their degree out of a Cracker Jack box or have been convicted of a crime. The bad news is that the only way to know if you have the wrong therapist is to sit with that person. And even then, you may not be sure if the problem is her or you…ever. But if the problem persists over months, it's probably time to stop—no matter where the fault lies. (You don't have to blame the oil *or* the water for not mixing.)

2 THERAPY IS NOT—BY AND LARGE—FUN
A shrink who has candy in bowls, music playing, handknit afghans on the couch, and a tendency to compliment you on everything from your outfits to your high I.Q. is not doing her job. (Unless you came into therapy saying, "I don't give a damn how I get in my own way, just make me feel better"—in which case, you have found the perfect therapist. You may also want to consider gigolos and recreational drug use.)

3 YOUR THERAPIST IS NOT A FRIEND
Don't get me started on how much your therapist is not a lover, or anything that even resembles a lover. Back rubs, lunch dates, and flirty e-mails are not part of the deal. The deal is: safety, security, and structure. A therapist who doesn't know this is an actual menace to you.

4 TIME IS OF THE ESSENCE
A therapist who can't start on time, can't end on time, who screws up your appointment more than once (you have to cut these people *some* slack), who needs to eat lunch while you talk, who takes phone calls during your session, or who in any way indicates that every minute of your session is not deeply important is not for you. If you really like the person anyway, bring this issue up. If things do not dramatically improve immediately, bail.

5 NOTHING WRONG WITH NUTS
An eccentric therapist (tatty old furniture, orthopedic sandals worn with leopard-skin bustiers, or walls decorated with elk heads) is not necessarily a bad one. People do not become therapists because they are profoundly normal. If what comes out is sensible and sensitive, don't worry too much about the trappings. (If what comes out is "In a past life, I was burned at the stake" or "On my planet, we do things differently," head for the hills.)

6 IMPASSE, PLATEAU, OR DEAD SHARK
Most little kids go through a period of regression before their next developmental spurt. Most adults do, too. (Remember the marriage-phobic, slacker boyfriend you dumped—who married a nice woman six months later and is now the father of three and a softball coach? You met him before his developmental leap.) In therapy, a longish dull period can precede a lot of movement. However, a very long dull period, in which you and the therapist seem both bored and bewildered, may signal that (a) you're done…for now, (b) you're done…with this person, or (c) you're done…until you're ready to try again. How to tell the difference? Bring it up with the shrink.

7 WHAT IF YOUR SHRINK SAYS STAY AND YOU'RE READY TO GO?
First rule: They work for you. Second rule: If you've always respected this person's judgment (not the same as liking them) and they say, "You're not ready to go," think twice. After you've thought twice, see the first rule. If you're wrong about stopping, you can go back—and you will have learned something.

8 HOW TO SUCCEED BY REALLY TRYING
Successful treatment should feature some resolution (you don't just talk about leaving the house and why you can't—you actually do leave the house), some understanding that holds up under pressure (even when you and your husband are having a terrible fight, you manage not to say the things that make his head burst into flames and your marriage collapse), and some self-awareness that helps you move the psychic furniture instead of stubbing your toe for the millionth time.

9 WHAT'S SO GOOD ABOUT GOODBYE
It's probably time to wrap things up when the two of you are happily, even cozily, chatting about this and that week after week. His Shar-Pei, your flower arranging, his kids, your kids. It's wonderful that you've come to enjoy each other's company and your problems have been resolved. That's why it's time to stop. It should hurt; you're ending something that has been valuable and significant.

10 WHERE'S THE ROPE LADDER?
Some therapies require an emergency exit: a therapist who makes sexual advances (whether in the name of repairing your self-esteem or his or her own uncontrollable desire); therapy that has gone on for 25 years during which you have changed nothing but your socks; therapy in which you're comforting/advising/reassuring your tearful/paranoid/anxious therapist; couples therapy in which the therapist has remarked, with some feeling, on how attractive your spouse is.

11 THE FUNNY THING ABOUT REFERRALS
You have to be your own Geiger counter. The guy who helped your friend overcome impotence, agoraphobia, and a fear of commitment may leave you cold and, worse, uninspired. It is best to check out the credentials (see #1) of anyone you seek treatment from, and it's great if someone you know and like has seen and been helped by that person—but it is never all you need to know. One man's Freud is another person's Froot Loop. ◖

Chilling out on the *Nova Spirit*, en route from Vancouver Island to Desolation Sound.

"MAKING THE DECISION TO LOOK AFTER YOURSELF IS THE ULTIMATE IN HEALTHCARE"

I had to give myself a break. My body was turning on me. First hy*per*thyroidism, which sped up my metabolism and left me unable to sleep for days. (Most people lose weight. I didn't.) Then hy*po*thyroidism, which slowed down my metabolism and made me want to sleep all the time. (Most people gain weight. I did! Twenty pounds!)

The thyroid, one of many body parts I'd never given a thought to, is a small, butterfly-shaped gland located at the base of your neck, just below your Adam's apple. It influences everything from digestion to metabolism to reproduction. When the thyroid is out of balance, so are you.

I craved balance. I was desperate to be somewhere in the middle of hy*per* and hy*po*—where, obviously, I'd been my whole life, taking it for granted because I didn't know any better. We often need a malfunction to appreciate all the things that function.

I decided to give myself July. Yes, the whole month—dedicated to myself, for myself. To regroup. Rejuvenate. Restore my soul.

By the end of my show season, in May, I was so exhausted, I was numb. But I still had commitments I needed and wanted to fulfill, like being in South Africa to take my girls to see their first stage play, *The Lion King*. That was a treat worth traveling for. One of the girls—Thando, whom you may remember if you watched our special—wants to be an actress. After seeing *The Lion King*, she told me, "It was so spectacular, my eyes didn't know where to land."

So I spent June with my 150 daughters, who are happy and thriving. But in July, I actively worked at doing nothing. I had no schedule. I told my office, "Call me only if someone or something is dying or burning."

I flew from Africa to Hawaii, which involves a 12-hour time difference that takes some adjustment even when you're well-rested. I made the transition by sleeping and waking when my body wanted to and not a moment before. It took a week for my internal clock to reset itself.

I took vitamins. Drank soy milk. Munched on golden flaxseed. I ate only fresh foods: grilled fish, corn, tomatoes, spinach, artichokes, broccoli from the farmers' market, mangoes from my neighbor's tree. I hiked with my dogs (who daily rolled in cow poop along the grassy trails), then came home and bathed them. I actually read the stack of books I'd chosen to read by summer's end. I dozed. And drifted into the afternoons waiting for the sun to set. I watched 28 consecutive sunsets. Took pictures and marveled at how each one was so different.

After 14 days, I started to feel my *self* returning. Not fully—just an awareness that I wasn't as tired and rote as I had been. By the end of the month I'd given myself, I was better in myriad ways. Not only was my physical health improved but I'd also become mentally stronger.

I won't tell you how many people challenged my decision to give time to myself. I have never gotten more requests to do something or be somewhere than I did the moment I declared that I was going out of circulation. And these were from people I normally would have said yes to.

But I was steadfast in my commitment to finding balance and reordering my life's priorities. So I said, "No, I can't come to Italy." And, "No, I can't be in Boston no matter how important you think it is." And, "No, I won't have you fly to Hawaii for a meeting here."

I may have lost a few friends, but I know for sure I saved myself. And learned that making the decision to look after yourself is the ultimate in healthcare.

As I write this, I'm wrapped in a blanket on the back of a friend's boat off Vancouver Island sipping a glass of nice red wine... watching the whales swim by. The earth has rotated to yet another sunset, and my balancing act continues.

Cheers!

Oprah

GETTING THROUGH IT

O'S BE-PREPARED, YOU'RE-TOUGHER-THAN-YOU-THOUGHT, WE'VE-GOT-YOU-COVERED GUIDE* TO SAVING YOURSELF FROM EVERY IMAGINABLE DISASTER. AND THEN SOME.

*BREATHTAKING TALES OF REAL-LIFE COURAGE INCLUDED

10 YEARS OLD, ALONE ON A HILL...

By Elaina Richardson

When you're 10 years old and wearing a new paisley-patterned pastel bikini, the top cinched, sophisticatedly you imagine, with a yellow ribbon, and you have your blanket spread out on the grass of the Cathkin Braes, over the hill from where everyone else has clustered together, and your dad's transistor radio, borrowed for the afternoon without his knowledge, is lying snugly in its brown leather carrying case, blasting out your favorite songs—when all of this is true, you just know it's going to be a great afternoon. This is how I found myself one sunny day in July in the middle of a Glasgow summer. The Cathkin Braes lay behind the tower blocks of flats (inspired by Le Corbusier but hopelessly inadequate to withstand the damp Scottish weather) where we had moved to start a new life when I was 5. The hills were steeped in history; it was from the ridge I sat on that Mary Queen of Scots had watched her troops lose the Battle of Langside, and with it all her hopes of claiming the English throne. I loved these hills, and loved to have them all to myself the better to indulge my sense of difference from the worker bees around me. I had climbed higher into the braes than anyone else ever bothered to do. I could hear the families gathered on the slopes below, hear their games of football, yells of laughter, and occasional screams from a baby. I wanted nothing to do with any of them.

I kicked off my new sandals, removed my shorts, and settled with a book I wanted to finish that day. I also had a sketch pad with me and imagined I would read for an hour or so and then draw some flowers. I'd just turned a page or two in the novel when I became aware that someone was watching me from behind. I sat up, turned, and saw a lanky man, short haired, ruddy in the way Scottish men sometimes are, ambling from the woods. Something in the certainty of his step told me he was heading for me, not just accidentally passing where I was. I watched him advance, noting the moustache, the slight bag of the trousers, the general air of purpose that enveloped him. He came and sat at the edge of the blanket and made a little chitchat about the day and how he wondered if I knew which bus he should take to get back into the center of town. I couldn't really tell how old he was—he looked oldish as everyone

over 18 does to a 10-year-old. He became very still and I could feel gooseflesh rise on my arms and thighs; his gaze was disturbing and in the stillness it crystallized for me that he was observing me in an unnatural way and that he liked what he saw. Instinctively I knew that something was *really* not right. With a calmness that came from God knows where and that completely belied the panic I was starting to feel, I moved onto my knees and started to gather my things together. He smiled as he watched this, and I said, politely I thought, "I have to go home now, but there are a lot of people just over there, grown-ups and dads, and they'll know which bus you need." He smiled again, then reached into his trouser pocket and asked, "If I gave you this two shillings, would you agree to be my girlfriend?" Everything cartoons suggest about fear now became my reality—I moved in slow-mo, my heart thumped, my words wouldn't come out. All I knew was that I needed to run very fast and right then. I clutched what I could and made to bolt, which is when he grabbed my ankle and twisted it so hard I guessed he'd just broken it.

We fought and struggled as he part-threw, part-dragged me toward the cover of the woods. I remember feeling tired at some point in this battle, tempted to just be very still and stop resisting, which was only leading to more force coming down on me. I let my muscles slacken for a second and then a huge rush of adrenaline coursed through my veins and I exploded into a frenzy of clawing and blow-throwing. I was a good fighter, a dirty fighter, my skills honed on the Glasgow playground, where girls swung a fist in each other's direction with hardly a thought. Eventually I did kick free and as I ran I saw and heard nothing. I must have run through the families picnicking on the lower hills, but I don't remember, and I don't remember crossing the grassy slopes, or the pain from the damaged ankle, or the chunks of hair that had been pulled out, or any of the other injuries. I do remember my bare feet hitting the concrete of the parking lot that sat in front of our apartments, and a surge of hope as I looked up and saw my mother waving from our 17th-floor balcony. She'd gone out to water her tomato plants, and as she saw me running helter-skelter, looking completely deranged, she wondered if I'd ever remember to be tidy and not to look, as she liked to describe me, "like you've been dragged through a hedge backward." When I reached her, the first thing I said was that I'd lost one of my new sandals, then the sobs came and I told her about the man.

Of course, the next scene involves the police and my dad petting my hand and my mother unable to resist saying, "You should never have gone off by yourself." That's one lesson I could have learned from the incident, and it's certainly the one that most fairy tales and parables endorse, but I didn't. Not even when I was told that my assailant was believed to be Scotland's most notorious serial killer, a character known as Bible John who terrorized women in the late 1960s, picking them up at the East End Barrowland Ballroom, asking them to be his girlfriend, then strangling, raping, and discarding them. He has never been caught, and to the best of my knowledge, I'm the only girl who ever got away.

So what did I learn? I suppose if I had to boil it down, I would say I learned to trust what Daniel Goleman would call emotional intelligence. I learned that when alarm bells are ringing, you should listen to them and act, that you should case out your surroundings and wonder if it's a good idea to be there, and that you should trust adrenaline to be your friend. But I didn't learn fear, because the central fact for me was that I survived, and with the knowledge that danger is real came the certainty that courage is, too. For a few years after the attack, and before I was told that the police believed Bible John was the assailant, I would imagine I saw the guy in all kinds of locations. I'd report these to my father—"I

think he's working at that new Chinese takeout," I'd say. And my dad would nod and say, "You do," and put on his shoes and head out to check. He'd often come home and say something like "It's not him. That's Sam White's son, he's only three years older than you." That my dad went each time filled me with an immense sense of safety and control, and after a few years, the sightings stopped and I realized I wouldn't really be able to draw his portrait if I was asked to. I'd been left with a belief in vigilance, and this is, I suppose, the final, mixed lesson of the incident. I notice a lot—how many people are in a room, where the doors are, what the mood is—to the extent that for a while I honestly thought my destiny was to be a spy. It would be really fine with me now and then to turn this habit off and be less vigilant on my way through the world. It's a bit tiring, you know? On the other hand, that vigilance has allowed me to feel very sure of myself, physically, and very confident that I could survive whatever came my way. I'd say that, in a way I'm hard pressed to define, the attack left me feeling safer than I might otherwise have done. When I came across Joseph Conrad's thoughts about how we project our vulnerabilities into the world and signal to others how we can be hurt, I was very taken with his whole theory, and reassured by it, too. I realized that I've chosen to interpret the event as proof that I'm not open to attack, I'm the lucky girl, the one who gets away. **O**

O'S WORST-CASE-SCENARIO HANDBOOK

Last time we checked, there was no burglar in the house, no quicksand in the yard, no drive-off-able cliff on the commute. But since we insist on clinging to fears even *we* know are irrational, Penny Wrenn found out what to do...just in case.

YOU'RE AT THE BANK AND A GUNMAN ENTERS

WHY IT PROBABLY WON'T HAPPEN The more secure the public place, the less likely that it will be held up, says J. Kelly McCann, president of Kroll's Security Group.

BUT IF IT DOES "There's an element of chance and risk in just waking up in the morning," says McCann. "You can mitigate some of the risk simply by being more aware." If you're in a bank, odds are the gunman's more interested in taking loot than lives. Follow his instructions, but try to stand behind something relatively bulletproof, like marble, stone, or concrete—not metal. And "if the gunman is a nut," adds McCann, "then un-ass that place!" In other words, run; a moving target is harder to hit.

YOU'RE CUTTING THROUGH A DARK ALLEY, AND YOU'RE JUMPED

WHY IT WON'T HAPPEN Because you know better than to cut through dark alleys alone.

BUT IF IT DOES McCann implores women to carry pepper spray in a coat pocket or other easily accessible place at all times. Failing that, use your hands. Pretend you're holding a grapefruit with all five fingers, then slam them into the attacker's face. If you don't get both eyes, you'll at least get one.

IT'S NIGHT, YOU'RE HOME ALONE, AND THERE'S A BURGLAR IN THE HOUSE

CONSIDER THE ODDS "A very small percentage of burglaries occur when somebody's home," says Michael R. Rand, chief of victimization statistics for the U.S. Bureau of Justice Statistics. "They want to steal things; they're not looking for confrontation."

BUT IF IT DOES HAPPEN If someone's coming in through your window or fire escape, run out the front door—and vice versa. If you can't get out, lock yourself in the bedroom, barricading the door if necessary, and call 911 from your cell phone, which you should keep by the bed at night. If he reaches you anyway, remember counterattack rule number one: Get 'em in the eyes. As McCann notes, if someone can't see you, he can't hurt you. Aim pepper spray, air freshener, or hairspray right where it counts.

YOUR PLANE IS IN TROUBLE…

WHY IT PROBABLY WON'T HAPPEN You've heard it before, and it's still true: You're safer when you board an airplane than when you get behind the wheel of a car. The chance that you'll be killed in a crash in any given year is only about one in 11 million for planes; one in 5,000 for automobiles. And according to the Aircraft Crashes Record Office, the number of plane accidents in 2006 was the lowest in 53 years.

BUT IF IT DOES Take the usual precautions—tighten your seat belt, and follow the instructions of the flight attendant, says Todd Curtis, PhD, founder of airsafe.com. Asked if there's a section of the plane where your odds of survival are greater, Curtis responds: "Tell me the kind of plane you're in and the kind of accident you're going to have, and I'll tell you where to sit." But, Curtis adds, the middle seating area near the wing is the strongest and most structurally stable part of most aircraft. And at the very least, you'll feel less turbulence when you sit there.

YOU'RE DROWNING IN QUICKSAND

WHY IT WON'T HAPPEN If you're a fan of the great outdoors, you might find yourself in quicksand—it's mostly likely to form near bogs—but you probably won't drown. A recent study published in the science journal *Nature* found that it's "impossible for a human to be drawn into quicksand altogether." Our density keeps us from going under.

BUT IF IT DOES The trick, says Gary Calkins of Texas Parks and Wildlife, who has worked around quicksand for almost two decades, is to "shuffle walk" to safety, wading through the muck (which he says will feel more like freshly poured concrete than a swimming pool) until you reach firm ground. The less moving around you do, the better.

YOU'RE WALKING DOWN THE STREET AND SOMEONE TRIES TO MUG YOU

CONSIDER THE ODDS In 2005 there were an estimated 625,000 robberies in the United States, or approximately 2.6 for every 1,000 people.

BUT IF IT DOES HAPPEN Give them what they want—your wallet, purse, keys, whatever. "There's not one material thing you possess that's worth dying over," says McCann. *But,* you're saying to yourself, *he has my keys and my license—he knows where I live!* McCann reports that criminals who make personal contact rarely come back for more. And he warns against the old "you throw your wallet, the mugger chases it, you run away" trick, which doesn't work and may invite violence. Don't try to talk sense into him, either; McCann says that's like to trying to coax a raging Rottweiler not to bite you. Final note: When the transaction is over, don't wait to be dismissed. Run.

A MADMAN HAS JUST ESCAPED FROM THE LOCAL JAIL—AND MIGHT BE HEADED YOUR WAY

WHY YOU SHOULDN'T FREAK OUT In some ways, "the closer you live to a prison, the safer you are," says Michelle Lyons of the Texas Department of Criminal Justice (which caught both of the Texas prisoners who bolted last year). The escapee wants to get as far from the prison as possible.

BUT IF IT DOES HAPPEN Lock your doors and try not to think about it. If you hear something, call 911, preferably while fleeing in your car or on foot. If you're trapped at home—the madman's footsteps ominously approaching—commence to McCann's grapefruit stance, and get ready to poke that fugitive creep's eyes out.

YOUR ELEVATOR SUDDENLY PLUMMETS

WHY YOU CAN RELAX Because modern elevators are equipped with so many fail-safes, it's almost impossible. On the extremely off chance the cables of your elevator get cut (as they did in 1945 when a plane hit the Empire State Building—the last time a traction elevator's cables were simultaneously severed and it started to fall), a brake-like device will quickly stop the car from free-falling.
BUT IF IT DOES HAPPEN Stay put. "Anytime you experience irregularities with an elevator, do not try to open the doors," says Dotty Stanlaske, executive director of the National Association of Elevator Safety Authorities. "The worst thing you can do is try to exit a moving elevator." If it's dropping, squat down in a corner, she says. That way you minimize the impact if you come to an abrupt stop.

YOU'RE DRIVING AT NIGHT IN THE DEAD OF WINTER, MILES FROM ANYWHERE…AND YOUR CAR BREAKS DOWN

WHY IT WON'T HAPPEN Because you don't drive in unfamiliar places after dark in a car that needs servicing.
BUT IF IT DOES (You should keep water and blankets in the trunk at all times.) Cut the engine, phone for help, and stay in the vehicle, says safety expert David Harkey. To stay warm, turn on your car every hour and crank the heat for ten minutes. As long as your exhaust pipe is cleared of snow or any other obstruction, there's no danger of carbon monoxide poisoning.

YOU'RE CRUISING ALONG AND YOUR BRAKES GIVE OUT

CONSIDER THE ODDS The brake systems in almost all cars are split into two circuits, so even if one malfunctions you can still rely on the other. Just pay attention to the brake warning light on your dashboard, and you should be fine.
BUT IF IT DOES HAPPEN William Van Tassel, PhD, AAA's manager of driver training operations, gives this advice: "First, pump the brakes. If that doesn't work, engage your emergency brake slowly. The goal is to gradually decrease your speed. You can also try downshifting one gear at a time (or put an automatic car into D2, then D1). As a last resort, if you're now going less than 20 mph, you can rub up against something—a continuous surface like a guardrail or concrete barrier. Ease into it, then maintain contact until you come to a complete stop."

YOUR CAR IS SUSPENDED HALFWAY OFF A CLIFF

WHY IT WON'T HAPPEN Because you're not 007. But Van Tassel is always up for a wildly improbable challenge, so…
IF IT DOES First, call 911. If the car is rear-wheel drive, try backing up. If you don't dare move your vehicle, carefully transfer as much weight as possible to the rear of the car, including any items from the front seat. But don't try to climb back yourself. Instead, gently pull up your knees and sit cross-legged, and wait for help. Whatever you do, keep your seat belt on, just in case the car goes down.

time. The average driver's perception-reaction time is about 1.5 seconds—often long enough to decide what to do—but that can double with the introduction of even a single in-car distraction. **BUT IF IT DOES** Hit the animal, says Harkey. If you try to avoid the impact by swerving to the left, you could collide with an oncoming car; swerve to the right and you'll meet greater risks off-road: drop-offs, trees, and utility poles. Then pull over and if necessary call 911.

YOU SKID AND PLUNGE OFF A BRIDGE INTO THE RIVER BELOW

CONSIDER THE ODDS "Bridge railings are designed with height and strength requirements to prevent cars from falling off," says David Harkey, director of the University of North Carolina Highway Safety Research Center. And only .1 percent of all motor-vehicle fatalities in 2004 were caused by immersion in water, according to the latest data from the National Highway Traffic Safety Administration.

BUT IF IT DOES HAPPEN The minute your car hits the water, open your door, unfasten your seat belt, and get out, says Harkey. As the car sinks and fills with water, the doors will become harder to open. (Don't even think about the power windows—they'll stop working seconds after impact.) **O**

YOU'RE KIDNAPPED AND HELD FOR RANSOM

WHY IT WON'T HAPPEN More likely than an open-ended capture for ransom, says McCann, is a "quicknapping," during which the victim is abducted for a short time, taken to one or more ATMs, and forced to give her captors cash before being released—usually unharmed.

BUT IF IT DOES At the moment someone tries to kidnap you, run and yell "Fire!" (which is more likely to attract attention than "Help!"). "A lot of people don't have an escape mentality," says McCann. "When you grab them, they stop thinking like a person who is free and start thinking like a prisoner." Look for an out—when your captor's attention is elsewhere. But if there's no chance of getting away, make him see you as a person, not a thing, by talking about how relieved your kids will be when you're freed, or about your ailing mother, who's depending on you—or whatever humanizing story you can convincingly muster that might induce empathy and get you released.

YOU HIT A ZERO-VISIBILITY SNOWSTORM

WHY YOU CAN RELAX Only about 4 percent of car accidents in 2004 occurred during snow and sleet conditions. According to Tom Moore, a senior meteorologist at the Weather Channel, your best bet is prevention: Plan your driving around the forecast. "If snow squalls are expected, be prepared. If you hear, for example, that there is a lake-effect snow advisory—where intense bands of precipitation occur from cold winds coming off warm water—know that conditions can change within minutes." Stay put, make some tea, and wait to get behind the wheel until the storm has passed. **BUT IF IT DOES HAPPEN** If there's less than 50 feet—or about two car lengths—of visibility, pull over, says Harkey. Then turn on your hazard lights to alert oncoming drivers to your location, and wait for visibility to improve.

AN ANIMAL SUDDENLY APPEARS IN YOUR HEADLIGHTS

WHY IT WON'T HAPPEN Actually, it might; nature is unpredictable. But if you drive at an appropriate speed and maintain your focus on the road—no eating, blasting Beyoncé, or talking on a cell phone, hands-free or otherwise—you'll decrease your reaction

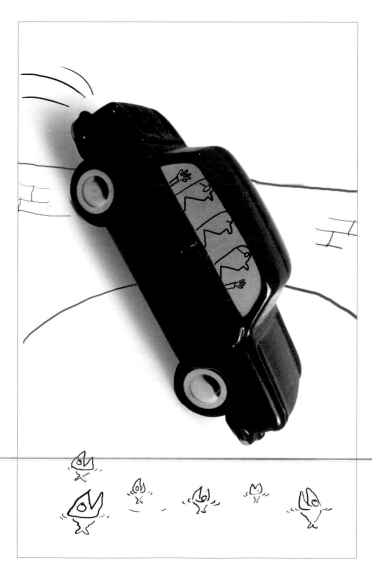

THE PLANE BEGAN TO PITCH...

By Sigrid Nunez

The week before I was scheduled to fly home from St. Louis, where I'd been a visiting writer at Washington University, there were periods of bad weather—severe storms and tornadoes—in several parts of the South and Midwest. I thought there was a good chance my flight to New York would be canceled. But that morning in St. Louis the weather was flyable. We took off only slightly later than scheduled. The plane was full, every seat taken.

We had not been aloft for long—the seat belt sign was still on—when the plane began to shudder. I travel often and have never been afraid of flying. I assumed we were going through what is normally called turbulence, though I had never felt such lurching.

I kept waiting to hear the familiar words: "Ladies and gentlemen, we seem to be experiencing some turbulence. Please stay seated with your seat belts on." But no such assurance came.

Instead there came a sudden gut-loosening dip. A cry of alarm rose from the passengers. I dropped my book in my lap.

"Are you all right?" asked the young man sitting next to me. He wore a billed cap with some sort of logo and looked to be still in his teens. I was grateful for his kindness and nodded.

"It's the clouds," he said. "Look how dense they are." There were only two seats in our row, and he was beside the window. He told me he had just joined the army, and that he was going to be a pilot. He began to explain what actually happens when an aircraft moves through a dense mass of clouds such as this, but I have no memory of what he said. He seemed excited, whether about joining the army or becoming a pilot or the fact that our plane was now pitching like a boat in rough seas I didn't know. Before our troubles began, he'd been listening to music on his iPod. But now his attention, like mine—like every passenger's, I have no doubt—was focused on our flight.

"Good thing we hit these clouds before the beverage service," he said, "or we'd all be soaked!" This was no exaggeration.

Now it felt more as if we were on a Ferris wheel than a boat. A rickety Ferris wheel. And still no word from the pilot.

There followed a moment or so in which the plane glided smoothly, and you could feel everyone start to relax. But almost immediately we began pitching and shuddering again—this time so violently anyone could have been forgiven for fearing the worst. A man across the aisle was gripping the bottom of his seat as if he expected to be ejected from it. He rolled his head rapidly from side to side against the headrest like a sleeper trapped in a nightmare. Another man nearby began hyperventilating. The young man beside me sucked in his breath. "Oh boy, oh boy," I heard him say as he rocked back and forth. My turn to ask: "Are you all right?"

Together, he and I checked for airsickness bags in the pockets in front of us. Turbulence severe enough to cause nausea: Oh boy, indeed, this was a first. I remember thinking what a blessing it was there were no children onboard.

But what did the continued silence from the crew mean? That the pilot was too preoccupied getting the plane under control to address us? What about the copilot? The flight attendants, it turned out, were strapped in their seats at the back of the plane, as helpless as the rest of us.

An unpleasant smell filled the cabin, like the stench of overheated electrical wiring. Then, somewhere below us and to the right, there came a rhythmic *ker-chunk, ker-chunk, ker-chunk*—exactly like the sound of a car whose right rear tire had just blown out. That's when I began thinking maybe it wasn't turbulence. Or at least not just turbulence, not anymore.

And that's when a woman began to wail. "Oh, God, no. Please, God, no, no, no." Hers was not the only terrified voice to be heard, and at least one person was sniffling.

I took a deep breath and told myself that even if the plane was damaged or there was some kind of mechanical problem, this did not automatically spell doom; there was such a thing as an emergency landing. And how often, after all, do large passenger planes crash? Everyone knows it's one of the least likely accidents to befall a person.

Nevertheless, my anxiety soared. At the same time, I was overcome by a piercing sadness, but this sadness was mixed with strong feelings of wonder and awe. It was as if every idea I'd ever had about dying had been faint or ambiguous, and now here it loomed, the real thing, stunning in its vivid clarity. Then I remembered reading about a Japanese man who, in the minutes before the plane he was traveling on crashed, managed to scribble a note to his wife and children.

And what if we, like that man, were only minutes away from crashing? Such presence of mind, such stoic control—I knew I would never be capable of that. But it struck me with the force of lightning that I needed a plan. If the plane started to go down—if nothing could save us—what should I do?

One thing I knew for certain: I did not want to go out in a blaze of terror. *I will not die screaming for my life!* my inner voice screamed.

Perhaps if I, like that Japanese man, had a spouse and children, I would have wanted my last thoughts to be only of them. But now, as thoughts of my family and friends—and even of the cat waiting for me to come home—crowded in, they were too much for me. Too much! They brought on panic and despair. I had to push them away, for I did not want to die with turbulence in my soul.

I told myself that if we started to go down, I must reach for the hands of the young man sitting next to me.

And that was my simple plan. To hold on to this kind young

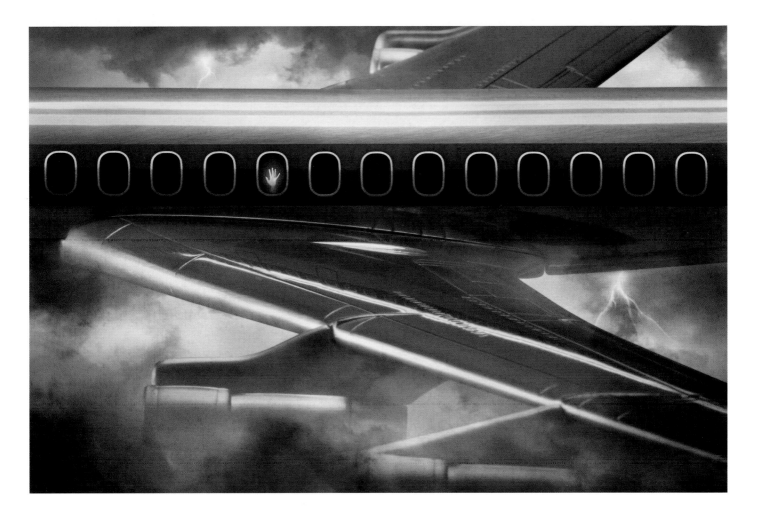

man, and to comfort him and be comforted by him. To be calm and present. To gather myself, and to distill my thoughts. This is how the story ends. So be it.

I had just time enough to make this plan when the plane stopped jerking, and I realized it was all over. Sighs and chuckles of relief all round, the flight attendants up out of their seats at last, moving along the aisle, speaking gently to passengers. I remember one of them stroking and squeezing my arm, and how everyone laughed heartily when the young man beside me shouted, "Hey, do we get our drinks now?"

"How long was that?" asked the man who'd been gripping his seat and rolling his head. "I think it must have been like 20 minutes!" I heard murmurs of agreement, but I'm sure this was wrong. Had it been that long, they would have had to carry some of us off the plane when we landed. I don't believe the entire episode could have lasted much more than five or at most ten minutes.

No satisfactory explanation was ever provided. The flight attendants told us the problem had indeed been turbulence, and when pressed about the bad smell and the knocking sound (both of which had mysteriously vanished, as if we had collectively dreamed them) they said, dismissively (but to me, at least, not entirely convincingly), that these things were also "turbulence related." And they said that they themselves had gotten the worst of it, sitting way in the back.

The rest of the flight was without incident. Our landing was smooth, the applause energetic. Leaving the plane, I thought the young man was right behind me. But when I turned to say goodbye,

I saw that several people had got between us, and I would have felt foolish waiting up for him.

At the baggage carousel, I heard various passengers telling people who'd come to meet them about our scare. ("I really thought I'd never see you again, hon." "I thought for sure this was it.") Then I caught sight of the young man, scratching his scalp under his billed cap while talking to an older man, and I felt my cheeks flush. A young soldier, a pilot in a time of war, headed for who knew what inescapable dangers, the likes of which I myself would never have to face. And I was ashamed of my fear and what now seemed like an exaggerated reaction.

I had thought that, in all likelihood, from now on it would be hard for me to fly. But happily this has not turned out to be the case. For a while I continued to feel resentment toward that pilot for his inexplicable silence. But since I don't know what really happened that day, I figured I might just as well feel gratitude: What if he'd saved all our lives? And though I hope never to have to go through another such episode, I can't say that I regret it, for it showed me a resource I was not sure I had.

I am used to thinking of myself as a nervous person, easily overwhelmed, the last one to stay cool in the face of extreme danger. And quite possibly, had the plane actually started to go down, I would have lost my head completely—to hell with my earnest little plan! But on reflection, I don't think so. I like to think I'll be able to find my way to that state again, in whatever challenging situations may come, when being calm and present is the best plan to have. ▢

THE RAPIST IN MY BEDROOM...
By Beverly Donofrio

I was raped one night in the summer of 2006 in San Miguel de Allende, Mexico, where I live. A friend and his sister had come over for dinner, and soon after they left, at 10:30, a neighbor came knocking. Water was gushing into her house from a construction site next door. I knew the builder, and the neighbor asked if I would call to tell him. I went upstairs, called the builder, then forgot to go back down and double lock the door. I was on the Internet, absorbed in looking up Benedictine monasteries, a recent preoccupation. I was investigating becoming a contemplative nun, trying to find a community that seemed right for me. At 12:10, shocked to be up so late, I put aside my laptop and promptly went to sleep.

At approximately 1 A.M., I was awakened by a rapist in my bed, his head inches from my own, a knife in his hand. I could make out the dark silhouette of a roundish man in a baseball cap, propped on his elbow beside me. I knew immediately who he was—the serial rapist who'd terrorized my town for the past eight months.

"Shhh, don't scream," he said in accented English. "I have a knife."

I recognized it immediately as the knife I'd cut limes with earlier and left on the counter. "Don't do this," I heard myself say. "This is not right. It's sick."

He told me I talked too much. He waved the knife closer to my face.

Now I will be raped, I thought.

And a worse thought: *I could lose my faith in God. After all my devotion, God has permitted this.*

I began to tremble.

"I'm going to be sick," I said. He knocked the heel of his hand on my shoulder. "Calm down," he said. "Look," and he placed the knife on the little altar beside the bed. "It's all right."

I will not write the details of the rape itself. Suffice it to say that I kept my arms crossed against my chest and my head turned away. The sexual ordeal lasted three minutes, the violating member was one inch long, the rapist never touched any other place on my body. Afterward he wanted to talk. "Are you Ingleterra?" he asked. "What's your name? Is your name Penelope? I see you on the street. You look good. Are you married? Where are you from?"

I am blessed to live in a community of strong women, four of whom had been raped by this man. They had not hidden away in shame but let the details of their rapes be known. And so I was aware that the first two women had fought him and been badly beaten. The next two women had not resisted and escaped physically unharmed except for the horrific sexual violation. I knew, too, that the rapist stayed for four or five hours, repeating his sexual assaults, that he liked to talk, to confess that he is a sick man who can't help himself, a confession that would arouse him again. So I decided not to answer one question, not to engage him in any conversation. I would pray in order to freak him out.

I said the first Hail Mary in English, then realized I should be using the language of this man's childhood: "Dios te salve Maria..."

"Stop it," he said. I said, "I'm praying for you"—which had not been true, but as soon as I said the words I understood that praying for him would be a very good thing to do, that I *should* be praying for him. So now, saying the next Hail Mary, I asked God, Jesus, the Virgin, the Holy Spirit, all the angels and saints and any other mystical agent of good to make this man see the harm he was doing. He kept talking as I prayed, patted my shoulder, told me everything would be okay, asked if I wanted wine or beer.

I switched to a Padre Nuestro, a loud one to let him know I was not listening to him. And I was struck by a new thought: I pray to the Virgin Mary for help every day, why wasn't I praying to her for help for myself right now? I began another Salve Maria, this time imploring the Virgin to get this man out of my bed and out of my house. Amazingly, seconds later, the rapist said, "Okay, I'm going," kissed me on the cheek, and backed out of the bed. I continued to pray as he said, "Goodbye, you'll be okay. Don't call the police."

As soon as I heard the door slam shut, I ran down the steps and locked the front door. As I walked back up the stairs, a dribble of sperm leaked onto my inner thigh and I considered the night ahead. The interrogation, the medical exam, the humiliating details confessed to strangers could feel like as much of a violation as the rape. It was possible, I realized, not even to call the police. Did I really want the whole town to know? Did I want to cause my son pain? Did I want to go through the rest of my life being known as a woman who had been raped? A victim? How I've always hated that word.

But before two minutes had passed, I understood I had no choice. People needed to know that the rapist had struck again, that he had not left town. It was my duty to report the crime.

I called my friends a block away, Caren and David Cross. Caren reached the police, and an army of them—on horseback, motorcycles, piled into trucks—arrived at my house even before Caren and David did. They were courteous and concerned. I was taken to the Ministerio Público, where, flanked by David and Caren, I told a competent and compassionate woman, a lawyer, the whole story.

Outside the office, a plainclothes detective pulled up a chair and told me to tell him every detail of what had happened. I began; moments later, feeling intensely irritated at having to relive it all, especially because this man was leaning in entirely too closely, I said, "I'm not telling you. I'm not repeating the story again."

I began in that instant to take back my power.

At dawn, after the report had been typed and the medical examiner had taken digital photos of my vagina along with a DNA sample, Caren and I drove back to my house, where 20 men combed through the rooms and the grounds, collecting evidence. A rope ladder still hung from my balcony rail.

Two state detectives arrived. It was very important, they said, that I tell them everything I could remember. "Read the report!" I said, then explained more calmly that I'd been traumatized enough for one night.

By the time everyone left, it was 10 in the morning. I had not slept and did not feel tired. In fact I felt rather energetic—and on a mission. The rapist had begun his attacks eight months earlier, scaling walls, lassoing balcony rails, removing skylights, cutting through glass. Women had installed alarm systems and put bars on their windows. They bought Mace and adopted dogs. One friend bolted herself into her bedroom every night and peed in a potty. Everywhere

we walked, we were aware he might be observing us. It was a reign of terror. But the rapist hadn't struck for four months and we had begun to feel safe, even complacent. I had to let the town know what had happened. Women needed to become vigilant again. I had been lax. I hadn't locked my upstairs patio door or double locked my front door. If I had, the rape might never have happened.

I asked Caren to post a notice on the town's Web site. And as weeping friends flooded into my house, I began to believe that if anyone had to be raped, it was good that it was me. The rape was just one more knock in a life of hard knocks. I could handle it. Plus I was a writer. I could write about it; I could be the messenger.

Virtually nothing had been publicized about the crimes in the local English-language paper. So I did an article sharing everything I'd learned from the other victims and the police. "The rapist has a pattern," I wrote. "He rapes women between 50 and 60 who live alone. He stalks them and attacks in their homes between 1 and 2 in the morning. The rapist needs to dominate, to feel powerful. If you fight you enrage him because you have ruined his fantasy, and if you act terrified you titillate him." At the end of the article, I wrote: "The outpouring of love and concern from both foreign and Mexican communities has been heartening and healing. I have always heard that we are all one. I never quite understood it the way I do now. Each time I'd heard how a woman among us had been raped, I felt sick and outraged. Now I am the one who was raped, and am the instrument of suffering. One person is hurt and everyone hurts. This is easy to see because we are a community. But it applies to the whole world. In our community, there is a sick member. That is all that he is."

The article was published exactly one week after the rape. Accompanying the article was the Hail Mary in Spanish. In shops notices appeared in Spanish and English saying that "a courageous sister" was raped and that by praying the Hail Mary she found strength. All over town English-speaking women kept the Hail Mary in Spanish by their beds, they carried it in their bags when they left home, they memorized it, and they prayed it.

People in town were saying that the energy felt different, lighter. People began to believe this man would be caught.

Meanwhile the police informed me that I was at high risk for a return attack. I stayed every night at Caren and Dave's. But during the day, even though it was scary imagining the rapist watching from the field beyond my courtyard walls, I lived in my house. I'd be damned if I'd let him keep me from my home.

Rapists are notoriously hard to catch. But five days after my article appeared, five days after everyone began praying, at 11 in the evening on the corner of my street, carrying a rope with a hook fastened to the end, he was caught.

I didn't have to be strong anymore, and I collapsed. I had no defenses. I cried because I'd been raped. And I cried at the drop of a hat. Strangely, while the rapist was still at large, it had not for one moment occurred to me to leave town. A friend had invited me to her cottage on Lake Huron, which I'd refused. Now I accepted. Walking all over the island, kayaking, skinny-dipping, canoeing, playing Scrabble with her other guests, I began to heal. One evening I wept to my friend. I needed to talk about what had happened, I said, but I felt that no one wanted to hear. She told me to talk as much as I wanted.

And so I did. As I write this article, it has been six months since the attack. It seems much longer. It was disturbing to be a celebrity because I'd been raped. But that has been more than made up for by the people thanking me for writing about it. Or the people who've approached me simply to say, "I'm sorry about what happened to you."

But most important, what happened has strengthened my faith in God and in prayer. When the rapist came into bed, I felt that God had betrayed me. But once I'd remembered to ask for help, I'd received it. Praying had turned despair into faith. And then the whole town prayed with me, and the rapist was caught. I am unutterably grateful that the rapist is behind bars.

I still talk about what happened to me once in a while, the way I might talk about having been caught in a tsunami. Rape has been a plague through all of history. It happens to women everywhere. It happens all the time. So why not admit that it happened to me?

Please, if you are ever raped, think of it as a physical attack that has absolutely nothing to do with sex as a tender act. Shout out loudly and open yourself to the respect due a survivor. You have done nothing to be ashamed of. The rapist has. **◖**

"SINCE HE'S GONE, I DON'T LAUGH ANYMORE"

Heart palpitations. Insomnia. Depression. Though far from the battlefields, the families of soldiers serving in Iraq suffer from their own war wounds. Usually in silence. But now a groundbreaking program is reaching out—and getting through!—to this traditionally therapy-resistant, tough-it-out population. Deborah Copaken Kogan sits down with shrinks, family members, and the brass....

The empty chairs—some two dozen of them—form a circle in the middle of a fluorescent-lit room in the Barnes Army Reserve Center in downtown Boston. The space is shared by a gym, where reserve soldiers, many of whom have done multiple tours of duty in Iraq, work out near a sign that reads—irony unintended—BE ALERT! THE FITNESS EQUIMENT IN THIS FACILITY PRESENTS HAZARDS WHICH, IF NOT AVOIDED, COULD CAUSE SERIOUS INJURY OR DEATH.

Mingling and chatting in the room are several volunteer psychologists and clinical social workers, a few absentmindedly pausing to check their watches and the door. Two reservists in full fatigues saunter in carrying boxes of cookies and colorful balls.

"What is this?" asks one of the shrinks, squeezing a ball in her palm.

"It's a stress ball, ma'am," says a soldier. "We thought, you know, they'd be useful."

"Wonderful idea!" says Jaine Darwin, PsyD, the smiling mother hen of the group, a positive-energy dynamo in her late 50s who is frantically ripping along the perforations of several pieces of cardboard, creating instant business cards bearing the acronym SOFAR—"I made them myself! On the printer!" She plans to give the cards to the people scheduled to fill her empty chairs: the wives, husbands, mothers, fathers, and children of the soldiers of the 883rd Medical Company, which shipped out to Iraq nearly three months earlier, in August 2005.

Established in 2004, SOFAR—Strategic Outreach to Families of All Reservists—is the brainchild of Darwin's partner and Harvard Medical School colleague, Kenneth Reich, EdD, and it aims to do what no other nonmilitary group has ever done—offer pro bono psychological care to family members of reserve and National Guard soldiers, a population that traditionally has not only lacked such care but shunned it.

The seeds of the organization were sown in the fall of 2001, when Reich was besieged by anxiety in his daughter's New York City apartment the night after 9/11. "I'd gone down there to comfort her," he says, "and I woke up about 2:30 in the morning, which is not my usual habit. I was trying to figure out what had woken me, and it was this horrible smell." The odor—the product of charred flesh, among other things—shook Reich, but its recollection would later spur him to action. If he, a trained psychiatric professional whose only connection to disaster was an unharmed child and an acrid smell, could be unnerved by the fear that he might not see his daughter again,

how much worse must it be for people who lived with the constant threat of a loved one's doom? "That's why we're doing this program," Reich says. "Because no one's really thinking hard about the families, that they are the invisible casualties of war."

In November 2003, eight months after the Iraq war began, Reich organized a conference—"War, Terrorism, and Children: Supporting Family Strength and Resilience"—to which he invited professionals from the therapeutic community as well as family members of New England National Guardsmen who'd been fighting in Afghanistan and Iraq. He targeted the group because, unlike families of career soldiers, who normally live on army bases with others undergoing the same emotional strains, the families of guardsmen (and likewise the families of reservists) live among the general population, without a system of built-in support.

"At the conference," Reich says, "family members talked about their experiences, and it was riveting and moving." There was the wife of a soldier whose children refused to get out of bed in the morning. There was the woman married to a Green Beret, who hadn't spoken to her husband in months and had no idea whether he was alive or dead. "I have to tell you: There was a roomful of shrinks sitting there, and most of us had no idea what the families go through or what the pressures are."

Reich left the conference determined to do more. He enlisted Darwin as his partner. He started doing research. In *The New York Times* he read that one-third of homeless men in America are veterans and that the number of homeless Vietnam vets has surpassed the number of U.S. troops killed during that war. In *The New England Journal of Medicine* he read the results of a Walter Reed Army Institute of Research study concluding that, as of July 2004, approximately one in six soldiers who had experienced combat in Iraq exhibited symptoms of major depression, serious anxiety, or post-traumatic stress disorder (PTSD). He read a surgeon general's report estimating that that number would soon climb to one in three. Because he is an expert in the field of family therapy, he began to wonder how all of this depression, anxiety, and post-traumatic stress would affect the families and friends of the soldiers upon their return. And then he did some math.

Having read that, by the end of 2004, an estimated 1 million American soldiers would have been deployed to Iraq and Afghanistan, Reich multiplied this number by seven (representing an estimate of each soldier's parents, siblings, spouse/fiancé, and children), and multiplied the result by six—what he calls the proverbial six degrees of separation, which could include grandparents, aunts and uncles, cousins, nieces and nephews, grandchildren, friends, and colleagues. The grand total: 42 million people with

Left: SOFAR founders Kenneth Reich and Jaine Darwin at a Veteran's Day celebration in Boston, 2006. *Right:* While her husband is on his second tour in Iraq, Shirley Burke talks with reservists and family members after a group therapy session in Boston, November 2005.

the potential to be psychologically affected by the war. Reich knew he couldn't help all of them, but what if he could help just a few?

Back at the Barnes Building, the families have finally started drifting into the room: a pregnant mother and her 7-year-old daughter; a few couples in their 50s and 60s; several younger adults, in their 20s, some dressed in army fatigues. They take their seats nearly silently, 25 in all.

After a brief introduction and an apology for my presence, Darwin begins to speak. "How do you worry?" she asks, pacing around the circle, directing her query outward, toward everyone. "Do you do the Scarlett O'Hara method—*I'll think about it tomorrow?* Or are you the type who thinks, *The more stories I read, the more Internet searches I do, the more TV news I watch, the better?* Or are you the kind of person who says, *I'm fine, I'm absolutely fine, nothing bothers me,* but then in the middle of the day you'll have a moment of intense panic?"

When no one answers, she turns to the pregnant mother, Kara Burke: "How are you doing?"

"Okay," says Kara, shrugging her shoulders, expressionless. Her daughter is sitting next to her, busy with crayons and paper.

After a long pause, Darwin says, "'Okay' worries me. When people say they're okay, sometimes it doesn't mean okay at all. Sometimes it means, 'It's hard for me to cope.' I guess the better question would be, how are you coping?"

Kara sighs. "It's pretty much what I expected. I mean, there's the surprise of being..." She searches for the right words. "I'm surprised emotionally, I guess. There's the new baby..." She looks down at her burgeoning belly but cannot express herself further. Her eyes start to well.

"AFTER THE FLAGS STOP WAVING AND THE BANDS STOP PLAYING, THERE'S AN EFFECT—WHETHER IT'S A PROSTHESIS, A DISABILITY, OR A MENTAL CONDITION—THAT THE SOLDIER AND HIS FAMILY WILL DEAL WITH FOR THE REST OF THEIR LIVES."

A friendly-looking, well-coiffed older woman named Shirley Boyajian-Burke (no relation to Kara) comes to the rescue. "I'll tell you what I'm feeling," she says. "This should have been my 25th wedding anniversary with my husband. I expected it to be fun, just the two of us, without the boys." Instead, her husband has just shipped off to Iraq for his second tour, the same month their two sons left for college. "I feel lonely. Empty. All the time."

Frank Ciaramitaro, dressed in fatigues, also has a spouse on a second tour of duty. "I've been over there," he says, "so I have a totally different perspective. I know what she's going through. I've walked across that burning desert with 50 pounds of equipment on my back. I can taste the sand."

"That's called heightened empathy," Darwin says. "It's a fancy term for being able to feel what your loved one is feeling."

"But it's not just the bad things," says Frank. "There's good things, too. Like playing Uno with the staff sergeant. Or"—he turns to Kara—"laughing with your husband. Jimmy always put a smile on all our faces."

Kara looks at her hands. "Since he's gone, I don't laugh anymore."

Frank seems to recognize a decisive moment in the discussion, a place to step in without the help of the professionals. Darwin remains silent, letting him find the words. Frank tells the story of the day Jimmy showed up in the barracks dressed, for no discernible reason, as Waldo (from *Where's Waldo?*), pretending to be the brigade general. "You should have seen him," Frank says, shaking his head and grinning. "It was so funny."

Kara laughs. Then she wipes away a tear.

Darwin nods at Frank as if to say, *Keep going.*

"I have the utmost respect for what

you're all going through," he says, glancing around, speaking to the group at large. "I'll tell you, now that I'm here, I realize that this is harder than being over there. There, you're just focused on your job, on staying alive. Here, every second of every moment of your existence, you're thinking, *What's happening over there?*"

Darwin, satisfied with the direction of the discussion, now takes over. "You're all engaged in a process that you're going to be changed by. The question is, how will you negotiate the journey?"

For many soldiers and their families, the answer to such a question is *not well*. Take the case of National Guard member John Crawford, who was on his honeymoon, one semester shy of graduating from college, when he was called to active duty in Iraq. By the time he returned, 15 months later, his marriage was in shambles, he had neither money nor home, and his psyche was deeply damaged. "I lose my temper if I can't get the key in the door," he told me in an e-mail, describing the constant anger he felt. "I've thrown my computer and broken it when it froze up. Stupid things like that become the norm."

He transformed his angst into a stunning memoir, *The Last True Story I'll Ever Tell*, a raw examination of the vast disconnect between the returning soldier and the friends and family who stayed behind. "Tell us a war story," he imagines a friend demanding in the final scene of the book. "Did you shoot anyone?" Crawford, unable to speak, flashes back to the day in Nasiriyah when he shot a young boy he thought was aiming an AK-47 at him, only to discover, after the boy was dead, that the weapon was a broken-off rifle barrel, as useless as a toy gun.

"Emotionally, it was strange for me, coming back," he says. "The average person disgusted me. I still have a hard time describing my animosity toward many civilians, whether they're retro-hippie types or the people who put yellow ribbons on their gas-guzzling SUVs." Crawford feels lucky to have his writing as a balm. "So many soldiers, I think, fail to realize they're even showing symptoms of PTSD," he says. "Or they choose to ignore the symptoms until, having burned their bridges, they have nowhere to turn. Unfortunately, the VA is about 600,000 cases behind, so

often there isn't much in the way of mental health or benefits when the time comes."

Major General Dennis Laich, a retired two-star general who, at the time this story was reported, headed the 94th Regional Readiness Command, understands these issues. And when he heard about Reich and Darwin's proposal, he was intrigued. Sitting in his office in Devens, Massachusetts, Laich told me, "When the soldier deploys, the soldier is deploying with his or her unit, with little flags waving and bands playing, to do the country's bidding. The family, on the other hand, has to turn around and go back to the daily trials and tribulations: Diapers still need to be changed, garbage still needs to be taken out, doctor bills need to be paid, pipes break."

Laich was instrumental in helping Reich and Darwin cut through the red tape separating them from the families. And while the army does not formally endorse any program not under the umbrella of the U.S. military, he worked hard to see that the families of his soldiers were able to take full advantage of the outstretched hand, facilitating contact between Reich and Darwin and the various networks of Family Readiness Groups (military-sponsored support groups meant to boost morale, improve communication, and help families deal with military life). Laich knows that when it comes to mental health, the military still has some catching up to do. "We made some mistakes," he says of the past. "Even in the first Gulf War, we were in denial as an army about Gulf War syndrome." When I ask him to elaborate, he talks about his two visits to the troops in Iraq, about the emotional difficulty of serving in a war with no front to speak of other than a "360 degree circle around your body that's about four feet out."

Of the troops, Laich says, "You can get into the argument however you want to about whether they are heroes, not heroes, but behind every one of those soldiers is a shadow of either an existing or a potential tragedy. After the flags stop waving and the bands stop playing, there's an effect—whether it's a prosthesis, a disability, or a mental condition—that the soldier and his family will deal with for the rest of their lives."

I ask Laich if he thinks it ironic that the army has joined forces with two liberal shrinks from Harvard, an institution that

Left: Retired Major General Dennis Laich, one of SOFAR's biggest fans, in Devens, Massachusetts, November 2005. *Center:* John Crawford (in Baghdad, 2003) was called to active duty while on his honeymoon. *Right:* As head of the 325th Transportation Company's Family Readiness Group, Lillian Connolly (Boston, November 2005) refers anxious family members of deployed reservists to SOFAR.

once famously kicked the ROTC off its campus. He smiles, then shakes his head. "This isn't a joining of Harvard and the army," he says. "This is some professionals who care enough to come out of their ivory tower to help the families of soldiers who are acting on their behalf."

Lillian Connolly appreciates how subtle the effects of war can be, how it has a way of creeping into the cracks of everyday life. When I first spoke to her, her husband, Joseph (then a butcher in civilian life, now a clerk at Lowe's), was in the middle of a yearlong deployment—his second—with the 220th Transportation Company. Recalling his first tour of duty, Lillian said, "While he was gone, everything was 'mine': my responsibilities, my children, my house. When he came back, I had to learn to switch back to 'ours.' I was acting out more. Picking fights. Yelling if I didn't get my way. He was quieter than usual." During Joseph's stint at home between his tours, it struck Lillian just how different their experiences during the separation had been. She realized that she would have to come to terms with the huge gap rather than try, futilely, to bridge it. "We'll never understand what they go through, and they'll never understand what we go through," she says with a smile and a shrug.

But even within Lillian's own experience, there are gaps—disconnects among feelings and emotions that are difficult to reconcile. On the one hand, she tells me how proud of her husband she is, how proud their four kids are, how she feels the media has been too negative in its reporting on the war. On the other hand, she tells me about her sister-in-law's brother, who was killed in combat; about deciding not to let her children attend the funeral; about how hard it was for her stoic 12-year-old son to have the fact of that death constantly rattling around in the back of his brain. Nothing is easy for the families of soldiers. And for that reason, Lillian is an enthusiastic participant in SOFAR. She's also in a position to be its champion. As the leader of the Family Readiness Group of Joseph's current company, the 325th Transportation Company, she fields phone calls and e-mails from anxious parents, spouses, and children of deployed reservists; in response, as well as in the newsletter she writes, she always provides the contact information for SOFAR. "What's great about them is that they don't take insurance, they don't take money, they don't take anything," she says. "There's no record. No paper trail."

"Without a doubt, the paper trail is a factor," John Crawford says, when I ask whether someone in his position would ever seek psychotherapy. In the military, he says, the mere fact of pursuing psychiatric help "follows you." One of the studies Reich consulted before starting SOFAR reveals that Crawford's opinion is widely shared. In a survey of more than 6,000 soldiers and marines (2,530 were surveyed just prior to shipping out to Iraq; 3,671 were surveyed several months after returning from combat duty in Iraq or Afghanistan), the Walter Reed Army Institute of Research found that taking advantage of mental health services was commonly viewed as having negative repercussions. Among respondents who met the criteria for major depression, generalized anxiety, or PTSD, 50 percent said seeking mental health services "would harm my career"; 59 percent said, "Members of my unit might have less confidence in me"; 63 percent said, "My unit leadership might treat me differently"; 65 percent said, "I would be seen as weak."

No doubt such attitudes are endemic to the military as an institution, embedded in military culture and perpetuated by old-school

commanders. But the anti-therapy bias hasn't come only from the top down; troops come equipped with their own prejudices. As Crawford says, people "attracted to military service are usually the types that don't run around asking for help"—and again the Walter Reed survey backs him up. Forty-one percent of those meeting the criteria for a mental disorder said seeking treatment "would be too embarrassing"; 38 percent said, "I don't trust mental health professionals"; 25 percent said, "Mental healthcare doesn't work."

The soldiers' attitudes tend to be shared by their families. "The culture of the military," Reich says, "is one of taking care of their own and not venturing to 'outsiders.' As a result, many family members view the idea of going to someone to talk about problems as a weakness rather than an act of valor."

By making SOFAR services confidential and free—25 percent of Walter Reed respondents who met the mental disorder criteria said, "Mental healthcare costs too much money"—Reich hoped to make talk therapy more palatable. But he and Darwin soon grew to appreciate the difficulty of reversing traditional biases. Despite the thousands of perforated business cards they handed out, their voice mailboxes remained strangely empty. "We were working away," Darwin says, "but our phones weren't ringing, and we were starting to get anxious. It finally dawned on us that we had to give people the service they wanted, not the service we thought they needed. And apparently the service they wanted was the opportunity to get together in group situations and have a supportive mental health presence there. That's what they were comfortable with. They were not comfortable with the idea of calling somebody and going to sit in that somebody's office."

"THE FAMILIES ARE THE INVISIBLE CASUALTIES OF WAR."

Lillian Connolly agrees. "We prefer to seek out support in our own communities," she says. And by coming into their communities, the SOFAR professionals have, she posits, allowed for a more open, more efficient, more profound free flow of ideas. "It gives family members a chance to speak their minds," she says, "so the soldiers can do their jobs overseas."

Major General Laich doesn't care if the therapists do their jobs one-on-one or in group situations or by simply waiting at their desks for a call. "I know one thing without question," he says. "By being there, they make a difference. Even if their phone never rings, I know—absolutely, without reservation—that by being there, they're making things better. The real measure of how well we're doing in taking care of our soldiers and their families will come not in the next six months. It's ten or 20 years down the road."

In 2006, Frank's wife, Kara's husband, Shirley's husband, Lillian's husband, and every other member of the 883rd and 220th came home alive, and Reich and Darwin were on hand to greet them. "It was incredibly gratifying to be invited to the return ceremonies," says Darwin, "to hear the family members say to us, 'These deployments were made easier by the help we received from you.'"

The doctors now have real business cards, along with a well-trafficked Web site (to learn more about, or donate to, SOFAR, go to sofarusa.org), and their phones ring for private consults outside the group sessions. In February 2007, the American Academy of Pediatrics formally endorsed SOFAR—thanks in part to a detailed pamphlet SOFAR produced to help teachers, caregivers, and pediatricians address the anxieties of soldiers' children. The pamphlet is now being distributed to every school in North Carolina. From the doctors' perspective, that means only 49 states to go. ◖

THE PANIC BUTTON

Your tire blew out on the freeway. Your wallet's been stolen. There's a deer in aisle one, next to the unsalted cashews. Don't just stand there—freak out! Martha Beck on the only rational way to weather life's big and little snafus.

The military has given the English language two words that brilliantly articulate different types of crises: The first is *snafu*, an acronym for "situation normal, all f---ed up." The second is *fubar*, which stands for "f---ed up beyond all recognition." As we travel the bumpy road of life, we must prepare to deal with both. Fubar situations are huge disasters, the kind that come with an implicit "get out of normal obligations free" card and often require a rethinking of where your future is headed. Smaller snafu crises—the broken toe, the stolen wallet, the babysitter quitting on short notice—can be incredibly disruptive, but usually they're not life changing; they're more likely month changing or ten-weeks-of-Vicodin disruptive. But a short-term crisis is still a crisis, so here's how to weather your next snafu:

1 GO AHEAD AND FREAK OUT

One fine day in 2006, a wild deer wandered into a Target store in West Des Moines. He skidded around like Bambi on ice for 20 minutes, until employees herded him through the automatic doors to freedom. On surveillance videos, the deer is wearing an expression I've seen on many human faces during minor crises—a look that says, "I feel fine, but *what the...?*"

I mention this because there's one way in which deer handle crises better than humans—at least according to *Waking the Tiger: Healing Trauma* author Peter Levine, PhD, who holds two doctorates, one in psychology, one in medical and biological physics. Early in his research, Levine noticed that when animals are traumatized—even a little bit—they react by trembling, running, kicking, and thrashing around, which is what that deer did. Meanwhile, human Target shoppers reacted with stiffness and consternation, because we generally try to subdue physical "emergency" reactions.

After falling down stairs or arguing with a coworker, we make every effort to keep our eyes, voices, and hands steady, determined to show through our physical motionlessness that we're in complete control of our bodies, moods, and lives (no matter how many Xanax this requires).

Levine noted that people who have physical emergency reactions often cope better with crisis, and show fewer symptoms of trauma afterward, than people who hold still. Stress compels action; in snafu situations, Mother Nature gives just one instruction to all her children, and that instruction is, "Move!" When the unexpected strikes, find a private space and let your body do whatever it wants. Heave, kick, shake your head like a wet cat. Then let that energy flow into constructive action, whether it's contesting a credit card charge, yanking cactus spines out of your child, or slapping duct tape on a broken pipe.

I got a chance to test this advice when one of my car tires blew out. After regaining control of the fishtailing vehicle, then coaxing it over to the freeway shoulder, I went a little crazy, shuddering and shouting incoherently for about ten seconds. Sure enough, this seemed to open up a channel to calm. Feeling very alert, I got out and changed that tire with my own profoundly nonmechanical hands. I drove away feeling so empowered, so conscious of life's fragility, that even the disruption of my schedule hardly bothered me. I do believe letting myself have those initial ten seconds of physical freak-out cleared my mind and body for positive action. Thank you, Dr. Levine.

2 RELEASE YOUR EXPECTATIONS

Not all problems are this quickly resolved. My flat tire rearranged my day, but you may have a disaster that lingers for weeks or months, such as your brother-in-law. The situation, whatever or whoever it is, will eventually be resolved, but in the meantime it requires accommodation.

Realizing this is like being turned upside down. We hear our plans falling out of our pockets and smashing into countless questions: "How will I meet my deadline?" "Who'll walk the dogs?" "Can I even tie my shoes with this cast on my arm?" Our knee-jerk reaction is often defiant refusal to let go of expectations: Somehow, we insist, we will stick to our schedule.

I've heard you can trap a monkey by putting a banana in a jar, then punching a hole in the lid just wide enough for the animal's hand—not wide enough, that is, for the hand plus a banana. The monkey's refusal to release the banana is what keeps it stuck. This is what happens when we hang on to expectations in the face of crisis, and it can turn a snafu into an utterly fubar situation. Working when you're sick, you end up in the hospital. Rushing tasks after a slowdown, you drop or break or miscalculate something crucial. Pushing yourself beyond emotional limits, you lash out and damage a relationship.

Conversely, learning to let go of expectations is a ticket to peace. It allows us to ride over every crisis—small or large, brother-in-law or end-of-quarter office lockdown—like a beach ball on water. The next time a problem arises in your life, take a deep breath, let out a sigh, and replace the thought *Oh no!* with the thought *Okay.* If it's hard to sustain this perspective, go immediately to step 3.

3 NARROW YOUR TIME APERTURE

It took me decades to learn how to surrender expectations. I wanted to let go; I just didn't know the procedure. Then a meditation teacher put it in terms I could understand. Imagine, he said, that your life is going badly—you're underpaid, and you've just discovered that your spouse has started smoking. You go for a walk in the woods, trying to clear your head. Anxiety eats at you: Should you demand a raise? What if your spouse gets lung cancer? Troubling scenarios spin out in your mind. You can't stop worrying.

Then you walk around a rock, and there it is: a bear.

At that moment, it becomes almost magically easy to stop obsessing about your lousy job and your spouse's lungs. You have no trouble surrendering your worries—in fact, as you sprint back to the safety of your SUV, you let go of verbal thought altogether. You've attained the enviable clarity meditators call one-pointed attention.

This is how you let go of expectations: by giving full attention to the snafu at hand. Forget about finishing your errands and focus on holding this bandage to this cut, right here, right now, until the bleeding stops. Do what is needed with full concentration: Find the spare tire, turn off the water valve, call your therapist. Be here now, and you'll realize there's nowhere else you ever need to be.

4 MAKE LOOSEY-GOOSEY PLANS

As you focus on the present, you'll find the next step arises almost automatically, and then the one after that. Your thought as you run from the bear is to reach the car. Your aim as you press on a wound is to stop the bleeding. Unlike plans made in calmer circumstances, which may be detailed, researched, and rigid, the ones you make when facing snafus should be so loose that they're almost floppy.

One year, when I lived in Cambridge, Massachusetts, I decided to run the Boston marathon. On a snowy afternoon, I took a bus to Wellesley, which lies at the halfway point of the marathon route. The idea was to run home, both training and familiarizing myself with the terrain. I overlooked only one thing: I have absolutely no sense of direction. After running for an hour, I noticed that Boston was not where I thought it was. After two hours, I was jogging past eerie, deserted factories. After three hours, my world was empty country roads in a pitch-dark blizzard.

Peter Levine would have been proud of the way I eventually freaked out, stomping, kicking, and, yes, using strong language. My tantrum freed me to release my expectations of knocking this off in a few hours and accept that I was well and truly lost. This allowed me to narrow my focus to the immediate situation, and I immediately formulated a plan: Retrace my route by following my own footprints. It worked for a half hour, until the falling snow obscured my tracks. By then I could hear the rumbling of motors, so my approach changed: Follow the noise. This took me to a freeway, from which I could see a distant glow of city lights. I followed them to downtown Boston, where, switching strategies one last time, I caught the subway home. Staying loose and flexible not only got me through a snafu but proved I could run for six straight hours. After that the marathon was a cakewalk.

THE PLANS THAT TAKE US OUT of short-term crises almost always proceed like this. A strategy that works well one moment is useless the next. That's okay. Keep moving. Keep letting go of expectations. Keep your attention on the here and now, and keep adjusting. And finally, refuse to contemplate the distant future until the snafu is over. Cancel lunch, obsess later about the social fallout. Look in the yellow pages under "flood repair" without wondering how much it will eventually cost to replace your carpet.

The difference between unthinkable disasters and short-term crises is that if you follow these instructions, life snaps back to being surprisingly normal surprisingly quickly. Think what that deer must have felt as he roamed the aisles of Target, wondering why the humans were forcing him toward a wall of glass and metal. Imagine his gratification when he finally triggered the door sensor. That's the way a minor crisis ends. It's almost anticlimactic: You look up from the one step that has your full attention and realize you're out of the woods. Or, if you're a deer, back in the woods. Back, in any case, to the world you're used to, where snafus are typical and things occasionally get fubar, but where you feel in your DNA that things are exactly as they should be. ◘

TO *BEAT* THE UNBEATABLE FOE

It hasn't been easy—or pretty. One of them has to inject herself in the stomach twice a day. The other came so close to dying that her father arranged—and paid for—her funeral. But Rae Lewis-Thornton and Sharon Lund, who were both infected with AIDS in 1983, when the disease was a virtual death sentence, are still here, still fighting, still working to help other women (now a quarter of all new cases) avoid their fate. And they have something to teach all of us about the art, craft, and sheer cussedness of hanging in. Liz Brody reports.

Sharon Lund says AIDS made her the woman she is—the woman Hector Parra fell in love with in 2001, photographed in the summer of 2007 at her home in San Diego.

She must be dead, Sharon Lund. I interviewed her—when, 1992? She'd already been HIV positive for nine years. Last time we talked, that virus was diabolically bungee jumping her in and out of her grave. The woman had three T cells, for God's sake.

So when the phone rings and a woman says, "Hi, it's Sharon Lund," my thoughts start splashing around in a mad, frantic backstroke until I finally manage: "Where are you?"

"I'm living in San Diego...it's beautiful." She practically sings it in that upbeat, holistic-healer voice of hers, as I try to wrap my mind around the *living* part.

"And your health?"

"Never been better," she tra-la-las.

"Are you living alone?" (Again, the *living*.)

Yes, but actually, there's someone in her life, a younger man.... And she's written a book, her daughter's great, the two of them are coming to New York....

At the time I wrote about Sharon in 1992, women made up 14 percent of Americans with AIDS, most casualties of IV drug use. Today, according to the latest statistics, women account for more than a quarter of all new HIV/AIDS cases; four out of five of them from plain old sex.

Very few female patients have been at it as long as Sharon, who was infected at the beginning of the epidemic, when there wasn't a single drug available and AIDS meant dying awfully and soon. As in: You could probably count the years on one hand. After hearing from Sharon, however, I met another long-term survivor, Rae Lewis-Thornton, who figured out she's been HIV positive since

1983. Both women—one white, one black—were blessed with the kind of looks that can make a man forget how to tie his oxfords and an unrelenting strength drawn, perhaps, from the fact that when they learned they had the disease, they'd already made it through worse. That grit has enabled them to hold themselves up through the worst of pain and social stigma, even to stare death in the face and say, "Not now, sorry: I've got other plans."

AIDS experts will tell you that women like Sharon and Rae, by participating in studies and speaking out publicly, have brightened the prognosis for the newly infected. But most of all, these two are heroes for fighting what was thought to be unfightable: They're models of resilience, whatever the difficulty might be.

"I THOUGHT I WAS GOING TO DIE. I THOUGHT, *I'M DONE WITH*," a frail, screened-out woman identified only as a "suburbanite" whimpered on the TV screen. "But my mom said, 'You're going to be fine, just get to the doctors.' ... That's what I did. So far everything's worked out okay."

Six weeks later she was dead, Dan Rather's voice trundled in on his 1986 CBS News special *AIDS Hits Home.*

Cut to: a man's profile, obscured for anonymity—the late suburbanite's ex-husband. As the tape rolled, he calmly admitted that she had no idea he was bisexual when he married her. Clearly she never imagined he could give her AIDS.

"Do you feel in some way as if you murdered your wife?" the interviewer asked uncomfortably.

"No," the man said with eerie confidence.

Rather's 1986 report was a wake-up call for many women watching: a husband on the down-low, not that we called it that then—the whole thing a chilling reminder of how you could get AIDS from someone you thought was totally safe. For one viewer, though, the program was a death sentence.

Sharon Lund, a soft-spoken single mother in Los Angeles, was watching because her parents had taped it for her. They knew she worked with AIDS patients and brought the video when they visited over Christmas. With everyone settled on the couch, a fire going, the tree all festively lit, Sharon didn't pay much attention until the man in profile came on, and then she started screaming.

"It's Bill, it's Bill," she shrieked. Her whole body shaking uncontrollably, she yanked the tape out of the machine before the program finished and scrambled into the bedroom. There she grabbed the phone and dialed Bill's number. She had been married to him after the frail woman. "Is it true you have AIDS?" she asked hysterically when he picked up.

By the time Sharon saw that CBS special, she was 37 and a veteran of tough times. Her two brothers died five years apart, both at age 23—Tommy in a motorcycle accident, Raymond from a heroin overdose. She'd been hospitalized with anorexia, lived (barely) through two suicide attempts. And her self-worth had been raked over by a childhood of abuse that started at age 3 and ended when she was 12, only because her grandfather, who'd been raping her, died. "And I felt responsible," says Sharon, "because I'd been praying for his death."

When she went into therapy as a young adult and told her dad she'd been molested all those years by his father, he turned livid. "I was so upset over it," says Tom Clark, a former navy captain who ran a ship-inspection business in Seattle. "If he hadn't already passed away, I'd probably have shot him."

The abuse left Sharon uncomfortable about getting physically intimate. Of her first husband, whom she married at 19, she says, "He's a wonderful man, but every time we had sex I screamed inside, became numb, and wanted to die." Three years before they split, they had a daughter, Jeaneen, who would become the reason Sharon fights to this day so fiercely for her life.

She had long been divorced when she attended an EST seminar in 1983 and met a new man—"Six-foot-two, silvery hair, a very nice-looking guy. We sat and we talked for a half hour and then he said, 'Can I call you?'" His name was Bill Geremesz, he managed the Rose Bowl Stadium in Pasadena, and he never tried to get her clothes off. "He doesn't like sex? I really like this guy; heck, this is perfect," she laughs, remembering. After six months, when he asked her to marry him, Sharon thought, *This is God sent—thank you, thank you.*

The couple was on their way to walk down the "aisle" at the Rose Bowl when he turned to her in the car and said, "You know what? You're ugly. I don't know why I'm marrying you." All dressed up in her wedding gown, she sat there shocked, marooned, and in tears. "Don't you start crying at me," he snapped. So Sharon gathered herself and, almost in a trance, made her way onto the field with him. "As I'm walking out, it was like a thousand voices shouted out, *Don't marry him,*" she recalls. "And I got to the 50-yard line and I said, 'I do.'"

That night would be their first time in bed together. "When we get to the hotel, I go into the bathroom and I put on a negligee," she says. "It was lavender satin and the V came down to my belly button so it exposed my breasts. And I come out and he's sleeping. I wake him up with kisses, and he looks at me and says, 'What are

you, some kind of a whore? You look like a tramp. Get the hell out of here.' I just lost it. I was crying and crying and crying."

After spending most of the night in the hotel lobby, she says, "the next morning we went home, and he acted like everything was normal. From then on, I could not do anything right."

Sharon left after four months and went to Hawaii, where her parents were living. "He called me every day and he said, 'I'm sorry; we'll go to therapy.' *Hey,* I thought, *'therapy'—that's a good word. We'll make it work.* So I said, 'Okay, okay, I'll come home.' I got to the airport and he wasn't there. And I called him and said into the message machine, 'Bill'—he didn't pick up. Call him again—'Bill, Bill'—he finally picks up the phone and says, 'Don't bother coming home.' I said, 'What do you mean? I'm at the airport.' He said, 'Don't bother coming home.'"

It turned out that Pat, his ex-wife—the woman on the AIDS special—had moved back in.

In December 1986, when Sharon saw the special, she and Bill had been divorced for two and a half years. On the phone that night, he flatly denied that he was the man on the show. But her instincts told her otherwise. She went to an anonymous test site, and the results were positive. She and Bill had sex only three times. (As he was dying in 1989, he called to admit he'd infected her. He hadn't told her about his HIV status, he explained, because he'd needed to marry her in order to get custody of his kids.)

> "EVEN ON BAD DAYS, I GET MY BUTT UP, PUT LIPSTICK ON. AIDS MAY CONTROL MY BODY. I CAN'T GIVE IT MY SPIRIT."

Anger doesn't suit Sharon; she doesn't like to put her immune system, weakened as it is, through the stress of it. From the get-go, she took a holistic and at times medically controversial path, using meditation to guide her treatment and visualization to help her immune system fight the virus. When AZT, the first antiretroviral drug for the treatment of HIV (it interferes with the virus's replicating process), was approved in 1987, she was told to get on it fast—if not, she would have only six months to live. A person with a healthy immune system generally has 500 to 1,500 CD4 cells (also called T cells), the "generals of our defense system," as one doctor puts it—but HIV takes them out. When the count drops below 200, the diagnosis shifts to AIDS and drugs are prescribed. Sharon refused, convinced she'd be better off without putting toxins into her system. Jeaneen changed the sheets as her mother soaked them with night sweats and cleaned up the diarrhea when she couldn't make it to the bathroom. "People freaked out once they found out she was infected," Jeaneen remembers, now 32 and a professional photographer. "They didn't want to have anything to do with her." That didn't stop Sharon.

In 1990 she started the Women's HIV/AIDS Support Group in Los Angeles. "One woman showed up," she says. "I thought, *There's got to be more out there.* So I changed the name to Women Faced with Life-Challenging Illnesses, and more started coming." With Jeaneen volunteering as a teen HIV peer educator, Sharon became increasingly active. In 1992 she testified before the Centers for Disease Control and Prevention to argue that women-specific conditions, such as cervical cancer, be included in the diagnostic criteria associated with AIDS, and the CDC issued revised guidelines in 1993. Until then, there had been no official acknowledgment that the disease can affect men and women differently. She also continued her work with AIDS patients, teaching them alternative healing techniques, and as an ordained metaphysical minister, performing many of their funerals. "These were absolutely the most compassionate, loving men that I'd ever met, and here they were, down to 100 pounds with KS [Kaposi's sarcoma, a cancer that causes purplish lesions] all over their body. Then in '93 we started seeing women die. Out of those who started right after me, I know only one who has survived."

In 1994, depleted by grief, she moved to the red rocks of Kayenta, a starkly serene suburb of St. George, Utah. Sharon felt at peace there until she was felled by a one-two punch of PCP (pneumocystis carinii pneumonia) followed by MAC (mycobacterium avium complex), both potentially deadly infections common to AIDS patients. Her doctor, Teresa Bowers, MD, started to worry that Sharon wasn't going to make it and summoned the family.

"After seeing her at the hospital," says her father, "I went right to the funeral home and made arrangements. I paid for the whole thing. That's how bad she was." Then he called a priest.

"What are you doing here?" Sharon asked the clergyman when he showed up the next day.

"Well, do you want your last rites?"

"No," Sharon said firmly. "I don't want my last rites."

But in truth, she had lost her will to live. The only thing she needed to do was to see Jeaneen, then 21, one more time. Her daughter flew from Los Angeles to the hospital as fast as she could.

"When I got there, I just stood in the doorway and thought, *Who is that?*" says Jeaneen. "My mom—I couldn't recognize her. I mean, she was probably 85, maybe 80 pounds, and she was lying there and I was—and it—seeing that was so heartbreaking"—she stops, apologizing, unable to hold her tears back even now. "It was such a shock to me that I couldn't even move.

"And then I went in there and jumped into the bed with her and held her."

Sharon says that's why she's alive. "I'll never forget how wonderful it was to have her warm body next to me, and she was just saying, 'Mom, I love you. I want you to get well so we can go home and I can take care of you.'"

The next morning, Jeaneen left the hospital briefly to take a shower. At that point, as Sharon writes in her 2006 book, *Sacred Living, Sacred Dying,* she had a near-death experience during which she was offered the option of living or continuing on into the tunnel of light, and she made the choice to come back to her daughter. By the time Jeaneen returned, Sharon knew she'd be home before long.

Her family, her doctors, everyone was stunned that AIDS didn't take her then. Bowers, who's now at Greenville Memorial Hospital in South Carolina, says, "I've never seen anybody who wants to live more than Sharon." She had only three T cells.

"Yeah, I call them Hope, Love, and Laughter," Sharon half jokes. "They're always with me."

Living back in Southern California now, Sharon has a T cell count of 205, barely above the AIDS line, "but at least out of the danger zone," she says optimistically. The best news is that the viral load in her blood is undetectable, an indication that the drug cocktail she's on is suppressing the HIV. (Imagine a train heading toward a cliff: The T cell count tells you how far away you are from death by AIDS; the viral load, how fast you're going, explains Monica Gandhi, MD, an assistant professor in the division of infectious diseases at the University of California, San Francisco.) Hoping at some point to get off medication, Sharon follows a regimen that includes acupuncture, visualization, meditation, and stress reduction—all in an effort to increase her energy level so she can go out on the talk circuit again to share her story.

"So many factors go into rebuilding an immune system," says Susan Wellborn, a holistic nurse practitioner at the Center for Special Immunology in Fountain Valley who cares for Sharon now and is amazed by her spirit. "I've been in this business long enough to see that the patients who do well are not depending just on medicine but are taking care of their whole being."

In her characteristic "bright-side only" way, Sharon will tell you how AIDS has been a blessing, making her who she is today—and with her 58th birthday on November 30, she couldn't be luckier. Hard at work on her next book, she's finally found herself in a loving relationship with a man she met almost seven years ago. He ran the copy shop where she went to do her xeroxing. "The first thing that moved when I saw her," says Hector Parra, "was my heart."

On their first date, before they went out, she tried to sit him down at her house: "I have to tell you something."

"I don't want to know about your past," he said.

"You have to know my past," she insisted. "I'm not going out with you if you don't let me tell you about it, Hector."

They wrangled back and forth like this until she finally said it: She had AIDS.

All he replied was, "Oh, okay."

"To me it's never been an issue," he says simply. "If I was in love then, I'm in love to the tenth power right now."

On a visit to New York from Chicago, where she lives, Rae Lewis-Thornton sits across the desk in a Manhattan office, smartly dressed in a fine-gauge wool pantsuit, and pulls out a swatch of fake hair from her purse. She's explaining how the elegant gray-accented mane that frames her face has just been installed by "the best" hair weaver in town. At 45, Rae doesn't mind exposing such privacies: She's used to hanging out the most intimate details of her life like jaunty bits of lingerie on a clothesline for all to see.

Verbally speed dialing through her résumé—magna cum laude from Northeastern Illinois University, national youth director of Jesse Jackson's presidential campaign—Rae periodically brushes the new long strands of hair off her face with the gesture of a woman who knows the power of her appeal. In the same sweep of hand she reveals a Rolex and a pair of Van Cleef & Arpels onyx earrings, which match her necklace, as well as a bracelet that leads the eye to the other jewelry on that wrist—a beloved antique diamond piece and the silver and gold bangle she calls her "until there's a cure for AIDS" bracelet.

Rae attributes her rapid-fire attention—which served her well as a young hot politico working presidential campaigns—to the Gemini in her. It could also be the legacy of starting life in a womb full of heroin. "My mom's white and my dad's black. They were two junkies. They hooked up together," she says, knocking back the information like a straight-up shot of whiskey. "My paternal grandfather took me from them."

Her story unfolds like a made-for-TV movie. When she was 6, her grandfather, the one steadying force in her early life, died, leaving her to the care of his third wife, Georgia, "the mama who raised me," as Rae calls her. "She told me nobody wanted me, 'Not even your white grandmama, and I'm stuck with your ass.'" Georgia, who worked as a maid, was a functional alcoholic, according to Rae. "My mother cooked a dinner every evening. My mother never staggered. My mother never slurred. But she beat me when the sun was shining, and she beat me when the sun wasn't shining.

Typically it was with an extension cord but it could have been a camera, whatever was close. And my mother was dark, so I was always 'a white bitch.' We never watched TV together, we never had family outings. It was a very troubled life."

At first the two of them lived on Chicago's South Side with a man who had seven children. One of the sons was about 19. "I was 9 or 10, and he abused me," Rae says. "I'd felt rejected my entire childhood, and then my stepbrother showed me attention. It started out slowly with sitting and watching TV, and it escalated to touching, then touching me with my panties to the side, and then eventually penetration. It was so normal that I thought this was something that *I* was doing. And I understood it as *I'm fast.* I was never told that people aren't supposed to be touching you at this age.

"It wasn't until I was 31 in a therapist's office and she said, 'How does a 9-year-old have sex with a 19-year-old, Rae?' I said, 'Oh, because I've been a sexual person my whole life,' and she said, 'No.' And I cried for two weeks. It was like, Oh my God, I wasn't participating."

In the riptide of family bonds generated by each of Georgia's men, Rae got caught in episodic abuse. By the time she was in seventh grade, she'd been molested by three different people, she says, at which point Georgia married a man "who never raped me, but he'd hem me in corners, push me up against the wall, kiss me, rub his hands all over my body parts, grab my breasts." When she told her mother, she says, "her explanation was, he wouldn't want to be with me if I wasn't a whore. He left in August, and she put me out in October. I had just started my senior year in high school."

The one upside to that last marriage for Rae was that they'd moved to the suburb of Evanston, which had a good school. She ended up finding a place to live with two of her former stepsisters, commuting an hour and a half each day to class, running to her job at a clothing store, and then hightailing it to her second gig, at McDonald's.

Sex with the right men, she realized quickly, could make things easier. In and out of relationships for the next few years, "trying to get validated, trying to find love," she turned her overachieving drive to becoming a sex goddess. Not that she was promiscuous; just choosy. "For me it was the richer and older, the better," says Rae wryly. "Got to pay rent. And you're pretty. With long hair. And you're high yellow. So you get your winter coat. And that's what I did. You screen very carefully: six-figure income, Giorgio Armani suit, Mercedes required."

Seriously?

"Seriously."

The move to Evanston exposed Rae to a new world of literature and arts and to black history and African-Americans with PhD's. She got into Southern Illinois University, Carbondale, which is where she first heard Jesse Jackson speak. It was at church on Easter Sunday, and she knew right then that she had to get politically involved. On campus she became the queen of activist causes, then quit school after a year to join Jackson's first presidential campaign, in 1984.

Piggybacking from one political candidate or organization to the next, in 1987 she found herself working for the peace action group SANE in Washington, D.C. That January there was a train accident, and she organized a blood drive. The Red Cross had started screening for HIV, and after donating, Rae was supposed to call in to make sure everything was okay with her blood, but she threw the number away. "I knew AIDS," she says. "AIDS was white. AIDS was gay. AIDS was IV drug abuse. It wasn't me."

In March she got a letter. It was from the Red Cross; she had to come in. She hopped into a taxi and sat down with a counselor. "The entire meeting took five minutes," says Rae. "I got up and went back to work. I said to myself, 'This is one more thing in my life. I can handle HIV. Just don't ever let me get AIDS.'"

That night she went home and washed her boyfriend's clothes; they'd been in a settled relationship and had been using condoms. "As soon as he came in the door, I said, 'I've got something to tell you. I have HIV.' He thought I was joking. And when it finally sank in, he said, 'You bitch.' And he took his clothes and left. If I knew he was going to leave, he would have left with dirty laundry." She was 24.

Rae called a number of ex-boyfriends. Only one phoned back to say he'd tested negative. "Everybody else was like, 'Wasn't me. Talk to you.'" The Red Cross counselor had told her about their HIV study with the National Institutes of Health, and though it was mostly on men, she enrolled, going in periodically to be monitored, which was all anyone could do at the time. Based on her T cell count then, she figured she'd been infected in 1983.

Rae tried to shove past *by whom,* and focused on her career. She kept her illness a secret: "Those first six years, I didn't read one article on HIV. I didn't watch one TV special. And when my buppie friends sat around and cracked jokes about AIDS, I sat there and laughed. I was not prepared to jeopardize all my hard work because of HIV." When Jackson ran again, in '88, she was his national youth director, mobilizing students across the country, becoming so close to the reverend and his family that she moved in with them for almost five years. When he didn't win, she campaign-hopped, working at one point for Mike Dukakis, at another for Carol Moseley Braun, the first African-American woman in the U.S. Senate. She went back to school and was two classes short of getting her master's when she made the transition to AIDS.

Unlike Sharon, Rae went on the first drug she could, AZT, though it made her nauseous and tired. Then, in 1992, just as she started having her first real symptoms—back-to-back yeast infections and staggering exhaustion—she got the call she'd been waiting a whole career for: The Clinton-Gore campaign was picking up Jackson people. "And I was way too tired to keep up the 14-hour days required to do advance work," Rae says heavily. "Clinton took all my friends to the White House. I had to say no."

Instead she got a job working at Physicians for a National Health Program, organizing doctors around healthcare reform. But she continued to decline as the virus literally consumed her, wasting her body from size 12 to 6 in a matter of months. Rae says, "I felt like I was dying."

And she was, according to Mardge Cohen, MD, who took over her care at Chicago's public Cook County Hospital, now called John H. Stroger Jr. Hospital. "She had no T cells. She had nothing."

Rae interrupts herself to fish around her purse, suddenly remembering she's forgotten to take her meds—ten pills plus Fuzeon, which she has to dilute and inject. It's a last-ditch drug for patients who have become resistant to other available medication and are in what's called deep salvage. The twice-daily shots are so painful and cause such huge welts that doctors prescribe it only when there's nothing left to lose. Rae is aware of that. "If you're on this," she says mixing up the solution, "you ain't got no place to go at all."

IN THE EARLY '90S, SEVERE WASTING was AIDS's macabre signature, and friends started asking Rae what the deal was. She realized the secret was killing her faster than the virus. So she started telling one

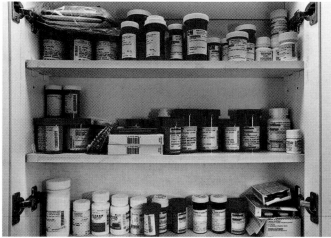

Left: After wrestling with the virus for 24 years, Rae Lewis-Thornton is resistant to most available medication. Fuzeon (she's preparing to inject it here in her Chicago apartment) is a drug of last resort. *Right:* Rae's medicine chest: Her regimen is "pretty intense," says her doctor, "but she's doing phenomenally well."

circle of people, then another. Before she could come out to her political friends, she knew she had to get honest with Jesse Jackson.

"Reverend, I got to talk to you," Rae said, standing in his kitchen one day.

"What's up? You pregnant?" he asked.

"I wish I was," she said, and then the truth started spilling out. After a few minutes, he stopped her.

"I loved you then," he said in his fashion, because he didn't like a lot of small talk, "and I love you now."

Jackson remembers that moment in his kitchen. "I was astonished," he says on the phone. "And I didn't know what it meant; I didn't know what the options were. At that time it was a death sentence for most people." Speaking fondly of Rae, he continues. "And so then she began this awesome journey to use her body and her experience as a living sacrifice, as a model. She declared the sickness. And she also declared war on AIDS. And no one has been a more informed advocate."

Rae started going into high schools to tell her story. "Sometimes I'd ask, 'How many of you guys would have sex with me?' They'd all raise their hands. And that's when the work would start: 'How did you get it, what did you do?'" With her telegenic looks and preacherlike delivery making her a popular speaker, she began traveling around the country taking on bigger engagements, appearing on TV and in magazines, determined to save others from her fate. "I heard her speak when I was a sophomore in high school, and it changed my life," says Luke Burke, now 27 and a senior coordinator for MTV news. "She doesn't sugarcoat anything. Point-blank, she scared me. When I casual date now, I don't generally have sex. If I do, it's definitely safe—it's a big deal to me."

As far as sex went for Rae, after being diagnosed, she didn't date for at least a year. "I was young, attractive, and had the worst disease of my century," she says. "And because of my past, I was not prepared for any more rejection." Deciding she was morally bound to reveal her status, she became much more careful; she had to really like a man, and condoms were required 100 percent of the time. When she met Kenny Thornton, she thought he fit the bill. Jackson married them in 1994.

With Kenny—a man around her age, way short of rich, forget the Armani or Mercedes—Rae broke all her rules. "I was so afraid to die alone. And I had no family," she admits. But Kenny was an

ace caregiver, which became crucial when she was on the road, because she suffered three bouts of PCP, going now from size 6 to 0, the virus taking her down to the bone. "She was as sick as you get," says Cohen, who became a principal investigator on the largest study of women and AIDS at the NIH—the Women's Interagency HIV Study (WIHS)—which Rae joined at the start. (One of its findings would be that a third of HIV-positive subjects, like her and Sharon, had been sexually abused as children, with twice as many suffering domestic abuse—a continuum of violence that, the researchers suggest, may increase the likelihood of behaviors that lead to infection.)

Not surrendering to the disease was all Rae could think about. "Even on bad days, I'd just get my butt up, comb my hair, put some lipstick on, and pop on some earrings, because a diva never leaves the house without earrings. There were no illusions that AIDS had control of my body. I couldn't give it my spirit." Still she knew her end was near. "I was literally keeping a breakneck schedule trying to speak to everybody I could before I died."

But 1996 became a swing year for AIDS patients like Rae who'd been hanging on by a few tattered T cells, planning their funerals. Suddenly, with a new class of medications—protease inhibitors—on the market, drug cocktails became the first regimens that were really effective. "We now had three classes of medications, so we could hit the virus lots of different ways," says Cohen. "That's when we saw real change. Instead of just keeping people bumping around for a while, the drugs helped them start living and working again."

That year, New York City therapist Robert Levithan remembers, "there was this kind of shock. People would come into my office saying, 'I've been waiting to die'—they'd gone into debt, sold their life insurance, lived out all their dreams—and nothing was organized around 'I could be here in 20 years.' For some, the idea of readjusting again seemed harder than dying." Levithan, who counsels HIV patients privately and at the nonprofit Friends in Deed, has been a patient himself since the early '80s, and was near death in the mid-'90s when he won a lottery and got early access to Crixivan, one of the first protease inhibitors. "I looked at it and went, 'That's what I've been waiting for,'" he says, today in good health.

For Rae, the ride was rougher. Just out of the hospital with her third round of PCP when she went on a protease inhibitor called ritonavir, she got so sick—"I'm talking about getting up at 5 in the morning and sitting in the bathroom bent over," she says—at one point, she called Cohen and announced she was quitting the drugs. "I had decided that the quality of my life was more important than how long I could live." A few weeks later when she went in for an appointment, her labs were bleak. Eight T cells. Cohen said, "You have to get back on the medicine."

Rae held fast; she was done. Cohen, usually matter-of-fact, went ballistic.

"You have to give me some more time. You have to do this for me," the doctor screamed. "There's another medicine coming soon and they say the side effects are not as bad. You can't quit now."

Rae had never seen her like this before. Through all their time together, they had avoided discussing the possibility of her death, but she could now hear it in her doctor's voice, and that got to her. She agreed to go back on ritonavir for a couple of weeks.

"Back then, Rae was at that brink where many people as immunocompromised as she was didn't make it," says Cohen, who after 31 years at Cook County left in the summer of 2007 to focus on the WIHS research and her HIV project in Rwanda, Women's Equity in Access to Care and Treatment (WE-ACTx). "We'd just be hoping each time a regimen was approved that it would help her get to the next place so we didn't lose her. Because we lost so many people. She knows how lucky she was to make it through that period."

Once Rae went on medication again, her labs improved. Finally the new drug, Crixivan, came, and she didn't feel sick on it. Her health rebounded amazingly. And as it did, she says, "Kenny stopped speaking to me. All his validation was wrapped into watching me die." Since they've divorced, she's had to depend on friends, "which is tricky," she says. "It's not that they don't love you, but it's like, 'Okay, what do you need now, girl?' If I had to say what scares me the most, it's the fact that I have no family and my support system is not as strong as I need it to be." She could have used help, for example, the time she was unable to walk for eight weeks due to severe nerve pain after Georgia died, and twice when monster herpes sores on her vulva and rectum ("Oh God, the most embarrassing thing on the planet") sent her to the hospital. "AIDS complicates everything else I have," she says. "It never stops."

Living in Chicago with two toy poodles, Rae is lonely. "In the 20 years I've known my HIV status," she says, "I've never had a man say no." But her last relationship ended two and a half years ago, when she discovered that the guy she thought was "wonderful" had a 28-year-old on the side (the woman got an earful from Rae about getting tested).

Still, she charges on. Busily writing her memoir, she trains hard—an hour of high-impact cardio five or six days a week plus three hours of lifting weights when she can make it—and watches her diet. And she believes in psychotherapy—"something the African-American community shuns"—which has helped her come to grips with her circumstances, including the blame. "I've had to work through my own culpability in my infection," she says, "to find the thin line where I don't beat myself up because of it but am able to say, 'Okay, it is what it is. This is what you did, and it left you with HIV. Get over yourself.' On my 45th birthday I said, 'Rae, you're forgiven. You did the best you could with what you knew.' And what I understand finally is, when you know better, you do better."

Rae fills a syringe with Fuzeon. As an effect of the medications, or possibly of the disease itself—scientists aren't sure—all her fat has redistributed to the top of her body as if blimped upward with helium, creating an AIDS "buffalo hump" and padding out her strikingly high cheekbones. ("When it first happened, I was so depressed," she says, poising

the needle.) She decides to inject it in her minimized thigh, even though it will be painful, because her stomach is covered with welts. As she pulls up her shirt to show me, I see her butterfly tattoo, an inky sigh to lost freedom and the cue for a whole other story about how one South Side parlor refused to serve her because of her HIV, and she sued them for discrimination. And won.

Cohen describes the salvage regimen that Rae is on as "pretty intense—sort of a wipeout in itself," but says, "she's doing phenomenally well. Fantastically." Her T cells are up to 449 and her viral load is undetectable—the most dramatic results Rae has ever had.

The fact that she's developed resistance to so many of the drug options is the curse she bears for being a guinea pig. "HIV mutates very frequently, and if you just use one or two of the drugs, the virus can overcome them fairly quickly," says Hiroyu Hatano, MD, an assistant professor of medicine at UCSF, who recently published a study on the topic. "And Rae took every regimen that came down the pike," says Cohen. "At first we gave people one drug at a time—we didn't have any other options. Now we give newly infected patients several drugs all together in one force, which has a much stronger effect and causes a lot less resistance."

And there are new medications. In fact, Hatano believes that 2007 may have been comparable to 1996 in seismically shifting the course of AIDS. On August 6, 2007 as Rae was injecting her drug of last resort, the FDA approved maraviroc, a CCR5 inhibitor, which represents the first new class of oral HIV drugs in more than a decade. Rather than fighting HIV inside the T cells, maraviroc thwarts the virus from even entering uninfected cells by blocking one of the main entryways. "So it's a whole different mechanism," says Hatano. Another novel class of drugs called integrase inhibitors has recently been approved by the FDA, as has a medication called etravirine, "which is exciting because it's effective against some viruses that have become resistant to the existing drugs in its class," she says.

Meanwhile, there's a lot of buzz around a group of patients called elite controllers, who have been infected with HIV for years without ever getting sick. "We thought these people were rare as hen's teeth. But now we realize that about one in 300 patients ends up like this," says Bruce Walker, MD, director of the Partners AIDS Research Center at Massachusetts General Hospital and a professor of medicine at Harvard, who is launching a multimillion-dollar study (elitecontrollers.org) to find out what's unique about their immune systems that could be applied to all patients—maybe even as a vaccine. "You want goose bumps?" he asks. "I look across the table at one of these people and feel like the answer is sitting right there in my office."

As it is, AIDS specialists say, with 22 drugs available, today's outlook for patients is so much better, and longer, than 24 years ago when Rae and Sharon were infected—to the point where, if a newly diagnosed woman comes into Monica Gandhi's clinic at UCSF asking how long she has left, the doctor is able to tell her, "We're going to try for a normal life span."

WHETHER ANY OF THE RESEARCH or new drugs will keep Rae or Sharon alive is a question neither chooses to dwell on. They have too much work to do to die anytime soon. With more and more women testing positive for HIV, their mission has intensified. They know they are in a unique position to change lives, and that in itself keeps them going. "I do it," says Rae, "so that my story will never become your story. I do it so you'll never have to walk in my shoes." ◐

"WHEN YOU KNOW WHO YOU ARE AND WHAT YOU STAND FOR, YOU STAND IN WISDOM"

The first time it happened to me, I took to my bed and cried for three days. A member of my family who has since passed away had gone to Florida, headquarters for *The National Enquirer,* sat in a room, told them the story of my hidden shame—and left their offices $19,000 richer.

Only my family and closest friends knew. Even Gayle, who knew everything about me, wasn't aware of my secret until several years into our friendship. The same is true for Stedman. I would tell no one until I felt safe enough to share my dark past: the years I was sexually abused, from age 10 to 14, my resulting promiscuity as a teenager, and finally, at 14, my becoming pregnant. I was so ashamed, I hid the pregnancy until my swollen ankles and belly gave me away. The baby died in the hospital weeks later.

I went back to school and told no one. My fear was that if I were found out, I would be expelled. So I carried the secret into my future, always afraid that if anyone discovered what had happened, they, too, would expel me from their lives. Even when I found the courage to publicly reveal the abuse, I still carried the shame and kept the pregnancy a secret.

The visit to the tabloids changed all that.

I felt devastated. Wounded. Betrayed. *How could this person do this to me?*

I cried and cried. I remember Stedman coming into the bedroom that Sunday afternoon, the room darkened from the closed curtains. Standing before me, looking like he, too, had shed tears, he handed me the tabloid. And said, "I'm so sorry. You don't deserve this."

When I dragged myself from bed for work on Monday morning (no matter what, the show rules), I felt beaten and scared. I imagined that every person on the street was going to point their finger at me and scream, *"Pregnant at , you wicked girl...expelled!"*

No one said a word, though—not strangers, not the people I knew. I was shocked.

Nobody treated me differently.

For 20 years, I had been expecting a reaction that never came. And I soon realized that having the secret out was liberating. Not until then could I begin the repair work on my spirit for the sexual abuse and damage done to me as a young girl.

I realized that all those years, I had been blaming myself. What I learned for sure was that holding the shame was the greatest burden of all. That, even more than the betrayal, is what had kept me in bed from Friday to Monday.

I've since been betrayed by others, most often by disgruntled employees trying to gain an extra buck. But although it's a kick in the gut, it doesn't make me cry or take to my bed anymore. What I learned from that first betrayal is that when you have nothing to be ashamed of, when you know who you are and what you stand for, you stand in wisdom. Insight. Strength and protection. You stand in peace.

No weapon formed against you shall prosper. Isaiah 54:17.

Oprah

SURVIVING THE UNIMAGINABLE:
OPRAH TALKS TO CHRISTINE McFADDEN

What's the worst thing that could happen to a mother of four? It happened to Christine McFadden the day her ex-husband slipped into her house and killed her children. For months afterward, Christine wished she'd died with her kids. But now, with a new husband and newborn twins, she's learning to live again.

When Christine McFadden, a veterinarian in Merced, California, went out for her early-morning walk on March 26, 2002, her four children were still sleeping. Melanie, 17, Stanley, 15, and Stuart, 14, were the kids from her first marriage; 5-year-old Michelle was from her second marriage, to a former sheriff's deputy named John Hogan.

Christine had divorced Hogan in 2001 but had made room for him in Michelle's life. And so while it was unusual, upon returning home that morning, to see his truck parked in the driveway, she wasn't alarmed. Having to deal with Hogan would be irritating, but Christine was used to that. Then she went inside and came upon Melanie, lying dead on the hallway floor.

While Christine was out, Hogan had shot and killed all four children with a .40-caliber handgun, then shot himself in the head.

"My whole life—it's gone," Christine told me when she appeared on the show two years after the murders. "There will be no grandchildren. I will never see my daughters walk down the aisle, never see my sons make any great plays. There really doesn't seem to be a lot of need for me in the world."

Three years later, at 49, Christine had emerged from that bleak

place. In April 2006 she married Gerald Corman, a family law judge. And on January 26, 2007, she gave birth to their twin daughters, Nicole and Claire. The decision to have more children wasn't one Christine made lightly, but it seems to have been the right one: Around the girls, she is joyous, doting, engaged—altogether a changed woman, ready to move forward.

Yet there remains an irresistible pull toward the past. The new family lives in Christine's Merced home—the house where Melanie, Stan, Stu, and Michelle lived and died—and for all the signs of new beginnings, loss is reflected everywhere. The dining room table and the refrigerator are covered with family photos, every one of which has the power to bring Christine to tears. Melanie's ballet slippers still hang on the door to her bedroom, which has sat practically untouched since 2002; the murder investigators' bright yellow "caution" tape is still attached to her bedpost.

When Christine first appeared on the show—beyond stunned, beyond hope—I told her I believed that her story would save lives. I told her that among all the people watching that day, there would be some who'd decided it was going to be their last day—but that seeing her would change their minds. Sure enough, out of the thousands of letters we got after the show, 16 were from people who'd been planning to commit suicide—and then didn't. I later invited Christine back to the show to meet three of these women, one of whom had told me, "I get up because she has the strength to."

That strength is why I flew to Merced when the twins were just

Oprah with Christine McFadden, holding Nicole (*left*) and Claire, in McFadden's Merced, California, home, February 24, 2007.
Below the portrait of McFadden's murdered children sits a photo of her first daughter, Melanie, preparing for ballet.

four weeks old—to talk to Christine again, and to hear what carried her through.

OPRAH: *So I sit here watching you hold your babies, bringing new life into the world, giving new life to yourself.*

CHRISTINE: Yes. It doesn't change anything with the other children, or lessen the feelings there. But it allows me to go forward and live a fuller, more normal life. Just going to the grocery store and seeing kids' cereal boxes is already easier.

OPRAH: *I've heard people say that sometimes it's the simplest things that bring back memories. For you, with four children, everywhere you turn, there must be a memory.*

CHRISTINE: Yes—from driving past their schools to seeing the plants they helped me pick out for the yard. They were involved in so many things. I spent nearly 18 years raising kids, and most of my friends had children my kids' age. Over the years, what did I talk about with the neighbors? It wasn't "I did a cystotomy and took out some bladder stones yesterday." We talked about our children. After my kids died, it was as if I had nothing else to say.

OPRAH: *How long after the murders did you begin dating Jerry?*

CHRISTINE: About eight months. I wasn't looking for a relationship. After I got divorced the second time, I wasn't going to have anything to do with men. Divorce is very painful, and I wasn't willing to put anybody through that again—not me, not another man, not my kids. But six months after they died—even though I was going around in jeans and no makeup, and not really going many places—men started coming out of the woodwork. I was floored!

Jerry had been married for 31 years; in 2000 his wife died from complications of diabetes. She'd been in a vegetative state for many years, and he was her caretaker. So when Jerry and I met, we were two emotionally shut-down people. The whole time we were dating, I was seeing a psychiatrist and a trauma therapist.

OPRAH: *What did you even do when you first started dating? Because when I saw you in 2004, you were definitely emotionally shut down.*

CHRISTINE: I don't think we knew it at the time. I wasn't demanding of him, and he was there for me. I thought if he was around, I might sleep three hours a night. So in some ways I probably used him. But we had good conversation, a lot in common. We certainly enjoyed each other. And the only time I was guaranteed not to think about the children was when we were having sex.

OPRAH: *Really.*

CHRISTINE: So it worked to see him.

OPRAH: *When did you know it was turning into something where you could actually say, "Yes, I want to be with you"?*

CHRISTINE: That was tough. He was spending pretty much all his time here, and I knew there could be no better man for me. At that point, I had two people left in the world: my mother and my sister, and my sister was dying of cancer. It's a scary thing to be totally alone. And I didn't question that I'd be happy with him. Even so, I panicked when he proposed—just the whole thought of getting married again. But I said yes.

We married two days after we got home from a trip to Paris. Jerry is a judge, so he got the marriage license on our first day back, and then a fellow judge married us the second day. I didn't want any press. In this town, talk spreads like wildfire. I've been a veterinarian in Merced for 25 years, and Jerry has been a judge here for the last ten, and we are both watched.

OPRAH: *Why are people watching you?*

CHRISTINE: Just for the sake of gossip. I didn't have to tell anybody

"HELL IS STILL ONLY A STEP AWAY. BUT I CHOOSE NOT TO STEP INTO IT."

I was pregnant. People told me! Everywhere I went—"Oh, you're pregnant!" I wasn't even showing!

OPRAH: *How many people live in Merced?*

CHRISTINE: About 75,000.

OPRAH: *Do you think the town has a vested interest in your story? Everyone must have been devastated.*

CHRISTINE: There has been tremendous support. Wonderful support. I feel a connection here. The neighbors knew my kids.

OPRAH: *If you packed up and moved to another city with your family, the new neighbors might not know that you'd had other children. Is that one of the reasons you've chosen not to leave?*

CHRISTINE: It's a big one. I would be completely lost somewhere else. That's why I've stayed in this house. I'm sure there are people who say, "How could she live there?" But where could you put me that I wouldn't be totally lost? All my kids' memories are here. Moving me someplace else would be like putting me in a room with white walls—a prison cell.

OPRAH: *I think people assume it would be too painful to live in the home where your children were murdered. Maybe they're projecting how they would feel. But Dr. Phil once said something I've never forgotten. He was talking with a woman who couldn't move forward after losing her daughter ten years before. He asked, "Are you going to let your daughter's life be remembered by the one horrible thing that happened to her on the day she died, or are you going to remember the 18 years of beautiful life she gave you?" The woman said, "I never thought of it that way." Nor had I. And it seems to me that you're in this house because the life of your children—and not just their death—is here.*

CHRISTINE: This is where they were born. I can still see their smudgy handprints on the walls. The plants they planted are here. Stuart's tree is out in the front yard. Stan painted the house. The few minutes it took somebody to come in and put bullets into them is not what my children are all about.

OPRAH: *I get that. I do. What did you do with all their stuff?*

CHRISTINE: I gave some of it to their closest friends.

OPRAH: *I just saw Melanie's cheerleading skirt hanging in her closet.*

CHRISTINE: Melanie's room hasn't been touched. But I'm not looking to maintain a living museum.

OPRAH: *Are you in contact with their friends?*

CHRISTINE: Yes. I've watched these kids grow up—I've known most of them since they were preschoolers—and they still drop in to see me.

OPRAH: *Has that helped?*

CHRISTINE: Tremendously. This house was a place where kids came together, so when it's filled with kids, that feels normal. Melanie's friend just drove up from San Diego to visit the twins. I also see Stan's and Stu's friends, as well as a couple of Michelle's classmates.

OPRAH: *And when will you tell the twins about what happened to their siblings?*

CHRISTINE: I don't have an answer. One of my fears is that when they're in preschool, someone will say something to them about it. I worry about that. So could that eventually mean leaving this house or leaving this town? Yes. I brought these girls into this world, so I'll do what I think is right for them—even if that means erasing the other children. And if I felt any resistance on the part of the community to connect with the girls, I'd also consider leaving. I want my daughters to have their own identities and not be overshadowed. That's why some of these family pictures are going to gradually be coming down. I have to do it gradually. To make a fresh space for the girls, we adjoined Stu's

McFadden and her husband, Gerald Corman, flanked by their month-old twins.

and Michelle's rooms, and it just erased them.

OPRAH: *It's interesting that you use the word erase. I understand what you're saying, because when I look at Nicole and Claire's new bedroom, there's no trace of Stu and Michelle. But obviously they can never really be erased from your memory.*

CHRISTINE: No. But I stopped seeing the trauma therapist because every week, all I did was cry as I revisited the whole thing. To move on, I had to put it to the back of my mind. I'm working hard to concentrate on other parts of life. That's the only way I can keep going. That's why I needed to have these girls. I was becoming an old person. You know why some older people sit around and talk only about what happened 20 years ago? Because that's when they were still doing things. That's what I was doing—telling the same old stories about my kids. When someone mentioned that it had been five years since they died, I was like, "Five years? That's impossible!"

OPRAH: *You were living in the past.*

CHRISTINE: Intellectually, I knew my kids were dead. But the first time I was on your show, it was still so unreal. If you'd said, "Look who we have behind door number two!" I would have believed that my kids were there. That's how bad it was.

OPRAH: *Did you cremate them all?*

CHRISTINE: Yes.

OPRAH: *What did you do with their ashes?*

CHRISTINE: I still have them. [*Long pause and tears*] I just can't let them go. In the crematorium, they ask you stuff like "Who do you want to go first?" What mom can answer that? I told them to send the boys first so they could protect their sisters.

OPRAH: *Did you want to kill yourself after they were murdered?*

CHRISTINE: I've never been suicidal. And when I married Jerry, I took on the responsibility of not committing suicide. But I wished I'd died with my kids. I wanted to be with them. We used to joke before we got on an airplane that if the plane crashed, we'd be fine because we'd all die together. There's probably some part of me that still feels that I won't be whole or happy again until I am with them.

OPRAH: *Still?*

CHRISTINE: I can't answer that fairly because of these two babies. I feel an obligation to be around for them—although if anything had gone wrong with them, that could have pushed me over the edge. But I would not do anything that would hurt them. I don't mean that I'm going to live my life for them, but bringing these girls into the world was a conscious thing. I have a responsibility to be a normal mother.

OPRAH: *Did you use in vitro?*

CHRISTINE: I'm not discussing my sex life.

OPRAH: *Did Jerry know you wanted more children?*

CHRISTINE: Oh, yes.

OPRAH: *You say that you wished you'd gone with your children. Do you think if you had been in the house that morning, you'd be dead?*

CHRISTINE: It's so clear that he wanted to kill them and have me survive.

OPRAH: *Because if he wanted to kill you, he could have.*

CHRISTINE: Yes.

OPRAH: *Had you feared him?*

CHRISTINE: No. There weren't any signs. He was invited to every major gathering—carnivals, Halloween, fairs—for Michelle's sake.

OPRAH: *Did he have a good relationship with your other children?*

CHRISTINE: It started out very well, then went downhill. I didn't approve of his way of disciplining the children. He'd have them write "I should not wrestle in the house" 200 times. I just don't think something like that has much value. He'd make them sit in their rooms for hours until I came home.

OPRAH: *I heard you sought a restraining order soon after your divorce.*

CHRISTINE: It was a year before the divorce, when we separated. It's not because I thought he was a danger; I just didn't want him coming over and bugging me.

OPRAH: *So you didn't fear him.*

CHRISTINE: No. In fact, he went out of his way not to be physical around me because I'd had some problems with that during my first marriage.

OPRAH: *Do you think he just snapped?*

CHRISTINE: That's probably a good word for it. I later learned that he'd been evicted from his apartment.

OPRAH: *When was the last time you saw him?*

CHRISTINE: He came over for Michelle's birthday party on March 9.

OPRAH: *Did he seem bitter, angry, resentful?*

CHRISTINE: I knew that he wanted to be back with me—so yes. I was in this nice house, with delightful kids. He looked unkempt. He was in his sweats. But the other parents didn't notice anything unusual. He helped with the piñata and played with the kids on the trampoline.

OPRAH: *Did you sense that he was missing this family life?*

CHRISTINE: Yes.

OPRAH: *But nothing that would lead you to believe he could commit such a heinous act.*

CHRISTINE: No. Why would I think that? He had talked about disappearing, so it had crossed my mind that he might try to commit suicide. But he never said anything that would lead me to believe he would hurt the children. He didn't have a close relationship with them, but he didn't dislike them. If he'd had a close relationship with all the children, I wouldn't have left him. I cared

THE FRIENDSHIP SCHOLARSHIP

To honor her four children, Christine McFadden created the MSSM (named for Melanie, Stanley, Stuart, and Michelle) Friendship Scholarship Foundation, which has already awarded 19 undergraduate scholarships of $4,000 each per year (renewable for three years). The chief criteria: Applicants must possess the characteristics of friendship—such as the loyalty, service, and compassion Christine's children exhibited. A friend of the applicant must write a recommendation letter. "I wanted the scholarship to encompass all of my children's lives," McFadden says. "That's why it's based on character and integrity. Any local child can apply—an applicant doesn't have to be class president or have top grades." Recipients, though, must maintain a 2.5 grade point average.

To make a donation, visit mssmfoundation.org or call (209) 722-MSSM.

OPRAH: TELL ME SOMETHING YOU LOVED ABOUT EACH CHILD.
CHRISTINE:

"MELANIE was very bright and secure. She was creative—you should have seen her in ballet.

"STAN had a sense of humor adults and kids loved. It got him benched in baseball. He was very popular, very good-looking—I was already trying to sit on that a bit.

"STUART was a little charmer, a gentleman. At school dances, he danced with every girl, whether she was popular or not.

"MICHELLE took all the love that she'd absorbed from being the darling baby of the family, and gave it all back."

more about my kids than I did about me—which he knew.

OPRAH: *When you came home that morning and saw John's truck in the driveway, what was your first thought?*

CHRISTINE: He had been showing Michelle the movie *E.T.,* and she was having nightmares. So she'd been sleeping with me. I figured that she'd awakened and called him on the phone next to my bed. Even though there were older children in the house, if John thought she wasn't being taken care of, I could see him coming over to be with her. I thought, *Oh, damn. Now I have to get him out of the house. What a pain.*

OPRAH: *And then you opened the door and went back through the kitchen and found Melanie lying dead in the hallway.*

CHRISTINE: [*After tears and a long pause*] Yes.

OPRAH: *On the 911 call, you said, "I think my ex-husband has killed my children." When you saw Melanie, did you immediately think all four were gone?*

CHRISTINE: It was just very quiet in the house. I figured I was the target. I thought he was still waiting for me. There was nothing I could do against a gun, so I ran to my friend's house to call 911.

OPRAH: *I don't know how the realization that one after another of your children has been murdered settles with you. How does it?*

CHRISTINE: I just had to pray that three of them really were asleep.

OPRAH: *You know Melanie wasn't. She fought.*

CHRISTINE: [*In tears*] She was so brave. Right before she was shot, she was putting on her brown eyeliner. She used to sit cross-legged on the bathroom counter to put on her makeup so she'd be closer to the mirror. She would have heard the noise that—it could have been the bullet going through Stu's brain. And then she must have opened the bathroom door, stepped out, and seen John.

OPRAH: *I know that John left a letter at the scene.*

CHRISTINE: I didn't read it.

OPRAH: *Ever?*

CHRISTINE: I think he said what he had to say when he killed my children. I'm not going to listen to one more word from that person. Not one more thought of his will enter my brain.

OPRAH: *Did the doctors put you on medication immediately after the murders?*

CHRISTINE: No. I wouldn't let them that day.

OPRAH: *Because you wanted to feel?*

CHRISTINE: I don't know what drugs would have done to me. In the end, I only wanted them so I could sleep.

OPRAH: *Are you still on drugs now?*

CHRISTINE: None at all.

OPRAH: *Even when you were, the drugs didn't diminish the pain.*

CHRISTINE: No—they only kept me feeling flat, with no highs or lows. What kept me going was the anger that my kids would die and not be remembered, not have their chance to make their mark on the world. I didn't want their lives to mean nothing.

OPRAH: *So you established a foundation in their names.*

CHRISTINE: Yes—the MSSM Friendship Scholarship Foundation.

OPRAH: *Didn't you refinance your house to contribute to the foundation?*

CHRISTINE: Yes! I'm laughing because I'm down to the last $10,000 I can borrow.

OPRAH: *It's clear that you've turned a corner. How would you describe your life now?*

CHRISTINE: I'm happily married. I'm thrilled to have these two babies, to live again. I'd like to work part-time again in my veterinary clinic. I still love the animals.

OPRAH: *Did faith play any role in your being where you are today?*

CHRISTINE: I've had a lot of battles there. In the simplest terms, I'm still so very angry.

OPRAH: *With God?*

CHRISTINE: With God. I miss what I felt was my relationship with God. My husband talks about the idea of a personal God being there just for you—that's what I used to think I had. Is that bad theology? Don't most people think God is there for them? But 9/11, for instance—do you think that the people who lived were the only people who believed in God? What about the people who died? Why did they have to die?

OPRAH: *So you still have more questions than answers. Will you ever find peace?*

CHRISTINE: I don't know. I'm still searching. I have friends of many different faiths, and so many of them have tried to give me encouragement. I appreciate all the prayers and thoughts. I welcome them. I'm more accepting now of all different faiths. But it's as if God still speaks to others but doesn't to me. That may not be the correct thinking, but I've seen my children with their brains blown out. And they all had Bibles. Stan's was in the bed stand. Melanie's was on a little table. Stuart's was at the end of his bed the morning he was murdered.

OPRAH: *Do you have hope?*

CHRISTINE: Yes. Yes, I do.

OPRAH: *After the tragedy, did you have faith that you'd one day be able to have more children?*

CHRISTINE: Initially, I wanted to have more kids because I wanted my other kids back. Crazy thinking.

OPRAH: *But you've gotten past that? You're not expecting these twins to be replacements for the other four?*

CHRISTINE: I'm trying real hard. I'm trying to be conscious of all those things.

OPRAH: *And yet how do you that? It must be hard not to think of your other four children every time you change a diaper.*

CHRISTINE: I don't. But reading them stories—people gave us books at the baby shower—*Goodnight Moon, Love You Forever...*

OPRAH: Love You Forever *is my favorite children's book.*

CHRISTINE: I put it away. That one I can't read. You know: "I'll love you forever, I'll like you for always, as long as I'm living..."

OPRAH: *"...my baby you'll be."*

CHRISTINE: "My baby you'll be." I'm not even going to try with that one.

OPRAH: *Did you think you would find the courage to love again?*

CHRISTINE: I wasn't looking for it. It just happened. It took a lot of time.

OPRAH: *I marvel at the kind of man your husband must be to handle all of this. How would you describe him?*

CHRISTINE: He's wonderful. Affectionate. Quiet. Thoughtful. And gentle.

OPRAH: *Thank you for your generosity in sharing your story again. The reason I keep coming back is that I so admire your strength.*

CHRISTINE: I attribute that strength to the children I lost. Melanie, Stanley, Stuart, and Michelle were the best things that ever happened to me. Even in their short lives, they exceeded any hopes I could have had for them. Yes, I know I have to go forward now. By marrying and bringing these two girls into the world, that's what I'm choosing to do.

OPRAH: *Do you feel like you've awakened from hell?*

CHRISTINE: No, it's been more gradual than that. Even now I still feel like hell is only a step away. But I choose not to step into it. ◖O◗

THE VICTIM

He was dark, smelled of gasoline, and held 32-year-old Ann Meng prisoner for nearly an hour while savagely and repeatedly raping her. Thanks to her "100 percent positive" identification, he was sentenced to five life terms. There was only one problem: She was 100 percent wrong. Melba Newsome on a heart-searing case of race, trauma, cutting-edge forensic science, and, most astonishing, forgiveness.

O n a Friday night in December 2002, Ann Meng arrived home to find the business card of a local newspaper reporter stuck in her door. The words *Call me* were scribbled on the back. She couldn't imagine why he'd want to speak to her until she went inside and played the message on her answering machine. It was from the commonwealth's attorney's office for the city of Norfolk, Virginia: "Please get in touch with us concerning a case you were involved in some years ago."

It had been two decades, but Meng knew instantly whom they were referring to: Julius Earl Ruffin, the man who had crept into her apartment early one morning and held her captive for almost an hour. The man who had raped and sodomized her. The man she later identified as her attacker and testified against in three separate trials. The man a third jury had finally convicted of burglary, rape, and sodomy. The man the judge had sentenced to five life terms.

When she spoke to the prosecutor, he said that the Virginia crime lab had discovered evidence thought long discarded and planned to test it for DNA. Did she have any concerns? Meng didn't especially want to go back to court and had to wonder at the lengths Ruffin was going to in order to prove his innocence. Still, she felt exactly as she had in 1982 when she'd testified to being 100 percent positive that he was her attacker. Nothing since then had made her any less sure.

But when the DNA analysis came in, it showed that Earl Ruffin was not the man who attacked her. The results were irrefutable. Although she'd been so certain, an innocent man had spent more than 20 years in prison. "I never believed I could make a mistake like that," she says. "Never."

With her glasses, close-cropped blonde hair, and somber demeanor, Meng comes across as a little schoolmarmish when I first meet her. But within minutes, she's poking fun as she drives me around in a stick-shift Toyota tagged with antiwar stickers. She is giving me a tour of West Ghent, the neighborhood where the rape occurred. Just outside downtown Norfolk, the area's tree-lined streets have become gentrified with rehabbed homes and condos. It's a nice place to live if you can afford it, a big change from 25 years ago when it was run-down and transient.

"That's the building," Meng says, pointing to a three-story brick colonial on the corner of Leigh Street and Westover Avenue. "The apartment is the one on the right-hand side of the first floor. There was a screen porch but no outlet from the porch to the street."

She was arriving home from her job as a surgical technician around midnight on December 5, 1981—a 32-year-old mother of three young children in the middle of a divorce. Her son and twin daughters were spending the weekend with their father, but Meng could not relax. "I felt really uncomfortable and I had this feeling that someone was there, so I went through the whole apartment, looked in all the closets first before I finally went to bed and to sleep."

Two hours later, she awoke to find a man leaning over her with a knife pressed to her throat. Her single shriek was muted when his large hand clamped over her mouth. "If you scream, you're dead," he said.

She believed him, so she stopped. She knew what would come next and prayed she would be alive when it was over.

For the next 45 minutes, he never stopped talking, alternating between threatening to come back and cripple her, or maybe kill her along with her children, and expressing his desire for her. "He said, 'I've fallen in love with you, but you probably wouldn't want a relationship with someone like me, would you?' I said, 'Maybe if we'd

Earl Ruffin, free at last, is mobbed by his grandchildren at an NAACP Justice Jubilee held for him in December 2003.

met another way,'" Meng recalls dryly, then rolls her eyes. I realize humor is one of the ways she copes with it all.

"He was a sick puppy, and I was trying to be very diplomatic, just trying to stay alive," Meng continues. Every time she turned toward him, he warned, "Don't look at me." She averted her eyes but stole glances and tried to take in as much about him as she could. After he was finished, he ordered her to take a shower and brush her teeth, then get back in bed and pretend nothing ever happened. She did, careful to preserve as much evidence as she could. When he finally left, he took what was in her wallet, including her ATM card, which she gave him the code for, and the $20 in pennies she had rolled with her son. Even now, remembering those pennies brings her to tears.

She lay there in the dark for 45 minutes to make sure he was gone. Then she sprang up and ran through the building pounding on the neighbors' doors for help. When the police arrived, she told them everything she could remember: He was a dark-skinned black man with some hair on the sides of his face, about a foot

taller than her (so at most 5'11"), and smelled strongly of gasoline. She was frustrated that she couldn't describe him in more detail. Trust yourself, the officers told her. You'll remember more with time. Things will become clearer, they promised.

Meng never spent another night in that apartment. "I was really freaked out," she says. "I had anxiety attacks and thought this guy was everywhere. When I'd see a group of people, I imagined he was among them." Haunted by his threat to find her, she was determined to find him first. She looked for him on crowded streets, at the market, in passing cars. And about six weeks later, she found him on an elevator. He was a maintenance worker at the medical office building where she worked at Eastern Virginia Medical School.

"He looked at me and smiled," she says, a memory that even now makes her tremble. She stood there frozen in fear, replaying every detail of that frigid December night. *It's definitely him,* she

First she suffered a brutal sexual assault, then the horror of putting the wrong man in prison. Now Ann Meng finds peace with granddaughter Sadie, 4, in Norfolk, Virginia.

"It was just an honest mistake," Earl Ruffin (*right*, in 2003) said of Ann Meng's rape accusation. DNA identified Aaron Doxie (*left*, in a 2003 mug shot)—already in prison for another rape—as Meng's attacker.

thought, but she needed to be sure, so she asked maintenance to send him up to the office on the ruse of checking out the radiator. Her visceral reaction to him up close confirmed her hunch. "It was a small office, and the whole time he was there, I had flashbacks and could hardly stay in there," says Meng. "That's when I called the detective and said, 'Maybe you should talk to him, because to me he looks like the guy.'"

From the moment the detectives confronted Ruffin, his story never changed. He had not raped anyone and he had three alibis for that night: He and his girlfriend spent the evening watching a horror movie on television with his brother and brother's girlfriend. Unfortunately for Ruffin, having a family member for an alibi ranks one step above having no alibi at all, particularly when the crime is rape and the victim is so certain and, in this case, so white.

Meng went to the police station for a voice lineup and picked Ruffin as soon as he began to speak. "That's the man!" she said with absolute certainty. He was booked and locked up.

There were a few problems. Ruffin was over six feet tall, not under. He was fair complexioned, not dark skinned. He also wore a beard and a mustache, not the hair pattern she'd described. And he had two gold front teeth, a detail Meng did not recall at all from the night of the attack. But by the time the trial got under way in Norfolk Circuit Court on May 3, 1982, Meng was surer than ever. And in the pre-DNA era, the best available science said Ruffin was a B secretor, which means he had type B blood that could be determined through his semen—as was true for roughly 8 percent of the male population, including the attacker. What were the odds it could be someone else?

Still, certain details—Ruffin's alibi witnesses and the description inconsistencies—created enough reasonable doubt for the black jurors, though not for the whites. They were hopelessly deadlocked, and the judge declared a mistrial. Two months later, prosecutors tried Ruffin again. And again, the jury (seven blacks and five whites) was divided. Meng was ready to give up. "I wanted to move on," she says, but the prosecution pushed for a third trial.

This time, the 12 jurors were all white. "I thought it was wrong but felt that if this is what they had to do to put the guy away so he wouldn't rape anyone else and come back and kill my children,

then okay," says Meng.

During that three-day trial, Meng told the court, "When I look at him, I know that's him, and when I hear him speak, I know that is his voice. He talked a lot. He was there a long time. He walked around. I was able to see his face and to see him completely, and when I saw him again I knew it was him." The jury filed out for deliberations around 4 P.M. They were back before the smokers finished their cigarettes. They found Ruffin guilty on the charges of statutory burglary, rape, and three counts of sodomy. He got five life terms.

Meng soon understood that putting the son of a bitch away for life did not guarantee that she would find peace or lose her fear. The trials had been the glue holding her together; afterward panic clutched the edges of her life. She moved several times, checked and rechecked the locks on every door, obsessed about burglar alarms, and would not allow the children to open the windows. Later she got a dog.

"For the first few years, I was suicidal most of the time," she recalls. "I hoarded enough sleeping pills for a lethal dose. I thought about crashing my car into the highway median almost daily. The only reason I didn't was because of my kids."

Over time, however, she managed to maintain a career and ultimately remarry, and was often able to minimize the rape in her memory, sometimes forgetting for days, even weeks, that it was there.

MEANWHILE, IN A STARK, CRAMPED PRISON CELL, separated from a loving family who never believed he was guilty, Ruffin aged from a 28-year-old man to a gray-haired grandfather. His mother passed away, and his two young children became adults with kids of their own.

Steadfastly proclaiming his innocence, he lost appeals all the way to the U.S. Supreme Court and was repeatedly denied parole, largely because he maintained that he had done nothing wrong. His only hope for freedom came in the 1990s, when DNA testing became increasingly available as a crime tool. But every time Ruffin sought to retest the evidence, the reply was always the same: There was nothing to test; the case file had been discarded after he exhausted his appeals in 1986.

As it turned out, however, that wasn't quite true. Long before *CSI* became the number one show on television, back in Virginia, forensic scientist Mary Jane Burton was taking procedural measures no one understood, taping bits of swabs containing blood, semen, and saliva from crime scenes into the files she kept.

It was Burton's testimony about the B-secretor evidence that had helped seal Ruffin's fate in 1982. In 2002, however—when she'd been retired for 14 years and dead for three—she would become his unwitting savior. His file was one of those still stored in boxes in a warehouse of the Virginia Department of Forensic Science. Finally, after two decades of trying to prove his innocence, Ruffin got a break.

Recently, as Meng and I sat at the tiny table in her kitchen leafing through the dozens of newspaper clippings she has collected on the case since it resurfaced in the news in December 2002, she said, "I've read everything printed, and followed it like crazy." During the two months after that first call from the prosecutor, she welcomed the certainty DNA would bring. But on February 12, 2003, when the prosecutor called again to say that Ruffin was innocent—the DNA matched a man named Aaron Doxie, a convicted rapist—she nearly collapsed.

I have to say, when I see the mug shots of Doxie and Ruffin at the time of the rape, I am stunned. "You've got to be kidding me!" I tell her. "They look absolutely nothing alike!"

"You don't think so?" she asks sincerely.

Not only is Ruffin taller, thinner, and several shades lighter, but the two men bear no facial resemblance at all. Being black men is the only thing they have in common. As an African-American, I can see this.

But such mistakes are surprisingly common. In an analysis of 200 prisoners exonerated by postconviction DNA in this country (there have been 205 cases to date), all but 15 involved rape and the leading cause of wrongful conviction (79 percent) was eyewitness misidentification. (Other reasons were faulty forensic evidence, false informant testimony, and false confessions.) Of the 200 exonorees in the study, published in the January 2008 *Columbia Law Review*, 14 had been sentenced to death, and 50 sent to prison for life. Almost all the eyewitness errors were made by strangers. When black men are accused of sexually assaulting white women, the odds of such errors are much higher—about five times the rate of misidentification within the same racial group, according to Peter J. Neufeld, cofounder of the Innocence Project, which works to exonerate wrongfully convicted prisoners through DNA testing. The reason has to do with how we respond to trauma, says Gary Wells, PhD, an eyewitness identification expert and professor of psychology at Iowa State University: "Under stress, the brain goes into fight-or-flight mode and devotes most of its efforts to survival, lessening its ability to form clear memories. When people visually process their environment, they're actually taking in much less information than we ever thought." In Meng's case,

WHEN BLACK MEN ARE ACCUSED OF RAPING WHITE WOMEN, THE ODDS OF EYEWITNESS ERROR ARE FIVE TIMES HIGHER THAN WHEN THE RACE IS THE SAME.

still traumatized by her ordeal, she ran into a man similar enough to her attacker, and he gave her a friendly look. "What luck," she says, "to smile at someone who's just been raped."

At first, when Meng learned Ruffin was innocent, she was terrified. "I was so afraid of what he might do to me," she recalls. "He had every reason to hate me."

But when she watched him on television walking out of prison a free man and he was asked what he would say to his accuser, he responded: "I don't fault you. I don't blame you. It was just an honest mistake."

"He called it an honest mistake," Meng repeats to me, her tone still incredulous. "He said he'd forgiven me because I'd made an honest mistake." (Ruffin told me he is writing a book about his experience and politely declined to comment for this article.)

After several months of sleepless nights, Meng wrote Ruffin asking for his forgiveness. He had already given it, but she needed to ask anyway. "I didn't think he could say anything worse than I'd said to myself," she recalls. Later she wrote the governor in support of Ruffin's petition for compensation and traveled to Richmond to testify on his behalf. That day the two came face-to-face.

"I was really scared, but Earl was great," she recalls. "He was as nice and gracious as can be. He said, 'Hello, how are you doing, and thanks for coming.' I apologized again. I can never apologize enough. I don't know if I've completely forgiven myself and if I ever will." Since going public with her story, Meng says she has received none of the backlash she expected, a fact that only exacerbates the deep remorse she already feels. "Frankly, it bothers me that people treat me so well," she says. "I point out that the big victim in this case is Earl Ruffin and his family. What happened to me was horrible and it caused me a lot of pain, but it's tiny compared to what he went through. I was allowed to move on, but he woke up every morning in that prison."

I ask how she lives with this. "I'm working on it. The only thing I can do is give something back by speaking out. We can't just say, 'Everybody in prison deserves to be there.' Let's look at what's wrong in our criminal justice system and fix it."

In March 2004, Virginia awarded Ruffin more than $1.2 million. "I think we owe him that," says Meng. "The all-white jury was just wrong. They looked at me and saw their daughter or sister and said, 'I don't want him to hurt somebody I love, so let's get this guy off the street.' There was nobody on that jury who looked at Earl and saw their brother, son, or husband. I take responsibility for my part in what happened. But the criminal justice system failed all of us."

As Meng tells me this, she stares at Doxie's mug shot. His face provokes no fear, no outrage, no anger. It means nothing to her. That is not the case with Ruffin. Glancing at his handsome profile in a newspaper clipping, she says, "This picture of Earl, looking at him at this angle, it sends chills through me—still." There is not a shred of Meng's conscious mind that believes Ruffin was her attacker, yet getting past this immediate visceral reaction may take years. For two decades, whenever she replayed the scenes from that cold December night, it was Ruffin's hand that clutched the knife, his face that pressed in upon her. In those fleeting subconscious moments, the memory remains that way today. It is yet one more thing to lament. ◖

MARTHA BECK'S ANTI-COMPLAIN CAMPAIGN

Face it: The only thing bitching does is make you bitchy, and whining just leaves you whiney. But according to Martha Beck, it's possible to take all that steaming frustration and convert it into the kind of energy that moves mountains and rocks worlds.

At 63, Minnie is one of the youngest people I've ever met. She sparkles, and not just because she's dressed in a fabulous buttercup-yellow tank top bedecked with rhinestones and sequins. Everything about Minnie, from her laughter to the successful businesses she's created, seems to shine.

This radiance didn't come easily. Minnie was once a young widow, grieving the death of her husband and one of her two children. When I ask how she rose from this desolation to her success as a mother and a professional, Minnie thinks for a minute, then says, "I just got tired of hearing myself whine. I harnessed my complaining energy and used it to create a really good life."

This isn't the first time I've heard such a story. While many people spend whole lifetimes complaining, most of the high achievers I know divert the energy of frustration away from complaint and into success. I've tried both paths. I can enjoy a good whine the way connoisseurs enjoy a good wine, but eventually, like Minnie, I get sick of my own petulance. Then I embark on something you might want to try: a "venting fast." It's not for the faint-hearted, but it's a powerful way to create a better life.

On the surface, a venting fast is a simple thing. Here are the instructions:

1. For a period of time, say a week or a month, stop complaining aloud about anything, to anybody.

2. When the urge to fuss arises, vent on paper. Start with the words *I'm upset about*. Then describe whatever's bothering you.

3. Think of at least one thing you can do to actually change the frustrating situation. Write it down.

If you can't think of any positive action steps, simply continue to resist venting out loud. Eventually, your frustration will increase until you think, *I'm so upset I just want to...!* Write down what you want to do.

4. Do it. Divorce the guy, cuss in front of your fundamentalist sister, put off lunching with the passive-aggressive "friend" until the end of time.

If you think that a venting fast requires willpower, you're half right. After a few whine-free days, you'll find that it also requires courage—possibly more than you've ever used. To understand why anyone would put themselves through a venting fast, it helps to know a little about the psychological dynamics of complaint.

■ ALL STEAMED UP

Complaining is as useful for people's minds as a whistle vent is for a teakettle. We use the phrase "let off steam" because frustration affects our behavior the way heat affects liquid in a container. As the level of negative emotion rises, we feel mounting pressure. We can handle this pressure in the same three ways we can handle steam: by letting it explode, venting it, or harnessing its power.

■ OPTION ONE: EXPLOSION

Many people try to deal with the hot vapor of irritation by simply choking it back. This leads to behavioral explosions, as you can learn from anyone who's ever tried to be the perfect, unruffled mother, only to find herself locked in the bathroom punching towels and using language that would make pirates faint.

Or maybe that's just me.

So here's another example: The nursing staff at an inner-city hospital once told me that although treating drug addicts and gunshot victims was a scary proposition, the most terrifying thing they ever had to face (no offense—I'm just repeating what I was told) was a partially anesthetized nun. Dramatic things happened, the nurses averred, when a holy sister from the neighborhood convent was "going under," drugged just beyond inhibition but not yet to oblivion. The nurses told tales of physical violence, of naked escapes from the OR, of destructive rampages through other patients' rooms—all perpetrated by brave, godly women who in their right minds never vented about anything.

Apparently, even those of us with the awesome self-control of religious renunciants occasionally need to release psychological pressure. You wouldn't want to emerge from an appendectomy to discover that you've decked the entire surgical team with your own IV rack, would you? That's where a strategy of controlled release comes in.

■ **OPTION TWO: VENTING**

The effect of emotional venting is to sustain an unsatisfactory status quo. Most people think the opposite, that complaining is part of an effort to change an unsatisfying situation. Nope. Complaining lets off pressure so that we neither explode with frustration nor feel compelled to take the often risky steps of openly opposing a difficult person or situation. Keeping emotional pressure tolerably low doesn't change problematic circumstances but rather perpetuates them.

For instance, Regina is a Mexican-American whose white racist parents-in-law treated her abominably. She complained about this to her husband every day. When I asked why she talked to her husband, she said she was starting an information chain: She would force him to force his parents to change. How long had Regina been employing this strategy? Twenty years. And the effect to date? Nada.

Mike worked for a pompous boss who gave his subordinates little direction and less support. The underlings spent their work hours muttering angry stories and following the soap opera of office conflict. Mike came home exhausted, not from working but from venting. And things at work kept getting worse, not better.

College sophomore Dinah spent hours with her friends ranting about a certain high-ranking elected official, who shall remain nameless. This, Dinah told me, was activism. I said it looked more like passivism—neither activism nor pacifism but an excellent way of feeling intelligent and important without studying.

These venters thought their chronic complaining was "powerful civil disobedience." Actually, it was disempowering uncivil obedience. By allowing emotional pressure to dissipate without action, these people were able to sit indefinitely in predicaments that pushed them to an emotional boiling point. Now, in situations you don't want to change, this can be a good idea. I was a better mother to my toddlers after a session of recreational complaining with other moms. Having vented about our sleep deprivation, boredom, and longing for adult company, we'd return to the field of battle—er, motherhood—able to focus on the sweeter aspects of parenting. In Minnie's case, venting helped ease the anguish of losing loved ones. Without it, she might not have survived her grief. But even she reached the point where venting felt excessive, like an illness rather than a cure. Then it was time for Option Three: creating a steam-driven life.

The effect of emotional venting is to sustain an unsatisfactory status quo.

■ **OPTION THREE: HARNESSING THE POWER OF FRUSTRATION**

"It is not that I do not get angry," said Gandhi. "I do not give vent to anger." On another occasion he wrote, "As heat conserved is transmuted into energy, even so our anger controlled can be transmuted into a power which can move the world." Gandhi was describing the power of a mind that refuses to vent frustration, channeling it into productive action the way an engine harnesses steam heat.

If you want to know how much change this can cause, consider the millennia that humans spent watching vapor rise from their cook pots before a 17th-century genius thought, *Hey, I think all that steam could drive a piston*. Et voilà: the Industrial Revolution. A mere 200 years later, people were walking on the moon. This is the level of transformation that can occur when we stop complaining about our circumstances and begin channeling our emotional pressure into positive action. Look how Gandhi changed the world. He was one of the great peacemakers in all history! Right up until someone shot him!

Oh, yeah. That.

Make no mistake, a venting fast is risky. Without the option of complaining, you'll have only two choices for dealing with emotional buildup: explosion or positive action. The first will damage you, your relationships, your life. The second will fundamentally alter the status quo, and the status quo, by definition, resists change. If you follow the venting-fast rules above, you're almost certain to break implicit or explicit social rules that now govern your life. Prepare to find this terrifying.

When Regina stopped complaining about her in-laws, her emotional steam pressure quickly rendered her unable to tolerate their company. One day, when her father-in-law made a racist comment, Regina stood up and took a cab home. "I was terrified," she told me later. "But I had to do something." The ensuing argument between Regina's husband and his parents was the beginning of overdue but impressive change. Faced with the choice of being respectful or losing their son, the bigots began showing respect.

Mike's story was simpler. When he stopped complaining at the office, he became so sick of his boss and bored with his coworkers' venting that he sought, and found, a job he liked better. The end.

Dinah stopped joining in college vent-fests, but her political discontent continued. She'd always been a mediocre student, but the energy she'd been pouring into complaint now drove her to study political science. Diligently. Dinah is now in law school, thinking up ways to create a just society, rather than simply criticizing the people in power. When she runs for office, I'm voting for her.

■ **I WILL VENT NO MORE FOREVER**

If you try a venting fast and survive, you may find yourself heading in new, exciting directions. You may even decide to do what Minnie did: commit to an entire life without complaining. "I have a rule," says Minnie, smile and sequins flashing. "I'm not allowed to whine about anything I can change. And since I can always change my attitude, I don't expect to find a really hopeless situation in this lifetime."

I admire this position enormously, though I don't think I'm quite ready to emulate it. Recreational complaining, the sense of steam leaving those emotional vents, is still perversely enjoyable for me. Maybe someday I'll be like Minnie, who's more vibrant and successful in her seventh decade than most people are in their third. Maybe I'll go on a venting fast that lasts the rest of my life. Until then, my existence will fail to match its potential. But I'm not complaining.

At least that's a start. ⬛

21 THINGS YOU CAN STOP WORRYING ABOUT RIGHT NOW!

Whatever's keeping you up at night—enough already! Suzan Colón checks in with a bunch of experts who'll convince you to give peace of mind a chance.

I used to worry. A lot. About things large and small, about what was happening with the world and with me, about the future, the present, the pie I ate the night before. I agonized over relationships—were they destined to break up? And my hips—were they fated to break down? Unfortunately, I got better at it: I went from stressing about garden-variety worries that anyone would regard as reasonable to logging many unhappy hours catastrophizing about the possibility of highly unlikely disasters.

I was hardly alone in this; I have friends who've also turned worrying into a second job. And so I wondered: Why *do* we worry so much? It turns out that we can thank, or blame, our evolutionary heritage. In prehistoric times, worry kept us from wandering into the lion's den. Today we're much safer, in the grand scheme of things,

but that sensitive warning system isn't easily dialed down. So it sits around wondering if so-and-so likes us, suspecting that the boss is being nice to us because we're about to get fired, and conjuring all the other doomsday scenarios that keep us up at night.

One day, after becoming paralyzed over what to have for lunch—too fattening? too much meat? were the vegetables full of pesticides?—I got fed up. I was sick of obsessing about my health, of feeling the pain in my shoulders from the weight of the world, of knowing that tomorrow's forecast was always going to be cloudy with a chance of regret.

I made a list of my worries, asked my friends for theirs, and took them to a group of experts to find out how we should handle them. What the pros had to say could soothe even the most nervous soul—and lead to a sudden surge in the world's population of "What, me worry?" types. All together now: Whew. —S.C.

SLEEPING, BEAUTY? If anxiety has given you insomnia, it's time to derail that train of thought.

⚡ THE CLOCK IS TICKING, BUT I'M NOT SURE I WANT A CHILD—YET I WORRY THAT IF I DON'T HAVE ONE, I'LL REGRET IT WHEN IT'S TOO LATE.

GAIL SALTZ, MD There are parts of life where you can compromise, but not here: You either have a child or don't.

The fear of regretting that you didn't have a child is not the best reason to have one. That said, rarely have I seen a patient who regretted becoming a mother, because once the baby is in the world, the woman loves it. Usually, the woman wants to be a parent and it's her spouse who isn't sure; he goes along with it because he listens to her fear of regret. Yet when the baby is born, he doesn't regret it either; he loves it, too.

On the other hand, I have had patients who've regretted not having children. The good news is, there are so many ways you can rectify that, including adoption and IVF.

(Dr. Saltz is a psychiatrist and author of Anatomy of a Secret Life.*)*

✝ I WORRY ABOUT MY DAD'S HEALTH—AND THE FACT THAT HE DOESN'T.

MARTHA BECK, PhD What we resist persists: When people are pushed, they almost always push back. The more you try to talk your dad into minding his health, the more he'll be able to ignore his physical symptoms and focus on pushing back against your "interference." Instead of nagging him or pointedly substituting steamed fish for steak, take excellent care of your own health and accept him without judgment—or accommodation. In other words, don't coddle him by holding back on normal activities. Let him experience the natural consequences of ignoring his health (breathlessness while playing with the grandkids, trouble concentrating during family poker games) so that he, not you, will be the one who decides he needs to be more conscientious.

(Beck is a life coach, author, and O *columnist.)*

💔 I WORRY THAT MY HUSBAND WILL CHEAT ON ME AND I WON'T BE ABLE TO FORGIVE HIM. AND I'M NOT EVEN MARRIED YET!

ESTHER PEREL, MA You're probably worried that your spouse will have extramarital sex or an emotional affair. But there are many ways to cheat: neglect, indifference, spite, refusal of physical intimacy, lack of respect. "Cheating" fails to describe the multiple ways people let each other down.

Before thinking about whether you'd be able to forgive him, it's important to understand what violations of trust mean to a relationship. Forgiveness doesn't mean acceptance but rather understanding, the ability to come to terms with a certain reality, and a willingness to live with it while it finds its place in our lives.

I once worked with a couple who had been together since high school. The man had an affair after his father died because he wanted to break loose from the constrictions he felt had been imposed on him by his father, and to rebel against being dutiful and responsible. While the wife was no less hurt, understanding that the affair had very little to do with her gave it a different meaning. The couple also gained new insights into each other: This strong woman showed a vulnerable side her husband hadn't been aware of, and this bold man was not the husband she thought she knew.

The thought that a partner can leave is not a baseless worry; it's a fact of love. There is no love without the fear of loss. Rather than becoming anxious about the possibility of your spouse cheating on you, think of your concern as an awareness that is part of being in a relationship.

(Perel is the author of Mating in Captivity.*)*

(WORRY ZAPPER)

"THERE IS NOTHING THAT WASTES THE BODY LIKE WORRY, AND ONE WHO HAS ANY FAITH IN GOD SHOULD BE ASHAMED TO WORRY ABOUT ANYTHING WHATSOEVER." —MAHATMA GANDHI

💔 I WORRY THAT IF MY HUSBAND AND I GET DIVORCED, HE'LL FIND A HUNDRED WOMEN WHO WANT TO REPLACE ME, WHEREAS I WILL NEVER FIND ANYONE. NO, WE'RE NOT SPLITTING UP...I'M JUST BEING PESSIMISTIC.

GILLIAN BUTLER, PhD, and **TONY HOPE, MD** If there's no real basis for your concern, there might be some low self-esteem issues you should divert your attention to. Or you may be an "imaginative worrier," someone who invents different possible futures. When negative events are unlikely but possible, some choose to focus on the possibility, while others don't give it a second thought. Being aware of this classification and shifting these scenarios from "possible" to "highly unlikely" is a useful strategy for combating this kind of worry.

(Butler and Hope are coauthors of Managing Your Mind.*)*

CANCER RUNS IN MY FAMILY. AM I DESTINED TO GET IT, TOO?

MEHMET OZ, MD Not necessarily. The top three things you can do to tip the odds in your favor are to maintain a waistline that's generally less than half your height in inches, eat low on the food chain, and not be a toxic dump—avoid exposure to cigarette smoke and asbestos, things like that. You can't control your genes, but they aren't as significant as how you affect them with risk factors you can control, such as smoking and obesity.
(*Dr. Oz is the coauthor [with Michael F. Roizen] of* You, on a Diet.)

I DON'T HAVE ENOUGH MONEY TO TRAVEL! I'M AFRAID I'LL NEVER SEE FRENCH POLYNESIA, CHINA, AND OTHER PLACES I DREAM OF.

PATRICIA SCHULTZ Waiting to have enough money will keep you securely ensconced at home. Consider the wonders of America that can be yours for a weekend and the price of a tank of gas (expensive, yes, but still cheaper than plane tickets). Tourists come from all over the globe to see our national treasures, but how many New Yorkers don't personally know the beauty of the historic Hudson Valley? How many Seattleites have never visited the Walla Walla wine region? How many folks in Dallas have yet to two-step their way through the old-time dance halls of Texas's Hill Country?

If you're still hungry for something exotic, you can find that frisson of foreign travel right here in North America. You can hear Cajun spoken in southern Louisiana, and French in the historic neighborhoods of Old Montreal and Old Quebec. The past is very much alive in the Gaelic culture of Nova Scotia and in the Amish communities of Indiana, Ohio, and Pennsylvania.

But don't give up your dream of a larger trip. Make a plan, and make it happen. Commit to a specific departure date, and put aside money regularly. Time passes quickly; better to spend it looking forward to your trip than allowing regrets to build.
(*Schultz is the author of* 1,000 Places to See in the USA and Canada Before You Die.)

WHEN I BUY CLOTHING MADE IN THIRD WORLD COUNTRIES, AM I EXPLOITING THE POOR? OR IN POVERTY-STRICKEN AREAS, IS ANY KIND OF ECONOMY GOOD?

NICHOLAS D. KRISTOF It'll surprise a lot of Americans to hear this, but in general buying cheap clothes from foreign factories actually helps the workers. True, there are problems with terrible facilities that use unsafe chemicals or lock the fire doors, but people in poor countries generally see factory jobs as better than many of the alternatives, such as peddling, farmwork, or day labor. East Asia has lifted hundreds of millions out of poverty by developing a model of export factories.

Americans usually focus on the low wages and bad conditions—workers earning 15 cents for making a shirt that will sell for $15. But for the person who makes that shirt, the alternative is usually a job that is more dangerous and pays less. I interviewed workers scavenging in a dump in Indonesia, and I'll never forget the mother who told me that she dreamed that her children would someday work in what we'd call a sweatshop.

Of course, if you want to pay more for a shirt that's produced by workers who get better treatment, terrific. But it's the poorest countries, where wages and working conditions are the worst, that most desperately need the jobs. And the most effective foreign aid is often to start a manufacturing industry in those countries.
(*Kristof is an op-ed columnist for* The New York Times.)

"JUST LET IT GO"—EASY FOR *THEM* TO SAY

You've scheduled the important health test, submitted your résumé for the job, or gone out on that first date… and some well-meaning friend says, "Now you have to just let it go." Gee, thanks—but how, exactly, do you do that?

JON KABAT-ZINN When people say "Let it go," what they really mean is "Get over it," and that's not a helpful thing to say. It's not a matter of letting go—you would if you could. Instead of "Let it go," we should probably say "Let it be"; this recognizes that the mind won't let go and the problem may not go away, and it allows you to form a healthier relationship with what's bothering you.

That's what mindfulness is all about: Paying attention—without judgment—to whatever is happening in the present moment. You can do this by thinking of your mind as an ocean. Just as waves are affected by weather, our emotions can be blown around by the winds of change and circumstance, and our troubled thoughts can create turbulence in our minds. However, if you went below the surface of the ocean, you would find calmer, gentler undulations. You can achieve the same thing with your mind. When you begin to feel anxious, take a moment to feel the breath in your body, preferably breathing down in your belly. Imagine your thoughts as waves; see them rise, linger, and pass. Keep breathing deeply and slowly, and keep watching your thoughts. You'll be able to live in the moment, even when it's difficult and scary, with greater calmness and balance. That is letting things be.

This exercise isn't easy, but the well-being that can come of it is huge. It lets you come to terms with reality—the good, the wonderful, and also the bad and the ugly—without being completely torpedoed by it. This doesn't mean that if your worries turn out to be justified, you'll hurt any less. But it will keep you from losing not only your mind but your common sense, just when you need it most.
(*Kabat-Zinn is coauthor of* The Mindful Way Through Depression: Freeing Yourself from Chronic Unhappiness.)

JOSEPH GOLDSTEIN Often we worry about things that don't materialize. But there are also times when we become lost in worry about real-life problems, either personal or global. Here we might use a reflection suggested by the Dalai Lama: "If you have some fear of pain or suffering, you should examine whether there is anything you can do about it. If you can, there is no need to worry about it. If you cannot, then there is also no need to worry."

As with all mental habits, the retraining of the mind takes patience and perseverance. But when we pay attention to how our minds are working, we can see how suffering is created, as well as the possibility of freedom from that suffering.
(*Goldstein is the author of* One Dharma: The Emerging Western Buddhism.)

I HAVE A BAD FEELING: I'M NEVER GOING TO LOSE THIS WEIGHT.

BOB GREENE You can't put all your emotional eggs in the weight loss basket. People say, "I'll be happy when I reach this size...," but that's a problem, because either you don't reach the goal, or you do—and you're no happier than you were 40 pounds ago. Then you ask yourself why you did all this work, you go back to the way you were before, and the lose-gain-lose cycle begins.

Instead of worrying about the future, work toward leading a fulfilled life today. That will naturally make you want to be healthy. Eating right and exercising are my two fields, but when I meet with a client, I ask her about the things that really hold the secret to her success—what the most important areas of her life are, and how she feels about each one.

So do a little self-discovery. Look at what brings you joy and what isn't going so well. Have a life plan as opposed to a weight plan. Next, figure out how active you're willing to be and how much time you can devote to exercise. Then balance the calories—but don't deprive yourself. I've never found anyone who should be eating fewer than 1,500 calories.

Finally, set realistic goals, or you're bound to fail. Adjust your thinking about what's healthy for you, given your genetics. Some of the healthiest people on the planet are heavier than what we claim is the ideal. Being realistic is not only important, it's empowering. *(Greene is the author of* The Best Life Diet.*)*

I DON'T THINK I'LL EVER SWIM OUT FROM UNDER THE PILE OF WORK I HAVE AT THE OFFICE!

JULIE MORGENSTERN You're right. The reality is that you'll never get to the bottom of your to-do list. The way our work world has evolved, it isn't humanly possible anymore. It's not just information overload; it's opportunity overload—there are always a million things to do. And please, forget multitasking. It doesn't increase efficiency at all, and it taxes brain cells in the frontal cortex, which has a terrible impact on performance.

Here's how to prioritize. I teach a concept called "dancing close to the revenue line." Evaluate the items on your to-do list in terms of their proximity to what will make money soonest for your company. Most people tackle the easiest tasks first so they can check off a lot of little things that don't matter at the end of the day. Instead, when you go into work, ask yourself, *If I ran out of time today, what would be the one thing that, completed, would give me the greatest sense of accomplishment and contribution?* When you take care of that, it won't matter if the rest of the day goes to hell in a handbasket. *(Morgenstern is the author of* Never Check E-Mail in the Morning.*)*

(WORRY ZAPPER)

"FINISH EVERY DAY AND BE DONE WITH IT.... YOU HAVE DONE WHAT YOU COULD; SOME BLUNDERS AND ABSURDITIES NO DOUBT CREPT IN; FORGET THEM AS SOON AS YOU CAN. TOMORROW IS A NEW DAY; YOU SHALL BEGIN IT...SERENELY, AND WITH TOO HIGH A SPIRIT TO BE CUMBERED WITH YOUR OLD NONSENSE."
—RALPH WALDO EMERSON

(WORRY ZAPPER)

"IT AIN'T NEVER NO USE PUTTIN' UP YOUR UMBRELL' TILL IT RAINS!" —ALICE CALDWELL RICE

SAVINGS BOUND Be smart about money now so you don't need to be streetwise later.

I'M AFRAID MY RETIREMENT HOME IS GOING TO BE A CARDBOARD BOX. HOW DO I KEEP FROM BECOMING A BAG LADY?

SUZE ORMAN That's a common fear: In a 2006 survey, nearly half the women respondents said they've imagined ending up homeless.

Concentrate on saving as much as possible for retirement. If you're 30 years old and you invest $250 a month for the next 35 years with an annual average return of approximately 8 percent, you'll have more than $575,000 by the time you're 65. Sock away $500 a month and you'll have $1.15 million. If you're 45 and can put away $250, in 20 years you'll have about $150,000; $500 a month will yield nearly $300,000. No procrastinating and no running up big credit card bills. If you are over 45 and own a home, aim to have the mortgage paid off before you retire. If anyone tells you you'll lose the mortgage interest deduction, set them straight: That deduction is most valuable in the early years of the loan. And in retirement, because you'll have total equity in the home, you can generate income to live on by doing a reverse mortgage (a loan that the lender pays you, based on the equity you have in your home, to be repaid only upon moving or death). To accelerate your mortgage payments, scale back your 401(k) investing so it is just enough to get the maximum company match. *(Orman is O's financial columnist.)*

I'M SO AFRAID OF TERRORISM, I CAN'T SLEEP. HOW UNSAFE ARE WE?

BRIAN MICHAEL JENKINS Terrorism is violence calculated to create an atmosphere of fear and alarm. It often works. Terrorist attacks are deadly, dramatic, and visual; how many times have we watched the World Trade Center's towers fall? And the terror is reinforced by a relentless message of fear in the form of Washington's color-coded alerts and announcements of imminent attack.

The terrorist threat is real, but we must distinguish between threats to our national security and danger to individual citizens—us. The threat we face as individuals is minuscule compared with the everyday risks we accept. Each year the average American has about a one in 7,000 chance of dying in a motor vehicle accident, and a one in 18,000 chance of being murdered, most likely by a relative or friend. Compare that to about a one in 600,000 chance of dying at the hands of terrorists. Yet, are we ready to toss the keys to the car? Avoid the family picnic? No.

As a nation, we will combat terrorism. As individuals, it is up to us to combat terror—our own—by putting terrorist fears in perspective.
(Jenkins is senior advisor on terrorism and homeland security for the RAND Corporation.)

(WORRY ZAPPER)

"I HAVE LEARNED TO LIVE EACH DAY AS IT COMES, AND NOT TO BORROW TROUBLE BY DREADING TOMORROW. IT IS THE DARK MENACE OF THE FUTURE THAT MAKES COWARDS OF US."—DOROTHY DIX

I PANIC WHEN I CAN'T REACH MY PARTNER. IF I CALL OR E-MAIL AND HE DOESN'T GET BACK TO ME WITHIN AN HOUR, I PICTURE HIM BEING WASHED AWAY BY A TIDAL WAVE OR RUN OVER BY A TRUCK.

BEVERLY ENGEL, MFCT There are several levels of questions I would ask. First, are you watching a lot of TV and focusing on disaster? If that's the case, turn off the TV and concentrate on the good things in your life. Next, do you worry only about your partner? If so, you may be too dependent on him and feel that if something really did happen to him, you'd be lost. Find ways to be more self-sufficient and widen your social network. If you worry about something bad happening to your child, parents, and other loved ones, look deeper for the cause. Are you obsessing about others because you're avoiding your own problems? Do you need to keep tabs on everybody because you have control issues? Was there a trauma in your life that causes you to fixate on bad possibilities? Or were you raised by worrying parents, such as a mother who said, "I thought you'd been hit by a truck!" if you came home late from school?

Whatever your reasons, try this exercise: Ask yourself if you're feeling angry about something; then ask if you're feeling sad, guilty, or fearful. Whatever the feeling, go to its opposite. For anger, that's gratitude; for sadness, it's joy; for guilt, it's pride; for fear, it's security. Now ask, what are you grateful for? Joyful about? What do you feel proud of and secure about? Focusing on positive messages, especially what you're secure about in times of fear, can help.
(Engel is a psychotherapist and author of Healing Your Emotional Self.*)*

I FIND ORGASMS TO BE OVERSTIMULATING, ALMOST PAINFUL. IS THERE SOMETHING WRONG WITH ME?

HILDA HUTCHERSON, MD First, talk to your gynecologist after a full checkup, especially if the contractions felt good in the past and have recently become painful. If that's not the case, it doesn't mean there's something wrong. If you're in your 20s, orgasms might seem painful simply because sex may be relatively new territory for you. Over time, you'll become more familiar with your body and what feels good.

For many women, riding the crest of the wave may be better than going over the top, which can be too intense. It could also be that your partner's stimulation is too direct. Showing your partner what you like and what doesn't work is part of being in a mutually enjoyable sexual relationship. Orgasm doesn't have to be the goal. It's more important, and fun, to figure out what works for both of you.
(Dr. Hutcherson is an obstetrician-gynecologist and author of Pleasure: A Woman's Guide to Getting the Sex You Want, Need, and Deserve.*)*

I KNOW HOW I SHOULD EAT AND EXERCISE. DO I DO EITHER? NO. HOW BAD IS MY HEALTH GOING TO BE LATER ON?

MEHMET OZ, MD You shouldn't just be concerned about health problems in the future. If you want to feel good, function better, and think more clearly, your quality of life will improve today if you do a few simple things—and the side effect is that you'll live longer.

For fitness, try walking. You won't dread it, and it's easy to incorporate into your daily life—walk to a lunch place a little farther from work, walk up stairs. Get a pedometer and aim for 10,000 steps a day.

To improve your diet, eat an ounce of nuts—about a palmful—daily. Walnuts, almonds, and hazelnuts have many of the nutrients you need, and they'll satiate you so you won't forage for doughnuts.

And finally, drink water. It's difficult for humans to differentiate between thirst and hunger. If you feel a desire to put something in your mouth, your first response should be water. If that's not enough, then get food—like nuts.

WHAT FREAKS ME OUT ABOUT TURNING 50: I'LL SPEND ALL MY TIME LOOKING BACK ON THE THINGS I HAVEN'T DONE.

MEL WALSH, MA I'm a grandmother of 12 who remarried three years ago at the age of 68, I've written books, and I host a radio show and write a column, both called *Second Wind.* That's the theme in my life—getting a second wind after 50.

Regrets are passions that aren't pursued: "I never got a chance to travel, or to be an artist." As you move toward retirement, you get the time to do these things. I was in my 60s when I thought, *What do I want to be when I grow up?* I went back to school to study gerontology and got my master's degree when I was 66. A friend of mine is writing her second novel at the age of 70.

Women had a revolution in the 1970s for liberation and equal pay, and now we're having another revolution about what it means to be older. Aging isn't the end of the road; it's the gift of another beginning.
(Walsh is the auther of Hot Granny.*)*

I WORRY ABOUT MY BONES DETERIORATING, MY BODY BREAKING DOWN, NEEDING HIP REPLACEMENT, KNEE AND ROTATOR CUFF SURGERY.... SHOULD I BECOME LESS ACTIVE IN MIDDLE AGE?

MEHMET OZ, MD If you're in your 40s, pick exercise that's gentler on your joints. For example, you can still run, but do it on the elliptical machine, which has no impact. Or swim, or do yoga.

The best way to maintain bone strength is to do weight-bearing exercises, either with weights or by using your body as the weight, which you do in yoga. Diet also matters. You want less alcohol and carbonated colas (which may interfere with the balance of calcium) and more vitamin D in your system. Exposure to sunlight converts cholesterol in the body into vitamin D, which in turn enables calcium to be deposited in your bones, so try to get 15 minutes of direct sun exposure at least two times a week. If that's not practical, take supplements that contain vitamin D and calcium. Start getting annual bone density screenings at 65; if there's a strong history of osteoporosis in your family, consult with your doctor.

I wouldn't stop doing fun sports for fear of breaking something. Yes, bad stuff happens, but as long as you're taking good care of your body, it's a remarkably versatile machine.

(WORRY ZAPPER)

"HE SUFFERS MORE THAN IS NECESSARY, WHO SUFFERS BEFORE IT IS NECESSARY."
—SENECA THE YOUNGER

AS I GET OLDER I'M TERRIFIED OF LOSING MY MIND—THE IDEA OF DEMENTIA SCARES THE HELL OUT OF ME.

MEHMET OZ, MD One of the best ways to prevent dementia is to challenge the brain. People tend to go for mental workouts like crossword puzzles, which are good, but exercise is better. It gives you a twofold benefit: First, whether you're learning a new sport or playing one you know, it makes your brain work in ways that it doesn't normally. When I play basketball, I'm calculating how to make a jump shot; when I jog, I'm daydreaming and brainstorming—things I don't do when I'm at my desk. Second, while crossword puzzles build your vocabulary, exercise builds your vascular system and promotes healthier blood vessels, so you can stave off the small strokes that are often part of the dementia picture.

IT FEELS AS IF I'M ALWAYS SHORTCHANGING EITHER MY FAMILY OR MY JOB. IS IT POSSIBLE TO BALANCE THEM?

PAUL WILSON It's not a matter of balance; it's a matter of attitude. All you have to do is follow a simple formula: Wherever you are physically present, be mentally present. When you walk out your front door in the morning, leave the kids' grades, your bills, your grocery list at home, and turn your thoughts toward your job. When you get there, bring 100 percent of your attention to your workplace. You will be more efficient for being completely focused on the tasks at hand.

When you get home, bring all your attention to whoever or whatever is before you. Listen to your kids; don't think about work. Do the same when you converse with your partner. Your relationships will be richer for it.
(Wilson is a meditation teacher and the author of Perfect Balance.*)*

I DON'T WANT TO GET WRINKLES, BUT I DON'T WANT TO HAVE PLASTIC SURGERY OR INJECTIONS IN MY FACE, EITHER. WORRIERS DEVELOP WORRY LINES, DON'T THEY?

RANELLA HIRSCH, MD You're right—our faces reflect where our minds are, so when we worry, that's what we show. There are a few noninvasive steps you can take to reduce lines. I know a woman who swears by Frownies, little pieces of tape you can put on your frown areas at night when you go to sleep to keep you from cultivating lines. Also, get your eyes checked. Chronic squinting can cause wrinkles to develop. If your eyes are okay, look into other ways to channel your stress, like exercise. And if you're going to worry, do it with sunscreen on!
(Dr. Hirsch is a dermatologist in Boston.) Ⓞ

ONE THING YOU REALLY *SHOULD* WORRY ABOUT
(THE GOOD NEWS: THERE'S SOMETHING YOU CAN DO ABOUT IT)

How fast is global warming going to happen? I own oceanfront property—should I sell? Will Antarctica—or penguins, outside of zoos—exist in 20 years? In ten?

SUSI MOSER, PhD The rise in sea level is going to happen over time; it won't be like a flood, where one day everything's fine and the next day you're wiped out. If we make no environmental changes, the ice pack on Greenland will probably melt down over the course of several hundred years, which could raise the global ocean by 18 to 20 feet. For the first few feet, we'll probably spend a lot of money trying to protect buildings near the water. But eventually, we'll have to make some hard choices, like giving up pieces of land.

It sounds like a doomsday future, but there are things we can do now to change that scenario—drive less, choose smaller cars, turn down the thermostat, buy energy-efficient lightbulbs and appliances. Another tip: Pay attention to where your food comes from. We can now get anything from anywhere in the world, but the amount of energy it takes to transport it is unbelievable, so eat local foods, in season.

Unfortunately, even with all those changes, the best we can say is that things won't get worse. So when people ask, "Why bother?" I say because we can benefit our children, our grandchildren, and their children. I think that's pretty good motivation to save the planet.
(Moser is a scientist with the Institute for the Study of Society and Environment/National Center for Atmospheric Research.)

LONG LIVE THE GREEN Convert the energy you spend worrying into saving the planet.

AGE BRILLIANTLY

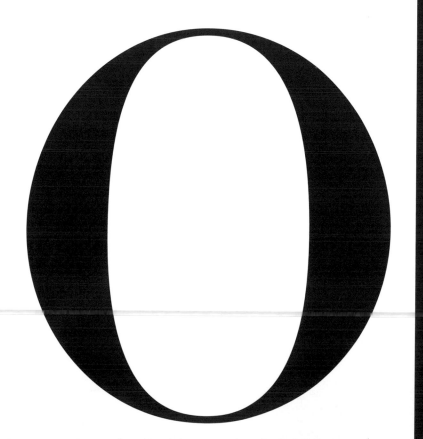

THE GRAY IS COMING! THE GRAY IS COMING!

What do you do when you see your first gray hair? Do you pluck it? Ignore it? Discreetly adjust your part—the way you might surreptitiously slide a chair over a slender imperfection in a rug? And when the gray starts coming in fast and furious: Do you dye, highlight, or throw up your hands and recklessly let it happen in a fit of gray abandon?

Since many people by the age of 50 have started to go gray, a quick glance around at the midlifers you know will tell you that in an effort to preserve a youthful look, most are choosing to dye. But a growing number of women—courageous, rebellious, or just exhausted by the tedium of coloring—are going brazenly, vividly gray.

Might that brazen route be right for you? "Gray or white hair tends to look best with pink, olive, and dark complexions," says Lisa Chiccine, a stylist and owner of the Lisa Chiccine Salon in New York City. "If you're sallow or very pale, you'll probably look washed-out and should consider highlights or lowlights," she says. Brown hair that looks mousy as the gray comes in can be brightened and enriched by weaving in highlights and lowlights of honey, tortoiseshell, or mahogany. Another good option if you're just starting to go gray is to use a vegetable dye or a semipermanent glaze. Both will stain a lot of the gray, and when the color starts to fade, you won't have a root line, says Chiccine. If your gray comes in wiry, it's because it's dry, so use a weekly deep conditioner (such as Aveda Damage Remedy Intensive Restructuring Treatment or Philip Kingsley Elasticizer) to moisturize and calm it down. To counteract any yellow tones, get a violet-based gloss at the salon every six to eight weeks; it coats the hair and gives it shine, says Mikael Padilla, celebrity colorist for Wella Professionals in Los Angeles.

Because we here at *O* take great pleasure in helping women look as terrific as possible, we found a handful who had decided to let their gray (or silver or white or salt-and-pepper) come in naturally (though one weaves blonde through her gray; another, black); they all needed some guidance about amping up their color and style. So we brought in a squad of experts on gray matters: for color, Rita Hazan, of the Rita Hazan Salon in New York City; for cut, Juan Carlos Maciques, who works with Rita; for makeup (because gray demands special attention to color on the face), Lisa Garner, a New York City makeup artist; and for brows (because brows can go gray, too), Eliza Petrescu, from New York City's Exhale Spa. Check out our eight transformations to see how our subjects went from gray to great.

YAMUNA ZAKE, 52, BODYWORK INSTRUCTOR
PROBLEM: FRIZZY, NO STYLE

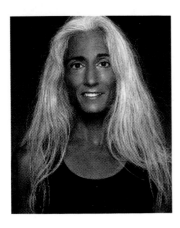

FIRST GRAY SIGHTING: "By the time I was 15, I already had an inch-wide streak in the front."

HER REACTION: "I always thought it was cool. It never occurred to me to dye it. But it occurred to everyone else. I can't tell you how many times people looked at my hair and said, 'You should do something about that.'"

WHEN SHE WENT COMPLETELY GRAY: "In my late 20s, the love of my life dropped dead. I turned gray very fast after that."

WHY SHE'LL NEVER DYE IT: "When my daughter was younger, she told me she was ashamed to be seen with me because of my hair. So I used a shampoo-in color, and it turned a hideous eggplant. It took me a year to grow it out; I just kept cutting it off till I was all gray again. I love it natural. It's who I am. I love being in my 50s and looking my age and being in great shape."

JUAN CARLOS'S SOLUTION: "Yamuna's hair has a coarse texture, so she needs to use a daily leave-in conditioner [like Logics DNA Leave-in Conditioning Protector] and then apply a serum or spray that controls frizz and adds shine [try Avon Advance Techniques Dry Ends Serum or Citré Shine Shine Miracle Anti-Frizz Spray Laminator]. She should use a deep conditioning treatment once a week, leaving it on for as long as possible, or even overnight." (We like Redken All Soft Heavy Cream or L'Oréal Professionnel Série Expert Age Densiforce Masque.)

Yamuna Zake has been going gray since she was a teenager: "I love it natural. It's who I am."

CATHY GUYTON, 52, ULTRASOUND TECHNOLOGIST
PROBLEM: LACKS VOLUME

FIRST GRAY SIGHTING: "I was 17. My boyfriend's mother saw the gray first. Then in my late 20s I started getting it around my temples and in the front. It looked as if my hair was frosted, with lots of colors—brown, gray, white. By the time I was 45, it was all white."
HER REACTION: "It never bothered me in any way. My grandfather was totally white at 30."

HER FAVORITE THING ABOUT BEING GRAY: "At least twice a day, every day, I get stopped on the street by someone telling me they love my hair. Twenty-year-old boys, men, and women my own age, hair stylists. I think I look good because I'm comfortable with who I am; that's powerful."
JUAN CARLOS'S SOLUTION: "Cathy's hair was heavy and limp. A slightly layered style—shorter at the cheekbone—and body-enhancing products give her hair a fuller, face-framing texture." (Try Phyto PhytoVolume Actif Volumizer Spray or Pantene Pro-V Sheer Volume Body Builder Volumizing Mousse.)

ALICIA CLARENS, 54, WRITER AND ADMINISTRATOR AT WEILL CORNELL MEDICAL COLLEGE IN NEW YORK CITY
PROBLEM: STRIPEY MIX

FIRST GRAY SIGHTING: "I was in my mid-40s. It started to come in around my temples and ears."
HER REACTION: "It amused me."
AFTER THE AMUSEMENT, WHAT SHE DID ABOUT IT: "I dyed it. I thought that was what I was supposed to do."
AND SHE CHANGED HER MIND ABOUT DYEING BECAUSE: "I've always loved gray hair. I think it's

elegant, smart, and sexy. So I quit dyeing and got black lowlights to kick up the contrast between my natural color and the gray. It keeps me from looking faded as more gray comes in. My hair is very thick and healthy, and I want to keep it that way. And I don't like to follow the crowd, so wearing my hair long is my way of showing independence."
HER FAVORITE EXPRESSION: "'Gray is the new black.' You remember when it wasn't considered appropriate to wear black? Then it became fashionable. I think it's going to be the same with gray hair."
RITA'S SOLUTION: "The contrast between the gray and the black in Alicia's hair was too stark; the color needed to be better blended. So I wove black lowlights evenly around her temples and gave her a clear gloss to boost shine."

SUSAN MCGRAW, 53, REAL ESTATE AGENT AND MODEL
PROBLEM: SEVERE CUT

FIRST GRAY SIGHTING: "In my early 30s my hairdresser handed me a mirror, showed me the back of my head, and said, 'Did you know you're going gray?'"

HER REACTION: "I just let it happen. About ten years later, I was divorced and getting very salt-and-pepper. My hairdresser kept telling me to dye my hair because it was making me look old. Finally I said, 'If you ever say that to me again, I'm not coming back.' He stopped. I thought my hair was beautiful. I still do. Instead of dark chocolate hair, I have this elegant silver mane."

SHE'LL CONSIDER DYEING HER HAIR WHEN: Hell freezes over. "I've never dyed it, and I never will."

JUAN CARLOS'S SOLUTION: "Gray hair can look harsh with a severe cut. A few layers around her face would soften her look. I used large hot rollers to give her body and waves, which bring out her beautiful cheekbones. Barex Gloss Mousse gives her hair volume and shine."

HELEN RUSSELL, 51, MUSICIAN AND PRODUCTION CONSULTANT
PROBLEM: FADED GRAY/BLONDE

FIRST GRAY SIGHTING: "About 12 years ago. My hair is fine, but the gray was an entirely different texture, wiry and coarse."

HER REACTION: "I tried covering it by combing my hair differently. That didn't work very well. So I started getting blonde highlights every six months or so."

HER HAIRCOLOR AMBITION: "Eventually, I want to go all gray. But for now, I wouldn't mind being a little blonder."

RITA'S SOLUTION: "There was no contrast between Helen's ashy haircolor and her complexion, so she looked completely washed-out. I gave her a warm, gold all over base color, with baby blonde, honey, and gold highlights to add dimension."

REGINA MUMME, 48
HOMEMAKER
PROBLEM: MOUSY SALT-AND-PEPPER

FIRST GRAY SIGHTING: "I was in my 30s. Gray hair has a way of making itself known: It was wiry and stuck up along my part."

HER REACTION: "I dyed it brown. Sometimes I dyed it red. I liked dyeing it different colors; it was fun."

WHEN DYEING STOPPED BEING FUN: "About four years ago, the gray hairs started changing color; they got orangey. And then my husband said to me, 'Just go gray.'

So with his encouragement, I cut off all the color and let my hair grow in naturally."

WHY SHE WON'T COMMIT TO GRAY FOREVER: "I've never been a platinum blonde!"

RITA'S SOLUTION: "Regina's color—a drab brown—can get yellowish and dull when it starts to turn gray. I used a violet shampoo [Clairol Professional Blonde & Silver Shimmer Lights] to remove dull yellow and enhance the silver. Then I applied a clear gloss to add shine." (Also try L'Oréal Professionnel Colorist Collection White Violet Shampoo or Keune Silver Reflex Shampoo.)

AMPING UP YOUR MAKEUP
Gray demands more color, more wattage...

■ **GO EASY WITH THE POWDER.** When you've gone gray, or white, or salt-and-pepper, your skin can look washed-out and dull. So use a luminizing, moisturizing foundation, and apply powder only where you absolutely need it, says New York City makeup artist Mally Roncal.

■ **WEAR BLUSH.** It makes every complexion more vibrant, says Roncal. If you're fair skinned, choose a light English rose; medium or olive, choose a bright peony; and if you're dark complexioned, choose a rich, candy pink. Sweep the blush onto the apples of your cheeks for an instantly brightening effect.

■ **LINE YOUR LIPS.** As you mature, lips lose their natural contour. Restore it by tracing your lips with a nude lip liner before applying gloss or lipstick.

■ **PICK A RICH LIPCOLOR.** Try juicy-looking lipcolors in pink, berry, peach, or apricot tones. (Avoid nudes and browns—they can look muddy.) Choose a color a few shades more intense than your natural lip tone.

■ **BRIGHTEN UP YOUR EYES.** Sweep a wash of linen-colored shadow onto your lids (this pale color reflects more light than a dark, smoky one), thicken the lashline with a stroke of liner, curl your lashes, and apply two coats of mascara. If your lashes are sparse, use a lash primer before mascara; the primer conditions and coats the lashes, making them look thicker, says Lisa Garner (the New York City makeup artist who did the makeup for this story). If black mascara looks harsh, try a brown or navy. Drag the wand outward and upward at the same time—your eyes will appear wider, and you'll look more awake.

■ **FORGET BASIC BLACK.** The stark contrast between jet black eyeliner and gray hair is more jarring than dramatic. So choose liners in softer, lava-like shades such as bronze and deep plum, says New York City makeup artist Trish McEvoy.

■ **PAY ATTENTION TO YOUR BROWS.** Fill in sparse brows with a pencil. If you're fair and your brows are light, choose a light to medium taupe shade; if you're olive or dark complexioned, and your brows are dark, try a deep, cool brown. For silver or salt-and-pepper brows, use a blue-gray pencil, says Eliza Petrescu, eyebrow expert at the Exhale Spa in New York City. And since brows lose their "tails" as you age, extend them in wispy strokes toward your temples.

YVETTE AND YVONNE DURANT, 54, EXECUTIVE ASSISTANT; WRITER. PROBLEM: GROWING-IN GRAY

FIRST GRAY SIGHTINGS Yvette—"I was 17. I couldn't really see it; it was underneath the top layer."
Yvonne—"I was 26 years old, and I saw a strand in the front near my face."
THEIR REACTION "We figured we were going to be like Mother, with a beautiful gray streak."
WHY YVONNE STOPPED DYEING: "The mascara I used to touch up the haircolor around my face came off on my boyfriend's jacket. That was it for me."

WHY YVETTE DIDN'T STOP "When Yvonne and I went out to dinner, people would ask if she was my mother. I thought, *Well, that's what happens when you let yourself go!*"
BUT THEN SHE DID STOP BECAUSE "My hair was breaking off from the coloring and the straightening. It was just very unhealthy. So I'm letting it grow out. It's about half grown out now, and I try to cover up the different colors with a headband, or at least by wearing it slicked back."

AND NOW SHE KNOWS WHAT YVONNE ALREADY KNEW "I get more attention from men. I think they like it."
RITA'S SOLUTION: "I would have liked to lighten Yvette's ends a bit to decrease the contrast between them and her growing-in gray, but because she's afraid of exposing her hair to more processing, I simply used a violet shampoo and a clear gloss on her [and Yvonne]. The shampoo brightens the gray and reduces yellow, and the gloss gives their hair a healthy shine." (At home, try John Frieda Collection Luminous Color Glaze Clear Shine.) ◐

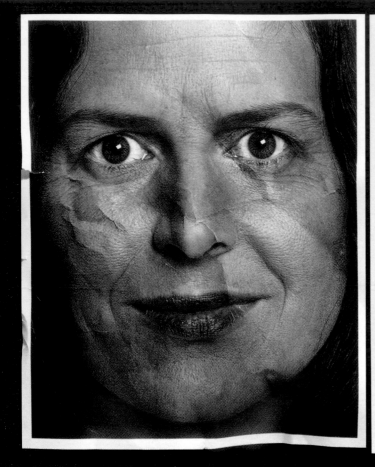
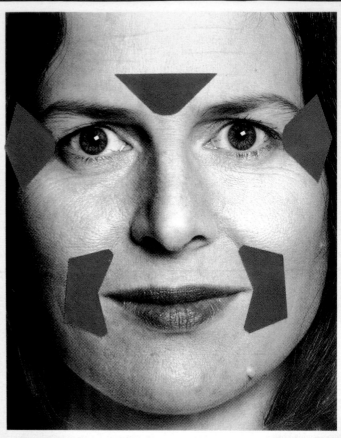

"My face looks as if it's been pressed onto the front of my head after getting wadded up and thrown to the floor like a Big Mac wrapper," says Newman.

UNCRUMPLING MY FACE

Crow's-feet: *No problem.* White hair: *Talk to me about something important.* But those irritating frown lines! Catherine Newman on the low-tech solution that smoothed out her brow—and her mood.

If a picture's worth a thousand words, then these are bad words. *Hag* comes to mind. *Grouch. Mean old lady.* My son, Ben, peers over my shoulder at the photograph in my hand. "I love that picture," he says—and of course he does. All he sees is his peachy 6-year-old self in the foreground, blurred with happiness and dancing with his little sister, both of them thigh-high in my old boots. They are pantsless and laughing and delicious, as short and sheathed in black leather as revelers in a gay jockey pageant. Who wouldn't smile to see them? Well, someone wouldn't—whatever that thing is in the background, hunched in its robe over a coffee mug. Even from here you can't miss the scowl lines, like the angry stomp of a pterodactyl foot between the eyes. It's the kind of face that would make you pedal your bike faster if you saw it in a window from the street. *Maybe that house really is haunted*, you would think.

And so I am struck with an epiphany that is both earth-shattering and obvious: The problem with aging isn't simply the looking older; it's the revealing of the ugliest parts of yourself to the whole world. As a person who gets a kick out of the white hairs springing from my scalp, who admires my own gorgeously wrinkled and silver-headed parents and thanks goodness every day of my life for the confidence and peace that come with the passing years, I'm shocked by this. I am a feminist, born of a long, proud line of crumply faced women. I had always secretly assumed that vanity about aging was for the duped, the narcissistic, the panderers to men. But for me, I see that it's about feeling exposed in all my creased crankiness. I don't mind looking mature; I mind looking like a bitch.

Because as this forehead plainly advertises, my generally joyful personality seems to have come packaged with Bonus Minutes of Irritability! Take one look at my face and you'll see that I'm aggravated by loud noises—such as yelling with a mouthful of macaroni and cheese—and also softer noises, such as humming with a mouthful of macaroni and cheese; you'll see exactly how much patience I have for some of your opinions when they straggle away from the straight and sensible path of my own (um, let me see—none); you'll see that I'm on the beach in the blaring sun with a bikini bottom full of sand and a belly full of nothing, peering at my watch because I'm restless and ready for lunch even though it's actually only 10:30; you'll see me grimacing over a Googled list of bird flu symptoms. Remember Dorian Gray? How he remained baby smooth and gym perfect (or the Victorian equivalent) while an old oil painting of him magically wrinkled up into debauched oblivion? It's like that, but on Opposite Day: Maybe somewhere in the attic there's a smooth and youthful portrait of me, my face a glossy bisque to reflect the contentment I feel inside. But my actual real-world face looks as if it's been pressed onto the front of my head only after first getting wadded up and thrown to the floor like a Big Mac wrapper from somebody's car seat.

And I know it's not the aging itself that bothers me, because the crow's-feet I love. I even love the smile lines that make me look like a daffy marionette, my hinged jaw clacking happily open and shut. Sometimes I climb from my marriage bed to the bathroom, and that long-loved look of my face—flushed and rumpled with pleasure—holds more beauty, I see clearly, than any of the plummy tautness of my younger self.

But those frown lines—they furrow my forehead so deeply that you could sow in them the very seeds of displeasure—go ahead, there's room for the whole packet! Oh, I want more than not having the wrinkles; I want not to be making the expressions that create them in the first place. "I'm getting Botox," I joke to my husband, Michael. "But not so I'll look younger—just to prevent me from scowling at all of you." I am totally kidding—and then, suddenly, not. What if I were actually physically unable to pull my face into negativity? Perhaps I would be paralyzed away from my own bouts of bad temper. Studies have proved this, or something like it: A facial expression doesn't simply reflect your moods; it actually shapes them. Frown and you feel sad; laugh and your spirits lift. To experiment now, I pull my eyebrows together and experience instant crabbiness; next, I smooth my forehead, smile, and plunk baby carrots onto my children's dinner plates. They smile back at me, our faces glowing lanterns of contentment. Is mood enhancement one of Botox's promises?

I can't say for sure, since I'm too proud and broke to consider it seriously. Also the word *botulism* unnerves me. I picture those swelled cans of vichyssoise from the seventies, imagine a kind of rotten-leeks injection puffing my face with poisonous, soupy off-gassing. Instead I choose a moisturizer from the mile of products as specifically designated as greeting cards—"retinol for nighttime fine lines," "retinol for light daytime protection," "retinol for the person who is profoundly grateful for her health and happiness yet prone to crankiness and deep creases"—but massaging it into my rutted forehead gives me not only a drop-in-the-bucket sensation but also a scattering of pimples. (Wrinkles and acne—together? Can this really be the natural order of things?) Plus the cream is thick and satiny, yes, but it does nothing for my personality.

This is where the Scotch tape comes in. In the privacy of home, I start smoothing an inch of it between my eyebrows, like an old lady protecting her cabbage-rose upholstery with clear vinyl. Will my face become like the parlor of a fancy house—the place you keep nice only for company? Maybe, but it's actually working: Taped into placidity, I can't really scowl. And Ben can't stop teasing me. "Take the chopstick out of your nose, Ben," he imitates, his eyes wide, his face pulled into smooth expressionlessness. "I said out of your nose." But the more I don't scowl, the more my family smiles back at me, and the happier I feel. It's crazy, but true.

When I pull the tape off in the morning, there's dead skin on it (bonus exfoliation!). There are also pale hairs: My eyebrows start to look like someone is waxing them with her eyes closed. But my wrinkles—I swear—are disappearing; my humor is improving; I'm onto something. In the bath one evening, I suddenly remember the *Old Farmer's Almanac* I paged through in the tub as a child—in particular, the ads for those old-fashioned "Frownies" beauty patches. The company still exists, it turns out, the Web site offering smiling head shots of women with papery beige triangles between their eyebrows and promises about safety and guarantees for happy results. Plus they're totally cheap. I order some, and they arrive in the mail, nestled in pearlized tissue paper inside an elegant little box sealed with a gold sticker—the fancy wrapping in hilarious contrast to the product itself, which looks like a stack of gummed corners snipped from manila envelopes. You're supposed to separate them at their perforations, lick them, and stick them to your skin. I smell one, and it has the gelatinous, faintly minty smell of envelope glue; maybe they really are snipped from envelopes. All in all they are as high-tech as pebbles or cheese.

But the kids don't care that I look like a recurring guest alien on *Star Trek: The Next Generation,* because they understand the beige triangle to be a symbol of my renewed benevolence. When I sigh one night over a pot of borscht, Ben asks if he can get me a Frownie—the way you might offer aspirin to someone with a headache. My daughter, Birdy, her own face aglow with toddler sweetness, touches it with a serious fingertip and asks, "If I pull this off, then you'll be grumpy?" (Since a triangle of skin will come off with it: Yes.) When I see the brown delivery truck, I open the front door to sign for my Lands' End swimsuit—am I trying to become a caricature of frumpiness?—and only when the puzzled UPS guy looks me right between the eyes do I realize that I've all but come outside with curlers and a blue gel mask. I would twist my face into embarrassment, but I can't—so I smile at him instead, and he shrugs, tucks his clipboard under one arm, and smiles back.

I'll tell you what, though: Slinking into bed with a nude-colored sticker between your eyebrows is probably very sexy if you're being initiated into some kind of Cult of the Foreheads, but with a regular old husband, it's just silly. "*Rowr,*" Michael teases. "That Frownie is hot!" Really, I could be as creased as an origami crone, or as wound around with tape and stickers as a mummy, and still he'd grope me while I was flossing. And if I were already the person I hope to become, I'd write that when Michael cups my face in his palms, I am cherished into a happy acceptance of my flawed person. *He loves me, wrinkles, irritability, and all!* I'd write, *And that's all I need.* I'd write about my renewed commitment to feminist politics and the reclaiming of my facial herstory. I'd write about my children's own taut and rosy faces, my realization that self-love is the most important thing I can teach them. The answer is not cosmetic, I'd write: It's cosmic! And it is—it's all true. But I'm still taping myself smoother and happier; it's like a dermatological bell of mindfulness, reminding me to smile even as I grapple with my own vanity. It's not exactly purgatory, this, but a kind of holding pattern: I'm circling around between conflict and harmony, between bad temper and blessedness. Or maybe I'm just stuck somewhere between youth and wisdom. ◐

YOU'RE MIDDLE-AGED. BUT ARE YOU DONE? DISCUSS.

Caitlin Flanagan invited six 40-something friends to spend an evening taking stock of their lives. The result: juicy, grown-up girl talk that could have gone on all night.

In 2006, at the age of 44, I published my first book, *To Hell with All That: Loving and Loathing Our Inner Housewife*. I had been planning to write a book ever since I was 19 and blurted to a boy I knew that I was going to become a "published writer." He was impressed and I was surprised—I wasn't majoring in English or turning out short stories or doing any of the other things that the future writers were doing. But come to think of it, writing seemed like something I probably *could* do—it wasn't as though I had said I was planning to climb Mount McKinley or become a lingerie model. I liked to read; I had a lot to say. How hard could it be? So I mentally added "write a book" to the to-do list I was making for my life. That's how it was when I was young: Everything seemed more or less possible. There was world enough, and time.

I got older, and my horses started coming in—or not. I never did get to have a job like Carol Merrill's on *Let's Make a Deal* or Betty Furness's on the *Today* show. But many of the other things I wanted to do—work in a museum, teach school, get married, have children—I've done. And with the arrival, one sunny day last spring, of the first copies of my book, the last of what my father used to call my "hopes and dreams" panned out.

Did I feel exhilarated, joyful, tickled pink? I did not.

I set the book on the edge of my desk, and then I propped it up on the living room bookcase, and then for a few months I wandered around in a funk, until I realized what was the matter: I had run out of dream.

For the first time in my life, I didn't have the pounding, driving sense of ambition that had always propelled me forward, the feeling that way up ahead were some things I wanted and was going to spend a lot of time lunging toward. It was as though I'd been in a speeding car that had suddenly stopped short. Here it was: middle-age. I know there are exceptional people who don't even get started on the great work of their lives until they're past the midpoint. But that's what makes them the exception.

Being Irish, I know a thing or two about how to deal with an identity crisis, or indeed any kind of crisis: Throw a party. And so I did. I asked some of my most accomplished women friends over to my house so that I could ply them with wine and hors d'oeuvres and ask them about their lives. Specifically, I wanted to know if they, too, had run out of dream, or if they still indulged in the kind of big, visionary thinking that comes so naturally to young people. And I wanted to know about how the daily traction of their lives—marriage and money and sex—shapes their ability to keep dreaming. It was going to be like a consciousness-raising session, except with catering and mood lighting and party favors in the form of fabulous $6 bath soaps from Target.

I issued invitations to a stay-at-home mom, a novelist, a performance artist, a television personality, a professional organizer, and a sidelined entrepreneur. Then I pushed my living room furniture around until it formed a big circle, and waited for my guests, who arrived promptly, grabbed glasses of wine, and started singing like canaries. Here's what I asked them:

I. When you were 18, what did you imagine your future would look like? How close does your life today come to that vision?

II. What is the one piece of advice you wish you'd been given as a young person?

III. What was the best money you ever spent?

IV. What was your biggest financial mistake—the complete waste of money that haunts you to this day?

V. Is sex with your husband a pleasure to savor or just one more item to check off your to-do list? If the latter, when did that change

"Maybe all we need are a few years to get out from under."

Sandra Tsing Loh, performance artist

Christine Schwartz, novelist

Jody Horowitz Marsh, TV personality

take place—and do you actually care?

VI. What has been the best surprise about married life? And the worst?

VII. What is the best thing about being a woman? The worst?

VIII. At this point in your life, is there a dream you will never get to fulfill? What is it—and what makes you so sure it's out of reach?

PART I: YOU CAN'T GET THERE FROM HERE—OR MAYBE YOU CAN...

To a woman, we could trace our current lives to the ideas we had about ourselves when we were very young. Consider Sandra Tsing Loh, a half-Chinese, half-German girl who grew up in Malibu in the 1960s and '70s and who was possessed of an unwavering conviction—unshared by anyone else—that she was born to perform. If there was a play, a ballet, a grade school staging of *Winnie the Pooh,* she was first in line for auditions and first to press her eager little face against the cast sheet, only to discover that once again she had been passed over. Her relieved father packed up his brainy daughter and sent her to Caltech, where she majored in physics. But a funny thing happened on the way to the jet propulsion laboratory. Sandra started performing. She played the grand piano by the side of the freeway during rush hour in Los Angeles; she serenaded spawning fish on a Malibu beach at midnight and a thousand people showed up to watch. She realized maybe ensemble productions of *Winnie the Pooh* weren't her thing; maybe she was more of a one-woman-show type. So far, she has written and appeared in six of them.

Christina Schwarz's dream was more vague but equally compelling. Her parents let her go far from home to college, but every vacation they reeled her back to Wisconsin, where she had a job at a big printing company just outside of town. The summer before her senior year, her boss offered her a full-time job, a career, really, with the company, when she graduated. "I was flattered and immensely excited at first," she said. "Here were all my scary questions about the future answered. I would live in the place my family had cleaved to for generations; I would surely rise into respectable middle management; and, since much of what I'd be doing would be technical writing, I'd technically be making my living with words." Maybe it wasn't glamorous, but it was serious and substantial, and it was real—unlike her niggling, unformed, and, to her mind, utterly unrealistic desire to experience new places and to write fiction. And yet in the end she decided to spin

the wheel on something more exciting. "I knew that if I took that job, I'd be closing the door on every vista I'd ever imagined. I couldn't do it." Since turning down a real career, she has lived in six cities and written three novels, one of which, *Drowning Ruth,* was an Oprah's Book Club selection.

My mother used to say, "Be careful what you wish for," and it did seem that some of our dreams, once realized, had not been as wondrous as imagined. Lynn Laws, a stay-at-home mom of three young children, says that she is living exactly the life she pictured for herself, "but I always thought I'd be more satisfied with it." She wouldn't trade it, but the days do not always unfold the way she had hoped. "There's too much time to think," Lynn said, "but not enough time to do anything besides take care of everyone. Your mind is always half on one thing—like folding the laundry or loading the dishwasher—and half on something else." Sarah Minot Gold, who imagined being a mom and staying home with her child, achieved both of those goals, but failed to factor divorce into her future: "I have never once regretted staying home with my daughter," she said. "But I wish I hadn't had to become dependent on a man to do it."

It was clear that the one thing none of us had fully been able to foresee when we were young was the ability of motherhood to reroute, fulfill, diminish, and improve us. "There was no way I was going to stay home with kids," said Andrea Williams-Green, who describes herself as "type A, type A, type A all the way." She attended UC Santa Barbara when only 2 percent of the students were, as she is, African-American, and she studied math and economics when even fewer women were enrolled in those classes. She roared out of college, worked in retail, then took a flier on something wonderful: opening her own shoe company. And then she had a baby. After which, the air began to leak out of the balloon of her professional life. She started going to the office less and less; the business began to falter and ultimately failed. It was a high price to pay—the loss of a dream and with it financial independence—but that's how babies are sometimes. They come in trailing clouds of glory, with havoc on their minds.

PART II: THE GREAT ADVICE WE NEVER GOT, AND WHY WE DIDN'T NEED IT AFTER ALL...

Jody Horowitz Marsh has been a television personality (she had a program called *Jody Horowitz Reports* on Showtime Networks for seven years), a humorist, and a correspondent for CNN, and is now a stay-at-home mom. She's so talented and accomplished that it was reassuring to learn she wasn't always that way. "It's the opening of Dr. Spock's book," Jody said about the advice she wished she had received as a young person. "'Trust yourself. You know more than you think you do.' It's a great piece of advice about going with your instincts rather than relying on others for validation. I wish I'd known that all my life—not just when I became a mother." Everyone nodded; it seemed that so often in our younger lives, the force we'd lacked wasn't ability or talent but simply the confidence to swagger our way into things.

On the other hand: "I never took anyone's advice about anything," Sandra said, and we realized, of course, that what we really wished was that we'd been able to distinguish good advice from bad, and learned how to act on the former. But who can do that at 21, when the mind is consumed by the world's great questions, such as how to fit into size 6 jeans by the weekend?

PART III: IN WHICH SIX SUCCESSFUL WOMEN REVEAL THEIR SECRET INVESTMENT STRATEGIES...

"The best money I ever spent was *maybe* on tooth whitening," Sandra said (we all leaned forward and realized anew how dazzling her teeth are, and I could sense six women secretly vowing to stick on their Crest Whitestrips before going to bed), "but probably the best was on my coat." Sandra has a fierce, black shearling coat that everyone admires; she bought it for $600, she told us, just before she had to go to the Sundance Film Festival one year. It's a coat that "raffishly and bad-boyishly covers a sloppy host of 40-something-mother fashion ills."

As the impartial moderator, I was abstaining from answering the questions, but when Sandra told us about the coat, I thought immediately of the dress I wore to my second wedding. It cost me most of a paycheck, and better money has never been spent. It was a Carmen Marc Valvo beaded cocktail dress that fit like a glove and banished forever the memory of myself as an '80s bride drowning in yards of tulle and marching purposefully toward a union that nobody was giving very good odds. That second dress rocked.

Then Jody averred that the best money she ever spent was on fertility treatments, and many of us hung our heads in shame. "Oh, yes, *definitely*!" I said, thinking of my own little boys and how they almost edge out that dress.

PART IV: AND ALSO THEIR FINANCIAL DISASTERS...

Lynn is the sort of prudent at-home mother who never makes a financial misstep, but just once she wanted to live as though money were no concern, and so it was that she revealed the shameful tale of her Anthropologie splurge. Just once, she wanted to buy an outfit—a whole outfit, not just a skirt or blouse—from her favorite store, and furthermore she didn't want to wait until it went on sale. She picked a beautiful green and yellow sweater with a matching skirt, but when she got them home, they never fit quite right, and she just about never wore them, and they're still hanging in her closet, compounding the misery.

Likewise, when Sandra was pregnant with her first baby, she came into a windfall, which she spent on a pair of expensive teak lawn chairs, on which she planned to sit while breastfeeding. But the chairs proved more demanding than the newborn; they were like a pair of young lovers who expected Sandra to be their handmaiden, oiling them and protecting them from any violation (sun, rain, a sweating glass of iced tea) that might in any way cause them harm. She ended up rarely sitting on them, and regretting every penny they'd cost her.

Now that we were letting our hair down, Jody made a confession: "I hired a decorator to do my house once. I hated everything he suggested, and while I was mustering up the courage to fire him, he quit! Unfortunately, not without first cashing my check." ("I realized that if you loathe someone, no matter how cleverly you think you're disguising it, the odds are they loathe you, too!")

Most of us know a lot about money, including how to manage it. When I was a schoolteacher, splitting the rent on an apartment and chronically broke, I nonetheless forced myself to put aside the maximum contribution to the school's pension plan—and it was that set-aside money that helped my husband and me, eventually, buy our first house. Sandra is on a one-woman mission to get parents to stop sending their children to ruinously expensive private schools, a mission that is helping thousands of families stay out of debt, and Sarah has hit the ground running after her divorce. We can all take care of business when we have to. But still, when we talked about money, the first thing that popped into our minds wasn't savings plans and investment strategies; it was dresses and lawn chairs. If we knew the answer to why women so often think about money on the small scale, we'd be...Suze Orman. And unfortunately we're not, so I changed the subject.

PART V: LET'S TALK ABOUT SEX...

Oscar Wilde is credited with saying there are no indiscreet questions, only indiscreet answers, and so it was that I asked my group of married ladies to tell me about the old hanky-panky. Jody,

Lynn Laws, stay-at-home mom

Andrea Williams-Green, entrepreneur

Sarah Minot Gold, organizer

Caitlin Flanagan, writer and host

mother of a ten-month-old, said that sex with her husband is "definitely something I savor...when I remember I *have* a husband."

"You always hear stories of married women going to the doctor because their libido is too low," Sandra said. "But how come you never hear about married men going to the doctor because their libido is too high?" At first some of us didn't quite take her meaning, but then she spelled it out: "Why are *men's* desires considered the norm? Maybe instead of us going to see doctors, they ought to see doctors to get their testosterone lowered!" It turned out that Sandra was reading a book—*I'd Rather Eat Chocolate: Learning to Love My Low Libido*—whose author, a married woman, had brazenly decided she wasn't very interested in sex, and had announced the same to her husband, who is apparently willing to put up with a greatly reduced schedule of amorous activities. There was, to put it mildly, a *lot* of interest in this idea. However, revolutionary though it sounded, it was far too depressing to consider at length.

PART VI: JUST WHEN YOU THOUGHT THERE WEREN'T GOING TO BE ANY MORE SURPRISES...

For Jody, the best surprise about marriage was how quickly arguments—the very same arguments that would have been grounds for a breakup in a dating situation—could be resolved, and that a marriage can move forward strengthened by these negotiations. Her worst surprise was the one every wife in history has had to face eventually: "discovering that everything I thought I could tweak and improve in my husband remains untouched and the same! I adore him, but somehow I always thought I'd be able to mold him to my will."

Lynn said that what had surprised her most was how expensive it is to raise a family on one income. "Even if your husband has a good job, and you send your children to public school, it still takes so much money to keep up a normal, nice, middle-class lifestyle," she said.

Sarah said she had never imagined that she'd get divorced, and I told her she was so much better off that she ought to write her ex-husband a thank-you note. Then there was a round of the kind of conversation that happens among women when a husband jumps ship. (Just because Sarah and her ex are being perfectly civilized about the whole thing doesn't mean the rest of us had to be. Take a side and commit to it—that's always been my approach to friends' divorces, and I'm not about to change it.)

PART VII: THE BEST AND WORST THINGS ABOUT BEING A WOMAN—A ROUNDTABLE DISCUSSION...

Jody said that the worst thing about being a woman is being judged so heavily on appearance, a truth so universally acknowledged and despised that we could have spent the rest of the evening expanding upon it. But then Christina brought up an idea that caught our attention even more forcefully—that the best and worst things about being a woman are the same: the way we feel drawn to caring for others, and the way this impulse becomes so much larger and stronger and more consuming once we have children. It's one of the truths at the center of my book: Motherhood brings with it a clear and compelling awareness of human vulnerability, and a sense of having been charged with the care of others. The dream that most women have—of having children someday, of being at the center of a family—is one of the most powerful impulses in the

world, yet it is also a destroyer of dreams, of ambition, and that fact is a hard and sometimes bitter truth about being female. Fortunately, there was more than enough Chardonnay—not to mention some sensational crab cakes—to take the sting out of the human condition, and we shored ourselves up, as women always do.

PART VIII: DREAMING...

So then I asked them the big one—what were their new dreams? What great, visionary things did they have in mind to do next?

Let this be a lesson: Don't get a group of mothers together, spend two hours talking about the hard work and exhaustion of raising children, keeping husbands satisfied, and balancing the books—and then ask them about the amazing, inspiring things they're planning to do with their lives. It's not going to go over very well.

Nobody was willing to call herself a woman without a dream; the very notion of doing so was deeply objectionable. But nobody had any dreams that they wanted to talk about, either. Maybe, as Jody suggested, part of getting older is learning to keep your trap shut until something actually comes true, so you're not left having to account for all your wretched failures and false starts.

I gave them their bath soaps and sent them home and felt a bit better for having seen them. And then Lynn sent me a photograph of some beautiful flowers arranged in a vase. It turns out that she is starting a little floral business, Posy, whose motto is "affordable style." She will undercut any other florists' prices, and stay up half the night arranging blooms she buys from the wholesale flower mart in downtown Los Angeles—if customers will only take a chance on a mom with no references. "It's just a little thing right now," Lynn admitted, almost bashfully, "but if I get a few more orders, I might buy a refrigerator for the garage so I can keep more inventory around."

Now, the reason this news got me excited was, number one—cheap flowers, hallelujah. And number two, I had just read an interesting statistic in Jack Canfield's book *The Success Principles.* Apparently, venture capitalists rarely invest in business start-ups because so many start-ups fail. But there's one exception: If the entrepreneur is 55 or older, the business's odds of success skyrocket. "These older entrepreneurs have already learned from their mistakes," writes Canfield. "They're simply a better risk because through a lifetime of learning from their failures, they have developed a knowledge base, a skill set, and a self-confidence that better enables them to move through the obstacles to success."

Lynn is 15 years short of an infusion of venture capital, but Canfield's observation captured my imagination. Maybe, as patched together and diminished by age and babies and grown-out roots as we are at this point—maybe we actually *know* something by now. Maybe all we need are a few years to get out from under, and then, just possibly, we'll be ready to take flight again. I tacked a picture of Lynn's flowers to my bulletin board, and next to it I put a picture of a beach I want to visit someday—and I found one that didn't have a 22-year-old bikini model ruining the view. Right next to that picture, I pinned up a photograph of the most beautiful older woman I've ever seen, the writer Alice Munro, to remind myself that whatever my next big venture is, I'll be doing it as a grown woman, not a youngster. And then, right before I left for carpool, I thought: *Maybe there's some dream in me yet.* ⬤

> AS PATCHED TOGETHER AND DIMINISHED BY AGE AS WE ARE, MAYBE WE ACTUALLY *KNOW* SOMETHING BY NOW.

NIKKI GIOVANNI'S AHA! MOMENT

She still thought of herself as a hip young babe at the age of 58. But when the poet discovered she was old, she realized she was even cooler.

WELL-VERSED: Nikki Giovanni's latest book of poetry is *Acolytes*.

For most of my life, I've thought of myself as pretty cool. I have a tattoo. I wear my hair short. Even at 58, even after being diagnosed with lung cancer several years earlier, I thought, *I'm in good shape. I'm young, and I'm healthy. I'm a babe.* That's how I felt when I left my home in Blacksburg, Virginia, late one night to drive seven hours to Princeton, New Jersey, where I was to attend one of Toni Morrison's birthday parties.

I drove my candy apple red sports car. A friend joined me on the ride. We had on our jeans. We looked good. But I am directionally challenged and can't read a map, so I got us lost. We were somewhere in the middle of Pennsylvania at around midnight when I was pulled over by a state trooper. He told me I was driving over the line; apparently, I'd fallen asleep at the wheel. Then he pointed his flashlight in the car to get a look at us.

Almost immediately, he backed up a bit and the tone of his voice changed. When he asked where we were going, he addressed me as "ma'am" in that solicitous way that people do when they're talking to an elder. I offered to get my license, sure that he would give me a ticket since he pulled me over, but he told me he didn't need it. Instead he gave us directions to Princeton and told us to "have some coffee, drive carefully, and just get where you're going safely." Then he left.

I turned to my friend and said, "We're *old*! If we were young, he would have ticketed me no matter what." I realized that when the trooper looked into the car, he didn't see what we thought he saw—two hip young women going someplace. He saw his grandmother. It was a depressing moment. I said, "You drive—I need to think about what just happened."

At Toni's party the next day, I shared the story with her and admitted, "Girl, I'm getting old." She responded, "Yes. You are." And she was right. It was time for me to embrace the moment I'd come to and see what "old" meant. I began exercising regularly, taking better care of myself. I joined AARP. I even started asking for my senior discount! And I left this message on my voice mail: "I am a little old lady, so please speak slowly."

Today I am 64 years old. I still look good. I appreciate and enjoy my age. While I have always liked my career, I have way more fun with it now. I've got nothing to prove, and I don't care what the critics say. When I finish writing a book, I don't push myself to start the next one; I enjoy having just written one.

A lot of people resist transition and therefore never allow themselves to enjoy who they are. Embrace the change, no matter what it is; once you do, you can learn about the new world you're in and take advantage of it. You still bring to bear all your prior experience, but you're riding on another level. It's completely liberating. Now, everything I do, I do because I want to. And I believe the best is yet to come. —*As told to Naomi Barr*

CONFIDENCE

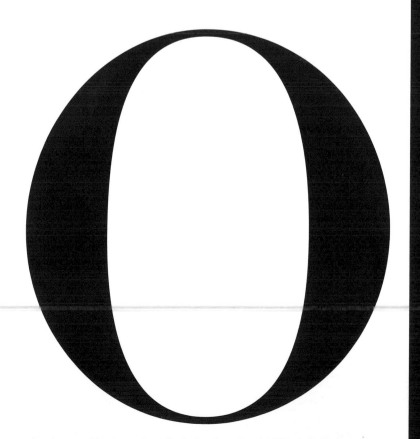

THE RELUCTANT HOSTESS

Okay, it's payback time—you owe the world an invitation. And you've got a gazillion reasons why you can't possibly have anyone over. Enough with the excuses! From an everything-but-dinner get-together to a last-minute personality potluck, Tish Durkin has four very entertaining solutions. Let the games begin!

I *don't have the time.... I don't have the glassware.... I don't have the flair....*

There are many, many reasons (or rationalizations) why the would-be-but-won't hostess hesitates to throw a party. But there is one reality that trumps them all: Talk yourself out of entertaining at home, and you will deny yourself one of life's great pleasures—and deny your friends one of life's great compliments. The pleasure, like the pleasure of making anything from scratch, is that of something of unique, imperfect charm. And the compliment is that of literally welcoming people into your space, letting people in.

You don't need money, a mansion, or an inner Martha to have a great gathering. You need friends and/or prospective friends. You need some sort of home; the cramped, cluttered, dog-hairy sort of home is perfectly fine. And you need a concept. Not a concept as in an all-girl luau or Christmas in July (although I keep meaning to do that...), but as in an idea that acknowledges any shortcomings you may be dealing with and turns them into selling points.

Take it from me, someone with absolutely no decorating, cleaning, or (until very recently) cooking skills of any kind: These are four parties that anyone can throw.

RANDOM RIGHT-NOW COCKTAILS
Actually, this originated as Poverty Cocktails—as in, "I'm in poverty, you bring the cocktails"—but the solvent can try it, too.

Sad story: I was headed for a 20-something birthday. I had just quit my job to become a freelance writer. I was living in a basement studio. None of my neighbors knew me, let alone my birthday, and there were no colleagues to drop hints to. So I decided I was one of those mature people who just hate a big fuss being made about their birthday.

Napoleon en route to Russia had fewer delusions. Around noon, dank little drops of sadness started to drip down like an overhead leak, and by sunset, I was up to my neck in it.

Down but not out, I started dialing. To anyone at his or her telephone, I posed the same question: "Can you come over and celebrate my birthday with me this very night—in a couple of hours, in fact? And, if so, um, might you perhaps bring a cake and maybe some wine or Champagne?"

Since no one had any notice, almost no one was free to fall for this. So I ended up with one ex-colleague, a 60-ish Irish friend of my mother's, the guy upstairs whom I had never met, and three or four others, none of whom knew each other. It was tacky, it was pathetic, it was one of the most hilariously excellent times I have ever had.

Now, unless you're really young, really poor, and really bummed about your birthday, I don't recommend making everyone bring everything. But I heartily recommend throwing very small, very low-stress, very last-minute parties—and doing so very often, as I did for years after that first foray. For, as I later realized, my original approach—desperate and accidental though it was—had several built-in virtues. One, it automatically weeded out anyone who stood on ceremony, as well as anyone who didn't really want to come. Moreover, the last-minute factor ruled out my finding a whole matched set of guests (colleagues or family) free to accept, and resulted in a refreshingly motley crew. People simply couldn't get caught up in the same old blather about work or politics or whatever; they had no "same old" anything in common.

Random, right-now cocktail parties free you to ignore the "Oh, if I invite this person, I have to invite that person" rule book, which swallows so many guest lists whole—and sucks the spark out of so many gatherings. This isn't a wedding; it's a whim.

THE SOIREE IN SHIFTS
While still living in that basement in which I could fit about eight people, I wanted to throw a Christmas party for about 50. Using the rule of thumb that one-quarter of invitees will decline outright, I calculated that I would actually need space for about 42 people. No problem: I invited everyone...just not all for the same time. Twelve (or maybe 13) invitations said 4 to 6 o'clock, implying a teatime kind of thing; nobody who showed up complained when offered cocktails. Twelve invitations said 5 to 7, 12 said 6 to 8, and so on. This way the place never got too crowded. Fresh blood was guaranteed to flow in once an hour. Yes, some people overstayed and overlapped, but only because they really wanted to...and there's always room for that.

BACK-TO-BACK DINNER PARTIES
Then again, perhaps you're in the mood for something less musical chairs. That's when I turn to the small, slow dinner. Phone up one

to three people or slip a note under their doors asking them to come over and brave your attempt at home cooking, and they will show up, tickled and touched to have been asked. So tickled and touched, in fact, that if the food—or anything else—is a disaster but you remain a delight as ever, they will actually like you better for it.

That said, you will inevitably go to some effort to get ready. You will put clean soap and towels in the bathroom. You will vacuum and dust. If you're going for an extra touch of class, you may put out some flowers or iron a tablecloth. And after your guests have come and gone—assuming that you have loaded the dishwasher and swept the kitchen floor—you will wake up with a house that still looks much better than usual and a refrigerator full of fabulous leftovers.

There is only one logical response: Have another small dinner party...that night.

All you have to do is (a) plan the first party for a Friday night, so you can have the second one on a Saturday night, and (b) make something that will not look or taste like leftovers—beef Bourguignonne or spaghetti Bolognese will actually taste better on night two. Whether you're making or buying the dessert, choose something that is served individually rather than something elaborate people are supposed to drool over before it's cut.

On Saturday all you have to do is inspect the tablecloth for any really bad stains; cover any not-really-bad stains with the dishes or some candlesticks. Open the dishwasher, and instead of putting the dishes, glasses, and cutlery away, put it all back on the table. Spritz the flowers. Reheat the leftovers. When the doorbell rings, open the door. Et voilà—you've doubled your entertaining, while barely adding to your effort.

THE SKIP-DINNER PARTY
But what if you want tons of people, tons of food, and tons of time?

The problem with a dinner is, unless you have a dining area of baronial proportions, it's very hard to seat more than six or eight people, or organize a buffet for more than ten or 12.

The problem with a larger, stand-up-and-

scarf-finger-food cocktail party is, it's only supposed to last about two hours. Apart from the one or two super-tipplers who can be counted on to be licking the salt out of the nut dishes while crooning "My Way" into the wee hours, everyone will clear out in time to go to dinner elsewhere—and that can be a real letdown for the hosts, who will have gone to tremendous effort getting ready, only to spend the night taking people's coats and then handing them back again.

The problem with a late-evening all-dessert party, which starts after dinner and at which numerous luscious sweets, coffees, and liqueurs are laid out on tables from which guests serve themselves, is...wait a minute, what was the problem with that one? Oh, I remember. It's at a weird time, it's only truly fabulous for the truly sweet of tooth, and nobody who's not Viennese will get it.

The solution: the Skip-Dinner Party. Lots of drinks, lots of hors d'oeuvres, and lots of desserts...all made ahead of time and strategically placed everywhere, along with any necessary forks, plates, or glasses. Granted, the host will still need to do some passing and replenishing of food, but that's intermittently over the course of a nice long party, not feverishly for two hours straight.

As for the guests, they will have great choice, in terms of tastes and timing: Those who want to come and go before dinner may do so. Those who want to come after dinner may do so. And those who want to talk and drink for hours on end can do so while continually filling their stomachs—on savories, on sweets, or on both.

At least that's how it's supposed to go. I won't tell you everything that went wrong at my last Skip-Dinner Party. Let's just say it involved small pieces of bread, small pieces of meat, and timing. It turns out that, although the recipe may say it takes just 30 seconds to flay the filet, one should allow considerably longer to flay enough of it for 50 people, lest one find oneself frantically plastering bits of meat to rounds of frantically buttered baguette and damning the Merlot glaze while the doorbell rings...and rings.... But I will get it right the next time. Or the time after that. **◖**

RANDOM, RIGHT-NOW COCKTAIL PARTIES FREE YOU TO IGNORE THE "OH, IF I INVITE THIS PERSON, I HAVE TO INVITE THAT PERSON" RULE BOOK, WHICH SWALLOWS SO MANY GUEST LISTS WHOLE.

THE CURE FOR SELF-CONSCIOUSNESS

It's one word—one *little* word—but it has revelatory power. Martha Beck spells it out for you.

You step into the party feeling reasonably confident. True, your favorite little black dress feels somewhat tight, but it's still elegant, and the wind outside only tousled your hair a little. Then, just as you're preparing to mingle, it happens: You pass a mirror and glimpse your reflection—your horrifying, horrifying reflection. The dress isn't just tight; it fits like Luciano Pavarotti's diving suit. Your hair looks as though a crazed weasel nested, bore young, and died there. Aghast, you wobble off your high heels and sprain an ankle. All eyes are glued on you. All conversation focuses on your disgrace. Everyone begins texting hilarious descriptions of you from their cell phones.

In your dreams, baby.

I mean this both literally and figuratively. Most of us occasionally dream about being embarrassed in social settings. But even in waking life, many of us operate as if Simon Cowell is doing a play-by-play of our work, wardrobe, and snack choices. One team of researchers has dubbed this phenomenon the "spotlight effect." In the beam of imaginary spotlights, many of us suffer untold shame and create smaller, weaker, less zestful lives than we deserve. Terrified that the neighbors might gossip, the critics might sneer, the love letter might fall into the hands of evil bloggers, we never even allow our minds to explore what our hearts may be calling us to do. These efforts to avoid embarrassment often keep us from imagining, let alone fulfilling, the measure of our destiny. To claim it, we need to develop a mental dimmer switch.

TURNING THE LIGHTS DOWN LOW

Thomas Gilovich, PhD, Victoria Husted Medvec, PhD, and Kenneth Savitsky, PhD, the psychologists who coined the term spotlight effect, also devised numerous ways to measure it. In one experiment, they had college students enter a room with other students while wearing an "embarrassing" T-shirt. (The shirt bore the likeness of a certain singer, whom I won't identify here. I will say that for days after reading this study, I was medically unable to stop humming "Copacabana.") When the mortified students were asked to guess how many people in the room would remember the face on their T-shirt, they gave a number about twice as high as the number of students who actually remembered the shirt.

Other studies support what this one suggested: The spotlight effect makes most of us assume we're getting about twice as much attention as we actually are. When Lincoln said, "The world will little note nor long remember what we say here," he was wrong—but only because he was president of the United States. If you are currently president, rest assured that millions will note and long remember if, say, you barf on the prime minister of Japan. However,

if you are not president, you're probably pointlessly blinded by the glare of imaginary social judgments.

These judgments aren't limited just to times when we mess up. Our distorted perceptions mean we not only exaggerate the impact of our errors but also undersell our inspirations and contributions. For example:

■ You modestly mumble an idea in a meeting, assuming that co-workers will be awestruck if they like it, appalled if they don't. Net effect: Nobody really hears the idea—until the annoying extrovert across the table repeats it more loudly, and gets all the glory.

■ You wear clothes a bit duller and more concealing than the ones you love, only to look back years later and wish you'd bared and dared more in your youth. (As one of my friends sighed about her self-conscious daughter, "If she only realized that at her age, you're beautiful even if you're not beautiful.")

■ You sing, swing, and mamba only in the privacy of your home, never with other people. Repressing the urge to sing "Copacabana," you miss the joy of sharing silly or sultry abandon with the people you love—and the people you may never get to love because inhibition robs you of the confidence needed to form a bond.

These self-limiting behaviors have no positive side; contrary to what many assume, they rarely save us from doing things we'll later regret. In fact, Gilovich and Medvec have found in other studies that, in the long run, people most often regret the things they failed to try, rather than the things they bombed at. Trying yields either success or an opportunity to learn; not trying has no positive result besides avoiding mockery or envy that (research shows) wouldn't be nearly as big or bad as we fear.

HOW TO FREE YOURSELF FROM THE GLARE

1 DOUBLE EVERYTHING

Just knowing that the spotlight effect is real and ubiquitous can begin to liberate us from its inhibiting clutches. I find it very comforting to have an actual number associated with my shame-based illusions: Spotlight effect studies suggest that people typically pay about 50 percent as much attention to me as I think they are. The first time I actually stood under a spotlight, in a high school play, the director told me, "Small gestures look embarrassed, so they're embarrassing. If you're going to do something, and you don't want to look foolish, do it BIG." Now, thanks to Gilovich, Medvec, and Savitsky, I know how big to make my actions—about twice as big as I think they should be.

I've been experimenting with this in many different circumstances: raising both my hands, instead of one, to ask a question of a lecturer I much admire; pausing twice as long for dramatic effect while telling a story to some friends; eating two servings of a fabulous dessert at a literary club luncheon. The result? I do seem to have attracted more attention, but rather than the disapproving judgment

the job, the person we love from afar.

The next time you feel performance anxiety in any form, remember that the negative attention you fear does not exist except in your mind—if this works with the hard, cold reality of my ice block, I guarantee it will work with something as vaporous as other people's opinions. Act as if there is no spotlight on you, even if there is one. Say, do, and be what you would if no one else were looking. It will be scary at first, but if you persist, there will come that liberating moment when you'll feel yourself sailing straight through your life's most inhibiting barriers without even feeling a bump.

3 ASK YOURSELF THE UNIVERSAL QUESTION.

Once, I had an intense, emotional cell phone discussion with a friend while riding in a taxi. At a certain point I fell into a strangled silence.

"What's wrong with you?" my friend asked. "Why aren't you talking?"

Covering my mouth with one hand, I whispered, "The driver can hear me."

At this point, my friend said something so lucid, so mind expanding, so simultaneously Socratic and Zenlike, that I memorized it on the spot. I've gained comfort by repeating it to myself in many other situations. I encourage you, too, to memorize this question and use it when you find yourself shrinking back from an imaginary spotlight. My friend said—and I quote:

"So?"

This brilliant interrogatory challenged me to consider the long-term consequences of being embarrassed (really, who cares?). It reminded me that failing to act almost always leaves me with more regret than taking embarrassing action. Here are a few instances where the Universal Question might help a person break through imprisoning inhibitions:

"If I say what I really think, people might disagree with me."

So?

"If I leave my drunken abusive husband, his crazy family will call me a bitch."

So?

"If I go windsurfing, I'll look like a klutz. Plus, people will see my cellulite."

So?

There are endless applications for the Universal Question. I suggest using it every time you feel yourself hesitating to do something that might deepen or broaden your life. The answer to the question "So?" is almost always "Well, when you put it that way...." It pushes us into the spotlight, showing us we can survive there and freeing us to act on our best instincts.

Today, remember that what you perceive as prudent social caution is probably limiting your life to about half its natural capacity; that if you did everything you long to do twice as often, twice as boldly, twice as openly, you wouldn't attract a shred more social pressure than you already think you're getting. Consider that vaulting well past the limits of your inhibitions will probably earn you more positive attention than negative judgment. More often than not, this will work out well. If it doesn't, remember the most enlightening of questions: "So?" Little by little, you'll feel and see that the worst consequences of living in the light are less oppressive than the best advantages of hiding in the shadows. And you'll have little to fear from the rest of us, who will only be inspired by your daring as we sit, blinking and bedazzled, in the private spotlights of our own attention. [0]

I expected, most people seem to feel pleased and liberated, made safer in their own skin by my willingness to live large in mine.

I believe this reaction is a major reason a lovely lady from Hawaii named Brook Lee once won the Miss Universe pageant. When asked what she'd do if she had no rules to follow, she replied, "I would eat everything in the whole world—twice!" That one word—"twice!"—struck a chord with me, the audience, and the judges, landing Ms. Lee squarely beneath the spotlight she actually wanted. Why not join her by doubling the social behaviors you usually limit: the energy with which you communicate, the intensity of the colors you wear, the number of times you laugh, the clarity of the opinions you voice. You may think this will attract massive disapproval from others. Actually, you'll be lucky to attract more than a passing glance, and my experience (not to mention Ms. Lee's) suggests it will be more approving than not.

2 THINK THROUGH YOUR LIMITS—NOT TO THEM.

"You can't break that board by hitting it," my karate teacher told me. "Hit something ten inches behind it. As far as you're concerned, the board doesn't even exist."

"But," I pointed out, "it does exist." (I am a trained observer.)

My sensei shrugged. "That's what you think."

Mentally noting that this man had been hit in the head many, many times, I proceeded to batter my hands to smithereens, trying to break that unbreakable board. When every knuckle was swollen, tender, and bleeding, I said, "My hands hurt."

"Yes," said my sensei. "Your mind is really damaging them."

I rolled my eyes and took my achy breaky pie hooks home, planning to pack them in ice. Unfortunately, my freezer had malfunctioned, and the only ice available was a three-inch-thick, rock-hard slab. I was so frustrated that I grabbed the ice in one hand, and with the other, punched the air ten inches behind it. The ice shattered into a thousand pieces. My hand barely felt a bump.

You get the metaphor: We smash into barriers of shame, embarrassment, and regret because we pull our punches in myriad social situations. Stopping at what we think is the limit of embarrassing behavior, we let others claim the credit, the opportunity,

RELAX....YOU...ARE... GETTING...BOLDER!

Beverly Donofrio was shy, mute at parties, and thought talking to strangers was a good way to ruin an evening. Then she had a session with a hypnotist, and she'll tell you all about it once she gets the lampshade off her head.

A few years ago, when I complained to my latest, greatest, and now past therapist that I didn't want to go to some party I was invited to, I'd be bored, have nothing to say to people—whom I wouldn't like and who wouldn't like me—she pinned me with her penetrating gaze and said, "You're a shy person."

I didn't believe my therapist. Even though I did remember suffering paroxysms of dread whenever I might be called on in elementary school, and how I would sit for an hour salivating in front of a candy bowl at a relative's and still refuse the candy once it had been offered because I was too shy. But that was a long time ago. Shy adults can't make eye contact; they dress plainly and turn red if you compliment them. I am not like that at all. I can be a flamboyant dresser, I meet your eye, and positively glow from attention and praise. I can even, if in the mood, be gregarious.

Sure, I often turned down an invitation, but I thought I was merely a recluse or maybe a wet blanket until the afternoon I took a beta-blocker and experienced what it is like to truly not be shy. A few of us had made up a song and dance routine to perform at a friend's wedding as a toast. Before the performance, I took a beta-blocker, offered by a musician who claimed she could not be a performing oboist without it. Beta-blockers are disinhibitors, often prescribed for people who have to speak or perform in public. I didn't take the pill sufficiently in advance to calm my nerves during the performance, but by the time I took my seat at the dinner table, it had kicked in. I am certain of this because of the outrageous idea I had: I should talk to somebody I *didn't* know.

After I talked to a dozen perfect strangers—and table-hopped to do it—instead of going home after the wedding reception, I went looking for a party I'd been invited to. I'd left the address at home because never in a million years had I expected to go. I couldn't find the party, so I drove into town to hear my friend Roland (who'd been inviting me for a year) play jazz at a bar. It felt a little awkward to walk into a bar alone on a Saturday night, but not awkward enough to stop me. As I sat down and ordered a lemonade—Sundays are my favorite days and I didn't want to risk a hangover—it occurred to me that I was having fun. It also occurred to me this was probably due to the beta-blocker. I felt calm and easy, curious. It wasn't like being drunk, when you might say or do outrageous things. On the beta-blocker, I was behaving in the way I'd always aspired to: I was open, spontaneous, friendly.

At the bar, I struck up a conversation with the couple sitting beside me. They were tourists in my town, and when they told me they were thinking of returning for a month in the summer, I suggested that they might like to rent my house because I'd be away then. We made a date for them to come by on Sunday at 2 in the afternoon.

The next morning, no longer under the influence of the beta-blocker, I had a mini breakdown. Strangers interrupting my Sunday? And I'd have to talk to them. The old panic rushed in. Talking was easy last night, but it wouldn't be today, and they wouldn't like me. I taped a note to my door apologizing for being unable to meet with them and then went about my solitary day—until 2 o'clock, when there came a knocking at my door. Actually, it was a banging. Evidently the note had blown away. I didn't answer, and the strangers didn't go away. Once I'd failed to respond, it was impossible to answer the door. They knocked on neighbors' doors. They waited on the stoop. I crouched on my bed, my arms over my head, like I'd been taught to do as a kid in case of nuclear attack.

I felt awful—selfish, mean, and a little nuts. I was beginning to suspect there was something wrong with me. A few nights later, I knew there was. I'd stopped in the middle of town to watch a procession, which in my Mexican town is about as common as cornflakes for breakfast is in the States. An attractive man on the other side of the street smiled at me. I smiled back, then immediately cast my eyes to the ground and turned my back. I sensed him cross the street to stand next to me. I thought to myself, *Say something. Talk to him.* I could not think of a single word, nor could I look at him. Eventually, he moved away and I went home.

That night I couldn't sleep for recalling all the times shyness had tripped me up. I'd gone to Guatemala to study Spanish for three weeks and never once struck up a conversation with anyone the entire time—in Spanish or in English. I'd noticed the starving street dogs and how they slunk around anticipating a kick, and on a particularly low day I decided I was like them. Afraid of people, anticipating a kick in the pants metaphorically. Shyness, I realized, was a defense mechanism, meant to place a distance between me and people, between me and hurt. But like most defenses, after a time it had turned on me and become the source of hurt.

I'd spent too many years and thousands of dollars to want to jump back on the therapeutic couch. And I didn't think even a Herculean act of will could make me flirtatious and friendly, open and at ease, but I did believe hypnotism could. A year earlier, my friend Amy, who had been complaining that she'd lost her soul ever since she became the president of her own company, had been hypnotized to "feel her feelings." The hypnotist put her under and spoke to her unconscious. "I know in the past there were very good reasons for Amy not to feel her feelings," he said. "But she'd like to feel them now. So can we let her feel her feelings

questions she would ask me. I was to answer quickly, the first thing that came into my mind. It didn't matter if it was true or not. I was to say the first words or memory I thought of. Half the time I didn't know if I was making things up.

"Where are you?" Debbie barked, "inside or out?"

"In."

"How old are you?"

"Two."

"Who is with you?"

"My father. He just pushed me off his lap, and I'm crying. I think he had an erection."

"Can you forgive him for that?"

"No. He thought it was my fault."

"Can you understand how frightened his erection made him feel?"

"Yes."

"Can you see that it wasn't your fault and that he was just frightened, that in his heart he didn't mean to hurt or reject you? Can you talk to him and tell him how you feel?"

In six hours we dealt with my mother, father, child, money, fiction writing, feeling stupid, a girlfriend I was having a problem with, my grandson to be. Shyness was never mentioned until I was about to leave. She asked if I felt that I would still be shy. I thought I might not, but that shyness had been a habit for a very long time. "Habits," Debbie said, "are easy to break once you've done this work."

That evening a friend threw me a cocktail party, inviting all the people I knew in Toronto and a few neighbors, more than 20 people in all. Normally, I would be filled with anxiety, thinking that small talk slays me, I will have nothing to say, people will think me boring, I'll want to leave in a few minutes and will be stuck for a few hours.

At one point, I sat on a bench in the garden between a woman and man who began talking about a person I didn't know. I had nothing to say, no entry into the conversation. I wondered if I should try to change the subject or if I should get up and talk to someone else. Then I realized I was quite comfortable on the bench and happy just to sit there. Nothing was required of me; I was fine. In that moment, I realized I really might not be shy anymore. I was no more skilled socially, but suddenly I didn't care.

Right after that I returned to New York. Walking in Brooklyn one day, I caught myself casting my eyes to the ground when I passed a man on the street. I decided not to do that anymore. Then I decided to smile at everyone I passed. I was now middle-aged and my smiles were not likely to be misconstrued as come-ons. People smiled back. It felt pretty good. It felt great. I wasn't smiling to be liked or to elicit a smile in return. I smiled as a gift. I spread a little joy. It hadn't been my intention, but it was the effect. And that's when I discovered something profound about shyness: It's a little self-involved. How can you ever think about the other person if you're so busy worrying about yourself?

I decided to knock it off. The hypnotism session was more than two years ago, and I have actually enjoyed social gatherings since. A few days after I came back home, I went to a dance and made a date to meet a man at a chocolate factory. The chocolate was deep, dark, and delicious. The man turned out to have a Mexican girlfriend.

Even conquering shyness didn't make life perfect, but it has made it more interesting, and now when I feel like being a wet blanket, I know it's my choice. ◻

for three months? If it doesn't work out, she can go back to not feeling them." Amy told me she immediately started feeling her feelings and she still did, although sometimes she wished she didn't. A few weeks after Amy told me about being hypnotized, I sat next to a Lacanian analyst at a dinner party who said, "Psychoanalysis doesn't work; hypnotism does."

Two positive mentions in two weeks were enough to make me want to give hypnotism a go. Amy recommended a hypnotherapist in Toronto. When I called Debbie Papadakis and said that I wanted to be hypnotized for shyness, she said, "Good for you. You're going to change in ways you can't even imagine. This will affect your entire life."

Even as I realized that Debbie had just planted a suggestion, the possibility of being comfortable in my own skin sent a tingly sensation right through me.

Debbie said, "If you want to take a long time and have somebody hold your hand, I'm not for you. I like results."

We met for six hours. I told her that one of my beliefs is that I am difficult and boring, and that people, most often men, don't like me.

Debbie explained that she would put me into a deep relaxed state. Then she would ask me questions derived from the exhaustive questionnaire she'd sent me. She told me that we probably wouldn't deal directly with shyness, since shyness encompassed so many issues. "Think of a circle," she said, and drew one on a piece of paper. "And all these little circles around the circumference are your issues. They're all connected, see?" she said, drawing lines crisscrossing from all the little circles to the other little circles. "What do you think happens if one of these little circles unravels? All the connections start unraveling. So you see, we don't have to unravel all your issues, only some."

I sat in a reclining chair as Debbie asked me to close my eyes and imagine walking down stairs toward a beautiful, peaceful scene. Each step I descended drew me deeper down and made me more relaxed. When she asked me to open my eyes, I couldn't. Maybe I could—I wasn't sure—but I was sure I didn't want to. When I couldn't count backward from 100 past 97, I was under. It felt like being all cozy in bed the moment before you drift off to sleep.

Debbie had coached me ahead of time about responding to the

Anxiety reducer: Private lessons with a pro.

BABY STEPS, OLÉ

How our dance-phobic beauty director went from I'll-look-ridiculous to "Ay, chica!" Rule # 1: Don't "think." Valerie Monroe sheds her last inhibition.

Just over a year ago, I wrote a story here examining how it felt to go out in public wearing the kind of extremely revealing clothing that was being touted as the height of fashion (and why a woman might choose to expose herself in it). For a week, I wore a lot of almost nothing: a scrap of black fabric only very generously called a dress, another dress, transparent, revealing my underwear as if behind a pale violet scrim, a pair of bloomers— yes, bloomers—so abbreviated they were interrupted almost before they bloomed. After the story came out, a number of people congratulated me on my courage. The thing is, I didn't feel courageous at all. I could walk down the street in a bra and panties and feel pretty comfortable (if I didn't think I'd be arrested). Nude beaches? Hand me the sunscreen and point the way. I'm just not very inhibited about my body.

But I have a secret: I won't dance. Don't ask me.

That wouldn't be a problem, necessarily, except that I *want* to dance. Especially at parties and weddings and bar mitzvahs and anywhere else I hear music that beats out a deep, pulsing rhythm that gets into the blood. I'm just too inhibited to take the floor; I'm afraid the moment I get out there, I won't know what to do. I'm even—and I hate, especially, to admit this—afraid to try.

That's why I decided to take a hip-hop class. And who wanted to join me but Gayle King, *O* editor at large, who claimed that

she'd been using the same dance moves since seventh grade and desperately needed an upgrade.

We decided on one of the Ailey Extension dance and fitness classes at Alvin Ailey American Dance Theater in Manhattan. It's called Hip-Hop for the Absolute Beginner. If there were a class called Not Even Anywhere Near *Approaching* Absolute Beginner, we'd have preferred that. But this is the best we can do. We're late to the first class, on a Monday evening after work. More than 20 people of all shapes and sizes are doing stretching exercises in a large room with a wall of mirrors and a cement floor. The class is led by Tweetie, a small, muscular, wildly energetic, fast-talking young woman. Gayle and I rush to a corner in the back of the class, where Gayle drops her stuff (she came in sweats) and I change from my heels into sneakers. As I'm tying my shoe, I get a terrific cramp in my side. (Not a good sign.) Neither Gayle nor I can do most of the stretches, and I notice that when we're asked to lie down on the floor, we both hold our heads up uncomfortably because we don't want to mess up our hair. (Another bad sign.) Tweetie starts the class by showing us in slow motion a simple kind of shuffle-off-to-Buffalo routine, and I'm thinking that if I have enough practice, I'll be able to get it. Things are looking up. Funky step, step, step, forward, slide, hop, slide, hop. "I don't know," says Gayle as she shuffles and hops along beside me, "this seems very vaudeville...." She does indeed look as if she could use a top hat and a cane. But we keep at it, as Tweetie, talking at warp speed and with a kind of hip-hop inflection I have to squint to understand, tells us we need some *attitude,* which she then demonstrates with a move, and another, and another, till it's obvious the hip-hop train has left the station while I'm still standing on the platform awkwardly juggling my bags.

There's a person in the class—gender unclear to me—who is doing a butt jiggling move in such a way that everything seems to be going in a different direction at once. It's completely fascinating; I can't take my eyes off it. Which might be why I keep losing my balance and can't keep up. (Imagine the Queen Mother at her 100th birthday party. Now imagine her trying to do the chicken noodle. That's me.) Gayle, ever curious and friendly, asks Butt Jiggler for advice about how to do the moves. BJ doesn't waste a second: "Get grimy," he/she says. At that moment, I know I'm never going to succeed at hip-hop. Though I think I know what grimy is—it's the hip-hop equivalent of dirty dancing—I have no idea how to get there. It's a state of being, a state of being for which I have enormous respect and admiration, but not one I will ever enter. I don't have the constitution for it. What I need is a dance that can be done with or without griminess. Like salsa.

Despite having failed utterly at hip-hop, I have learned a helpful lesson. A private class is more my style; for someone as hopelessly self-conscious as I, learning to dance in a room full of strangers is just too hard. (Every single time Tweetie had said, "Whatever you do, don't do *this,*" and then demonstrated with great flair a move exactly, and I mean exactly, the way I had done it, all the lucky grimy people in the class burst out laughing and nodded at one another. Really, I just couldn't handle the humiliation.) So I sign up for a lesson at Dance New York with Jose, a competitive Latin dancer recommended by a friend. She said he'd be great, and he is. He's tightly wound, graceful, a sleek young Latin cat, and remarkably patient. He introduces me to the basic steps, going over and over them till I can master them. Even with the endless repetitions, I make lots of mistakes. But I hardly mind at all. Because whenever I mess up, Jose, with the kind of loving, indulgent laugh a parent has for his child when she does something adorably wrong, tells me it's okay. He calls me lover and *mamasita* and baby, and, if I make a really egregious move, baby lover. So I'm pretty fine with egregious. "Bup, bup, bup, *mamasita,* do it this way!" he says as he shows me a new step. With his hand lightly touching my back, he guides me, not quite pushing me along but suggesting. He shows me how to do a turn, and when I finally get it right, he murmurs, "*Gorgeous,* lover." He gives no indication of how bored he is till the end of the first lesson, when he starts a crazy, loose, kicking and scooping thing all around me, like he's street fighting with a little person, and I abruptly stop my back-and-forth to ask him what he's doing. "Don't mind me, lover," he says, fondly, "I'm trying not to get bored. Keep dancing." And I do.

As I'm slipping on my jacket after the lesson, I ask Jose brightly, "Should I practice at home?" A cloud passes over his face. "No," he says, "I don't think so." Why not? He stares off into the distance behind me, as if he were visualizing something. Something unpleasant. Finally he says, "You might do something wrong, again and again, and then I'll have to teach it out of you."

But later that evening, I can't resist trying out the steps. And someone at the office has given me a salsa exercise DVD, which

promises not only a tighter "core," which I could probably use, but a few good moves. One Saturday morning before I start cleaning my apartment, I remember the DVD and put down the vacuum. A minute later, I'm standing in front of my computer, trying to follow the hip swiveling and grinding. I add a couple of Jose's moves. This scene, ridiculous as it is—and, catching a glimpse of myself in the mirror, I see that it is very ridiculous—is also a breakthrough. I've never been able to dance, even alone, in the privacy of my home.

At my second class, we take up our positions—Jose, with his right arm around my back and his left hand holding my right—and, surprising myself, I immediately assume the correct stance. "Okay, baby, let's go!" says Jose, and we're off. We practice the old steps and then we start on some turns. There is a waltz playing in the background: Other couples are swirling gracefully around the dance floor to the three-quarter beat. Trying to keep to a salsa rhythm isn't easy. I'm about to give up, when the music changes. Now it's a tango. I notice a couple to my right: I can't tear my eyes away, they're so magnetic. "Don't look at them," says Jose, compassionately, but with some urgency. "You'll lose your focus and your place." It makes me feel as if he understands my shyness; I realize that I trust him, even after only two lessons. Why? For one thing, he hasn't once asked me to do something I couldn't do. Though he's obviously a very skilled and talented dancer, he seems to want to *share* his skill with me, rather than use it to show me how good he is.

When I get home, I'm so jazzed that I search for some salsa sites on the Net, and watch a few competitions on YouTube. Then I find myself trying to imitate the salsa stance, keeping the upper body still while moving the hips and legs and feet. I even look in the mirror while I do it. (This would have been excruciating a month ago.

> JOSE KEEPS TELLING ME TO STOP *THINKING,* TO SIMPLY FOLLOW HIS LEAD, AND WHEN I DO, FINALLY, IT'S SMOOTH SAILING.

Today it makes me laugh, and reflecting on my progress gives me a small sense of accomplishment. Very small, but still.) I start thinking about parallels to my work: How did I learn to write? By reading other writers, trying to figure out how they did it, and by writing myself. The more I wrote, the more comfortable at it I became. Dancing isn't very different. The more I do it, the more comfortable it feels. It requires trust (in my teacher) and focus. I notice that whenever I lose focus on what Jose and I are doing, by looking at other (far more experienced and graceful) dancers in the room, not only do I forget my place but my self-esteem slips and falters. Then my inhibition, returning in full force, gives it a nasty shove, and I might as well just take a chair. Jose keeps telling me to stop *thinking,* to simply follow his lead, and when I do, finally, it's smooth sailing: He navigates me breezily through turns we haven't even practiced yet. There is magic to the letting go. Every time I become less a spectator and more engaged, my dancing improves. My engagement with Jose helps, too. You might have thought I knew this before I tried it, but I discovered that hip-hop is more about performance, while salsa—though it can also be about performance—thrives on the connection between the partners. I guess I'm more comfortable sharing responsibility on the dance floor; I *know* I'm comfortable when I'm relating to a guy (even, I find, a sleek Latin cat a couple of decades younger than I). A woman dancing salsa, Jose tells me, can be kind of low-key if she chooses, letting her partner show off all around her. I'm happy to let Jose do that (as I'm still more Queen Mother than Rita Moreno), but step-by-step, I hope I can learn to do some showing off myself. ◑

"WHEN YOU GET THE CHANCE, GO FOR IT. YOU CAN'T ACCOMPLISH ANYTHING WORTHWHILE IF YOU INHIBIT YOURSELF"

Robin Williams joins Oprah on the show in 1999, 21 years after their electrifying first interview.

Many years ago, as a young television reporter at WJZ in Baltimore, I was given what was considered a plum assignment. I was sent to Los Angeles to interview the stars of ABC's new fall season.

At first I was thrilled. Here was a chance to prove myself a good interviewer—alone, without the help of my usual coanchor. And a chance to add some celebrity cachet to my world of local news reporting. But by the time I arrived in California, I felt like a small fish dropped into the Hollywood fishbowl. I started to doubt myself: Who was I to think I could just walk into their world and expect them to talk to me? Reporters from every other ABC affiliate in the country had been invited. There were throngs of us local newscasters, entertainment/lifestyle reporters, each given five minutes to interview an actor from the network's upcoming lineup.

This was 1978—I was 24 years old and I'd been a TV reporter since I was 19. I'd interviewed hundreds of people in difficult situations and prided myself on being able to break the ice and establish rapport. But I wasn't accustomed to real "stars." I thought they had some mystique, that being famous made them not only different but also better than us regular folk. I started to feel nervous. Uncomfortable. Inept. Not good enough to be there with all those other reporters from much bigger cities with more experience than I.

To make matters worse, a representative for Priscilla Presley, who was there for a new show she was hosting, told me—as I was 11th in line to talk to her—"You can ask her anything, but whatever you do, don't mention Elvis. She'll walk out on you."

So now I wasn't just intimidated by this new world of "stars" and their handlers—I was feeling completely inhibited. I knew my only saving grace lay in finding a way to be real, but I was having difficulty figuring out how I'd pull that off in a five-minute time frame with the most real questions being off-limits.

For some reason—some would call it coincidence, but I call it grace in action—I was switched from the Priscilla Presley line to interview a young comedian who was starting a new show called *Mork & Mindy*. What followed were five of the most exhilarating, wild, off-the-charts minutes I'd ever spent in an interview, with the most uninhibited, out-of-the-box, free-falling-in-every-second celebrity/human I'd ever met.

I don't remember a word I said (but I know I hardly said any). He was newly released energy. I remember thinking, *Whoever this guy is, he is going to be big.* He wasn't afraid to be his many selves. I had great fun playing with Robin Williams, and I learned in that instant to go where the interview takes you. He's all over the place, and you have to flow with it.

So when my turn came to talk to Miss Priscilla, I for sure had gotten the lesson. You can't accomplish anything worthwhile if you inhibit yourself. If life teaches you nothing else, know this for sure: When you get the chance, *go for it.*

I asked about Elvis. She didn't walk out. She obliged me with an answer. Shortly after my trip to Hollywood, I was no longer doing newscasts but was offered a job as talk-show host. Some would call it coincidence....

Oprah

WHAT YOUR HAIR SAYS ABOUT YOU... (AND HOW TO CHANGE THE MESSAGE)

Sometimes your hair just gets away from you. You put in a few highlights, next thing you're sprouting colors previously unseen on humans. You declare war on your curls—until you realize you're spending 70 hours a year working out with the blow-dryer.... Four women talk about the moment they realized their hair wasn't *them* anymore. And what they did about it. And how they feel now.

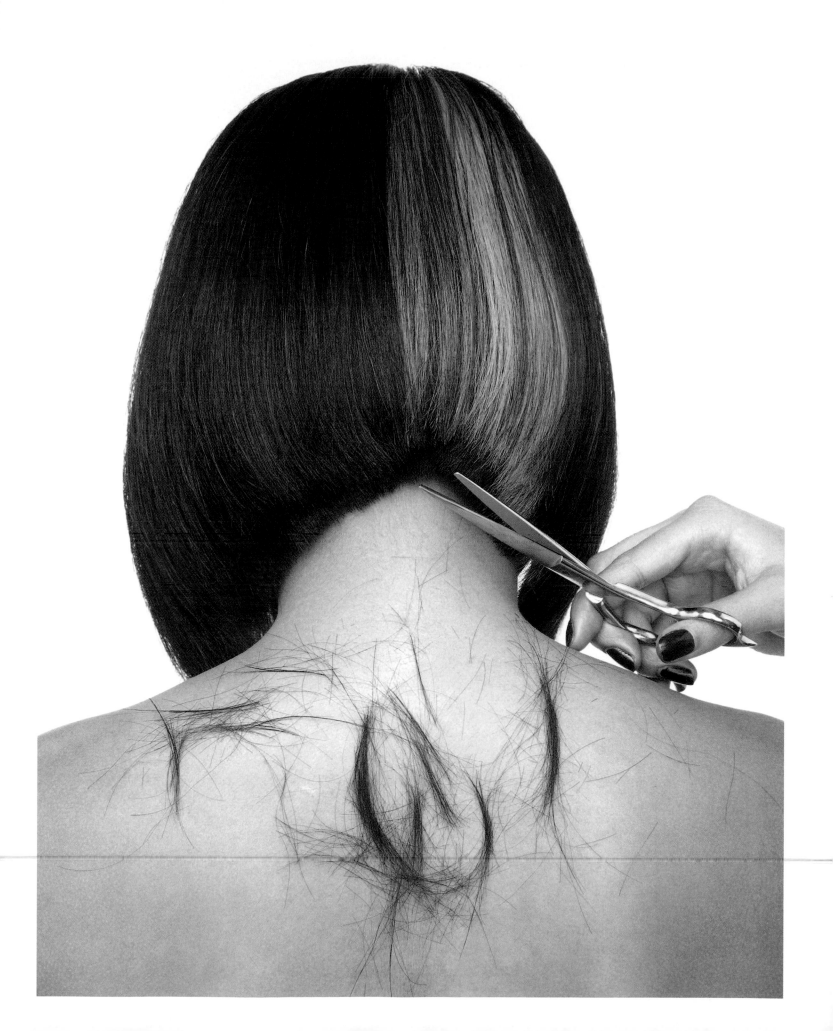

(NOW)

(THEN)

GOING SHORTER
BY WHITNEY FULLER

Every morning when my alarm goes off, I reach over and feel around my nightstand until I find the offending object and the button that will buy me exactly eight more minutes of peace. And then eight more. And then eight more, until I know that the consequences of another eight—being late to work, skipping my morning coffee—would sabotage the pleasure of that last snooze. Wakefulness seeps in, and thinking about the challenges and the pleasures of the day ahead, I see my safe, dream-filled cocoon for what it is—a thread-bare down comforter—and the world beyond as a place immensely more interesting. So I cast off my blankets, brave the chill of the hardwood against my bare feet: I get up.

In the past seven years, I've scheduled as many appointments with the intention of cutting my hair. And the first six times I sat down in that swiveling chair, I backpedaled, opted for only an inch, then asked my stylist how she would cut it if, the next time, I went through with it. Then last October I found myself, black smock on, hair wet, with the pedals locked in place, because my long blonde hair had become a bit like my comforter: safe and snug to the point of stifling.

My wake-up call came in the form of someone from my past—a fling who had never been more than a crush but who, in the two years, nine months, and 21 days since I'd moved to New York, had morphed into a symbol of everything my life wasn't. He worked on an organic farm in Hawaii; I work on the 36th floor of a skyscraper on an island of an entirely different ilk. One autumn Thursday, Casey bounced back into my present, putting my current life into

sharp relief: I recognized how much I'd grown, and how young Casey seemed, the same idealistic, airborne soul he was when I first met him. I also recognized my reluctance to accept that fact. In looking back at what things could have been, I'd failed to see what they had become. I'd failed to see that my life was interesting—fascinating, really; it was just waiting for me to catch up. All this was running through my head the following Saturday afternoon; my hair happened to be the metaphor of the day. So I placed any trepidation I'd had about chopping it off—my mother's words of warning against doing something I'd later be sorry about ("Boys don't like short hair!"), my own insecurities over whether she was right—behind me.

My new hairstylist, a compact man with Zenlike focus, actually giggled when I told him it was my first time going short. "Change is good," he said before he made the first cut. I nodded in agreement, apprehensive nonetheless. But my nerves steadied; as Kaz snipped and the dead ends fell to the floor, I surrendered. By the time he was done, I was the one laughing—at my new sense of freedom, at my understanding of how ridiculously exaggerated my hesitation had been. By the time I walked out the door with hair clear up to my chin, I was so exhilarated by my new cut that I'd forgotten what long hair felt like.

People complimented me for the next couple of weeks, whether out of a sense of duty or sincerity, I don't know. I didn't care. Someone could have said I looked like a middle-aged man, and it would have rolled off my shoulders—because they were newly bare, and it was a pleasure to show them off.

(NOW)

(THEN)

BEING NATURAL
BY CHEE GATES

Every black girl I knew—whether she was ebony-skinned or the color of butternut squash—wanted the same thing I did: hair that hung silk-straight. Our collective desire was rooted in the self-deprecating mentality that kinks were gross and had to be concealed, if not corrected. Straight hair promised romance, laughter, abounding beauty. If I wanted to be happy, I had no choice but to unravel every nap on my head. There was only one method that would do it: I'd have to get a perm, also called a "relaxer."

That first perm is like a black girl's bat mitzvah. It's a coming out—a rite of passage into womanhood. What's different is that the initial relaxing doesn't happen at any set age. And waiting too long could retard a girl's social progress. Here's why: Before your hair is relaxed, you're viewed as a child. (Or even a dope. Or you aren't viewed at all.) Because being invisible doesn't jibe with an only child whose astrological sun is in Leo—I could barely wait ten minutes to be in the spotlight—I got my first relaxer before I was even old enough to wear deodorant, thinking it would accelerate my path to stardom.

I was a follower—mimicked whatever was deemed of-the-moment. But then I started reading books like *The Bluest Eye* and *The Autobiography of Malcolm X.* I saw footage of the Watts riots and Al Jolson's blackface act in *The Jazz Singer.* I began asking myself questions: *Is straightening my hair just another kind of minstrel show? Can I really love myself if I don't embrace my kinks, my authenticity?* I felt as if I'd been bamboozled. I'd spent the last decade idolizing an image that undermined me. Just as I came to this realization, my hair started falling out.

Stress on the hair begets breakage, according to my beautician, Yvette. She explained how overprocessed relaxed hair is "damaged beyond repair." The chemical opens the cuticle on the hair strand, gets underneath, and causes the hair to lose its strength. We shine it up with jojoba products, and though our hair might look all sleek and glossy and buoyant, the whole thing is really a sham.

My original plan was to cut back my perm gradually, while I eased into my new mind-set. Patience isn't my virtue, though. One Saturday in the summer of 2002, I woke up with an itch to do something colossally big. I called Yvette and spoke two words: *I'm ready.* Three hours later, hair was all over the floor—14 inches, in fact. It took 21 years to grow it that long.

Touching my short little Afro for the first time was like sticking my fingers into thick carpet. I couldn't even believe the stuff was mine. I wouldn't look at myself in the mirror for longer than four seconds. *Who's that stranger in the black woolly cap?* I'd think.

Gradually, I got used to the natural look; I even "Chee'd" it up by donning supa-flair jeans and "Rock the Vote" buttons on my jacket. At school, people would hold up their closed fists when I passed by. I'd nod to them, aggressively. Friends started calling me Angie, short for Angela Davis. Men got all melodramatic, pulling out lines like "I truly do beg your pardon, my sistah" or "Have a gorgeous day, empress." One time the president of the Black Student Union walked up to me and asked why I hadn't been to any of their meetings or joined the movement, because "it's obvious that you care," he said. Then it hit me: Wearing my hair without a chemical had become as much of a statement as wearing it straight. I was just promoting another stereotype that came with its own potentially disenfranchising expectations. I had thought "natural" was a hairstyle, but it's really a state of mind. Doesn't matter if I rock my hair straight or kinky, as long as I'm doing it for me.

Now I can get playful with my do: Afro in the back, perm in the front, and honey blonde streaks everywhere. I may switch it up in a few months. There are too many choices to stick with any for too long. And I'm open to every single one.

(NOW)

(THEN)

THE RIGHT CUT
BY SUZAN COLÓN

Other people have bad hair days; I thought I was going to have a bad hair life. In every other respect, my Irish-French–Puerto Rican heritage had been very good to me. I got big hazel eyes and skin that doesn't automatically burn in the sun. I was exposed to both corned beef and cabbage *and* pernil and platanos, and both cultures were forgiving of the hips I developed as a result of my family's multicultural cuisine.

But my appreciation for my little United Nations ran out when it came to my hair. My mother's fine blonde coif perfectly complements her blue eyes and pink glow; my biological father has thick, dark, Latino waves. I ended up with a brownish, kind-of-wavy-sort-of-curly-but-not-quite-either mop, and both sides contributed a propensity to frizz on even the driest days.

As a teenager, I didn't like to brush it; a hundred strokes every night may have worked for Marcia Brady, but it took my hair from a vaguely triangular shape to a full-on pyramid. I was in my 20s in the '80s, the era of straight, spiky hair; new wave meant no wave, and I was stuck with a classic rock shag. Since a trendy style was out of the question, I had it chopped off into a short back and sides, long bangs look. It wasn't great, but I didn't know what else to do with it.

Neither, it turned out, did any of the stylists I went to. For years they cut my hair as though it were straight and blew it out that way, as if they were correcting a mistake. A hairdresser in Miami gave me a Louise Brooks bob and sent me out into the humidity with a jar of pomade and a prayer (neither of which prevented my hair from frizzing into the shape of an orange slice). When I went to a woman who later became famous for her expertise with curls, she just sheared all my hair off and gave me a pixie cut.

It was incredibly chic and easy. Dazzled by this new hair perfection, I forgot about the rest of me—specifically, my hips—until I realized that, with my close-cropped hairdo, I was shaped like a bowling pin.

In an effort to balance my top with my booty, I started growing my hair out. This felt like reuniting with a difficult ex; I expected problems and took precautions. In the case of an ex, it means extra time with the therapist. With my hair, it meant more time with the blow-dryer.

Having a lot of hair is a blessing, except when you're trying to blow it all straight. It took 40 minutes and three different kinds of brushes, and then I would discover I missed a wavy section in the back and had a bump. To avoid frizz and waves brought on by humidity, year-round hats became a necessity. Plus, a woman with a blow-out is the least romantic person on the planet: There's no sex in the shower, and she's always extracting herself from her lover's embrace because he's breathing on her blow-out and making it curl.

It wasn't for any of those reasons that I stopped struggling with my hair. I was tired of all the work, and I calculated the amount of time it took me to blow-dry my hair. It came to almost 70 hours a year! Life, or at least nearly three days a year for the rest of my life, was passing me by as I singed my scalp.

So I put down the blow-dryer. In their natural state, my shortish curls made me look like a half-Irish, half-Spanish poodle. But people said it was cute, and a few months later it was even cuter…almost hot. The pixie I'd been growing out had layers all around; this time, the waves and curls fell gradually, naturally, sexy-shaggily.

When it got long, I found a stylist who kept me in curls with multiple layers and the tricky diagonal slices that keep thick hair pouf at bay. Daily styling is almost as easy as my old pixie cut: Along with a little scrunching, the wind is my blow-dryer. And I discovered a great trick one night: Not wanting to sleep on wet hair, I piled it at the top of my pillow, Bride of Frankenstein–style. When I woke up, I had va-va-va-*volume*.

Recently, a woman asked who did my perm. "This is what my hair does naturally," I said. Her envy nearly killed me. It felt great.

(NOW)

(THEN)

CONFESSIONS OF A BLONDAHOLIC
BY LAUREN IANNOTTI

Hi. My name is Lauren and I'm a blondaholic. I've been blonde-free for going on six months. I know it's not the color that's to blame. I know plenty of people can handle highlights, show restraint, enjoy small amounts of the ivory (or ash or golden) stuff, whose lives are enhanced by it. But not me. Moderation is not within my capacity. Overdose is always imminent.

I remember the turning point. It was a late-fall day nearly two years ago, and I had just spent almost three hours getting highlights at a chic New York salon. I felt out of place among the socialites and CEOs there, but I enjoyed a mind-boggling professional rate from my days as a grooming editor at a national magazine. Here's where my habit took hold: Every three months I'd put on my most presentable threads and visit a brilliantly talented colorist for foils. And, for reasons I hadn't reflected on, I always begged her for more than the last time.

"Don't you think it's time to just go for a single process?" I'd ask, trying to hide my desperation. She'd respond by gathering around the other lab-coated stylists and presenting them with my question. It was always met with frowns. "Your natural color is too dark. It will look brassy." "You'd have to come in once a month for maintenance. You don't even make it as often as you should for highlights." So I'd convince her to at least bump up my dose, and she'd send me off with incrementally more wheaty strands in my otherwise boring, fade-into-the-background, medium mouse brown.

That October day, I probably walked out with more blonde streaks than not. But I couldn't see them. I went to the drugstore the same night and bought a box of single-process dye described, no kidding, as "Bleach Blonding." And I used it.

Natural blondes make up approximately 2 percent of the world's population. They are as rare as albinos. But you can't toss a cat without hitting a golden ponytail these days, because the bottle-amplified ilk are everywhere. Sales of at-home blonding kits held steady last year, while in-salon lightening saw an unprecedented leap, according to every stylist I spoke to. No matter that celebrities seem at the moment to be exploring their dark sides. For every Cameron there's a Scarlett, a Gwyneth, and a Nicole. We are a nation that loves to be blonde.

The impulses that lead us to lighten up are as varied as the summery shades available at your local CVS. Natalia Ilyin, author of *Blonde Like Me,* a memoir of blonde addiction, says that for some the color signifies innocence, youth. For others it's the platinum seductress, she says, and still others are looking to be a sun-blonded mom or moon-blonded goddess. And there's a shade for every purpose under heaven.

"Once the marketers can get a woman thinking, *What I am is not quite right,* they've got her by the narcissism," says Ilyin, who was studying symbols in graduate school when, she says, "I realized I had a cult symbol right on my head." So maybe you're at the salon, or strolling the aisles at the drugstore, and you're thinking, *What do I want to be? More innocent? Nurturing? Sexy?* "You read the names of the colors on the box, like Glamour Gold and Beach Baby Blonde," says Ilyin. "And you decide, here's how I can pump that up in my persona."

I started getting highlights after college, and I was always conservative about them, looking for a natural, summery, all-American blonde. But then I got married (which I'd never intended to do), and I suddenly felt distinctly conventional. Appearance and identity are linked, for better or worse. So it was during our turbulent second year of marriage—as my husband and I attempted to figure out what being married meant, and how we were expected to behave—that I decided to rebel against my good-girl image and change my look. I bought some very snug pencil skirts and fishnet and crochet tights, tore open my blonde-in-a-box, and made myself into what I imagined was a Hitchcockian heroine—all snug sweaters and chignons. My husband didn't care for it.

Others did, not that I was looking. But it was fun to dress like I was on the make when I knew I'd be spending the evening reheating roast chicken for two.

Plum Sykes, author of *Bergdorf Blondes,* the literary ode to expensive dye jobs, adds, "When you achieve that white blonde, it's noticeable from anywhere in the room. Carolyn Bessette Kennedy was the perfect example. You couldn't stop looking at her. It was like a halo."

Carolyn was the iconic blonde of a generation, one in a long line of glamour girls, many of whom had lit up the silver screen. But the appeal of the towhead is much older than Hollywood, according to Peter Frost, PhD, a Canadian anthropologist and expert in the evolution of skin and hair color. He believes women had to compete for men in Europe during the Ice Age, and the brightness and rarity of their hair may have given blondes the edge in survival. "The less common the haircolor, the stronger the male preference for that color," he says.

I love it when I can excuse my own strange impulses as evolutionary urges. Especially to my dubious husband, who, a few months into my peroxide dependence, moved out of our apartment. It wasn't because of the hair. But off he went. At that point I was using a trick an enabler/stylist friend had told me about: For more dramatic results, leave the stuff on for double the time recommended on the box.

Many women hit the bottle now and then without harming themselves or their hair. But for the obsessive among us, highlights are the root of the problem: Though you might start with a reasonable dose, it's easy to lose perspective. "At a certain point, there are so many highlights, the client simply doesn't see them anymore," says Marcy Cona, haircolorist, and creative director of color and style for Clairol. "The color relies on contrast to have any impact." Sometimes intervention is the only hope. Cona has staged them in her salon, surrounding the client with stylists who gently explain that the contrast underneath was why the hair looked so good the first time. "You don't talk about going darker. It's the worst thing you can say to a blonde addict. You just try to get her to tone it down in steps."

Twelve steps?

"It doesn't usually require 12. Just six months or so of slowly reintroducing lowlights until you're back to the beginning. More often than not, they'll relapse," she says. "And we'll intervene all over again."

After a year of progressively lighter hair, I looked in the mirror and didn't like what I saw. Bleached out and strung out, I decided to go cold turkey. I called an old friend and stylist I'd been avoiding since I'd stepped off the precipice. When she saw me, she contained her horror and gave me a stain that would restore my natural color without hurting my hair. After a few more visits, she said, I'd be back to my brunette self.

Six months on the wagon and I feel as if I'm there. The chaotic year of being a confused-about-who-she-was bleached blonde has passed into a new one of relatively solid-ground brunettehood. My husband's back in the picture, too. I love how he calls me Sister of Mercy, after an old goth-pop band from the '80s. He used to call me Blondie, but I never really liked that. As any New Yorker will tell you, too much sunniness can be oppressive. It feels good to be in a warm, dark, all-natural groove. At least for now. ◘

> I BOUGHT SOME VERY SNUG PENCIL SKIRTS AND FISHNET TIGHTS, TORE OPEN MY BLONDE-IN-A-BOX, AND MADE MYSELF INTO WHAT I IMAGINED WAS A HITCHCOCKIAN HEROINE.

FAITH

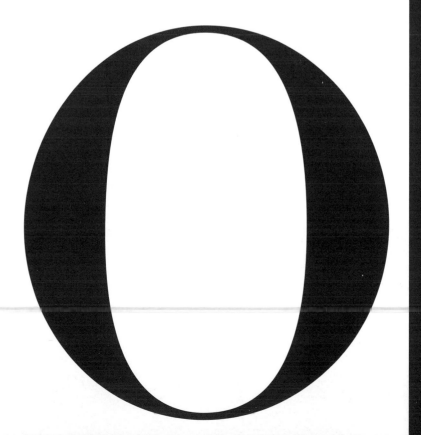

THE HARDEST QUESTION

How do you not abandon God when it feels as though God has abandoned you?
By Chris Adrian

As a divinity student, I spend my time in a state of near perpetual confusion. I have not read a tenth of what my classmates have. Immanuel Kant and Friedrich Schleiermacher were the friends of their youth the way the Bionic Woman and Marie Osmond were the friends of mine. And my theological vocabulary, compared to that of my peers, is so impoverished as to make me practically a divine mute.

During my second semester, I took a course on literature and theology, and at one of the first few sessions I woke from a daydream to discover that my classmates were eagerly discussing *The Odyssey*. I panicked, figuring that even though for once I had done the reading, I had done the wrong reading. But when I fiddled in my notebook to check the syllabus, *The Odyssey* was nowhere to be found. I poked my neighbor at the seminar table, gently, in the rib. "We were supposed to read *The Odyssey*?"

"Huh?" she said. "What are you talking about?" When I'm not in class, I work as a pediatrician, and I noticed pretty early that though divinity school, like pediatrics, is full of large-hearted, patient people, during intense intellectual discussions my fellow students can get a little testy.

"Why are we talking about *The Odyssey*?"

"Not *The Odyssey*," she said. "*The Odyssey*. Leibniz. Bayle. Polkinghorne. Those guys."

"Oh," I said, but she could tell I was still confused, so she wrote the word on my notebook, which was blank except for a half-finished doodle of a pony.

Theodicy.

"Oh," I said, as if I recognized the word. The class discussion moved on without my ever deciphering what exactly they were talking about—everyone lamenting the problem of theodicy without ever saying what it *was*—so I walked to the library after class to consult the dictionary and discovered that, like anyone who has ever felt afflicted by existence, I was already familiar with the concept, if not the word. It means an attempt to reconcile a God who is thoroughly and supremely good with the undeniable fact of evil

in the world. It was as strange and embarrassing as the episode in class had been, to stand there and learn a word I suddenly felt I should have known all my life.

You don't have to have your cookies stolen in kindergarten too many times before you start to perceive that all is not right with the world. My cookies were stolen so often that I learned to offer them before they were demanded; my tormentor was a girl whose name I have long forgotten but whose face, round and sweet and utterly at odds with her dreadful disposition, has remained with me forever. I was raised Catholic, but was at that age more a dreamy little pagan, and it was indicative of my particular brand of religiosity that I prayed to Big Bird and not to Jesus to deliver me from my freckled oppressor. When nothing changed, I continued to believe in Big Bird, but I gave up on the notion that he cared very specifically about what happened to me.

AS I BECAME AN OLDER CHILD and then a teenager, and dogs died and family members died and did not return to life no matter how hard I prayed to alter the fact of their death, I reconciled miserable reality with faith in an all-powerful and entirely benevolent God by telling myself that it wasn't that God didn't care to intervene, or didn't have the power to—my grief was just too particular to attract his attention. And as I grew still older and began to notice that we are accompanied throughout history by all sorts of unspeakable suffering, I amended this view, too, telling myself that the sum of these miserable parts must add up to something I could never apprehend while alive, and that although the fact of evil in the world might speak against God's scrutability, it said nothing about his existence or beneficence. But the older I became, and the more unhappy a place the world revealed itself to be, the more difficult it became to accept the idea of a personally invested, personally loving God.

Most days it's not the most pressing question in the world—how God can be good and allow terrible things to occur. It's when something really bad happens to you, or collective cataclysm descends, or some really wretched piece of news falls out of the television or slithers from the papers that this question that has vexed generations becomes all of a sudden quite present and personal. I would venture to guess that there are certain obsessive

sorts of personalities who dwell on it even on sunny days and during Disney ice shows (maybe even especially during Disney ice shows), but for people with certain jobs—theologian, divinity student, vice detective, physician—it becomes a professional hazard. By the time I got to residency, I understood that I needed to come up with an answer to the question people kept asking when I told them I wanted to be a pediatric oncologist: "How can you stand to work in a field where you see such terrible things?"

I did see terrible things, but in fact it was those terrible things that seemed to enable me to get up and go back to work every day. If the parents and children who were actually suffering with the illnesses could be as gracious as I discovered them to be, the very least I could do was get myself back to the hospital to be with them as they labored through the process of getting well or dying. Sometimes it seemed that the failure of drugs or technology reduced the practice of medicine to a ministry of accompaniment. I say reduced, but you could argue that it's an elevation of our practice as physicians. I came to divinity school largely because I thought the experience and education would make me better able to accompany patients into their adversity, and I think I'm in the right place for that. But it turns out that I have already learned things as a doctor that make me if not a smarter divinity student, at least a less agitated one.

Every parent and child I meet who overcomes or succumbs to illness is challenged to reconcile their fate with their faith in the goodness of the world. They never reason or parse like theologians, and by no means do they all express a faith in any kind of God, but they all find strength and will to wake up every day to a job tremendously more difficult than mine. A child complains one morning at the breakfast table of numbness in one arm, and then collapses from a catastrophic cerebral bleed (or pulls a steaming rice cooker down upon her head, or rides a scooter headfirst into a speeding taxi), and a parent's world suddenly collapses. It's a privilege and a burden to be witness to other people's tragedies, to watch them proceed from stunned disbelief to miserable acknowledgment to stoic acceptance and then beyond to the place I can't quite enter myself, a place in which they are both fully aware of how completely horrible life can be and yet still fully in love with it, possessed of a particular buoyancy of spirit that is somehow heavier than it is light.

I can't say if I believe in the God who knows us and cares for us down to the last hair of our head, and so I don't feel obligated to reconcile such a being with the ugly facts of the chromosomal syndrome trisomy 13, or teenage myelogenous leukemia, but I am pretty sure one need look no further than people's responses to adversity to find evidence that there is something in the world that resists tragedy, and seeks to overturn the evils of seeming fate.

The last and least of my professions, after physician and student, is fiction writer, and I'd like to think that the little tragedy-resisting organ in me is the one that generates stories. They are ghastly, depressing stories for the most part, about ghosts, and zombies, and unhappy angels managing apocalypses, and people attempting to bring the dead back to life, but they are a great comfort to me. I write fiction mostly to try to make sense of my own petty and profound misery, and I fail every time, but every time I come away with a peculiar sort of contentment, as if it was just the trying that mattered. And maybe that's the best answer to the patently ridiculous problem of trying to reconcile all the very visible evil and suffering in the world with the existence of a God who is not actually out to get us: We suffer and we don't give up. ⬤

THE FLASH FROM HEAVEN

NOVELIST ALICE SEBOLD PUTS HER TRUST IN HER UNCONSCIOUS…UP TO A POINT.

In some sense, faith is what I'm all about and also what can disappear in the blink of an eye. For a writer, it is as simple as words coming easily one day and failing you the next. During bleak times, when my characters sound like so many holiday-drunk relatives—and not the garrulous kind—I reassure myself that writing, like dreaming, is a function of my unconscious and will never leave me entirely on my own. I wake in the very early morning and like to start an hour or two before sunrise as if to catch the tailwind of my dreams. Also, pragmatically, I prefer to start when all the judges are still sleepy, including the harshest one—myself.

A difficult lesson, which I fought at every turn, is that what often must substitute for faith is discipline. Faith has a lovely ease about it, an ethereal ring. Discipline is the rod, the staff, your insecurities internalized and spouting rules and limits on your life. Why can't I just have faith that books will be completed? Why isn't faith alone enough? I hear my Southern roots respond. Faith doesn't dig ditches, they say; faith doesn't scrape the burn from the bottom of the pot. Ultimately, faith gives freedom, and discipline, its sister, makes sure the job gets done. Authors, when alone, often talk of page counts or word counts or how many hours they spent working that day. Rarely do we discuss our own attempts at poetry even though it is the poetry of others that routinely charges us with enough faith to go on.

Waking at 4 A.M.—3 A.M. when I am truly driven—is surely no fun for anyone, but having an image sneak up on you before the rest of the world wakes up is heaven. A small and precious secret that no one can see in the dark. Hours later, when the house stirs, and I hear my husband making a fresh pot of coffee in the kitchen, I begin to feel the pressures of the day invade. I feel as if the air around me literally changes, and the work that comes then is harder and driven by will, not grace. I finish up for the day—always in the middle of something with notes jotted down that make no sense to anyone (and if I leave my desk for more than a day, that often includes me)—and go into the world of responsibilities where that necessary if often oppressive goddess of discipline takes center stage.

The work I leave behind in my study is unfinished and unknowable almost every day. Characters come alive and die in an instant, metaphors wobble, and sentences shift meaning without my fully understanding how. After all, conscious thought is the death of creativity and to have faith in one's unconscious is the ultimate need of a writer—at least this one. Dreams go unfinished while we sleep but can be completed upon waking if we both have faith and are willing to do the grueling work of follow-through. In this way faith is a figment, a dream, a creation—something beautiful I never hope to lose. ⬤

WHAT IS YOUR LIFE THE ANSWER TO?

IF YOU'RE SUDDENLY FULL OF QUESTIONS (*WHERE AM I GOING? IS THIS ALL THERE IS?*), RABBI AND ALL-AROUND WISE WOMAN JENNIFER KRAUSE GIVES YOU A NEW ONE TO CHEW ON.

"I'm stalled," the young woman said, sitting mannequin-still in the bustle of the café where we met. Although grateful for a wonderful husband, beautiful children, and the valuable work she did each day, something was making her engine falter, and nothing could give it a jump. She called it a crisis of faith. Yet for her, as with many people I encounter in my work, it did not involve God or religion. It had to do with a broken trust in the meaning of her life—a struggle that transcends church, mosque, yarmulkes, and yoga mats; age, geography, and tax bracket. It's a trust that can break not only when you end up in a place you hoped you'd never be but also when you have everything you ever dreamed of.

"What's the point?" she asked.

"I know you want an answer," I said, "but what you need is a new question."

When you get stranded, the way to start moving again is not to search for an answer but to find a new question to which your life can be the answer. Whether you're celebrating the birth of your firstborn or marveling at her graduating in cap and gown; whether you've landed a dream job or hit retirement, are getting married or mourning the loss of a longtime love—every one of these moments is a starting line. Feeling stuck doesn't mean the meaning has gone from your life. You've just outlived one question and need to find the next—and the possibilities are endless.

True, it takes some searching to find your new question, but everyone has what I call an SPS—a Spiritual Positioning System—to guide them. This SPS is the instinct that makes you stop multitasking and lean in closer to hear what someone's saying because a sentence suddenly gives you the chills. It's the impulse to keep hitting replay on your iPod when John Legend sings "Ordinary People," daring you to wonder what you're afraid of if you trade a "fairy-tale conclusion" for the "confusing" reality of everyday love. It's the headline that stays in your mind long after it fades from the TV screen, prompting you to think, *Do I have a talent or an idea that could turn this problem into yesterday's news?* It's the photo of you as a girl, writing a story on your grandfather's typewriter, that turns up in a drawer and makes you consider, *Is there someone I forgot I wanted to be?* As long as you keep letting life ask you another question—and reveal that there is always more for you to be and do—you are unstoppable.

The stalled woman who came to me for "the answer" didn't receive one that day, but she did get the jump-start she needed with a new question. While we sipped our coffee, her SPS suddenly engaged as the conversation turned to an organization she had created. I was marveling at how she'd grown it from a staff of one to a team of devoted people when she realized she was putting in the same amount of energy now as she had when its existence depended solely on her. The organization had become what she'd worked for so tirelessly, but it didn't need her in the same way—and although she certainly hadn't stopped caring about it, the passion that had driven her was gone. "I've been trying to find what's missing, figure out what I need," she said, "but the question is, What else really needs me now?"

It was only a beginning, but just sensing that there was a new answer for her to live out was the start of finding her faith—and her fuel—again. ◖

ONLY CONNECT

WHEN YOU TAP INTO THE WORLD'S GOODNESS AND YOUR OWN INNER STRENGTH, YOU'RE NEVER ALONE. AND THAT, SAYS SHARON SALZBERG, MAKES ALL THE DIFFERENCE.

After the bomb fell on Hiroshima, even greater panic swept the city when rumors spread that the cherry blossoms would never bloom again. The thought that nature's cycle had been destroyed added a sense of hopelessness to the devastation people were already suffering. In times of trauma or loss or fear, we look to a world not defined by our pain in order to heal; we try to find a context of still-existing goodness. We turn to nature or relationships or a belief in God, seeking strength in our connection to what is unbroken. We look for affirmation that growth and restoration are possible.

Faith is the quality of the heart that impels us to seek what is constant and whole. The sense of connection can be found in vastly different ways: in classically religious pursuits or ones that are completely secular; in music or art, meditation or service to others; with groups in city rooms or in the forest on one's own.

We need faith because despite our desire for the center of our lives to hold firm, we see that it never does. We're planning a career move, when suddenly illness threatens everything. We've settled comfortably into being alone, when we meet someone and fall in love. In life there is always change, and change can be uncomfortable, even terrifying.

We may try to deny the dynamic nature of change, telling ourselves, "I know it will all work out exactly the way I want it to." We may call this faith, but in fact it is no more than hope—a hope that is no longer energized and alive but has become fixed and brittle. And in reality, this hope is a subtle form of fear.

To be open to life, we need to first acknowledge what we cannot control. We can then begin to value—and trust in—our own inner strength and wisdom, which can remain unbroken no matter our circumstances. We can develop faith in a bigger picture of life, one that recognizes that whatever we face, we are held in a web of interconnection—we're not cut off and alone.

Conventional wisdom says the opposite of faith is doubt. But doubt, applied in the right way—as curiosity and a willingness to question—can enrich and enliven our faith. I believe the true opposite of faith is the sundering of connection, the desolate certainty that the cherry trees will never bloom again. It is the experience of utter isolation, or despair.

In contrast, faith helps us approach life with a sense of possibility rather than foreboding or helplessness. It dares us to imagine what we might be capable of. It enables us to reach for what we don't yet know with a measure of courage. It gives us resilience in times of difficulty, and the ability to respond to challenges without feeling trapped. My own faith has taught me that whatever disappointments I might meet, I can try again, trust again, and love again. ◖

"I DON'T BELIEVE IN ACCIDENTS. I KNOW FOR SURE THAT EVERYTHING IN LIFE HAPPENS TO HELP US LIVE"

Weeks have passed. And the pain has not subsided. Every time I think about it, my heart starts racing and I feel like I just got stabbed in the chest. It's a jolt, still. Gracie's death.

Gracie is the smallest of the golden retrievers photographed with me on *O*'s January '06 and '07 covers. She had just turned 2 on May 21. I thought we'd grow old together.

She choked to death on a plastic ball she found in the grass (it belonged to Sophie, my 12-year-old cocker spaniel). The goldens were not allowed to play with those clear little balls that light up. I feared they'd chew them, or worse.

The worst happened on May 26. Gracie was out with her dog walker, on a walk I often do myself after their evening meal. On this sunny Saturday, having just returned from a late lunch with friends, I decided to let the caretaker do it—walk all three.

I hugged them all goodbye, leaving a lipstick print on Gracie's furry white forehead, where she loved getting kisses. Twenty minutes later, I got a call: "She's down and isn't breathing."

I ran barefoot out of the house and found the dog walker and one of my security guys pumping her chest. Just as I reached them, the security guy looked up and said, "I'm sorry, ma'am. We tried everything. I'm sorry. She's gone."

Gone??!! I couldn't believe what I was hearing. Yes, I saw it. I saw the caretaker rocking back and forth on the ground, his arms wrapped around himself, crying hysterically. My brain took in the whole scene, but it wasn't tracking properly. The first thing I remember saying is, "It's okay. It'll be okay. Tell me what happened." Through his sobs I heard: "...choked on a ball."

And I knew, this was real. *Gracie is gone, Gracie is gone, Gracie is gone* kept repeating in my head.

I stood there dazed, stunned, crying—and watched as they placed her in the back of a golf cart, her still-warm body with the lipstick stain on her fur.

But even in my stunned state, I knew this was not what it appeared to be: a freak accident with a clear plastic ball that lit up inside. I don't believe in accidents. I know for sure that everything in life happens to help us live.

So through my tears and stabbing pain and disbelief and wonder and questions about how and why this happened, I leaned over my sweet and wild and curious and mind-of-her-own Gracie, and asked, "Dear Gracie, what were you here to teach me that only your death could show me?"

And this is the answer: This lovely little runt whom I'd brought home sick—on his first visit with her, the vet told me to return her and get my money back—did more living in two years than most dogs do in 12. She never stopped moving. Was energy in motion. Chasing squirrels, hop-leaping through the pond like a rabbit. Finding anything she could to play with, chew, run with. Dashing, frolicking. Speeding across the lawn as though she were in a rush for life. I was always saying, "Gracie, slow down." She gulped her

Gracie (*circled*), Luke, and Layla at 3 months on *O*'s January 2006 cover and a year later for the January 2007 cover.

food. Gulped treats. Would let you hug her for a second, then race off to—where? She was the only dog I was always looking for. Going out on the porch calling, "Graaaacie! Gracie, come!"

The day after she died, I went to the spot where she took her last breath and called again, "Graaaacie! Graaaacie!" I was hoping security wouldn't hear me and think I needed medical—or psychological—attention. Of course I knew this time she wouldn't come running through the brush. Out of the pond. Shaking her wet fur and racing to my arms with a smile. She was always, always smiling.

Not until I knew there'd be no response did I realize how much pleasure I had taken in calling for her. So I called and cried. Called and cried. "Graaaacie!" Tears of sadness for the shocking loss. Tears of joy for the pure happiness she'd given me for nearly two years. I have never seen a being, human or animal, always so full of joy. This dog lived every moment as though it were her last.

Her life was a gift to me. Her death, a greater one.

Ten days before she died, I was getting a yearly physical, and to lower my blood pressure I'd think of Gracie's smiling face.

Just days before the "freak accident," the head of my company came into my office to have a serious talk about "taking some things off your schedule—you're doing too much." Maya Angelou called me to say the same thing. "You're doing too much. Don't

make me come to Chicago," she chided. "I want you to slow down."

I'd broken a cardinal rule: The whole month of May I'd had no day off, dashing from one event to the next. But though I appreciated everyone's concern, I still had to finish the season. Wrap up the year's shows. Have foundation meetings. Meet with auditors. Review plans for a new building, and on and on. So many people on my list. I literally forgot to put myself on the list for a follow-up checkup.

When the doctor's office called, I confessed. I hadn't heeded what I know for sure. I said, "Doctor, I'm sorry. I had so many meetings with different people, I forgot to put myself on the list."

The next day, Gracie died.

Slow down, you're moving too fast.

I got the message.

Thank you for being my saving Gracie.

I now know for sure angels come in all forms.

Oprah

151

BREATHING SPACE

LONGNOOK BEACH, CAPE COD, MASSACHUSETTS, 1983

Photograph by Joel Meyerowitz, courtesy of Edwynn Houk Gallery

DATING, MATING, RELATING

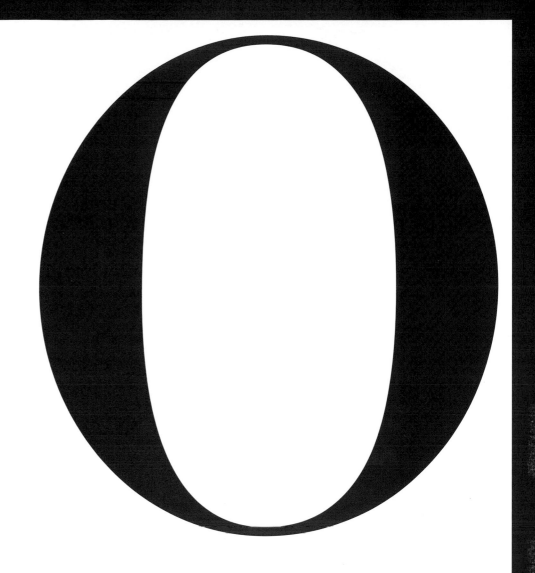

COUPLES

LOVE: THE LATEST

EXPLORER Oh, they're appealing, these life-loving, adventurous, independent souls. Think: Angelina Jolie, Jane Goodall, Jim Morrison. But lover beware: Intimacy isn't their strong suit, and they get bored easily.

BUILDER Mothers-in-law adore them. So do their buddies. Tom Hanks is the type (versus Jude Law); Gwyneth Paltrow, too (versus Gina Gershon). Not likely to whisk you off to Pago Pago on a dare, the Builder is as dependable as a Volvo.

Who are these four people and what can they tell you about your love life? According to relationship wizard Helen Fisher, PhD, they're the four basic personality types, and once you know which you are (take her test on page 163), you'll know why you're attracted to some types, left cold by others—and who might be your best bet for the long haul. We've also got the smartest love advice you've never heard (turns out needy is *good*); a roundup of startling love statistics; and, because nothing is forever, a kind word for change.

DIRECTOR Touchy-feely they're not, but Directors are the go-to folks when you need a quick decision or someone to organize a movement. The CEOs and political leaders of this world, they play to win—and if it's you they love, they're often devoted.

NEGOTIATOR Starbucks owes its success to this highly verbal type, happy to sit for hours with a mate soul searching, analyzing the relationship (think *Sex and the City*'s Carrie Bradshaw). They see all sides of an issue, too: Bill Clinton is a classic.

LOVE TYPES

Her bags are always packed. His bliss is Barcalounging with the TiVo and family puggle. Do they have a future together? Helen Fisher, PhD, says you can predict a couple's chances of happiness based on which of four personality types they fit into. And she's got a 500-couple, *O*-sponsored survey to prove it.

"They went quietly down into the roaring streets, inseparable and blessed…" So wrote Dickens in *Little Dorrit*. We all want a happy partnership, but what is that? And how can we differentiate between an intoxicating attraction that will end in a flameout and the kind of chemistry that makes for long-term compatibility? Using my latest research (the subject of my next book), I designed a survey for *O* magazine to explore why—and how—certain couples click so well, and why others are plagued by tension and misery.

I began with a theory. Since antiquity, poets, philosophers, and physicians have classified people into four styles of temperament. For Plato, they were the Artisan, Guardian, Idealist, and Rational. I have come to call them the Explorer, Builder, Negotiator, and Director. Each basic type, I suspect, is associated with a distinct cluster of genes—along with the expression of certain brain chemicals and a unique collection of personality traits. When people pair up, I propose, they tend to fall for a type different from their own, pulled by an unconscious biological appetite to create more genetic variety in their young and to raise their children with a wider array of parenting skills. Furthermore, each kind of pair will have its own joys and challenges, so a Builder married to a Director might face one set of highs and lows; a Negotiator-Explorer couple, another.

To see how these ideas play out in the real world, we e-mailed thousands of married *O* readers and asked each spouse to complete our online survey independently (once partners hit "submit," they couldn't read each other's answers). Part of the survey consisted of questions I had originally developed for the new dating/relationship site chemistry.com to determine a person's love type. Other questions addressed issues that might cause friction in the relationship—money, sex, respect, boredom—as well as levels of general happiness.

Then I studied the hundreds of pages of data collected by Beta Research Corporation, the company that carried out the survey for us, on 500 couples who answered our questionnaire.

With some respondents as young as 21 and others in their 60s, the average age for women was 47 and for men, 49. Some 83 percent of couples had children, many still living at home. And on average, the spouses had been married 16 years. Were some pairings more compatible than others? Are certain types better left unwed?

WHAT'S YOUR TYPE?

We're each a mix of all four broad genetic categories, but we express some traits more regularly than others. I, for example, am primarily an Explorer and secondarily a Negotiator. I don't have much Builder in me (I never follow schedules unless I have to; nor do I have traditional values, and I'm not at all cautious—a trait I should cultivate). I am even less of a Director (my need for social harmony far exceeds my desire to be direct or, sometimes, even pragmatic). As you read on, you'll probably guess both your primary and secondary types, as well as those of your mate. To be sure, take the test on page 163.

■ THE NEGOTIATOR

Negotiators have specific personality traits that have been linked with estrogen. Although estrogen is known as a female sex hormone, men have it, too, and there are plenty of male Negotiators. As the name suggests, this type is superb at handling people. Negotiators instinctively know what others are thinking and feeling. They artfully read facial expressions, postures, gestures, and tone of voice. Their interest in identity extends not only to others but to themselves. So they are introspective and self-analytical—men and women who take pleasure in journeying into their thoughts and motives. As a result, when they form a partnership, they like to delve deeply into the strengths and weaknesses of the relationship.

Not only do Negotiators connect psychologically, they also have the ability to remain mentally flexible. When they make decisions, they weigh many variables and consider various ways to proceed; they see things contextually, rather than linearly—I call it web thinking. As a result, they tend to be comfortable with ambiguity. Negotiators can be highly intuitive and creative. And they like to theorize. Perhaps

49% OF MEN ALWAYS FEEL "IN LOVE" WITH THEIR PARTNERS. ONLY 36% OF WOMEN SAY THE SAME. TWICE AS MANY WOMEN AS MEN SAY THEY ALWAYS OR OFTEN THINK OF LEAVING THE RELATIONSHIP.

their most distinctive characteristic is verbal fluency, the facility for finding the right words rapidly. With this skill—alongside an agreeable and accommodating nature, compassion, social savvy, and patience—the Negotiator can be very friendly, diplomatic, and authentic.

But as with all qualities, these traits can warp. Negotiators sometimes become such placators they appear wishy-washy to the point of spinelessness. Because they're not willing to confront, they can turn to backstabbing. With their need to examine all the possibilities, they can get bogged down in rumination as opposed to action. And in a relationship, their desire to connect and dissect all the subtle meanings between the two of you can become cloying and invasive.

■ THE DIRECTOR

Specific activities in the testosterone system are what distinguishes this type. Again, although we think of the hormone as male, it is shared by both sexes, and there are many full-blooded women Directors. Whatever the gender, people of this type are competitive. They strive to be top dog and have many skills to get there. They are pragmatic, tough-minded, and most notably decisive, able to make up their minds rapidly, even when faced with difficult choices. Rational analysis, logical reasoning, and objectivity are their core strengths. They also pay attention to details and can focus their attention to the exclusion of everything around them—an ability that enables them to weed out extraneous data and progress on a straightforward path toward a specific goal: the solution. Many Directors are also ingenious, theoretical, and bold in their ideas. Moreover, they are willing to take unpopular, even dangerous paths, to get to the truth. So they persist and often win.

Directors are particularly skilled at understanding machines and other rule-based systems, from computers and math problems to the details of biology, world finance, or architecture. They excel at sports, and often have an acute ear for all kinds of music. Their interests can be narrow; but they pursue them deeply and thoroughly. And they can captivate those who share their hobbies.

Placating leaves the Director cold. He or she often chooses to do a good job rather than please others. In fact, Directors are the least socially skilled of the four types. When preoccupied with work or personal goals, they can appear aloof, distant, even cold, and are generally not interested in making social connections, with the exception of those that are useful or exciting to them.

As with the other types, the traits that make Directors so successful may become grating: For example, their confidence can veer into bragging, their exactitude turn uncompromising, and their forthrightness simply seem rude. And because they often see issues in black and white, they miss the nuances of social, business, and personal situations. But thanks to their dedication, loyalty, and interest in sharing ideas, Directors make close friends. And they can be fiercely protective of those they love.

■ THE BUILDER

Calm, affable, and people oriented, the Builder's personality is influenced by the serotonin system. Social situations are often fun and relaxing for Builders; they like to network.

Because duty and loyalty are their strong suits, they often acquire a devoted pack of peers and pals. And they're true guardians when it comes to family and friends.

Builders are cautious—but not fearful. They think concretely. They have a clear memory of yesterday's mistakes, so they prepare. These people are not impulsive with their money, their actions, or their feelings. Security is important to them. Structure and order are, too. Taking particular pride in upholding social norms, many are traditional, and they often have a strong moral streak. Builders don't get bored easily, which enables them to be methodical, hardworking, and dependable. Thanks to all these solid qualities, they tend to be regarded as pillars of the community.

But Builders can go overboard. In their quest to do things the "proper way," they can be intolerant of other ways. Indeed, they can be stubborn. And with their need for order, rules, and schedules, they can stifle spontaneity. Their stoicism can turn into pessimism, their conformity into rigidity, and their concrete thinking sometimes makes them too literal. Normally, however, Builders are community minded, industrious, and popular with colleagues and companions.

■ THE EXPLORER

Explorers have a very active dopamine system, a brain chemical associated with the tendency to seek novelty, among other qualities. An Explorer might look up from the newspaper on Sunday and say, "Want to go to Warsaw?"—and by Wednesday you're in Poland. Champions of "never a dull moment," these adventurers live to discover new people, places, things, or ideas, often on the spur of the moment. Friends, family, and colleagues frequently regard them as highly independent and autonomous.

Explorers have more energy than most people; they tend to be restless, sometimes fast-paced. And they are highly curious—"For always roaming with a hungry heart," as Tennyson put it. Constantly generating new ideas or creative insights, they easily shift their attention from one thing to another. Although the classic Explorer is a race-car driver, South Pole trekker, or bad-boy rocker who lives hard, taking drugs and having risky sex, I know many who exercise their passion for adventure by reading several hours a day; collecting stamps, coins, or antiques; or walking through the byways of a city.

People quickly like most Explorers. Generous and sunny, they tend to be playful, sensual, sometimes hedonistic, often unpredictable, and regularly amusing. But they can be difficult to take—especially in a marriage. They do not tolerate boredom well. So they are generally not interested in routine social or business events. In fact, Explorers try to avoid routine of almost any kind, and can trample on another person's cherished beliefs and habits—not to mention be impatient.

Their drive for novelty may make them unreliable (I know several, for example, who are always late—so caught up in their adventures, they simply disregard the time), impractical, even reckless. Some are so irreverent they can appear cynical. And they are also more susceptible to addictions. Finally, Explorers often lack the self-consciousness and introspectiveness of other types. And their self-reliance can inhibit deep intimacy with a partner. ◗

33% OF MEN STRONGLY AGREE THAT SEX IS AN IMPORTANT PART OF MARRIAGE. THIS IS TRUE OF ONLY 20% OF WOMEN. SEX MATTERS MOST TO MALE EXPLORERS AND LEAST TO FEMALE BUILDERS.

WHO MATCHES UP?

Can a thrill-seeking Explorer find happiness with a down-to-earth Builder? A people-pleasing Negotiator with a driven Director? Here's what our survey says....

Explorer

Director

Builder

Negotiator

Among our 500 couples, the most popular couplings are between a Builder and a Director, followed by a Negotiator and a Director. As I hypothesized, partners for the most part married someone with a different set of primary social and cognitive skills. Interestingly, three of the four most prevalent marital combinations involve Builders, which makes sense. These people build families, homes, and solid careers. They're good marriage—not to mention parent—material. On the other hand, a strikingly small percentage of our couples include Explorers. I'm not surprised. The primary gene (in the dopamine system) associated with risk-taking occurs in only a small percentage of the world's population. So it's reasonable that only 9.5 percent of the 1,000 respondents in our survey—59 women and 36 men—scored in this category. (I particularly like these numbers because they undermine the smug belief that women are less adventurous than men.) Rarer still are Explorers who marry each other: only 5 couples, or 1 percent of our sample. As for other same-type unions, a mere 7 percent of marriages are between two Directors and 4 percent between two Negotiators. The one exception is the double-Builder pair: 14 percent of couples. But the world may have a special need for these marriages, a theory I'll tell you later. For now let's explore each type of match:

BUILDER AND DIRECTOR

This was the most popular combination (25 percent of the couples in our sample), which is interesting because each type brings such different qualities to the relationship. Both share a loyalty to home and family, so the Builder is likely to admire the Director's ingenuity, competence, and workaholism. And the Director, who is less socially skilled, may be particularly drawn to the Builder's charm and ability to provide a social life. In addition, the Director may find the Builder's need to uphold traditions comforting, while the Builder values the Director's decisiveness.

Any friction in this couple is likely to occur around relating to others. Because Directors tend to shy away from routine social commitments, they may feel annoyed by the Builder's drive to nurture extensive networks of companions and colleagues. Conversely, Builders probably find the Director's aloofness frustrating at times. In fact, according to our survey, Builders in these couples were more likely to say their partners "never" or "rarely" satisfied their "deepest psychological needs" (23 percent versus 10 percent for Directors). Diverging interests in sex might also be an issue for this couple. When asked, "Is sex an important part of your marriage?" the Director was more than twice as likely to say "always" (36 percent) as the Builder (15 percent). This isn't surprising considering that Directors express more testosterone, which is associated with sexuality for both genders, and Builders' high levels of serotonin can dampen the sex drive. Even so, when it comes to feeling "in love" with their spouse, Directors are far more likely to say they do (44 percent) than Builders (28 percent); Directors are also the ones to agree, "If I could marry again, I'd marry the same person" (45 percent versus 32 percent). Bottom line, this is a strong pair for raising good citizens of tomorrow.

BUILDER AND NEGOTIATOR

This is another promising and popular combination. The Builder's dedication to home and family life is shared by the Negotiator, who—unlike the Director—is socially skilled and inclined to connect with others. Both are naturally quite nurturing, loyal, and dependable. They each also have a proclivity for religious faith or spirituality, a need to help others, and a deep belief in moral behavior. As for their differences, they can complement each other nicely: The Builder is most likely drawn to the Negotiator's enthusiasm, creativity, and flexibility, and the Negotiator is grounded by the Builder's orderliness and ability to meet deadlines.

There are downsides. Builders are likely to become irritated by what they consider their partner's self-absorption and idealism. Meanwhile the Negotiator can long for more depth and meaning in the relationship and come to find the Builder's lack of passion and romance disappointing. When asked, "Does your partner satisfy your deepest psychological needs?," significantly fewer Negotiators said "always" or "often" (55 percent) than Builders (75 percent). Also, not surprisingly, the tenderhearted Negotiator has a lot more respect for the way the frugal Builder partner "handles money" than the Builder has for the Negotiator's more casual financial style (51 percent versus 30 percent).

DIRECTOR AND DIRECTOR

Although a rare match (only 7 percent of our couples), these mates no doubt see eye-to-eye—and each lets the other pursue his or her goals. Two Directors are likely to enjoy their time together immensely, talking earnestly and in great detail about their interests. They are both logical, focused, exacting, critical, and competitive, and neither is terribly interested in casual social engagements. Moreover, they probably share a deep trust in and respect for each other.

The pitfall is likely to be time. Both are workaholics. And neither is socially skilled. So they can fall into a pattern of barely spending time together and misunderstanding each other when they do. I hadn't predicted this, but male Directors seem to have some dissatisfaction when it comes to sex: Only 24 percent of them say their partners are sensitive to their sexual needs, while over half the females (51.5 percent) say that's the case.

BUILDER AND BUILDER

As the exception to the rule that people are drawn to genetic types different from their own, this couple has great strength, precisely because Builders are enormously interested in family stability. In fact, this is such a fine match for raising children, I suspect Mother Evolution gave Builders a trait to overcome their potential boredom with one another: They thrive on predictability.

Women in these marriages seem particularly content. The female Builder is more likely than the male to say her spouse is sensitive to her sexual needs (38 percent compared to 19 percent) and respects her (57 percent versus 35 percent); she's also more likely to admire the way her husband handles money than vice versa (44 percent versus 28 percent). The main downside of the couple is that while Builders make a powerful team when they agree, they can lock horns if they don't. Still, I would guess that this combination is the least likely of all marriages to part company.

BUILDER AND EXPLORER

Only a small number (6 percent) of our respondents were this kind of couple. Almost polar opposites, the responsible, family-focused Builder may feed off the Explorer's energy and sense of adventure and fun; and alternately, Explorers undoubtedly benefit from their partner's calm, cautious nature, their pragmatism, security, and sexual fidelity. Moreover, Builders have an opportunity to care for someone, while Explorers get a chance to amuse and charm, to make their partner laugh and shed life's burdens.

But each will likely have complaints. The financially practical Builder may sense that the far less frugal Explorer is trying to undermine his or her drive to behave sensibly. Meanwhile, the Explorer may feel stifled by all the rules and schedules that the Builder constructs—wanting to push off and do new things while the Builder prefers to see old friends or follow traditions. When asked, "How often do you feel bored in your relationship?" the Explorer was more than twice as likely to say "sometimes" than the Builder (41 percent versus 17 percent). Fortunately, with the Explorer's easygoing tolerance and the Builder's determination, this match can work.

NEGOTIATOR AND EXPLORER

This is the only type of marriage for whom no particular problems came up in our survey. But there were so few of these couples (only 4 percent), the data might be misleading. I'd venture to say that the Negotiator's traits—enthusiasm, morality, empathy, insight, and imagination—all appeal to the Explorer, who probably also values his or her win-win attitude and interest in the big picture. But the Explorer could easily become impatient with, even cynical about, the Negotiator's spiritual quests and constant desire to delve into the psychological underpinnings of the relationship. And although Negotiators are captivated by the

(Except where otherwise noted, numbers refer to answering the statement "always.")

Explorer's impromptu adventures and romantic drama, they may never fully accept their partner's genuine need for autonomy and freedom. In fact, the Negotiator is likely to long for more intimacy. As to how these two might overcome their differences, I can only guess that the Negotiator's deep need for harmony and the Explorer's tolerance—along with their shared flexibility and mutual craving for romance—enable both to sustain their positive illusions about each other.

NEGOTIATOR AND DIRECTOR

This was the second most common combination in our sample (18 percent of couples), and I can see why. Although Negotiators and Directors are extremely different, they think alike. Both are abstract and creative, and turned on by books and ideas. Both like to talk at length and in detail about their insights. And they bring complementary skills to their conversations as well as to other parts of their lives. While the Negotiator tends to see the large picture, the Director focuses on a smaller piece of the world. Also, because Negotiators live in a complex inner world full of options and ethical knots, they appreciate the Director's directness and decisiveness, not to mention technical prowess and ability to provide. On the flip side, the Director is drawn to the Negotiator's warmth and insight into people.

The problems arise when the Negotiator begins to construe the Director's aloofness and any preoccupation with work as being thoughtless and indifferent. And when accused of not caring, the self-contained Director can feel misunderstood. Sex could be an issue for this couple, too: Directors in our survey were significantly more likely to feel sex is important to the relationship than were Negotiators—29 percent versus 16 percent. Also, when asked about money, four times as many Directors said they "never" or "rarely" have respect for the way their partner handles it, compared with the other way around. No surprise here. Directors are typically far more skilled at making money than the idealistic Negotiator. But these differences may not matter so much to the Director. In answer to the question, "How often do you think: If I could marry again, I'd marry the same person," Directors were much more likely—33 percent versus 15 percent—to say "often." Overall, this is likely to be a happy match.

NEGOTIATOR AND NEGOTIATOR

Superb at communication, and deeply introspective, these like-minded souls can talk for hours, indeed years, about ideas, family relations, and spiritual beliefs. Both value morality, are concerned about community, and appreciate the flexible, giving spirit in the other, and both are highly romantic. Negotiators bond deeply.

But I suspect these lovers can wear each other out with their constant analyzing. They are likely to give each other too little privacy as well. And both can be anxious and prone to depression. Most important, Negotiators tend to put a high premium on having a profound, meaningful relationship for all eternity. And because they look for the perfect mate, they can easily become disillusioned and eventually part. Perhaps this is why only 4 percent of the marriages in our sample were of this type. The survey

picked up one notable discrepancy between two Negotiators: Only 45 percent of the males in these couples reported that their partners were "always" or "often" sensitive to their sexual needs, whereas 80 percent of the female Negotiators said that their husbands were responsive in this way.

DIRECTOR AND EXPLORER

This is a curious match. A Director and Explorer can be highly compatible lovers, because both dopamine and testosterone stimulate sex drive. And they share the ability to be creative, even ingenious. The Explorer is likely to respect the Director's focus on work, logical inventiveness, irreverence, and pragmatism. And the Director probably enjoys the Explorer's daring and curiosity. But Explorers may have difficulty dealing with Directors' frank and doubting natures, as well as their dedication to deep knowledge on esoteric topics, competitiveness, and serious approach to life. And the Director may feel that the Explorer is, at times, unfocused and out of control. When asked, "Do you and your partner have the same goals," only 38 percent of Directors said "often," compared with 65 percent of their Explorer spouses.

EXPLORER AND EXPLORER

As for Explorers marrying Explorers, there were so few—only 5 couples—it wasn't possible to do any real analysis. But I suspect I know a few of their pleasures and their problems, in part because I'm an Explorer who's gone out with another Explorer for some nine years. This pair has a huge amount of fun together. Both are independent, resourceful, impulsive, creative, high energy, adventurous, and interested in sex. So for a while, two Explorers are likely to feel as if they have slipped into Nirvana; each has found someone who will play as hard and fast as they do. But Explorers are so independent that they have difficulty working as a team or discussing the problems in the relationship. Interestingly, in our sample, Builder-Builder couples had many more children than did Explorer pairs. Natural selection is at work before our eyes: The steady, dependable, family- and community-oriented Builders are sending more of their DNA toward eternity.

AS A GREAT SAGE ONCE WROTE, "Happiness is like a butterfly. The more you chase it, the more it will elude you. But if you turn your attention to other things, it will come and sit softly on your shoulder." Perhaps we will never know which matches make the happiest marriages. What we do know from our survey is that compatibility comes in many varieties and couples get along—and don't get along—in different ways. Most striking to me, though, is that when asked, "How often do you feel in love with your partner?" 80 percent of our survey takers said "often" or "always." And 82 percent stated that they rarely if ever think about leaving the relationship. I have long maintained that we humans have evolved an intense drive for romantic love—far more powerful than the sex drive. Songs, poems, and legends about love bedeck the world. Everywhere people live for love, kill for love, and die for love. And most important, when we choose the right person, we can keep this passion percolating for years. ◧

> "DOES YOUR PARTNER SATISFY YOUR DEEPEST PSYCHOLOGICAL NEEDS?" 29% OF MEN SAY ALWAYS. ONLY 18% OF WOMEN AGREE: MOST CRAVE MORE EMOTIONAL CONNECTION.

THE LOVE-TYPE TEST Here's the way to determine what personality type you are—Explorer, Director, Negotiator, or Builder. As you go through the quiz Helen Fisher developed, keep in mind that there are no wrong answers. Also, the truer you are to yourself, the more useful the test will be for you. When you're finished, have your partner do the same.

1 I find unpredictable situations exhilarating.
- ☐ Strongly disagree
- ☐ Disagree
- ☐ Agree
- ☐ Strongly agree

2 I do things on the spur of the moment.
- ☐ Strongly disagree
- ☐ Disagree
- ☐ Agree
- ☐ Strongly agree

3 I often try new things.
- ☐ Strongly disagree
- ☐ Disagree
- ☐ Agree
- ☐ Strongly agree

4 I have more energy than most people.
- ☐ Strongly disagree
- ☐ Disagree
- ☐ Agree
- ☐ Strongly agree

5 I get interesting thoughts when I am half asleep.
- ☐ Strongly disagree
- ☐ Disagree
- ☐ Agree
- ☐ Strongly agree

6 I open gifts early that say "Don't open until your birthday."
- ☐ Strongly disagree
- ☐ Disagree
- ☐ Agree
- ☐ Strongly agree

7 I experience déjà vu.
- ☐ Strongly disagree
- ☐ Disagree
- ☐ Agree
- ☐ Strongly agree

8 I place a high degree of importance on how other people view me.
- ☐ Strongly disagree
- ☐ Disagree
- ☐ Agree
- ☐ Strongly agree

9 I think it is more fun to do things with friends than with just my partner.
- ☐ Strongly disagree
- ☐ Disagree
- ☐ Agree
- ☐ Strongly agree

10 I play the role of peacemaker between feuding friends or coworkers.
- ☐ Strongly disagree
- ☐ Disagree
- ☐ Agree
- ☐ Strongly agree

11 In general I think it is important to follow the rules.
- ☐ Strongly disagree
- ☐ Disagree
- ☐ Agree
- ☐ Strongly agree

12 Taking care of my possessions is a high priority for me.
- ☐ Strongly disagree
- ☐ Disagree
- ☐ Agree
- ☐ Strongly agree

13 I am the first one to step up when family and friends need protection.
- ☐ Strongly disagree
- ☐ Disagree
- ☐ Agree
- ☐ Strongly agree

14 My friends and family say that I have traditional values.
- ☐ Strongly disagree
- ☐ Disagree
- ☐ Agree
- ☐ Strongly agree

15 I am more idealistic than most people.
- ☐ Strongly disagree
- ☐ Disagree
- ☐ Agree
- ☐ Strongly agree

16 I generally try to avoid work that includes math.
- ☐ Strongly disagree
- ☐ Disagree
- ☐ Agree
- ☐ Strongly agree

17 I believe that the solution to most problems is somewhere between black and white.
- ☐ Strongly disagree
- ☐ Disagree
- ☐ Agree
- ☐ Strongly agree

18 In most situations, from expressing feelings to solving work problems, I can find the right words rapidly.
- ☐ Strongly disagree
- ☐ Disagree
- ☐ Agree
- ☐ Strongly agree

19 When a waiter clears the table, I usually hand him/her the hard-to-reach items.
- ☐ Strongly disagree
- ☐ Disagree
- ☐ Agree
- ☐ Strongly agree

20 I vividly imagine dramatic things (wonderful or horrible) happening to me.
- ☐ Strongly disagree
- ☐ Disagree
- ☐ Agree
- ☐ Strongly agree

21 I can see many different ways to solve a particular problem.
- ☐ Strongly disagree
- ☐ Disagree
- ☐ Agree
- ☐ Strongly agree

22 I understand complex machines easily.
- ☐ Strongly disagree
- ☐ Disagree
- ☐ Agree
- ☐ Strongly agree

23 I think it is more important to do a good job than to make friends.
- ☐ Strongly disagree
- ☐ Disagree
- ☐ Agree
- ☐ Strongly agree

24 I prefer to work independently rather than with a team of coworkers.
- ☐ Strongly disagree
- ☐ Disagree
- ☐ Agree
- ☐ Strongly agree

25 I make up my mind rapidly when faced with a difficult decision.
- ☐ Strongly disagree
- ☐ Disagree
- ☐ Agree
- ☐ Strongly agree

26 I wait for someone to prove himself before I trust him.
- ☐ Strongly disagree
- ☐ Disagree
- ☐ Agree
- ☐ Strongly agree

27 It takes a lot of evidence to make me change my mind on an important issue.
- ☐ Strongly disagree
- ☐ Disagree
- ☐ Agree
- ☐ Strongly agree

28 I like to cut through the uncertainties to get to the point.
- ☐ Strongly disagree
- ☐ Disagree
- ☐ Agree
- ☐ Strongly agree

TO SCORE, FIRST GIVE THE FOLLOWING POINTS TO EACH ANSWER:
Strongly disagree = 1
Disagree = 2
Agree = 3
Strongly agree = 4

Then add up the points in each of the following four sections. (Do not add points of each section together.) Whichever is the highest is your dominant type; the next highest is your secondary type. In fact, our secondary types can play an important part in our relationships (for example, an Explorer/Negotiator may have an understanding of social skills that an Explorer/Director doesn't).

■ Questions 1–7 measure the degree to which you are an *Explorer*
■ Questions 8–14 measure the degree to which you are a *Builder*
■ Questions 15–21 measure the degree to which you are a *Negotiator*
■ Questions 22–28 measure the degree to which you are a *Director*

Keep in mind that personality is complex, and romantic love, ever mysterious. Looking at patterns is merely an opportunity for insight.

8 ENTIRELY NEW IDEAS ABOUT LOVE

Forget everything you've been told. Like: Don't be picky; plan dates with your mate to Keep Love Alive; don't even try to change his annoying habits. Wrong, all wrong. In this eye-opening and incredibly useful report, researchers stand conventional wisdom on its head.

1 IT'S GOOD TO BE PICKY. VERY PICKY

Single women the world over will thank God for these two researchers: In a study of speed daters, Paul W. Eastwick and Eli J. Finkel, PhD, of Northwestern University, found that people who selected a large number of candidates for follow-up meetings were less likely to be picked themselves for another round. People who chose only a few contenders were more successful in getting attention and responses. It turns out that singles who show interest in every partner they encounter may come off not as eager and open but as just plain desperate.

"What's interesting about that is it actually differs from platonic liking," says Finkel. "In nonromantic contexts, if I like everybody, then everybody likes me back. After all, who doesn't like the guy who likes everybody? But in a romantic context, if I say, 'Yeah, she's hot! And *she's* hot...and *she's* hot...and that other girl over there is hot, too,' there's now hard statistical evidence that, in general, the women I meet will not find me sexually desirable."

Does this mean that grandmothers who've warned single women not to be too picky have been wrong? "I don't think your grandma meant, 'You have to go on dates with everybody under every circumstance,'" says Finkel. "But in a situation in which there are a bunch of eligible men, like a party, be selective." Finkel warns against interpreting this data as an invitation to sit home

or play hard to get: "What you want to do is be easy for one person to get and hard for everyone else, which will increase the likelihood of that one person's liking you."

2 IT'S NOT THE JOURNEY, IT'S THE PREPARATION

What people look for in a marriage partner is another topic Finkel has investigated. "Basically they think, *The sex is good, we love each other, we're good friends...,*" he says. "You'd go pretty far down the list before you'd get to '*We get in sync effectively.*'" But he's learned that the ability to coordinate day-to-day tasks like shopping for food and running errands is a crucial component of a couple's happiness.

"Married partners are co-managers, and as the marriage progresses, it involves more logistical organization, especially if kids come," he says. "If you're not in sync with your partner, research suggests, you'll find yourself depleted, exhausted, and less effective, and if the problems are serious enough, it's difficult to imagine the relationship continuing to function effectively."

A courtship affords few opportunities to engage in the sort of knotty tactical tasks that fill a marriage. To test a relationship, Finkel suggests that you "throw it into challenge, so that if there's a problem, you can develop a system. Expose it to stressful coordination experiences. Instead of watching TV together or doing something comfortable, take a road trip that requires a lot of collaboration. Put one person in charge of six things, the other in charge of six other things, and then ask yourselves, 'How well do we do these things?'"

3 BETTER TO CELEBRATE THAN COMMISERATE

A new study has found that the way you respond to your partner's good news may be more important than how you react to his disappointments. Couples who celebrated each other's happy events (like promotions or raises) reported greater satisfaction in their relationship and were less likely to break up than those who offered support only during rough times, says lead study author Shelly L. Gable, PhD, an associate professor of psychology at UC Santa Barbara.

She and her researchers videotaped 79 couples as they talked about negative and positive events in their lives, then categorized the partner's responses in four ways: active-destructive ("Are you sure you can handle that job?"); passive-destructive (silence, changing the subject); passive-constructive (an absentminded "That's nice"); and, the most helpful, active-constructive ("I'm so proud of you" or "I know how important this was to you"). The finding that praise boosted a relationship more than a sympathetic response to bad news surprised Gable—as did the results concerning passive support, like smiling vaguely, saying, "Great," and returning to your newspaper. "We assumed when we started this research that passive support would be good—not as good as active-constructive, but certainly not bad," she says. But time and time again, Gable's team saw that passive responses negatively affected relationship satisfaction.

So when your mate bursts through the door with good news, "make an effort to notice these events and act on them in some way," says Gable. A partner can sense false enthusiasm, so if you're not able to have a genuine reaction, she suggests asking questions about why he's so happy. "This will help him," she says, "because you're giving positive feedback, and it will help you because it gives you insight into what makes him click." She isn't saying couples need to celebrate every event with a five-course dinner; simple and sincere praise is enough. "It's the thought that counts," she says. "Although I'd never turn down a five-course dinner."

4 IT TAKES A STRONG WOMAN TO BE NEEDY

You'd think John Gottman, PhD, who founded the Gottman Institute (otherwise known as the Love Lab) with his wife, Julie, wouldn't make dumb mistakes in his own relationship. But he always remembers the time he harangued his busy wife for neglecting him: "I said, 'You're so emotionally unavailable; everyone else comes first; what is wrong with you?' And I found when I said that, she didn't want to spend time with me." He laughs. "So I learned from the couples we studied to say, 'You know, I'm getting that lonely feeling again. I just need more of you in my day.'" And it worked.

The trick was employing what Gottman calls a soft start-up, which involves telling your partner "what you need and giving

them a way to succeed." His team had found that even in happy relationships, partners reciprocate anger with anger, so the easiest way to de-escalate a conflict was not to escalate it in the first place. For instance, instead of saying, "I'm sick to death of cooking dinner, you lazy slob," Gottman suggests telling your spouse, "You know, I'm sick of my own cooking. I think we need to go out to dinner, or have you take charge of dinner for a while."

Many Love Lab participants find it difficult to make themselves that vulnerable. "A lot of people feel shame about having a need," he says. "Our culture tells us that to be needy is to be weak, but it's really a tremendous strength to know what you need and to be able to ask for it." Beginning a conversation with what you need, rather than the more aggressive "You never..." or "You idiot," is a way to complain that's easier for your partner to hear and act on. "You can't listen to somebody if they're attacking you... well, maybe you can if you're the Dalai Lama," Gottman says. "Then again, he's not married."

> COUPLES SHOULD ASK THEMSELVES THREE QUESTIONS EVERY YEAR: DOES MY PARTNER FEEL SAFE BEING EMOTIONALLY VULNERABLE WITH ME? DOES MY PARTNER FEEL ACCEPTED? CAN I GO TO MY PARTNER FOR NON-JUDGMENTAL SUPPORT?

5 60 SECONDS TO A BETTER RELATIONSHIP

For the overworked, overcommitted, and all-around overwhelmed couples, Peter Fraenkel, PhD, has one piece of advice: "Don't try to schedule time together. Schedules are more work. And you don't need any more work."

Instead, Fraenkel, the director of the Center for Time, Work, and the Family at the Ackerman Institute for the Family, in New York City, tells couples to come up with a list of things they can enjoy together that can be done in less than a minute: telling a joke, one long kiss, etc. These 60-second pleasure points, as Fraenkel calls them, don't all have to be face-to-face. He even suggests using the tools that make many individuals feel overextended—a Black-Berry or cell phone—for private matters. Couples are encouraged to send a quick text message or e-mail links to a funny Web site or a restaurant review (and a note: "Let's do takeout from here tonight?"). He asks clients to each initiate three pleasure points a day. Couples report that this practice not only instills a better sense of connection throughout the week but, as Fraenkel says, "also greatly relieves each partner's concern that they could never find any time for the other." And it lowers the couple's expectations for a vacation—suddenly, they don't look at those two weeks in Bermuda as their only chance to connect but rather as a chance to lengthen those pleasure points, stretching that 60-second kiss into something more.

6 AND BABY MAKES…TROUBLE

In a series of studies over 13 years, John Gottman and his researchers observed couples from the first few months of marriage through the birth of a child. In 2007 he announced that 67 percent of the couples in his studies experienced a drop in relationship happiness in the first three years of a baby's life (and were twice as likely to divorce).

Gottman stresses that it's crucial for couples to tackle major marriage problems before the infant arrives. Couples who did well became a team early on, he says. The successful men were easy to spot: They helped with housework and loved the way their pregnant wives looked (whereas supposedly funny comments like "She's a whale" were a warning sign). In his new book, *And Baby Makes Three* (cowritten with his wife, Julie), Gottman teaches couples ways to improve their teamwork.

Renowned child development expert T. Berry Brazelton, MD, is familiar with times when a child's behavior stresses her parents' relationship—usually when she is moving from one developmental stage to another. When parents prepare for these phases, he says they do better together. He also says that children naturally register their parents' reactions—for instance, *Dad doesn't freak when I crawl to the stairs; Mom does*—and when those responses contradict each other, children act out. Most parents, though, don't realize that this conflict can start as early as nine months. Like Gottman, Brazelton encourages couples to find a workable, united parenting style early on.

7 COMING SOON: A DIVORCE VACCINE

Marriage researcher James V. Córdova, PhD, has become haunted by a disheartening statistic: Fifty percent of couples who finish marital therapy get better (and stay better), but the other half either do not improve or relapse. "It's better than nothing, but not as good as we could be doing," says Córdova, an associate professor of psychology at Clark University in Worcester, Massachusetts. The problem, he recognized, is that couples usually see a counselor when the relationship is already breaking down.

"We take care of our physical health by going in for checkups," he says. "The point is not to wait until you get sick but to keep you well." His team created the Marriage Checkup, a program he has tested twice before that's now part of a third major study being conducted through 2010. The program starts with an hour-long series of questionnaires that rate satisfaction levels on fraught topics like sex and parenting.

"We give the couples feedback, the way a doctor would from a blood test or an X-ray," Córdova says. His early studies have shown that the majority of couples have reported a significant uptick in relationship satisfaction as well as higher intimacy levels. He hopes to devise a program that can be replicated across the country, using local therapists to give the tests and feedback. In the meantime, he recommends that couples ask themselves three questions every year: Does my partner feel safe being emotionally vulnerable with me? Does my partner feel accepted? When I feel that life is yanking the rug out from under me, can I go to my partner for nonjudgmental support? Answering no to even one can signal a fraying relationship. Córdova also tells couples to avoid one very toxic behavior: withdrawal. "It's the equivalent of bingeing on Twinkies," he says. "Talk—even confused, lost, sometimes frustrating talk—is always better."

8 YOU *CAN* CHANGE YOUR SPOUSE

For more than 15 years, Richard A. Mackey, professor emeritus at Boston College's graduate school of social work, studied heterosexual couples who have been married more than 20 years but have never seen a couples therapist. He found that the long-marrieds instinctively learned not to insist their partner make big behavioral changes. They asked for tiny modifications. (For instance, instead of saying, "Can't you stop being such a slob?" or "Will you *ever* learn to pick up after yourself?" they ask, "Can you put your clothes in the hamper?")

But what surprised him—and gives hope to anyone stuck in a small house with an unrepentant slob, control freak, pack rat, *Star Wars* figurine collector—is that over two decades of asking each other for small alterations, many spouses had nudged their partners into making significant changes without alienating them. This technique was particularly effective, Mackey says, when used on men. **O**

LOVE'S DILEMMA:

It's the wish to be together forever versus the inevitability of change. Trish Deitch finds the way through.

Years ago my boyfriend Geoff and I sat on the old twin bed we'd bought from the Salvation Army, crying so hard our noses ran and shirtsleeves grew wet with tears. At 17 it had never occurred to me that I'd ever be without him, my first love. But that evening—I don't remember why—we suddenly realized that death would one day separate us. Imagining my future without Geoff felt like imagining the planet without light and air. Still, three years later, I was in love with one of my professors, and Geoff was living by himself in a tiny apartment a good mile uptown. Life is like that: unexpected, fluid, fleeting, temporary—each fraction of a second of experience fresh and vivid, but then gone, replaced by the next fraction of a second of experience. Moment by moment we meet and are met by everything new—sensations, sounds, smells, tastes, sights, textures, feelings. And they change us. And we change them.

It is only by our powers of habit, and the strength of our will, and our attachment to the things we want and don't want, love and don't love, that we create lives that seem continuous and solid, the same from day to day. But that sameness is fabricated. Look: In my 50 years, gone are the Javan tiger and the West African black rhino, the Caribbean monk seal and the Arabian ostrich; gone are the Italians from Little Italy; gone is cheap housing. My father is long dead, and so is Kevin, the boy who taught me how to ride a bicycle. Eight of my pets are dust. Nothing is left of my youth but my memories of it, and those, more and more, are dissolving like clouds in the sky. There are bags under my eyes and wrinkles around my mouth. My hair is mostly silver, and my daughter, who it seems was just being born, is now grown. We are all, as the poet Galway Kinnell put it, "forever in the pre-trembling of a house that falls."

And so, perhaps in reaction to all this change, and as if to forestall loss, we lean toward cozy lives. We gravitate toward the familiar. We grow almost insistently attached to the people we love. The very last thing I want, after all, is for my lover to leave me, to be captured by some *new thing* because he or she is vivid and fresh and I'm not. Nor do I want to chase whatever siren calls me. There's so much to be said for partnering up and making a commitment. There's so much to be said for trying to make a life with someone, even if that life will never turn out the way we plan.

So that's the dilemma: the wish to be together forever, and the inevitability of change. We need to stay aware of that dilemma because it's the truth of how things are. And staying aware of how everything—*everything*—is impermanent brings its own gift: the possibility of real love.

IF YOU'RE ANYTHING LIKE ME, you have grown so used to your mate, so sure of who they are and what they want, that you can't see them anymore. Your idea of who they are eclipses who they *really* are (though they're always changing too, and not really anyone for long), and you lose sight of them. They become like the tree outside your window or the old painting on your wall. And if you can't see them, you can't really love them.

I knew a woman who declared every Sunday a silent day. One Sunday her husband came home from the gym, having had his wallet stolen. He spent an hour freaking out, pacing in front of his silent wife, waving his arms and ranting, not only repeating the story of what had happened but providing her reaction: "I know what you'd say," he told her. "You'd say, 'It's okay—just cancel the cards and get on with your life.' But I can't—I'm angry. And I know you hate that about me. You'd say, 'What's the point of wasting time being angry—the wallet's gone....'" The woman, listening, was surprised and a bit miffed at how wrong her husband was about her. But that's what we do with the people we love: In large part, we make them up, based on past experience. We bring the past into the present, and fail to experience, in any given moment, the people we love unencumbered by our projections.

It's our wish for continuity and cohesiveness that gets in the way, and our fear of starting over every moment, as if it were the first. I knew a couple who had been married 30 years when the wife died of a heart attack. They'd seemed content enough, but after the wife died, the husband felt very guilty: His wife, it turns out, had been miserable for most of their time together. He kept asking himself why they hadn't done something early on to change that—even if it meant splitting up. But he knew why: They'd grown attached to their routines, which had quickly become ruts. And they viewed this situation as Their Life. Someday, the husband had told himself, they'd change things, break out, have fun. And then she was gone.

I have a girlfriend now, Julia—that's how much things have changed for me. Julia, who's much younger than I, was married to a man who died four years ago, in his early 30s, of a brain tumor. She and I don't talk about forever—about love being permanent—because we know that it's not. Though we love each other, we know that our inclination toward getting too attached, the way Geoff and I did, inevitably causes us pain—makes us clingy, jealous, angry, resentful, and afraid. As much as we like each other, we start to dislike each other, threatened by loss.

The trick is coming back to this moment with Julia, whoever she is right now. It's hard work, cutting off the last moment and entering this one, but when I remember to, I practice doing just that: I look at Julia as she comes toward me in the morning, and drop all my projections. There she is, unknown to me, with a cup of coffee dangling from her hand, and an armful of laundry, and she is alive and beautiful and brand-new. Most times I fall in love with her all over again. But then, whether I want to or not, I have to let her go. ◗

TO STIR, WITH LOVE

Music isn't the food of love. *Food* is (though never, ever soup or pheasant). Celia Barbour uncovers the most seductive sauce on earth.

Beef, milk, tomatoes—and a generous dash of passion—are the key ingredients of an unforgettable Bolognese.

A slice of bread can be sexy if it's handled right; toasted, for example, and spread with pale butter and honey, and brought to you in bed by a man with whom you have just spent the night. Oysters on the half shell are seldom so potent an aphrodisiac.

All too often, people confuse romantic food with elaborate food, and believe that only money, sweat, and four-star culinary skills can produce a meal good enough to win someone's heart. But romance is a delicate thing, as easily ruined by too much effort as it is by too little.

I have overreached on countless occasions. I once roasted a pheasant for a man I was greedily and desperately in love with. The bird came out of the oven tough as an old crow, and I cried through dinner, convinced that our relationship was doomed. (It was, but not because of my cooking.) Another time, I burned my fingers trying to make tortillas for a boyfriend who had to be somewhere else that evening and ate impatiently and distractedly while I dunked my singed hands in ice water.

The fact is that if someone is madly in love with you, you can serve him almost anything and he will lap it up like a cat, purring all the while. And if he isn't, no filet mignon will change his mind.

But what about the man who is not sure yet, who thinks he might be falling for you but still has one foot on the brakes? He is the one who needs seducing. And not just into bed, either—most men I know need very little arm-twisting in that department; a bucket of day-old KFC would be sufficient foreplay. No, you are only going to bother cooking a nice, romantic meal for a man who's worth hanging on to for more than one night. And that's where things get complicated, because your goal is a very subtle one: You want it to occur to him—as if by chance, as if he just happened to think of it himself—that when he's with you, everything tastes a little better; that being with you is like visiting a land where life is brighter, easier, and just a bit exotic, and to which he might want to consider relocating permanently someday.

You need to make a meal, in other words, that will leave him hungry not for sex but for you.

If only there were a single, surefire recipe. But food is a deeply personal thing, and the first home-cooked meal you prepare for a man is, among other things, a key to your idiosyncrasies, and a map to the kind of relationship you want to be in. If you serve your grandmother's brisket, for example, it sends a message that you are thoroughly wrapped up in your own family and would like him to become enmeshed in it, too. If you serve something challenging like calves brains, it announces that you plan to change him—or else. If you serve pheasant...well, let's just agree that you should not, under any circumstances, serve pheasant.

Indeed, there is only one thing I know of that can kill a budding relationship faster than pheasant, and that is soup. Many years ago, I developed a woozy kind of crush on a man who worked in the office next door. He had his eye on me, too, and one night, wonder of wonders, he invited me to a show. The following week we went to a movie. After that, he took me out to dinner, and the very next night, to another, nicer dinner. Everything was progressing swimmingly: The evenings ended with kisses that grew in duration and passion, but nothing more.

A few days later, he called. I was home, making soup. He missed me, he said, and wanted to see me—right away, please, and was I free? I said, "Sure, come on over; I'm cooking dinner." I had a feeling after we hung up that this was *it:* Things were about to heat up. I was excited, scared, happy. I showered, brushed my hair, and put on lip gloss. I made myself look nice, in an offhand, sexily-at-home sort of way.

The buzzer rang. I opened the door. We kissed hello, smiling. And then he sniffed the air. "What are you making?" he asked. "Soup," I said.

"Huh," he said, a scowl creeping across his face. "What kind?"

"Vegetable?" I said, starting to feel the evening sinking away. "It's good. Really. You'll like it."

"Uh, okay," he said. He ate the soup quickly and did not have seconds. Our conversation was terse and awkward. He left shortly after dinner. A few days later, he called and left a message on my answering machine. "Look," he said, "I like you and everything, I do. But I think you're more serious about me than I am about you. I mean, I'm not ready to get into a committed relationship just yet, and, um, so, well...thanks for everything! Oh, yeah, and thanks for dinner the other night. See you around."

For a moment, I debated calling him back and shouting: "It was just *soup*! It didn't mean anything!" But I was too irritated to bother. Besides, it did mean something. Food always does. In this case, it meant (to him, anyway) that I was auditioning for the role of Mom. He wasn't interested.

Fortunately, I began to wise up. For one thing, I got to know my neighbors Julie and Kevin. Julie was achingly beautiful, and Kevin was the lead singer in a rock 'n' roll band. One afternoon, I stopped by their apartment on my way home from work and

YOU NEED TO LEAVE HIM HUNGRY NOT FOR SEX BUT FOR YOU.

found Julie standing over her stove, cooking something that smelled better than anything I'd ever smelled before. She told me it was Bolognese sauce, and that she made it only once a year, for Kevin's birthday. "It takes a whole day to cook," she said. "He gets it only on special occasions."

Just then Kevin burst through the door looking ravenous, eyeing the sauce, eyeing Julie. I quickly excused myself, but not before coming to two important conclusions: one, that I would learn to make Bolognese sauce, and two, that I would find a man worth cooking it for, preferably in that order.

AND, LO AND BEHOLD, I did. Peter and I were barely an hour into our first date when I realized that he might warrant a day at the stove. But there was no hurry. No, I was going to wait, take it easy, order takeout. In fact, the first home-cooked meal we ate was made not by me but by him, on the tiny stove in his 400-square-foot apartment.

Still I bided my time. We ate bread and cheese and apricots in bed in the middle of the night. We ate eggs in the morning, or toast with butter and honey. Summer turned to fall and the weather grew cool. At last, one bright morning I took down my cutting board and began to cut some onions. I chopped two carrots in tiny pieces, and two stalks of celery just the same. I put them in my heavy, red Dutch oven and lit the stove. The Bolognese was underway. All day it simmered, filling the apartment with its warm, rich aroma. At 7 o'clock, Peter whistled up to me from the park across the street. I waved to him out my kitchen window.

"Wow," he said, coming through the door a minute later. "It smells amazing in here. What's for dinner?"

I shrugged. "Pasta," I said casually. He looked at me sideways, as if to say, *Hey, wait a minute—pasta never smelled like this back on my planet.* I just smiled mysteriously, set the table, tossed the salad. And then we sat down to the dinner that I had made just for him—just for us—and I don't remember a single bite of it. I am certain, however, that it was delicious. Of course it was. We had fallen in love. **◑**

BOLOGNESE SAUCE

This sauce takes a lot of time—it should simmer for four to five hours—but it does not require much skill or effort. Once the vegetables are chopped, all that's left to do is add ingredients and stir. This gives you plenty of time to shower, tidy up your house, and do whatever else you need to do to prepare for your dinner guest.

1 medium onion
1 large or 2 small carrots
2 to 3 stalks celery
1 ounce pancetta, very finely chopped
1 pound ground beef (not lean)
1 tsp. salt
⅛ tsp. freshly ground pepper
Pinch allspice
1 cup whole milk
1 cup dry white wine
1 (15-ounce) can diced tomatoes with their juice
1 pound pasta, such as rigatoni
Parmigiano-Reggiano cheese, for grating

1 Finely chop onion, carrot, and celery. In a heavy-bottomed saucepan or Dutch oven over low heat, cook pancetta until all fat is rendered and pancetta is just beginning to brown. Add chopped vegetables, raise heat to medium, and cook, stirring frequently, until onion is translucent and soft.

2 Add ground beef, breaking it up with a spoon, ¼ tsp. (to start) salt, plus pepper and allspice. Cook until meat is brown.

3 Add milk. When it begins to simmer, reduce heat to low and cook at a gentle simmer, stirring occasionally until milk has mostly boiled away, about 30 minutes. Add white wine and cook as with milk, until it has mostly boiled away. Add tomatoes and juice; bring to a simmer. Cover pot, reduce heat to low, and allow sauce to cook very gently at barest simmer, 2½ to 3 hours. Season to taste with remaining salt.

4 Just before sauce is done, bring a pot of water to boil, salt it generously, and boil pasta according to package directions. Drain, mix with a third of sauce, then serve with remaining sauce on top with lots of grated Parmigiano cheese. *Makes 4 cups sauce.*

Her funny valentine: The author rethinks romance.

LISA KOGAN TELLS ALL

Some couples will always have Paris; some hit the occasional iceberg. Our ever-loving columnist goes in search of *real* romance.

Ever hear the one about the guy who had peachy-pink peonies imported from Chile every February? Apparently, he wanted to guarantee his sweetheart a touch of spring each morning. Then there's that story of the man who kept his wife's kindergarten picture in his wallet, because they met on the first day of school and (even after 66 years together) that photo never failed to make him smile. Oh, and let's not forget my personal favorite: This one involves a woman who thought her boyfriend was taking her for a weekend in East Hampton. Work was high-stress and they were both pretty beat. "You know what? I don't feel like driving," the man said casually. "Let's head for LaGuardia and catch a puddle jumper." But as they approached the airport, he announced a little change of plans. "You'll be needing this," he said, and put a passport in her hand. The very surprised woman and her boyfriend didn't go to the Hamptons that weekend. Instead, he jetted her off to Paris, and there, in the courtyard of the Louvre, he got down on one knee and proposed.

All three stories sound like urban boyfriend legends. But Peony Guy does exist—he colors my hair. And yes, Virginia, somewhere outside Tucson there lives a 71-year-old gentleman who is still madly in love with the girl who taught him to hopscotch. As for Mr. Ooh-La-La, I saw the engagement ring with my own two eyes and—so help me God—that diamond was bigger than my high school.

When I recount the tale of my friend's Parisian proposal to Johannes (a.k.a. the father of my child, the love of my life), there is a thoughtful pause. I know he must be doing what I did—picturing the giddy hand-in-hand walk along the Seine, the caviar on toast points at dinner, Notre Dame glowing against a blanket of stars in the night sky. I sigh. He sighs: "Hey, do you remember the time I went out and bought the stuff that turned the water in your toilet that cool ocean blue color?" "Yeah, honey," I said. "I remember."

I am a sensible woman. I keep Bactine in my medicine chest, an umbrella in my office, $200 in my sock drawer. I'd sooner remove my own spleen with a grapefruit spoon than buy a set of sheets that require ironing. I believe in practical shoes, low-maintenance hair, and whichever frozen peas happen to be on sale. I'm not entirely sure what a bodice is, but I can tell you that I don't want mine ripped. Still, I can't help feeling that there's something to be said for moons and Junes and Ferris wheels. I believe in the power of marabou, the brothers Gershwin, bubble baths in claw-footed tubs surrounded by a bazillion twinkly white candles. I believe in strawberries coated in dark chocolate and raspberries floating in pink Champagne. I'm glad Victoria has a few secrets. I think fireplaces should be lit, compliments should be paid, *La Bohème* should be sung, legs should be shaved. I want Lassie to come home, I want Ali MacGraw to live, and I want Gene Kelly to dip Cyd Charisse straight into next Thursday. I'm not proud of this, but in the interest of full disclosure, here it is: I am deeply relieved when Tom Hanks and Meg Ryan finally kiss. My name is Lisa, and I am a romantic.

THE TRUTH IS that I fell for someone who prefers a blue toilet bowl to, oh, I don't know, let's say Wuthering Heights. Here is the worst (and by far the stupidest) fight Johannes and I ever had:

J: What are you reading about?

L: Ida and Isidor Straus. They were an amazing couple! Instead of getting into the lifeboat, she decided to die with her husband on the Titanic. Of course, if Julia were grown, I'd do the same for you.

J: What do you mean?

L: What do you mean, what do I mean?

J: You're not getting in the lifeboat?

L: No, I love you too much to let you drown all by yourself.

J: But I won't be by myself—I think they were playing poker and getting drunk.

L: So you're saying that you'd rather play poker with John Jacob Astor than cuddle with me?

J: That's not what I'd be doing, because if you're not getting your ass into that lifeboat, then I am. We are not leaving an empty seat.

L: Oh, you're getting into that boat over my dead body.

J: Where the hell is the Tylenol?

L: Try the bathroom...you know, the place with the ocean blue toilet water.

J: You mean like the ocean you want both of us to sink to the bottom of?

Things kind of spiraled downward from there, and I still break into a cold sweat every time Céline Dion starts wailing about how her heart will go on.

SO JOHANNES and I won't be taking a cruise together anytime soon. And no, those weren't his arms around me as I perched on a dune watching the sun come up over the Sea of Galilee; he wasn't the man who sent me a basket of French damson plums or the one who wanted all babies to have my nose. The slow dances are few and far between these days, and walks in the rain usually involve him running up ahead with the stroller. But he did teach me how to fly a kite last summer, and we have been known to share steamed dumplings in a little East Village dive he discovered a few years back, and sometimes early in the morning I overhear him playing "tea party" with our daughter, and sometimes late at night I overhear him playing Blackbird with his guitar. He has genuine integrity, he has serious style, and he's pulled me through more than one bout of the stomach flu. Anybody can sprinkle rose petals across a big brass bed, but only a real man will hold your hair while you're throwing up.

Now, there are those who will say that references to intense nausea don't belong in a column about romance, but I'm thinking maybe it's time we broaden our definition of what constitutes romance. Ask yourself this:

When the man you love realizes that half the screws are missing from the Ikea bookcase he's attempting to assemble for you, does he:

(a) Complain bitterly about herring and Volvos—vowing to forsake all things Swedish for the rest of his natural days?

(b) Leave the shelving in a heap on the living room floor and question your need to read in the first place?

(c) Complete construction using a combination of rubber bands and Krazy Glue while suggesting you fill the thing with pamphlets rather than actual books?

If you answered c, then, my friend, life is good—because it means somebody out there loves you enough to try to get your bookcase together. That creative effort is the kind of everyday gesture on which great romances are built. I wouldn't be surprised to hear that while at the drugstore picking up the amulet of poison, Romeo also picked up a copy of *People* for Juliet. I like to imagine Abelard taping *Grey's Anatomy* for Heloise. I bet a day didn't go by that Mel Brooks wasn't funny for Anne Bancroft.

Don't get me wrong, I'll always want the chubby little cupids and coconut bonbons, but lately I find myself drawn to something richer, deeper, sweeter. Provided nobody decides to do a remake of *Titanic,* with Johannes each day is Valentine's Day. ⬤

LOVE TRAPS 101

How did you find him, the guy who pushes all your wrong buttons? Liesl Schillinger reports on an amazingly effective new therapy that just might transform what we think about when we think about love.

Not long ago, Jeffrey E. Young, PhD, a cognitive psychologist and clinical researcher at Columbia University Medical Center, met with a couple in crisis. The woman, let's call her Chloe, was brutally critical of her boyfriend, let's call him Dan. She thought Dan's teeth were ugly and wanted him to get them whitened; she thought his back was too hairy and complained that he wouldn't get regular waxing. It sent her into a rage when he was a few minutes late to pick her up on dates, even though Dan lived an hour away and traffic made exact arrival times nearly impossible. As Chloe continued with her onslaught, Young realized that Dan agreed with Chloe: Dan believed himself to be horribly flawed and thought Chloe was right to be angry with him. Although she was terribly critical of Dan, Young noted, Chloe loved him and was terrified of losing him.

If Young had been a Freudian therapist, he might have encouraged Dan and Chloe to speculate on the painful effect of childhood problems without suggesting specific ways to change their behavior. But Young began his career in the early '80s as a new therapy was gaining popularity—cognitive therapy, which teaches that how people think about events in their lives determines how they feel about them. Young, who studied with the man behind the therapy, Aaron T. Beck, was excited to be a part of a dynamic new method. But early on, he found that this approach alone was not enough to help clients with lifelong relationship troubles. "It was fine with people who'd been healthy and had problems only recently, but the majority of patients had problems that stemmed from their early life, and those people didn't respond well," he says.

Young began to spot a number of distinct, recurring patterns in his patients' psychological profiles—patterns laid down in early childhood that continued to shape their adult thoughts, actions, relationships, careers, and life choices. He called these habits "schemas," borrowing the ancient Greek word for "form," and he nicknamed them "lifetraps" to make it easier for his clients to understand both the concept and the risk of letting their schemas define them.

ALTHOUGH SCHEMA THERAPY BEGAN as an individual therapeutic strategy, it quickly turned into a couples therapy technique. "More than half the people we saw were coming in with problems with their relationship," Young says. "We thought, *What if we got the partner in?* Once we did, we began to notice there was an interplay between them that was creating problems. One partner's schema would trigger the other's schema, and tensions would escalate." Some of the schemas dovetail—in a catastrophic way—each exacerbating the other. In fact, Young says, head-over-heels romantic attraction is often a sign of bad schema chemistry.

Young suspected that Dan suffered from the Defectiveness schema, which means that, when he was a child, his peers or family put him down, criticized him, and made him feel inferior. By asking questions in further sessions, he learned that Dan's mother favored his older brother and his father told him he was incompetent.

Chloe, on the other hand, was plagued by Unrelenting Standards. As a child, her family made her feel that, unless she was completely above reproach, she was a total failure. These are two of the 18 schemas Young has identified; a person may be affected or defined by any number of schemas—just as in astrology, people speak of an Aries who has a Cancer moon and Virgo rising. For instance, a patient may have the core schema of Emotional Deprivation, and also be affected by the Abandonment and Self-Sacrifice schemas (for a quiz on common schemas, see page 176).

Young's work has a curious parallel with recent developments in the field of interpersonal neurobiology, which suggest that our personal relationships affect the way the mind builds neural pathways. Your emotional memories—of a parent you adored or feared, of a partner you loved or lost—create pathways in the limbic part of the brain. Every time you revisit those memories, positive or negative, you reinforce the path, deepening a trench of emotional connection. Throughout life, your unconscious mind embraces any new person who reminds you of those older paths. They exert an almost irresistible pull, compelling you to make decisions that feel like choices but are actually automatic responses guided by the map of your past: It's like a ghost road that lures in passersby. "We think what we call schemas are really what some people call neural pathways," Young says. People who want healthy relationships but have a history of unhealthy ones must work hard to resist the pull of habit and strike out along new pathways, literally and figuratively.

Young's first step is to help his patients recognize that they have schemas: "They've affected their view of everything," says Young. "But they don't see that there's anything wrong with the way they look at the world." He began by asking Chloe about her parents. She described them as high-level professionals who had been extremely critical of her. If she came home with an A- instead of an A+, for instance, her mother would withdraw her affection for a week, withholding kisses and kindness.

"I tried to get Chloe to remember what it felt like when her mother would withdraw from her, and to remember how bad she felt about herself," Young says. As an adult, Chloe remained stuck in her schema, clinging stubbornly to her childhood fear that if she or anyone she was associated with was less than perfect, she would be a disappointment. Young knew that she had internalized her parents' harsh judgments and was not aware they weren't her own. His questions helped her make the connection that the way her mother hurt her was the way she hurt the men in her life—at which point, Chloe

got it, saying, "I don't want to make Dan feel the way I felt."

Young also helped Dan realize that he was repeating his unhappy childhood cycle with Chloe: trying to prove that he was good enough. Young spent the next several sessions helping Chloe and Dan understand that when they upset each other, it was not out of deliberate cruelty but often because one partner had set off the other's core schemas.

"Chloe had to become more aware of when her Unrelenting Standards were being triggered, making her critical and mean," Young says. "Dan had to become aware of when he was starting to feel inadequate and trying to prove himself to her." When a fight began to escalate, Young instructed, they should say out loud, "Schema clash!"—as unnatural as it might feel—and then call a time-out. They should retreat into separate rooms, and read through a flash card to remind them of the havoc their schemas were trying to unleash (Young helps couples create a variety of notes, tailored to common issues of discord—arguments over money or parenting, for example). A card for Chloe might read in part:

Even though I feel as if my criticisms are valid, it's almost certain that I'm being much too hard on Dan and too judgmental, the same way my mother was with me. Therefore I need to let up on him, stop criticizing him, and apologize for what I did.

Young admits this technique can seem awkward in the beginning. As therapy progresses and communication improves, the flash cards can be left behind. "Eventually, the partners catch their pattern much more quickly, and they don't have to have time-outs," Young says. They can head off the conflict before it arises. "When therapy is successful, it doesn't mean the schema inside each person isn't being triggered," he says. "But they learn that they don't need to let it out." As patients come to recognize their schemas, they realize that, although they are not entirely to blame for their strong feelings, they are responsible for learning to control them better.

SCHEMA THERAPY SAVED CHLOE AND DAN'S RELATIONSHIP. "We have a very high success rate with couples like this," Young says. Both partners genuinely wanted to change, and, still more important, both of them were willing to accept the idea that there was something wrong with their behavior. (Young estimates schema therapy succeeds with about 70 percent of couples he and his colleagues see.)

Those who have benefited from schema therapy have one thing in common: They felt the thrill and relief of learning that there was a name for the impulses that had directed their actions for so long. They could see there was a more accurate explanation for the unhealthy patterns in their lives and relationships than the one they'd been telling themselves. They stepped back from their lifetraps and studied the map of their behavior. And slowly, but perseveringly, they dared to set out on a different course, with a new understanding not only of the direction they wanted to take but of themselves. **O**

To find a schema therapist, e-mail institute@schematherapy.com.

THE GRAND SCHEMA OF THINGS

The test here evaluates the schemas Jeffrey E. Young sees most often. To find out if any apply to you, choose the most accurate reading from 1 to 6 that describes you and write the number on the line provided. For info on the other ten schemas, go to oprah.com/omagextras.

1 = Completely untrue of me
2 = Mostly untrue of me
3 = Slightly more true than untrue
4 = Moderately true of me
5 = Mostly true of me
6 = Describes me perfectly

1_____ Most of the time, I haven't had someone to nurture me, share him/herself with me, or care deeply about everything that happens to me.

2 _____ For much of my life, I haven't felt that I am special to someone.

3 _____ For the most part, I have not had someone who really listens to me, understands me, or is tuned in to my true needs and feelings.

4 _____ I hate to be constrained or kept from doing what I want.

5 _____ I feel that I shouldn't have to follow the normal rules and conventions other people do.

6 _____ I can't tolerate other people telling me what to do.

7 _____ I find myself clinging to people I'm close to, because I'm afraid they'll leave me.

8 _____ I don't feel that important relationships will last; I expect them to end.

9 _____ I feel addicted to partners who can't be there for me in a committed way.

10 _____ I'm unworthy of the love, attention, and respect of others.

11 _____ I am inherently flawed and defective.

12_____ No matter how hard I try, I feel that I won't be able to get a significant man/woman to respect me or feel that I am worthwhile.

13_____ In relationships, I let the other person have the upper hand.

14_____ I worry a lot about pleasing other people so they won't reject me.

15_____ I will go to much greater lengths than most people to avoid confrontations.

16_____ I must be the best at most of what I do; I can't accept second best.

17_____ I feel there is constant pressure for me to achieve and get things done.

18_____ My relationships suffer because I push myself so hard.

19_____ I feel that I cannot let my guard down in the presence of other people, or else they will intentionally hurt me.

20 _____ I have a great deal of difficulty trusting people.

21_____ If someone acts nicely toward me, I assume that he/she must be after something.

22 _____ I put others' needs before my own, or else I feel guilty.

23 _____ I'm the one who usually ends up taking care of the people I'm close to.

24 _____ I'm only happy when those around me are happy.

Numbers 1 to 3 are indicators for Emotional Deprivation; 4 to 6, Entitlement; 7 to 9, Abandonment; 10 to 12, Defectiveness; 13 to 15, Subjugation; 16 to 18, Unrelenting Standards; 19 to 21, Mistrust/Abuse; and 22 to 24, Self-Sacrifice.

SCORING
3–8: Low; this schema probably does not apply to you
9–11: Medium; this schema may have some relevance to you
12–13: High; this schema is probably very significant to you
14–18: Very high; this is likely one of your core schemas

In schema therapy, some combinations feed into each other, constantly triggering tensions within the relationship. Young calls these the worst matches:
• Abandonment and Subjugation
• Unrelenting Standards and Approval Seeking
• Self-Sacrifice and Entitlement
• Defectiveness and Punitiveness
• Subjugation and Enmeshment
• Emotional Deprivation and Emotional Inhibition

DR. PHIL: "HE'S GIVING YOU EVERY SIGNAL IN THE WORLD HE'S NOT INTERESTED"

Philip C. McGraw, PhD: A woman is stuck in a dead-end affair and a marriage is stalled.

Q. I've been dating a guy for the past two years. He says he really likes me but isn't ready for a commitment. We see each other every week, often for overnight stays, but sometimes he doesn't answer my calls or want to talk to me. I believe we're meant to be together and that maybe he's just scared of being with a good woman. When I tell him I love him, occasionally he says the same, but most of the time he says, "Thank you." I know I should probably call it quits, but I've grown to accept the way he treats me. Do you think I should continue in this relationship?

DR. PHIL: Did you ever hear the old saying "There's a sucker born every minute"? You need to recognize that this guy thinks of you as nothing more than a fling. He doesn't answer your calls or want to talk because he's probably with someone else. When you say "I love you" and he says "Thank you," he's thinking, *Oh, great, here she goes again. Beam me up, Scotty, and get me out of here. This is so awkward. Why won't she take the hint already?*

You say that maybe he's scared of being with a good woman, but you're just making excuses for him. Even if that were true, let's take that statement at face value: A man who's afraid of being with a good woman has a pretty major flaw. Forgiving his behavior tells me you have so little self-esteem that you have been not only settling for this but trying to rationalize it so you can *continue* to settle for it. No one with any dignity would say "I've grown to accept" such lousy

treatment. So you need to ask yourself why you're putting up with it, and why you don't seem to think you're worth more.

If you want to date him casually, then go ahead and keep sleeping together—with the understanding that it will happen only when it's handy for him. But don't kid yourself that you two are "meant to be." He's giving you every signal in the world that he's not interested in the long haul. If you're looking for a committed relationship, end it with this guy before you finish reading this sentence.

Q. My husband and I have been together for eight years. One day, out of the blue, he told me he wanted us to separate because I'm not affectionate enough. When we went out in public, he needed us to hold hands; every time he'd come home, I was supposed to kiss him; whenever we hung up the phone, he had to hear "I love you." He also said he wanted more sex (about every other day). At first I begged him to stay, so he gave me a chance. But now I cringe whenever he touches me. He calls me at work to talk about nothing. When I'm home, he has to be in the same room. I feel smothered and am starting to regret wanting him back. I do love him, but he's worse than my kids in terms of neediness. The thought of losing him was scary because I felt I needed a man around and I wanted to be married—but lately, I don't want to bother anymore. It seems to me I shouldn't have to try so hard.

DR. PHIL: It's possible that you're resentful because you feel overwhelming pressure to be affectionate on your husband's terms. Alternatively—and this is the subject you need to examine—you may not have the kinds of feelings that are the foundation of a marriage. Two people who are in love typically want to touch base during the day and have physical contact in public or private. In my opinion, you're resisting appropriate levels of intimacy.

Only you can determine what the problem is, but it seems to me there's enough confusion here that you're probably not ready to end the relationship without doing some more work. I don't think you should stay out of fear, but I also don't think you should quit until you've thought through some questions:

■ Why did I marry this man in the first place? Obviously, I was attracted to him at one point. What drew me to him, and what dreams did he fulfill in me?

■ Has something shifted since then? Have I changed, has he changed, or have we changed as a couple? What's missing? Are these things fixable?

■ Does he know with certainty what my wants and needs are? Have I been clear about what I require from him?

■ What can I do to give this relationship a chance to breathe?

After thinking carefully about where you are, you might then consider going to counseling before making a decision about whether it's time to bail. **O**

LOVE AT LAST

Whether you're 35 or 75, it's never too late to fall madly (or gently and even sacredly) in love. Just ask actress Ellen Burstyn and a host of other women who found themselves in the heat of romance when they least expected it. Sara Davidson reports.

My mother met the love of her life when she was 84. A widow for nine years, she spotted Harold Lapidus, a retired doctor, standing alone at a bridge club. She asked if he wanted to play, and they became inseparable.

"He's a younger man," she told me.

"How young?" I asked.

"Oh...," she said. "I think he's 80."

They're still devoted to each other as my mother moves into her 90s, which fills me with awe. But do I have to wait that long?

I've been unattached for seven years and have become very good at it. I love my house, my work, and my kids, and every day I'm grateful for good health and what I see as a fortunate life. But sometimes I ache for a partner to check in with, talk, snuggle, and grow spiritually with. I'm afraid that in my 60s, after two divorces, such love may be behind me, as the pickings get slimmer every year. When I go to parties or events, there are 13 single women and one single guy, and he's usually gay.

This depresses me, and I wonder if my mother's experience was a fluke. But during the past month, I've talked to a dozen women, ranging from their late 40s to their 90s, who've found deep love—a soul mate—long after they thought that was possible.

Ellen Burstyn was alone for 25 years before she fell in love, at 71, with the man with whom she now lives, who is 23 years younger. Jane Fonda, 69, recently started a relationship with Lynden Gillis, 75, a retired management consultant, and wants to make a "sexy erotic movie about people over 70."

As I listened to these stories, I felt...hope. And I wanted to explore whether this kind of love happens because of luck, karma, or accident, or if there are interior changes one can make or steps one can take to connect with a partner at any age.

What surprised me was that the women's stories were remarkably similar. All had been afraid they were too old. They all relished their independence and had come to terms with the fact that they might never find another mate. At the same time, they'd done inner work that enabled them to feel worthy of love, ready to accept a man as he is and be accepted unconditionally by him.

Most see their relationship as a spiritual practice, an opportunity to work on hurtful patterns and expand their capacity to forgive. There's less drama, they report, and more peace. Each woman feels her current partner is her *beshert*—Yiddish for "destined mate"—and that all her experiences, past relationships, and heartbreak were necessary to prepare her for this union.

LESSON 1: MAKE FRIENDS WITH SOLITUDE

For 25 years, Ellen Burstyn did not go out on a date.

Why not?

"Nobody asked me," she says.

I find that hard to believe, I say. "In 25 years, weren't you attracted to a man, or pursued by one?"

"I was busy living my life," she says. She worked constantly around the world, won an Oscar for *Alice Doesn't Live Here Anymore,* and was nominated for five other films. She enjoyed being with her son, Jefferson, her friends, and her animals. Every so often, she would look around and think, *Where are all the men?* "I thought it would be great to go home and curl up in someone's lap after a job, but I didn't sit around crying about it. I made a friend of solitude," Ellen says.

But this ease took her decades to attain. In her 20s, she'd been "promiscuous," she says. "I'd gone from man to man since puberty and had three marriages that were all painful and ended in divorce." She knew she had to heal the wounds that kept her repeating the same pattern with men, "so that aspect of myself closed up shop. I think I built an invisible shield that no one could penetrate."

She worked with a therapist, studied Sufism, and reconnected with her Christian roots, which she describes in her book, *Lessons in Becoming Myself.* When she finally believed she knew how to "do it right—attract a man who would treat me well and whom I could love"—she feared it was too late. On a whim, she asked a woman friend if she knew a man who might be suitable.

"I'll have to think about that," the woman said.

Shortly afterward, this same woman was approached by a Greek actor who had auditioned for Ellen at the Actors Studio when he was 25 and she was 48. He confessed to Ellen's friend that he'd been in love with her for the 23 years since they'd met.

"What?!" Ellen said, when the message was relayed. The Greek kid? But he was 48 now, attractive and a successful acting teacher. (She won't disclose his name.) He sent her an e-mail, which she answered, guardedly. He wrote back, "I don't see the word *no* in this."

They've been together for three years, living in her house on the Hudson River in New York. She says it's been an easy fit, "which is startling because he's from a different culture and a different generation." One reason for that may be her new approach. "Most of my life, if a man did something totally other than the way I thought it should be done, I would try to correct him. Now I say, 'Oh, isn't that interesting? You do that differently than I do.' It's the biggest thing I've learned. It allows for a stress-free relationship."

Ellen's greatest challenge has been working with her fear of abandonment. "I had so much anxiety in my former relationships—I was scared of losing men, all of them." She believes there are patterns we can work on only in a relationship, and this is one of them. "Right now, he's in Greece, teaching, and that brings up anxiety. *He's away—what will happen? Somebody else will grab him!* I have to see that and keep releasing those thoughts."

LESSON 2: BE OPEN TO REUNIONS

As I get older, I hear more frequently about people who fall in love again with boyfriends from the past. This strikes me as auspicious: You already know the person, and presumably you've attained more wisdom to make the relationship work.

Marta Vago, an executive coach in Santa Monica, California, was 62 when she received an e-mail from her first love, Stephen Manes, whom she'd started dating the summer she was 14, after meeting him at a piano master class in Vermont. She and Stephen were a couple for three years, parting when she was 17 and he was 21.

Forty-six years later, Stephen wrote to Marta saying that his wife of 43 years had died of cancer, he was coming to Los Angeles to rehearse with his chamber music trio, and could he take her out to lunch? Curious and amused, Marta suggested that he come to her house and she'd order in sushi: "I want to hear you play."

Marta lives in a cottage filled with art and antiques. Her piano is in her bedroom, so after lunch, Stephen played a Beethoven sonata while she sat on the bed. "It was exactly how it had been when I would visit him at his apartment near Juilliard," she says. "He would play, and I would sit on the bed. In some ways it felt as if no time had passed, and in some ways I was with a stranger."

They'd been apart all their working lives. Stephen had pursued one calling—performing and teaching music—and he'd loved only two women: Marta and his wife. Marta had left music, earned a PhD in psychology, and lived with different men, sometimes marrying them and sometimes not.

In 2006 she'd been alone for five years when she traveled to Budapest and found the city alive with culture and vibrant people. "I thought, *If I'm not married or engaged by my next birthday, I'm going to retire in Budapest,*" she recalls. "That statement told me that I really wanted to be married, and if I wasn't, I would make a big change in my life."

She hired a matchmaker, who arranged a few dates that fizzled.

The matchmaker told her: "My dear, you look too old. That's not gonna fly." Because Marta coached executives, she'd always worn her hair severely short and dressed in "scary-looking suits." By the time Stephen's e-mail arrived, she'd ditched the suits and let her hair grow out soft and curly. Five months after their reunion, she and Stephen were engaged.

While Marta's teenage love had made the first move, Sally Grounds, 72, set things in motion at her 50th high school reunion. Sally had run with the most popular girls and football players at University High in Los Angeles. At the reunion, Sally, who's 5'1", spotted a man who was 6'5", trim, strong, and tan as a surfer—Gene Grounds. He *was* a surfer, and also a banker, who had flown in from Hawaii.

Sally went up to him and asked, "Do you remember me?"

"Of course," Gene said. He'd asked her out once, for grad night, and had been nervous she'd say no because he didn't belong to her crowd. Sally remembers Gene as "kind of intellectual, and he wore braces." But at the reunion, Gene, at 71, was a standout. "All the other men had potbellies," Sally says.

In January of this year, Sally closed up her home in Palm Desert, California, and flew to Honolulu, carrying two suitcases. "I felt like a war bride," she recalls. Gene was barefoot when he picked her up at the airport and placed a lei around her neck. They'd spent a few months getting to know each other, sailing on his trimaran and visiting each other's homes; then he proposed.

Sally and Gene hadn't been in love before, but they had much in common now: Both had lost their spouses to illness, and they shared a zest for adventure and hunger for spiritual fulfillment.

When she moved into Gene's house, where his 39-year-old son and new wife (who happens to be my niece) live in an upstairs suite, Sally started to cry. She'd known the house was a bachelor pad, but now she had to learn to live in it. Gene and his son Daniel surf ten-foot waves and do long-distance swims between the islands. They had surfboards on the walls, and a boat in the garage, along with mountains of boxes filled with junk, Sally says. The paint was peeling, the bathrooms were moldy, and cockroaches were on parade. As Daniel put it, "We had a roof over our heads. A dead gecko in the closet? Whatever. My dad said he'd rather live with dirt than use chemical cleaning products."

Sally put on rubber gloves and went through the house with Clorox. Slowly, she's been sorting and discarding boxes—"I had to fight for space," she says—painting walls and, with Gene's help, picking out fabrics to reupholster the furniture. "I gave up my perfect little house in the desert, my friends, my style of living," she says. "But I would do anything to be with Gene. I've never loved anybody like this and never thought I could. I feel such a bond because we went to school together, and we can really communicate. You know how very few men can communicate? This one tells you everything."

Sally's lifelong passion has been dancing, and she's always been afraid of the water. Now she's learning to swim, and Gene is learning to dance. They pray together daily and attend church meetings. "Are we soul mates?" Sally asks. Gene answers: "Yes."

LESSON 3: SAY YOUR PRAYERS

Well, what is a soul mate? Not someone who's identical to you, I've found, but a partner with whom you share values and a commitment to bring out the highest good in each other. As Ellen Burstyn puts it, "There's a coupling of two people's development into one path—so his development is as important to me as my own."

Two of the women I met prayed for such a partner. Verlean

Holland, 65, who lives in the Bronx, New York, lay down on her bed one night and said out loud: "Lord, I am *sooo* lonely. Please send me someone who will love me just for me, and I will love him for himself." She prayed for a husband who shared her faith and "could go to church with me. That's what I wanted most."

The answer to her prayers was right under her nose. Verlean had been alone for 13 years, but she was always busy with her work for the board of education, her church, and her grandchildren. But in 2003, because of budget cuts, she lost her job testing vision and hearing in special ed children. That's when she began to feel lonely.

Around the same time, a man in her extended circle, Rodney Holland, called "Pop" by friends and family, lost his son in a car crash. Pop had befriended Verlean's youngest son, Tyrone, when her second oldest son was killed in a shooting. Pop, a retired postal worker, came to Verlean's house on Thanksgiving and New Year's, but she paid him no attention. "He was a friend of my baby's," she explains. Her friends teased her: "That man likes you." Verlean would say, "No, he don't."

On New Year's Eve 2003, Verlean, her son, and Pop went to church and then a party. Verlean couldn't stand the loud rap music, so Pop escorted her home. Then he started calling and taking her to the movies. After a few weeks, he said, "We're too old to be dating. I want a wife, not a girlfriend."

Did you accept right away? I ask.

"Oh, yes, I wasn't going to let him get away," Verlean says. "Looking back, it was like a cake that had to be baked up. The man knew me, and I knew who he was. I liked his gentleness, and he treated me with high respect."

At their church wedding, all their offspring and siblings walked down the aisle. Pop moved into Verlean's apartment, "and that was the worst part," she says. "That first year was *haaaard*. I'm used to doing things my way. I'm used to cleaning and picking up; he doesn't clean and pick up. He likes to watch TV; I don't," she says. "Then I realized: I love him a lot, and he loves me a lot. Let me accept him the way he is—that's what I asked for. Stop screaming about little things and just adapt."

They set up a day room for Pop with his TV, "and I have my own room where I can pray and listen to gospel music," Verlean says. She's grateful to have someone "to grow old with. I escort him to the doctor and he escorts me. And we go to church together. I like to dress up, but at first he was casual. I told him, 'A man needs to be in a suit on Sunday.'"

Donna Zerner, who lives in Boulder, Colorado, also prayed for a spiritual partner. In 2003 when I met Donna, an editor in her 40s, she said she'd never been in love and didn't think it was possible. She had dated men but never felt she could be all she was or give herself completely to the relationship. She thought she might be "perpetually single" because she felt flawed. She also suspected that what other people call "being in love" was an illusion and that

As long as we both shall love: Sally Merrill, 71, and Gene Grounds, 71.

Marta Vago, 63, and Stephen Manes, 67.

Alice Davidson, 90, and Harold Lapidus, 85.

eventually they'd get their hearts broken. Despite these thoughts, she was still trying to find a "beautiful, healthy relationship."

On New Year's Eve 2005, Donna and I made a list of the qualities we desired in a mate. "Jewish" was at the top of her list. She's a leader in the Jewish Renewal community and founded the Kosher Hams, a Jewish comedy improv troupe that performs at services and conferences. She had dated only men who were Jewish and couldn't imagine sharing life with someone who wasn't.

Not long after drawing up the list, Donna went to a multifaith conference. She found a chair beside David Frenette, who she thought was the "cutest guy in the room." During the three-day conference, they sat together, talked, and went for a walk. David invited her to a movie, and "by the second date, we realized something amazing was going on," Donna says. They seemed a perfect match: They made each other laugh, they liked the same books and films, they both craved solitude, neither drank alcohol, and both are gluten intolerant. It was perfect, except...David wasn't Jewish. He was a Christian spiritual counselor who'd lived like a monk for 12 years. It was his intense spiritual devotion that made their union possible.

"He was much more interested in and open to Judaism than any of the Jewish guys I'd dated," Donna says. She brought him to Jewish Renewal services, which he loved. "And I became interested in his path of contemplative Christianity," she says. They found they could meet "in that place beyond religion. For both of us, religion is a path to God, and our commitment to God goes beyond any organized structure. That's what really bonds us."

Unlike the other couples, Donna and David haven't had any conflict. "Not even a moment of irritation," Donna says.

That defies credulity, for me. Neither had been married or had children. What are the odds they could connect in their 40s and not have a single argument?

"No one will believe it," Donna says. "I don't believe it. It's like grace." They haven't lived together and don't wish to marry yet, but this past August, they invited their friends to a "commitzvah" ceremony to celebrate their interdependence. "We wanted to publicly express our gratitude for this relationship, and set intentions for our future," Donna says. "We both know this is it—we're done looking."

LESSON 4: TRY, TRY AGAIN

What about people who've been married multiple times? Do they see this as failure and throw in the towel? Do they privately fear, as I do, *I'm just not good at relationships—I lack the gene?* Or do they acquire knowledge and skills that make later relationships more fulfilling?

I explored this and other questions about love after 50 in my book *Leap! What Will We Do with the Rest of Our Lives?* I wrote about my friend, Joan Borysenko, the spiritual teacher and author of *Minding the Body, Mending the Mind,* who'd just divorced her third husband when we met. Shortly after, she began telling friends that she was getting married for the fourth time to Gordon Dveirin, an organizational psychologist who'd also been married three times before.

The women's posse mobilized. They cornered her and said, "What the hell are you doing? I'm sure he's terrific, but you said good things about your other husbands at the beginning." None of them had met Gordon, but that was irrelevant; they were upset at what they considered the delusion of taking vows she'd already broken three times.

Joan and Gordon, who were 57 and 59 respectively, had to ask the question themselves: Why is this wedding different from all our other weddings? They'd both felt instant sparks—physically, mentally, and spiritually—when they ran into each other at the general store in Gold Hill, Colorado. They seemed well matched. They began teaching and writing together and their latest book, *Your Soul's Compass,* was published in 2007.

They decided that what would be different about a fourth wedding was them. "We're mature individuals who've learned a lot and know who we are," Joan says. "When I was younger, I couldn't have articulated the vows I want to take. This time I will vow with my whole heart: *I will walk the rest of the way with you. I will walk into the mystery with you. I know there will be difficult times, and I vow to see them as grist for the mill.*"

Joan knows—as do the other women—that infatuation burns out and deeper affinities must rise. "At first it's like you're drugged," she says. "You have seen the promised land. You can't sustain that bliss forever, but after four years, we're still in it a lot of the time." She says they've cultivated ways to return to that state.

How? I ask.

"Being in nature together, sharing spiritual practice, creating together—like writing or designing a garden, when all of a sudden ideas are flowing and you're in that magical space."

She says what's different about love when you're older "is that we're so damned grateful. I'm even grateful for my previous marriages—I don't consider any of them failures—because you get honed in the process. They readied me for this."

LESSON 5: KEEP AN OPEN MIND

What's liberating about late love is that you don't have to follow convention or anyone else's ideas; you can design what works for you. Marry, or not. Live together, or not. Have sex a lot or a little.

Peggy Hilliard, 80, met John Morse, 84, through an Internet dating service in

Verlean Barnes, 63, and Rodney Holland, 62.

David Frenette, 48, and Donna Zerner, 44.

Joan Borysenko, 58, and Gordon Dveirin, 59.

John Morse, 83, and Peggy Hilliard, 80.

2006. They lived in different cities, and after a year, Peggy left her house in Oregon and moved in with John at a retirement village in Washington State. She says that 50 years ago, "I would never have lived with a man without being married. At 80 you have more freedom."

I tell her some of the women I've met are having glorious sex, but others say erotic desire lessens as you get older.

"Wrong!" Peggy says. "We have a wonderful sexual life—very fulfilling." She admits there are physical challenges, "but that doesn't stop us. You just have to relax and be creative."

LESSON 6: ENJOY EVERY MOMENT

I take heart from these stories, even if some seem a bit mushy. They offer evidence that love can come to people at all ages and stations. They inspire me to let go of my tendency to be pessimistic and think, *They're writing songs of love, but not for me.* What good are such thoughts? Donna Zerner had never been in love before, and the joy and sacredness at her commitzvah ceremony with David were so palpable, people couldn't stop smiling. Those who were single felt there was still a chance for them, and those who had a partner were inspired to strengthen their bond.

Donna and David set the bar high, vowing they would always see challenges between them as an opportunity to deepen their love and their relationship to God. When I heard them voice this, I thought, *That's the reason I want to be in a relationship again. Not for sex (alone) or even companionship, but for the opportunity to go deeper with another and draw closer to the light—especially at this age, when time seems to be speeding up.*

Ellen Burstyn talks about how, around age 65, "I experienced my mortality. Not like 'Oh yeah, I'm gonna die,' but it's a possibility that's there all the time. And once that happens, everything becomes more precious.

"And to be in love!" she says. "To experience the joy of intimacy in the presence of death—that is delicious. When you're in love you feel so young, and at the same time, you're summing life up. So it's beautiful and rich, and you have to be aware that it's impermanent." She says that she and her partner joke all the time about funerals and ashes. He told her recently that he was driving home and a song on the radio threw him into a terrible dark place....

"Oh, was I dead again?" Ellen said with a laugh. "Will you stop already?"

She says they don't plan to marry. "We have being in love right now. We know that life is short. Death is certain. And love is real. We're going to enjoy every moment of it." **O**

HOW TO IMPROVE YOUR MARRIAGE WITHOUT TALKING ABOUT IT

Forget everything you've heard about frankness, sharing your feelings, getting him to express *his*. New research into the male mind makes it clear that discussion may be the fastest way to shut down communication. (Oh, you've noticed that, have you?) Barbara Graham reports.

When I first heard about the book, I thought it was a gimmick. *How to Improve Your Marriage Without Talking About It* sounded like a title somebody's prankster husband dreamed up after a rocky couples' therapy session. When I mentioned it to Hugh, my own husband—who in 22 years of marriage has never once said, "Honey, we need to talk"—his face lit up like the Fourth of July. Needless to say, I was suspicious. What about the vast repertoire of communication skills women have spent decades perfecting? Were Patricia Love and Steven Stosny, the psychotherapists who coauthored the book, advising us to forget everything we've learned and rethink how we relate to our partners?

The answer is yes—and they're not kidding.

"The number one myth about relationships is that talking helps. The truth is, more often than not, it makes things worse," says Love, a tall, lean redhead with a down-home Texas twang and a generous smile. She is cofounder of the Austin Family Institute, and leads workshops around the country when she isn't making television appearances or cowriting books, including the best-selling *Hot Monogamy*.

"Talking about feelings, which is soothing to women, makes men physically uncomfortable," says Stosny, the Maryland-based author of *You Don't Have to Take It Anymore* and an expert on male aggression. "There's literally more blood flow to their muscles. They get fidgety, and women think they're not listening."

We're relaxing in the sunroom of my house in Washington, D.C., on a golden autumn morning. I learn that it was Stosny's research into the core emotional differences between the sexes that radically altered his thinking, as well as the way he works with clients. When he shared his findings with his friend and colleague Pat Love, they rang true to her, even though they flew in the face of the verbal problem-solving approach she'd been using for 30 years.

According to Stosny's analysis of several hundred human and animal studies, male and female responses to stress are distinct from birth. "When a baby girl hears a loud noise or gets anxious, she wants to make eye contact with someone, but a baby boy will react to the same sound by looking around, in a fight-or-flight response," he says. What's more, while newborn girls are much more easily frightened, boys have five times as many "startle" reactions, which are emotionally neutral but pump up adrenaline. Boys need to intermittently withdraw into themselves to keep from becoming overstimulated. These differences hold true for most social animals and correlate with our biological roles: The female's fear response is an early warning system that serves to detect threats and alert the males of the pack to danger.

As girls grow, they go beyond needing eye contact and refine a coping strategy identified by UCLA psychologists as "tend and befriend." If there's a conflict, girls and women want to talk about it. Boys and men, however, need to pull away. A man's greatest suffering, Stosny says, comes from the shame he feels when he doesn't measure up—which is why discussing relationship problems (i.e., what he's doing wrong) offers about as much comfort as sleeping on a bed of nails.

So, I wonder, does this explain why, when I reach out and tell Hugh I'm feeling isolated from him—on the assumption that this will foster closeness—he gets defensive or withdraws? Do my verbal attempts to reestablish intimacy make him feel inadequate? Is that why he gets that glazed look in his eye and is suddenly compelled to watch men tossing balls on TV?

Yes, yes, and yes, replies Love. And our responses aren't all in

A touch can be worth a thousand words.

our heads. When a man feels shamed by a woman's criticism, his body is flooded with cortisol, a stress hormone whose effect is decidedly unpleasant. A woman experiences a similar cortisol rush whenever her husband shouts at her, ignores her, or otherwise does something that scares her and seems to threaten their bond. Love compares the sensation that accompanies the sudden release of cortisol to sticking your finger in an electric socket, followed by the sort of "sugar blues" crash that occurs after you polish off a few too many glazed doughnuts. "A cortisol hangover can last for hours in men and up to several days in women," Love says. "It's no wonder both sexes try to prevent it."

Okay, this makes sense, but if talking about relationships makes men twitchy and drunk on cortisol, then what's the alternative? Charades?

"It's the connection, stupid!" exclaims Love, quickly adding that it's not me personally she's calling stupid. "Everyone—men, women, myself included—needs to learn that before we can communicate with words, we need to connect nonverbally. We can do that in simple ways, through touch, sex, doing things together. The deepest moments of intimacy occur when you're not talking."

Stosny puts it this way: "We need to stop trying to assess the bonding verbally and instead let the words come out of the bonding." Interestingly, he adds, "When couples feel connected, men want to talk more and women need to talk less, so they meet somewhere in the middle. Being aware of the fear-shame dynamic helps."

To illustrate the point, Love tells the story of an afternoon when she and her husband were lying in bed naked after showering. "I was wondering if he'd initiate sex, when all of a sudden in my mind I crossed over to his side of the bed and got a sense of what it was like to be him, never knowing if he's going to be accepted or rejected. It was terrifying. I understood then how deeply ashamed

that must make him feel," she recalls. "It was an epiphany that changed my life." She immediately began emphasizing compassion in her work with clients, and has come to believe—as does Stosny— that it's even more crucial to the success of a long-term relationship than love.

The tricky part is that men and women must empathize with vulnerabilities they don't feel to the same degree— namely fear and shame. To do this requires what the authors call binocular vision, in which each partner makes a conscious effort to consider the other's point of view. "The problem is that when you're angry, you're wrong even when you're right because you can't see the other person's perspective," Stosny says. "That's when you lose the thing you long for most, the connection."

Okay, I get it: Connection rules. But it's hard to imagine most people being capable of reaching out to their partners in the heat of an argument. Love and Stosny acknowledge that it's a tall order. Still, they say, for couples to productively address the hurt that underlies anger, it helps to have a previously agreed-upon signal such as a hand gesture to keep disagreements from spiraling out of control. This doesn't mean they should try to ignore their feelings, but instead find a way to convey that the other person matters more than whatever they're resentful or anxious about—and then talk. The beautiful part, Love says, is that "it takes only one person to make the gesture. The partner will feel the impact, even if he or she can't drop the anger right at that moment."

Admittedly, this approach is most effective for couples in a precrisis state, Stosny says, "when there's still time for the man to step up to the plate and stop withdrawing or being reactive, and for the woman to understand that her husband really does want to make her happy and to stop being so critical. Men are better able to stay in the room and listen to women if they don't think they're being blamed for their distress."

But ultimately, Love adds, "couples have to decide that the relationship is more important than all those things they do that annoy each other."

"Even when Hugh throws his sopping wet towel on the bed, forgets to put gas in the car, or stares into space when I try to tell him something that really matters to me?" I ask, only half joking.

"If you give him positive reinforcement instead of criticizing him, he'll start doing more of the things you want him to do," Love says.

The next night over dinner, I give it a whirl. "I love it when you put gas in the car and hang up your wet towel," I say. He looks at me like I've gone off the deep end. "What's up?" he asks suspiciously. "Why are you being so nice?"

But a few days later when I'm distraught over a potentially scary mammogram report and he jumps in too quickly to reassure me that everything will turn out fine (it does), I decide to try out the binocular vision that Love and Stosny recommend. That's when I see that Hugh feels like a failure because he wants to make things better and he can't.

So instead of my usual knee-jerk irritability at what I perceive as his lack of sensitivity, I say, "I'm terrified and I just need you to listen." Which he does, patiently, lovingly. After I've finished reciting my laundry list of fears, he holds me close and neither of us says anything for a long time. We don't need to.

It's the connection, stupid! ◙

A LITTLE MOUSE MUSIC

Love is in the air—even if you can't quite hear it. Cathleen Medwick listens in on a tiny, touching serenade.

I heard it on the radio late one night, just as I was drifting off. The news came in on the lips of a BBC reporter, through the salt spray of an impending dream. Mice can sing. To one another, when they want to mate. You can't hear it, the reporter said.

But now I was awake, I was floating. They sing! Even though you can't hear it—you can only hear them skittering across your kitchen counter on winter nights, leaving tiny black, perfectly formed pellets in your fruit bowl.

What do they sing? Can birds hear it, and does it make them cock their heads in the early morning, just before dawn? Is it operatic, what the mice sing, a full-throated invitation to couple madly on your kitchen floor? Is it a love duet, a trilling affirmation of consensual desire? Do they nibble on a pear while they're singing, and does the soft fruit moisten their palates and put them in robust voice? Do girl mice sing, too, or do they lick their whiskers and wait?

I checked the local newspaper in the morning. There was a small item in the Lifestyle section:

> Scientists have long known that male lab mice produce high-frequency sounds—undetectable by human ears—when they pick up the scent of a female mouse.... Audio recordings of the sounds, modified for human ears, reveal that the vocalizations are patterned songs, not random twittering....

How long have scientists known? While the rest of us were marveling over whale songs, were scientists coyly bobbing their heads to modified mouse ditties? After they finally gave up on the music of the spheres, did they start randomly listening to the least vocally flamboyant of creatures? What if the expression "quiet as a mouse" set off a chain reaction of urgent questions, jotted in notebooks in the dead of night?

I turned to Google. "Mice can sing," I typed, and there arose a chorus of affirmations. PICKING OUT THE FAINT NOTES OF DIE FLEDER-MOUSE headlined an article at Canada's globeandmail.com. ROMANTIC RODENTS GIVE SECRET SERENADES led off a jaunty piece from newscientist.com. And, darkly, from someone at the white nationalist stormfront.org, a posting that read, "This is of limited use to the cause..., but I cannot be alone in feeling that it is obscurely encouraging."

I hurried on, arriving at last at an online journal from the Public Library of Science. And there it was, the report from a team of researchers at the Washington University School of Medicine in St. Louis, Missouri. It turned out that "Ultrasonic Songs of Male Mice" was number one in the journal's top ten articles viewed within the past week, besting "First Observation of Tool Use in Wild Gorillas" (number two) and "Cro-Magnons Conquered Europe, but Left Neanderthals Alone" (number five), an event apparently auguring a global peace that so far has not materialized.

Still, mice can sing. Or so posit Timothy E. Holy, PhD, and his coauthor, Zhongsheng Guo, who, like many scientists before them, began their experiment by dipping cotton swabs into mouse urine. They wanted to study how male mice responded vocally to the intoxicating scent of females. The mice were obliging, crooning into the mike placed inside their test chamber, and Holy's team was listening hard. But how could their indelicate human membranes pick up signals meant only for the quivery ears of a female rodent? Unless the scientists took the recording they had made and processed it on a computer, slowing down the audio track and dropping the pitch so the mouse sounds would be audible to the human ear...

Moments of inspiration can come quietly, even casually. When they slowed the mouse sounds, Timothy Holy later wrote, they heard something unusual, "like a series of breathy whistles," and when they dropped the pitch several octaves, they didn't hear grunts or whines or frantic yodels of lust. They heard something wonderfully like music. A melodic trilling. A rhythmic thrumming. An ultrasonic welcome to the dance of life.

"There was joy in this discovery," Holy told Associated Press reporter Cheryl Wittenauer. "We didn't expect it." And yet, and yet...he was ready to hear *something*. Imagine a darkened room, the needle poised above the vinyl record, silence about to give way to exquisite sound. Think of a hushed opera house, where not a creature is stirring as the tenor gathers his breath. "The first moment I heard them," Holy told the British newspaper *The Guardian,* "I thought they sounded like songs, and they really do." He listened to one mouse, then another and another. All their songs were different. Were some better than others? Did the Pavarotti of rodents always get the girl? Holy didn't know. "Whether a male gains an advantage when it comes to mating by singing well is something nobody has yet looked at," he said. Was there a twinkle in his eye when he said it? Will the rewards of scientific inquiry never end?

I had to hear the music. And I could—there were actually links in the online research paper. I just needed to click once, twice with my...well, my mouse...and the computer would download two tracks. The first one would play the mouse opus four octaves lower than the mouse had actually performed it, but just as fast. The second track would play it lower, too, but 16 times more slowly, an adagio for mice and men.

I clicked on the first track, and into my waiting ear came a sweet and silvery warbling, a delicately insistent twitter, a refreshing spritz of sound. It was beautiful. It was endearing. It was relaxing, though it made my neutered Labrador hide beneath the desk, and my black cat look up from snoozing and primly lick her lips.

I clicked on the second track. It began with a long slow stroke, then a shorter one, and then a glide and a swoop, with intriguing variations in timbre. It was rich, it was undulating. It was melancholy, too, but under that was something, oh, sweet and resonant, like the last drop of wine decanted straight to the back of the throat. It was desire under the floorboards, everywhere and nowhere. It was mousy me afloat in my bed, under a night sky scurrying with stars. ⦾

SEX

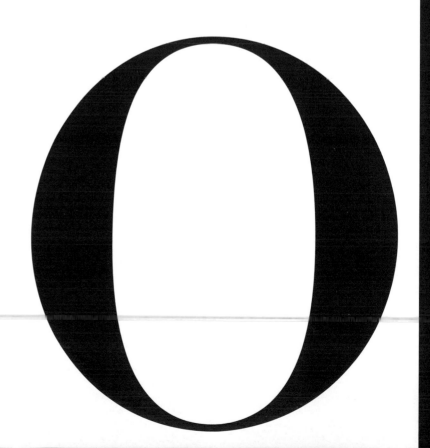

DON'T DO IT IN THE DARK!

Lights on, clothes off—for Sarah Broom, that's the best practice for risk-taking, forgiveness, passion.

And so it came as a shock to me. I'd gotten ready for bed and stood stark naked in front of the man with whom I had undressed. We went tit for tat—he removed his shirt, then I removed mine, lest either of us feel the need to outdo the other. I loved what I saw. I made my way toward bed; he made his way toward the lamp. I heard him say, "On or off?" and before I could get sarcastic with him, say "Are you kidding?," I was staring into blackness. For a second I did not know where to direct my eyes, did not know where in the room he stood, and this reminded me why I have nearly always made love with the lights on. Not because I am afraid of the dark, no, but because to be intimate with someone I have chosen and to miss laying my eyes on their physical geography is like eating my mother's shrimp creole with a clothespin shutting my nose. Certain things, like crying, do not need light, I know. Sex, for me, is not one of them.

My mother liked to tell us 12 children that those things done in private are preparation for how one might show oneself in public. I do not know that my mother meant for me to go as far as this, but I have long felt that the bedroom was the perfect training ground, a microcosm of the world, since so much is exposed there, given and sometimes taken away. The thinking is this: If I can get naked in front of you here, stand fully in this body, with its inadequacies and niceties, its multiplicities, then how much more will I be able to do that fully clothed, out of doors.

I grew up in a humid city where one tried to minimize body heat by moving as little as possible, so that arriving at any one place took time. This taught me one good thing: No big and important place can really be arrived at tomorrow. Without the momentum of small movement, the bigger thing may never come. One must begin somewhere, and besides, in the bedroom there is so much to behold: I want to see the particulars of the person I am touching, notice what shadows the body can make, want to acknowledge the space this person takes up in the world and let them do the same for me.

In a few weeks, I will be leaving this country and living in Burundi. This move began as a germ of an idea. I know that the courage of it came partly from the small moments of affirmation in bedrooms with the lights on. Here I am, I said, and here is where I'd like to go, and so I will make steps toward that thing, and when I am almost to the end, the thing I'm headed toward might move or change shape and I might feel like a baby tottering and holding my diaper so it won't fall down, but even yet, even yet, I will be moving. ◙

DR. PHIL:"PLAN A DATE, FARM OUT THE KIDS, LIGHT SOME CANDLES, AND SEDUCE HIM"

Philip C. McGraw, PhD, on sex: A wife craves romance…a tired mother loses interest in intimacy…and a woman wishes she desired her husband.

Q. My husband and I used to make love all the time. He would play soft music, give me massages, and kiss me endlessly. Then, three years ago, he was unfaithful. We worked things out, but ever since, we've just had sex: no romance, no fire. I've been trying to tell him how I feel and explain what I'd like him to do, but I'm not getting through to him. How can we rekindle our passion?

DR. PHIL: There's a line from the song "Careless Whisper," by Wham!, that goes, *I'm never gonna dance again / Guilty feet have got no rhythm.* My guess is that your husband still feels a strong sense of shame, and that's why he can't "dance." It's difficult for your husband to immerse himself in lovemaking because he may feel that he's let you down terribly and doesn't deserve such closeness. That's why now it just feels like sex, which isn't necessarily intimate and can often be out of a sense of duty or a need for physical release. Guilt is a very selfish emotion because a guilty partner isn't good company. I imagine that's what's happening with him, and you're getting the brunt of it.

I hate to tell you this, but what may also be going on here is that he did the same things with her that he used to do with you, so he feels that making love to you in that way would be compounding the betrayal. As with post-traumatic stress disorder, it triggers the memory of his misconduct and makes him feel worse.

So what do you do? This isn't 1950 anymore; you don't have to let him set the tone in the bedroom. I believe in the principle of reciprocity: You get what you give. If you want more passion, make it happen. Plan a date, farm out the kids, light some candles, and seduce him. Be the spark that creates the fire. You can do it with a sexy negligee, a bottle of wine, a night in a hotel…there are many tactics for turning sex back into lovemaking. He's lost his way, but you haven't. So let's follow the one with the working compass and get moving in the right direction.

Q. Since having my three children (the oldest is 9, the youngest is 3), I've stopped caring about sex. I used to love sleeping with my husband, but these days I hope he doesn't bring it up—it's one less thing I have to do! Honestly, I'd rather go to sleep, but I'm worried that he will start looking for love elsewhere.

DR. PHIL: The question you should be asking yourself isn't how to keep your husband from straying but why you don't feel any desire for the man you love, the father of your children. You say that you were hot for him at one time, so what's changed?

I'm not blaming you for your lack of passion, and you shouldn't blame yourself, either. You're not alone—in one study, about a third of women complained of low sexual desire. Issues in three main areas can contribute to a waning sex drive: lifestyle, relationship, or physiology.

You suggest that the source could be your lifestyle. There's no question that having three young kids is demanding and probably leaves you exhausted. Also, I suspect that when you and your husband became parents, you stopped being friends and lovers. Between family, work, and chores, sex can get crowded off the schedule.

But I would also ask you to look at the relational factor. While one couple can vastly differ from another, we're all prewired for intimacy. After 30 years of counseling people, I've learned that when a couple doesn't have sex, there's a really good chance that there are problems in other areas of the relationship as well. What's going on in the bedroom—or what's not going on—is symptomatic.

Last, and by no means least in terms of importance, are the physiological complications. Having three kids can certainly change you hormonally, or you could be experiencing some degree of depression. I recommend that you see a physician and get some blood work done to determine whether biochemical imbalances could be playing a role.

While it's up to you to change your "one less thing to do" internal dialogue, this isn't just your problem. This is a challenge to your marriage. Both of you need to start making a conscious commitment to increasing intimacy. At first you may not be particularly motivated. But you will be soon, because there are emotional, physical, and mental rewards for having sex. Above all, be up front with your husband. You might say something like the following.

SCRIPT:
DISCUSSING YOUR DIMINISHED SEX LIFE

It's important to me that we have an honest talk about the intimate aspects of our relationship. I don't feel motivated in that area anymore, and I want to find out why. I'm concerned on many levels, including my fear that you'll turn to someone else. I'm not trying to force celibacy on you, and I don't want you to resent me. This situation isn't okay with me, either, and I'm committed to resolving it. Maybe we've simply gotten so busy in our lives, or maybe something's out of balance with me physically. Whatever it is, I want to be closer with you, so can we try to figure out what's going on together?

Q. **I married my husband because he's a good, kind man, and I knew he would be a great father and partner. But I have never been physically attracted to him. Is there any way to develop those feelings? He'd like more physical interaction, and I feel guilty for not wanting the same.**

DR. PHIL: You've probably heard me say that when you choose the behavior, you choose the consequences. What I mean is that when you make a decision, you're accountable for everything that comes with it. You picked some important characteristics in a mate, but clearly you knew that you were settling for less than the full package.

That said, to be honest, the phase of infatuation that marks the early stages of a relationship seldom lasts a long period of time. We tend to morph into a much more relaxed, predictable love. I'm not saying that's better or worse, only that it's different. So even if you had experienced that initial heat with him, it probably would've evolved into something closer to where you are now than to what it is you think you're missing.

The good news here is that you truly like this guy. There's nothing about him that precludes you from feeling affection; it's just not an instant reflex for you. But you can choose to feel differently. There is no reality, only perception—and you control your perception. You can become more attracted to your husband simply by changing your thinking. Concentrate on the things in him that you deem attractive and that you would miss if they were gone.

Then get active in your fantasy life and create some situational romance to help you bond at that next level. Would it be less forced if you had an instantaneous chemical attraction? Sure. If that were the case, sex would be fun in the backseat of a car, in the middle of a field, practically anywhere. Without that reflexive pull, you're going to have to work a little harder. When you start setting up circumstances that are exciting for you both, you'll begin to create a romantic history. You may even surprise yourself. ◗

IT'S A FAMILY AFFAIR (*from left*): Khrystian Wilson, 19, Christy Parcha, 18, and Anna Holt, 19, open the Purity Ball ceremony in Colorado Springs, November 10, 2006.

THE INNOCENCE PROJECT

A lot of fathers hope their daughters will be virgins until they walk them down the aisle. But some are going a step further—taking pledges to support the girls' commitment to chastity. And formalizing those pledges at what are called purity balls. Amanda Robb gets herself invited.

Three days before her 15th birthday, Elise Forte is at a formal ball. She's radiant in a spaghetti-strapped white tulle gown. Brilliants scattered in her updo catch the soft light of Colorado Springs' five-star Broadmoor hotel. In between dinner and dancing, Elise sits demurely across from the tuxedoed man who brought her here—her father, Jerry Forte. Elise's mother, Denise Forte, accompanied them and kneels by Elise's side. She hands her daughter a box.

Elise opens it to discover a piece of jewelry she knows well—her mother's confirmation ring. To explain why she's chosen to pass the heirloom along, Mrs. Forte reads Elise a letter.

"Dear Elise. This is the day of the Purity Ball.... We are so excited.... This ring is made of gold..., a precious metal, and shaped into a heart, and it signifies how precious your heart is to God, to us, and to your future husband, who God is preparing you for.... The diamond chip is a sign of purity, a reminder that you are committing to purity in heart, soul, mind, and body until marriage.... You will be able to give your husband the gift of purity, rare and precious."

Mr. Forte slips the band onto his daughter's ring finger. With a tender smile, he hands her another box. In it Elise finds a man's ring. Her creamy brow furrows in confusion. Mr. Forte explains that just as Elise now wears a ring representing her promise to be pure until marriage, he will wear one, too, as a sign of his dedication to the same goal. "It is in the form of a shield," Mr. Forte reads, "symbolizing my commitment to protect and shield you from the enemy. Inside the shield is a heart, which is your heart, which I am covering. Across the heart are a key and a sword—the key is the key to your heart, which I will safeguard until your wedding day, and the sword is the protection I pledge to you.... On your wedding day, I will give this ring to your husband. I love you, my jewel, my princess. Daddy."

Elise slips the ring onto her father's right-hand ring finger, then falls into his arms, crying. A few minutes later, the family returns to the festivities at the seventh annual Colorado Springs Father-Daughter Purity Ball. During the evening, the girls present white roses before a cross under swords held aloft by two fathers, the attendees watch a "celebrate fathers" ballet choreographed to Natalie Grant's "Always Be Your Baby," and all the fathers sign a covenant that reads:

I, (daughter's name)'s father, choose before God to cover my daughter as her authority and protection in the area of purity. I will be pure in my own life as a man, husband, and father. I will be a man of integrity and accountability as I lead, guide, and pray over my daughter and my family as the high priest in my home. This covering will be used by God to influence generations to come.

The first purity ball took place in 1998 at a nearby Marriott. Randy and Lisa Wilson, a Colorado Springs couple with seven children, hosted about 100 daughters and their parents, primarily from Evangelical Christian churches in the area. In 2006 the National Abstinence Clearinghouse, the ten-year-old nerve center of the U.S. virginity-until-marriage movement, sold 750 packets that outlined how to host a purity ball, and events were held in 48 states: Nearly 200 people attended the one in Tucson, about 150 people gathered in Spearfish, South Dakota, and around 600 fathers and daughters celebrated at a ball in Peoria, Illinois.

The balls are an outgrowth of the purity movement, which began in the 1980s when American teens, mostly girls, began taking abstinence pledges in their local churches and community groups. The campaign was largely a grassroots Christian response to the AIDS epidemic, high teen pregnancy and sexually transmitted disease (STD) rates, and the cultural mores of the sexual revolution. Pledging spread by word of mouth and went national in the 1990s, with programs such as True Love Waits, which encourages teenagers and college students to sign commitment cards that obligate them to remain pure and sexually abstinent by saying no to "sexual intercourse, oral sex...sexual touching...and pictures that feed sexual thoughts" until they enter "a biblical marriage relationship," and Silver Ring Thing, which encourages middle and high school boys and girls to think of their sexuality as a car engine that is safest not to "turn on."

Today Peter Bearman, PhD, the Columbia University sociologist who codesigned the largest, most comprehensive survey of adolescent health ever taken, estimates that one in six Americans between the ages of 12 and 28 has taken a purity pledge.

The growing emphasis on abstinence is no doubt fueled by the increasing support the government has provided the abstinence movement. In 1981 conservative Republican senators Jeremiah Denton and Orrin Hatch sponsored the first legislation "to promote chastity and self-discipline." President Ronald Reagan signed their bill into law, and Congress put $11 million behind it. In 1996 congressional social conservatives attached language to the welfare reform bill that required newly federally funded abstinence education classes to teach that "sexual activity outside the context of marriage is likely to have harmful psychological and physical effects."

In President Bush's first six years in office, annual funding for abstinence-until-marriage initiatives more than doubled to $176 million. This money is earmarked despite a 2004 congressional investigation that found that 11 of 13 federally supported abstinence programs contain misleading or flat-out-incorrect information—for example, that 5 to 10 percent of legal abortions lead to sterility, that 50 percent of homosexual male U.S. teens have HIV, and that touching another person's genitals can result in pregnancy.

The comprehensive sex education some of us remember from public health classes—covering various methods of birth control and how sexually active people can reduce their risk of getting STDs—receives no federal money. (If a school wants to teach beyond abstinence, administrators must use local or state funds; poor schools often can't afford to offer additional classes.)

Supporters of abstinence-only initiatives claim their programs are largely responsible for the fact that between 1990 and 2002, the U.S. teen pregnancy rate declined by more than 30 percent and the number of abortions went from about 1.6 million to just under 1.3 million. The Heritage Foundation, a conservative think tank, further bolstered the abstinence movement when it reported in 2005 that teens who are virgins when they graduate high school are nearly twice as likely to graduate from college than their sexually active classmates. "Obviously, teaching kids to be proud virgins works," says Leslee Unruh, the president of the National Abstinence Clearinghouse.

But social scientists who've researched these numbers don't agree that abstinence programs are the driving force behind either those declines or the academic successes. For instance, Peter Bearman says that virginity has no effect on school achievement,

THE PLEDGE: Jerry Forte watches as his wife, Denise, gives a ring to their daughter, Elise. The ring, Denise explains, "signifies how precious your heart is to God, to us, and to your future husband..." *Right:* Khrystian stands by her father, Randy Wilson, who organized the first ball in 1998.

explaining that the Heritage Foundation analysts are "confusing causality."

He compares the situation to that of a Swedish town that simultaneously had a lot of storks and babies. "They decided storks bring babies," Bearman says. "Actually, though, storks breed in chimneys. So when there's an increase in population—i.e., babies—there's an increase in houses, chimneys, and thus storks. Babies and storks are independent things that occur in this particular town simultaneously—like virginity and good grades in a certain kind of person."

In addition, Bearman discounts the influence of virginity pledges on those declines in teen pregnancy and abortions. He explains that pledges succeed at delaying sex only within an extremely narrow set of circumstances: if an adolescent is between 14 and 16, and if she's part of a group that consists of no more than 30 percent of the population where she's growing up. "The only way the pledges work is if they draw kids into a moral community and give them a sense of identity," Bearman says. Under these circumstances, teens delayed having their first sexual experience by an average of 18 months.

The problem, Bearman says, is that 88 percent of pledgers wind up breaking their promise. "And you can't take a purity pledge and carry a condom in your pocket," he says. "From what we can tell, pledgers have fewer partners than nonpledgers and they are sexually active for a shorter period of time; however, their STD rates are statistically the same as nonpledgers. Pledgers are much more likely than nonpledgers to engage in substitutional sex—including acts that may put them at higher risk for STDs, such as oral and anal sex."

It's interesting to note that at the same time that abstinence programs were on the rise, another statistic shifted—one that many experts believe had a larger impact on teen pregnancy and abortion rates. Planned Parenthood Federation of America president Cecile Richards points to the increased use of condoms by teenagers, from 46 percent of sexually active high school students in 1991 to 63 percent in 2005. In fact researchers at the National Campaign to Prevent Teen Pregnancy have found that some of the most effective programs to get teens to put off having sex offer them information on both abstinence and contraception, or sex education in combination with activities that don't have anything to do with sex—sports, arts, or mentoring.

Teen pregnancy, STDs, and public policy were not on Randy and Lisa Wilson's minds when they held the first Father-Daughter Purity Ball in Colorado Springs nine years ago. They love creating rituals that bring families together, particularly ones that give fathers ways to be involved in their children's lives.

Their passion is born of personal pain. When Lisa was 2 years old, her dad walked out on her family. Although he later tried to establish a relationship, she says, "I felt as if my father ripped my heart out and threw it on the ground and said, 'Deal with it.'"

Randy says his dad "unintentionally abandoned" him. "He was a great provider, but we didn't do relationship well. Dad worked nights, so he wasn't there for my football games or basketball games. He never saw any of that, so he never saw me."

Randy, now Family Life Pastor at Colorado Springs' Mountain Springs Church, has done a lot of research on the importance of fathers in their daughters' lives. It's true that studies have shown that girls with involved fathers get better grades, are less likely to use drugs, and have better self-esteem than those whose fathers are uninvolved or absent.

Randy takes it a step further: He considers abstinence a fundamental piece of the father-daughter relationship. It's in the Bible, he says. It's the only 100 percent effective method to prevent STDs or unintended pregnancy, and he believes it will protect his daughters from getting their hearts broken.

"Guys out there are about themselves," Randy says. "They're not about the girl. They're out only to get what they want from the girl, that pleasure. There's an incredible risk of abuse. A guy I know—his sister-in-law, at 18, in a bad relationship, unmarried, was pushed out of a car and killed."

Judy Kuriansky, PhD, an Adjunct associate professor of clinical psychology at Columbia University Teachers College and a board member of the American Association of Sexuality Educators, Counselors, and Therapists, has worked with a number of women who've made purity pledges. "Certain

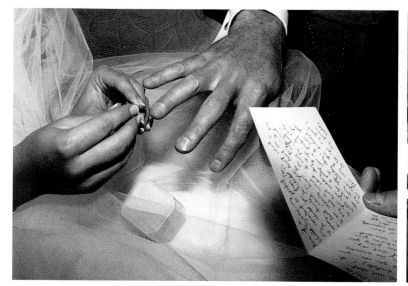

ELISE FORTE PLACES A RING ON HER FATHER'S FINGER, signaling his role in helping her keep her pledge. Allison Smith, 18 (*far right*), and her father Kevin take part in the procession, followed by Kevin Moore, daughter Claire, 12 (*left*), and friend Alissa Edwards, 16.

aspects of purity balls are highly appropriate and laudable," she says. "You want better family relationships, you want kids to make wise choices. Dynamite." But Kuriansky finds some aspects of the ball troubling. "It's controlling—it's overinvolved," she says of fathers promising to be their daughters' "authority and protection in the area of purity." She wonders, "Whose needs are really being met by making such a pledge?"

That's a question Jessica Decker (not her real name), 23, wished her mother and father had asked themselves. At their behest, she began taking purity pledges in kindergarten at her south Florida Baptist school.

"You got a purity ring when you got your period," Decker recalls. "I got mine when I was 9 years old."

At the beginning of every school year, she renewed her purity pledge, even after she began having sex with her boyfriend when she was 15. "I wanted to save myself for marriage because it was what I had been taught," Decker remembers. "But in the heat of the moment I was thinking, *I'm 15 and I'm horny, and my boyfriend is 18 and he's hot.* I didn't use a condom because I didn't know what a condom was. No one ever told me. If we told our school counselor we were sexually active, she would tell our parents and we would be expelled. There was no place for me to get information. My parents were like, 'You are never allowed to let a boy touch you there!'"

Decker believes many of her classmates were sexually active, but says, "You just didn't talk about it." Not even when Decker was certain one of her friends was in the middle of miscarrying. "I'm not sure if it was self-inflicted. I was at her house, and she was sitting on her toilet and blood was pouring out of her, and I was thinking, *Hmm, this can't be good.* We ended up never telling anybody."

When Decker was 17 years old, her mother took her for a gynecological exam. "I was like, 'Please don't tell my mother I had sex!' The doctor told me I had HPV. I thought I was going to die, because I didn't know what it was. I couldn't tell my friends, because they were all going to think I was a slut."

The physician agreed to tell Decker's mother she had an "abnormal Pap smear," and her mother asked no further questions. The physician himself didn't counsel Decker to use condoms if she was going to continue to be sexually active. It wasn't until a few years later in college, when she enrolled in a women's studies course, that Decker learned that most types of HPV are harmless. Today Decker works as a community educator for Planned Parenthood.

Marjorie Holmes (not her real name), 35, took a virginity pledge through her Presbyterian congregation in Atlanta when she was 17 years old. "I loved my church youth group," Holmes says. "It was fun. Whether or not I really understood what I was doing wasn't a big deal to me because I wasn't very involved with guys."

After Holmes earned her nursing degree, she moved to Southern California. There she met Clark (not his real name either), a model. A Christian from the Bible Belt, too, he is "a big, strapping boy who cooks better than anybody I know. He's also a woodworker— great with his hands. He's just an amazing guy," Holmes says. Like nearly nine out of ten virginity pledgers, Holmes didn't keep her vow. She slept with him while they were still dating. She thought their sex life was normal, she says. "But our honeymoon night was a disaster. Nothing happened. It was horrible." When the couple returned home, she said, there were some weird things that took place and odd requests. Six weeks into her marriage, Holmes discovered her husband was sleeping with his best male friend. "I didn't tell anyone I was leaving him until the day that I filed for divorce," she says.

Holmes has since remarried and is now trying to get pregnant. She believes that the culture around the purity movement kept her from knowing what she wanted in a partner or what she needed for herself. About purity pledges, she says, "I would never do that to my daughters. Never. It's a setup for shame and ignorance."

Among the women who took purity pledges, kept them, and married happily is Amber Davidson, 27. She made virginity vows at home and through her nondenominational Sioux Falls Christian High School in South Dakota. "On my 16th birthday, my dad took me out on a date and gave me a purity ring. He told me how much he loved me and how beautiful I was." He spoke about how purity is a big part of "ultimate love and ultimate trust."

Even though she was a popular, outgoing student, Davidson didn't date at all during high school. "There were so many girls in these drama relationships, it was ridiculous," she says. "I thought about my

Todd Anderson guides daughters (*from left*) Claire, 6, Ariana, 9, and Katelyn, 6, under the crossed swords of Steve Holt (*left*) and Randy Wilson. *Far right:* Karlyn Leander, 9.

future husband—how I wanted to give him the very best of me. I wanted to be able to come to him without all these memories of past guys. To be able to give him the ultimate. Give him myself."

After her senior year, Davidson met and fell in love with a young man at a summer camp. They dated for three and a half years and never once kissed.

"We talked for more hours than any couple I've ever known because of that," she says. "And the day I got married, I felt so honored. Here's this man who respected me despite what his desires of the moment were, who has been strong, who hasn't taken advantage of me."

Davidson believes she has a better sex life than friends who had sex with multiple people before they got married. "It's very hard for them," she says. "They have all those memories they can't get rid of when they're in bed with their spouse. And they don't have that level of trust. My husband showed me his self-control before we were married, so I don't have to worry about it after."

Davidson swears there need be nothing awkward between two virgins on their wedding night. "I can't explain to you how beautiful it was when we saw each other for the first time in our hotel room," she says. "It was amazing. I knew beyond a shadow of doubt that he loved me for who I am. For my heart and my mind. The emotional and mental part was so deep, which made the physical part out of this world."

That's the kind of intimate relationship Jerry Forte wants his daughter, Elise, to enjoy. It's what he feels he has with his wife, Denise. Raised a Catholic, Jerry had a conversion experience when he was 19 years old. He took the strictures of his new Evangelical Christianity seriously. He was 32 and still a virgin when he met Denise, who was also raised Catholic and became a born-again Christian at age 29. Before they met, she had been engaged.

"But," as Denise Forte tells the story the day after the ball, "my dad said, 'I don't really think he's the right one.' And I thought, *You've got to be kidding.* Everything seemed like it was great. And my dad said, 'I just love you so much. I don't know if I can walk you down the aisle.' I ended up saying, 'Okay, Dad. Because I want you to be proud, I will postpone it for six months.' And then I found

out that my fiancé was not faithful. He was not what I thought he was. But my dad knew that. I think God gives the fathers that kind of insight."

Jerry and Denise's daughter, Elise, is grateful for her parents' input. "I think your life is kind of like a flower," she says. "And every time you have a relationship or a boyfriend or something, you're taking a petal of your flower and giving it to that person. So you're giving all these petals away. Pretty soon you're not left with anything to give your husband."

Until Elise marries, Jerry sees his job as protecting that flower. "I want Elise's heartstring to be tied to me. Then on her wedding day, I'll be able to give her to her husband with a whole heart." Jerry adds that, when the time comes, he'll "train this guy in Elise's heart.... I'll be working with him and getting to know him and mentoring him and loving him." Jerry says that he wants Elise "to be attracted to that person—but she would want me to be able to bless that."

Asked if she doesn't ever just long for a boy to like her, Elise's Roman lips curl into a dazzling smile. "I want my dad and brother to like me," she says.

BACK AT THE BALL, Elise straightens the new ring on her hand. She gets up from her chair and brushes wrapping paper and ribbon from her tulle skirt. "Come on, Dad. Let's dance." Jerry leads Elise to the ballroom, where they join the other couples—born-again, Catholic, Presbyterian, Caucasian, African-American, Hispanic, military, even a few fathers who brought their daughters as well as girls whose dads were not in the picture.

The girls are giddy about purity. "I'm 13," Gabrielle Perkins says. "And I want to save myself for my husband. I would want him to do the same thing. I don't want my husband to already have seen a bunch of other girls. I don't know who he is, but right now I pray that he will be able to remain pure, too." Her dad, an air force lieutenant colonel wearing his full dress uniform, looks on and beams.

Twelve-year-old Claire Moore just wants to dance. "Come on, Dad," she says. Now all the fathers lead their daughters to the dance floor as a song plays:

I like the way ya make me feel about you baby / Want the whole wide world to see / Whoa, whoa, you got the best of my love. ◑

TALKING AND LISTENING

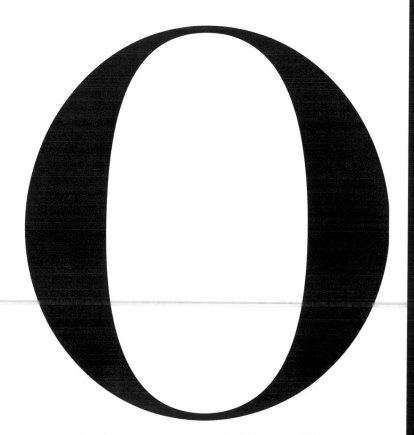

HOW TO GET WHAT YOU WANT FROM ANYONE
(AND WE MEAN THAT IN THE NICEST POSSIBLE WAY)

She'd been a roaring success in her old job but was running into walls in her new one. Why wouldn't her colleagues respond to her e-mails? Answer: She wasn't speaking their language. Enter a laserlike coach with a talking cure that's transformed her life—on and off the job. By Amy Hertz

You know that feeling you get when you say something you weren't supposed to say and it comes out a little louder than you anticipated? It's a naked moment, and there's nothing you can do to cover up. You goofed, everybody heard, and how you fare from here on out depends on what you do next.

When I started a new job three years ago, that's how I felt all the time. I came from a publishing company where the communication style was pretty loose. There were cupcake birthday parties, plenty of pranks, exciting meetings with loads of brainstorming, but there was also a lot of yelling, and a good dose of humiliation. When a very junior person offered an opinion at a meeting, a very senior person responded, "Can someone who matters please speak?" Tears flowed freely. It was an overworked, understaffed, underpaid, frantic environment in which the only way to get I.T. to help with a dead computer was to throw a fit and threaten to call the president.

I'd spent ten years at that company before moving to my new job. Somehow I didn't pay attention to the fact that everything—and I mean everything—was different at this office. People were busy but not frantic. Nobody snapped at anyone else, at least not in an obvious way. I didn't realize that all you needed to do to get I.T. to come was simply call and leave a polite message.

Not surprisingly, my requests were falling to the bottom of most people's list of things to do. I couldn't get anyone to cooperate. I had a rough time with one young man who told me about a decision that was made on one of my books when I wasn't in the room. "Over my dead body," I exclaimed, not intending anything other than to express my dismay at what I thought was a bad decision. But for the first time, I saw the intimidation embedded in that remark: His eyes popped open and for an instant fear flashed across his face. I saw clearly the effects of my own brashness and his sensitivity at the same time. I never wanted to see that look on anyone's face again, and I couldn't believe I hadn't seen it before. To continue to work with him, I'd have to climb out of the hole I'd dug for myself, but I couldn't see a ladder. Although my boss and I had frank discussions about the need for me to adjust my style of interaction, he had no practical help to offer.

I called my friend Tony—a management and branding consultant—and told him what was up. "Did you think about asking them for a coach?" he said.

"A what?"

"A communications coach. Your HR department probably has a list, and I bet they'll even pay for it."

I couldn't imagine that my company would—publishing is not known for having extra money for this kind of thing—but I asked, and my boss said yes right away. And that's when I met John Artise, my communications sensei.

A big Italian-American bear of a man with a love of jazz, Brazilian music, and Eastern philosophy, Artise has been in the business of communication for close to 30 years. He developed the system he works with now after an experiment he conducted as a career coach to try to help his clients crack the code of getting hired: He spent eight years posing as a job applicant, during which time he sat through 300 interviews. "The process was a mess," Artise says, because each person was speaking a different language. He administered more than 5,000 communication style assessments to people in corporate outplacement and training to investigate language styles. After analyzing the results, he identified four types of communicators: The Feeler uses language to express emotion. The Sensor is driven by the drumbeat of constant deadline; she's interested in getting things done quickly. The Intuitor thinks in terms of the conceptual and long-range plans; he's a problem solver but not necessarily interested in sticking around to implement solutions—he'd rather move on to the next puzzle. The Thinker operates on logic: She loves organization and systems, and unlike the Intuitor, she likes to see projects through to the bitter end.

"Once I saw how hard it was for them to communicate with each other," says Artise, "it became clear that we needed to learn to recognize and even speak in each other's styles if we ever wanted to get what we needed at work and in life—cooperation." Success, Artise explains, isn't a matter of Sensors hiring only Sensors, or Intuitors working only with Intuitors. It depends on recognizing what is necessary for each person to do his best.

I took the assessment test. I came out a Feeler, and thought I was stuck there but found out that under different circumstances, we shift into other communication styles. Under stress my Thinker takes over. That's good news because the Thinker is clear and logical—balancing my emotional Feeler tendencies. Artise says that other people under stress might slip into Sensor mode. You know what I'm talking about: You walk into a meeting with your boss, and he makes you feel as if the clock is ticking before you've even opened your mouth. Sensors are very efficient, but when pressed, they become abrupt. The best way to drive a stressed-out Sensor crazy is to throw an Intuitor in her path—someone who is abstract, idealistic, and can take a while to get to the point. On the other hand, an overwhelmed Sensor can appreciate Thinkers and their habit of sticking strictly to the facts.

Artise explained that each type has its good and bad traits. As I read the list of characteristics for a Feeler, I was a bit pleased with myself: They're empathetic, concerned about others, they like to help people solve their problems. But when stretched, Feelers can be manipulative, impulsive; they can overpersonalize, become too subjective, and stir up conflict. I felt the sting that only recognition brings. Fortunately, Artise says Feelers are the most interested in making changes and the most willing.

My next task was to put this new knowledge into practice and try to get the cooperation I was hoping for. I messed up a lot, and my days were punctuated by phone calls to Artise, before things started to improve at work.

"I'm getting stonewalled by H."

"Don't forget he's a Feeler," Artise replied. "End every e-mail with a question he can answer. It'll make him feel good about himself and good about working with you. Every chance you get, remind him he's great, and you just couldn't function without him. Feelers love that." Indeed H did. After a few interactions using Artise's techniques, H said yes so quickly to my requests, it made my chair spin.

"I'm getting nothing but impatience and dismissiveness from R."

"She's in Sensor mode," Artise said. "Give her what she needs to do the work. Go in prepared with what you're going to say. Then get out fast." Soon, whenever I needed information from R, if she took more than an hour to get it to me, she included an apology.

"G starts every sentence midthought, and I have trouble understanding him. He gets irritated when I ask questions."

"He's an off-the-charts Intuitor. He thinks what's in his brain is also in yours. Let him speak for a while and then ask your questions. He'll feel he's had a chance to be heard, and you can locate yourself in his thinking process. Let him know that you love his ideas and want to know more—you're just having trouble absorbing them so quickly." This person became a treasured mentor.

I felt a bit manipulative using these techniques, until one day the veil lifted: I was giving people what they needed to feel safe working with me. They were happier and that thought made me happy. The method had fallen away.

Call me stupid, but it was only then that I noticed my dramatic style was a little too present in my personal life as well. I'd surrounded myself with people who were, I thought, tough enough to take my unfiltered style of self-expression, but I hadn't noticed that my behavior could be shocking to those outside my nice little coterie of family, friends, and colleagues who somehow found it worthwhile to put up with me. And even within that circle, my vociferousness could wear a little thin.

So I started using the tactics Artise had laid out—identifying someone's type, speaking their language, then asking for what I needed using the style that meshed best with their type (see "Can We Talk?" below). If my husband was overwhelmed at the office but I wanted him to do something right away because we were on a deadline for our taxes, I had a choice. I could say, "I need you to do this now" and begin a battle of wills in which he lets me know he's too tired to think about it. The other option would be to try to move him into Feeler mode. Artise has noticed that's where people are more empathetic, more emotional, and more likely to help you. If I began with, "I'm sorry things are rough," my husband would then be more willing to cooperate when I said, "but I know you're the one who can figure out whether or not these accountants are the right people to hire."

I've found that this kind of attunement works even on strangers. Say there are ten people behind you in line at the drugstore, the register won't accept your $5 cash-back reward, and the credit card reader is down. You can push the cashier to hurry up and figure it out—likely leading her to tell you where to stick it and you can forget your cash-back reward. Or you can recognize that she's under pressure. She's probably in Sensor mode, and you try to draw out her Thinker by saying, "Boy these machines are terrible. Is there another one that's working? Maybe the manager can help us." She'll likely begin to come up with a way to fix the problems and make sure you get your five bucks.

It can be difficult to show restraint—especially if you're like me and you have none—but the discipline pays off. Alice, a friend who went through the same training, was having a tough time with her Sensor fiancé, Tom. She wanted to change wedding planners—the one they hired was giving them her version of a wedding, and Alice's own dream was going down the tubes. Tom was stressed at work and felt it was too late in the game to start from scratch. Instead of arguing that he wasn't respecting what she wanted, Alice recognized that a Sensor would respond best to a plan for making the switch easily—which she came up with. Once she showed him her outline, he agreed to the change right away.

It might seem that when you give up arguing for your point of view ("I want this done now," "I want you to finish ringing up my purchase and give me back my money," "I want to change wedding planners and you have to agree"), you're sacrificing your needs. But the opposite is true: By shifting gears to speak in another person's emotional language, you're dropping the impulse to get your way by imposing your style on them. This isn't easy, but the surprise is that by giving up, you get even more of what you want. ◑

CAN WE TALK?

Yes, but first know your audience: Are you dealing with a Feeler, a Sensor, a Thinker, or an Intuitor? Consultant John Artise teaches people to listen for clues to the other person's communication style—or the style they've slipped into for that particular moment—so you know how to get compromise and cooperation from anyone, at work or at home. To become a black belt communicator, take a look at the following cheat sheet:

THE FEELER She's an empath and wants to connect, make you feel comfortable. If you're not doing so well, she'll try to figure out a way to help you.
HOW TO GET A FEELER TO COOPERATE: Listen for signals that she is overwhelmed or exhausted. The Feeler needs to hear two things: One, that you understand she's having difficulties—something like: "I'm sorry you're having such a hard time. I don't want to make things more difficult for you." Second, explain that she's the best one to help you: "I'm in trouble and I need your advice; you're so good in situations like this." Being a rescuer is the role she lives to fill, but she wants to be acknowledged for it. When she feels appreciated, she'll be ready to jump in.

THE SENSOR A Sensor labors under the constant pressure of deadlines and does everything—including communicating with you—in bursts of very intense energy. She has a short attention span and can make you feel as if you're taking up too much of her time just by saying hello.

HOW TO GET A SENSOR TO COOPERATE: She responds best when she knows you have a plan for getting a task done fast. You need to communicate in easily digestible sound bites, so prepare ahead of time. If you don't get to the point quickly enough, the Sensor will consider you an additional source of stress. What you want the Sensor to know is that you can help reduce her workload.

THE THINKER These people play by numbers and facts. They are logical and realistic, and they will pop any idealistic balloon by citing a similar situation in which someone failed.
HOW TO GET A THINKER TO COOPERATE: A Thinker loves systems and organization and solving problems. So when she points out inaccuracies or mistakes, let her know that you understand and will fix the problem. She needs to be reassured that you'll stay grounded in reality and that you'll be very careful about gathering your research.

THE INTUITOR She's the one with the big ideas that you have a hard time understanding. She presents information as though you're supposed to know exactly what she's talking about. She doesn't give any context—no last names of people to whom she's referring, no company names even though she's discussing a problem specific to that company. When you ask questions, she gets impatient. She doesn't realize that you don't know what's in her brain.
HOW TO GET AN INTUITOR TO COOPERATE: Let her talk out her ideas for a while before you begin asking questions. They should be phrased to show her you like her ideas but simply need more details to understand the full picture.

HOPE DAVIS'S AHA! MOMENT

Being cursed doesn't usually trigger an enlightening experience. But for the star of *Charlie Bartlett,* a stranger's harsh words led to a wake-up call.

Every summer my husband and I pack our suitcases, load our kids into the car, and drive from tense, crowded New York City to my family's cottage in Maine. It's on an island, with stretches of sea and sandy beaches, rocky coasts, and pine trees. We barbecue, swim, lie around, and try to do nothing.

We were on one of these vacations about two years ago when my husband, Jon Patrick Walker, and I decided to go out for a movie date. We left our then 6-month-old and 2-year-old daughters with my sister and went to town, which consists of some fish restaurants, one bar, a general store, and a movie theater. It was a Friday night, so all the tourists who flood the island in the high season had taken over, but we didn't mind. We ate lobster rolls on the bay, sat in the theater with our popcorn, and poured out with the rest of the crowd to get to our car.

The tiny main street was clogged with traffic. My husband saw a shortcut and made a left onto a quiet lane. We chitchatted about the movie; we were relaxed, distracted, and removed from the stresses of the city. And it was during this pleasurable little moment that a young woman passing by us screamed, "This is a one-way street, *you asshole!*"

In the silence that followed, I felt a fury overtake me. But there's a reason my husband's nickname is the Zen Master. Before I could think of a suitable comeback, he'd stopped the car, smiled at the woman, and said, "Hi."

She looked surprised. "Uh…hi," she said.

"Just so you know, I'm really not an asshole," Jon began. "I didn't realize this was one way because I didn't see the sign."

The woman's complexion, previously tan, turned crimson. "It's on the edge of the entrance," she said quietly. "It's easy to miss."

"Okay," he said. "Well, I'm sorry about that."

"No worries," she said. "I'm sorry, too."

"See you around, then," my husband said. "Take care."

"You, too," she said. And we drove off.

Had I been alone when she yelled, I would have cursed under my breath and sped off, feeling mad at her and stupid about driving down the wrong road. Instead, what could have been an ugly moment between strangers became something…elevating. I had seen the woman as a rude and bitter local, and she had figured us for two selfish, careless tourists, but when we took the time to look one another in the eye, it turned out that we'd all made a mistake. We were three people with stories very different from the ones we'd made up about one another. We were human.

It's too easy to sum up a person's character in one negative instant, and it doesn't put anything good out into the world. I certainly have my moments, but ever since that night, I don't shoot nasty glares at the man fumbling for his wallet at the cash register, or yell at the driver who doesn't go the moment the light changes. If someone is walking slowly on the sidewalk or cuts in line at the supermarket, I try to imagine her situation: Is she just having a really bad day? I try to remember that we're all in this together.

I like to look back on that brief exchange on a one-way street in a small town, at the moment when I saw that people are so rarely what we make of them in snap judgments. And when I do, I realize how a little understanding of that can go a very long way. —*As told to Justine van der Leun*

For Hope Davis, making a wrong turn led her to a better path.

DO: If you're going to blow up your relationship, find a nice, quiet table and an easily accessible exit.

THE DEAR JOHN TALK AND OTHER DREADED CONVERSATIONS

Eight ways to make them easier, kinder, gentler.

Fill in the blank: "I'm sorry to say this, but… ("You're fired," "I don't love you," "I don't know how the cat got out"). Donald Trump and Anne (*"You are the weakest link; goodbye"*) Robinson have no problem ruining people's days, but for the rest of us there's got to be a way to make delivering bad news more bearable. Actually, there are a few things you can do:

1 SHOW UP IN PERSON. Tempting as it may be to e-mail or have a one-way conversation with an answering machine, talking face-to-face shows respect, especially if you're discussing the loss of a job or relationship. Also, an e-mail or voice message is easy to misinterpret, whereas when you're physically with someone, you can explain or clarify immediately so there's less room for misunderstanding, according to Judith Bram Murphy, PhD, a Manhattan clinical psychologist who also does executive coaching.

2 CONSIDER THE SETTING. There's never a great moment to have a tough talk, but you can avoid undue hurt by finding the least terrible time (New Year's Eve is not the night to ask for a divorce), says Linda Sapadin, PhD, author of *Now I Get It! Totally Sensational Advice for Living and Loving*. The place, too, can make a difference: It should offer relative privacy, the option for a quick exit, and an atmosphere that will allow the other person to feel comfortable and react safely. (Sitting in a well-chosen restaurant, for instance, can be more conducive to a sensitive conversation than driving in a car, where both of you are stuck after you drop the bomb.)

3 REHEARSE (BUT ONLY A LITTLE). The impulse to memorize exactly what you're going to say is understandable (all the easier to just spit it out and make a beeline for the door). But scripting the entire speech as if it's a state of the union address will make you seem insincere, Sapadin says. Also a brusque, agitated delivery can cause both of you to feel worse, says Dana Bristol-Smith, president of Speak for Success, a business communications firm in San Diego. It's not a bad idea to practice the first few sentences to help you through the initial awkward moments, but after that, try letting the words come naturally.

4 REMIND YOURSELF THAT YOU'RE NOT THE BAD GUY. The truth is, you don't want to hurt anyone. Nor did you likely cause the situation—you may be keeping it from becoming worse. Continuing to lead someone on, for example, will only create more heartbreak in the long run. If you have to fire an employee, it's probably because she's not performing up to snuff or the budget was cut and she's the least useful to the company. If the other person will be disappointed by what you have to say, perhaps it's because of her own expectations—ones that you don't share.

5 ACKNOWLEDGE HOW HARD THIS IS. If you're stumbling over how to start, Sapadin suggests an opener like "I don't know how to say this, but I must tell you something" or "I don't want to scare you, but there's something you need to know."

6 SLIP IN SOME PRAISE. You can soften the blow by paying tribute to the other person's strengths. In the case of breaking up, says Bram Murphy, you might sandwich the negative between positive statements, as in: "You are terrific—generous, kind, and funny. I've enjoyed our time together, and I've really grown as a person. But I just don't see us going forward together, and you deserve to be in a wonderful relationship."

7 LET THE OTHER PERSON REACT. Uncomfortable as this can be, keep in mind that most people wind down after an initial outburst. Remaining conscious of your breathing, keep it slow and steady—that will go a long way in helping you stay calm. (When you're nervous, you tend to breathe very rapidly or hold your breath.) Try not to interrupt or respond emotionally to the other person's upset. If their anger escalates and feels unsafe, announce that you are providing some time to cool down, and leave the room.

8 EXPRESS EMPATHY. For someone who is visibly crushed or sobbing hysterically, acknowledging your role in her distress ("I'm really sorry this is making you so upset") lets her know you care despite the circumstances. If there are tears, offer Kleenex or a glass of water, and ask if she would like a few minutes of privacy, Bristol-Smith suggests. If she's angry, something like "I hear you" at least offers some validation of how she's feeling. Just make sure your empathy is rooted in reality, Sapadin cautions. "Saying, 'I can understand that you're angry with me because I disappointed you, and that was not the way I wanted it to work out, either,' shows concern without giving false hope." —Kathryn Matthews

DON'T: Scripting the whole speech will detract from the sense of sincerity you want to convey.

DO: Sandwich a compliment in between the bad news.

WAIT—ARE YOU IMPLYING I *NEED* TO READ THIS ARTICLE?

Tread carefully around thin-skinned people—they'll bite your head off if you don't. (And of course we don't mean *you*.) Martha Beck on defending yourself against the defensive.

"I want your honest opinion," said my friend Joanna, handing me her unpublished manuscript. "Don't whitewash; tell the truth. Promise!"

So I promised—apprehensively. Joanna's very talented, but I know she also takes criticism hard. To my relief, I loved her book, and I fired off an e-mail saying that the only way she could possibly improve it would be to make it a little more personal. "You're so amazing," I told her. "Putting more of *you* in the book would take it from great to sublime."

Joanna didn't write back for nearly a month. When she did, it was to tell me that my "attack" had left her "inconsolable."

Oy.

I'd made a crucial mistake when I agreed to be Joanna's critic: I ignored my knowledge that she is a highly defensive person. People like her (let's call them HDPs for short) can be found in almost every family, workplace, or crowd. Dealing with them requires a special set of skills, a defense against defensiveness. I recommend keeping these techniques handy for dealing with the HDPs in your life—or for minimizing your own defensiveness, should it ever raise its touchy little head.

■ THE DARK SIDE OF SENSITIVITY

Joanna describes herself as sensitive, and she is. But her reaction to my comments wasn't sensitivity; it was defensiveness. The two may feel identical to the person experiencing them, but actually they're worlds apart. Sensitivity is born of careful attention. It involves looking closely, understanding deeply, and therefore not causing harm. Defensiveness, on the other hand, is the bastard child of shame. For people who have survived harshly judgmental environments, shame—the sick sense that they're basically inadequate—dominates the psychological landscape. They're sensitive the way a truckload of TNT is sensitive. Virtually any bump or jostle causes them to explode, often harming others.

Knowing an HDP's destructive behavior comes from shame doesn't excuse it. But at least it helps me understand why one of my clients dumped her boyfriend for "implying she was ugly" because he closed his eyes when they kissed, or why I once saw a party guest respond to the question, "Would you like some wine?" by snapping, "Why, do I look like an alcoholic?" From the outside, defensive behavior is disproportionate, bizarre, often appalling. But from the perspective of the HDPs, these actions are justifiable—no, necessary!—self-protection. I've spent a long time thinking about the best way to deal effectively with such people.

■ HOW TO HAVE A FUNCTIONAL, TRUSTING, RELAXED, MUTUALLY SATISFYING HUMAN RELATIONSHIP WITH A HIGHLY DEFENSIVE PERSON

Short answer: You can't.

Long answer: You really can't. Don't even try.

The reason one can't look to defensive people for top-quality relationships is that such relationships require two human beings. But defensive people don't think like humans. They think like reptiles. I mean this literally. Beneath the elaborate neural structures that mediate our subtle social interactions, we all possess what scientists call a reptilian brain. This ancient biological structure, which evolved in reptiles, isn't capable of nuanced emotion or logical thought. Its primary driving force is fear. Two fears, to be specific.

The first worry of all reptile brains (including yours and mine) is "I don't have enough!" Not enough love, money, food, credit, glory—the subject of our deprivation obsessions varies, but the theme "not enough" pounds away like a monotonous drumbeat. The only thing as loud to the reptile ear is its other major concern: "Someone's out to get me!" An HDP perceives threat coming from lots of sources; one day the Enemy may be a coworker, the next a relative, the next an entire nation. But to the reptile brain, someone, somewhere, is always about to attack.

This makes evolutionary sense. Lizards live longer if they obsessively acquire more food, shelter, and mates, and if they expect predators to jump them at any moment. Sadly, however, reptiles are blind to nondefensive emotions; to the glow of love, the tickle of amusement. The only thing playing on their mental screens, all day every day, is *The Lack and Attack Show*. The same is true of HDPs. When humans are gripped by primal fear, they become their inner lizards—and HDPs are virtually always gripped by primal fear.

Remain fearless in the face of hostility: Handle a difficult person firmly but lovingly.

So the best relationship you can hope to sustain with a defensive person is the sort you might have with a reptile. As a doctor here in Arizona once explained to a man who was bitten on the lip while kissing his pet rattlesnake (it made the newspapers), you simply cannot expect a loving connection from a reptile, even if you raised it from the egg. Remembering that these people are basically giant talking lizards will keep you from futilely trying to please them, persuade them, or explain yourself to them. That's a key step. But a solid defense against defensiveness requires you to go further—to manage the fear that may put *you* in HDP mode.

■ HOW TO AVOID BECOMING A HIGHLY DEFENSIVE PERSON

Defensiveness is extremely contagious. When Joanna "forgave" me for what I thought was glowingly positive feedback, I felt a jolt of angry defensiveness myself. If I'd followed my own inner lizard, with its worries of being insufficiently loved and excessively criticized, I'd have accused Joanna of being paranoid—which would've sent *her* inner lizard into all-out combat mode, triggering still more defensiveness in me, resulting in a relationship catastrophe I call War of the Dinosaurs (*dinosaur* means "fearfully great lizard").

It's easy to say that we should stay out of reptile mode, but that's hard advice to follow when some HDP launches an attack—especially if the person has any power over you. When your highly defensive parent, boss, head nurse, or gang leader launches a dinosaur attack, you may not be able to stop yourself from getting upset in return. But if you can't help slithering into reptile mode, there's still one option left: Don't go lizard. Go turtle.

■ THE SHELL GAME

One reason the Roman Empire conquered most of ancient Europe was a military maneuver called the turtle. In battles a regiment would clump together, the soldiers in the center holding their shields above their heads, while those on the periphery shielded the unit's front, back, and sides. They'd march along that way, pretty much an indestructible human tortoise. You, too, need such tactics for engaging with HDPs who loom above you in the social-power landscape.

"Going turtle" means putting up an emotional shell. This isn't easy, because mirror neurons in your brain fire in resonance with the feelings of people around you. If you and I were talking, part of your brain would organize itself to match part of mine, and vice versa. When you're with a loving person, this is wonderful; with an HDP, it creates wars straight out of the Mesozoic era. To avoid conflagration, you must pull your sensitive social neurons back into a shell.

It isn't all that hard. Try this: Think about an occasion when an HDP blew up at you. Remember the shock, the anger, the urge to lash back. Got it? Good. Now picture your living room painted kumquat orange. Then figure out whether 713 is a prime number. Do you notice how your mind lets go of emotional reactivity as it attacks visual or analytical problems? Artists and scientists are notoriously eccentric because their mental work diverts brainpower from social connection. When I'm listening to an HDP's rant, I am also, almost always, thinking about painting. Desert landscapes, usually. They help my inner turtle feel safe, so that I don't mirror the aggression of the HDP.

■ NEXT STEP: THE HIGH ROAD

Pulling into an emotional shell is better than engaging in dinosaur warfare, and can allow you to converse with HDPs without being destroyed. An even higher goal than turtling, however, is to remain fearlessly human in the face of hostility. My idol, in this regard, is dear departed Steve Irwin, the crocodile hunter, who loved reptiles unabashedly and unilaterally, even as he grappled and sidestepped to avoid their violent attacks. There are many HDPs in my life I really enjoy, the way Steve Irwin enjoyed his crocs. Joanna, for example, is a good friend and wonderful writer, especially for a lizard.

You can learn a lot about handling HDPs by studying the way Irwin treated his beloved reptiles: firmly but lovingly. "You're all right, sweetheart," he'd croon as a sea snake tried desperately to envenomate him. "Aren't you gorgeous!" he'd exult to a charging one-eyed alligator. And you could tell he meant it. I think HDPs all over the world must have felt strangely happy watching Steve lovingly disarm reptiles like themselves.

If you're feeling brave enough, try the crocodile hunter's techniques on a highly defensive person. See something beautiful in them, and steadfastly mirror that instead of their antagonism. I've used the above Irwinisms—"You're all right, sweetheart" and "Aren't you gorgeous!"—and found them very effective, even in business negotiations. But my favorite reptile-wrangling skill, the one I used with Joanna, consists of three ridiculously simple words: "All is well."

Try saying this, warmly, the next time an HDP lashes out at you. "You attacked my writing!" All is well. "You're implying I'm ugly!" All is well. "Do I look like an alcoholic to you?" All is well. It may sound off-point, but since extreme defensiveness is itself off-point, this actually works better than following your HDP's arguments. When I assured Joanna, "All is well," she instantly relaxed. Keeping "All is well" on the tip of your tongue can disarm bullies, mend marriages, stop fistfights. It's a three-word de-defensivizer.

Say it now, to feel it in your mouth and mind. Repeat the whole classic mantra: "All is well, and all will be well, and all manner of things will be well." Feel how this soothes your inner lizard. It works so well I don't even care if it's true—though I suspect it may be, in some mystical realm that mortal eyes see only through a glass, darkly. But one thing's for sure, even in the workaday world, where friends may turn into dinosaurs and you're stuck with an exploding coworker: If you have a few reptile-wrangling tricks under your belt, all will be a heck of a lot better. ◑

FAMILY

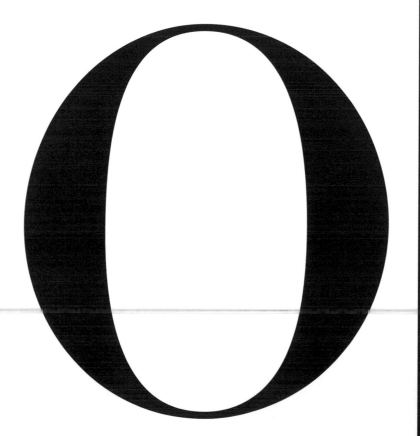

8 THINGS NEVER TO SAY TO AN ADOPTED CHILD

Willa and Josey are her daughters; they're from China, and they're her heart, her soul, her life. Any other questions? Unfortunately, yes. Elizabeth Cuthrell has a few words for well-meaning strangers.

There's no story my daughters and I love more than how we became a family through adoption. My 9-year-old, Willa, asks me to recite the details over and over again. Josey, my 4-year old, listens intently to her story and makes me go back and start over if I leave anything out. Willa is so amused by a certain part of her story that she once asked me to come to her kindergarten classroom to tell it: how her father, Steve, and I, about to meet her for the very first time, found ourselves racing around our tiny hotel room in Nanchang, China, trying on and taking off some combination of the three outfits we had each brought along. We'd look at ourselves in the mirror, nod disapproval at our reflection, and bump into each other racing back to the closet for a more suitable option.

"I look like I'm going out dancing!" my husband said.

"All I have is black pants," I moaned. "Kids like color!"

"Just wear a bright top," my husband said. "Do you think she'll notice I'm losing my hair?"

"You look great," I replied, perkily applying lipstick from the credit card–size makeup palette I had packed in lieu of my normal arsenal of beauty supplies. "Oh, damn it!" I said.

My husband looked at me and burst out laughing. "Honey, your lips are blue."

"I put eyeshadow on them!"

"You're just nervous!"

"Well, obviously I'm nervous!" I said, scrubbing my mouth with soap and water. I looked over at my husband, who had finished shaving with a trembling hand and was now applying tissue to the multiple bloody nicks he'd inflicted upon himself. "And you cannot meet our daughter with toilet paper all over your face!"

Our costume drama served to distract us from the enormous affect welling in our throats. We had spent a solid year and a half preparing to become Willa's parents—months of paperwork, shopping for every imaginable baby item, getting fingerprinted to prove we weren't wanted criminals, and a lot of staring at the ceiling at 3 A.M., wondering if the little baby daughter we called Willa, whom we already madly loved but knew only from a health report and two black-and-white photographs, was safe and sound. One of the very last bits of advice our adoption agency gave us as we set out on our 18-hour plane trip to China was, *No matter what, when you meet your child, do not cry. You'll scare your daughter if you cry.* So here we were,

doing everything possible to keep our minds off the emotion beating like a tom-tom in our chests.

When the phone rang and Mrs. Chen, head of Willa's children's home, told us our baby daughter was waiting in a hospitality suite, we held each other for 20 quiet seconds, then screamed for joy, jumped up and down on the bed on the way to the door, and ran for the elevator. We knew it was the best day of our lives so far, and when Willa hears her story, she knows it, too. "Tell the part again where Daddy had toilet paper on his face! Tell the part where you jumped on the bed and almost broke it! Tell the part where you looked into my eyes and felt like you had known me forever, and you reached for me and held me, and I pointed to my nose because I was sick and I wanted you to know. Tell the part where you were afraid that you were going to cry but then you didn't because you were too happy."

Ours is the remarkable story of how two luminous girls born across the world in the southern portion of rural China became our daughters. But it's also our private story, our own family history, and sometimes we choose to share parts of it and sometimes we don't. So if you approach me in public and I don't want to discuss personal details of my daughters' lives, I hope you'll understand.

Interracial adoption becomes a public event because it's obvious: My children are racially Chinese; my husband and I are not. Sometimes people stare at us, sometimes they smile, and sometimes—when we're with our children—people ask us questions they would be unlikely to ask any other parent.

The staring part I understand. In my early 20s, I often stared at what I thought to be interracial adoptive families. I would want to follow them. I can't explain why, except that imagining myself in a family like theirs made some kind of bone-deep sense to me. Sometimes they would catch me staring, and I would smile warmly in an effort to convey my support. Now I realize that they didn't need my approval, or my enthusiastic smile. What they needed was for me not to notice, or at least not to make a big deal out of noticing. The thing I didn't understand at the time is that frequently what interracially adopted kids and their families long for is privacy: just to be treated like any other human being whose history the public doesn't assume it knows or assume it has the right to know.

The first time I was approached by a curious stranger was in Babies "R" Us. I was looking for a teething ring for Willa. "Where'd you get her?" a voice said, and I turned to find a woman staring at my daughter sitting serenely in her stroller.

Willa, at 8, and Josey Cuthrell Tuttleman, at 3, December 2006.

I was startled. "Excuse me?"

"Where'd you get the baby?"

"Oh," I said. I touched my daughter's foot. "You mean where was she born?"

"Yes," she said. "Where's she from?"

"She was born in China."

"I thought so—so cute. Do you mind my asking how much she cost you?" I mumbled something like the name of my adoption agency and pushed the stroller in the opposite direction. Luckily, Willa didn't comprehend this exchange, but she's 9 now, extremely alert, and, like all of us, never more so than when someone asks intimate questions about her or her sister. She has also absorbed some of the negative theories people have about adoption. A few weeks ago, having lunch, she looked at me and casually asked, "Did you buy me and Josey?" I took a deep breath.

"Why are you asking that?"

"Because that's how you got us, right?"

"Did somebody at school ask you if you were bought?"

Willa wriggled in her chair. "I don't remember."

"Willa, adopting you—getting you and Josey—required a long list of things to do, and part of that was to pay a fee to the adoption agency for the work they did to make it possible to bring you and Josey into our family. But there's almost always the exchange of money when children come into a family."

"How?"

"It can cost a lot of money to have a baby in a hospital, or even at home with a midwife. And there are also other tests and things moms and dads have to pay for before the baby comes. Sometimes parents have trouble making a baby, and they have to pay the doctors a ton of money to help them, and on top of that they still have to pay a big hospital bill." Willa got out of her chair and sat on my lap. "So if anybody ever does ask you that question, you can tell them it always costs money to make a family. And really, Willa, kids who ask things like that are just misinformed and have to be educated. I'm sorry you have to be their teacher. It must get exhausting."

"It's a little tiring," Willa said. "But not so bad."

Since that initial Babies "R" Us incident, I've learned to handle strangers' questions with a breeziness and body language that usually informs the stranger that I'm uncomfortable answering personal questions about my kids, but simultaneously reassures my girls that I'm proud of how we became a family. Sometimes it works better than others. Recently, at the airport waiting for a flight, I noticed a woman staring and smiling at my children. After a while she came over and told me how beautiful my girls were. She asked, "Is their father Chinese?"

"Their biological father is Chinese," I said, "but their daddy is German and Russian."

"Do they speak English?"

Willa sighed loudly and slapped the page of her book. I think the slap was meant to draw the woman's attention to the English words that were clearly written across the page. "Of course," I said.

"How long have you had them?"

"We've been a family for a long time," I answered and turned my back to her.

"Did you get them through an agency?"

I turned back around and looked into her eyes. "Why do you ask?"

"Just curious," she said. "I think what you've done for those children is so great. They're so lucky."

I gathered up our bags. "What I've done for my children is minor compared with the joy they've given me. Come on, girls, we have to use the restroom."

"We just used the restroom," Willa complained, then shut her book, zipped up her backpack, and rolled her eyes.

"You're one lucky little girl," the woman said to Willa. "I hope you know it."

"No," I said, "I am one lucky mama." I guided my girls to another section of the gate.

"Why are people so nosy?" Willa fumed.

"Sometimes rudeness, sometimes racism, sometimes ignorance—there are a lot of reasons, but mainly it's because our family is interracial and that makes people notice us and want to know all about us."

"It's annoying!" Willa said, stomping her feet.

"I know it is," I said, and took Willa's hand. "It's the downside of being so interesting."

"I'd rather be boring."

"Sometimes I'd rather be boring, too, but I wouldn't want to change a single thing about us, so for now, or until the world gets its act together, we're stuck with being fascinating."

Most likely, no one who has approached my family and asked us personal questions has meant any harm, but they do assume that an adopted child's background is available for public discussion, and not subject to the same sensitivity or restraint due any child. My girls are not immune to the self-consciousness all children feel being scrutinized. The best expression of support for my family is to respect our differences by not calling attention to them. There are many adoption agencies and adoption Web sites with tons of information. Unless you are a friend or relative of an adoptive family, it's best to look there for answers.

Someday, I hope, we'll live in a world where racial or sexual or familial differences don't matter because we'll have achieved the understanding that one kind, or one way, is not necessarily better than another. As for now, I fear we routinely call unneeded attention to these differences. For example, why are Nicole Kidman and Tom Cruise's kids described as their "adopted kids"? Why aren't they just identified as "their kids"? Or why did the press write that Angelina Jolie and Brad Pitt were expecting their *first* child when they already have a son and a daughter? What's next? "Angelina and Brad's biologically born child joins their adopted son and adopted daughter." Or "So-and-so's donor-egg-born son joins their gestationally carried, IVF-born daughter." We don't refer to how biological children become a part of their families, so why do we point out adoption?

There are exceptions. A few weeks ago, Willa was a flower girl in my sister's wedding. At the beauty parlor where the bridal party was having their hair done, I introduced Willa to the hairdresser. She looked at my daughter and said, "Hey, Willa, are you adopted?"

Willa answered, "Yes, from China."

I touched Willa's shoulder protectively to remind her that, if needed, I was there to help navigate the encounter.

"So am I," beamed the hairdresser. "Isn't adoption the coolest?"

Willa looked at me and smiled. "Yep. It's totally cool." **◐**

HOME FOR THE HOLIDAYS (WHEREVER *THAT IS...*)

She'll be home for Christmas—you can count on that. But whose home? Her mother's? Her father's? Her stepmother's? Her grandparents'? Her boyfriend's? Maile Meloy confronts the now-classic holiday question.

For a few years after I moved to Los Angeles from Montana, my mother gave me tree ornaments when I went home for Christmas—delicate glass icicles and handmade silver stars. She wasn't trying to encourage me to spend the holidays somewhere else; she was just acknowledging that I was now an adult. Baffled, I hung the ornaments right back on her tree. What else would I do with them? Christmas paraphernalia lived in my parents' attics, because Christmas happened at home.

Gradually, though, I started to develop a fantasy about staying in L.A. The weather is tauntingly spectacular in the last week of December, the skies clear and blue from winter winds. After a few parties, everything shuts down and the freeways empty. I could swim in an outdoor pool with all the lanes free, and surf without stealing anyone's wave. I could go to brunch, see a movie, open no presents, cook nothing.

What I was avoiding, in my fantasy, was crowding onto an overloaded plane, then changing to a tiny second plane in Salt Lake City to arrive in Montana late at night. I was avoiding the cold I always catch, and the tension about exactly how much time to spend at my father's house, my mother's house, my stepmother's house (long story), and my grandparents' house with my uncles and aunts and cousins. I was avoiding the marathon of presents, each more difficult to pack.

I was also avoiding the schlepping of Christmas stockings from one house to the other, which my brother and I still do in our 30s because my mother's face crumples when we occasionally forget, and because my father spends all year collecting small stocking-friendly gifts. You'd think we could own two sets, but my mother knitted the stockings when we were babies, with our names and birth dates and Santa's face with a fuzzy angora beard, so we tote them back and forth like Halloween loot bags. Refills on stockings once seemed like an accidental bonus of divorce, but how many knick-knacks and oranges does one person need?

If I stayed in L.A., I wouldn't see my old friends, but I also wouldn't end up racing from one party to another on slippery streets. I wouldn't have to make, at my mother's house, the peanut brittle my father still loves—a strange ritual that annoys my stepmother, who doesn't like having first-marriage confections around. I need my mother's help to make it because I never know when to take the pot off the stove (too soon and the brittle will stick to your teeth, too late and the nuts will burn). My mother does it by smell, rushing in with the pot holders while I'm still dropping test globs of candy in ice water.

Just to complicate the algorithm by which holiday time is apportioned, my mother's family also gathers in Oregon every other year. My mother (like my father) has three brothers and a sister, and they all have children, and now their children have children. The flights to Oregon from Montana—two or three, through Salt Lake or Seattle or Portland—are cramped and turbulent, and they're often delayed or canceled. My grandmother becomes a nervous Border collie with an incomplete flock until that brief, happy moment when everyone has arrived—at which point she starts worrying about departures.

We go to midnight mass in Oregon, and on Christmas Day we eat tourtières for breakfast, as my grandparents did when they were children. The recipe is a relic of medieval French cooking, a flaky piecrust filled with ground pork, spiced with cinnamon and cloves, served (this part isn't medieval) with Del Monte dill pickles. The pickles are not negotiable; they've been Del Monte as long as anyone can remember, presumably because they were cheap, and now the flavor combination is seared into everyone's brain. To refuse a piece of tourtières is to be suspected of an eating disorder. But I'll risk saying in print that I could survive without them.

The thing I would miss, if I didn't go home, would be the ice-skating. The wild, friendly outdoor hockey games with my Montana

Christmas 1973: Meloy, age 1, searches the hand-knit stocking she still uses.

cousins, who were little kids pushing child-size wooden chairs across the ice for balance when I was in high school, but who now skate circles around me, stripping the puck away anytime I get near it—that would be a real sacrifice. Everything else could pretty much go.

Or at least that's what I used to think every October, when it was time to book the flights on those bouncy small planes.

Two years ago, I opted out and flew to New York for a stripped-down Christmas with my boyfriend's family. His mother, brother, and sister usually go upstate with friends, but that year they were having dinner at home in the city. The trip had some of the appeal of my fantasy—no small planes, no presents, no parceling out time equally between my parents. And it would be glamorous Manhattan: people bustling around in boots and coats, under the holiday lights. There was always Rockefeller Plaza if I needed a skating fix.

Things started off well. We went to a cocktail party with writers and architects and an Irish poet I'd read in college. The hostess was English, and handed out sheet music for English carols no one knew; sight-reading around the piano, we all sang gamely anyway. We had drinks at my agent's apartment, and I was interviewed for a magazine story about my new novel. If I had been told, when I was 22 and wanting to be a writer, that I might someday have such a Christmas, I wouldn't have believed it.

My boyfriend had learned to knit in order to make his mother a scarf, but he'd run out of wool on the plane, midway through the last-minute matching hat. So we spent an afternoon wandering the city, looking for a matching skein. A woman in a shop gave us a tip on a knitting store a few blocks away. They couldn't match the yarn, but sent us to another narrow building, with a small room full of knitting supplies on an upper floor. Someone there suggested a third shop. It was like trying to buy drugs, except drugs must be easier to find. We never did track down the yarn, but it was lovely to walk around in the pale winter light without anywhere we had to be.

Christmas Eve, we went to Rockefeller Plaza but couldn't even *see* the ice; people were packed against the rail 20 deep. So many men were dressed as Santa Claus, it looked like he had hired decoys for protection. We searched for a carol service and failed; the midtown churches weren't going to waste their bumper crowds on kiddie songs. Still, there was snow in the air and the lights were pretty, and a million jolly people walked the streets.

Christmas Day, I went for a run in Central Park, where people wandered, walking off meals. Opening presents took no time: I got two books. The homemade scarf was a big hit, even without the hat.

It was everything I had wanted in a holiday, but I wanted everything else. When I called home to Montana, everyone was together, all my uncles and aunts and cousins. My brother was home, his first baby about to be born. They passed around the phone, and I could hear someone pounding noisily on the piano, and my sister singing. (She's my half sister, my father and stepmother's daughter, so her stocking gets to stay in one place.) I don't know what song it was—it seemed like multiple songs—but it was the death knell of my L.A. fantasy. It wasn't just that I missed my family. I missed all the attendant madness. My brother, who is two years younger, said, "I wish you'd been here to decide when to move from Mom's house to Dad's house. When you're not here, I don't know when to go."

I called my grandparents' house in Oregon, and it was the same—loud and crowded, the little kids playing in a cardboard box, preferring it to whatever had been inside. I'm sure there were annoying things going on, but I couldn't hear them. My advice: If you decide to escape from a family holiday, don't call home.

Last year there was no hesitation about going to Montana. My boyfriend—he's now my husband—loves it there, too. It was an off year for Oregon, which made things simpler. We even skipped the stockings, out of pure weariness of presents. My father, who keeps a secret stash of embarrassing artifacts from our childhood, gave me an autobiographical poster I'd made in school at 7 or 8, a self-portrait with ketchup-colored hair framed by spiraling text: Something special about me is I am helpful. I feel nervous when I have something that I think will be hard. My mother made tourtières. My sister had a new boyfriend everyone loved. My brother wasn't home, but we crowded around the computer to watch a video of his baby playing with a giant plush monkey.

At the big lake outside town, the ice had expanded in thick sheets up onto the beach, jutting at an angle into the air, so we had to clamber over and slide down the other side before putting on our skates. Someone sailed an iceboat by at 50 miles an hour. We played hockey with no lines, racing after loose pucks, my uncle guarding the makeshift goal in his snow boots. The mountains turned pink on the other side of the lake as the sun started to go down; the ice was black underfoot with fine white cracks, and silvery blue in the distance.

This will be our first married Christmas, and we're going to horrify some people by spending it apart. For my grandparents, the essential thing about Christmas is midnight mass, and the birth of a child who shall be called Prince of Peace. For my mother, I think it's the solstice and the fact that the days will get longer, the light will return. For my father it's Santa Claus, the spirit of abundance and generosity. But for me, it seems to be something at once simpler and more complicated than all these things. So my husband will go to New York while I'm in Montana, and then together we'll brave the little flights to Oregon. I'm slow, but I learn. Someone else can have the empty freeways and the waves; I'm going home. ◑

MOTHER'S NATURE

It's usually about nurturing her child—not swilling vodka, hitting on her daughter's boyfriends, and setting her up with frat boys by stranding her at the bar. P. Hunter relives her stormy relationship with her mother and the way she finally found the calm within it.

Lots of daughters have difficult mothers. I knew that. So I didn't spend a lot of time questioning my own mother's eccentricities. The Thanksgiving I went to stay with her and my stepfather, Butch, at their Florida vacation condo, for instance, I was only hoping the change of scenery might distract her from her usual mission of trying to get it through my head just how much I was screwing up my life.

Instead my mother directed Butch to drive straight from the airport to a noisy college bar. She ordered a double vodka and struck up a conversation with the baseball-capped frat boys at the next table. "They're nice! And good-lookin', too!" she shouted across the table at me. "Why don't you move over here by me and talk to them? You're not going to get a boyfriend sitting there waiting for Prince Charming to find you!"

"Mom," I feebly protested. "They're too young for me."

"Bullshit!" she declared and launched into a boilerplate tirade, which might have been titled "Why You Are a Dumb-ass Who Wouldn't Know an Eligible Bachelor If He Hit You on the Head with a Dead Polecat."

My mother never met an adult male I wouldn't have been better off marrying rather than doing whatever it was I thought I was

doing up in New York. I excused myself to go to the ladies' room. I'd sat through the speech. All I had to do now was sit through a plate of chicken wings and some nachos.

When I came back, my mother and Butch weren't at the table. I looked around. They weren't anywhere in the restaurant.

One of the frat boys leaned over and said, "Your mother said she had to go. She asked if we'd give you a ride home."

My mother was right about one thing. The frat boys were nice. But I had only a vague notion of where "home" was (I'd visited the condo briefly once before) and had no phone number or address. I sat in on the boys' night out for hours, feeling as though there was a large rock in my rib cage, trying to let them carry on the kind of conversations 20-year-old guys usually have, instead of the kind they have when an older woman has been foisted upon them by her mother. Sometime much later, a couple of them drove me around for an hour or so, until eventually a road looked familiar, and then another road, and then another.

The next day, my mother greeted me with a cheery "Did you have fun?" With all the gumption I could muster, I said, "Not really."

"Well, that doesn't surprise me," she said. "You're not a people person like me. You're more like your daddy—as mean as a snake." This snake business was a favorite leitmotif of Mom's. I had never thought my father was mean. It's true that I didn't spend as much time with him as with my mother (his second wife didn't much welcome my brother and me), but to my mind the man bore more resemblance to a Labrador retriever than he did to a snake.

My mother, however, is a people person—if being a people person means loving an audience. She's a flamboyant former Southern belle, Tallulah Bankhead playing the role of Carol Brady. As you'd expect, the miscasting did make for moments of comedy. My friends thought my mother was a blast, since she told dirty jokes and smoked and drank with us. The local society portrait painter—adored by my mother's country club friends for portraying them as, say, wood nymphs in paintings with titles like *Starshine* and *Raindance*—pretty much nailed our relationship: She

painted my mother as the sun, smiling and surrounded by a dazzling nimbus of gold rays. I became the moon, looking wan on a blue background and draped in ghostly white. My mother hung her portrait over the mantelpiece in her living room. She hung mine on the landing of the stairs leading up to the spare bedroom.

For years I asked her advice, hoping for a word of encouragement. Instead I'd hear her say, "I always thought sending you to that college was a huge waste of money." Boyfriend broke up with me? Must have been because I was something of a slut.

If I brought a man home, her opinion was never in doubt. Joe, for instance, returned from a trip to the bathroom a bit ruffled to report, "Your mom just grabbed me and French-kissed me." (He was her all-time favorite.) Upon meeting Eric, she tousled his hair and told him she thought he was so cute she could just eat him up. He dumped me shortly thereafter. She got his number from directory assistance and called him up sobbing, begging him to take me back. Needless to say, I stayed dumped.

I also got a steady stream of phone calls from strange men my mother had met in bars who seemed to think I'd be dying to go out with them. Apparently, she had pressed my phone number on them, saying I desperately needed a decent man to knock some sense into me.

Once, when my mother came to visit with friends, she took me out to a nightclub where the waiters took turns lip-synching to tunes like "Rock Around the Clock" and a gargantuan fiberglass Chevrolet appeared to have just plowed through one wall. I watched her knock back cocktails and shimmy with anyone who would shimmy back.

Eventually, I left, telling her friends I was tired. She arrived home an hour later and came through the door like a jet-propelled wolverine, grabbing me and shaking me as I lay on the sofa.

"I will not tolerate your being rude to my friends!" she shrieked, eyes bulging, fingernails digging into my arms. "When I take you someplace, you stay there and have fun!" I kicked her away, and she slapped me, hard. I fled to the bathroom, locked myself in, and sat crying on the toilet. When one of my mother's friends returned a few minutes later, I heard her ask, "What's the matter with her?"

"Aw, she's just crying over some guy," my mother said.

The next day it was as though nothing had happened. I wondered whether she even remembered it.

> WHY DID I NEVER JUST STOP AND THINK, "WOULDN'T MY LIFE BE MORE PLEASANT IF I INTERACTED LESS WITH MY MOTHER?"

Why did I never just stop and think, *Wouldn't my life be more pleasant if I interacted a little less with my mother? Why couldn't I give up expecting her to be the parent I wanted?*

It never crossed my mind. I was 28 years old and had no idea why I was so unhappy. I quit my job in book publishing to try my hand as a writer, bartending for a living. But as the pitch of my mother's disapproval became ever more shrill, I couldn't seem to see the way forward. The rock that had sat in my rib cage during the night out in Florida was now a permanent fixture. I found myself choking back tears all day long.

Fortunately, in New York people never stop talking about their shrinks, so the thought finally occurred to me, *Maybe seeing a professional is a better idea than the one I had the other night about throwing myself from the window of my 12th-floor apartment.*

After a year or so in therapy, I started to think that I could handle my mother a little differently. I continued to put myself in the line of fire, but now I fought back. For a while it just made things harder. I would end up in tears, ground down by my mother's viciousness. "You are a worthless piece of shit!" she'd yell through the phone. "I'm doing you a favor. You need to be broken! You need to hit rock bottom."

I said some horrible things, too. I told her she'd never done anything for me except to sleep with my father (and I phrased it a little more forcefully). I sleepwalked through my days, consumed by hatred. I lay in bed at night entertaining myself with visions of my mother being squashed by a falling baby grand or mown down by a crosstown bus.

One night I did hit rock bottom, if not in the way my mother had meant. She was telling me what a failure I was, that I'd never amount to anything. Suddenly, I found myself screaming into the phone, "Mother! I'm not you! I'm a separate person! I have my own life, and it doesn't matter what you think of it!" I remember a silence at the other end of the line. From that moment, I saw that I had never really thought of myself as me—I had only been a blank screen, the moon feebly throwing off a pale (and entirely unsatisfactory) imitation of her personality.

I hardly spoke to her on the phone after that. I stopped asking her advice, and at holidays I made the decision—why had I not done it sooner?—to stay at my father's house. I'd always known that my mother qualified as a serious drinker, but now I realized she was suffering from a clinical condition. And that it was her problem, not mine.

The changes seemed to bewilder my mother. I knew something had shifted between us when I took a boyfriend home and he laughed at my mother's four-letter words and sozzled escapades as you would at any harmless eccentric. And she didn't lay a finger on him.

I married that boyfriend, and we had children of our own. We literally distanced ourselves from my mother by moving thousands of miles away. It seemed, finally, as if I had figured things out.

Except motherhood didn't come easy to me. Listening to my daughter cry for hours as an infant or trying to handle her defiance as a toddler was too much for me at times. I'd suddenly snap and start screaming like a madwoman at my little girl, clutching her by the arms as I shrieked. My husband would say, "Everyone loses their temper with their children from time to time." But I remembered similar scenes from my own childhood. I couldn't believe that after all that effort to become myself, as a mother I was back to reflecting her.

That was a terrifying time, to be at home with a small child, knowing I wasn't keeping it together. After another round of therapy, I saw that separating myself from my mother wasn't enough. I needed to try to understand her. Her own mother, I recalled, had been an alcoholic, and, faced with my own failures as a parent, I saw that she must suffer from the same shaky sense of self I had.

I knew that some women were able to fix their relationships with their difficult mothers—but I also knew that was impossible for me. I'd met people who, like me, had decided that cutting their

MY MOTHER GOT AN EX-BOYFRIEND'S NUMBER FROM DIRECTORY ASSISTANCE AND CALLED HIM UP SOBBING, BEGGING HIM TO TAKE ME BACK. NEEDLESS TO SAY, I STAYED DUMPED.

mothers out of their lives was for the best. But that hadn't worked, either.

Now I'm trying a third way: I don't depend on my mother for support or encouragement, but I no longer spend time or energy pushing her away. We talk about once a month for no more than ten minutes. She tells me tidbits of hometown gossip—mostly thrilling anecdotes about bridge tournaments and the gall-bladder surgery of people I've never met—and I tell her cute things her grandchildren have done. She comes for a visit once a year, and maybe because I have a little more of the emotional distance I always needed, I don't feel the impulse to duck and cover the moment she rings the doorbell.

I look at my children, and I'm glad they know their grandmother, especially since with them her famous sense of fun comes into its own. On her last visit, she unzipped her bulging suitcase to reveal a mountain of pink tulle, feathers, and sequins with which she planned to fashion a to-die-for fairy costume. Underneath she'd managed to squeeze in a rocking horse—she'd only had to dismantle it and cut up the insides of the suitcase a bit to get it to fit, she explained. I couldn't help noticing she'd also packed a handy thermos full of vodka, but she had the kids, like my erstwhile teenage friends, in hysterics. In fact, we all laughed. **O**

DR. PHIL: "IT'S TIME TO PUT AN END TO THE PHONINESS"

Phillip C. McGraw, PhD: A woman can't win over her stepdaughter…a widow wants her kids to accept her boyfriend…and a mother talks to a child about cancer.

Q: **I just attended my stepdaughter's wedding with my husband of 18 years. As usual, she did subtle things to let me know I wasn't welcome. For example, she addressed the invitation to only her father and feigned surprise that I was at the rehearsal dinner. She's coming for a visit soon, and my husband said he'd like me to be there. I can already imagine how uncomfortable I will feel. If I don't point out her slights, he pretends not to notice. I'd always hoped his daughter would grow up and we could be friends. After the wedding, though, I reached my limit. I'm sorry my husband is caught in the middle, but what am I supposed to do?**

DR. PHIL: You call addressing an invitation to only one person in a couple subtle? I wouldn't call that subtle at all. I think that's an intentionally in-your-face message that says, "I don't want you around." I can understand why you've had enough. Your husband ignores his daughter's insults because he's afraid to jeopardize his relationship with her. He doesn't seem to realize that he has other options.

Let's take a look at what's going on with your stepdaughter. Like any adult, she has the right to pick the people she surrounds herself with. Sure, most of us fantasize about being part of a perfect family. But it's her prerogative not to like you, and her father can't make her. It's time to put an end to the phoniness. He needs to spell out that anyone who disrespects his wife is disrespecting him. An insult to you by omission, exclusion, or outright hostility is an insult to him, too. I suggest you convey this to your husband by saying something along the following lines.

SCRIPT:

GIVING UP ON GETTING ALONG WITH A STEPCHILD

I want to have a candid conversation with you about your daughter. She's made it clear over time that she dislikes me. I don't blame you or hold you responsible for that, and I'm not demanding that you broker peace. At this point, you can't tell her what to think of me. Of course I want you to be in each other's lives, and she doesn't have to like me for that to happen. I would never demand that you choose between us. All I ask is that you stand by my side and stick up for me. I expect you to tell her that you won't tolerate insensitive behavior and that her unkindness toward me is offensive to you as well. It isn't too much to ask for some civility. She's old enough to pick the people she wants to be friends with. I'm not one of them, and that's okay. Go spend time together, but don't ask me to participate and to act like everything is fine when we know it isn't.

Ideally, your husband will get onboard with you. It's your call as to whether you see your stepdaughter, so if the prospect makes you uneasy, don't be around when she comes by. When you find yourselves in the same place, take the high road and be polite. But there's no need to force the issue.

Q: **I'm 46 years old and have been widowed for three years. My husband had been ill on and off for a while, and my children and I went through a very hard time at first. About a year ago, I started seeing a kind, loving widower. My college-age children are not taking well to the idea of my being with someone** besides their father; they say they want me to be happy but aren't ready for this. They refuse to even meet him. I love my children and this man very much. He's willing to do whatever it takes to make the situation easier on them. How can I bring these two worlds together?

DR. PHIL: We've got an example of the tail wagging the dog here. This is your life, and to be blunt, your college-age kids don't get a vote. Would it be nice if they were excited about your relationship with this man? Sure. Would it be wonderful if you could all go to Sunday dinner? Yes, and maybe that will happen one day. But at 46, you have many years ahead of you, and they shouldn't amount to a life sentence of solitary confinement. Why are you letting your kids dictate how you spend your time?

Waiting two years after your husband died before getting involved with someone was appropriate and respectful. Your kids are being selfish. They're expecting you to be in the same place in the grieving process that they are, though you have different needs. It sounds like they're judging you, and while you sit home alone, they go about their business. That's not fair. You teach people how to treat you, and you'd better stand up for yourself because nobody else will. You need to do what you want, when you want, with whom you want. It would be different if they were young kids wondering who this stranger is who might become their stepfather, but that isn't the case.

Once your children learn that they don't get to shame or control you, I suspect they'll start coming around. Until then, you may need to keep these worlds apart. You can have a loving relationship with your kids, and you can have an intimate relationship with this man. That doesn't mean there has to be a bond between them. If your grown kids want to act like babies, that's their choice. But let them know that you're no longer going to tolerate their judgment by saying something like the following.

SCRIPT:
RECLAIMING YOUR LIFE

I understand that you and I are in different places with regard to handling the loss of your father. You have the freedom to date and be social, and you're asking that I deny myself the same. I refuse to do that. I loved your father, and he'll always have a prominent place in my mind and heart. But life is for the living. I'm not going to spend the next 40 or 50 years keeping vigil so you don't have to deal with the fact that I'm moving on. It's not going to be any easier for you five years from now than it is today, so I need to do what's right for me. I've met someone I care about. He's never going to replace your father, but he means a lot to me and I would be grateful for your support. I understand if you can't give me that. Either way, I love you.

Q. How do I tell my 10-year-old son that my life expectancy is two to ten years at most? He knows I have cancer, but he doesn't really understand its dark side. I've tried explaining to him that I might go to heaven before he does. These conversations induce stress and nightmares. Last time, he told me he would cry himself to death if I died. I didn't want to traumatize him any more than necessary, so I stopped talking about it. I feel incredibly guilty that my child has to go through this. While I can accept my fate, how do I prepare him for my passing?

DR. PHIL: First of all, I'm sorry for you and your family about your diagnosis. Second, I have two rules for dealing with kids: Don't ask them to handle situations they have no control over, and don't ask them to grapple with adult issues. Having candid conversations with your son about your passing is, in my opinion, ill advised.

Children his age have some concept of death, but they don't yet have the tools to manage it constructively. You say that you could die in the next two to ten years; that means your son is going to be between 12 and 20 years old. His ability to cope will be exponentially greater even two years from now, let alone a decade. Allowing him to mature in this time span is a gift. If you were on your deathbed right now, you'd be forced to explain this in a timely manner. But that doesn't appear to be the case, so don't get ahead of yourself.

I think you may be premature in burdening your son, not only because he's young but also because so much progress is being made in cancer research. Your broad window for survival leads me to assume that you may not have a fast-moving, aggressive cancer. With every passing year, the chances improve that a treatment that could dramatically impact your life expectancy will become available.

All I can do is encourage you to stop talking about what might happen at some point and start preparing your son for life. In other words, rather than discussing the gravity of your circumstances, you can help him be a strong, independent young man—mentally, emotionally, and spiritually. You haven't mentioned his father, and to the extent that it's possible, I suggest you talk to him to make certain your son will have at least one adult around to see him through difficult times.

You've already said a lot to your son, so I have mixed emotions about your saying anything further. If, however, you feel you need to raise the issue again, you might try to undo the anxiety he's feeling in the following way.

SCRIPT:
TALKING TO A CHILD ABOUT CANCER

I know you and I have discussed the fact that I am sick, and that I may pass before you do. You have to realize that I'm a lot older than you are, so that's likely going to happen one day no matter what. I want you to understand that I'm working very hard to stay healthy. All my doctors are working hard, too, and our hope is that we're going to find a cure for this. In the meantime, I think it's really important that you and I focus on the present. Nobody knows what's going to happen tomorrow, but here's what I do know: I'm here, you're here, and we love each other. So let's make the most of every day we have together and not worry about what might be. If you have any questions, please come and ask me, because I won't keep secrets from you. But for now, let's be optimistic and enjoy life. **O**

THE $60,000 DOG

Lila was a shedding, drooling, romping bundle of fur, and the light of her human companion's life. Then she went blind, and the first vet bill was a ferocious $3,338. So...what was it going to be: summer camp for her daughter or meds for the dog? Lauren Slater faces a bitch of a question.

PUPPY LOVE A Shiba Inu—Lila's breed, albeit a younger stand-in.

My dog Lila is 40 pounds packed with muscle and grit. Her hide is as rough as the rind of a cantaloupe, covered with coarse hair that is nevertheless somehow soft to the touch. She is a dumb dog in the sense that all dogs are dumb; driven by genes and status, she will willingly fight any mammal that threatens her alpha position, and she delights in bones, big greasy bones she can crunch in her curved canines and then swallow, splinters and all.

My husband disparages Lila, and, to his credit, there is much there to disparage. She lacks the capacity for critical thought; she has deposited in our yard an estimated 4,000 pounds of feces during her ten-year tenure with us; her urine has bleached our green grass so the lawn is now a bright yellow-lime, the same shade as the world seen through a pair of poorly tinted sunglasses. Lila farts and howls. Lila sheds and drools. Lila, in the past year or so, has cost us more to maintain than does the oil to heat our home. There is her food, her vaccinations, her grooming, the four times yearly palpating of her anal glands, her heartworm medications, her eye medications, her chew toys, her city leash, her second, country retractable leash, the dog bed, the emergency veterinary visits, the maintenance veterinary visits for eye pressure checks, the sheer time it takes to walk her (my husband estimates the value of my time at 50 bucks an hour, which I personally think is a little low for

someone of my age and experience, but there you have it). Picture him, my husband, at night, the children tucked in bed, punching the keys on the calculator. Picture Lila, unsuspecting (and this is why she charms us, is it not?), draped across his feet, dreaming of deer and rivers as he figures the cost of her existence meshed with ours. He presses "=" and announces the price he claims is right: $60,000. I look out the window. The sky above the lawn she's bleached is as dark as a blackboard, scrawled with stars the weight of which I cannot calculate. I love my husband. I love Lila, too.

There are by some estimates two million tons of dog feces deposited annually on American sidewalks and lawns and in American parks. The volume of the canine liquid in this country has been estimated at four billion gallons, which, writes author Stephen Budiansky in his book *The Truth About Dogs,* "could fill all the wine bottles from a full year's output of the vineyards in France, Italy, Spain, and the United States combined." Dogs are the carriers of more than 65 diseases they can pass to their human counterparts: Some of the more well-known ones are rabies, tuberculosis, and Rocky Mountain spotted fever. Each year about a dozen people in the United States die from dog bites, and about 386,000 are injured enough to require a visit to the emergency room. Seems a no-brainer, right? Knowing these facts, you would have to be as dumb as a dog to have a dog in your home.

My own dogs were puppies when we got them, puppies like my husband and me. Now, 12 years later, I've begun to read the obituaries in the paper, I worry about osteoporosis, I experience occasional sciatica. Musashi, the elder of our canines, appears blessed with youthful genes, but Lila, like me, is going gray, her hips eroding, clumps of fur falling from her hide.

Until recently, I viewed Lila's decline as I do my own, an unfortunate inconvenience auguring a foreboding future that was still a way off. Then, a few months ago (it was spring then, a beautiful soft May day), I came downstairs to find my feisty dog crouched by the front door, her eyes squinted shut, her breath hot and fast. I called to her. She struggled toward me, then keeled sideways. I rushed her to the 24-hour veterinary hospital located ten miles from our house. *Why,* I thought, as I waited at a series of interminable red lights, my dog panting in pain, *why are there no ambulances for animals?* While an ambulance for animals may strike some as absurd, it is likely no more ridiculous than a pet ER would have seemed to the general public 100 years ago.

Perhaps of all the 20th century's advances, veterinary medicine ranks among the greatest, not too far behind the combustible gas-powered engine. As barnyard animals disappeared from mainstream American life, so too did the barnyard vet, his primitive tools replaced with the antiseptic power-driven appliances that characterize so much of modern medicine, his sheep and goats and chickens now shampooed lapdogs and fine-boned huskies with bead-blue eyes and soap-white coats. And whereas in the 19th century "vets" had minimal education if any at all, they now are required to slog through four years of training more intense than an ordinary doctor's owing to the sheer quantity of species whose structures and metabolisms they need to master. And yet despite the difficulties of a veterinary education, the fact is that the number of vets and veterinary hospitals have, over the course of the 20th century, exponentially increased. Experts seem to agree that this increase reflects the pet's phenomenal rise in status, from a lowly creature consigned to the outhouse or no-house to honored family member with her own Eddie Bauer bed.

Or her own hospital bed, as the case may be. The hospital we arrived at that day is a 25 "bed" facility, a piece of prime real estate amid a row of biotechnology companies on a tiny road just off the highway. I carried my panting puppy in through the pneumatic doors. A Burmese mountain dog lying sideways on a stretcher was whisked past me by two masked attendants. On the wall above the reception desk hung pictures of the vets, each coiffed and poised, below gold plaques inscribed with their specialties: neurology, oncology, pediatrics, psychology. The Burmese mountain dog was stalled outside the OR doors. He lay on his side, his front paws politely, precisely, crossed. His yellow eyes met mine. I had the distinct feeling he was from a fairy tale, a prince put under a spell, his carcass canine, his mind man.

A doctor ushered me into a small examination room. With thumb and forefinger she peeled back Lila's clamped lids, and I could see it then, how her normally amber eyes were filled with milk, glinting a dull bluish color, all opaque. Her eyes were oozing, and when I touched the fluid dampening her fur, it felt gluey.

The doctor called in the staff ophthalmologist, who brought in a huge machine and pressed its probe right up against Lila's pupil in a way that made me wince. "Seventy-five," the ophthalmologist said. The two doctors looked at each other grimly. Lila had gone still, stunned or dead I could not tell. They peeled back her other eye and again pressed the probe right to its center. "Eighty-three," the ophthalmologist said again. They turned to me. "Your dog has glaucoma," the ophthalmologist said. "The pressure in her eyes has risen well beyond normal."

Glaucoma. I had heard of that before. It did not seem so bad, I thought. I was wrong. In people glaucoma is manageable. In dogs

it's devastating. The pounding pressure winches the canine's much smaller skull, causing a migraine well beyond what humans can conceive. Lila lay rigid with agony, her snout and fur hot to the touch. "The pressure has gone so high," the ophthalmologist said, "it has crushed both optic nerves. Lila is permanently blind."

I left Lila at the hospital that day—and for two days following. I left distraught. On my way out, the receptionist presented me with the first half of my bill: $1,400—money we didn't have. I looked again. My eyes, after all, were working. Fourteen hundred dollars for the ER visit, the emergency ophthalmology consult, the 48-hour boarding fee. The projected costs were on the second page. The only one I recall is the $1,800 charge for some advanced interventions that might be necessary. "Does everyone pay these charges?" I asked. "What happens if people don't have the money?"

"That hardly ever happens," she said. "People find a way to pay."

Owning a dog or a cat was relatively rare up through the 17th century. Now, however, 63 percent of American families own pets, while, according to a survey by the American Veterinary Medical Association, 72 percent of childless couples under 45 have companion animals in their households. Sociologists hypothesize that the rise in companion animals is due to the phenomenon so well described by Robert Putnam in his book *Bowling Alone,* discussing the decline of community in the United States during the 20th century. Pets, it seems, are filling a vacant space in our society, a space that used to be occupied by people in relation to one another and is now occupied by people petting pugs. Still, we could think of this another way. It could be that pets have risen in status for reasons rooted not in decline but rather in progress—in this case progress toward a more sophisticated understanding of ethics and the relative value of life. Traditionally, we have held human life to be of utmost comparative worth, but who's to say that stance is right, or even productive for our planet? A shifting ethos is reflected in the fact that the term "pet owner" has become disagreeable to enough people that it has been virtually banned in a number of jurisdictions as well as the entire state of Rhode Island and replaced by the phrase "animal guardian." According to a 2006 Purina survey, 73 percent of cat owners said they went to a doctor only when very sick or injured, while 96 percent said they would call or visit a vet immediately at any sign of their pet's ill health. Since Katrina, animal activists have succeeded in getting legislation passed that requires rescue personnel to include companion animals in disaster planning. And stories of devoted (or insane—this, the core question) pet owners spending tens of thousands of dollars to fund advanced cancer care for Spot are becoming ever more common.

I drove home. My dog was neither dying nor dead, but the fact of her pain was almost beyond what I could bear. And what would her life become once the pain subsided? A blind dog. How could she understand what was happening to her? It was late in the day, the clouds like cataracts spreading. Inside the house, my 7-year-old daughter was riding her scooter in our hallway. "Lila has gone blind," I said to her. I started to cry. I told my husband when he returned from work. I did not mention the veterinary bill. Instead, I called the bank, cashed in a CD, paid the penalty.

Two days later, I drove back to the hospital. The final bill was $3,338. I figured this was a onetime cost that my liquidated CD could cover. They brought Lila to me. She did not come out on a

Lauren Slater and her dog Lila at home, May 26, 2007.

leash. She came out carried, and when they set her in my lap I could see, immediately, that a dog can be devastated. The medications had brought the pressure down, so her eyes were open, but they were thickened, blank, like opaque sea glass, reflective but not receptive. "Lila, Lila," I whispered. She moved her whole head in the direction of my voice, but gave not the tiniest tail wag, not the slightest ear prick.

Back at home, I set Lila on the floor of our living room, but even here, amid familiar scents, she would not move. Musashi bounded forward in his typical greeting style, but something, some smell, stopped him short. He skidded to a bunched halt, then cautiously extended his snout to sniff his companion of 11 years— where had she been all these days? Lila stayed stone-still. Musashi backed away, then clattered, fast, up the steps. "Lila, Lila," I called, my daughter called, even my husband called, but the dog was too terrified, or despairing, to move. At last I picked her up, carried her to our bed. I slept with her for one week straight, my face buried in her fur, her pee soaking the sheets, her eyes weeping pus and drops.

I ordered a book about blind dogs. I watched a video that demonstrated training techniques. I stroked Lila's skull, moved my fingers through her dense fur, sent my husband to the pharmacy to fill the prescriptions, four tiny tubes of glaucoma drops. "Four hundred dollars," he said when he returned, holding the paper bag. "Four hundred dollars for a month's supply of this stuff."

What choice did we have? While the medication would not restore a single stripe of sight to Lila's world, it would prevent the pain of the pressure crushing her head.

"Maybe," my husband said, " we should put Lila down."

"Put Lila down," I repeated mechanically. "Put her down."

"She's had 11 good years," my husband said. "Look at her now."

Yes, look at her now. Lying in a puddle of pee on our marital bed. I called the ophthalmologist. "Lila's depressed," I said. "She won't move."

"Put her on her leash," the doctor said. "Take her out. Do not baby her. I've seen blind dogs climb mountains. If you teach them toughness, they'll be tough."

I brought Lila outside. I made a Hansel and Gretel path through the woods by our home, using beef instead of bread crumbs. That got her going. She found the shreds of roast, tasted baked blood, and remembered the meaning of life.

Slowly, over the weeks, Lila began to make her way.

A month passed. We needed more medication.

It was June then. School ended. My daughter's day camp was $3,000, its high price reflecting its high quality. Now I had to choose: Clara's camp or Lila's eyes. To my husband it was clear. To me it was not. If Clara did not go to the fancy camp, she could still enjoy her summer. If Lila did not get her medications, she would not only not enjoy her summer, she would pass it in agony.

A dilemma such as this one is new in the history of pet owning. Sixty years ago, the average pet owner could expect to spend at most a couple of hundred dollars for care during the entire life span of his or her pet. Now the lifetime cost of the American pet could reach $60,000, and this isn't due simply to inflation. As veterinary students train in specialties and subspecialties and subspecialties of those subspecialties, Fido, should he need it, can receive a kidney transplant, chemotherapy, back surgery, a titanium hip replacement, radiation, neurological correction—you name it. Add to this the fact that dogs and cats are living longer than ever before because of improved nutrition and vaccinations. In an earlier era, my Lila may very well have died before reaching old age and its complications, like glaucoma, and I would thus have been spared the difficult game of weighing the relative value of my daughter's summer camp versus my dog's comfort.

My husband felt I was being led like a blind donkey on the string of sentimentality, and that if I took a hardheaded view of things, I would see that spending $400 a month on a decade-old dog was wrong—wrong for our family, wrong for our marriage, wrong for the world. To get the money, I took on every extra work assignment I could. According to my husband, everyone would be much better served were I to donate the monthly medication payments I was earning by working overtime to the starving continent of Africa, to the Green Party, to victims of lymphoma. His beliefs are echoed by Dr. Bruce Alexander, professor emeritus at Simon Fraser University and the author of an upcoming book on globalization gone awry: "If Americans were to take all the money they spend on dog food, it would be enough to make a significant dent in the problem of world hunger." In other words, dog lovers are baby killers. Shame on us.

Shame on Darrell and Nina Hallett, a couple from Washington who in 2004 spent $45,000—which included a stem cell transplant—on their dog with T-cell lymphoma. Shame on Pauline Wilson of Manhattan, who spent $50,000 in less than half a decade in an attempt to keep her "Baby Cat" alive. Shame on families who spend more than $4,000 for end-of-life hospice care to ensure that their pets die in more comfort and with more dignity than far too many human beings who have no one to help them through. In much of the Third World, people tend to feel that doting on one's pet is a sign of Western excess. Wrote Aleetha al-Jihani in a letter to *Al-Madina* newspaper in Saudi Arabia, "One bad habit spreading among our youths is the acquisition of dogs and showing them off in the streets and malls...this is blind emulation of the infidels."

I know I am an infidel, in more ways than I care to mention. I can discuss my deficits, but I am not yet ready to admit to the particular one of which we are speaking, even as I state it as a possibility. Because perhaps valuing nonhuman animals as much as, if not more than, our own kind is not wrong at all. Perhaps it's in fact right. What, I have to ask, in the Darwinian theory of evolution, which has more proof to it than any holy book, posits human beings at the top of the heap? As the planet erodes, and as our role as its destroyer becomes harder and harder to deny, might we not be considering, or reconsidering, the idea that the human species is far from sacred? Might we, in losing the sense of our own importance, be better able to see our kinship with species outside of ours? A long, long time ago, Copernicus suggested the earth was not the center of the solar system, and by doing so he shook the souls we say we have to their ethereal roots. Roger Fouts, comparative psychologist at Central Washington University, told me, "It is a fundamental misperception to think human life has more value than any other life form."

I like to touch my dogs' paws. Their paws are rough, scaly, the skin cracked like quaked earth, the nails smooth and curved in their sharpness. A dog's nails can be difficult to cut because, unlike humans, they have veins, and if you snip too deeply, a bead of blood wells up and the animal winces in a way that is hard to bear. I did this to Lila once, cut too close to the quick, cut the blue-violet vein that threads the nacreous nail of this beautiful beast I call mine. I call her mine not because I own her but because I love her. I call her mine as I call mine my children, my husband, my self. She is mine for as long as she is Lila, which amounts to no more than a nanosecond of time in the scheme of things, and when that second passes, she, like us all, will undergo the phenomenal changing of categories that we call death. But until she does, I will care for her with everything I have. I will struggle to divide up my limited resources in the best way I can. I will admire her daily, as I do all those I love. And why? That is the question I have not answered here, the question my husband always asks. He no longer asks if it is right to so love a dog, because he knows how I will answer. "Yes, it is right," or "Someone has yet to offer me any scientific proof that animals mean less than we do, so it is certainly not wrong." His question for me now is simply, why?

Why? I don't know. What I do know is that when I look into Lila's blind eyes, I see amazing things. I see the wildness of the wolf; I see humans finding fire, the Pliocene plains, millions of molecules, the softest snout, a single cell split. I see an animal walk out of the water; I see the engine of evolution, and if I listen closely, I think I can hear it, too, a low continuous hum—a sound that doesn't stop, I must believe, even if, or when, we do. ◖

HOW MUCH IS THAT DOGGY IN THE WINDOW?

Average cost of a dog: $331

Number of U.S. households with at least one dog: 44.8 million

Number of pet dogs in U.S.: 74.8 million

What Americans spent on pets in 2006: $38.5 billion (nearly double the $21 billion they shelled out a decade ago)

What they ponied up on veterinary care in 2007: an estimated $9.8 billion, up 6.7 percent since 2006 ($9.2 billion)

How much the pet industry could ring up by 2010 at the current growth rate: $50 billion

Percentage of 379 human resource departments surveyed that offer pet health insurance as an employee benefit: 5

Cost of MRI pet scan: $2,200 to $2,700

Cost of radiation: $6,000 for 19 treatments

Percentage of 580 dog owners who would buy an urn for their deceased dog's ashes: 15

Percentage who would buy a memorial stone for their yard or garden: 23

Minimum cost for a taxidermist to freeze-dry a dog: $1,000

Number of states where judges have administered financial trusts set up in a pet's name: 25

Sampling of pampering services and products available: pet spas, doggy day care, pet steps and denture products (for elderly dogs), personalized bones, organic pet food, massage, acupuncture

Percentage of 8,000 pet owners who said their pets sleep in bed with them: 56

Annual estimated cost of dog-walking service in Brooklyn: $5,200 (at the rate of $20 per solo walk, five days a week)

Minimum lifetime cost of a medium-size dog, including food, supplies, boarding, and basic veterinary care: $4,500 to $5,500

Number of states in which cruelty to animals is a felony: 42

Souces: American Pet Product Manufacturers Association, Veterinary Pet Insurance Company, *The Wall Street Journal*

THE MAN WHO GOT AWAY
(THANK GOODNESS!)

Her father ran off when she was 12, leaving behind a wife, four children, 50 unmilked cows, and a trail of questions. Amy Dickinson, who grew up to write the unflappable advice column Ask Amy, gets to see what she's been missing.

Amy and her daughter, Emily, summer 2006 in Freeville, New York—the hometown she's come back to.

My father called me one day last summer. "Um, it's your father," he said. "I shot a bear and now it looks like I've got to go to court." I replayed his message a few times. His voice is nasal and gravelly and full of flatness and diphthongs. I hadn't heard it in a long time. He asked me to call him back and left his number.

His wife, Pat, answered. I realized I had forgotten her name, so I just introduced myself and asked for my father. "He's out back with his bees, but I'll call him," she said. I heard her Marjorie Main voice sail out the back door. "Charles!!" I had never heard him called Charles before—it was a bit of a surprise. Back when I knew him, everyone called him Buck, the nickname his mother gave him as a child. He couldn't sit still, just like a buck, the story went. I think of bucks as being majestic, many-antlered royalty of the woods, so his nickname never quite made sense to me, until I realized that the reference was most likely not to a buck but to a bucking bronco. Regardless, his nickname suited him. It is the name of someone who doesn't want to be a Charles.

My parents were married for 22 years. They had four children. We were raised on a crumbling dairy farm on the fringes of a tiny village in the Finger Lakes region of New York State. The landscape I know is one of crags, waterfalls, and glacially formed lakes alongside low hills called drumlins, tumbling and overlapping. It is sprinkled with tough-looking villages scarred by severe winters and ringed by farms and trailer parks strung along beside unruly creeks. Homely as it is, the countryside of my childhood brings

tears to my eyes. I love it beyond my understanding. When I see news reports about heartbroken Albanian refugees who can't wait to get back to their muddy villages, I understand.

Several years ago, after living in various cities, I bought a little house on Main Street in my hometown, and my daughter and I now divide our time between there and Chicago. My extended family, who make up about half the population of 450 in our village, laughingly deride us as "summer people," the joke being that this is a place no one comes to on purpose—my hometown is the kind of place people dream of leaving.

I have a persistent vision of my father making his way across the field in back of our barn. Going somewhere! His step was springy and enterprising. He drew his bucket from a bottomless well of energy and cultivated a tough restlessness that got him into trouble. He loved shortcuts and windfalls and wayward moneymaking projects, sometimes involving other men like him, who, when things went sour, tended to punch each other in the nose. He was handsome like a B movie star, in the manner of Glenn Ford, but with the ego of a Caribbean despot. I loved to watch him but not, I think, in the way daughters commonly love to look at their fathers. He was like an animal. Unpredictable. He would crouch beside the belligerent Holsteins in our barn during the evening milking, a hand-rolled cigarette hanging between his lips, urging milk out of their udders and calling them goddamn filthy bitches when they shifted their weight and threatened to crush him. He would hop around on his haunches. He had springs in his work boots.

To make ends meet on our ever-failing farm, in between the morning and evening milkings, Buck laid iron with Iroquois Indians recruited from nearby reservations. He said he loved the work—being outside, climbing and dangling from the substructure of a building. One day my mother and I stopped at a muddy construction site outside Ithaca. What looked like a medium security prison but later turned out to be a Howard Johnson was going up along Route 13. We pulled in and checked around for a sign of my father. Scanning the skeleton of the building, I saw his unmistakable silhouette skipping along an iron beam, two stories up. His arms were flying out from his sides like a tightrope walker in the circus. He seemed lighter than air.

My father left when I was 12. It was a sudden thing, and as far as I know, beyond his travels to increasingly far-off construction jobs, he had given no warning that he would leave home permanently. Our 50 cows were in the field, needing to be milked. A neighbor helped out in the mornings, and my sisters, brother, and I did the second milking when we got home from school. Evening chores had always been a warm, antic time. In between hoisting milk pails, my sisters and I practiced cheerleading routines on the long concrete alley between the cows and sang Three Dog Night songs at the top of our voices. But now the milking became quiet. My 16-year-old brother handled the heavy lifting, and my sisters and I silently went about our business.

We didn't know where Buck was, but after a few weeks he called from Lowville, a town along the Black River in the North Country. He had taken up with a woman named Joan, who waited tables at a truck stop he frequented while working a construction job in Watertown.

My father told my mother that he had sold our herd of Holsteins. The next day two huge cattle trucks belonging to the Gunzenhauser Dairy in Cortland drove in and took the cows away. It was April and raining a cold, hard rain that was sluicing the last vestiges of dingy snow into the creek. I watched from the driveway as our cows slipped and slid through the mud and were prodded with electric shocks onto the trucks.

Like most farm kids, I had a love-hate relationship with our cows, but when they were gone I found I missed them terribly. They showed up in my dreams, roaming through my mother's flower beds, lowing quietly, and letting me know that we had failed them. Our old red barn was like a cathedral looming over the landscape. It was the size of an ocean liner with enormous rooms, milking parlors, and lofts. After the cows left, I couldn't go inside it.

We had an auction. The Munson family ran all the auctions in our area, and they handled things. About 100 people crowded onto the property just outside the entrance to the barn. Glenn Munson, who was a junior at our high school and had muscular dystrophy, called the auction in a speedy high-pitched singsong auctioneer voice, swaying back and forth in his wheelchair like Stevie Wonder at the piano. Our neighbors bid on our rusty farm implements, milking equipment, even the leftover hay stacked in our barn, and loaded our worldly goods into their pickups.

Later in school, whenever Glenn wheeled by in the hallway, I felt him looking at me compassionately.

The summer after my father left, my brother quit high school and hitched his way to Scandinavia. My sisters and I continued with high school, all ambitious, high-strung overachievers. We were cheerleaders and athletes and student body presidents. We starred in the school plays. Our mother went to work as a typist at Cornell University. She typed very fast, almost 100 words a minute. She would come home from work and lie down on her bed, still wearing her coat, and then rise with a sigh in the dusky half-light to make dinner. After years of cooking and baking large meals of meats, preserves, breads, and pies for her big family, she stepped down to hot dogs served from a pot on the stove and buns pulled out of plastic sleeves. All spring and summer, she sat out on the front stoop in the warm evenings, listening to the peepers on the creek, smoking cigarettes, and playing the same Three Dog Night song, "Out in the Country," over and over on our record player.

One night about a year after my father left, Joan—now his second wife—called. "Where is that bastard?" she asked. My mother said she didn't know.

My father surfaced again several months later. He had taken up with Jeanne, a family friend. Buck and Jeanne started moving around. They lived on Long Island while he worked construction. They lived in Vermont and Connecticut, where he found jobs on farms; sometimes he trimmed trees. Then they moved to Port Allegheny, in North Central Pennsylvania. Jeanne was sick for a long time and then died of emphysema. My brother told me she smoked right next to her oxygen canister. He thought she might blow herself up.

When I went to college, my mother quit typing and enrolled at Cornell as a full-time undergraduate. After she got her bachelor's degree, she went on to get an MFA at Cornell. She taught at Cornell and later Ithaca College.

Our old red barn fell down, a victim of decay caused by a hole in the roof that my father had always been meaning to patch. The absent barn left an enormous empty space next to the house that I couldn't look at. An elderly neighbor who lived up the road left his house to my mother when he died, and she moved away from the empty farm to that little place, which is lovely and ghost-free.

Like the man himself, my feelings about my father seemed to wander. There were the years when I avoided thinking about him because remembering him made me too sad. There were the times when I actively fled from the memory of him because I was worried that his hard luck would rub off on me. There were the men I avoided because they reminded me of him, and the men I wanted because they reminded me of him.

Buck did what he did best. He kept moving. The marriages increased in frequency, if not duration. After my mother, Jane, he married Joan, then Jeanne. After Jeanne died, he married Jean. That one didn't last long—her children intervened.

Then came Pat. Pat worked at the bottle factory in Port Allegheny and retired on disability.

My father had become the many-married protagonist of a George Jones song. Remember the old joke about country songs—that if you play them backward all the hard luck reverses itself and the dog comes back? Sometimes I fantasize about playing my father's song backward. The wives fall away, one by one. The barn rights itself, our possessions return to their rightful owners, the cows back themselves off of the cattle trucks and into their assigned stanchions, and I look out the window and see my father striding across a field, going places.

Buck took to driving around in a gigantic rusty delivery van. One day about 15 years ago I was drinking coffee with my mother on her porch. He drove slowly by. I caught a glimpse of his profile. It was shockingly like my own. "Isn't that your father?" my mother asked. "Yup. That's him," I said.

He drove past the house, turned around down the road, and then came back.

I hadn't seen him in many years, but he was the same kinetic man I remembered. He crossed his legs at the knee and his free foot dangled and jangled as he spun out his schemes. He was looking

Buck Dickinson with his family in 1963 (*clockwise from top left*): Amy (age 3), wife Jane, Rachel, Charlie, and Anne. *Right:* Amy, in her backyard with Emily.

into emus. He was thinking about livestock or maybe soybeans. He'd read an article about Nova Scotia and thought about maybe moving up there for apple picking season. I pictured him driving to Nova Scotia and sleeping in the back of the delivery van, parked in an orchard—which turned out to be exactly what he did.

I realized that I was relieved he'd left us. All I had to do was look at my mother, the college professor, sitting on the porch in the house she owned. More than once she'd said that if Buck had stayed, she'd be living in a trailer, and I knew this was true. My father's life tended toward chaos, and he didn't like to be alone.

I married the most un-Buck-like person I could find, but the marriage ended anyway. I resolved to be the kind of mother that my own mother was, and I succeeded. My daughter and I spend our summers in the little house on Main Street, next door to my aunt and just up the street from my mother, my sister, and various other aunts and cousins.

Over the past ten years, once or twice a summer I'll look out of the front window to see Buck standing on my porch. He'll stay for the length of time it takes to drink a cup of coffee, talk maniacally about his latest venture, jump up suddenly—and leave. A few years ago, he started keeping bees at his place in Port Allegheny. Sometimes on a visit he'll leave me with a jar of honey, which is the palest yellow, like sunshine in deep winter. I try to make the honey last, since I never know when I'll see him again.

I hadn't heard from my father in over a year when he called and left his message saying that he'd shot a bear.

I decided to make the drive out to Port Allegheny on the day after Thanksgiving. The cartoon topography of low hills and valleys was awash in tints of brown and gray; it was Andrew Wyeth season, a sadly beautiful but depressing time of year brightened, for some, only by the prospect of venicide. Gunfire

rang out all morning in the field surrounding my house, and Toad's Diner was filled with camouflaged deer killers swapping hangover lies over their morning coffee.

Fortunately, the three-day-long bear hunting season in Pennsylvania had just ended, and deer season didn't start for another day in Port Allegheny. I figured that if I made it out of my home county alive and raced for the state border, I had a chance of completing the trip without being taken down by a stray bullet.

As I neared Port Allegheny, I stopped for coffee at a gas station and picked up a local paper: No bear deaths were recorded from the latest three-day shooting spree; my father's off-season August kill had been the only bear felled by man in the area all year.

I crossed the Allegheny River at the edge of town, following his directions. The country was rough and rolling and it reminded me of him. I knew his place from the number of vehicles in various states of repair parked beside and behind the house. When I turned in to the driveway, a large Ford flatbed truck followed me in.

My father hopped down from the cab and said hello. He looked old. Tired. His hair was close-cropped, as if he had cut it himself looking at his reflection in the kitchen window. He'd had some health problems, including a small stroke the previous year, but after a few days, he'd hitchhiked home from the hospital. A blood clot in his leg was killing him, he said. He had a pronounced limp.

Pat was waiting for us inside. She was boarding three hunter brothers from Ohio. They slept in bunk beds upstairs but were now out stalking game on the state land. I heard gunfire ring out occasionally, bounce back and forth off the hills, and carom through the valley.

Over tuna sandwiches at the kitchen table, Buck started to tell the bear story. He produced some papers, which he said illustrated his claim of self-defense. The bear wasn't his fault, he said. The bear was the bear's fault. But I had a feeling that both of them were simply being true to their natures.

Buck told me he first saw the bear when it ambled down off the ridge by the house and helped itself to a garbage can full of cat food on the back porch.

In defiance of every known stereotype, my father is a cat man. The few times from my childhood when I can visualize him being still, he is sitting cross-legged in a ladder-back chair, smoking a cigarette and stroking a house cat, Godfather-style. Here in his kitchen I noticed he had at least two cats that periodically curled around his ankles.

After the bear had its fill of Friskies, my father told me, it scrambled back up the ridge and disappeared. It was a male. Young. Big. My father said he was a beauty. The bear had a tag pinned to his ear—this was not his first taste of kibble; he'd been caught and tagged before by the game warden. Buck had a feeling that this bear had been released into their back woods the previous week. The game warden had a habit of taking captured bears on tours of Boy Scout troops and schools before releasing them— Buck felt that this bear was particularly bold and was probably used to being around people.

He called the game warden, who came out, and together they baited a barrel trap with rotted meat and honey. The warden told my father to fortify his beehives.

Buck spent the morning installing fencing at his apiary. His biggest fear was that the bear would destroy or permanently disrupt his hives. As he told me this, he gestured out to the back field, where wooden trays of beehives stacked waist high were surrounded by a low electrified fence. It looked like a stalag in miniature. I imagined groups of worker bees smoking cigarettes and hanging around the prison yard, planning their escape from the queen.

After working on the fencing all morning, he and Pat went into town. On their way back to the house, a neighbor who kept goats flagged them down and said that the bear was back and had been lying in the road. The neighbor had to get out of his car and kick him out of the way. "That bear wasn't afraid of anything. He was crazy," my father said.

Buck raced back to the hives to finish the fence. He said the bear was watching him from the edge of the tree line.

That's when my father's instincts, running as they do toward the hair-brained, violent, and adventuresome, made him decide to take matters into his own hands, so he went and grabbed his 20-gauge shotgun.

When Buck got to this next part of the story, he started to sound wounded and practiced, like a man on the witness stand. He said he called the game warden a second time. Whatever. He got tired of the whole business.

The next time the bear came down the ridge, my father was waiting for him. He says he waited until the bear got close enough—about 25 feet—and then he shot him in the chest. The wounded bear fell down but then managed to scramble back into the woods.

That's when the game warden showed up. He asked my father what happened to the bear.

Buck said, "I just shot him."

They went into the woods and found the bear, crumpled in a heap—dead.

The officer wrote up a ticket. Buck showed me the receipt. I recalled how my father had always railed against the system. He was a refusenik when it came to taxes, licenses, permits, paperwork, child support, insurance, credit cards, and savings accounts. Somehow he managed to square his feelings enough to cash his Social Security checks, but paying for a dead bear? That's where he drew his imaginary line.

Buck decided not to pay his $800 fine, $2 per pound of bear. He called one attorney who said she wouldn't take the case because she sided with the bear. In the end, he retained the services of an old, retired lawyer in town. I pictured the two of them shambling up the steps of a courthouse, each wearing his only suit, my father managing to look somehow handsome with his necktie knotted thickly against his throat.

The argument was self-defense: The young bear, a menace, not only damaged his hives but charged down the hill at him. My father was being scrappy, his favorite attitude.

The judge said they could take payment in the form of a money order.

There would be an appeal. My father pulled out some papers to show me and started shuffling through them. There was a precedent. He thought a lawyer for the farm bureau over in Harrisburg might agree to represent him.

I asked my father if he'd learned anything from killing the bear. I asked him if he saw the bear as a metaphor for something else and if he could explain that to me. The questions I really wanted answers for went unasked. I wanted to know who he was, what he longed for, and why he left all those years ago, cleaving my childhood in two.

"Ummmm, I don't see things as metaphors for other things," he said.

I asked Pat what she thought of all of this. She said she had cooked bear meat before and that it could be very tasty as long as it was not old and tough.

My father walked me to the car. We had spent the bulk of the day together. I realized that in my whole life, I had never spent so many hours all at once with him. We said goodbye and Pat came out. I waved to them both as I drove away.

I wondered if I would ever see my old man again. I guessed there was a chance I wouldn't. I reflexively looked in the rearview mirror, but he was already gone.

My father doesn't see things as metaphors for other things, but I do. As I drove away, I tried not to think about the jobs, the wives, and the children that he left, but about the bees and the honey they make. The honey stands for the sweetness of life, while the bee brings the sting. My father, the self-aggrandizing bear killer, was both the bee and the honey to me.

A few days ago I got an envelope in the mail. Inside was a tear sheet from a notice put out by the Pennsylvania Farm Bureau about a new state regulation that expands the means by which farmers can legally kill game, including bears, "...causing or about to cause damage to farm crops, fruit trees, vegetables, livestock, or beehives...." That part was underlined. My father attached a note:

I made enough noise that the state changed some of its rules. Now we have a right to protect ourselves and our stuff.

Love, Buck
your dad. ◑

Counterclockwise from top left, October 11, 1974, Frances and Ben in Nashville, the day after his birth; 1976, Ben listening to music as a toddler; 1979, in the yard at home in Wisconsin; 1988, preparing for a dance; 1994, his first year at West Point.

FOR MY SON, IN IRAQ

As long as men have gone to war, mothers have wept for their sons. For poet Frances Richey, whose only child serves in Iraq, words are her only weapon against a near-unspeakable fear.

KILL SCHOOL

That was the summer he rappelled
down mountains on rope

that from a distance looked thin
as the dragline of a spider,

barely visible, the tension
he descended

into the made-up
state of Pineland

with soldiers from his class.
They started with a rabbit,

and since my son was the only one
who'd never hunted,

he went first. He described it:
moonlight, the softness

of fur, another pulse
against his chest.

The trainer showed him
how to rock the rabbit

like a baby in his arms,
faster and faster,

until every sinew surrendered
and he smashed its head into a tree.

"They make a little squeaking sound,"
he said. *"They cry."*

He drove as he told me:
"You said you wanted to know."

I didn't ask how he felt.
Maybe I should have,

but I was biting
off the skin from my lips,

looking out
beyond the glittering line

of traffic flying
past us in the dark.

FRANCES RICHEY'S SON,
Ben, is a 33-year-old army captain who was deployed twice to Iraq and remains on active duty. "Ben's graduation from West Point in 1998 was a huge celebration," Richey recalls. "These young men and women were ready to serve." She hesitates. "We had no idea what was coming." Now she finds herself unable to turn away from the ever-present news coverage and horrific images coming from the war zone. The poetry editor of the Bellevue Literary Review, a journal of fiction and nonfiction affiliated with New York City's Bellevue Hospital, Richey began writing these poems after Ben was called to action. "This is how I keep myself together," she says. Her poems are blunt, and Ben has read them all. "They tell him how I feel without my saying, 'I support you, but I'm scared you may never come home.'"

WAITING

In my dream a girl
floats on a raft.
She bends,
pulls from the river
a small dark
winged thing,
brings it to me,
a stone, John
(my son's first name,
the one we never use)
chiseled into it.
I'm half awake:
5:15am; 1:15pm in Iraq.

*

On the way to the doctor,
I carry the dream in my body
over the snowy walk
past Wollman Rink...
8am; 4pm in Iraq

Ben has asked for warm clothes,
lip balm. I'd forgotten
it could get cold in the desert.

In the beginning,
all the stories were about
the heat, anguished
faces; that Iraqi man
on his knees, caught
in crossfire, the futile container
his arms were
around his small son.

*

9am; 5pm in Iraq
As the cold dime of
the stethoscope sweeps
my back, I imagine Ben
underground in a
concrete room, maps
spread out on tables,
tacked to walls. He moves
from map to map,
never leaves the room.
This is how I keep him safe.

*

The vertigo started in March
when he told me
he would be deployed.
I sat down on the sidewalk
at the corner of 43rd
and Broadway, waited
for the spinning to stop.

12pm; 8pm in Iraq
The technician gives
me earplugs, presses
the button that slides
my body into the white
tunnel, where harsh
knocks and alarms
hammer out the map
of my brain, hidden
in its burning pigments,
the memory of my son
when he was three, sitting
by a window, waiting for
the rain to stop so
we could walk through
the mud to the lake
where we would place
our hands on stones,
let ladybugs crawl all over them.

*

I believed if I was present
for his football games,
he wouldn't get hurt;
that if I made the two hour drive
from Stamford to Ramsey
in half the time
that day he ran into a tree,
I could keep him
whole in his body.

Mid-afternoon, September,
after Beast, that first
training Plebe year, I fixed
him in my mind,
and he called
later that evening: *Mom,
were you at West Point today?*
And I said no.
        *But I thought
I saw you on the Plain.*
I said no, but what time
did you see me?
And he named the moment
I'd prayed for him.

I thought it had something
to do with our
heartbeats, like clocks
placed in the same
room. Once

I believed I could
close my eyes and know,
even when my son was
on the other side of the world,
if he was alive. ◖❶◗

From left, 1990, Ben playing high school football; 1998, graduating from West Point; 2004, hiking in Colorado Springs just before his first deployment.

BREATHING SPACE

"ROBIN'S ROSE," FROM *ONE HUNDRED FLOWERS*

Photograph by Harold Feinstein

DREAMING BIG

WORKING

SCARY WORK SCENARIO #1:
THE VERY BAD BOSS

If coming to the office every day feels like entering a war zone (with a crazy person as your commander in chief), you might want to ask yourself four crucial questions. As Suzy Welch reports, the answers could save your career—or jump-start a whole new one.

About a year ago, I bumped into a friend whose daughter, Amanda, used to drive me a little crazy when she was in high school. Not because she committed any of the typical teenage transgressions but because she was perfect. She got great grades, made captain of two teams, played violin in the school orchestra, and was completely down-to-earth and cheerful to boot. So it was with trepidation, as the mother of mere mortals, that I asked after this girl—by then a college graduate working at a well-known company.

"Oh my God, she is terrible," came the grief-stricken reply. "Her life is in ruins. She has a bad boss."

Instantly, my heart broke for Amanda. She had joined the ranks of humankind.

"Well, it happens to all of us," I told her mother sadly.

"I know—I went through it," she said with a sigh. "But I just quit and married Bill. Amanda doesn't have a Bill. She has only herself."

Exactly. Some of the most successful careers I've seen have been born of women who overcame one of life's scariest job situations, the very bad boss. The experience changes you, but it can also help you become more at home—and at peace—with yourself and your work.

That may sound Pollyanna-ish. I know bad bosses can make each day feel like a little battle for your soul, but my research into women's careers has convinced me that there is a viable road from office hell to happy ending. It's not an easy process—it requires focusing more time and attention on a very frustrating situation and, hardest of all, taking yourself out of the vortex of victimhood.

Yes, victimhood. Because I would make the case that bad bosses are a choice. They can put your "life in ruins," to quote Amanda's mother, only if you let them. To prevent that, you can start by answering four questions.

1 WHO'S THE BAD ONE—REALLY?

This question requires an unnatural act: a brutally candid conversation with yourself. Bad bosses obviously exist, but most managers are not critical, bullying, or withholding with people they like and respect. If your boss is being a jerk to you, the first thing you need to do is ask yourself if there is something about your performance or attitude that is engendering the behavior.

Start with the monster in the middle of the room—your results. If you're not performing up to expectations, even if you believe something outside your control is to blame, know that your boss has had to explain your underperformance to his bosses, an unpleasant experience that can quickly turn to resentment toward you.

Next you need to double-check your self-examination by tactfully extracting information about your performance from your boss. Prepare to be shocked. I once had a coworker with tremendous results who complained to our boss that she felt underappreciated. She emerged from the meeting reeling. "He said I lied to him three years ago," she said, "about a little thing on my expense account. He never forgave me."

On the other hand, you might come out of your review having been told that your performance is acceptable. He may even say he likes you, and be completely unaware that his disorganization or

temper is a problem for you. Nevertheless, you've confirmed that your boss's behavior is not about you. He or she is just a bad boss, and you must ask the following question:

2 WHAT IS THE ENDGAME FOR MY BAD BOSS?

In other words, how much do you trust your company's senior executives and human resource managers? If they're any good, they know about your bad boss and are working on an exit strategy. All you need to do is keep your head down and wait patiently. This process always takes longer than everyone wants, so you'll have to fight the completely human urge to form a cabal with your coworkers to bitch about the situation. Complaining will only drain and distract you. Instead, focus on the work and keep a positive attitude. That will hold you in good stead with the higher-ups when your boss (finally) moves on.

It's a different situation entirely if your company appears to tolerate destructive behaviors. Too many companies turn a blind eye to difficult managers as long as they're delivering the numbers. A friend of mine was an analyst at an investment firm where the manager of her 60-person department routinely screamed at people for "incompetence." Even though his rages were widely known, the CEO of the company often singled him out for praise on his financial results. It was clear he wasn't going anywhere but up.

If that sounds familiar, it's time for a serious career evaluation.

3 DO I WANT TO WORK FOR A COMPANY THAT TOLERATES BAD BOSSES?

The simple answer is no. I don't know anyone who likes the idea of giving half her waking hours, if not more, to an organization she doesn't respect. Most people realize (sooner or later) that it's time to start looking for a new job.

This is hard to accept, and it's tempting to consider the infamous end run: complaining to your boss's boss. I don't necessarily recommend that choice. Given the way most companies work, this option will fail 80 to 90 percent of the time, and will likely lead to your own demise, if only in slow motion. (If you're determined to go over your boss's head, have a job offer elsewhere ready.)

Whether you leap or get pushed, leaving your company will be hard. But it can open up surprising opportunities, as it did for a single mother I met four years ago. She had supported herself and her son as a hairdresser for nearly a decade, until one day, pummeled into a depressed mess by an abusive boss, she quit. Broke and living in her former stepfather's basement, she started a knitwear company that just earned its first million dollars. "My bad boss was the best thing that ever happened to me," she said, "because he forced me to create a life for myself that makes me proud."

Too often, however, the answer to the question, "Do I want to work at my company?" is anything but simple: Your job may be the only game in town. Or it pays you too well to leave. Or it gives you the flexibility you need to take care of your kids. If so, there is one thing left to ask....

4 WHAT IS MY PASSWORD?

By the time most people hit 25, they've come up with a single password that gets them into everything from their bank account to their e-mail box. If you decide to stay with a bad boss, you need to come up with a password that lets you into an emotional place where you do not ride your bad boss experience like a roller coaster every single day.

A friend who worked at an intensely political company once ended up working for a man who ardently wanted him to fail so his own guy would get ahead. After a few months of punching the dashboard of his car every morning, my friend's password became "Deliver and this will pass." For three years, during every grueling day, he stayed focused on building his own team's morale and new product innovation, not his boss's scrutiny. It worked: He was promoted to another division (and a good boss).

I myself had one terrible boss, who was moody and secretive. My password became "You cannot have it all, all at once." My job had enormous flexibility. I got through the rough weeks by reminding myself that by staying, I was able to be a better, more present mother. It didn't make me like my boss, but it made me tolerate her, a much more sustainable emotional alternative.

With a password, you may still have bad days, but you will have taken yourself out of the vortex of victimhood. This brings me back to Amanda, the young woman whose life had been thrown into disarray by a bad boss. She's still at the same company, working for the same person. "But you'll never believe it," her mother told me recently, "things are really looking up."

I do believe it. Back in the days before Amanda bumped into messy reality (as we all eventually do), she had believed the future was hers for the making. No doubt there was now a dent in that youthful optimism, but Amanda's perseverance could mean only one thing. She had made a choice: No one could take her happiness, or her success, away. ❑

SCARY WORK SCENARIO #2:
AND I HAVE TO SPEND ALL DAY WITH THESE PEOPLE?

Whether they're pushy, lazy, boss hating, self-promoting, or haven't done any actual work since 1973, dysfunctional colleagues can make everyone look bad. Suzy Welch on how to win at work with a losing team.

Her name was Margaret. She had an answer for everything, even questions I didn't ask her. She dominated team meetings, nearly jumping out of her chair with "Look at me!"–type comments aimed directly at the boss. The rest of us sitting there, jaws slack with amazement and disgust—we were merely a load she had to carry on her back.

His name was Mike, and he hadn't done a full day's work in years, but he sure knew how to draw us into his life of woe. One night at 10 P.M., I found myself finishing his report on deadline. He couldn't be there, he said, because his father was sick. By that point, I wasn't even sure he had a father. But there I was, alone, frustrated, and exhausted, in a state of loathing for work so intense I wished I could ditch it all.

And that is exactly where a dysfunctional coworker—or as I call them, an "un-teammate"—can put you. It's a crying shame, because working alongside a good team player is one of life's most fulfilling experiences. She makes work enjoyable; she makes it feel like something bigger than a paycheck. Working with team destroyers, well, destroys all that. They slow work down; they sap its fun, trust, and creativity. And in the process, they invariably undermine the candid and energized debate that characterizes any successful group.

So why aren't they all sent packing? In good organizations, most are—eventually. But many team destroyers are like workplace Houdinis, escaping damage to their own careers while making everyone else look bad. These are the people you must survive. But how?

The answer depends on the type of un-teammate you're dealing with. Generally speaking, there are five: Boss Haters, Stars, Sliders, Pity Parties, and Self-Promoters. Each species has its own way of poisoning the environment, and its own antidote. The first thing you can do is start with the assumption that virtually every team destroyer is an unhappy person. No one tries to damage coworkers, a team, or an entire organization without being a bit emotionally damaged themselves.

LET'S START WITH BOSS HATERS—you know the type. Harry will tell you his disdain for authority is a reasonable reaction to the tyranny of incompetent bosses. Elizabeth will tell you she refuses to be oppressed by corporate lackeys. Other Boss Haters have personal issues behind their nitpicking resistance to every directive from above. I once met a manager who told me, "For a long time, I hated all my bosses because my father was a cruel authoritarian—I almost ruined my own career. Thank God I came to my senses."

Such conversion experiences are rare, however. Most Boss Haters persist, using every kind of subterfuge from eye-rolling to outright belligerence, until management loses patience and ousts them. Some Boss Haters are hard to extricate because of union rules or special skills. If that's your situation, your best approach as the peer of a Boss Hater is a freeze-out. Don't belabor Harry's resistance or try reasoning with Elizabeth. Simply isolate; refuse to listen to their ongoing complaints. Once they're cut off from the group, Boss Haters tend to lose their energy.

Now for Stars. Make no mistake—organizations could not survive without their results. Fortunately, many key players are Stars largely because they are the best kind of employee, inclusive and inspiring, but some Stars can develop into real bullies. My team at a consulting firm had to endure Chad, an articulate (and, yes, brilliant) economics major from M.I.T. whom our clients adored. (Like other people in this piece, his name has been changed.) Sensing he was untouchable, Chad would bulldoze his ideas through the team process and ridicule anyone who dared to disagree. Another group I worked with suffered through Gwen, a marketing "guru" who'd been stolen away from another firm to bestow her genius on us. She passively disrupted our discussions by not participating, her silence sending the message "This nonsense is beneath me."

We didn't have much recourse. Few bosses want to hear nattering about a goose that's laying golden eggs. Your best option in terms of self-preservation is to accept Stars for the good they do and ignore the bad. I've seen only one other approach work, but it's hard to recommend. This technique involves playing to a Star's weakness—the need for constant praise. As strange as it may seem, many Stars are deeply insecure and cannot receive enough ego stroking from bosses. Coworkers can play the same game, thereby drawing a Star back into the team process. But don't try this unless you really feel the love for your own Chad or Gwen; a phony intervention won't work.

Sliders are former Stars, resting on their laurels and undermining their teams with apathy. Their unspoken excuse is "I've proven my worth around here; I don't need to scramble anymore." Take John Smith, a crusty old newsman who had won the Pulitzer Prize for his reporting in Vietnam. I met him when we were both assigned to the same investigative team 20 years ago. The young reporters, myself included, fairly trembled in John's exalted presence, but within weeks, it became obvious to us that he had no interest in interviewing sources or late-night stakeouts. He preferred to sit

around the office drinking coffee and telling war stories to his in-house fan club.

Fast-forward to the end of the project: a front-page article under the byline—you guessed it—John Smith and the newspaper team. The editors knew John had done minimal work, but in the newspaper business, one way of keeping score is by the number of Pulitzer Prize winners on staff.

My solution at the time was to moan and groan with my teammates about the injustice of it all. What a waste. Sliders will always live inside a protective bubble that no peer can pierce, because they deliver tangible value to an institution. Don't bother griping; instead, buck up and join the Slider's fan club, respecting him for contributions you can only imagine making. With that mind-set, you might even be able to turn your Slider into a mentor. To this day, I remember what John Smith taught me about reporting—when I finally dumped my pointless indignation and asked him.

Pity Parties are those un-teammates who have an excuse for every act of inaction. Their computer melted down. Their elderly aunt came to visit, or like Mike, their father is sick. The most expert Pity Parties concoct long-running sympathy stories: bad backs, bad marriages, bad childcare, and so on. I don't want to sound harsh. Sometimes people really do need time off or special accommodations, but Pity Parties make an art form of wriggling out of responsibility, and you're left wondering if you're a heel for resenting them—or a dupe for helping them.

Your best strategy is to steer clear of Pity Parties and their appeals for help. You'll need to steel yourself to say no as often as humanly possible, even if they promise you, "This is the *very* last time." The line I ended up using with Mike was "I'm in a bind, too. Did you ask Rory for help?" (Rory was our boss.) That response did not put an immediate end to Mike's ways; he went looking for other enablers. Still, it sent the signal—both to Mike and my coworkers—that I would not cut side deals. When

enough of us started saying no, he left us alone.

The final form of dysfunctional coworker is the Self-Promoter, like "Look at Me" Margaret, who saw every team assignment as an opportunity for personal advancement. In their pursuit of fame and glory, Self-Promoters occasionally sabotage peers. I once had a coworker who used staff meetings, with the boss in attendance, to vociferously attack every other writer's work as "hackneyed" or, her favorite word, "superficial." If we pushed back against her critiques, she accused us of being competitive with her. There was no way to win.

Usually, that's the case with Self-Promoters. They can drub you with their narcissistic "logic"—they're right; you're just defensive—and wear you down with their egocentric career campaign. But they can't smite everyone forever. After a few promotions, the moment comes for every Self-Promoter when they need a favor or help, and there is no one left to ask. So keep your head down and wait. And most important, keep overdelivering, even if your local weasel tries to steal all the credit. Self-Promoters might get more praise than they deserve, but in any good organization, real team players ultimately get what they deserve: respect and admiration.

IF YOU HAVE ANY DOUBT ABOUT THAT, you might ask Margaret. I stopped working with her years ago, but I recently heard that the company asked her to move on—just when she thought she had achieved the position of vice president, the goal she'd been gunning for. Colleagues tell me she interviewed for jobs for a year afterward, but with less than enthusiastic references, she couldn't land one. She ended up going out on her own as a consultant, and I just learned she's a tireless and admired mentor for young women in a leadership program in Boston. I don't know what she tells them, but I can venture a guess: Do everything you can at work to be a great team player, and learn to survive (and thrive) around those who are not. ⬭

THE SELF-PROMOTER SEES A TEAM ASSIGNMENT AS A CHANCE FOR PERSONAL GAIN.

SCARY WORK SCENARIO #3: THE UH-OH FEELING

A boss asks you to do something iffy. You see a colleague doing something that runs counter to everything you believe in. What's your best move? Suzy Welch has some advice for the morally befuddled.

Here's a tricky one for you: Imagine that one day, you start to suspect that a woman you work with, the one with the new baby and the newly unemployed husband, is padding her expense account. What would you do? Report her to HR? Admonish her yourself? Probably not. Instead, if you're like most people who find themselves entangled in an ethical dilemma at the office, either as a participant or an observer, you'd do nothing. That is, except agonize and flail, searching for a clean escape from the ambiguous moral mess you've found yourself in.

If there is one.

I have a file in my desk drawer filled with e-mails from people I've met while traveling as a business journalist, all seeking advice about ethical dilemmas at work. Not that they call their problems by that term. Usually they just describe something that has happened on the job that has made them feel vaguely compromised. Something that has given them a gnawing sensation in their gut that will not go away.

Now, to be clear: This "Uh-Oh" file is not filled with letters from people who have stumbled into cases of egregious wrongdoing, like what happened at Enron and Tyco. Those whoppers weren't ethical dilemmas—they were ethical violations in black-and-white. The situations I hear about exist in shades of gray.

Take, for instance, the woman who contacted me from San Francisco, where she worked at a bank. "My manager is extraordinarily political and very adept at covering his back," she wrote. "I admire him for his intelligence, but I am having some discomfort lately doing what he is asking of me, which amounts to suppressing the opportunities of those who work for him. I would love to stay at this company and move out of my boss's department. But I'm not sure I can. I think I am stuck 'screwing' people who don't deserve it."

Or consider the woman from Detroit—the head of operations at an automotive parts supplier. "As you can imagine, we have been through many rounds of job cuts over the last few years," she wrote. "I used to be able to let go of my poor performers first, but now I am being told by the legal department that I have to make cuts based on seniority. It's not fair, and the effect on the performance of my team is devastating. Should I just look the other way?"

Both of these women—and others in the Uh-Oh file—share in the belief that there isn't a good way out. I can relate. I'm a veteran of a few ethical dilemmas myself, as are most people who have worked for any stretch of time (in my case, 26 years). But it is the poignant and sometimes painful stories of the women who've written me and whom I have met across the country that have taught

me how common these predicaments are, and how treacherous. Although I've learned that almost no one walks away from one unchanged, I've also come to a three-step approach that makes it possible to emerge from the experience with your nervous system and self-confidence relatively intact.

That's a far cry from what usually happens—as I found when I was a 23-year-old newspaper reporter on the crime beat in Fort Lauderdale, Florida. Driving to work one day, I recognized several policemen hanging around my neighborhood. They weren't in uniform, so I figured an undercover operation was under way. I called my best source in the department, who told me a rapist had struck in the area five times and that if my paper reported on the sting, the rapist would skip town, and no cop in the city would ever speak to me again.

"But women are in imminent danger," I protested. "Someone has to warn them."

"Any publicity and we'll lose this creep," came the answer. "He'll go to another city and rape more women. You cannot let that happen."

Today I'm not sure exactly why I did what I did, which was obey the detective. I'd like to believe it was because, after covering the police for a year, I'd come to trust their judgment. But I'd be disingenuous to say my career didn't figure into the decision. It must have. That night, as I lay in bed with my stomach twisted in a knot and my heart pounding through my eyeballs, the police caught their prey breaking into a first-floor apartment. His intended victim was a 15-year-old girl.

Now, you might think my anxiety would have vanished with the rapist's arrest. But to this day, I still get an uh-oh feeling every time I let myself think, *What if they hadn't caught the rapist that night and a woman had been attacked because of my selfishness?* I still wonder if my decision in Fort Lauderdale was more lucky than right.

What I don't wonder about is why my choice confused me so much at the time. I've learned that most ethical dilemmas are difficult because of insufficient information and overheated deductions. And when the dilemma occurs on the job—the source of your mortgage payment, retirement fund, and medical benefits—it's even more challenging to get to a place where you can make a dispassionate, informed decision about what to do.

That's why your first step, should you find yourself in this particular work nightmare, must be to get all the facts. Because of their very nature—their inherent ambiguity—ethical dilemmas at the office are usually rife with rumor and worst-case-scenario hypothesizing. That coworker padding her expenses? Turns out she's following new tax guidelines for calculating mileage. That

had discovered that the people on her boss's list were, in fact, about to get fired without adequate warning, her choice would have been a true moral quandary. But other so-called ethical dilemmas are made of fuzzier stuff.

I know a corporate executive, a woman I'll call Margaret, who was forced out of her job after a coworker accused her of not following the company's procedure for picking a firm to handle regional distribution, saying she blatantly favored a firm where she had close friends. Margaret strongly denied the charges, but, concerned about looking soft on integrity issues, her boss asked her to go. And guess who immediately made a quiet and successful play for the newly vacated job? Margaret's accuser, of course.

Maybe his motives were pure. I don't believe Margaret is the only one thinking they were not, and in some cases it will be difficult, if not impossible, to determine if a person is acting out of self-interest. But in other instances, it might be apparent that the conflict isn't about ethics; it's about ambition, payback, or other interoffice jockeying. In loaded situations, it never hurts to pull back and ask, "Is this about principles or a power play?"

The third and final step in handling an ethical dilemma is the most straightforward: It's taking your dilemma to a "Yoda"—a confidant with wisdom and insight but no skin in your particular game. The fact is, ethical dilemmas can be so fraught, it's often impossible to make sense of them alone—even after fact-finding and asking yourself who stands to benefit most.

Your instinct, of course, will be to sort it all out with a trusted ally, like your husband or a friend from work. Forget that. They're about as close to the fire as you are. What you need is someone at a cool distance. In Fort Lauderdale, for example, I could have called an old journalism professor for advice, or my best friend in Boston, who was in the process of earning a PhD in ethics. Either could have provided the 20,000-foot view and helped me focus on my choices and their consequences. Maybe I still would have elected to remain silent, but at least I would have understood why.

As for the women in my Uh-Oh file, they too might have benefited from a Yoda. Unable to find another position in a different division, the bank employee from San Francisco who felt compromised by her "extraordinarily political" boss eventually quit. She is running her own small consulting firm now, happy but still occasionally haunted by the unplanned way her corporate career ended. "I love being my own boss," she wrote me recently. "Sometimes I think that leaving was the luckiest accident that ever happened to me. But sometimes, usually when I am at my computer still working at 10 at night, I wonder if I should have just stuck it out." As for the operations manager from Detroit who was forced to conduct layoffs by seniority, she ceded to the company's lawyers. When I contacted her recently, she simply explained, "I'm used to it now. I need my job." I asked if she still had an uh-oh feeling. She paused for a long time, then finally said, "When I'm driving home."

Happy endings? Well, real ones. Ethical dilemmas rarely wrap themselves up, with loose ends neatly tied. Like life itself, they are usually messy and complex, and many of us muddle through until a messy and complex ending emerges from the ether. Sometimes, however, we can find better endings if we take charge instead of muddling through. With careful fact-finding, the thoughtful sorting of real agendas, and sound outside counsel, an ethical dilemma doesn't have to disrupt your career or linger in your gut.

That uh-oh feeling may sure feel like it is telling you to run or hide. You can answer it back by rising to the occasion. ⬤

threat in Fort Lauderdale about my sources drying up? I later discovered that many police officers on the force, including an assistant chief, wanted to go public with the story. Had I done that, I might actually have earned a few new "friends" in high places. I just didn't know enough.

Nor did a secretary I'll call Carol, whose boss had asked her to prepare severance documents for about a dozen people in her division. The request tormented her. "It's just wrong to give employees one week's notice," she said. "I know the right thing is to let these poor people know what's coming."

Not long after, a sheepish Carol contacted me. At lunch one day, she had confided in a friend in HR that she was thinking of quitting because she couldn't bring herself to collude with her boss's ruthless severance plan. Her friend had burst into laughter. The "poor people" on her boss's list, she said, had all elected to take a generous early-retirement package from the company. Carol's conclusion: "You can only do the right thing when you're not looking at things all wrong."

Obviously, fact-finding isn't always easy. It involves discretion, patience, and savvy. Think more Nancy Drew than Spanish Inquisition. Focus your "investigation" on the people at your company who aren't gossips, but insiders. You know them: Often they're longtime employees, trusted by management and colleagues alike, experienced enough to tell a fire drill from a conflagration, and emotionally invested in keeping the organization on an even keel. Approach these individuals not like a prosecutor ready to go to trial but like a detective new to the case. And remember, such insiders usually don't give information; they trade it. Be prepared to engage in that process without revealing confidences. HR can also be a source of reliable information, if you work in a large enough company. At the very least, like Carol's friend, they can steer you away from significantly misconstrued conclusions.

Once you've completed your fact-finding mission, it's time to move to the second phase of this process, determining whether this is an ethical dilemma or a crisis that is more personal or political in nature. Yes, some instances are about principles. If Carol

WHAT DO YOU *REALLY* WANT TO DO WITH YOUR LIFE?

That's the question the eight women here asked themselves at a point when their days were filled with the same old, same old. And then they jumped—sometimes without a clue as to where they were heading. The upshot was, each found herself one step closer to connecting wholeheartedly with the person she was meant to be. Mary South, for instance, pulled up anchor on her career and her life as she knew it…and sailed into entirely new waters. Three years later, she writes about the three myths of starting over.…

FROM PUBLISHING EXECUTIVE TO SAILOR AND AUTHOR

Several years ago I had notions of myself that I wore like clothes: I was a book editor. 39. Single. Relatively successful. Stable. Secure.

Not unhappy.

Double negatives gnaw at an editor, though. *Not unhappy* became increasingly not acceptable. As the walls of my office slowly disappeared behind a fleet of fishing vessel photos, I became increasingly obsessed with the dream of salty freedom. So after one bad day at work, I did it: I quit my good job, sold my tiny weekend house in Pennsylvania, packed a duffel bag of clothes, and put everything else into storage. I then sank every penny from the sale of my home into the *Bossanova,* a 40-foot, 30-ton steel trawler that I moved aboard without a clue as to how to run it. Nine weeks of seamanship school later, I pulled away from the dock on my very first trip: a journey up the Atlantic coast from Florida to Maine.

The happiness I found at sea, the sense of accomplishment I felt, made it clear that I was more myself, more me, standing at the helm of my little ship than I had ever been sitting in a conference room. And even though the *Bossanova* now spends as much time at the dock as she does at sea, the lessons I learned on her pitching decks continue to color my days.

I can't count the times that someone has heard my story and said, "Oh, someday I'd love to [insert their fantasy here]." I'm not able to tell them how to make that happen, but I can offer what I now understand about many of the great go-for-it clichés.

Take the maxim "Do what you love and the money will follow." Unless you happen to love being a stockbroker, this is not necessarily true. I, for instance, abandoned a six-figure job with an expense account, bonus package, full medical and dental benefits, and a 401(k) plan for…genteel poverty. (Taking the proceeds of a house sale and putting them all into a 40-foot, 30-ton steel boat is probably not what Warren Buffett would have advised as an investment strategy.)

Mary South on her boat, the *Bossanova*, in Sag Harbor, New York, with Heck (*in her lap*) and Samba, June 6, 2007.

I can honestly say, however, that buying the *Bossanova* was the smartest thing I ever did. In the end, my adventure thrilled me in a way that a fat paycheck and job security never could. And I noticed how much less *stuff* I needed to be happy. I stopped compensating myself for my boredom with expensive things I didn't really need and inevitably lost interest in. So by all means, do what you love, but be prepared for that to be its own reward.

No one prizes reckless abandon more than I do, but "Carpe diem" is another adage that should never be taken literally. Seize the day if you must, but do so gently and never, ever shake it. All days are not alike, and some of them are just not meant for seizing. Some days you wake up with a headache, a dentist's appointment, and a long to-do list. But that's okay. Seize tomorrow instead and today follow the path of least resistance—because deciding *not* to seize this particular day is also a form of seizing the day, if you follow my drift.

Likewise, whoever came up with the bright idea that you should live each day as if it were your last has probably never taken this advice. Even the most self-controlled among us might become hopelessly self-indulgent as we faced our final chances—gorging ourselves on our favorite rich foods, emptying our savings accounts for that crazy extravagance we'd always postponed, quitting our jobs, blurting out our long-suppressed dislike for a particular colleague, or confessing our inappropriate crushes to the unsuspecting. What this cliché fails to address is that the day *after* your imagined last day quickly arrives and transforms your grand exit into an unmitigated disaster. Now you're chubby, broke, jobless, and have really spooked your cute UPS driver. And you're supposed to live this nightmarish new day as if *it's* your last. You see where I'm going with this—it gets old very fast.

Better advice is to live each *year* as if it's your last. Pace yourself. Prioritize. Most of all, enjoy the constructive daydreaming it takes to plan your fantasy, because if you don't, you're missing the whole point: Living each day as if it's your last is really about enjoying *now*. Even if you're not exactly where you want to be yet, there really is a ton of pleasure to be had in stopping to smell the rugosas along the way.

And how do you know where to go? That's easy: Follow your heart. Just remember that a heart is not a GPS, and it can lead you to some pretty unexpected places. For instance, I set off to navigate the eastern seaboard. But I also wound up falling in love, working as a dockmaster, and writing a book. None of these were ports I had planned on visiting, but I am who I am because of them.

Adventure comes with no guarantees or promises. Risk and reward are conjoined twins—and that's why my favorite piece of advice needs translation but no disclaimers: *Fortes fortuna juvat.* "Fortune favors the brave," the ancient Roman dramatist Terence declared. In other words, there are many good reasons not to toss your life up in the air and see how it lands. Just don't let fear be one of them. ◖

FROM CORPORATE FASHION EXECUTIVE TO CLOTHING COMPANY FOUNDER

Jordan Veatch-Goffi, 30 (*right*), with her business partner, Lisa Pidge, on the beach in St. Petersburg, Florida, June 5, 2007.

JORDAN VEATCH-GOFFI CLIMBED THE RANKS AT GAP for five years before she leveraged her corporate experience into Doce Vida Fitness. Her advice to office workers: You can make the jump in six (sort of) easy steps.

1 **TREAT YOUR JOB AS AN MBA PROGRAM**: To get the full picture of how to run a retail business, I applied to the Gap's retail management training program. Essentially, the company paid me to learn design, marketing (which is how to get publicity for your products), planning (meaning, have enough money on hand to pay the bills), and production (how to buy zippers from one factory and buttons from another and ship them to a third where they make the garment).

2 **FIND A PROBLEM**: I'm a very athletic, big-boned person, and I like my body. I want to look great when I work out, but nothing I bought in the United States ever fit right.

3 **LET YOUR IDEA BE THE SOLUTION**: I'm half Brazilian, and I visit the country at least twice a year. The women there are very curvy and very body confident. They show off what they've got. Brazilian fabric and design reflect that. I wanted to create athletic gear here that makes you look better, feel better, and work out better.

4 **STRETCH YOURSELF**: Our fabric, which is made in Brazil, has 12 percent stretch—that's more than most American athletic fabrics. It really hugs your body. The compression not only makes you look smooth but also expands and contracts as your body changes. Expecting moms wear our V-top pants before, during, and after pregnancy.

5 **CELEBRATE YOUR SUCCESS**: The Dallas Cowboys cheerleaders hired us to create their fitness wear—we celebrated by doing high kicks!

6 **MAKE ALTERATIONS**: We modified the Cowboys cheerleaders design before putting it in our catalog—their inseams are really short. No one but cheerleaders could *ever* wear those.

Chandra Greer, 49, in her store, Greer, in Chicago, June 19, 2007.

FROM MARKETING EXECUTIVE TO STATIONERY STORE OWNER

KNOW WHEN TO FOLD 'EM: I was an executive at an ad firm, and I felt as if the space between who I was and who I had to be for my career was huge. In 1997 I quit with no idea what to do next. I spent several weeks in despair, convinced I'd ruined my life. Then I went shopping. I was drawn to paper stores, places that sold all the things you needed to make greeting cards or little books.

PUT YOUR STAMP ON THINGS: I started making my own cards because they're such a positive product. You send them to make people feel better. When I took my designs to retailers, I was rejected. I knew I needed my own place. In 1998 I opened Greer in a tiny space in a wealthy suburb north of Chicago, with money my husband and I had saved up.

PLAY YOUR CARDS RIGHT: The store did well enough, but my taste wasn't completely resonating with my suburban customers. My sales weren't as good as they could be, and the people who were buying had come up from the city. Obviously, I needed to move downtown—but Chicago has a lot of great stationery stores, and rents aren't cheap. Still, in 2005, I did it. My sales went right up. We started getting press, which generated even more business. Today we sell stationery and paper goods as well as soaps, pillows, vintage scarf button pins, even a little book called *George Washington's Rules of Civility & Decent Behaviour*. I should never have been in business anywhere else.

239

Rosanne Haggerty, 47, in the lobby of the Prince George, with Common Ground residents, May 31, 2007.

FROM NONPROFIT STAFFER TO NONPROFIT FOUNDER

IN 1982 ROSANNE HAGGERTY TOOK A VOLUNTEER JOB with Covenant House New York, a shelter for at-risk youth. Eight years later, she would create Common Ground, an innovative solution to housing the homeless in Manhattan.

DID YOU KNOW THIS WOULD BE YOUR LIFE'S WORK WHEN YOU STARTED VOLUNTEERING? No, I kept thinking I'd do it for one more year, then go back to a conventional career path. I bought an updated LSAT study guide every summer.

WHY DIDN'T YOU GO TO LAW SCHOOL? When the 735-room, filthy, decrepit Times Square Hotel (a.k.a. Homeless Hell) went bankrupt in the late 1980s, I wanted someone to turn it into quality supportive housing—with employment services, a clinic, and caseworkers right in the building. Not a shelter but permanent,

dignified housing. Because I'd been development coordinator for Catholic Charities of Brooklyn, I knew what questions financiers, tenants, and the city would need answered, and I wrote up a plan. Everyone I talked to was too overcommitted to take it on. They all agreed, though, that someone really ought to do it. Finally, I thought, *Oh, someone is me*. In 1993 the first new tenants moved in. It became the largest example of permanent, supportive housing for individuals in the country. We've opened four others in New York [including the Prince George, *above*] and are helping to create similar projects in Los Angeles, New Orleans, and Australia.

EVER THINK ABOUT BECOMING A LAWYER? No, I bought my last LSAT guide in 1985.

FROM STAY-AT-HOME MOM TO ADVENTURE-TRAVEL COMPANY OWNER

Karen Berber, 41, at Crandon Park in Key Biscayne, Florida, June 4, 2007, with fellow kiteboarders.

IN OCTOBER 2000, KAREN BERBER—PREGNANT WITH HER THIRD CHILD and busy with a small but demanding business importing children's clothing that blocks UV rays—meant to run a quick errand. Instead, driving along Miami's Rickenbacker Causeway, she found a new career. Her transformation hinged on four questions that surfaced at just the right time.

WHAT'S THAT? I saw two guys on the ocean, riding boards attached to beautiful kites. I love anything you can do in the water or on it, so I pulled over and waited for them to come in.

HOW CAN I DO THAT? They explained they were kiteboarding—a cross between windsurfing and kite flying—and one of them was starting a school to teach it. I would've signed up right away, but I waited until I delivered to enroll.

WHERE CAN I DO THAT? Being out on the water with the wind as your engine is so many things at one time—beauty, freedom, control, power, fear, and awareness. But it's often not windy enough to kiteboard in Miami. I was totally willing to travel, but no one could tell me where to go.

HOW CAN I GET PAID TO DO THAT? I knew how to use the Internet, and I knew what kiteboarders needed (wind and a beach hotel where the staff doesn't mind if you lug wet, sandy gear through their lobby). In 2004 I started Ozone Travel to create custom trips. European destinations had been scoped out, so I researched windy locations and hotels in the Caribbean and South America. Then I sent a press release to three influential magazines: *Kiteboarding, SBC Kiteboard, and Kite World.* They listed my business in their news sections. We've created about 300 vacations to more than a dozen different destinations. The best part? I have to check out the places we recommend.

FROM EXECUTIVE RECRUITER TO RENOVATION AND DESIGN MANAGER

Robin Wilson, 37, at the Peninsula hotel in New York (she managed the renovation of its Mélange salon), May 31, 2007.

REAL ESTATE IS IN MY BLOOD, four generations back. I got into it with my grandfather, who owned several Texas "shotgun" houses—studios where oil workers lived. He let me choose their exterior paint when I was 7 years old. I made one block the "rainbow" houses: one blue, one violet, one red, and so on. It made caring for property seem like art. On Sundays we collected rent. That made real estate seem like an ATM—you can get money out of it.

After college, I went into management consulting and then executive search. But I felt as if I only got to start projects—finding people jobs—never finish them. I might not learn until years later if it was a great match. When my firm went public in 1999, I instantly sold my shares and used the money to go to graduate school to study real estate finance.

I wanted to go into commercial property management, but no one would hire me. Most people suggested I become a broker, which is the real estate job "for girls." I wanted to be like my grandfather, so when a professor suggested I try residential property management, I talked my friends into hiring me to do their kitchen, bath, and baby nursery renovations. I said, "I'll be like the wedding planner of your project. You won't have to worry about one thing." And they didn't. Now I do whole apartments, homes, law firms, even former president Clinton's office. My budgets run as high as $7 million.

Women, especially Southern women, are taught to be demure. When I first opened, I didn't want to be a show-off and name my company after myself. Instead I called it WSG (Wilson Services Group) Consulting. Huge mistake. No one could remember it. Plus, my expertise and talent are what clients are buying. We rebranded in 2007 as Robin Wilson Home. Business is booming.

ATTORNEY PLUS BAKERY CO-OWNER

IN 2004 NORRINDA BROWN AND HER MOTHER were both feeling a little empty: Norrinda had just started practicing law and missed the creativity of school; her mother and father had split up after more than 30 years of marriage. Baking became their sweet weekend escape—then their business plan. We took down Norrinda's not-so-secret recipe for success...

THE BASIC INGREDIENTS: Many of our products are based on my grandmom's recipes. We wanted to see if our cakes would sell, so for months we held tasting parties for friends and family. We asked guests to write comments anonymously on cards. Mostly, people said nice things, but they also said "too moist," "too sweet," and "needs to be more pineapple-y"—which sort of got my mom's back up.

SIFT GENTLY: My mom worked on the recipes until people thought the cakes had just the right amount of moistness, sweetness, and flavor. Now she's meticulous about her instructions—down to the number of minutes you mix things and how much you sift them.

SET IN A COOL PLACE: We took out a home equity loan to buy equipment and rent a space. We picked the Northern Liberties area because we could afford it, and it's the Philadelphia neighborhood that's supposed to grow the most in the next ten years.

WATCH THE DOUGH RISE: My mom and I are both very risk averse, so she has kept on teaching and I still practice law. She works in the bakery after school and we both work on weekends. We're tired a lot. Four employees hold things together when we're not around. It's working. Last year we were voted Best of Philadelphia by a city magazine and a newspaper.

THE ICING ON THE CAKE: Opening the business gave everyone in my family a new way to talk to one another during a difficult time. Even my dad helped out with construction and finance.

—Interviews by Amanda Robb

Norrinda Brown, 29, at the Brown Betty Dessert Boutique in Philadelphia, with her grandmother, Betty, and mother, Linda, June 17, 2007.

Holly Brubach (at the Granite Building in Pittsburgh, June 18, 2007) writes about the strange turn her life took.

STYLE MAVEN PLUS REAL ESTATE DEVELOPER

AFTER YEARS OF LIVING IN NEW YORK CITY, I thought of real estate developers as greedy megalomaniacs who mowed down entire city blocks and erected architectural atrocities with low ceilings and cheap kitchens in order to maximize their profit per square foot. It was not a line of work to which I had ever aspired.

I was: (A) a writer by default, after my first career, as a dancer, didn't go according to plan; and (B) a design consultant, dispensing advice to corporations on brand strategy and product development—this had started out as a day job, to support my writing, but turned into something I actually liked doing. I was not looking to leave either of these occupations. Nor, to be honest, was I in search of some new job that would take up what little time and brain space I hadn't already allotted to A and B.

Nevertheless, I bought a building in Pittsburgh, my hometown. I wasn't planning on buying a building. I just wanted an apartment. After 30 years in New York and abroad, I was looking for a place where I wouldn't have to work overtime to meet an overhead that had turned into a heavy monthly burden, and it seemed like moving back to Pittsburgh might be a good idea, based on the easy access to both culture and nature, the fact that real estate there is tremendously undervalued, and the prospect of a life less frenetic and trendy than the one I was living out of a loft in lower Manhattan.

In the course of my search for an apartment in Pittsburgh, preferably a raw space that I could design to my own specifications, I came across a vacant nine-story architectural landmark, which, as

it happened, offered everything I was looking for: a large, uninterrupted space, high ceilings, abundant natural light, character, charm, an ideal location. Built in 1889 and '90 as the German National Bank, with a massive facade entirely handcarved by Italian stonemasons, it had gone down in the guidebooks as an outstanding example of the style dubbed Richardsonian Romanesque, after H.H. Richardson, the famous architect who had designed the county courthouse a few blocks away. When the bank left the premises, sometime in the 1930s, the name was changed to the Granite Building, and over the years a succession of office tenants proceeded to subdivide the capacious interiors until the original grandeur was gone. What I found—coffee-stained wall-to-wall carpeting and a maze of makeshift cubicles—might have deterred some, if not most, people. But I was too busy seeing what wasn't there: a continuous expanse of dining and living areas, a kitchen overlooking the steeple of the church across the street, a master bedroom with a big bay window. I would wake up to the sounds of the carillon playing hymns on Sundays. I would grow rosebushes in little pots on the balconies.

But first I would have to buy the whole building, and that would leave me with six more floors than I could use, to say nothing of the payments on the financing. I kept looking. Surely there was someplace else to live that I could love as much.

As it turned out, there wasn't. Everything else I saw only served to make me appreciate the Granite Building even more: It had what all the other buildings lacked. And the price was right.

(When I told a friend in San Francisco what it cost, he asked, "Do you get a roof with that?") The timing seemed right, too. Developers from Philadelphia, Cleveland, Chicago, and elsewhere had been circling, buying up properties and setting off a long-overdue revitalization of a downtown that over the course of the past 20 years had become the hollow core of a city on the skids.

I would keep two floors for myself and sell the rest as luxury condominiums, one 3,000-square-foot unit per floor. I asked friends who are more financially astute than I am to run the numbers and see if the project made sense. One came back and said, "Let's put it this way: I couldn't do it." Well, of course he couldn't do it—he's a conservative guy who orders the same thing for dinner at his favorite restaurant every night. What was the worst that could happen? I asked him. "You could lose your shirt," he said. Well, that *would* be bad, I agreed.

My option on the building was about to expire. I needed to come to a decision. I recalled a magazine article I'd read in which some self-help expert urged people to list the best and worst decisions they'd ever made, as a way of taking responsibility for their mistakes and understanding the faulty logic that had led to them. I got out a legal pad and drew a line down the middle. "Best Decisions," I wrote at the top of the left-hand column.

Uh. Let's see. Well, there was the time I refused a marriage proposal from Mr. Wrong—I figured that was to my credit. And yet, a few months ago when I was unpacking some moving cartons, I came across a packet of letters he had written me and thought what a shame it is that two people who once had so much in common could fall completely out of touch. So, though I don't for a minute doubt my decision, it did have some rather sad ramifications. There must be some other decisions I made that were better than this one. I let it stand, but I put it in parentheses.

Next I wrote: "1. Moving to Paris." Now that was absolutely the right thing to do. Although it was only a few months later that my father was diagnosed with a terminal illness, and I'm still sorry that I didn't spend more time with him in the years before he died. So I put that in parentheses, too. Then I sat for a while and tried to think of another good decision I had made, but nothing came to mind, so I decided to move on and come back to this part.

For "Worst Decisions," there was no shortage of material. "1. Choice of college." For years I'd been wondering how different my life might have been if I'd gone to that fancy Ivy League school I got into but didn't attend because I found the students so intimidating. I would know things that I don't know now and have friends in lofty places. On the other hand, I would never have met two friends from my freshman year whom I now consider family. So maybe that wasn't such a terrible decision after all. I crossed it out. New number 1: "Staying in the wrong job too long." Okay! No doubt about it that was a mistake. And yet. I walked away with skills that helped me nail the next job. I gave this some thought, then crossed out that entry, too.

This exercise was turning out to be harder than I expected. Doodling, I drew circles around the two entries on the right and arrows, as if to move them to the middle of the page, somewhere between best and worst. Then I drew circles around the two items in the left column and did the same. It was becoming apparent that both the good decisions and the bad ones had some mitigating consequences. Staring at my sheet of paper neatly bisected by a line where decisions from the left and right sides now converged, I came to the conclusion that there are no "right" decisions and no mistakes—or, anyway, not very many, and not as many as you might think.

And that gave me courage.

I tried to imagine how my life would change when I became a real estate developer. A few more phone calls, maybe. I could handle that. Design meetings with architects. Fun! There I'd be in some showroom, picking marble for the showers, choosing faucets. If you've read Daniel Gilbert's *Stumbling on Happiness,* you know that people contemplating future choices are limited by their own experience, and so we project our own distorted vision of things as we would like them to be, unable to foresee the grisly details and complications that will undermine the happiness we imagine. If only I'd read Gilbert's book before I bought the Granite Building.... But not even Gilbert could have changed my mind. I still would have done what I went ahead and did.

Because, in the end, I had one thought that put all the others to rest: My life will be more interesting if I do this than if I don't.

I signed the papers. The word was out. For every person I met who congratulated me and wished me well, there were two who said Pittsburgh was hopeless, nothing would ever change, I must be nuts. I thanked them for their support.

There have been some glitches that I didn't foresee—that, quite frankly, no one could have foreseen. Any number of people with more experience in the field have come forward to volunteer their help. Sometimes this takes the form of free advice, much of it welcome. More often it has proved to be a bid to take the building off my hands. Some of these white knights turned out to be other developers who had been lined up behind me, back when I had the building under contract, waiting for me to come to my senses and walk away. They were still waiting. Just as soon as I realized that I was in over my head, desperate to get out, they would swoop in and buy at a discount. They gave me a few months to stew, and then the offers started coming in.

There was the developer who wanted to turn the building into student housing: People with the means to afford the condominiums I was offering, he contended, wanted to live in fancy suburbs. There was the developer sporting a dark tan in January, who prefaced our conversation by informing me that, although he was a Pittsburgh native, his success had enabled him to escape to Boca Raton. There was the developer who tried to frighten me by saying he'd be afraid to cross the street at night after parking in the garage directly opposite. "You would?" I asked, incredulous. Pittsburgh's crime rate is low, and my building is situated in the Cultural District, where there's plenty of activity in the evening. "Well," he said, "I wouldn't be afraid, but you should be—you're a woman." Like bad blind dates, these meetings confirmed my resolve to go it alone.

What my self-appointed white knights had failed to understand is that, although I had bought the Granite Building to live in it, that was by no means the only reason. In New York, Paris, Milan, I was a mere spectator, standing by and looking on while the landscape in which I lived was transformed, for better and for worse, by billionaires and corporations. But in Pittsburgh, I can call on my experience of other cities and make something happen.

Sometimes I wake up in a cold sweat before dawn and think about what my life will be like if I lose my shirt. I picture myself in some hovel, freezing in the winter, with nothing to my name but a few sticks of furniture donated by the handful of friends I will still have left (I know who you are). But alive, nonetheless, and able to read and write and go for walks along the river and do many of the other things that I enjoy. There are worse fates, I remind myself. And worse ways to lose your shirt. ◻

YOUR BRILLIANT (NEXT) CAREER ...AND HOW TO FIND IT

The puzzle: a successful woman who felt that something in her life was missing—but what, precisely? The answer: Marcus Buckingham, an expert in what works at work, believes that the power to transform your life is much closer than anyone realizes. Susan Choi reports on a surprising (and profound) lesson in getting unstuck and on track.

One day at work, the computer system Kylie (not her real name) depends on to get her job done collapsed in a total meltdown. The tech support people, five states away in Virginia, wouldn't pick up the phone. Kylie's colleagues wouldn't get off her back—they were literally hanging over her shoulders, demanding to receive what she had no way to give them until the system started up again. In the end, she was glued to her chair for six unbroken, miserable hours. For Kylie, who grew up in Midwestern farm country, who loves to hike and ride horses and work with her hands, this six-hour imprisonment in her chair was the worst thing of all. At home that night, she felt as if she'd been beaten up. "I looked ahead at the next 20 years and thought, *If it's more of this, I'll slit my wrists.*"

More alarming was that lots of days felt like this. There hadn't been a single last straw, Kylie realized; there were haystacks of them. At some point in the past two or three years, the job Kylie had worked at for more than a decade had become not just unsatisfying but intolerable. Something had to change. But what? Kylie was well into an online master's degree in psychology, because she'd always loved helping others through transitions in their lives. Yet the course wasn't helping her transition at all. It was "geared toward research and academia," she says, and that wasn't her style.

On the surface, Kylie's life looked pretty great, even glamorous. She owned her own apartment in Manhattan. She had a job at a newspaper, working in design, an activity she'd loved ever since she was a teenager making her own jewelry. She wasn't one of those women who are afraid of change: She'd had success singing jazz and

the blues before switching to news. She'd been married and divorced. She'd moved from her native Midwest to California, then to New York City, then to California again, then to New York City again. "I guess that might sound kind of flaky," she worried.

Marcus Buckingham could not have disagreed more. "She's so specific, so focused, it's great," he confided to me, not long after *O* magazine brought him and Kylie together to try to figure out what she should do. A former Gallup Organization researcher, Marcus is a management consultant and the best-selling author of *Go Put Your Strengths to Work* (a handbook for improving performance to achieve maximum success in the workplace); most important, he's devoted his life to helping other people decide what to devote their lives to. He completed a 26-city tour, where he spoke with hundreds of executives and human resource professionals about what he's learned from years of researching people who've excelled at their careers.

"I was so afraid," Marcus added, "that I was going to be working with one of those people who, when you ask them what they like, say 'Ooooh, I don't knooow.' What do you wish you were doing? 'Ooooh, I don't knooow.' What interests you? 'Ooooh, I don't knooow!'" Marcus was making me laugh, but he was also making a point. Kylie did know what she wanted and needed.

For all his success helping people refocus their lives, the most crucial materials he uses—the clues for solving the mystery of anyone's unhappiness—are never furnished by Marcus but by the people themselves. One of his fundamental beliefs is that all of us, even at our most confused and unhappy, like Kylie, have very good instincts about what we should be doing. Even the person who, when asked what she likes, wails "I don't knooow!" does know, in her gut. She's just not noticing, amid all the dispiriting moments when she feels overwhelmed or unsatisfied or bored, those other

Everything is illuminated with the help of a few specific questions.

moments—perhaps less numerous, but far more significant—when she feels good. Absorbed, so time flies. Excited. Everyone, Marcus maintains, has such experiences, even during the worst sort of week. Kylie felt completely out of her element, miles off course from where she was supposed to be, but Marcus believed that she was actually in the vicinity of real happiness. Her instincts had led her to the ballpark, but she wasn't hitting homers. She was wandering around in the stands, or stuck in line for the restroom.

What was keeping her there was that she'd forgotten, or maybe she'd failed to discern from the start, what she was passionate about. Most people, Marcus says, make the mistake of speaking of their passions in overly general, grandiose terms. "I'm passionate about making the world a better place." "Well, who isn't?" Marcus would say. He calls this kind of vague talk "skywriting"—it's way up there, far from the specific conditions of our lives, and it tends to melt away. Marcus prefers a more concrete, muscular way of discussing our passions: in terms of strengths.

Our strengths are the actions that make us feel energized and optimistic, eager for the chance to do them again. We're not just good at our strengths—I'm good at paying bills, but that doesn't mean I like doing it. We're also nourished by them as by nothing else. When Marcus works with people like Kylie, the first thing he wants them to do is the most basic: He wants them to define their strengths, as narrowly and concretely as they possibly can. *I feel strong when I close the deal and shake the buyer's hand. I feel strong when my explanation makes my students' faces light up with understanding. I feel strong when I've hit "print" and I see my own words in black ink on the page.* Our strengths, Marcus says, are those situations in which we are intensely, happily, completely engaged. And because he believes our instincts are good—because they've gotten us into the ballpark—the place to look for clues to our strengths isn't way up in the sky but right where we're sitting, right in that office chair Kylie hated so much. Her hatred of that chair was real, but something important—some glimmering of passion—had led her to be sitting there in the first place.

Marcus asked Kylie to start generating raw material—to pile up clues to her strengths. For one week, she was to write a list of things she loved and things she loathed about her job. She was to be as detailed as possible, to pay exquisitely close attention to her own frame of mind in the course of a typical week: When did she

247

feel energized, satisfied? When was she miserable?

Kylie's list was disheartening, if unsurprising. She could only come up with eight "loves," and she had more than twice as many "loathes." But Marcus noticed right away that six of Kylie's "loves" were in the passive voice. In other words, six were things that other people did to her. Kylie had written, "I felt strong when people sought my advice...when I was included in the planning stages...when I was given the go-ahead...when my contributions were acknowledged...when given the opportunity...when allowed to assume..." Only two were things Kylie did: "I felt strong when interacting with my colleagues one-on-one rather than through e-mail," and "I felt strong when I developed a good working relationship with a colleague that turned into a friendship."

Kylie, the former singer, had always thought of herself as the opposite of a wallflower. But now she and Marcus saw that there was something not just wallflowerish but positively wilted about her professional self. She had given away all her power, Marcus told her; she needed to start taking it back. "Marcus turned a light on," she later told me. Together they worked out a list of things she would do to make the best of this job. Even if Kylie found that she wanted to do something radically different with her life, she had to sort out the problems in her current situation. She needed to find a way to act instead of being acted upon, or she'd find herself passive and likely unhappy in the next job.

Right away, Kylie vowed never to let that chair claim her for six hours again: She was going to get up every hour and a half, no matter what crisis had erupted around her, and take a walk. She craved movement and freedom, and there was no one better to bestow it than herself. Second, she was going to stop letting herself be at the mercy of her coworkers when it came to being gainfully occupied. One of Kylie's "loathes" about her job was the downtime—it was either crisis central or the doldrums, with little in between. Instead of waiting for the next cataclysm, Kylie would go find herself something to do. Third, she was going to start connecting face-to-face. The sheer size of the newspaper meant that many of the people she most needed to talk to communicated everything via e-mail—a medium she found draining. But her supervisor had recently asked for her feedback on something, and though Kylie had assumed she should give it in writing, she realized she could respond in person.

All these changes might have seemed minor, yet each one put a little more control back in Kylie's hands and even helped her perceive that in some ways she did like her job. Marcus asked Kylie to go back to her list of loves and loathes and cast them in more active terms. She'd felt strong when her advice was "sought"; now she saw how simple—and welcome—it might be if she *offered* her opinion at appropriate moments. Slowly, she and Marcus hammered out descriptions of her strengths that, when Marcus read them back to her, she responded to with a flood of recognition. Kylie felt strong, she and Marcus concluded, when she took an idea of her own and made it tangible—whether laying out a page or crafting a necklace. And she felt strong when she forged a trusting relationship with a coworker.

The more clues to her strengths that Kylie and Marcus gathered, the more Marcus's early suspicion was borne out. Miserable as she was, Kylie really was in the ballpark. She loved to design. But her job at the paper didn't afford her as much opportunity to do it as she craved. Often she was executing someone else's vision—just inputting. Now Marcus gave Kylie another assignment: to list ten things she could do over the next five weeks to gain more opportunities to do the work she loved best. Her managers had given her outstanding performance reviews. They clearly had no idea she was unhappy. It was up to her to give them the chance to use her even more effectively by telling them what her strengths were. "One of the most insidious myths people suffer under in the workplace," says Marcus, "is this idea that we should all be team players and do what the team asks of us. It's a moral myth, but it misunderstands our moral duty. Our real moral duty is to offer our greatest strength to the team—to give it the opportunity to use us where we're at our strongest."

But Marcus also could see that Kylie's current job, even with substantial reengineering, might never make her happy. The list of "loves" had offered crucial information, but there were still all those "loathes" to confront. Kylie had told Marcus that she'd always loved jewelry making—except for one part at the very end, when the slightest of goofs, like tying a knot badly, could "make the beads fall all over the floor." Marcus had noticed that this same intense dislike of things falling apart at the last minute came up when they spoke of her job at the paper. Kylie's beautiful layouts were forever being messed up at the very last minute by events she couldn't control. And this wasn't unexpected—news has a way of changing all the time. It also wasn't likely that e-mail culture would ever reverse, returning Kylie to the face-to-face collaborative atmosphere that she craved.

If Kylie really did need to start fresh in another job, how would she know where to go? How could she both follow her instincts and avoid the mistakes that her instincts had made the last time? At this juncture, Marcus sees people fall prey to the same four pitfalls again and again. First, we're so close to our own strengths, we don't see them; or if we do see them, we don't value them. Kylie wouldn't necessarily label her love for engagement with others as a strength to be utilized in the workplace; she'd be more likely to assume everyone felt that way. Yet the world is full of people who do their best work in isolation. Second, we suffer from "should" syndrome: We should love doing layouts at a newspaper because we love design, and news is important and exciting. Or we should stay at our job because it's irresponsible not to. Third, we tend to pile our work misery into a big, mushy lump that we then allow to crush us. We don't ask ourselves the questions that Marcus was asking Kylie. We don't patiently tease apart the many strands of our daily existence, distinguishing those that actually make us happy—the lump has made us forget there were any of these—from those that we have to eliminate as soon as we can.

The last pitfall is perhaps the most complex, yet addressing it can tell us not only what's wrong with our current job but how to avoid falling into the same trap again. It's the failure to have asked, of any current or possible job, the three questions of *why, who,* and *what: Why will I be doing these things?*—the job's broader purpose. *Who will I be working with?* And finally, *What precise activities will I be performing every day?* Often people who seem to be doing something suited to their needs—who, in theory, should be happy—have nailed one or even two of the three answers through instinct alone. But such a partial fit will never feel right, no matter how much we think it should. Kylie had been on the right track when she'd embarked on her online psychology degree; she knew in her gut that she loved engaging with people. The *why* of that degree resonated. But the *what* was all wrong—the degree wasn't preparing Kylie for actual human engagement. It was preparing her to write papers on psychological theory.

Such near misses, Marcus says, are particularly baffling. He once worked with a woman who had always longed to work in healthcare. ("I have a passion for helping people," would be skywriting to Marcus: very noble and surely true, but way too vague to be of any real use.) She became an ER nurse and was incredibly unhappy. That made no sense to her—she was doing what she'd always longed to do. She loved the *why* of healthcare, and here she was, living it. But when Marcus pressed her to detail her passion, it turned out that what she really loved was seeing people get better. And an ER nurse rarely gets to do that; they see patients at their most dire moments, and then the patients are whisked away. The thing that made this woman feel strong—the thing she was passionate for—was missing. She found it as soon as she transferred to one of the hospital's pediatric wards.

The questions of *why, who,* and *what* don't work just in these situations. They can also rescue that rare person who really is lost. This had been the case with a copy machine saleswoman Marcus worked with. She was quite successful—always in the top 10 percent of the sales force—but at some point she couldn't bear the idea of getting up every morning, every day, and doing more of the same. How had she ended up there? Her list of strengths yielded clues. She felt strong when sensing another person's emotions. And she felt strong when she told another person what to do—and they did it! The *what* of selling copy machines had, in fact, played to these passions, making her a very good saleswoman. Unlike the ER nurse, she had her *what* nailed, but she didn't have the ghost of a *why.*

This was when Marcus began casting his net beyond the workplace, but with the same basic principle in mind—that we have good instincts about our needs and wants. He began asking the saleswoman a series of questions. What were her hobbies and special interests? What did she think about early in the morning and late at night, when she was alone? What stories did she find herself always reading in the newspaper— the ones about rescues? About making money? About big fancy parties? What were the last two books she'd read, and why had she chosen them? What prizes, if any, had she won in her life, and for what?

"What you're getting at is yearnings," Marcus says. "The activities that make us feel strong express these, but we can also find them through the subjects that interest us." The saleswoman, it turned out, always read the obituaries in the paper; she was especially drawn to the part at the end, where those left behind by the deceased were listed. She would find herself thinking about them— the wives and husbands, the parents and children, who had lost someone.

For the saleswoman, the eureka moment didn't come when she realized she was drawn to stories of grieving; she'd always known this of herself. But after working with Marcus she was able to look at this interest in a new way: as a unique strength that she could and should offer the world, and for which the world, in turn, might pay her. That strength summed her up at her most valuable, not just because she was good at it but because she enjoyed it—and when we enjoy doing something, we don't just stay good. We get better and better. The copy machine saleswoman, a naturally empathetic person who liked telling people what to do, knew that the grieving are often overwhelmed with decisions to make. Now she knew she might love guiding them through those circumstances.

She was right. Once she finished volunteering at a hospice, she learned what credentials were required to be a grief counselor,

WE TEND TO PILE OUR WORK MISERY INTO A BIG, MUSHY LUMP THAT WE THEN ALLOW TO CRUSH US.

obtained them, and in so doing found real fulfillment for the first time in her life.

After the strengths exercise, Kylie was a step ahead of where the copy machine saleswoman had been at the same point in the process. Kylie was in a job that somewhat let her do what she wanted: bring an idea of her own into tangible form. But the *why* of her job, which she'd initially thought was important to her—she'd found working in news exciting at the start—turned out not to be as crucial as the *what* (the ability to control and complete her own designs without unforeseen circumstances disrupting them). And she learned that the *who*—the presence of people with whom she could speak face-to-face and form bonds—was just as indispensable.

Marcus and Kylie subjected other potential jobs in the design industry to the three questions. "You have the wisdom within you to find the place where you can be your best self. That wisdom isn't out there—it's in there," Marcus says. Of any potential new job, Kylie had to ask, *What will I be doing? Will I be taking an idea of my own and bringing it to fruition—in an atmosphere free of the sort of constant flux that messes things up?* Kylie had told Marcus that she felt strongest when deeply immersed in the work of design; at those times, she said, "it's like a meditation." Clearly, Kylie needed to be designing in a peaceful environment. Next she had to ask, *Who will I be doing it with? Will I be on a small team of collaborators who talk to each other, or will I be lost in an impersonal hive?* Finally, she had to ask, *Why will I be designing?* Now that she knew how important the *what* of any future job was— this was where her passion lay—the *why* seemed far more flexible. Kylie might find greater happiness designing a gorgeously produced jewelry catalog than pages of a hectic daily newspaper.

Wherever Kylie wound up professionally, she also had to remember that life is not work alone. The big lump of Kylie's professional unhappiness had expanded well outside the workplace, squeezing the things she most loved to the margins, if not out of existence completely. Singing was one of her passions—one of the new strengths she'd defined was, "I feel strong when I accurately express an emotion through song." Long ago Kylie's desire for order and stability had led her to leave music as a profession, a decision she didn't regret. But she needed passion in her off-hours as well; she needed to get music back into her life. Even if she did end up leaving the paper, she would take advantage of the company's resources while still there and post on a message board for fellow musicians. She was hiking as much as she could. When she was living in rural Michigan, she had loved gardening; now she noticed there were untended plots by her Manhattan building, and she was going to plant flowers in them. "I've been finding my way back to the person I was a long time ago," she told me.

Incremental changes like these, Marcus feels, are far from small. They're powerful, because they're deliberate and insightful and true to ourselves. "Even if things seem like a disaster, don't leap," Marcus says. "Build a bridge and walk over. Build it out of today. In everybody's week, there are things they look forward to." Our unhappiness might make those things seem insignificant, like nothing more than scattered planks and nails. But start hammering them together, and you'll find yourself, as Marcus says, with just the bridge to transport you from a place that you loathed to a place you can't wait to return to. ◖

YOUR GREAT IDEA, WHOSE TIME HAS COME

You have a brainstorm...but now what? Polly Brewster's six-part guide to going from concept to reality.

1 FIND YOUR INSPIRATION

■ **CREATE YOUR OWN SERVICE DEPARTMENT.** You don't need a billion-dollar idea—like sneakers with wheels—to start a company. The Small Business Administration (SBA) reports that 55 percent of women business owners are in a service profession, like interior decorator, personal chef, or art buyer. These industries are appealing, says Linda Pinson, coauthor of *Steps to Small Business Start-Up,* "because you don't need a lot of start-up cash and your customers pay right away."

■ **TEST-DRIVE YOUR IDEA.** If you want to open a jewelry store, says Victoria Colligan, a founder of Ladies Who Launch, "make a necklace. It costs very little to do that." One choker may be fun but tying 500 knots by hand at 3 A.M. would require a Zoloft prescription. "It's okay to hate your idea," says Beth Schoenfeldt, cofounder of Ladies Who Launch. "It means you've ruled something out."

■ **APPRENTICE YOURSELF.** For dreams that can't be tried out on a small scale, you might investigate a VocationVacation, which matches you with someone who's happy to help you determine if you, too, are meant to be an alpaca farmer or coffeehouse owner (starting at $549). Volunteering is another option—and free. If you think you want to be an event planner, for instance, help organize your local March of Dimes Walk. (Volunteermatch.org lists opportunities by zip code.)

■ **FIND A MENTOR.** Log on to networking sites like ladieswholaunch.com, mominventors.com, or makemineamillion.org, where you'll find profiles of women entrepreneurs. If a story strikes a chord, send the owner an e-mail. "I've found that people are happy to tell you how they did whatever they did," says Nell Merlino, founder of Make Mine a Million $ Business.

2 IDENTIFY THE NEXT STEPS

■ **DO YOUR HOMEWORK.** "With the Web, no one has an excuse for not doing research," says Mary Cantando, author of *The Woman's Advantage.* "If you're starting a service, like a doggy day care, do an Internet search in your zip code. If there's competition, leave your dog at one of the places and see what it's not offering."

■ **DEVELOP A PROTOTYPE.** Shapelock.com sells ten- and 20-ounce jars of plastic pellets that you can heat in the microwave and form into the shape of a gadget. If your first try doesn't pan out, put it back in the microwave. For more complicated designs, look for a machinist in the Yellow Pages, says Tamara Monosoff, author of

Secrets of Millionaire Moms, who's sold thousands of her invention, TP Saver, which holds toilet paper in place so toddlers can't pull the roll off the rack. She also suggests logging on to thomas.net, where you enter the materials you need for your product and it provides a list of factories that work with those components.

■ **FIND A WORKSPACE.** Incubators let you rent space and equipment, from fax machines to industrial mixers, at a low cost. They usually require tenants to attend mentoring sessions, says Dinah Adkins, president of the National Business Incubation Association, "so, if you don't like to take advice, then an incubator is not a place for you." (To find one, go to nbia.org.)

3 CREATE AN A-1 BUSINESS PLAN

Writing a business plan will force you to consider the what-ifs (what if you get sick, need a trademark, need worker's comp insurance) and the tiny costs that you might overlook: "Like the cost of a cup of coffee—the cup, the java jacket, the lid, the napkin, the stirrer, the sugar," says Liat Cohen, co-owner of Cocoa Bar in Brooklyn. "A business plan forced me to figure out exactly what I would have to charge to make money."

■ **GET PROFESSIONAL HELP.** Two groups operating under the umbrella of the Small Business Administration can provide guidance. The Women's Business Center program (sba.gov/womeninbusiness) provides training and counseling, usually at very low fees (or free). For example, the Central Alabama Women's Business Center offers a course, Writing Your Business Plan: Your Business Roadmap, for $15.

SCORE (score.org) is a network of working and retired executives who freely share their expertise. They try to match their members' specialties with the needs of a new entrepreneur—like pairing an artist who wanted to open her own gallery with a finance executive. If you can't get to a SCORE chapter, one of their members will work with you via e-mail.

■ **REVIEW THE PLAN.** "A few months down the road, compare what actually happened to what you projected," says Pinson. Use this time to modify your forecasts and tweak your strategy. (Go to oprah.com/omagextras for one of Pinson's sample business plans.)

4 MARKET LIKE A GENIUS

■ **TAP INTO YOUR NETWORKS.** You want to get the word out, so start by sending a short e-mail about your new business to friends

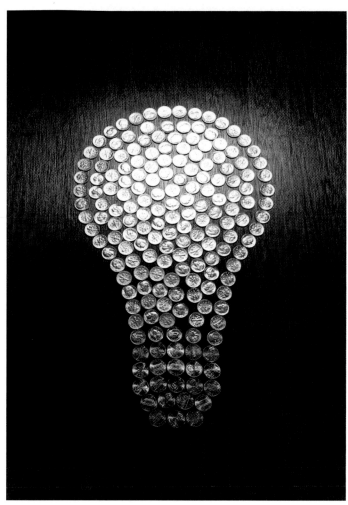

Transform your bright idea into a moneymaker.

samples to a local gourmet store. "Flatter the buyer by asking for their opinion," she says. "But call in advance to busy stores—they usually have specific times set aside to review new products."

■ **BUY GOOGLE ADWORDS.** You choose words—say, *flowers* and *Cincinnati*—and every time someone enters those search terms, your company may appear in sponsored links. The ads we researched ranged from 30 cents to $1 per click (though the cost per click can be as little as one cent). Google will also help you set up a Web page free of charge and can help local businesses zero in on clients by having ads appear strictly to people searching in a certain area. As your company grows, you might place ads on Web sites that are already attracting your customer base. For instance, if you make one-of-a-kind lingerie that's popular among honeymoon-bound brides, you might contact the advertising sales department of theknot.com.

5 SECURE FUNDING

It's almost impossible to get a loan based solely on an idea. But once you have your product (or service), a business plan, and a cash flow (no matter how small), you can start to look for funds to expand your business. You'll need to be clear about exactly how much money you need and what specifically you'll use the loan for. "We just lent to a woman who makes organic pet food," says Merlino. "She needed to buy a freeze-drying machine so she could ship her product." If you aren't sure how big a loan is necessary, you can contact an SBA Women's Business Center or SCORE counselor. Then seek funding at the following places:

■ **FOR AMOUNTS UNDER $500**: "Put it on a credit card or borrow from friends and family," says Schoenfeldt, of Ladies Who Launch.

■ **FOR $500 TO $45,000**: Contact a microfinance institution, which is more open to entrepreneurs. Accion USA gives $500 credit-builder loans to people with no credit history, META in Boise, Idaho (a local group), lends up to $2,000 to first-time business owners, and Make Mine a Million $ Business lends up to $45,000 strictly to women business owners (for more see oprah.com/omagextras).

■ **FOR AMOUNTS UP TO $1,000,000**: You can apply for an SBA-backed loan—where the SBA acts as a guarantor for small-business owners—available through a commercial lender; the SBA expects entrepreneurs to have enough equity to cover 25 percent of a start-up loan. If you need $10,000, then you must have invested about $2,500 in your business.

6 STAFF UP LIKE A PRO

■ **KNOW WHAT YOU NEED.** Is it someone with a highly developed skill, like Web site design? Or are you looking to train your employees from scratch? "I don't care about experience," says Cohen, co-owner of the Cocoa Bar. "I can teach someone how to make a great latte; I can't teach someone to be proactive or friendly."

■ **IDENTIFY ATYPICAL HIRING POOLS.** If you're opening a doggy day care, post a HELP WANTED sign at the local dog run. Want a professional voice for your answering machine's outgoing message? Contact a local acting school or high school drama teacher to see if they can recommend a student who might want to earn extra money.

■ **START WITH TEMPS.** "I always suggest hiring on a part-time or project basis," says Merlino, of Make Mine a Million $ Business. You can see if their skills match what you need, and if there is enough work (and revenue) coming in to support a full-time employee. **O**

and family, encouraging them to forward it. Then turn to organizations you're already involved with, including the PTA, your over-30 soccer league, Neighborhood Watch, etc. "Most entrepreneurs tell us, 'That first client came in because I knew so-and-so,'" says Erin Fuller, executive director of the National Association of Women Business Owners.

■ **ADVERTISE WITHOUT BREAKING THE BANK.** You can put up flyers at the grocery store, have a friend post a review of your business on yelp.com or citysearch.com, or place a free online classified. "A woman in our program wanted to do event planning for dogs," says Adele Foster of the Plan Fund in Dallas, which develops entrepreneurs from low- and middle-income areas. "She posted an ad on craigslist.org. Someone immediately responded, and that was her first client."

■ **HAND OUT FREE SAMPLES.** "Instead of spending money on fancy advertising, put the product in your trunk and get it out there," says Stephen Hall, author of *From Kitchen to Market*. You can rent a booth at a local greenmarket, attend an industry trade show, or host a special event in your community. Immaculate Baking, a small cookie company in Flat Rock, North Carolina, staged a free art workshop for local kids and served their baked goods. "The workshop got our name out there," says Ann Marshall, Immaculate Baking's director of marketing. Anyone trying to launch a food product, says Kathrine Gregory, owner of Mi Kitchen Es Su Kitchen, a food industry incubator in New York City, should bring

MAKING FRIENDS WITH YOUR MONEY

SUZE ORMAN ON…

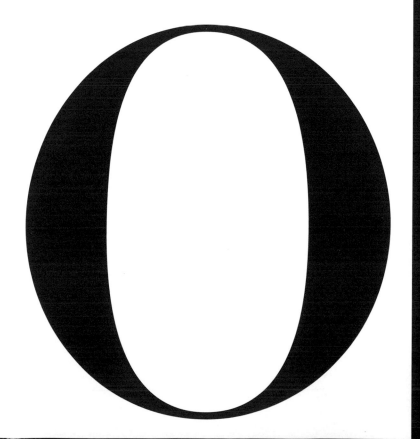

SUZE ORMAN: "GO AFTER YOUR DREAM RATIONALLY, NOT RASHLY"

LOVE AND MONEY

Q. I'm 36 years old, and my husband and I have three children. My job is stressful and unfulfilling, but it pays very well. After a serious illness last year, I started to see life differently. I created a plan to get us out of debt and want to embark on a career change that requires returning to college. I would continue in my current job for three more years while attending school part-time to help pay off our credit card balance, establish an emergency fund, and save for my children's educations and my own. However, my husband is completely unsupportive of my "siphoning off funds" for an interior design degree that, according to him, "you can't do much with." The average salary for graduates in that field is less than half of what I'm now earning. We already have some money put away for retirement. Do you think it's irresponsible to pursue this dream?

SUZE: Your mental and physical health are, in my opinion, the most precious gift you can give yourself, your children, and your husband. What does he want you to do, stay in a situation you hate just so you can continue to make more money? There is nothing—I repeat, *nothing*—irresponsible about how you're preparing to achieve this goal. You've given yourself a three-year buffer to clean up your balance sheet and enact your plan. I'm so impressed at the care you're taking in anticipation of this life-altering move. So many women who hate their jobs come to me ready to quit tomorrow without a penny saved. You're a great example of how to move toward change in a sensible way. (For more tips, see "Getting Set to Start Over," *right*.)

Your husband is the one being irresponsible. He should value your dreams over your paycheck. Besides, even though you were earning a lot, you still had credit card debt and no emergency savings. Unhappy people often spend, spend, spend; people who are satisfied with their lives don't need money to create a false sense of well-being. If you follow your passion for interior design, you'll be more content in your professional and personal life. That's good for your health, good for your head, and ultimately great for your family. Will you have less money? Only time will tell. But even if your income decreases, I bet you'll find you can make more out of less.

By the way, don't be angry with your husband. My sense is that he's just fearful of change and worried about making sure the family will be okay. Over the next three years, you'll have plenty of time to talk about how to make this leap.

GETTING SET TO START OVER

Yes, there is a financially responsible way to make a midlife career change. Walking into work one morning and resigning is not it. I wish everybody would follow the lead of the woman in the first question: She's going after a dream rationally, not rashly. Here are some financial tactics to keep in mind before making a move.

■ **Get rid of your credit card debt.** If the change entails going back to school, you can't afford to be paying high interest rates. The right time to make a switch is when your credit card debt is paid off, and not a minute before.

■ **Make sure you'll have health insurance.** If your spouse has a plan through work, that solves your problem. Or you can look into COBRA—you are entitled to continue receiving health benefits from your old employer for 18 months, but you'll be required to pay the entire premium. You can also shop for your own policy at ehealthinsurance.com.

■ **Boost your cash savings.** It's imperative to have the equivalent of at least eight months' living expenses in reserves. Put the money into a high-yield, risk-free savings account like the one offered by emigrantdirect.com.

■ **See what training you can get right now.** Many employers will help pay for employees to continue their educations. Granted, classes typically need to be in a field related to your job. Call human resources and see if they can finance some of your course work.

■ **Fund a 529 college savings plan for yourself.** You may have heard about these for your kids, but they can work for you, too. If you're making long-range plans to go back to school, any money you withdraw from a 529 plan will be free of federal taxes if you use it for eligible school expenses. Learn more at savingforcollege.com.

Q. I'm 25 years old and have been dating my college sweetheart for almost seven years. We've been living together and splitting all our expenses—we each have our own car, loans, and savings and checking accounts. Our arrangement has worked well so far, but our friends think it's ridiculous that we don't pool our resources. My mother stayed at home for most of her life and never had any money; I'm terrified of losing my career and financial independence the way she did. I love this man and want to share my future with him, but not necessarily a checking account. Does this mean I'm not marriage material?

SUZE: As far as finances go, you're perfect marriage material. You love this guy, yet you're smart enough to hold on to your identity. The only problem is that you're taking an extreme approach by

keeping *everything* separate. The solution is to merge some of your money. Here's the strategy: Both of you are to keep separate checking accounts and open a joint account from which you'll pay all shared expenses. This joint fund will be a testing ground to see how you commingle your finances.

The division of your cost of living should be based on your incomes. To determine how much you should be paying, add up your combined take-home earnings, then figure out what percentage each of you brings in. Let's say your take-home pay is $3,500 and your boyfriend's is $2,800, giving you a total monthly household income of $6,300. Your income is 55 percent of that sum and his is 45 percent. So if your mutual expenses are $3,000 a month, you pay $1,650 and he pays $1,350.

Next up is an emergency savings account. Again, I want you to have both a joint *and* a separate one. The former ensures that you're protected as a couple; the latter is where you find the certainty that you'll never be dependent on somebody else. Your personal reserve should equal three months of your living expenses, while the joint account should cover six to eight months. I recommend a hefty joint fund so that if one of you were to lose your job or become ill, you would have enough to get by for a while. At the same time, if the relationship doesn't work out, you will have your own nest egg to fall back on.

Q. I am married to a man who has no financial ambition. He's the nicest guy, and at first I tried to ignore the fact that he had a dead-end job. Later I helped him start a business, but without the motivation to learn new skills, he closed it down. Now he's settled into another $10-an-hour job; meanwhile, I cover 80 percent of the bills. I'm 56 years old and trying to pay down our mortgage and save for retirement. I've tried telling my husband how his lack of drive puts a huge burden on me. I love him, but sometimes I feel like a meal ticket. Should I divorce him over this?

SUZE: You're asking the wrong question, my dear. What you need to figure out is why you married him in the first place. By your own admission, you knew from the get-go that he wasn't financially driven, so why are you mad at him now for being exactly who he's always been? Is he really such a burden, or are you falling back on the old notion that a husband is supposed to be the breadwinner, and you resent him for not fitting into that traditional mold?

Clearly, the big mistake here is that you chose to overlook some troubling facts. If you expected that he would cover more than 20 percent of the bills, then you should have made sure you were both on the same page about what you wanted him to provide financially.

It sounds like you had expectations for him that he never had for himself.

But that doesn't mean the relationship is doomed. It seems as though his strength lies in offering you emotional support rather than financial. That's what attracted you to him in the beginning. It's up to you to decide whether that's enough.

MINE, YOURS, AND OURS

These women are struggling with the same root problem: how to mesh love and money. That's why it pays to have a clear strategy.

■ **As I explained, every woman needs her own savings in addition to a shared account.** If you're married and don't earn income, you can still build your own savings. After paying the bills and putting away for retirement, I think you should be entitled to an equal share of any household income left over at the end of each month. Yes, it's *household* income, not your husband's. That's an important distinction many couples fail to honor. Just because one of you earns the paycheck doesn't mean that person should lord over how the money is handled. Use your portion to fund a high-yield savings account. (Check out emigrantdirect.com or ingdirect.com.)

■ **Every woman also needs one credit card in her name only.** If you become divorced or widowed, an individual credit history will enable you to get a loan and open utility accounts without leaving a deposit, and may even help you land a job (some employers check applicants' credit during the hiring process).

■ **Debts you had prior to marriage are yours alone**—unless you actively merge them. When you wed, don't automatically rush to combine everything. You can help each other out by chipping away at your loans without becoming officially responsible for each other's.

■ **Be pragmatic about the assets you bring into a marriage.** Think long and hard, for example, about adding your husband to the title of your great-aunt's lake house that you inherited. Should you ever separate, it would be tragic to lose your family treasure. This is doubly important in remarriages, as you may have property you want to leave to your children from an earlier relationship. Work with a qualified estate lawyer to make sure you have the right documents set up to protect you.

■ **After you marry, every asset either of you acquires is jointly held.** That's why you both need to be in sync on your long-term financial goals, from paying off the mortgage to putting away for retirement. Ideally, you should talk about all this before you wed. If you don't, you can end up deeply frustrated and financially spent. Discussing money with the man you hope to spend the rest of your life with doesn't mean you don't love him. It means you love him *and* yourself.

IDENTITY THEFT

Q. A representative from my bank called recently to ask whether I had received my new credit card. Since my current one wasn't due to expire for five more years, I asked why they sent a replacement. The agent said there had been a copyright problem, and they reissued all the cards without notification. I never got mine, but apparently someone else did. That person tried to use my card to buy a report from an online data

ARE YOU FALLING BACK ON THE OLD NOTION THAT A HUSBAND IS SUPPOSED TO BE THE BREAD-WINNER, AND YOU RESENT HIM FOR NOT FITTING INTO THAT TRADITIONAL MOLD?

broker that would include my name, my parents' names, and my Social Security number. I asked the bank representative how the charge was processed when I never activated the card, and she said it was declined. Should I have my credit report frozen?

SUZE: At the risk of making you more worried, are you sure that was your bank calling? Scammers are infamous for getting people to cough up personal information by posing as concerned customer service agents on the phone or by sending official-looking e-mails.

I want you to be doubly safe if this ever happens again: When you get a call or an e-mail from a financial institution, politely hang up or walk away from your computer. Then call customer service and explain that you just received an inquiry and want to confirm its legitimacy. The representative can pull up your record to see if anything warrants your attention.

While it sounds like you dodged a bullet this time, you're smart to be concerned. A credit freeze is indeed the ultimate protection. Unfortunately, not all states allow consumers to freeze their reports. In "Identity Crisis" (*below*), I explain the rules, along with steps you can take to better safeguard your financial information.

IDENTITY CRISIS

Identity theft has been the top consumer fraud complaint lodged with the Federal Trade Commission for seven years straight. Here's how to avoid becoming a statistic:

■ **Scour your accounts.** Identity theft comes in two basic flavors. Someone either gains access to an existing account or poses as you to get a loan or open a new account. To protect yourself, closely monitor your accounts for anything fishy—a charge you didn't make, a withdrawal you didn't take out. Spend a few minutes each month reviewing your statements to make sure your accounts haven't been invaded. If you spot a problem, call customer service immediately.

■ **Check your credit reports.** Most likely, you have a report on file at one of the three major credit bureaus: Equifax (800-685-1111), Experian (888-397-3742), or TransUnion (800-888-4213). If an identity thief has opened any accounts using your personal information, it will show up in your report. Get a free copy of your records from all three credit bureaus every year at annualcreditreport.com or 877-322-8228. You can receive them all at once or request a report every four months to monitor your accounts throughout the year. If you have children, run the same check using their Social Security numbers. Identity thieves love to open accounts under children's names because the crime can go undetected for years. It's also smart to make sure your parents' reports are in good shape; again, thieves love to prey on the unsuspecting.

■ **Make life harder on would-be criminals.** Placing a fraud alert on your credit report can slow down thieves. An alert serves as a signal to potential creditors to be extra careful granting any new cards or loans on your account. But it's important to understand that alerts don't force the creditor to go the extra mile to protect you; they're merely a suggestion. You can put a free 90-day alert on your accounts by calling one of the credit bureaus, which is required to send your request to the other two. It's up to you to renew your alert every three months. A seven-year fraud alert is available only to someone who has already become a victim of identity theft.

■ **Freeze out thieves.** A security freeze is the most powerful way to protect your personal information, but not all states allow you to set one up. To put a freeze on your credit reports, you must contact the three credit bureaus separately in writing. Unless you've been victimized, there may be a charge to put a hold in place. And because it keeps prospective creditors from looking at your accounts, they won't have access to the information they need to grant new loans or issue new credit cards. If you're applying for one, you will first need to call the credit bureaus and have the freeze lifted so creditors will be able to check your record. And be aware that a freeze locks you out, too.

See oprah.com/omagextras for more information.

PASSING ON AN INHERITANCE

Q: My aunt told me that she was going to leave me more than $100,000 when she died. We made a will because she wanted to be sure I got all the money, which was in mutual funds and IRAs. After my aunt passed away, I found out she had a beneficiary listed from many years ago. I've called several lawyers, but no one will talk to me; they all say, "Give up, you're wasting your time." Is there any way this money can still be mine? I was counting on investing it for my retirement.

SUZE: I am so sorry to tell you that the lawyers you've contacted are correct. The beneficiary stated on your aunt's accounts overrides what's written in her will. If she hired a lawyer to draw up that document, you should be mad. Any professional knows this basic rule of estate planning and should have worked with your aunt to make sure that the names listed on every single one of her assets were in sync with what she said she wanted in her will.

Though you don't have any legal recourse, if you know the recipient identified on the accounts, perhaps you can try appealing to him or her. This person probably loved your aunt as much as you did and would want to honor her intent.

At the very least, I'd like to help others learn from your predicament. In "Leaving a Legacy" (*below*), I discuss how to ensure that one's wishes are carried out.

LEAVING A LEGACY

This may come as a surprise, but guaranteeing that your loved ones get the inheritance you meant for them requires more than a will. As the woman in the above question learned, conditions in a will are superseded by the beneficiaries listed on financial assets such as IRAs, life insurance policies, and bank accounts.

Our lives are so busy, we forget to pick up milk at the grocery store, let alone change our beneficiaries. You may divorce, for example, and fail to remember that your ex is the recipient on the IRA you set up 20 years ago, or that his name is on the title to the home you supposedly won in the settlement. Here's how to protect yourself and your heirs:

■ **Do an annual review.** If you've married, divorced, or had children, you'll want to update your beneficiaries. Contact the account administrator at the bank, brokerage house, or mutual fund company and ask customer service to confirm who is currently listed. If you need to make a change, request the proper form, write down the new designation (typically, you need that person's Social Security number and birth date), and sign on the dotted line.

■ **Set up a trust.** We've covered this before, but it bears repeating: Create a living revocable trust, and make that trust the beneficiary of all your sizable assets (including your home). This will ensure a smooth transition. While you're alive, your assets remain completely in your control.

■ **Designate wisely.** Never make an underage child the beneficiary of your life insurance policy. If you die, the insurer will force your relatives into court to get someone appointed as a guardian of the estate (this is separate from any guardian you may have specified in your will to care for your children). That's going to take time and money, and your heirs will still have a major headache: The court may demand that the funds be placed in a "blocked" account that requires approval for withdrawals. Every time your children's guardian needs money, she'll have to go to court (that usually means hiring a lawyer and spending more cash) to request it. Again, the solution is to make your trust the beneficiary. Insurers will happily transfer the money to the trust, and the distribution of assets will be handled exactly as you specified. That's going to be a serious benefit for your heirs.

CAN I AFFORD TO BE A STAY-AT-HOME MOTHER?

Q: I am a married mother of three, and I've been at home with the children for the past four and a half years. My youngest will start kindergarten soon. I would really like to return to work because our mortgage is pretty high, and it's hard for us on one income. But I also love the fact that I'm home when the kids get out of school, dinner is ready, and the house is clean. Paying for a babysitter is so expensive that I'm not sure whether it would be worth going back. What do you suggest?

SUZE: It may surprise you to hear this, but I'm in favor of families having a stay-at-home parent if it works for them financially. I think it's so telling that you say you love being home for the kids, because good things come when you follow your passion.

The key here is to stay at home only if you and your husband can handle all your expenses. If you find you're getting deeper and deeper into debt on just one income, then you need to return to work. But who says it has to be in an office or full-time? Think creatively about ways you can earn a living and still be there after school for your children. For example, people can make great money as sellers on eBay.

Even if you previously worked a five-day-a-week office job, see if there's part-time or consulting work you can do in your field—perhaps for your former employer. Companies are always looking to save on the cost of benefits; your willingness to act as an independent contractor means you may be able to negotiate flexible or reduced hours.

> SCAMMERS ARE INFAMOUS FOR GETTING PEOPLE TO COUGH UP PERSONAL INFORMATION BY POSING AS CONCERNED CUSTOMER SERVICE AGENTS.

CREDIT CARD REWARDS

Q. My brother is determined to wring as much value as possible from his credit cards. He goes so far as to write in permanent marker on each of his and his wife's cards exactly what they should be used for—gas, groceries, morning coffee—so they can rack up airline miles, points, or cash back. When issuers try to up his interest rate or charge him a monthly fee, he gets on the phone and threatens to cut up the card until they give in. He makes me feel as though I'm not vigilant enough about my credit. Is this worth my time? Can he really be saving all that much?

SUZE: I admit the permanent marker sounds a bit intense, but there's a payoff for being credit card compulsive. Assuming he hasn't crossed the line from focused to fanatical—meaning he isn't driving his wife crazy—then I think it's great that he works to get the most from his plastic.

My main concern is whether he's read the fine print to determine how beneficial his rewards cards really are. Quite often they carry substantial annual fees that can decrease or wipe out the value of any perks. For example, an ad might promise 5 percent cash back, but in reality, you have to charge thousands of dollars before you can get it, or the rate might not apply to most of your everyday purchases. One of the hidden traps of many rewards cards is an extrahigh interest rate, so if he and his wife occasionally carry a balance, a rewards card isn't a smart bet.

When it comes to interest rates, being vigilant is worth your time. A recent survey found that more than 75 percent of people who called their credit card issuer to push for a lower rate were given a better deal. Let's say you had a $3,000 balance and reduced your interest rate from 15 percent to 10 percent. You could shave more than $1,000 off the total interest paid if you were to send in just the minimum amount due each month. With a strong credit rating (a FICO score of 700 or higher), you might be able to go even lower than that. In "Play Your Cards Right" (*below*), I review the moves everyone should make.

PLAY YOUR CARDS RIGHT

Thanks to recent congressional pressure, some credit card issuers have become a little more consumer-friendly. Citigroup, the world's largest card company, has quit using "universal default," which permitted it to raise users' interest rates even if they slipped up on payments to other creditors. Chase has decided to stop using "two-cycle billing," a practice that enabled the company to charge interest even for periods in which cardholders didn't carry a balance. But don't think for a minute that creditors have become altruistic. They can still make plenty of money off your account if you aren't paying attention. Here's how a little effort can help:

■ **Request a lower interest rate.** If you've been a reliable client with a solid credit profile, there's no reason to settle for a card with a rate of 15 percent or more. Call customer service and be polite but firm: "Given my strong credit history and the fact that I pay my bills on time, I think the interest rate on my card should be reduced to 8 percent. If you can't do that, I intend to take my business to a lower-rate card and cancel this account." (You can shop for a better deal at bankrate.com, but don't actually cancel the card. It's best to get the balance down to zero by transferring it to a new card or paying it off. Then don't use the card again.)

■ **Pay on time.** According to a study by the Government Accountability Office, 35 percent of cardholders paid at least one late fee in 2005 and the average cost was $34, compared with $13 a decade earlier. This is too expensive a slipup to make. Even if you can't cover the bill in full, send in the minimum payment by the due date.

■ **Eliminate your highest-rate balance first.** To deal with multiple credit card balances, always pay the minimum due on each, and add *more* than the minimum onto the one with the highest interest rate. Concentrate on getting rid of the debt on that card, then move on to the card with the next highest interest rate, and so on, until you're in the clear.

> AS LONG AS THERE ARE PEOPLE AND CAUSES THAT CAN BENEFIT FROM YOUR ALTRUISM, THERE IS NO TIME LIKE THE PRESENT TO GIVE.

DO SMALL DONATIONS MAKE A DIFFERENCE?

Q. I try to donate money to a few different charities I believe in—$100 here, $50 there. The subject came up at a party not long ago, and one of the guests said my approach is pointless. He said that smaller contributions don't have as much of an impact as one large donation. Is he right? Should I be setting aside money in a savings account or investing in a mutual fund to give away at the end of my life?

SUZE: I sure wish I had been at that party so I could tell that guest how wrong he is. There's no such thing as an insignificant donation. As long as there are people and causes that can benefit from your altruism, there is no time like the present to give.

If you happen to run into that guy again, you might want to point out that small donations can make a big difference. A $10 donation to Habitat for Humanity buys a box of nails that will help to build a home for a needy family. According to UNICEF, $17 can immunize a child against the top six childhood diseases. The American Red Cross reports that $115 will buy a week's worth of groceries for a family of four.

Sure, the billions of dollars the Bill & Melinda Gates Foundation disburses have a global reach, but that doesn't diminish the fact that your charitable contributions, at any size, are helping someone somewhere to live a better life right now. No one can belittle the value of that. **O**

TURNING POINTS

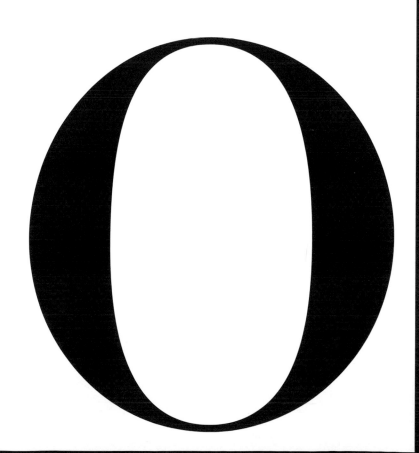

FIRSTS

Remember your first day of school? Your first job? Your first crush? Your first broken heart? On the next six pages, a few extraordinary ordinary people tell the stories of all kinds of milestone moments in their lives. How did Barack Obama land his first date with his wife? What did Colin Powell do on his first day off? (It involved a wrench.) And just how disastrous was Anthony Bourdain's first cooking disaster? (See how bad things can get, at right.)

MY FIRST COOKING DISASTER

ANTHONY BOURDAIN, CHEF, AUTHOR, HOST OF *NO RESERVATIONS*

Back in the 1970s, flush with a little knowledge and a lot of youthful enthusiasm, my catering partner and I took on a new client. The job was a large wedding reception— big money—and, eager to close the deal, we had assured the customer that there was nothing we couldn't do: pâtés en croûte, truffled galantines of poultry and veal en gelée, decorative chaudfroids, whole poached salmon adorned with Escoffier-era garnishes.... All these were things we could pull off with reasonable competence. So when the client inquired about a wedding cake, I didn't flinch: "Yes, of course! We'd be happy to provide a cake!"

The fact that outside of a few baking classes in culinary school I had never in my life made any baked good, not even a from-the-mix Bundt cake, did nothing to diminish my faith in my abilities. But perhaps sensing in some dim, instinctive way that a classic, sky-high, round cake adorned with intricate pastillage work was beyond me, I opted for something different. I filled sheet pans of various sizes with batter (a recipe I'd cribbed from Julia Child). When these had baked, I stacked them in jelly-smeared layers like a Flintstones version of a Mayan temple, then iced them with buttercream that, in a disco-era moment of chemical-inspired lunacy, I'd dyed blue. For the finishing touch, I used a pastry bag to add what I believed to be avant-garde patterns of more blue icing and studded it with blueberries, raspberries, and strawberries.

My catering partner was skeptical. "It looks like Betty Crocker on acid." But it was too late to do anything else. And frankly, we thought young guns like us didn't have to follow convention—we *made* conventions.

We sent the cake out to the expectant crowd, where the bride and groom were poised with a knife.

Total silence.

The bride said, "Ewwww!"

The groom said, "Honey, it looks like Carvel! You like Carvel!"

And in the cold light of near-universal repulsion, I realized that I had created an abomination. I hope the happy couple is still together—though somehow I doubt it.

I never baked again.

MY FIRST DAY AT SCHOOL
CLAIRE MESSUD, AUTHOR OF *THE EMPEROR'S CHILDREN*

We moved around a lot when I was a kid, and I'd been new at school a bunch of times—in Canada, in Australia, in Canada again. But in 1980, it felt harder: We were moving to yet another new country—the United States—and this time my new school was a boarding school outside Boston, hours from home and worlds away from the Toronto public school I was leaving behind. Worst of all, I was 13.

Nineteen eighty was the year of preppy mania. *The Official Preppy Handbook* was a best-seller. *Seventeen* magazine ran a cover story highlighting preppy fashion. My parents, indulgent of my adolescent anxiety—negotiating bad skin, breasts, and boys seemed hard enough, without a whole new society of scary, well-heeled Americans to decode—had allowed me new items for my wardrobe. I was used to making my own clothes on my ancient Singer portable, out of Vogue patterns and cheap fabrics, but I knew they wouldn't be right for my new life. So I'd spent weeks planning my first-impression outfit, and when I climbed out of the taxi that late summer morning, I wore a green woolen kilt, knee-high argyle socks, Bass Weejun loafers, and a pale gray button-down shirt, with a Fair Isle sweater draped strategically over my shoulders.

Of course I'd got it all wrong. It was 85 degrees in the shade. Even before I walked into the large white clapboard dormitory, I was sweating like a pig. Perspiration poured down my temples, down my back, in the crooks of my knees. Worth it, I thought, if it meant that my Canadian bumpkinness didn't show and I could slip into the crowd like someone who was, if not born to boarding school, at least plausibly American.

But inside I grasped at once that my trouble went beyond the damp patches on my clothes. Girls—so many blonde girls—milled about, chattering as if they'd always known one another, all of them

Messud at 13, before her boarding school makeover.

wearing Indian-print T-shirts, floaty tiered skirts, and flip-flops. My new roommate, a six-foot myopic blonde, too cool to wear her glasses, apparently couldn't even see me when I said hello. Worse than wrong, I was invisible. Even the other new kids ignored me. Only one girl, a kind black girl from St. Louis, asked where I was from and whether I didn't want to change into something less stifling. The shame of it lives in my memory as only shame can, as if it were yesterday.

Still in my kilt but without the socks and sweater, I stuck to the kind girl like a pet and trotted along mutely beside her to the opening-day events. She didn't shun me, but she laughed at me, which actually made me feel better. A few weeks later, I would buy several 1960s psychedelic print shift dresses at a garage sale for 5 cents apiece, and stuff my preppy clothes in the back of my closet. It would all, eventually, be more than okay. But I've never forgotten the early shock of it, and the pain, imperfectly repressed, remains a useful lesson in misery, a reminder of how lonely and foreign it feels when you don't belong.

MY FIRST BROKEN HEART
DAVID SEDARIS, WRITER

Sedaris in London, 2003.

I've never gone in for clothing with writing on it. Team jackets, T-shirts kitted out with goofy slogans—I can't even bear a discreet logo. At some point, though, I must have owned a pair of pants with KICK ME embroidered in bright letters across the ass. How else to explain "M," whom I met while in my early 20s. We worked different shifts in the same small-town restaurant, and what attracted me, aside from his looks, was an unspoken guarantee that he would never return my feelings. Unlike myself, M was sexy and popular. He liked clubs and dancing, and had once gone to Studio 54 on the arm of a wallpaper designer.

I could not have fallen for anyone more unsuitable, yet still I pursued him. We slept together only twice, and when he gave me the inevitable brush-off, I acted as though he'd ended a 30-year marriage. My crying and begging were completely uncalled for, but what really shames me are the letters I sent—60 in all. Roughly amounting to five pages for every hour we spent together, they were the ravings of a certified crazy person, and I can only hope that he threw them directly into the trash can.

A broken heart is a rite of passage and, looking back, I must have wanted one pretty badly. "Kick me," I demanded, and when somebody finally did, I burst like a cheap piñata. It's been almost 30 years since I last slept with M, but sometimes, when bending to tie my shoe, I can still feel his ghostly footprint, booting me into adulthood.

MY FIRST DAY OFF

COLIN POWELL, FORMER CHAIRMAN OF THE JOINT CHIEFS OF STAFF, FORMER SECRETARY OF STATE

When I retired from the army in 1993, there was a huge ceremony at Fort Myer in Virginia. President Clinton was there, as well as Vice President Gore; there were 1,000 people at the reception. I had served 35 years. I'd had a staff of 1,500. I ran wars. I commanded more than two million soldiers, sailors, airmen, and marines. Now, after all those years, it was suddenly over. I was in charge of me. No more alarm clock. No more name tag. And I was ready. I was looking forward to being normal again—getting to the point where I could maybe even go to a garage sale. It's important to get back to being normal.

The first morning, I slept a little later than usual. Then I went downstairs for breakfast, and my wife, Alma, said to me, "The sink is clogged." I was delighted.

I got under the sink, took it apart, cleaned out the trap, put it back on, and made sure it didn't leak. An accomplishment.

The same thing happened after I left the State Department, when I had to replace a toilet—which, by the way, involves more than what they give you at Home Depot.

Before I decided to become a plumber, I used to rebuild Volvos. There's something invigorating about working on an engine. You know something is wrong, and by the process of elimination, you figure it out. Plumbing is the same way. You do the work, and you can test it. Either it holds water or it doesn't. The problems you deal with as chairman of the Joint Chiefs or secretary of state are usually not that amenable to rapid analysis and solution.

MY FIRST CASUALTY

GENERAL PETER PACE, UNITED STATES MARINE CORPS, CHAIRMAN OF THE JOINT CHIEFS OF STAFF

I was 22, a rifle platoon leader in Vietnam. It was a great platoon, great guys. Chubby Hale, Whitey Travers, Little Joe Arnold—everybody had a nickname except Guido Farinaro. Having Guido for a name was good enough.

I was lucky: In my first six months, we had folks wounded but not killed. It was a blessing to make it that far without losing anyone. But one day, 35 or 40 of us were walking through rice paddies and small villages, patrolling. There was an exchange of fire, and Guido Farinaro was shot by a sniper.

He was the first marine I lost. We were waiting for the medevac chopper to come in and pick him up, and he died while we were waiting. I had rage inside me. We did a sweep through the village, trying to find who shot him, but we saw only women and children.

Guido had a great smile and a great sense of humor. He was born in Italy and came to the United States. He lived in Bethpage, New York, out on Long Island, and went to Chaminade High School. Most, if not all, of his classmates had gone on to college, but he determined that he was going to serve his country—his adopted country—first.

After he was killed, I wrote to his family, but I didn't try to contact them further. I figured if they wanted to be in touch with me, they would. I didn't want to impose myself on their grief. Then about two years ago, I found out that Guido's parents had died but

General Pace in his Pentagon office.

that he had a sister out west. I wrote to her, but the letter came back, and the phones had been disconnected. I just thought that if there was anything she wanted to know about her brother and what a great marine he was, I would have been happy to share it with her.

I keep his picture on my desk at the Pentagon, to remind me of the cost of war. But I don't need the picture to see Guido's face. You don't forget. I decided that I would stay in the Marine Corps as long as I could, as long as I was adding value, because I felt I owed more than I could ever repay to Guido and the other young men who followed their second lieutenant into combat and died doing so.

MY FIRST DAY OF FREEDOM
DENNIS MAHER, INNOCENT MAN, EXONERATED AFTER 19 YEARS IN PRISON

Maher and his daughter, Aliza, at home in Massachusetts.

I was sentenced to life in prison for three sexual assaults I didn't commit, and I served 19 years, two months, and 29 days. Not that I counted.

On April 1—April Fool's Day—2003, I got the word that I was going to be released. Unbelievable. Aliza, my lawyer, called and said, "When do you want to go home? You can go tomorrow if you want."

I said, "Let's make it April 3." I wanted my family to have time to adjust. Plus I wanted time to say goodbye. I'd been with some of these guys 17 years. I had made a lot of friends.

I started crying and got all emotional. I had come to the conclusion I was going to die in prison. When I called my mother, she said, "I'll believe it when I see it."

I remember going out in the yard to walk—thinking how, on the outside, I'd be able to walk in straight lines instead of squares or circles. Having to wait for cars to go by, dealing with the hustle and bustle of people—I was looking forward to it.

In prison I ran the staff kitchen, and later that day the cops were saying, "What are we going to eat now?" The whole staff was glad I was leaving. Quite a few of them believed I was innocent.

The night before I got out, my friends and I went up to the prison library to sit and say our goodbyes. These were all hardened criminals, and they were crying. Some of them I worked with, some I lifted weights with. Everyone knew my story.

On April 3, the guards woke me up at 5 A.M. I was strip-searched, then I changed into a suit. Of course we got stuck in the beautiful Boston traffic on our way to the courthouse. As we pulled up, I could see the camera crews. I thought, *All those crews are for me.* They took me to a holding cell, and my lawyer came in and said, "Are you ready?" I started crying again. It was something I never thought would happen and here it is staring me in the face.

In the courtroom, my mom didn't recognize me. She hadn't seen me in a suit in 19 years. I was clean-shaven. I still had chains on my ankles and wrists, but I looked good. The guards took off the chains, and I hugged my parents and my lawyer. Then J.W. Carney, the man who had prosecuted me 19 years earlier, asked to speak with me. He said, "I'm sorry, Dennis. I did not know." He said, "Can you forgive me?" I said, "I forgive you, Jay." He had the guts to step forward and apologize. And he still gets picked on for

it. I was one of the first exonerees to get a face-to-face apology—which went a long way toward helping me get through this.

They had a reception for me in the attorney's office—Brie cheese and all this food I had never eaten. And then we drove to Lowell, which is where I was arrested and where my parents live. There was a new train station, new parks, new bridges. The whole face of the city had changed. My parents lived in a different place now and had set up a cot for me. I was 42 years old, and my mother joked, "You're grounded." But for the next week or two, I went out and walked in a different direction every day, just exploring. On my way back to the house, I'd stop at McDonald's to get an Egg McMuffin. That was the only thing that was the same.

I went to renew my driver's license. I gave them my old license, and the clerk said, "You've got a speeding ticket from ten years ago." I said, "I just got out of prison yesterday after 19 years, two months, and 29 days. There's no way."

My Sears credit card still worked. That really freaked me out.

When I was arrested, I was a soldier. I had planned on doing 20 years in the military, but I ended up doing almost 20 years in prison. I was a defender of freedom, and they took my freedom away.

In prison I had to be in a treatment program for sexually dangerous people because I had denied my "crimes." I had a hard time with the program. I had to deal with sex offenders talking about what they did, and therapists who said I was in denial. As part of the program, you were supposed to write a release plan. I told the woman who was leading the group, "My plan is I'll get released through DNA testing, take two months off, find a job"—which I did; I got hired as a mechanic for a waste management company—"meet a woman and get married and have children." And that's what happened.

I knew the DNA was not going to match; I just didn't know when the results were going to come. I'd fought the bureaucracy for years trying to get the DNA tested, but the judge wouldn't release the evidence. The day the judge retired, I called the Innocence Project in New York, which referred me to the New England Innocence Project. Those were the first lawyers who ever took my case. Aliza Kaplan was the lawyer who got me out. My daughter is 11 months old now, and her name is Aliza Maher.

Barack and Michelle Obama at the Democratic National Convention, 2004.

MY FIRST DATE WITH MY WIFE
BARACK OBAMA, U.S. SENATOR

I met Michelle in 1988, after my first year of law school, when I took a summer job at Sidley & Austin, a law firm in Chicago. A year earlier I had been working as a community organizer in some of Chicago's poorest neighborhoods, and I struggled with the decision to go to a large firm. But with student loans mounting, the three months of salary they offered wasn't something I could pass up.

Michelle worked at Sidley, too, and, in the luckiest break of my life, was assigned to be my adviser, charged with helping me learn the ropes. I remember being struck by how tall and beautiful she was. She, I have since learned, was pleasantly surprised to see that my nose and ears weren't quite as enormous as they looked in the photo I'd submitted for the firm directory.

Over the next several weeks, we saw a lot of each other at work. She was kind enough to take me to a few parties, and never once commented on my mismatched and decidedly unstylish wardrobe.

I asked her out. She refused. I kept asking. She kept refusing. "I'm your adviser," she said. "It's not appropriate." Finally, I offered to quit my job, and at last she relented. On our first date, I treated her to the finest ice cream Baskin-Robbins had to offer, our dinner table doubling as the curb. I kissed her, and it tasted like chocolate.

I had known those student loans were going to get me a great education, but I had no idea they'd get me my first date with the love of my life. **O**

JOURNEY TO THE CENTER OF YOURSELF

Sixty women won the chance of a lifetime: A five-day retreat at Miraval Resort and Spa with Oprah, Gayle, and a dream team of advisers for mind, body, and spirit. What they learned could change their lives—and yours. Aimee Lee Ball brings the experience here for you.

Why are you here?" Oprah is talking to the women joining her and Gayle King for five days at Miraval Resort near Tucson with Oprah's top health and wellness advisers, Bob Greene, Martha Beck, PhD, Mehmet Oz, MD, and Jon Kabat-Zinn, PhD. From almost 50,000 applicants, 60 women deeply in need of respite and renewal have been selected. Women like Erin Leigh Mergil, from El Paso, Texas, who used the phrase "empty arms, tired heart" to describe her angst following the death of a newborn; Valerie Smith, from Oakdale, Connecticut, who returned from her deployment in Iraq to face abdominal surgery and to bury her husband, who died suddenly of a pulmonary embolism; Jennifer West, from Richmond, Kentucky, a war widow whose grief-stricken image in a newspaper led a stranger to enter her in the Miraval contest. There's a mother who has two adult children in wheelchairs. A woman who took in a homeless family, despite her own financial chaos. A bride whose mother died on her wedding day. A psychiatrist for mentally ill prisoners. Two survivors of Hurricane Katrina.

Their stories are unique, but the situation is universal: These are women who have come to a crossroads. They can no longer dwell, safe and numb, in weight or grief or whatever their lives have become about. They are here to find both a way out and a way back to themselves.

On the first night, the group has gathered for Oprah's welcome. Her opening question is a doozy, because she doesn't just mean here at the spa. "If you don't know the answer to why you are really here," she says, "your whole life will be out of sorts. The job I go to every day is in alignment with why I'm here. Your purpose is the spiritual thread that connects all of your life experiences."

She gazes around the room at women whose responsibilities and experiences have left them depleted. It will be easy for them to feel nourished and pampered at Miraval—warmed by the Sonoran Desert, cooled by the Santa Catalina mountains, a fresh smoothie at their beckoning, a massage before going to sleep on a downy bed.

But they didn't come here for a quick fix. If this trip is to have a lasting effect, they must learn, as Oprah says, that they are more than the roles they play in their lives—wife, mother, sister, daughter, caregiver. They must see themselves in ways they never imagined. And they must use the tools they will be given on this trip to take them through the journey.

"I know about the grace and kindness you give to everybody else," Oprah says. "But there is a greater purpose than your sacrifice to others. This week is devoted to the you that needs to be empowered to move forward."

Left: Gayle King flying high during Swing & a Prayer, an exercise in learning to let go—literally. After you're strapped into a harness and attached to a cable, you're hoisted 40 feet in the air; it's up to you when to let go of the rope and drop in a dramatic arc to the ground. After many expletives, the group renamed it Swing & a Swear. *Right:* Oprah and friends start the day with an exercise class.

Left: Oprah cracks up while Gayle swings and swears. *Right:* She did it! Congratulations after the perilous plunge.

Left: O reader and Miraval winner Wendy Wiebell in the Cardio Box class. *Right:* The women at Zen Boot Camp, a workout that emphasizes body awareness.

MONDAY MORNING: BOB GREENE

"A NUMBER ON THE SCALE ISN'T NECESSARILY THE KEY TO HAPPINESS...."

Exercise physiologist Bob Greene motivates a roomful of women with weight loss on their minds by comparing his two passions: personal training and house renovation. "You start with a home that has unlimited potential," he says. "What are you willing to invest in it?"

Greene asks everyone to draw a pie chart, labeling each wedge with some aspect of a fulfilled life—family, career, friends, travel, health and fitness, or whatever they choose. Then he instructs them to put a plus or minus sign next to each part, indicating whether that area of life is going well. The exercise is designed to show them that the reason for overeating probably has less to do with a love for pasta or chocolate and is more likely about an emotional roadblock. "Everyone here knows what she should and shouldn't be eating. The answer to losing weight is often somewhere other than health and fitness," Greene explains. "The folks who are successful at keeping pounds off are those who understand that a number on a scale isn't necessarily the key to happiness. If you try to move forward without figuring out what the issue really is, it's like building a house with a bad foundation."

Greene references a psychological phenomenon known as happiness anxiety. "People get a kind of satisfaction in living out negative core beliefs," he says. "You might think you want to be a certain size or fall head over heels in love, but unconsciously you're fulfilling a conviction—maybe it's 'I'm unlovable.' It defines you, puts you in a box. But if you feel you deserve something, you're going to find a way to get it. You must believe that you're deserving of what you want and that you have the skills to get it."

As Greene speaks, there are clicks of realization around the room as each woman sees clearly, for the first time, the root of the problem—not the weight but the why. Kathy Cinquemani Shields, from University Park, Texas, recognizes her bigger body as armor; after her third (yes, third) breast cancer diagnosis, she was told to eat anything she wanted, her doctors assuming she would become too thin while undergoing chemo. But she gained the pounds and kept them. "I became invisible," she says, "and it was a safe place to be." Kathy S. Anderson, from Windsor, Colorado, remembers soothing herself with red wine and potato chips for months after her son was murdered. Jesse Hennen, from Paynesville, Minnesota, gave up a baby for adoption. She may have forgiven the birth father for refusing to be involved, but she is now sabotaging herself with food because she feels unworthy of a relationship with a good man.

And then, of course, there is the most common reason: no time. Joanne McColm, from Pleasanton, California, contends that she has none for herself, much less for fitness, since 1998, when she became the mother of quadruplets, along with two older children. But Greene won't let her off the hook. "I've never met anybody who couldn't free up the amount of time it takes to be fit—at least 20 minutes a day, five times a week," he counters. "As the flight attendants on the plane say, put on your own oxygen mask before you help your children. If you take care of yourself, you'll be of greater service to the people in your life."

An exercise pointer from Bob Greene: Watch your "results zone." On a scale of one (easy) to ten (almost impossible), stay at seven; "You should be able to talk, but not for long." *Above, left:* Bob coaches Sofia Taylor-Edwards during the group's morning workout at the gym. *Middle:* Oprah, Amanda Hendon, and Gayle. *Right:* Gayle urges Oprah on during resistance training in Cardio Box.

BOB GREENE'S TOP 5 RULES FOR WEIGHT LOSS

1 Understand the reasons you eat when you're not hungry.
2 Start moving, as often as you can, so that you rev up your metabolism before you start cutting calories.
3 Toss out the five troublemaker foods: soda, anything with trans fats, fried foods, white bread, and high-fat dairy products.

4 Bring in foods that are high in fiber: fresh fruits, vegetables, and whole grains.
5 Quick weight loss programs can eventually inhibit losing pounds. Your body doesn't release more than about three pounds of fat a week. If you lose more than that, you're really losing water weight and, to a degree, the body's capacity to burn calories.

"THIS IS A ROOM FULL OF SAMURAI SWORDS...."

Life coach Martha Beck, PhD, stands at the front of an auditorium addressing the women, each of whom has a story, a history, a wound that has inspired her to use a metaphor. "Japanese swordmakers start with the best material they can find," she explains to the women. "Then they beat it, over and over, until the sword is so strong and sharp, it can cut through anything. You are all swords—made of fine stuff, pounded but powerful."

Powerful is not the word these women would use to describe themselves, though it's apt, considering how they have been holding themselves and their worlds together. Now Beck wants them to see themselves that way.

To that end, she doesn't focus on why Wendy Wiebell, from Westerville, Ohio, stayed in an abusive marriage for 11 years, or her guilt about her children watching it all happen. "There are a lot of reasons we put up with bad treatment," she says. "If somebody has an arrow sticking out of her, I don't ask about its design." Instead, she concentrates on what must be done now. Children model what we do to ourselves, not what we do to them, she says, so Wendy must be fairly transparent about her own psychological process. She must let her kids know that she's angry because she has been hurt but is going to use her anger to make their lives better. "It's amazing how healing it is for children to know that their mother is taking authority to protect herself," Beck assures.

Many of the women say fear is their main impediment to making the changes they feel are necessary. Beck dismantles the emotion with a scientific tidbit: The brains of mammals are elaborate expansions of what is essentially a reptile's brain, where fear lives. "Are you really going to take advice from a lizard?" she asks. "I encourage you to name your inner lizard. Mine is Mo. He sits on my shoulder, and when fear comes up, I know it's Mo."

Many of the women have been telling the people around them that everything is just fine for so long that they've lost the ability to be honest with themselves. Judy Mathews, from Lee's Summit, Missouri, was widowed last November, leaving her to raise five young children alone. "I want to be everything to my kids," she says, "and I know I'm up to it."

"Oh, honey," says Beck sympathetically, "no, you're not." Judy realizes that perhaps a truer statement would be "I need help."

Beck reminds the women of the infinite possibilities ahead of them. "What will happen to you this afternoon is as unknown to you as the moment of your death," she says. "Here's how to figure out whether your mission in life is done yet: Are you dead?"

Martha Beck (with Patricia A. Ringgenberg, *right*) tells the women, "You are all heroes."

MARTHA BECK'S 3 RULES FOR FIGHTING FEAR

1 Make a list of the things you have to do today. Drop anything negative that you can, and sweeten what you can't. Listen for that inner voice, and go toward the good whispers.

2 For five minutes every day, go to a treasure chest of pleasing thoughts in your mind. If you have trouble filling the chest, answer these questions: I love the smell of _____. I love the sound of _____. I love the taste of _____. I love the sight of _____. I love the feel of _____.

3 While doing the exercise above, clasp either pinky finger with your other hand; this creates a state-dependent memory and will take you back to this blissful mood whenever you hold your pinky.

MONDAY AFTERNOON: MEHMET OZ, MD

"THE GOOD NEWS IS THAT YOU HAVE THE ABILITY TO ALTER THE AGING PROCESS...."

Mehmet Oz, MD, knows that pictures are worth a thousand words when it comes to illustrating his point. He projects onto a screen a computerized image of himself going through a typical aging process, and, despite the fact that he was once on *People* magazine's list of the sexiest men alive, it is not a pretty sight. "The real battles against the debilitating aspects of aging are not going to be won by me in the operating room; they're going to be won by you in your homes," he says. Though he's professor and vice chair of surgery at New York Presbyterian Hospital–Columbia University Medical Center and performs more than 300 heart operations a year, he'd really like us to stay away from doctors and hospitals.

Oz introduces a rather shocking idea: He replaces the idea of weight management with *waist* management. What's important, he says, is the omentum, the organ connected to the stomach that catches and stores fat. This fat is chemically active and can lead to irritation of the arteries, putting you at risk for blockages. "Measure your waist at your belly button. It should be no more than half of your height in inches—that goes for all genders, all races. If you reduce the size of your waist with exercise and healthy diet, you also reduce your risk of heart disease, hypertension, diabetes, high cholesterol, cancer, joint disease, and kidney failure."

According to Oz, waist size can be a measure of stress. "Belly fat is our adaptive system to stress," he explains. "It was a great system when that meant famine, as it did for our ancestors a thousand years ago. Now not so much." Cannabinoid receptors (which scientists have nicknamed the "can't avoid" receptors) help calm the body after stress. When activated, these receptors, found in the omentum as well as the brain and other parts of the body, also trigger feedback that tells us to eat—even foods we wouldn't normally crave—so our bodies will store fat for future emergencies.

The diversity of modern-day stresses in the room is striking. Cicely Douglas, from Louisville, Kentucky, works in a 911 center and "can't" lose weight, even though she teaches her children that *can't* is a bad word. Amy Hutchinson, from Philadelphia, is working through the aftermath of an intruder assaulting her as she held her 2-year-old daughter in her arms. Patricia A. Ringgenberg, from Las Vegas, is an asbestos inspector who overeats to null the sexism and difficulties she encounters in her work; she nostalgically whips out a photo of herself 30 pounds thinner.

Women are the caretakers in our culture, only now they're without the community of support available to previous generations, says Oz. He explains that when the heart pumps out blood, it immediately circulates back to the heart itself. Eventually, that blood will go to the liver and the kidneys and the nose and the knees, but the heart must take care of itself first—a reminder to the women who neglect their own needs.

Mehmet Oz, MD, makes a dramatic connection between stress and weight gain.

MEHMET OZ'S 4 SMALL CHANGES FOR BIG HEALTH BENEFITS

1 Big food decisions should be made in the market, not in the kitchen.

2 There is no healthy breakfast option at fast food places—you have to make it yourself. It should include high fiber (such as oatmeal or bran cereal) and protein.

3 Trans fats were originally created to be a cheaper version of candle wax. Do you want to eat wax?

4 People have the longest life spans in Costa Rica, Sardinia, and Okinawa, Japan. The inhabitants of these areas do things like carry wood in a bag or water in a bucket—in other words, they get regular physical exercise, which helps to slow the rate of senescence (the frailty associated with growing old).

"MINDFULNESS IS REALLY PAYING ATTENTION, ON PURPOSE, TO THE PRESENT MOMENT...."

To anyone who has tried—and failed—to "clear the mind" for meditation, this simple definition comes as a huge relief, and it comes from an impeccable source. The author of *Full Catastrophe Living*, Jon Kabat-Zinn, PhD, has been at the forefront of bringing mindfulness-based stress reduction to the Western world; having him as a meditation instructor is rather like having Lance Armstrong teach you how to ride a bike.

On a clear, very still morning, the group listens as Kabat-Zinn mentions a twist on a traditional postcard message that has particular relevance for a session on being mindful and aware: *Having a great time. Wish I were here.* "The next time you're in the shower, check and see if you're really in the shower," he says. "You may already be in your first meeting of the day. How many times have you eaten a whole meal without knowing it, or complained to a loved one, 'You never listen to me'? You can taste without tasting, hear without hearing," he says. "You don't want that to happen when you're with your children because you're so preoccupied."

Though it sounds somewhat counterintuitive, mindfulness, says Kabat-Zinn, is not about thinking. "Throw out the word *meditating*—how about *awarenessing*? The awareness that holds a calm mind is just as good as the awareness that holds a chaotic mind. A beautiful meditation practice can happen when you wake your children, gaze at them, and remind yourself how deep that relationship is."

Kabat-Zinn goes on to destroy other myths of meditative perfection that are themselves the antithesis of what mindfulness can accomplish. "Don't push anything away, and don't pursue anything. Calmness is available, but not if you try to force it. Think of the mind as being like an ocean: Its surface can be turbulent, and you can't clear your mind any more than you can still the water's current by putting Plexiglas on top of it. But you can drop down into it, drop down into your breathing." To get away from "doing" and into "being," he suggests a mindfulness exercise (*below*).

"We turn thoughts into facts, and facts into stories, and we carry these stories around as if they're truth," says Kabat-Zinn. For each of these women, their own truth may have been obscured by these distorted thoughts. Meditation and awareness may help them to see this more clearly, perhaps even see themselves more compassionately. "Why not befriend the body as it is?" he asks. "What about loving yourself at every weight? The Tibetans call this nonmeditation—the real meditation is living your life. Mindfulness is a radical act of love."

Jon Kabat-Zinn keeps the meditation instruction simple: Focus on breathing.

JON KABAT-ZINN'S 4 STEPS TO MEDITATION

1 Lie on your back in bed. Feel where your breathing is most vivid—in the belly, at the nostrils—and bring your awareness to those breath waves.

2 Expand your awareness to include a sense of the whole body breathing. When you notice that the mind wanders, remember that's what minds do, so there is no need to judge.

3 Note what's on your mind if you're no longer in touch with the breath or the sensations of the body. Always come back to your breath. Repeat as necessary.

4 You don't have to be in bed to cultivate mindfulness; you can do it while sitting, standing, walking, cooking, eating, brushing your teeth, picking up the kids, making love. Just be aware of whatever is unfolding in your life in the present moment.

Clockwise from top left: Yvette Hornsby (in white tank) and Evelyn Rauen (in t-shirt) try a different kind of workout in Miraval's Belly Dancing class; a group goes for a morning hike on a desert trail; a framed message from Oprah and a personal journal were among the gifts each winner received; Wyatt Webb leads Miraval's Equine Experience, in which participants recognize patterns in fear and uncertainty by working with horses.

THE LAST NIGHT: OPRAH

"The life experience of every woman here says what is possible," Oprah says to the group after dinner. "When you're faced with a challenge—cancer, divorce, death, murder—and you can still hold yourself upright and continue to move forward, it shows that it is possible to keep standing in grace."

For Oprah, the most moving realization of all during this retreat was that of a woman who said that she remembered thinking as she walked down the aisle on her wedding day, *I guess it's too late now,* but didn't act on that thought until 37 years later. "That was the saddest story. That's 37 years of mediocrity, where no part of you can be what it needs to be. I think all pain is the same, but regret is different. What I wish for her is that she now live a life with intensity and fire. That's why this is such a wonderful week: It gets to be a wake-up call. Let her story be an example for everybody." O

LISA KOGAN TELLS ALL

Quick, name the most awful thing you ever did! Our columnist confesses a sin that led to her cousin's worst hair day—ever. But don't try to guilt her...she'll do it herself.

How long have you and I known each other? Well, by my calculations we go back 13, maybe 14 columns now. This can mean only one thing: It's time for the monkey story.

There are those who will suggest that even to hint at the monkey story is to bring immeasurable shame upon the good Kogan name, that its mere mention invites the sort of familial acrimony and heartache seldom witnessed outside *King Lear*. Still, I will tell the monkey story not because I want to—but because I must.

The monkey story takes place in the late 1960s. It was, as Simon & Garfunkel used to sing, a time of innocence, a time of confidences. I wore a "That Girl" flip and white vinyl go-go boots. Those boots were made for walking, so I'd walk two doors down the street to the Sapersteins' house because the Sapersteins had the biggest color TV on the block, and it was impossible to fully appreciate a masterpiece like *Batman* in black-and-white. Anyway, at some point between Nixon's election and Elvis's comeback concert, my mother and father, brother, and cousins all went to visit the grandparents in Miami Beach...but not the Miami Beach you're thinking of. You see, before Miami was filled with fabulously sexy models eating fabulously sexy food at fabulously sexy boutique hotels, it was filled with old people who had dinner at 5:30 and worshipped Eleanor Roosevelt. As for entertainment, a kid could check out Ponce de León at the wax museum, play a rousing game of bingo, and still be bored silly by noon. And that, my friends, brings us to the monkey story.

There was (and I believe there probably still is) a place in Florida called the Monkey Jungle. It had funny little monkeys swinging from vines overhead, it had monkey memorabilia that made monkey memories last forever, it even had a monkey that was trained to put his hairy little arms around your neck and smile for the camera. I could go on, but suffice it to say the place was lousy with monkeys, and my cousin Suzie Gale and I thought we'd found paradise, complete with souvenir shop and snack bar. Then it happened.

Fact: Suzie was holding a peanut.

Fact: There, high above a large cage of spider monkeys, hung a gigantic sign that read DO NOT FEED THE MONKEYS.

Fact: I was always an inquisitive child, a sucker for an educational science project, if you will, and... Hell, I wanted to know what would happen if I fed the monkeys. Okay, strike that, I wanted to know what would happen if *somebody* fed the monkeys.

And there was sweet Suzie with her cherry pink cheeks and her enormous angel eyes and her layers of dark, curly hair that rioted around that innocent freckled face, tangling and untangling according to the humidity, and, lo and behold, there was her peanut. "Suzie," I whispered with perfect nonchalance, "go see if that monkey wants your peanut."

This next part happened rather quickly, and my recollection is a little hazy. If memory serves, Suzie walked over to the monkey cage and held the peanut up to the bars. The monkey took the peanut, and I could see Suzie beaming with pride as she turned to look at me. Unfortunately, I could also see the monkey toss the peanut over its shoulder, reach its menacing monkey paw between the bars, grab a chunk of Suzie's hair, and yank it out of her terrified little head.

I don't know how many of you have ever had to act as lookout while your mother crouches in a closet as she attempts to hide from her mother-in-law while phoning every pediatrician in the Greater Miami area to inquire about any potential issues that might arise, "if, say, for example, your 5-year-old niece happens to be mauled by a deranged monkey." Wait a minute, I do know. *None* of you have had to do that, because I'm the only person in the universe who's ever sent her darling cousin out to be attacked by a monkey.

In any case, the name of the column is Lisa Kogan Tells All, and now I've told you all the monkey story. It was the first bad thing I ever did—and I remember being shocked that Walter Cronkite didn't lead with it that night on the evening news. I guess Paul Simon knows his stuff—it really was a time of innocence. My family hadn't yet been touched by debt or divorce or death, and betrayal never amounted to more than a little bit of monkey business. The grown-ups smoked, the children tanned, we all ate red meat, and everybody thought they would live forever. But by the summer of '67, my hometown of Detroit was burning around us, and—thanks to James Earl Ray, Sirhan Sirhan, and a war we were assured was winnable—the shelf life on forever officially expired in 1968.

Suzie Gale eventually became Suzanne Rubini, an Atlanta attorney with a lovely husband, two terrific kids, and a major aversion to Curious George. Because my cousin is a charitable soul, and because she understood that I would do a much better job of beating myself up than she ever could, and mostly because her hair grew back, Suzie still speaks to me. Of course, these days the conversations tend to include a lot more about politics and eye lifts than we ever would have imagined back when we played shuffleboard at our grandparents' condominium. The monkey story does occasionally come up, because it turns out you can't really have a monkey take a swipe at your head without mentioning it from time to time, but for the record, Suzie laughs when she tells the story. She's always been slightly sunnier than me—on a bad day, I can make Sylvia Plath look like a rodeo clown. And I've always been slightly funnier than Suzie—though she might argue that this is because I've never been attacked by a giant spider monkey. I still struggle with impulse control and guilt and the deeply unsettling truth that I am actually quite capable of hurting the people I adore, that, given the right set of circumstances, we all are.

Suzie and I are both a lot older and a little wiser now, and we've learned to pay close attention when a warning sign is posted right there in front of our eyes. We fasten our seat belts, we leave the tags on our mattresses, we refuse to operate heavy machinery after a tablespoon of Robitussin—and under no circumstances do we ever feed the monkeys. O

BERNIE MAC'S AHA! MOMENT

His mother was crying. Then laughing. The comedian knew, right then, what he had to do (his best, forever).

It was rough being dark. I got heat from my own people more than anyone else. I remember going to my mom and saying, "Why am I so black?" And she said, "Because *I'm* black. You just gotta always work harder than the average bear." She taught me that if you give your best, you can always walk away. You won't have to worry about how well you did. You'll just think, *I did my best.*

We lived in Chicago, in an apartment on 69th and Morgan. One time when I was about 5 years old, I was sitting on my mom's lap watching *Ed Sullivan* with her, and she was crying. I was on her lap, crying, too, and wiping her face with my little 5-year-old hand. I kept asking, "Why you cryin'?" And she said nothing. What I didn't know was that she had breast cancer. She would lose both breasts and wear a prosthetic bra. She took care of all of us kids and her mother, and so many others, though she was sick herself. And she never told a soul.

So we're watching *Ed Sullivan,* and he calls out Bill Cosby, who starts doing this routine about Noah's ark. And my mom started laughing and crying at the same time. When I saw this, I started laughing. And when Cosby was finished, I looked at my mom and said, "Mom, that's what I'm gonna do. I'm gonna be a comedian, so you never cry again."

I became the storyteller of South Side Chicago. I used an old Kiwi liquid shoe polish as a microphone. I'd go around the house interviewing everybody, telling stupid jokes, doing voices. I mimicked Sidney Poitier, Sammy Davis Jr., people on *Laugh-In,* Flip Wilson. I'd make up stories at the drop of a hat, then sometimes get a whipping because they'd say I was lying, but I just loved entertaining people. I was good at keeping my mother from crying. And I stopped crying, too, even when she died, because I was 15 and that's how I thought it was done.

When I hit my 20s, I struggled to make it. I got married at 19, and my daughter, Je'Niece, was born a year later. I worked blue collar jobs during the day and comedy clubs at night, and I was earning about $25 a year doing stand-up.

One day, when I was selling beer at Soldier Field, I fell down a flight of stairs. The way I fell, I should've been dead, so I went home, even though I really needed the $150-a-week paycheck. I sat in the apartment worrying about the light bill and the rent and wondering why I was wasting my time and energy in those clubs. And then I started thinking about my mom and what she taught me. I heard her words: *Always give your best.* And I wept. It was the first tear I'd cried over my mother's death, and I couldn't stop. I cried until my head hurt.

After that, whether I was playing to one or 1,000 or 10,000 people, I gave them everything. I got roughed up. I was the butt of a lot of jokes. But I kept on, because I knew what I was doing it for. My mother had it right. I wanted to be the best that I could be, first for myself, then for an audience. I love to see a smile on somebody's face, like I saw on my mother's that night. If I can tell someone a story that makes them bend over and laugh, that's bigger than anything else. —*As told to Scott Frampton*

Enjoying the view: Oprah, Luke, and Layla take a break from climbing, Hawaii, July 2007.

"IT MAKES NO DIFFERENCE HOW MANY PEAKS YOU REACH IF THERE WAS NO PLEASURE IN THE CLIMB"

I just came in from a hike up the mountain in back of my house in Hawaii. Funny thing about a mountain: It always looks easier to climb when you're at the foot of it. My goal was to reach the top of the tree line—about 3,000 feet up from my house—in less than an hour. I started out strong, with good intentions, two bottles of water, sunscreen, my hat, and my golden retrievers, Luke and Layla.

A mountain, I realized more than ever today, is one of the great metaphors for life, reminding you that:

1. Challenges are often more difficult than they seem at the outset.

2. An ascent that at first looks smooth turns out to have unseen dips and ridges and valleys.

3. The higher you climb, the thicker the weeds.

4. You need a clear vision of where you're going if you want to avoid getting disoriented by the clouds that roll in and block your view.

5. You have to be determined to make it to the top. Otherwise every slip, stumble, and fall (all of which happened to me today, within that first hour) will give you an excuse to turn around and head home.

But I made a decision: I was going to make it to the eucalyptus grove at the top, no matter how long it took me. So I slowed down and stopped trying to meet a self-imposed timeline, forgot about how far the top was, and just focused on one foot in front of the other. Breathe in. Breathe out.

The result was that each step became its own accomplishment, and I took the time to look at the view from every level. *Wow,* I thought, *I need to do this more often in the daily meshugas of my life.*

I've been so focused on getting to the next level, I haven't enjoyed enough of the view from where I am. Years are a blur to me, and that's not just because September 2007 marked my 22nd season of the show and I have talked to thousands of guests along the way.

It's because when you live life in the fast lane, as I have for most of my career, you end up speeding through, just moving to the next thing, doing more and more and filling your schedule until there's no time even to *think* about what you're doing. And as busy as I am, I often look in wonder at those of you who do all that you do *and* raise children and prepare meals every day and run a household.

I bow to your endurance.

As we're all blessed to witness another season here on planet Earth, I hope you're reading these words and thinking about your own life on adrenaline. And about how you, too, can manage with more attention to things that matter. Because with all that I know for sure, today I added this: It makes no difference how many peaks you reach if there was no pleasure in the climb.

I'm going to spend more time enjoying the view from here.

Oprah

THE POWER OF AUTHENTICITY

THE AUTHENTICS

We know it when we see it, and we love the people who live it—the ones we can count on, always, to be brazenly, exhilaratingly themselves. In the age of spin and truthiness, authenticity is the real deal: speaking up for what you believe in, refusing to be ruled by the desire for acceptance, listening for the difference between the impulses that move you and the fear that holds you back. Authenticity is funny, it's provocative, it slices through the bull. In its company, you're inspired to be truer to yourself. We start by talking to the great authentics, from Chris Rock to Molly Ivins, Grace Paley to Spike Lee...

CHRIS ROCK

There's an adage among stand-ups that says it takes ten years to come up with a good ten-minute set. Every three or four years, Chris Rock delivers an excellent hour of fresh material—what he calls his state of the union address.

Like all great comedians, Rock is an acute observer of the human condition and a serious man. His stand-up confronts uncomfortable issues, among them race ("Every town has the same two malls: the one white people go to and the one white people used to go to") and class ("There are people who would like to get rid of minimum wage. But we have to have it, because if we didn't some people would not get paid money. They would work all week for two loaves of bread and some Spam"). He's funny, but he doesn't hesitate to serve up the provocation straight: "The government doesn't give a fuck about your safety. They sell guns at Wal-Mart; they don't give a fuck about you!" His voracious performances do triple duty, enlisting, dissecting, and amusing his targets—us—all at once.

Rock grapples with what strikes him: A hunch turns into a premise, a stranger's gesture suggests a character, the two—over months—become a bit. ("I need to get it out, and it takes me a long time to get the material to the level I feel.") Right now he's mulling over America's devaluation of intelligence. "We have no idea who's smart; we only know who's rich," he says. He's worried about the chilling effect of the "gotcha!" culture of cell phone films. He's disturbed by how our national obsession with celebrity distracts us from the war. His bits may start off quietly, but by the time they reach an audience, they're fierce.

When he writes, he cranks up Prince for inspiration. "He reinvented himself," says Rock. "Different albums, different sounds." Rock's own versatility cuts across genres, including successful scripts for TV and film. His goals are as expansive: "I am into showing black people in any way that we're not being seen." But while he gleefully eviscerates the media—the culprit behind stereotypical portrayals of black people—no one is spared his scrutiny. ("Get real! When I'm looking over my shoulder at an ATM machine, I'm not scared of the media!")

Rock feels an artist's obligation is to express, unhindered, his God-given gift. Fame is incidental. The common man's church is the comedy club. Words are powerful, and Rock labors hard to get the most from them. "You spend your whole life biting your tongue," he says. "You're married, you're biting your tongue. You go to work, you're biting your tongue. So it's nice to go someplace to see some guys and women exercise free speech. And if it's funny, even better."

—Adrian Nicole LeBlanc

Chris Rock in Hollywood's Kodak Theater.

MOLLY IVINS

Of the millions of words written by and about the last American political columnist with balls, the seven most famous are the title of her first book: *Molly Ivins Can't Say That, Can She?* In fact, during a career that's spanned nearly 40 years, the 62-year-old has said pretty much what she wants on whatever subject she wants, niceties be damned, and woe to the poor schmuck who's tried to muzzle her.

No one can stop her—not the powers that be at *The New York Times* when, as their Rocky Mountain bureau chief in the early eighties, she described a chicken-killing festival as a "gang pluck"; not the pickup-driving Texans who claim her as one of their own, even when she says of George W. Bush, "He's a terrible president, and I knew he would be"; not the freshly minted media moguls who carry her syndicated gems in nearly 400 of their once-great properties ("It just infuriates me to see newspapers' response to their own death, which of course is being decided by some 24-year-old genius on Wall Street who's never even worked at a newspaper in his life"). Ivins has never suffered fools—not gladly, not at all—but unlike the rest of us, who candy-coat our scorn, she is who she is, as comfortable in her own skin as anyone alive, so there's no point in wondering whether she'll hold back. It's just not in her nature.

Being funny, fortunately, is, and it's one of the keys to her staying power. Like another liberal Op-Ed icon, Maureen Dowd, she wins over her enemies with a wit so sharp that even the man she

Molly Ivins in Austin.

routinely derides as Governor Goodhair—Bush's successor in Texas, Rick Perry—must have a hard time suppressing a laugh.

And she takes it as well as she dishes it out. At a roast of Ivins to benefit her beloved *Texas Observer,* the muckraking biweekly she once upon a time edited, speaker after speaker mocked her clothes, her shoes, even her hair—a touchy subject, since an ongoing third bout with breast cancer has left her bald. "She is the first woman in history whose hairdo was actually improved by chemotherapy," cracked pundit Jim Hightower. The guest of honor beamed, and the audience did, too, in appreciation of the bravery and spunk with which she's battled the disease. Ivins refuses to wear a wig, true to form and, as ever, to herself.   **—Evan Smith**
Molly Ivins passed away on January 31, 2007.

HARVEY FIERSTEIN

If there's any greater example of fearlessness than Harvey Fierstein in a dress on a stage, it's Harvey Fierstein in a rage on a soapbox. His résumé includes Broadway star turns (*Hairspray, Fiddler on the Roof*), playwriting (*Torch Song Trilogy,* the musical *La Cage Aux Folles*), and impromptu political jeremiads.

"I've yelled at Al Gore, lectured poor Ned Lamont—at an antiques show—about gays in the military, and taken Joe Lieberman to task when he was running for vice president," Fierstein recalls. "Lieberman said, 'Now, don't you worry, we're going to get you civil unions,' and I said, 'Civil unions? Fuck you; you've been married twice. Am I any less a citizen than you?'"

One of the reasons politicians can seem so out of touch is that no one dares to touch them. As an actor, Fierstein knows all about taking risks to make contact. The biggest risk isn't the size of the gesture; it's the authenticity. His performances, even in outrageous drag, are meticulously genuine. Partly that's because of his sexuality: There was never a closet big enough to contain him. And partly that's because of his burning commitment to the "sacred bond" of drama, largely or narrowly defined. "When people come into the theater, it's an act of faith no different from a sacrament in a church," he says in that famous fey-grit rumble of a voice. "They are willing to go where you take them, and you have the duty to take them where it will do the absolute best."

Lots of celebrities speak up about causes, but often they're looking nervously at the effect it might have on their careers. Not Fierstein, even though he's probably lost work because of his widespread advocacy for gay rights. He doesn't care: "It's not worth it, otherwise." In an age of calibrated political positioning and small theatrical personalities, Fierstein crashes every fourth wall he can find. "When they were planning a Broadway salute to Cardinal O'Connor, I had a hand in getting the whole cast of celebrities to

cancel until they were left with Lee Meriwether. I said to O'Connor: 'You condemn homosexuality because the Bible says it's a sin for two men to lie together. Well, turn back one page, where it says it's the exact same sin to eat pork.'" And then he made a rude and rather startling link between the two "sins." Well, did you expect Fierstein to be cowed by a man in a red muumuu? "I was brought up to be a proud American," he says defiantly, "which means opening your friggin' mouth."   **—Jesse Green**

Harvey Fierstein on the stage set of *Hairspray*.

Spike Lee in New Orleans's Lower Ninth Ward.

SPIKE LEE

For 20 years now, filmmaker Spike Lee has been treading the racial and social fault lines that divide and consume us. He has not stepped lightly. The name of his production company—40 Acres and a Mule, a nod to the reparations assigned freed slaves and then revoked—threw down the gauntlet early on. And when *Do the Right Thing* dared us (to a hip-hop beat) to fight the power, "a Spike Lee Joint" came to be known as an explosive cultural artifact. Often using sly humor and relying on his sharp eye for the ridiculous, the prolific auteur looks beyond black and white to a prism of taboo issues, from black-on-black discrimination to the motivation behind interracial dating to "minstreling" in the entertainment industry. Even when his movies shift to less dangerous ground—as with his recent heist flick, *Inside Man*—they're subversive in their resolute portrayal of African-Americans as they truly are.

The nickname his mother gave Shelton Jackson Lee has by now, at 50, become destiny. Whatever the prickly filmmaker has to say, he says it loud (it's fitting that one of his next projects will be the James Brown biopic)—and the confrontational style in which he purveys his truth (calling Mississippi senator Trent Lott a "card-carrying member" of the Ku Klux Klan; calling out 50 Cent for glorifying the pimp and gangsta ethos) has inspired extreme reactions. But his indignation is necessary. *When the Levees Broke: A*

Requiem in Four Acts, Lee's definitive documentary account of Hurricane Katrina, chronicles the government apathy and incompetence that amplified the tragedy, and the dignity and grace of those who survived it. For Lee the personal is inexorably political, and this masterwork is as much an epic act of filmmaking as a public service for posterity.

Lee has always spoken his mind, and recently, on the phone, in lieu of answering questions about his career, he stuck to his own, more pressing script—his words as emphatic, their intent as clear, as the jazz notes that so often score his films. "Right now I am in Atlanta, Georgia, making burial arrangements for Zimmie Shelton, my grandmother," he said. This was the woman who used her saved Social Security checks to put him through college and film school and finance his breakout debut, *She's Gotta Have It.* ("It was too racy for her," he said, laughing as he recalled his grandmother's reaction to his comedic take on female sexual freedom. "But she believed in me and what I wanted to do, absolutely.") And as he eulogized her, channeling feeling through the facts of a life well lived—"She was born August 2, 1906.... She was a graduate of Spelman College.... She taught art for 50 years.... She worked hard"—it was clear that doing the right thing comes from a place deep in Lee's soul, as does the need for all he has to say to be heard. —Suzanne Boyd

A LIFE THAT'S TRUTHFUL

"You don't want to show off. You want to just be who you are." The inestimable Grace Paley sits down with Genine Lentine.

Open any page of Grace Paley's cherished and acclaimed stories, poems, and essays, and you'll hear people talking, often directly to you; Paley's voice is unmistakable: startling in its diamond compression, its encompassing heart, its honesty and humor. I visited Grace in the Vermont farmhouse where she lives with her husband, Bob Nichols. Even in delicate health, Grace Paley radiates a stainless well-being born of her avid engagement in the flux of living into her ninth decade. Speaking with Grace is like a spell check for the spirit; any burdensome illusion you didn't even know you had hauled up her long driveway suddenly lights up in her presence, giving you the chance to drop it right then and there. At every turn, she speaks out of the deepest kind of knowledge: that which can be found only in plain sight.

GENINE: *So, is it okay if we talk for an hour?*

GRACE: We can talk for two hours. I mean, I'm a talker, you're a talker. We talk. We can talk as long as we feel like talking. We can stop and we can have tea and we can begin to talk again.

GENINE: *Great, so, let's talk about this word authenticity, this idea of leading an authentic life.*

GRACE: But I don't know what that means! I'm not the person to ask about that. I don't know what an authentic life *is*. I guess a life that's truthful, where you don't bullshit. You're alive. You don't do work that you hate. You do things you believe in. That's authentic. I don't know if that's what *authentic* means; I just think it's a new word that's flown into the vocabulary. It's just being yourself, that's all.

GENINE: *Like what Auden said to you when you were 17. Could you tell me about that?*

GRACE: I went to Auden's class—there were 200 people there. I went four times maybe. That was that. No big deal. I made a big deal of it because he said at a certain point, "Would anybody like me to see their work?" and I found my hand going up. I still feel the miracle of it. I was with a friend who was about two years older than me. And she was so amazed because she was terrified to put her hand up. And *I* was! So anyway I put my hand up, and I brought him my work. He looked it over and he said, "You're using words you don't use. You're using British English. Do you use words like *trousers?*" I said, "Yes." And he said, "I don't think you do. And *subaltern*. Do you use the word *subaltern?*" I laughed. I wouldn't say yes. "Why don't you try writing in your own language?" he asked. What he did was, in one short period, he pointed a way for me to be myself.

GENINE: *Did you already have a sense that you wanted to use the language around you?*

GRACE: I did have a sense that I was doing something wrong, as far as that's concerned. I could have found the road myself, but it would have taken me another two years.

GENINE: *The most incisive teaching moments often simply affirm an instinct a student already has.*

GRACE: That's right.

GENINE: *He said, Do what your instinct tells you.*

GRACE: He didn't say that.

GENINE: *I know he didn't say that exactly, but he freed up your incredible capacity for listening. You already had this fine-tuned ear and he said, I'm restoring this gift to you.*

GRACE: Right, that's a good way to put it.

GENINE: *When people allow themselves to be themselves, they're getting back something they already have.*

GRACE: That's good. I like that.

GENINE: *"Using your own language" has such profound implications.*

GRACE: It does relate to your whole life, in which you really learn to be yourself more.

GENINE: *I've noticed that when you enter the room to give a reading, the level of joy palpably rises, before you've even said a word.*

GRACE: Reading to an audience, they're like people I know, friends. You want to be truthful to them. You want to read to them. You don't want to do a lot of bullshitting. You don't want to show off. You want to just be who you are. It seems no matter what the audience, or who the audience is, I really try—I can't say I try to be myself, because I'm now myself. There may have been years when I tried to be myself. But I'm me now. I'm just who I am. There's no other way to be. No way out.

GENINE: *I read about your uncle who was killed in czarist Russia for carrying the red flag of the working class in a demonstration. And your aunt told you, Don't—*

GRACE: She said, "Don't carry the flag. You can be in the parade, but don't carry the flag. You'll be noticed. Don't be noticed."

GENINE: *Not exactly advice you've followed.*

GRACE: No, but it was very touching.

GENINE: *You've gone to prison several times. Could you talk about your willingness to be arrested for standing up for your principles?*

GRACE: Oh, well, in the first place, it's not prison, it's jail. The longest I ever did was only about two weeks. I never was afraid to go. It seemed like the natural thing to do. I was in the United States of America, where they weren't going to beat me up or anything. I was still an American citizen. I was in a women's jail.

Why are women so afraid of getting arrested? It was not a terrible experience by a long shot. I mean, you're in prison with other

Grace Paley near her home in Thetford Hill, Vermont, December, 1997.

people! You were meeting people, mostly not white, mostly black, who lived there, who were in prison a lot, who were there for months and months, and years, so they really—God, I had the most enlightening days of my life. It was very worthwhile meeting them. It was worth every bit of it. Couldn't have been better. I could do it again as easily as pie.

GENINE: *You've forged deep friendships in commitment to social action.*

GRACE: I've never been without friends. Never. I've never not had a best girlfriend. I can go through their names from the time I was 5 years old: Betty, Charlotte, Sylvia. I've always had a best friend, best girlfriend. Later on, boys, but the boy thing was totally different. And as time went on, they really became best political friends. Vera and Eva. They were political friends. I can't understand women living without women friends. I don't know how they do it.

GENINE: *You said that you like going to the hospital for chemo because you've made friends with the people there.*

GRACE: When you go to the infusion room, the people are all talking to each other, so it's nice.

GENINE: *You have a knack for finding opportunity in adversity. It seems like that's one of the main tricks in life.*

GRACE: Yes. Yes. To use what you're handed. I'm not afraid of being sick. I'm really not. I have no fear of it.

GENINE: *Do you have any advice for people living with a serious illness?*

GRACE: They proceed out of their own natures. I think I'd have a lot of nerve to give advice. It depends entirely on their own natures. Either they take things the way they are or they get upset about everything. It's who they are.

GENINE: *What have you found helpful as you've been living with cancer?*

GRACE: I'm still interested in everything. I like to read. I like to talk to Bob. I'm interested in my grandchildren. I'm not so ill that I can't be interested in the whole world. I'm just not that sick, that's all. All I feel is I'm more tired than ever. I complain about having no energy. That's my big complaint.

This small period's very hard for me. It isn't that it's the cancer, it's all kinds of odd things that have stepped in that have nothing to do with my major illness.

GENINE: *I'm thinking about your poem "Walking in the Woods," those last lines,* A terrible stretch to sun / just to stay alive but if you've / liked life you do it. *I see you here right now living those lines.*

GRACE: Yes.

GENINE: *How does that feel?*

GRACE: Well, I don't know exactly what that means because right now I feel really rotten.

GENINE: *"A terrible stretch to sun / just to stay alive."*

GRACE: It is. You do it. You do it. You have to go through illness as well as health. If you like life, you stay with it. That's how people stay alive who are quite quite quite ill.

GENINE: *You radiate a tremendous abiding love for being alive.*

GRACE: Yeah, I like it. It's a nice place to be. ◻

Grace Paley passed away on August 22, 2007.

FINDING YOUR VOICE

If you've ever harbored a secret ambition to sing, listen in as Barbara Cook, one of our greatest cabaret artists, teaches Patricia Volk a lesson in emotional honesty.

Barbara Cook is teaching a Master class. I'm in the first row. We are at the Orange County Performing Arts Center in Costa Mesa, a California town world famous for its mall. Klieg lights focus on where Ms. Cook will stand. The theater is packed with college students. Not one was born when Barbara Cook was Broadway's beloved ingenue Marian the librarian in *The Music Man.*

Ms. Cook will be 79 in a few days. The first 78 were the hardest. Her baby sister died when Barbara was 3. That same week, her mother's brother was murdered. Then her parents divorced. Cook's mother clung to her remaining daughter. They shared the same bed until 1948 when, after a visit to New York, Barbara waved goodbye at the station. Success came quickly. So did marriage, motherhood, divorce, depression, alcoholism, and a weight gain that led to starring offers in *Tugboat Annie.* Two years ago, Wally Harper, Ms. Cook's accompanist of almost 31 years, died.

At 2:05 P.M. a door opens. The auditorium goes silent. Ms. Cook sweeps in. She gets a standing ovation.

"Now, who's going to sing for me?" She takes in the house.

Hands shoot up.

"This is not a performance," Ms. Cook cautions. "This is a class. What this is about, what I respond to most, is someone being their authentic self."

Authentic self? I thought her publicist told me she loves imitations. I'm having a private class with her tomorrow. Will she like my imitations?

A tall cherub starts to sing "Smile": *Smile though your heart is aching / Smile even though it's breaking / When there are clouds in the sky, you'll get by / If you smile....*

He sings as if he's already absorbed the advice in that last stanza. Ms. Cook interrupts. "You're showing us the result, not the process. Put yourself back to when the loss occurred."

He begins again. Ms. Cook interrupts again: "If you try to move me, you won't."

On the third try: "I hear no difference. Would you just bloody sing it more, get into the song more?"

Demonstrating, she sings "Smile." It could break your heart. "Do you see what I'm saying?"

He tries for the fourth time. She holds up her hand. "We put on a fake cloak because we think that's what's needed. What we really want is you. Take off your emotional clothes and be naked. It's scary. But this is where safety lies. The core place. If we can sing, dance, paint from that place, we cannot be wrong. Got that?"

The cherub takes "Smile" from the top. I hear no difference. Ms. Cook stares at him. After the final note, she puts her hands on his shoulders. "That was sweet." She turns to the audience. "Wasn't that sweet?"

Clarissa Lecce, a pretty girl in a flippy polka-dot dress, sings a song from *Ragtime.* Oh my God. Her voice is perfection. What could Barbara Cook possibly say?

"You're very talented. You sang that beautifully. Now sing it and let us come to you. Simple, simple, simple."

Miss Lecce gets it. The song is even better.

Dressed head to toe in black, Barbara Cook moves like a cat. As a student sings "Someone to Watch over Me," she paces, tilts her head, stops, walks, stops again, turns, tilts. She shifts her weight, holds her chin, cocks her head, gets closer, moves back. Listening, for Barbara Cook, is physical.

"Play 'em like a fish," she tells one girl. "Keep 'em on the line. 'I want you in bed with me.' C'mon. We're all adults. That's what this song is about."

Ms. Cook invites a boy in the audience to stand in front of the girl so she can look in his eyes while she sings. "Hold hands," Ms. Cook says. The song takes off. When it's over, the boy continues to hold the singer's hands. His cheeks are flushed. His chinos bulge with what the writer Gerard Shyne used to call a 10 to 6.

I'm learning so much! Everyone improves! Even students who start in the stratosphere! I can't wait for my private lesson. I'm a singing fool. My mother perched me on the piano when I was 3. I'd sing "Bewitched, Bothered and Bewildered" for company, waving a chiffon scarf. In camp I was Dorothy in *The Wizard of Oz.* Wait till Ms. Cook hears my voice. I can hold my breath for two laps in an Olympic-size pool.

I make a list of favorite songs; the ones I sing straight are on

Sweet music: The singer prepares for her new students.

the left, my impersonations on the right. We meet at noon in a hotel banquet room, the rehearsal pianist, Barbara Cook, her assistant, me.

She studies my list. "I don't like imitations." She points to a song on the left. "How about 'The Nearness of You'?"

We get right into it. I'm doing my fabulous breath-control thing, singing the first eight bars without coming up for air.

Ms. Cook's eyes bug.

"Uh, why don't you try it a bit lower?" she says. "And don't hold your breath so much."

This time I channel Billie Holiday with a little Chet Baker. Ms. Cook stops me.

"You let these phrases run together in a way you wouldn't do at all in conversation," she says.

"Oh." I decide not to tell her that's my specialty, my jazz heritage, my *technique*. So I say: "I grew up on jazz. It was almost as if the voice were an instrument and not about the meaning of the words. Do you ever scat?"

"No. It's not what I do. My God, Ella, that's in her bones. It's not in my bones. I sing soulful ballads as well as anybody's ever done them, you know? That's what's really the meat of my talent, I think."

She thinks? Barbara Cook has won every award available to a lyric soprano who sings the American songbook. She triumphed as Cunegonde in Leonard Bernstein's *Candide*. She owns "I've Got the World on a String." She is widely considered the grande dame of cabaret. Her evening of song, *Mostly Sondheim,* played to packed houses internationally. Barbara Cook was the first woman invited to sing pop tunes in concert at the Metropolitan Opera. She's recorded 19 solo albums and sung for four presidents. *The New York Times* calls her voice transcendent.

"That song," she says. "How does it begin, sweetie?"

She sings "The Nearness of You" looking me in the eye. I am speechless. I almost blurt "Wow!" What to say? Who knew that song could touch so deep?

"Now, that doesn't come out of anything other than memory," Ms. Cook breaks the silence.

"You're saying that amount of feeling is accessible to everyone?"

"I've been in love a lot of times," Ms. Cook says. "Yeah. So that's what you use."

I've been in love a lot of times, too. I'm rarely not in love. Does that show in my voice? Does Ms. Cook love more profoundly than I do? My first husband used to turn on the radio when I sang.

"Are you sure you wouldn't like to hear my Jimmy Durante?"

"I don't want to hear you do impersonations. I want the authentic you. Durante doesn't have a wonderful voice. But when he sings, you're moved. He sings in tune, and he has a great sense of rhythm. *You must remember this,"* Ms. Cook does Durante singing "As Time Goes By." She doesn't do his gruffness, just his timing and sincerity.

"And he doesn't hold the note, and it doesn't matter." She demonstrates: *A kiss is just a kiss....*

"It's about the ability to be true to yourself and communicate that truth. As an audience, you know immediately whether you believe somebody or not. Don't you?"

"Um-hmm," I say. It's clear I'm not going to get to do Durante's "You Gotta Start Off Each Day with a Song" or my much-in-demand "Can't Help Lovin' Dat Man" à la Helen Morgan.

Have I come here to find out what Barbara Cook thinks of my voice? Did I come to see if I could entertain a great entertainer? Nope. I'm here because I love to sing. Singing makes me happy.

Or, when I'm happy, I sing. And if I can learn to sing better from Barbara Cook, I'd be nuts not to try.

I launch into "The Nearness of You" again. This time I interrupt me.

"I feel as if I can't keep up with the piano. Like I'm not matching the notes."

"You are missing a few," Ms. Cook says in a kind way. If King Kong tried to sing, she would critique him with respect.

"Could I try it without the piano? If I can sing at my own pace, I know I'll sing it with more feeling."

"Tell you what," Ms. Cook says. "Speak the lines. Speak the words."

It's not the pale moon that excites me, I say, as if Barbara Cook and I were having coffee.

"Slowly."

It's...not...the...pale...moon...that...excites...me,...that...thrills...and... delights...me....

She interrupts. "It has to be backed up emotionally. You talk about somebody having sweet conversation: 'Oh my God! Your conversation knocks me out!' Okay? You use those words, those feelings."

"I'm worried I'll get hammy," I say.

"The only way it could get hammy is if you're on the outside doing it. But if it's really coming from a real place in you, there's no way it can be hammy. We all have these feelings. You're saying, I'm human, too. I'm like you. We're not alone. Hmm? And it heals. It's important. It's not a little thing."

I ask Barbara Cook if she'll sing my father's favorite song: "Younger Than Springtime." I want to know why it made him cry.

She sings: *And when your youth / And joy invade my arms / And fill my heart as now they do / Then younger than springtime, am I....*

My eyes well up. The song is a short story. A story about the power of love to triumph over time. I've sung this song all my life. I'm hearing the words for the first time. I'm seeing the words in the context of my father's bountiful love. I'm learning something that will make my life smarter. All that, from one song, sung directly to me, by Barbara Cook. Is this what authenticity can do?

"Did you ever feel in your life you were inauthentic?" I ask.

"You bet. I still do sometimes. And I say, 'Barbara, what the hell are you doing?' Because I get awed like everybody else, particularly around people who are famous. And I catch myself doing something ridiculous and I—'Jesus! Calm down, you know, come on.'"

We spend two hours singing together. I don't want this lesson to end. Ms. Cook tries on my shoes. I promise to send her a pair in orange to match the faux Bottega Veneta bag she got online from Korea. My plane is leaving in 45 minutes, but I'm only 15 minutes from the airport. There's a song from *Carousel* that I love. I saw the revival at Lincoln Center a few years ago. What can someone intimate with disillusion do with a song about innocence?

"Would you consider singing a little something from *Carousel* before I go? Would you sing 'When I Marry Mr. Snow?'" Barbara Cook says yes. The years fall away. She is a bride-to-be, pert, full of hope, ready for love. Barbara Cook is almost 80. It's baffling how she does this. It's magic.

A month later, at an informal gathering at a friend's house, the tenor Robert White is singing by the piano. Robert White has sung for five presidents and is taking requests. I ask for "Younger Than Springtime." Midway through, he extends his palm toward me and curls his fingers. I look into his eyes. I sing from a place I've never sung. We finish our duet. Everyone applauds. Robert White blows me a kiss. O

Master class: Cook (*above*) coaches Carina Morales (*below, left*) and Caitlin Macy-Beckwith (*below, right*).

QUEEN LATIFAH'S AHA! MOMENT

Growing up, the singer-actress formerly known as Dana Owens didn't look like anyone else. Then one night, she found a perfect role model: herself.

I'm a statuesque woman and have been for most of my life. I developed early, and I was always one of the tallest girls in my class. By the time I was 13, I had a *body*. I was one of those girls whose daddy wanted to keep a shotgun by the door, because it was *all* there.

When I was younger, my size didn't bother me. My mom had to make me wear a bra, because I wasn't even paying attention. I just thought, *There are these things coming up on me; I know what they are, but who cares? I'm going out to play.* But then when I hit my teens, it became a big deal. Boys started zoning in on certain parts of me—which made me feel cool and totally embarrassed at the same time.

Like any girl whose body is changing, I felt unsure of who I was becoming. I was having mature emotions for the first time, I had a crush on a classmate, and all of these things made me suddenly conscious of my body. Plus, the images I saw in magazines and movies weren't women who looked like me; they were thin white girls, for the most part. There were some people I admired—the Patti LaBelles of the world, Diana Ross—but most weren't thick and big-boned like I was.

Then my eighth-grade class put on the musical *The Wiz*. I went to a small Catholic school in Newark, New Jersey, and in order to be fair the teachers cast three students as Dorothy. There was one girl who resembled Dorothy—she was petite and spry and looked the part. The second Dorothy was a really good actor. And then there was me. I was a big, tall Dorothy, but I guess the teachers thought I had a good voice, because I got to sing the finale, "Home."

I performed the song in front of all the students, as well as parents, teachers, and guests. It was a large audience, but I latched on to my mother's smiling face in the crowd. I sang, *When I think of home, I think of a place where there's love overflowing....* I was totally in the moment, and, suddenly, I became Dorothy, not Dana. When I finished, I got a standing ovation. It was the first time in my life I'd gotten that kind of mass encouragement. For the audience to receive me like that, to enjoy the song so much that they were moved to stand up and clap, I knew they saw me as more than just the "big Dorothy."

I realized in that moment that I didn't need to change. I felt comfortable—strong, beautiful, talented—in my own skin. I had the same feeling years later when I was onstage at Madison Square Garden and 20,000 people were singing along with me to my song "Ladies First," and again when I was nominated for an Academy Award for my performance in *Chicago*. I've never molded myself to fit other people's ideals. Who I am works for me, and it's working for my career.

I'm a realistic person. If there's something I can't do, I know that. But if there's something I love, something I'm willing to put 150 percent into, then nothing—especially not my body—can limit me. —*As told to Rachel Bertsche*

Drama Queen: Latifah learned an important lesson in a school play.

WE VS. ME

Not knowing where one of you leaves off and the other begins sounds romantic, but, Valerie Monroe asks, how do you stay true to you when you're also half a couple?

Have you ever found it difficult to be authentic in a relationship? Have you ever wondered why?

"Well," says Laura Kipnis, author of *The Female Thing,* an account of the conflicted state of the female psyche at the 21st-century point, "we *are* the sex that wears concealer...." And the one that has been encouraged (historically, at least) to act weak when we feel strong, strong when we feel needy, guarding our real feelings against scrutiny in case they make us look like a harridan or a baby or a bitch. Actually, femininity and authenticity are often at cross-purposes, says Kipnis. Women have relied on artifice for centuries (and more), and it's only a fairly recent development—which Kipnis attributes to the culture of psychotherapy—that authenticity has taken on value. (*The Importance of Being Earnest,* a celebration of artifice if ever there was one, was written only a little over a hundred years ago.) I happen to be (for better or worse) the kind of person who prides herself on straightforwardness, which is why I felt a little troubled one evening when I asked a new friend if he'd like to read a book I'd written. "I only read historical nonfiction," he replied, at which point, with the sociable timidity of an Edith Wharton character, I demurely murmured, "Oh, I see," rather than say what I was thinking: that he was being radically, maybe terminally rude. Why didn't I say, "My book is a kind of historical nonfiction; give it a try?" Or "Wouldn't you like to broaden your horizons, literature-wise?" Or even "It's the story of my life, pal, so if you ever hope to get into my pants, you'll buy the book on your way home and read it before you hit the sheets." But all I could manage was "Oh, I see." And I felt as if I'd betrayed myself.

That feeling of self-betrayal isn't uncommon among women, says Esther Perel, family therapist and author of *Mating in Captivity.* "Girls in our culture are socialized with a strong emphasis on connectivity—establishing and maintaining relationships—so that as women, we may find it difficult to hold on to a sense of self in the context of a relationship," she says. A woman's feelings of responsibility about keeping a connection going smoothly can lead her to ensure everyone else's needs are being met, which often means that she falls short of taking care of her own. She's the one who darns the holes and knits up the loose ends of the relationship and is most likely to feel that she's subverted her authentic self in the service of coupledom, says Perel. Sometimes the partners polarize, each becoming frozen in their behavior, which makes it harder and harder to find a balance of responsibility.

So what's the key to maintaining your sense of self and not getting lost? Space, says Perel. The more you can leave the relationship to explore your own interests, the more likely you'll be to bring your authentic self back to it. She compares this exploration to the process a mother and young child go through when the child is learning how to feel safe away from her anchoring parent. "You see the child jump off her mother's lap and run away, checking back every once in a while to be sure that her mother is still there," says Perel. "Eventually, the child feels comfortable enough to explore for longer and longer periods because she trusts that her mother will be available to her when she returns."

It's not so different with couples. Each "trip" away—whether it's a hiking excursion to Hawaii or a pottery class—has the potential to strengthen the individual partner, so that he or she returns to the relationship with a greater sense of self to share. This may seem like a no-brainer, but the urge to merge can be very powerful, blurring a couple's boundaries. The deeper the trust when partners are allowed to roam freely, says Perel, the more secure they feel to go out and explore. If partners can temporarily leave without either one feeling anxious, then they can be independent without fear. And they're less likely to betray their partner's trust if they don't feel controlled, Perel says (typically, control doesn't restrain people—it fuels their rebellion). Perel talks about a woman she met recently who had conflated her whole sense of self with her marriage; she did nothing separate from her husband. Never having given herself permission to go out on her own once in a while—even though her husband traveled extensively for business—she had begun (unsurprisingly) to feel lost and trapped by the "we-ness" she'd created. Finding a solution wasn't complicated, says Perel; once the woman gave herself permission to basically have a life of her own, she became not only increasingly interested in the world but also increasingly interesting to herself and to her husband. For her, and for anyone—you, maybe?—looking to be happy and comfortable and fulfilled in a relationship, it's an excellent idea to try to maintain separateness and togetherness in a way that feels flexible and balanced. Easier said than done, of course.

I GAVE THAT GUY A COPY OF MY BOOK. I didn't tell him that I thought his initial response was rude. But I did suggest that he might know me a little better if he read it. I'm not sure he got the double entendre, but I felt more like myself in our exchange. O

WE LOVE TO READ

THE STORY OF MY LIFE

For Peggy Orenstein, it was one of those books—the kind you keep forever and read again and again. It taught her about dreams, about love, and—in a remarkable plot twist—about the courage it takes to really live.

I happened across *Mrs. Mike* when I was in sixth grade; it was buried under a stack of tattered comic books in my older brother's room. I'd snuck in there to snoop for contraband issues of *National Lampoon*, which my mother insisted he hide from me (already possessed of a journalist's curiosity, I took that as a challenge). But *Mrs. Mike*, with its cover illustration of a parka-clad girl on a dogsled, stopped me. The manila library pocket, its checkout card intact, was stamped SUSAN B. ANTHONY, the Minneapolis junior high my brother had attended. I didn't stop to wonder why he would have boosted a love story, first published in 1947, about a plucky 16-year-old girl who married a Mountie. Figuring that if he'd swiped it, it must be juicy, I hightailed it to my room, slid under the covers of my canopy bed, and dug in.

That was 35 years ago. *Mrs. Mike* has sat at my bedside ever since—traveling with me from Minnesota to Ohio to New York and, finally, to California. After all this time, it's held together with rubber bands and Scotch tape, the pages weathered and dogeared. I pick it up about once a year, intending merely to leaf through, and end up as engrossed as the first time I read it; the themes of resilience, a woman's indomitable spirit, of living a life of purpose, and doing so with gusto and courage, still hook me.

A classic girl's adventure yarn, *Mrs. Mike* is the real-life tale of Katherine Mary O'Fallon, a turn-of-the-last-century Boston lass who, stricken with pleurisy, (one of those literary wasting diseases about which one no longer hears) is sent to Canada to take in the bracing fresh air at her uncle's cattle ranch. She weds Mountie Mike Flannigan after seeing him a mere handful of times and joins him in the wilds of British Columbia. Yet this is no happily-ever-after trifle: Every tender moment is offset by tragedy, every triumph booby-trapped with loss. Kathy announces she's pregnant, and shortly afterward a fire levels her town, destroying her home, incinerating her neighbor's son. In the absence of doctors, Mike must assist in amputating a man's leg (without anesthesia). Tension simmers among whites, "'breeds," and Indians. Mosquitoes drive men mad.

When the couple's own two children perish from diphtheria—a disease that would have been treatable had they lived closer to civilization—Kathy breaks. She leaves Mike to return to Boston. But the harsh country, as much as her husband's love, has changed her, and eventually she goes back. They adopt the children of friends (who also died in the epidemic) and begin again, knowing they may well lose this family, too. By the book's final page, Kathy is barely 19 years old.

As a girl, I was inspired by Kathy's determination. It was the early 1970s, and the feminist movement was crashing headlong into the traditional expectations I'd been raised with. I knew I wanted something different for myself, and even if I wasn't sure what that might be, I suspected that it would involve breaking free of my family and community as Kathy had. She had defied convention and her mother, leaving behind everything she knew, perhaps forever, for a questionable future. True, she was simply following her man (the book isn't called *Ms. Kathy,* after all). But given the parameters and proprieties of the time—before meeting Mike, she'd never even worn pants—hers was a radical act. I wanted to be that fearless, that confident of my convictions, that willing to create a life on my own terms. It was Kathy I thought of at 21, when my father warned me that I'd never make it as a writer. It was Kathy I thought of when I quit my day job with no money in the bank. It was Kathy I thought of when I moved to San Francisco, where I didn't know a soul.

In my late 20s, with my career blossoming, the appeal the book

Left: Benedict and Nancy Freedman in 1943, and, *right,* in 2007, after 66 years of marriage.

held for me shifted: Now I was more taken with the passionate, collaborative partnership Kathy and Mike had formed. I was hoping to find my own soul mate, someone who would engage me, heart and mind. When I found that man, just to be sure, I read him *Mrs. Mike* during late, lazy nights in bed. I noticed that the story was a tad schmaltzy, its portrayal of native people often problematic. But luckily—for him as well as me—he saw past that. He compared the book to his own all-time favorite, *Jude the Obscure,* another tale of near-inexplicable perseverance.

I'm not saying I wouldn't have married him if he didn't love my favorite book, but that certainly clinched the deal.

Mrs. Mike caused a sensation when it was published 60 years ago, selling more than a million copies in the first year. Since then, it's been continuously in print, though often just barely. I'd assumed its authors, husband-and-wife team Nancy and Benedict Freedman, were long dead. Even if they'd been as young as 30 in 1947...well, you do the math. Still, they'd had such a profound effect on my life, I wondered what theirs had been like. So one afternoon in the fall of 2002, I did the contemporary version of sneaking into someone's bedroom: I Googled them. Immediately, I found a newspaper article about the way that much-loved but obscure books had been given new life via amazon.com. *Mrs. Mike* was example A. The dozens of reader reviews—mostly from women like me who'd treasured the story in their teens—had prompted a major reissue. Interesting. But there was more: The Freedmans had been interviewed for the story. Interviewed! That meant they were alive. And not only were they alive, but in a miraculous coincidence, their home was just a short drive from mine. It felt like fate. I quickly banged out a fan letter explaining what their book had meant to me—the chance to have a similar impact on even a single reader is, as much as anything, why I became a writer—and asking if I could

meet them. Within days I received an invitation to tea.

By then, my husband and I had been married for ten years, the last five of which had been spent—more and more miserably—trying to have a child. We'd been through three miscarriages, months of soulless sex, invasive tests, pills and shots, two cycles of in vitro fertilization using my eggs and a third using a friend's. Nothing had worked. Along the way, I seemed to have lost the ability to feel joy; my husband was angry that his tenderness couldn't restore it. Now, when I reread *Mrs. Mike* before visiting its authors, it was the tragedies that stood out, the cost of Kathy's willfulness. I recognized myself in the flat grief of her losses, the way pain eroded her capacity for love. I, too, dreamed of starting over somewhere else, making different, perhaps safer, choices. Even my usual refuge—my work—was suffering. How could I trust my instincts as a writer, as an observer of human nature, when I'd so screwed up my own life?

I don't know what I wanted from the Freedmans. A little distraction, perhaps, a reminder of a better time. I was eager to quiz them about what had happened to Kathy and Mike after the book's final page. Had things gone well? Were they happy? After so much sadness, had they found peace? I felt personally invested—maybe too invested—in the answers.

Nancy Freedman, then 82, met me at her apartment door. A tall, slender woman, she carried herself like the actress she'd trained to be. Her hair was a dramatic white, her eyebrows dark above pale blue eyes, her features wide and vibrant. The beauty in the lines of her face was the best argument I'd seen yet against Botox. She greeted me as if we were old friends. Later I'd realize that full-throttle was the Freedmans' approach to everything—during their courtship, which took place almost entirely by mail, Benedict wrote "page 40" at the top of his first letter, as if they were already mid-conversation. "You gotta love a guy like that," Nancy would tell me. At that point they'd been married 61 years.

Benedict was on the couch in the living room, facing a window that overlooked a canal dotted with rowboats and waterfowl. At 83, he had difficulty walking, though you'd never have known it; he made his way across the room by leaning casually on the backs of strategically placed chairs. His mind, however, was still nimble: He had just finished his day's work on a nonfiction book titled *Rescuing the Future,* which he described as a plea, for the good of humanity, to focus on looking forward rather than bickering over past wrongs.

"What appealed to us about Katherine Flannigan's story," Benedict told me right off, "was how it paralleled our own." He and Nancy had met briefly in Los Angeles in 1939. He was a junior writer on Al Jolson's radio show; she was a 19-year-old ingenue about to move to New York. But after a few months of hoofing around Broadway, she was diagnosed with a lethal heart infection (now treatable with antibiotics) that forced a retreat to her native Chicago, where she was confined to bed. Benedict followed her there and, though he'd seen her a mere five times, proposed marriage. Nancy burst into tears; her father, who was a doctor, explained that she probably wouldn't survive three months. Benedict didn't care. "I just didn't believe she was going to die," he said. "Also, I felt even if it's only three months, we've got three months. Better than lying in bed staring at the ceiling."

Like Mike, who fashioned a bed on a dogsled for Kathy out of boxes and fur blankets, Benedict folded back the seat of his jalopy—a convertible with a beach umbrella for a roof—to make a chaise for his bride before they headed West for their honeymoon. For years, first in Chicago and later in Los Angeles, he would carry Nancy up every flight of stairs. "She couldn't walk," he said. "On the other hand, she was always full of life."

And like Kathy, Nancy never saw another doctor. Benedict took care of her himself. Three months turned to six, turned to a year, turned to eight. Slowly, she improved. The woman who should never have seen 1942 now has four great-grandchildren. She credits her recovery to Benedict's love—"He hauled me back to life," she said, "he really did"—and to *Mrs. Mike,* which they wrote together from her sickbed. I could have swooned from the romance of it all.

After Mike Flannigan died, in his 40s, from a ruptured appendix (another preventable loss, I thought grimly), Kathy went to L.A. and tried to peddle her story to the movies. No one bit. But an agent introduced her to the Freedmans, who thought her life might be the stuff of literature (*Mrs. Mike* was eventually adapted for the screen; the film is truly ghastly). They invited her to their tiny apartment, a converted garage on what had once been the actress Mary Pickford's estate, and spent two days listening to her talk. "We were enchanted by her story," Benedict recalled. "Here was this girl, very young, incapacitated—but willing to fall in love, *really* fall in love, passionately, without any care for anything else. That reinforced our own determination to live the life we wanted to live regardless of the clouds on the horizon."

I knew the feeling. "Did any of their children survive?"

Nancy shook her head. "No. They had adopted an Indian girl. But not the ones that are in the book. I dreamed those."

I must have looked confused. "*Mrs. Mike* is a novel," Benedict explained.

"A *novel*?" My stomach clenched. I felt an abrupt, almost physical sense of displacement, the way you would if, say, you found out at age 45 that your mother was actually your aunt. I'd based my life on this book. It was a core part of my identity. As an 11-year-old I'd accepted each word as gospel; it had never occurred to me to question that assumption. Now I looked at my ancient library copy, which I'd brought with me: Sure enough, a red *F* was taped to the side, indicating it should be shelved in the fiction section.

"But did she really live in that town that burned down?" I asked, my voice rising.

"Yes," said Nancy.

"No," said Benedict.

Yes? No? Which was it? I'm sure I looked as stunned as I felt. "What's true is her spirit," Benedict added, firmly. "She was a person afraid of nothing, willing to take on anything. And the most important scenes—for example, when she leaves Mike and goes back to Boston—we didn't invent that. But we also didn't check her account of things."

Part of me wanted to rush home right then and try to retrace the story, to follow the Flannigans' trail north. I could Google the town of Grouard. Or look up Mike's name in the records of the Royal Canadian Mounted Police. But even as I plotted my search, I realized its results would be irrelevant. *Mrs. Mike* might have played a lesser role in my life had I known it was, at least in part, fabrication. But Kathy—the reality, the invention, the symbol—had been there when I needed her most. And if I still needed proof that real, ordinary people could choose bold, unconventional lives, all I had to do was look at the Freedmans, whose story was as enthralling as Kathy's—maybe more so. They had lived so fully, experienced so much, crossed paths with so many great names of their day. Nancy had played Juliet in a production of Shakespeare's play staged by Fanchon and Marco, the brother-sister dance team who'd launched the careers of Cyd Charisse, Judy Garland, Doris Day, and Bing Crosby. Igor Stravinsky himself had chosen her to dance in *Petrushka.* She had studied under the director Max Reinhardt.

Meanwhile, Benedict's father, David, had created the character of Baby Snooks for Fanny Brice, written a Broadway hit, and was head writer of Eddie Cantor's radio show. When, at age 13, Benedict needed a date for a school dance, his father tried to fix him up with the burlesque queen Gypsy Rose Lee (who, informed of the boy's predicament, responded, "Well, for Dave's son…" and flipped a breast out of her bra; Benedict did not pursue the opportunity).

David died when Benedict was 16, leaving gambling debts that bankrupted the family. They left their tower apartment in Manhattan's swank Beresford building (the unit is now owned by tennis star John McEnroe), and Benedict, the eldest of three, dropped out of school to help support the family. He worked for an actuary by day, and wrote scripts at night and on weekends. Eventually, he snagged a job as a junior writer on the Marx Brothers' film *At the Circus* and headed off to Los Angeles. He wrote gags for Mickey Rooney, Bob Hope, Jimmy Durante. He spent 12 years with *The Red Skelton Show,* moving with it from radio to television, and wrote episodes of *My Favorite Martian and The Andy Griffith Show.* He and Nancy collaborated on writing eight books. They still spend

> I'D THOUGHT TRUE LOVE WOULD PROTECT ME FROM PAIN. I'D CLEARLY MISSED THE POINT OF THE BOOK.

Left: The author's 35-year-old copy of her all-time favorite book. *Right*: The Freedmans, Katherine Flannigan, and agent Laura Wilck compare *Mrs. Mike* with the *Atlantic Monthly*'s serial version, 1948.

hours a day working side by side, Benedict on his humanitarian manifesto and Nancy on a novel.

"Tell her about the time you met Howard Hughes," Nancy said during that first visit, and I listened, rapt, to how the famous eccentric instructed Benedict to shower, sponge himself off with rubbing alcohol, then shower again before their meeting. It was a fine anecdote, but I was more impressed that, at 44, with three kids and a wife to support, Benedict had walked away from his Hollywood paycheck—with Nancy's blessing—to pursue an early dream, the one he'd abandoned when his father died: studying advanced mathematics. He enrolled at UCLA, eventually earning a PhD in mathematical logic and teaching for 35 years at Occidental College in Los Angeles. The man had the courage to reinvent himself at midlife, to refuse to be ruled by regret. Maybe, I thought, I could do that, too.

Nancy and Benedict spent their entire *Mrs. Mike* windfall on a house in the Pacific Palisades designed by the architect Richard Neutra—only to see the house severely damaged in a mud slide. A second home, in Malibu, went up in flames. At times over the years, they were penniless; once when their kids were young, Benedict had to tend bar until a writing job came through. None of it fazed them. As children of the Great Depression, they never much trusted wealth or stability. "One of the things we learned from all of it was to celebrate bad news," Benedict said. "If a book is turned down or something goes very wrong, you go out and have a party."

"Good news, you're happy anyway," Nancy added. "But bad news, you've got to have a great dinner and kick up your heels.

"Benedict and I have had difficult periods," she continued. "And we always faced serious, scary problems. But I have a theory about courage. I don't think it's a moment of bravery when you have a rush of adrenaline. Courage is something level, a kind of force that sustains you. And that's what it takes to face difficult things, to make it through life successfully."

Maybe Nancy was right. It's easy to congratulate yourself on your wisdom, your bravery when things are going well. The challenge is to trust in yourself, your work, your marriage, your gut, when they aren't. I'd thought, as Kathy had, that seizing my destiny and finding true love would protect me from pain, bad luck, mistakes, failure. I'd clearly missed the point of the book. Those things aren't avoidable; they're actually the hallmark of a life richly lived.

One meeting with my favorite authors did not erase years of struggle. There were still plenty of nights in our California home when the atmosphere felt as chilly as the Yukon's. But over time, especially after the birth of our daughter, my husband and I found our way back to each other, just as Kathy and Mike had. Last summer, we celebrated our 15th anniversary, and we marked the occasion by rereading *Mrs. Mike*. This time, I felt new appreciation for the bittersweet finale—the couple's courage to forgive and their leap of faith in reconciling. I asked my husband what he had taken away from the book. "That's easy," he said, with a half smile. "Life is hard. But love is strong."

I already have plans for my next rereading: It will be in another few years, snuggled up in bed with my daughter. Maybe *Mrs. Mike* won't be the book that changes her life. But when she hears Kathy's story, and especially how it influenced my own, I hope she'll be inspired to find the book that will.

A RIVER FLOWS THROUGH US

Her worldly 12-year-old wasn't the sort to read *Tom Sawyer.* Or was he? So his mother pulled a fast one. Sneaky girl! Andrea Lee forms a classic bond with her boy.

Reading rapture: Lee and son Charles in Turin, Italy, 2007.

It was with a certain timidity that I began reading *Tom Sawyer* to my son, Charles. We live in Italy, and Charles at 12, with a smudge of nascent mustache, is one of those jaded bicultural kids now produced in such quantities by this shrinking planet: Half Italian on his father's side, half African-American on mine, he spends vacations in the States or traveling in Asia and Africa on a passport that has more stamps than *Grand Theft Auto* has cheats. He's a passionate reader, both in Italian and English, but compared to the sensational premises of the books he suddenly started devouring after *James and the Giant Peach, Tom Sawyer* seemed parochial, overly homespun, just plain small. Yet it seemed to me that a childhood without this book had a dead spot in it. I certainly didn't want him discovering it on a reading list for a college course entitled something like "Myth and Platonic Motif in Mark Twain."

So I resorted to trickery. One September morning, as we waited down at the end of our driveway for the bus from the International School to appear down the road, I pulled *Tom Sawyer* out of my pocket and said that though he was far too old to be read to, I needed practice for an upcoming book tour. As Charles gave me a cut-the-crap look, I added craftily that it would be useful in his often-described future career as dictator of the Western Hemisphere (12 is a power-hungry age), as it was an American classic, a key to the hearts and minds of future subjects. Then I quickly started reading, not at the beginning, not even at the whitewashing episode, but at a point that instantly chimed with our immediate situation. "Monday morning found Tom Sawyer miserable. Monday morning always found him so—because it began another week's slow suffering in school."

My son, his eyes still clogged with sleep, sat hunched on his backpack on the ledge by the driveway, fiddling with a castor bean pod, the dog gnawing the toe of his running shoes, and listened to Tom's encounter with Huck Finn on the way to school. "Say—what is dead cats good for, Huck?" "Good for? Cure warts with."

This is the kind of conversation that, in spite of contemporary distractions posed by *Medal of Honor,* YouTube, *Borat,* and André 3000, still sings to the youthful soul. I saw a glint in Charles's eye.

"Mark the page," he commanded, as the bus pulled up and he slouched out of the gate. And the next morning he asked me to start all over again, at the beginning.

After that our morning appointments with *Tom Sawyer* became a ritual. I read aloud in the dank Northern Italian fog that rises off the Po River at the foot of our hill; on blazing clear days where the snowy line of the Alps gleams in the distance; in the rain, huddled soggily under an umbrella. As weeks passed and the oak and castor leaves turned brown and fell around us, and the school bus chugged past withering vineyards up the winding road, we made our leisurely way through the whitewashing, the pinch bug in church, Tom's staged death and glorious resurrection at his own funeral, the terror of Injun Joe, the ordeal with Becky Thatcher in the cave, the finding of the treasure. I recalled my own first reactions to the tale, which I read, like many other books, lying on a creaky glider on my sunporch in a black bourgeois Philadelphia suburb that spiritually was nearly as far from Samuel Clemens's Missouri as our aerie in the Italian Piedmont hills—farther, perhaps, because my parents regarded the book with the severity with which politically minded black people, in the fraught 1970s, regarded any literary classic by a white author whose prose lightly dealt in the word *nigger*. I myself, at 10 or 11, was completely unmoved by the occasional *nigger,* though the word had angered and embarrassed me in other books, skimming over it as I partook of a series of adventures that seemed less like fiction than like some part of me that I was just discovering, page by page. Like my other favorite books at the time, *Tom Sawyer* had an ecstatic familiarity, as if I had somehow grown the story myself; it seemed exactly calibrated to assuage my chronic boredom, to feed my dreams and obsessions.

And though I was a black girl growing up in a nest of civil rights activists, and Tom was a white boy at home with slavery, it was easy to imagine myself into his barefoot anarchic self, as it was easy to translate the Mississippi riverfront into the backyards, creeks, tree houses, and vacant lots of Delaware County, Pennsylvania.

My husband, who was born in Venice during the Second World War, and whose childhood experience of Americans was mainly limited to Gary Cooper movies and a standing maternal order to avoid GIs and their offers of chocolate, was pleased by our reading, and confessed that *Tom Sawyer* had been his favorite book as a boy. When Charles and I challenged him as to what he remembered, he listed everything precisely: whitewash; funeral; Becky; cave; treasure. He said it reminded him of days he'd spent on the lagoon with his friends, messing around in boats, fishing, swimming in canals (Venice was cleaner then). "I always thought of the Mississippi as looking something like the Giudecca," he added dreamily.

I could see that our son, too, had constructed his own mental *Tom Sawyer* landscape. He slid over any racism with the matter-of-fact attitude of an expatriate kid who has grown up being lectured ad nauseam on African-American history. From a few comments he made, I guessed that he envisioned the plot as unfolding in the woods in back of our house, a forest with a long history of military occupation, from Caesar's legions to Napoleon to Italian partisans, which is now frequently host to my son and his cronies, who have built a fort along a stream, where they spend time getting wet, hunting for Roman coins, smoking pilfered cigarettes, trying to kill small mammals, and plotting raids on other bands of boys.

And when we got to the desperate search for Tom and Becky lost in the cave, Charles compared it to a case we'd all been following in the Italian press a year earlier, in which the inhabitants of Gravina di Puglia were combing the caverns of the surrounding stony wilderness for a missing pair of 11- and 13-year-old boys.

It's beyond a trope that great books are universal, but I was struck by the ability of this slender tale to grasp subjects of abiding interest to any reader just on the verge of growing up. One of these, of course, is the friction between the safe, constrained world of childhood and the terrible joys of mature freedom, lawless adventure, romantic love, the heroic pleasure of cutting a figure in the eyes of the world. I found unexpectedly touching the scene in which Tom and his friend Joe Harper, who have run off to live in a boys' paradise on a Mississippi island, begin to sicken of freedom, to feel the pangs of desire for rules, home, the small boundaries imposed by their mothers. "Swimming's no good," says Joe. "I don't seem to care for it, somehow, when there ain't anybody to say I sha'n't go in." I've seen it many times at the end of the day, how boys who at the height of their energy seem like supermen, with their alarming sophistication, their rumbustious strength, their overweening need to push limits, suddenly, almost pathetically, ask to be children again.

> THE STORY EXPLORES THE FRICTION BETWEEN THE SAFE, CONSTRAINED WORLD OF CHILDHOOD AND THE TERRIBLE JOYS OF MATURE FREEDOM.

But what most strikes an adult revisiting *Tom Sawyer* is how dark it is, how filled with peril and death. I'd remembered the book as tame by contemporary standards, but compared to it, *Harry Potter* is almost Pollyannaish. Clemens well understood the preadolescent fascination with mortality in all its forms, how just at the time one approaches the fullness of life, one becomes obsessed with the inevitability of its end. After the dead cat, Tom Sawyer encounters grave robbers, witnesses a moonlit murder, attends, in a sublime evocation of the ultimate 12-year-old fantasy, his own funeral, narrowly escapes a horrible end with Becky in the cave, and then bears witness—with an astonishing surge of compassion, which is perhaps a greater treasure than the mass of gold coins he and Huck discover—to the true horror of the protracted, tortured death of his archenemy, Injun Joe, accidently imprisoned in the same cave. Both Charles and I sat riveted the morning I read Clemens's chilling expansion into oratory as he describes the dying villain's futile attempts to gather drinking water from a dripping stalactite. "That drop was falling when the Pyramids were new; when Troy fell; when the foundations of Rome were laid; when Christ was crucified... when Columbus sailed.... It is falling now; it will still be falling when all these things shall have sunk down the afternoon of history, and the twilight of tradition, and been swallowed up in the thick night of oblivion."

Some time later, Charles said: "You forget that all this stuff is happening to just one boy in a tiny little town. It's a big story."

Big. That's just what I thought, and at the end of our reading, I felt oddly triumphant, pleased that an American river, a small-town tale, could reach over time and space. Over continents and generations. ◖

INSIDE THE WRITER'S MIND

If you've ever thought maybe you had a book in you, six terrific novelists are here to tell you about the art, the craft, the isolation, the listening, the mysterious energy, and the sheer, termite-like determination that go into making a world out of words.

O: WHAT'S THE BEST THING ABOUT BEING A WRITER?

JEFFREY EUGENIDES: The best thing is also the worst thing. It's that, no matter how long you've been at it, you always start from scratch. Henry James said, "We work in the dark—we do what we can—we give what we have. Our doubt is our passion and our passion is our task. The rest is the madness of art." Unless you're the kind of writer who works with a template, where the narrative strategies remain more or less constant and the job consists of filling in the boxes with new material, then what you have to do, with each new book, is discover all these things anew. Your material determines your narrative strategy and your tone of voice rather than the other way around. You change from book to book. You begin always knowing nothing. You remain forever an amateur, a first-timer. Sure, you might cobble together something akin to a methodology after a while, a working method, a sense of pacing yourself through the seasons. But that's about it in terms of the pleasures and wisdom of the veteran.

What makes this worst thing also the best thing has to do with the agelessness of aspiration. When you're always starting out, always trying to learn to do what you don't know how to do, you remain close to the place (college dorm room, Prague café) where you first set pen to paper. You remain in touch with that crazy, dreamy kid who spent so much time in the library. You persist in being impractical, idealistic, naive, and brave. Your body ages, but your imagination remains young, and on your deathbed, if you're lucky, you might be prideful enough to say to yourself, *I'm finally getting the hang of this.*

MARY GAITSKILL: The best thing about writing is being able to clearly express things in a way you can't express in conversation. This is especially true if you are socially awkward and a little inarticulate, which I was when I first started to write seriously (at age 23) and is still how I occasionally feel. In countless conversations I have had, someone has said something and I have had several responses at once, sometimes responses that were nonverbal, coming to me in confused masses of feeling, images, and half-formed thoughts that I could not refine into words until, say, sometime the next day. Anything I did say would feel partial to me and often sounded just plain dumb.

Writing is in some way being able to sit down the next day and go through everything you wanted to say, finding the right words, giving shape to the images, and linking them to feelings and thoughts. It isn't exactly like a social conversation because you aren't giving information in the usual sense of the word or flirting or persuading anyone of anything or proving a point; it's more that you are revealing something whole in the form of a character, a city, a moment, an image seen in a flash out of a character's eyes. It's being able to take something whole and fiercely alive that exists inside you in some unknowable combination of thought, feeling, physicality, and spirit, and to then store it like a genie in tense, tiny black symbols on a calm white page. If the wrong reader comes across the words, they will remain just words. But for the right readers, your vision blooms off the page and is absorbed into their minds like smoke, where it will reform, whole and alive, fully adapted to its new environment. It is a deeply satisfying feeling.

O: BESIDES TALENT, WHAT ARE THE PARTICULAR HUMAN QUALITIES IT TAKES TO BE A NOVELIST?

WALTER KIRN: At the beginning of a novel, a writer needs confidence, but after that what's required is persistence. These traits sound similar. They aren't. Confidence is what politicians, seducers, and currency speculators have, but persistence is a quality found in termites. It's the blind drive to keep on working that persists after confidence breaks down.

This breakdown usually happens in chapter five or so, but sometimes it comes as early as chapter two. The book's characters have been introduced by then and given a world to live in, creating atmosphere. The challenges they face have been described and made to seem monumental, creating tension. Finally, the novelist's friends and family have been pushed away, creating loneliness. Now what? The mind is powerless to answer, leaving the nerves and glands to do the job, assisted at times by caffeine and other substances.

But such chemical helpers only help so much. The mysterious energy required to turn silence into words and roll those words perpetually uphill originates deep within the soul—so deep that its sources resist analysis. Novelists who pretend to understand what keeps them scribbling are really just guessing. A profound, unmet childish need to be acknowledged? Maybe. It hardly matters, though. The termite that asks itself why it keeps chewing risks becoming sluggish and inefficient, as does the writer who grows self-conscious in the middle of chapter five. Stopping to think is fine for characters, but not for their creators. They have to work.

JOHN EDGAR WIDEMAN: Novelists must learn the skill of listening, practice listening as discipline and discovery. The best novelists hear their subjects, and their writing bears witness to a conversation with presences real as a friend, an enemy, a stone in a shoe, a sword poised over the writer's head, a person or place unrecoverable yet never quite absent. Which is not to say writers are necessarily nuts. Cervantes, unlike his creation Don Quixote, could distinguish windmills from dragons. Most of the time, anyway.

To hear a subject requires a novelist to develop an acute aural consciousness. Special muscles must be honed for listening not only to what other people say but for tuning in and gauging the immense silence in which speech, action, and time resonate. Good writers learn to understand they inhabit a world full of unheard music—music analogous to the dense, unfathomable welter of sensations animating creatures like dogs, birds, and fish, whose biological makeup enables them to experience perceptions outside human reach. Echoes, traces of this separate, elusive, overarching music, infiltrate and saturate the best fiction, dancing around the edges of characters and ideas. Based upon the singularity of what they discipline themselves to hear of this mix, individual writers generate a signature prose rhythm that plays inside the reader's head. A kind of ground-noise, barely rising above silence, though close enough to the threshold of audibility so you know when it's there, know when it's missing. Music less intrusive, more subtle than a Hollywood soundtrack but equally as informative and supportive of a story's narrative flow.

Part of the pleasure, the instruction, of reading a novelist who achieves the gift/burden of hearing a subject is learning to listen to the writer's act of listening. Attentiveness doubled. Give and take. Call and response. In Duke Ellington's sense, the prose *swings*. The matter communicated literally moves a reader's body and mind. We share what a story's talking about, feel the tangible presence of the many, many *things* it embodies.

SUSANNA MOORE: We writers are very interested in, if not obsessed with, the idea of what is true. (Ivy-Compton Burnett wrote: "It is not true that people have nothing to fear if they speak the truth. They have everything to fear. That is the reason for falsehood.")

It is a commonplace that autobiography is particularly vulnerable to untruth, whereas it is said that fiction never lies. Facts may be altered and reordered. Facts may be used to conceal the truth. In fiction the opposite is true. The artist must lie in order to tell the truth. Every word a writer writes has as its purpose a function of truth in that it is a choice—each word eliminates an endless number of possibilities. Style itself is a manifestation of what is true, a heightening of meaning, if we take for truth something more delicate, more fascinating than the not telling of a lie. There are, of course, endless layers of truth; style is one way to get to the heart of the matter. The seemingly untrue—the illogical, the absurd, the magical—are not exceptions to this. (Words themselves may be ambiguous, even mysterious, but not ambiguously so.) Illusions, fantasies, deceptions, fevers—these things are possible in a writer, even desired, all in the service of what is true.

JOSHUA FERRIS: It takes no particular human quality for one to become a novelist save this: the ability to endure long stretches of time at one's desk. Not even that: Short bursts of intense time at one's desk will do. You don't even need an actual desk. You can be at a desk on the subway. You can be at a desk in the bathroom stalls. Wherever you give yourself over again to sustained meditation. Sustained meditation, specifically on your preoccupations, obsessions, overriding curiosities. Preoccupations and curiosities you believe best served not by the casual anecdote, the emotive e-mail, the journal entry, or the autobiographical essay, but through the variegated freedom that comes from making people out of words. People and planes landing on tarmacs and lost tourists at nightfall in a land of casual murder. Words spoken in a voice you search for and hold like water in your hand. A voice lost and recaptured over and over during your hours at your desk. A voice once borrowed from a chorus of voices you like best, now distilled from that chorus and distilled and distilled down to your specific range and harmony. A range and harmony that coalesce with your preoccupations and curiosities into a story of people made with words inhabiting a world inimitably yours. The people and the tarmacs and the tourists anxious to find their hotel in the dark. Inimitably yours because you shaped them hour after hour, at your desk. Their conflict, their destiny, in your inimitable voice, confronting the vagaries of your imagined world. Will they survive? The two hooded figures are approaching. The moon-dark beach is endless. What they would do to be home right now. What they would do to be at your desk, determining the fate of their world. ◙

CONFESSIONS OF A SELF-HELP-BOOK READER

For years she thought self-help books were only for nincompoops. Then she read one. And another. And another. Now she can't believe the hands-on wisdom about love and sex! The timely advice about breaking up! The illuminating psychology about men and women! Liesl Schillinger on some self-help books that she actually found helpful.

L et me admit it. There was a time, not so long ago, when I thought self-help books were for ninnies. It's not that I believed that people didn't need help. But having grown up among literary-minded college professors—my father taught Russian literature, my mother taught journalism and social theory, and most of their friends were academics and book lovers—I assumed that any coping strategies I might need as I blundered through life could be found in the novels that I devoured. By the age of 6, I had absorbed pioneer stoicism from the Little House series: Where there's a will, there's a way. In *Jane Eyre,* I saw that a bookish loner who was ostracized by coddled children could educate herself into a richer life than her blinkered peers imagined. Later, reading Dostoyevsky, Naipaul, Flaubert, Balzac, Fitzgerald, Graham Greene, Anne Tyler, John Irving, and...um, Tom Robbins (*Even Cowgirls Get the Blues* was a teen favorite), I anticipated the freighted entanglements of romance, sex, adulthood, and parent-hood—with their joys, despairs, perfidies, and compromises. What torments could I possibly face that my literary heroes and antiheroes hadn't already thrashed out for me on the printed page?

Besides, my own family background predisposed me to keep a stiff upper lip. Descended from a long line of German-American Midwesterners, I instinctively adopted the family motto: If you're looking for a helping hand, look at the end of your own arm. This didn't mean that any of us, or all of us (I have two brothers), did not melt down from time to time (well, not my dad...). It meant that when we did, we sorted ourselves out without the benefit of any dime-store manual about the color of our parachutes, or about which planets our romantic nemeses came from.

Furthermore, as someone who wanted to write, I superstitiously

believed that psychological knots in the mind were best left tangled. I feared that if I were to avail myself of over-the-counter psychology, my thoughts would become so clear to me that my own inner life would bore me. Childhood is the writer's bank balance, Graham Greene had written. What if organizing the accounts emptied it?

And then, early in 1999, in the wake of the old-fashioned husband-hunting manual *The Rules*—volumes 1 and 2—I came across a breathtakingly elegant, jaded, and useful book called *The Technique of the Love Affair*, published in 1928 by a sultry British newlywed in her early 20s named Doris Langley Moore. (She later divorced, I read in an online biography.) In her author photo, she looked like the luscious, sly heroine of a Noël Coward play. Her book begins with a dialogue between a sophisticated minx named Cypria and a naive damsel named Saccharissa. "It is desirable for the happiness and well-being of a woman that she should be frequently, or at any rate constantly, pursued," Cypria declared. At the time, I was young, divorced, and enmeshed in my first serious postmarriage relationship. I wondered: Could I follow Moore's instructions so that, as Dorothy Parker had written when she reviewed the book decades earlier, I might become "successful instead of just successive"? Cypria's lessons were pointed and unsentimental. Chastity was not necessary to earn a man's loyalty, she explained, but teasing and reticence were de rigueur. "We dare not give rein to our generosity," she said, "for men, like children, soon tire of what is soon obtained." Saccharissa, Cypria's sappy sidekick, was horrified. "Your cynicism has shocked me," she whimpered. But before long, she was won over.

I took less convincing.

Captivated by Moore's antique Realpolitik on the battle of the sexes, I proposed an essay to my editors at *The New York Times*. The piece appeared on Valentine's Day. "At last," I wrote, "a self-help book for women who don't need help, not for women who are past it."

Then the phone began to ring. My friends wanted to be walked through *The Technique*. (They already had *The Rules*.) I lent my marked-up book to one friend; she kept it. I bought another, and soon lent that out as well (it also failed to find its way back to my library). I am currently on my sixth copy. Later that year, my editors called. Would I review a book called *A General Theory of Love*, on the neurological basis of romance? I was leery of falling into a "love" beat. I wanted to write on general, gender-neutral subjects. Would writing about relationship books twice in 12 months pigeonhole me?

But *A General Theory of Love* beguiled me. Like Moore's book, it was written in an artful literary style—the authors began their explanation of the workings of the limbic brain by reaching back to Pascal's *Pensées*. See? Not for ninnies. Also, my post-divorce relationship had just ended, and I was soothed by the doctors' news. The brain forges neural pathways in response to anyone you love, they explained. Over time, the pathways are reinforced by repeat exposure, and before long, tributary associations begin to connect with the main path, deepening and expanding its tracks. Their message was clear: To haul yourself out of the limbic rut of a lost love, you must forge new neural paths with new people. This insight was useful. It also helped explain why my friends and I had found it so difficult in the past to shake memories of previous relationships. Even when you want to forget, the limbic brain remembers. Sheepishly recalling the cocky essay I'd written about Cypria and Saccharissa, and the people who "don't need help...," I thought to myself, *Now, just who might that be?*

I had always shunned the self-help section in bookstores, but my respect for the wisdom in those two books began to erode my suspicion of the genre. When a friend confided to me that she was enduring a rending crisis with her parents and siblings, I went online, plugged in some of her concerns, and found a relevant book called *How You Can Survive When They're Depressed*. Walking to my local Barnes & Noble, I mumbled the title to the clerk, afraid of being overheard. He directed me to the proper section. Once there, I looked around furtively to make sure no friends were nearby—being seen would have felt like being spotted in a particularly sordid aisle of an adult boutique. Spying the title, I whisked it under my elbow and hustled it to the register. My friend loved the book. It lacked the lyricism of the bellwether titles that had lured me, and had none of the style of the 19th- and 20th-century novels that paint such a detailed map of human woes. But my friend was not a character marching through a predetermined series of imagined events; she was a real person who needed up-to-date strategies to address problems no novelist could resolve.

> LITERATURE ALONE IS NOT ENOUGH TO SORT OUT CONTEMPORARY MORES. "THE END" IS A FICTION. THE REALITY IS: WHAT'S NEXT?

This is not to say that I am a complete convert. As a critic, I read a number of books a week, nearly all of them literary novels, biographies, or books of social commentary. A self-help book makes it into the mix perhaps once a month. But in 2005, I became a columnist for the Styles section of the *Times*, reviewing books on lighthearted, provocative, or glamorous subjects that fit the Styles brief. As word went out to publicists, shipments of unsolicited books, many of them volumes of self-help, began to land on my doorstep. Reader, I read them.

Some I laughed at and threw out: smug men preaching the virtues of open relationships; supermodels sharing man-catching tips (as if anyone so magically endowed had secrets that could be transferred to mere mortals); or scarred veterans of the war between the sexes writing screeds about how to dump pond-scum partners. Others I thumbed through, getting hooked against my will. These books were, well, helpful. From Dalma Heyn's *Drama Kings: The Men Who Drive Strong Women Crazy...* I learned to identify certain kinds of boyfriends I was susceptible to. One was the "Easygoing Guy," or EGG—"so friendly, so attractive, so subtly, characterologically mysterious," who's "present, but not entirely, not all the way." The EGG, she concluded damningly, was "a performer acting casual in order to ward off relationship." Wised up by Heyn, I informed my then boyfriend (an EGG) that I had noticed his evasiveness. "You're in the shower with a raincoat on," I said. "I think it's time to either take off the raincoat or get out of the shower." We are still friends, though we are not "involved."

From Debbie Magids and Nancy Peske's *All the Good Ones Aren't Taken*, I learned about women who sabotage their own romantic chances—the "Old Faithful" who hangs on to an old love and never makes room for a new one; the "Standstill," too shy and cautious to step into the fray; and the one I recognized myself in, with a sting of regret, the "Whirlwind Dater"—busy and social, prone to serially monogamous relationships that have little likelihood of working out long-term. Anna Karenina left her husband for Vronsky, I thought. If she'd had a career in New York at the turn of the 20th century, would she have put her head on the tracks when the liaison soured, or gone on to...the next Vronsky? Literature alone is not enough to sort out contemporary mores. "The end" is a fiction. The reality is: What's next?

Last summer, while I was visiting friends at a beach house, the hostess, who'd recently landed her hard-to-get boyfriend after a complicated courtship, sat next to me poolside, explaining what had turned the tide in their affair. The relationship had been touch and go for a long time, she admitted. But a year before, she had read a review of a book titled *It's Called a Breakup Because It's Broken,* which had convinced her that she needed to kill her relationship to save it. Talking further, we realized it was my review that had led her to the

book. She never had believed in self-help books before, she said, but with my apparent sanction, she had dared. "I was too proud to buy it, so I was reading it in the Barnes & Noble coffee shop, concealing the cover," she told me. "Afterward, for weeks, I did just what the book said, avoiding the places I knew I'd see him, not calling, not being available. I would repeat after myself like a mantra, 'It's called a breakup because it's broken, it's called a breakup because it's broken...'"

It's not broken now, for her. I'm delighted if my tardy embrace of the relationship genre can help any of my friends; and with any luck, someday I'll acquire the ingenuity to make it work for me. For the moment, though, I'm still struggling to keep EGGs at bay, and waiting with curiosity (not unmixed with dread) to see what wisdom the next unsolicited manuscript on my doorstep may contain. If it's not a self-help book, that's okay: It's high time I reread *The Technique* anyway. ◖

WITH A LITTLE SELF-HELP FROM MY FAVORITES

Liesl Schillinger's advice: Read these titles. Be wowed. Pass them on!

■ **If You Can't Live Without Me, Why Aren't You Dead Yet? by Cynthia Heimel.** These essays are packed with uncensored advice that's both sensitive and saucy. For instance, Heimel explains what to do to get the right man: "Nothing." The right man will adore you, she writes, even if you have "greasy hair, spinach in your teeth, and your skirt on inside out." Why accept anything less?

■ **I'm Too Sexy for My Volvo: A Mom's Guide to Staying Fabulous, by Betty Londergan.** Funny, frank, indulgent, and packed with helpful baby care tips, this guide is free of the earnestness that weighs down so many advice books for new mothers, and includes practical suggestions such as: Buy bracelets before your due date, because so many photos will soon include your forearms.

■ **The Worry Cure: Seven Steps to Stop Worry from Stopping You, by Robert L. Leahy.** A pep talk on paper, this book lays out the ways in which

worriers tend to sabotage their happiness, and provides a seven-step strategy for coping with common crises. Leahy helps men and women address their anxieties and overcome them.

■ **The Mystery Method: How to Get Beautiful Women into Bed, by Mystery with Chris Odom.** Hadn't you better acquaint yourself with the tactics members of the opposite sex can use to hoodwink you? This DIY Casanova primer provides useful insights into the masculine art of seduction.

■ **Our Lady of Weight Loss: Miraculous and Motivational Musings from the Patron Saint of Permanent Fat Removal, by Janice Taylor.** It takes a kooky kind of genius to turn weight loss into an art project, and Taylor's soaking in it. Several years ago, she began to turn food into collages and dioramas. She shed 50 pounds in the process and has kept it off. See if her idiosyncratic diet plan will work for you.

DO SOMETHING!

OPRAH TALKS TO BOBBY KENNEDY JR.

The ardent environmentalist opens up about his family, politics, the worrisome state of our planet, and how a few changes in the law could make us all healthier, wealthier, and safer....

The front hallway of Bobby Kennedy Jr.'s home in Mt. Kisco, New York, bears a framed letter from former president Richard Nixon. "While your father and I were political opponents," Nixon wrote, "I always respected him as one of the ablest political leaders of our time." The note—dated June 24, 1985—hangs across from a letter Bobby sent his uncle Jack in 1961 requesting a visit to the White House. Once there, Bobby presented then president John F. Kennedy with a salamander.

Four decades later, Bobby, 53*, is one of the country's most passionate environmental activists. Protecting nature isn't just about saving the fish and the birds, he says; it's about tending to our own deepest values and our children's basic needs. "Our landscapes connect us to our history; they are the source of our character as a people, as well as our health, our safety, and our prosperity," he tells me. "Natural resources enrich us economically, yes. But they also enrich us aesthetically and recreationally and culturally and spiritually." Never before have I heard someone speak with such clarity and conviction about protecting our earth.

Born into a political dynasty (the third of Robert and Ethel Kennedy's 11 children), Bobby didn't always plan to work in environmental law—his career grew out of personal adversity. In 1983, when he was a 29-year-old assistant district attorney in Manhattan, he was arrested for possession of heroin. Sentenced to community service following rehab, he volunteered with Riverkeeper, a group fighting industrial pollution in New York's Hudson River. He quickly became the organization's chief prosecuting attorney. Today he is also chairman of the Waterkeeper Alliance, an international network of groups protecting the world's waterways.

He is also clearly a family man, married to second wife Mary Richardson and the father of six kids: Robert F. III, 22; Kathleen, 18; Connor, 12; Kyra, 11; William, 9; and Aidan, 5. On the day of our visit, he has just returned from taking Connor to hockey practice. The Kennedys' miniature long-haired dachshund, Cupid (born on Valentine's Day), scurries through the living room, where a chair cushion reads BORN TO FISH. Home is a priority, which is why he has never considered a bid for public office—until now.

All ages from February 2007.

OPRAH: *Nearly every American who's old enough can tell you where they were when they heard your father had been shot [after he'd won the California Democratic presidential primary in 1968]. Where were you?*

BOBBY: I was asleep. I was in boarding school, and I was woken up and told to get in the car.

OPRAH: *Did they say why?*

BOBBY: No, but when I got home, I found out.

OPRAH: *And you were flown immediately to California?*

BOBBY: Yes. I was brought to the hospital.

OPRAH: *Were you there when he died?*

BOBBY: Yeah.

OPRAH: *Before he was assassinated, did you fear he'd be killed?*

BOBBY: No.

OPRAH: *You and I are the same age. And I remember that I was 14 and living in Milwaukee, and I was worried that your father would be assassinated because Martin Luther King and John F. Kennedy had been killed. But you were never afraid?*

BOBBY: No.

OPRAH: *I just recently saw the movie Bobby [directed by Emilio Estevez], about your father. Have you seen it?*

BOBBY: No. My sister Kerry saw it. The filmmakers were very considerate of my family. I think most of my family won't see it because parts of it are so painful—it's just not worth it. But I'm very happy that Emilio made the film. Everything I've heard indicates that it's a wonderful tribute to my father.

OPRAH: *It makes people think about what the world would have been like if he hadn't been shot down. Do you ever think about that?*

BOBBY: You know, I think about that a lot as it applies to the kinds of decisions being made in our country today. To the fact that America is now involved in torturing people; that habeas corpus, which is a fundamental civil right guaranteed since the Magna Carta, has been abandoned; that we're imprisoning people without proper trials. My father thought of America as the last best hope for humanity. He believed we had a historical mission to be a paragon to the rest of the world, to be about what human beings can accomplish if they work together and maintain their focus. He was never afraid of debate; he was willing to debate with Communists because he believed this country's ideas were so good that we shouldn't be scared of meeting with anybody.

Oprah and Bobby take a friend's falcon, Race, for a flight on the Kennedys' 12-acre property in Mt. Kisco, New York.

Above left: Bobby at home with sons Aidan, 5, and Connor, 12 (holding Cupid). *Above right:* Bobby, 3 (*second from left*), with his family in McLean, Virginia, 1957.

When I was boy, my father took me to Europe—Greece, Czechoslovakia, Poland, Italy, Germany, England, France. Everywhere we went, we were met by huge crowds, sometimes hundreds of thousands of people who came out because they loved our country. They were starved for our leadership. They looked to us for moral authority. They proudly named their streets after our presidents: Washington, Jefferson, Jackson, Lincoln, Kennedy. And I remember after 9/11, the headline in the French newspaper *Le Monde* was WE ARE ALL AMERICANS. For two weeks after 9/11, there were spontaneous candlelight vigils in Tehran, initiated by Muslims who loved our country. It took more than 200 years of disciplined, visionary leadership by Republican and Democratic presidents to build these huge reservoirs of public love. We were the most beloved nation on the face of the earth. And today—in six short years, through monumental incompetence and arrogance, this White House has absolutely drained that reservoir dry. America has become the most hated nation on earth. There are five billion people who either fear or just don't know what to think about the United States. For me that's the most bitter pill to swallow.

OPRAH: *Can we turn this around?*

BOBBY: I think we can, but it's going to take a generation to recover, particularly in the Muslim world. In Tehran there was a nascent democratic movement; most observers were betting that Iran would be a democratic nation by now. But after the war in Iraq, that movement disappeared. The war allowed the radicals to say to the moderates, "Here's proof that all the bad things we've been saying about the United States are true." The radical, Islamofascist leaders were empowered.

OPRAH: *Do you fear for our country?*

BOBBY: I think the worst thing this White House has done is to use fear as a governing tool. No, I don't fear for our country in terms of an attack. They've used the excuse that 9/11 suddenly put us in the most dangerous part of our history. That's nonsense. When you and I were raised, there were 25,000 nuclear warheads pointed at America, and we faced absolute annihilation. That was a dangerous time.

When George Washington fought the British and his troops didn't have shoes, that was a dangerous time. And during the Civil War, if we had lost Gettysburg, the United States of America would have disappeared.

OPRAH: *That's right.*

BOBBY: Lots of countries, like Israel, live with terrorism every day, and it doesn't impact their integrity. The big threat to America is the way we react to terrorism by throwing away what everybody values about our country—a commitment to human rights. America is a great nation because we are a good nation. When we stop being a good nation, we stop being great.

OPRAH: *Why haven't you run for office?*

BOBBY: I've got six reasons running around this house. But at this point, I would run if there were an office open because I'm so distressed about the kind of country my children will inherit. I've tried to cling to the idea that I could be of public service without compromising my family life. But at this point, I would run.

OPRAH: *For what?*

BOBBY: I would run for the Senate or for the governor's office [in New York]. But my friends are in those offices, and I'm not going to run against them.

OPRAH: *Why didn't you run for New York attorney general?*

BOBBY: Because I really didn't want to be attorney general. I have the kind of life where I can take my kids on trips with me. I can involve them in my work. I've always avoided politics because I didn't want to make commitments that would take me away from raising these children. But now America has changed so dramatically that I'm asking myself: *What's going to be left of this country?* I'm spending time with my kids, but maybe my time would be spent just as well if I tried to save the country.

OPRAH: *What kind of father would your children call you?*

BOBBY: You can ask them.

OPRAH: *Your wife's not here with us today. What kind of husband would she call you?*

BOBBY: I think Mary would call me a pretty good husband. And by the way, Mary remembers you as a great sport, because she once

Presenting his presidential uncle with a salamander, 1961.

picked you up in Boston to take you to Maria [Shriver]'s wedding....

OPRAH: *We were in a convertible....*

BOBBY: She said you'd just had your hair done. The convertible top wouldn't go up, so she drove you at 76 miles an hour with an open roof. She says you were gracious and good-humored about it.

OPRAH: *I remember that day. Do the Kennedys still have all those big family gatherings?*

BOBBY: Yes.

OPRAH: *If one of your children told you they wanted to run for office, what would you think?*

BOBBY: I'd think it was fine. My son Connor [age 12] is very interested in politics. He reads the papers, loves history, and knows what's going on.

OPRAH: *Would you ever run for president?*

BOBBY: I don't know what the future will bring. I really just try to live my life one day at a time and do what I'm supposed to on that day. But if opportunities came up for me to run for office, I would probably do it. If that doesn't happen, then I'll happily continue doing what I'm doing.

OPRAH: *An opportunity—meaning if none of your friends were running?*

BOBBY: If Hillary left the Senate, I might run for that seat.

OPRAH: *If you could create the perfect presidential ticket for 2008, what would it be?*

BOBBY: I can't answer that question now. The candidates are my friends, and I like all of them.

OPRAH: *Do you think this country would elect a woman for president?*

BOBBY: Yes.

OPRAH: *Would this country elect a black man for president?*

BOBBY: Yes. I think Barack Obama and Hillary Clinton are terrific candidates. A lot of candidates are three questions deep on the issues. But Hillary is thoughtful. She's a problem-solver who has more than just surface knowledge. Though I disagree with her position on the war, I think she has an impressive depth that a lot of other candidates don't have.

OPRAH: *Including Obama?*

BOBBY: I don't know Obama that well, but I know him well enough to really like him. My father's best friend in Africa was a man named Tom Mboya, a labor leader from Kenya. I met him right after my father died—and a year later, Tom was assassinated. During his life, he was completely committed to human rights and democracy. His heroes were Abraham Lincoln and Thomas Jefferson. He was from a tribe called the Luo—lake people who are very gentle. When I met Barack, I asked him what tribe he was from, and he said he was Luo. I told him about my father's friend. He said Tom Mboya was the man responsible for his being in the United States.

OPRAH: *That's amazing. For two decades, you've taken a strong stand against what you call pollution-based prosperity. What does that term mean?*

BOBBY: Good environmental policy is identical to good economic policy 100 percent of the time. We can measure the economy in one of two ways. We can base our assessment on whether the economy produces jobs of dignity over the long term and preserves our community assets. Or we can do what the polluters are urging us to do: treat the planet as if it were a business in liquidation and convert our natural resources into cash as quickly as possible. This is pollution-based prosperity. It creates the illusion of a prosperous economy, but our children will pay for our joyride. They'll pay for it with denuded landscapes, poor health, and huge cleanup costs. Environmental injury is deficit spending. It loads the cost of our generation's prosperity onto the backs of our children.

OPRAH: *Don't three of your children have asthma?*

BOBBY: Three of my boys. We have an asthma epidemic in this country. A 2003 study done in Harlem indicates that one in four black children in America's cities has asthma. The principal trigger is bad air—notably ozone and particulates that primarily come from the hundreds of power plants that burn coal illegally. It has been against the law for 17 years to burn coal without removing these two pollutants. But in states where corporations dominate the political process, the plants were not forced to clean up. The Clinton administration was prosecuting the worst 51 plants. But this is an industry that has donated more than $100 million to President Bush and the Republican Party since 2000, and one of the first things this White House did was to get the Justice Department and EPA to drop all those lawsuits. The top three enforcers at the EPA all resigned their jobs in protest. These enforcers weren't appointed by Democrats. They were people who'd worked through the Reagan and Bush administrations. Then the White House abolished the New Source rule, which was the heart and soul of the Clean Air Act. Now that there's no requirement for plants to clean up the ozone and particulates, the plants that already did it are at a competitive disadvantage in the marketplace. So the good guys are being punished! Plus I'll be able to watch my children gasp for air on bad air days because somebody gave money to a politician. The decision to abolish the New Source rule kills 18,000 Americans every year—six times the number killed in the World Trade Center attacks.

OPRAH: *Why is asthma so predominant among urban black children?*

BOBBY: There's a lot of suggestion that urban black neighborhoods are often next to incinerators, sewer plants, and highways, so children are breathing in diesel fuel. They don't put those coal-burning power plants in Beverly Hills. They don't put them next to golf courses. The poor always shoulder a disproportionate burden of environmental pollution. Four out of five toxic waste dumps in America are in black neighborhoods. The largest dump in America is in Emelle, Alabama, which is more than 90 percent black. The highest concentration of toxic waste dumps is on the South Side of Chicago. The most contaminated zip code in California is East

L.A. Navajo youth develop sexual organ cancers at 17 times the rate of other Americans because of the thousands of tons of toxic uranium tailings that have been dumped on their reservations.

Environmentalism has become the most important civil rights issue. The role of government is to protect the commons: the air we breathe, the water we drink, the fisheries, the wildlife, the public lands. Those resources are our social safety net. During the Great Depression when thousands lost their jobs in New York, they went down to the Hudson River to catch fish so they could feed their families. New York's constitution says the fish of the state belong to the people. Whether you're young or old, rich or poor, humble or noble, black or white, you have an absolute right to go down to the Hudson, pull out a striped bass, and proudly feed it to your family. But we don't own the fish anymore—the General Electric Company owns the fish. Because they put PCBs in the river, it's now illegal to sell those fish in the marketplace. So the battle is over whether we're going to continue allowing the commonwealth to be privatized by powerful political entities.

OPRAH: *I hear you don't even eat fish these days.*

BOBBY: No, I eat fish. I don't watch my diet. I eat fast food and potato chips.

OPRAH: *Didn't your doctor warn you about fish, though?*

BOBBY: Listen, one out of every six American women has so much mercury in her womb that her children are at risk for a grim inventory of health issues, including autism, blindness, mental retardation, and heart and kidney disease. I had my levels tested recently, and they were more than twice what the EPA considers safe. Dr. David Carpenter, a national authority on mercury contamination, told me that a woman with my levels would have children with cognitive impairment—a permanent neurological injury and an IQ loss of about five to seven points.

OPRAH: *I know you became an environmental advocate after beating a heroin addiction. How did you get hooked?*

BOBBY: Pretty soon after my dad died, I started taking drugs. I was part of a generational revolution that looked at drugs almost as a political statement—a rebellion again the preceding generation, which had opposed the civil rights movement and promoted Vietnam. At the time, I don't think any of us were aware of how damaging drugs could be.

OPRAH: *When did you first know you were in trouble?*

BOBBY: When I was a kid, I'd always had iron willpower and the ability to control my appetites. At 9 I gave up candy for Lent and didn't eat it again until I was in college. After I started taking drugs, I earnestly tried to stop. I couldn't. That's the most demoralizing part of addiction. I couldn't keep contracts with myself.

OPRAH: *I think every addiction is a cover for an emotional wound.*

BOBBY: I'm not sure if I agree with that. I don't know whether addiction is principally genetic, a result of emotional injury, or a combination of both. But all that matters is what I do today. Insight doesn't cure the addict any more than insight cures diabetes. You may understand perfectly well how diabetes works, but if you don't take your insulin, you're dead. The same is true with addiction. It doesn't matter what got you there; it's how you conduct yourself today, day by day.

OPRAH: *Once you broke the habit, did you still crave heroin?*

BOBBY: No. I've been sober for 23 years, and I'm one of the lucky ones: I've never had a single urge since. Once I completed a 12-step program, the obsession I lived with for 14 years just lifted. I would describe it as miraculous.

OPRAH: *I've heard that you carry a rosary in your pocket. Do you use it?*

BOBBY: Yes. I say the rosary every day.

OPRAH: *I know that you have a genetic neurological condition called spasmodic dysphonia, which is straining your speech. Does it hurt when you talk?*

BOBBY: No, but it's an effort. The disease didn't hit me until I was about 43. I used to have a strong voice.

OPRAH: *So you just woke up one day and your voice was different?*

BOBBY: It began as a mild tremble for a couple of years. After people would hear me speak, I'd get all these letters, almost always from women: "I saw you on TV and you were crying—it was so good seeing a man share his feelings!" I'd think, *Oh God.* I knew for every woman who wrote, there were ten men saying, "Look at this friggin' crybaby!" [*Laughs*]

OPRAH: *Did your voice worsen?*

BOBBY: I've been told that it's not supposed to, but I think it has. There's a treatment for it: Botox shots. They put a needle into your voice box every four months. They still haven't gotten my dose right.

OPRAH: *It's fascinating talking to you. What is the number one thing Americans need to focus on in terms of the planet?*

BOBBY: Global warming. The good news is that we have the technological and scientific capacity to avert the most catastrophic impacts. All the things we need to do to stop the globe from warming are also the things we ought to do for our national security and economy. For instance, if we raised fuel economy standards in American cars by one mile per gallon, we'd generate twice the oil that's in the Arctic National Wildlife Refuge. If we raised fuel economy standards by 7.6 miles per gallon, we'd yield more oil than is now being pumped in the Persian Gulf. We could eliminate 100 percent of our Persian Gulf oil imports simply by raising fuel economy standards! That's a tiny investment compared with the $2 trillion we're on track to spend in Iraq and compared with the $60 billion a year we spent on military protection of the Gulf before the war. It would preserve us from entanglements with Middle Eastern dictators who hate democracy and are despised by their own people. It would keep us out of humiliating and expensive wars like the one we're quagmired in now. It would reduce our national deficit by $20 billion a year. It would make us all healthier, because we'd be breathing cleaner air. And we'd all be richer. I used to drive a minivan that got 22 miles per gallon. I spent more than $2,000 a year on gasoline. I now drive a Prius, which gets 48 miles per gallon, and I spend less than $1,000 a year on gas. What if every American had an extra $1,000 in their pocket every year?

OPRAH: *Why is it so hard to get this message across?*

BOBBY: In part it's because the press in our country is sick. They don't explain the important issues. They appeal to the prurient interests at the reptilian core of our brains—the craving for sex and celebrity gossip. So they give us Laci Peterson and Kobe Bryant and Michael Jackson, Brad and Angelina, Tom and Katie. We're the best entertained and the least informed people on earth. You can't even get foreign news in America unless you go to the BBC.

OPRAH: *Let's end with the issue you've devoted so much of your career to—protecting our environment. What are the consequences if we don't?*

BOBBY: The environment is the infrastructure of our communities. As a nation, as a civilization, it's our obligation to create communities for our children that provide them with opportunities for dignity and good health. When we destroy nature, we diminish ourselves and impoverish our children. We ignore that at our own peril. ◧

Sally's talismans: a photo of her son Peter, and Afghan prayer beads.

THE AFTERLIFE

When her son Peter was killed on a hijacked plane on 9/11, Sally Goodrich concluded that life as she knew it was over. But then she found a new mission—building schools in, of all places, the harsh, violence-ridden land of Afghanistan. Peter Trachtenberg on an amazing woman who's risen triumphantly from the smoke and ashes of her own bereavement.

In April 2006, Sarah Goodrich, a 61-year-old school administrator from Bennington, Vermont, paid a visit to a newly constructed girls' middle school in Logar, Afghanistan. Logar lies an hour and a half from Kabul, in a broad, fertile valley encircled by the arms of the Hindu Kush. When Goodrich, whom everybody calls Sally, had come here the year before, children were attending classes in tents set up in an open courtyard. Now it was a two-story building whose 26 rooms could hold some 500 k through eighth graders. It looked, Sally thought, like a Comfort Inn, and it had no heat or plumbing. Still, she was proud of it. This school for girls is one of the first in a region where

they were once illegal and where girls who pursue an education still take their lives in their hands. And it was built largely with funds—some $236,000—that Sally raised herself.

On this visit, she'd come with several boxes of backpacks for the schoolchildren. She'd also brought a gift for the principal: an English-Arabic Qur'an. The village elder, a ferociously bearded, grandly turbaned man named Haji Malik, was astonished by it. He'd never heard of the holy book being printed in any language besides Arabic, the language in which the angel Gabriel is said to have dictated it to the prophet Muhammad. Sally told her hosts that she'd brought the bilingual Qur'an because that was the edition her son Peter used to read. He'd read the Qur'an the same way

311

he'd read the Bible, avidly and with attention, marking passages that interested him with brass book darts. Peter Goodrich was killed on September 11, 2001, when the plane on which he was traveling for business, United Airlines 175, was hijacked by al-Qaeda terrorists who, 20 minutes later, flew it into the south tower of the World Trade Center.

Before then, Sally says, "I was pretty all-American. I was a grandmother, I was a wife, I was a dutiful daughter. I was a teacher, I was an administrator, and I was not a world citizen in any respect." On September 11, however, Sally Goodrich's life, and that of her husband, Don, was changed as catastrophically as a life can be. In a sense, their lives ended. For more than a year afterward, she couldn't drive her car on the winding roads near her home without wanting to swerve into the oncoming traffic. But over time, the Goodriches found a new life. This new life—or afterlife—is centered on Afghanistan, the country that once sheltered Osama bin Laden, the man who planned Peter's murder, and that is now under renewed threat from his old allies in the Taliban. Over the past two years, Sally has traveled there five times for the charity she and Don founded, the Peter M. Goodrich Memorial Foundation, which raises money to build schools and fund development projects. Although the trips are arduous and increasingly dangerous, she says that Afghanistan is the place where she feels most at home. "When I'm in Afghanistan, I feel like I'm in Peter mode. I feel connected to him. I'm fortunate to be there, I'm fortunate to be where people are good to me. They're so warm. What a great place to be heartbroken. Anyone who's in pain should have the experience of being plunked down in a place where everyone is heartbroken."

A small, energetic woman with a dazzling smile and watchful blue-gray eyes, Sally grew up in Bennington. She met Don when she was 18 and fell in love with him because he could do a handstand on the back of a horse and acted as if he wanted nothing to do with her. They married in 1964. After law school, Don went into practice. Peter was the first of two sons (his younger brother, Foster, is now 35, and his adoptive sister, Kim, 40). He was a fragile, dreamy boy who suffered from dyslexia; bigger kids picked on him. As he grew older, though, he discovered talents for chess and math. He began running cross-country. By the time he graduated with high honors in math from Bates College in 1989, he was a strapping 6'1" track star who'd made all-American six times. With his girlfriend, Rachel, whom he married in 1992, he moved to Cambridge and got a job as a programmer.

What struck everyone who knew him was not just his brilliance but his generosity and warmth. His hugs were enveloping. He couldn't pass a homeless person on the street without giving him money. When Peter's bosses told him that he had to cut $200,000 from his departmental budget, he eliminated his own job rather than break up his team. A while after that, another company bought out his firm and promptly rehired him. He was still a dreamer, someone who could get lost watching insects or thinking about quantum theory or poring over the sacred books whose pages he marked with those brass darts. Increasingly, he was the person who held his family together. "Peter was the caretaker," Sally says. "He'd tell you he was going to be the rich uncle. I was going to live

near him. There was a little house near his. He'd say, 'That's where I'm gonna put you, Ma.' And truthfully, he would have."

He was afraid of flying and even more afraid of terrorists. "He'd been that way for three or four years," Sally remembers. "He just had it in his head. I used to make fun of him." She pauses. "He died the worst death I could imagine for my child. I imagine him as being so anxious and impaired by fear that he couldn't understand what was happening; what was happening had no place in his consciousness. He would've tried to protect the other passengers, but it would've been another instance in which he was helpless before other people's brutality. When he used to get bullied in school, he'd tell me, 'My arms won't work.' It would have been like that all over again."

The last time she saw Peter was on the weekend of September 7, when he helped her and Don move from their old home in Massachusetts back to Vermont so that they could care for her elderly father, who was ill with Alzheimer's. She still remembers the way he hugged her goodbye. On the morning of the 11th, the phone rang as she was leaving the old house. She didn't answer it and for months afterward was tormented by the thought that it might have been Peter trying to call her from the plane. Sometime later she recalls sitting with her father and watching footage of airliners slamming into the Twin Towers. She felt a quick thrill of anger pass through her. Still, it wasn't until the afternoon, when Don showed up along with her brother and their minister, that Sally realized she'd been watching her son's death. The rest of that day and night she passed in a trance. They drove to Peter and Rachel's home in Massachusetts, half expecting him to be there. The next morning, the Goodrich family found themselves at Boston's Logan airport, Peter's point of departure, along with dozens of stunned men and women whose loved ones had gotten onboard a routine flight from Boston to Los Angeles only to disappear in a ball of flame.

"THE ONE CERTAINTY, THE ONE COMFORT, WAS THAT I KNEW OUR SON LOVED US WITHOUT ANY RESERVATIONS. AND HE KNEW THAT WE LOVED HIM IN THE SAME FASHION."

Sally says, "Of course, the first question you ask yourself after you absorb the shock is, *Why? Why did they hate us so much? And why did my good kid have to die such a horrible death.* And just, *Why?*"

No answers were forthcoming. Between the secrecy of the FBI, which didn't want to compromise its investigation, and that of the airline, it was a year and a half before Don and Sally could even find out Peter's seat assignment. A month after the attacks, some of the shattered men and women who'd gathered at Logan met in the Boston suburb of Newton. They called themselves Families of September 11, and Don and Sally were elected to the board. Today Don, a scholarly, soft-spoken man who resembles a New England Atticus Finch, is the chairman. Sally, however, had to step down from the board. She was still going to work every day and taking care of her father as his Alzheimer's worsened. She was also drinking too much. "I could not feel anything," she recalls. "I would just try to get through a day and then a night and then another day. I remember going home and drinking a bottle of wine at night, and then going to work. I had a very tight path. It would be work, church, home, work, church, home. I would tell myself to just breathe, and we divided the days into the light and the dark.

Peter Goodrich, age 27, in Greensboro, Vermont, July 1995.

Sally with Afghan students at a girls' school built mostly with funds she raised.

"The one certainty, the one comfort—the only comfort—was that I knew our son loved us without any reservations. And he knew that we loved him in the same fashion.

"And the other certainty was that I wanted to kill myself. There's a part of you that just dies, and it doesn't come back."

In November her father entered a nursing home, where he died three months later. A month after that, Sally stopped drinking. She's been sober ever since. In August 2002, she was diagnosed with ovarian cancer and began chemotherapy. A year later, her cancer in remission, she went back to school to do graduate work in language and learning disabilities. She was starting to engage with the world again. But both she and Don still felt lost, like expatriates in a country whose language they will never speak fluently. Everything reminded them of Peter. Simple interactions became ordeals of awkwardness or incomprehension. Sally was afraid to go to the supermarket because she might run into a neighbor, who might ask her how she was. "I was afraid that if I answered, I would fall apart. You think, *If I cry, I will never stop crying, I will not exist. I* will *try to kill myself.* How can I answer that question, 'How are you?' And that's not what they're really asking. They're really saying, 'I'm sorry. I'm concerned about you.' But just to go into a grocery store feels like an assault."

Don was once introduced to a new colleague who knew nothing about his connection to September 11. Somehow the subject came up, and the stranger told a melodramatic story about having been in New York that day and almost meeting his wife at the World Trade Center. In the telling, it was about a brush with death. Don listened silently, torn between his own pain and his embarrassment for the young man, who would eventually find out whom he had been telling his story to. "As a country, we have been so spoiled in our isolation from suffering and injustice that we have no cultural norms for them," Don says. "Those around us see us as a curiosity. And no one wants to be a curiosity."

> "BEFORE PETER WAS KILLED, I WAS NOT A WORLD CITIZEN IN ANY RESPECT," SALLY SAYS.

Then, in 2004, Sally got an e-mail from the parents of Rush Filson, a childhood friend of Peter's who was now a marine major serving in Afghanistan. In Logar he'd been introduced to a village schoolmaster, a man of great probity and courage, who was trying to round up supplies for his pupils; the Filsons wondered whether Sally might be able to help. She started out collecting supplies and shipping them via Kathleen Rafiq, an American TV producer in Kabul. Then Kathleen suggested that Sally build a school. The idea seemed crazy, the money beyond anything she could hope to raise. But at some point, Sally realized that for the first time since Peter's death, she felt she was doing what her son would have wanted her to do. "It was a door opening. We just followed Pete's lead." She raised funds in dribs and drabs. The Berkshire School, Peter's alma mater, donated the proceeds from its bake sale. The 200 backpacks Sally would bring to Logar were gifts from an Eagle Scout troop. Speaking before small audiences, she told her family's story. She often had to remind her listeners that none of the 9/11 hijackers had been Afghan.

She came to the country for the first time in spring 2005. It was, she says, like traveling into the biblical past. The land was harsh and jagged, with unexpected green places that reminded her of Vermont. Baked-mud houses seemed to rise out of the earth and tumble down the sides of the valleys. Five times a day, the call to prayer echoed through the still air. Women rarely appeared outside or did so only shrouded in chadors or burkas, the enveloping head-to-toe garments—like a body bag for the living—that were obligatory under the Taliban and are still widely worn. The people were desperately poor, but their hospitality was overwhelming. Wherever Sally went, she was feasted. With the help of David Edwards, a professor at Williams College, and his former research assistant Shahmahmood Miakhel,

The power of connection, *above left:* Don and Sally holding their grandchild Gavin in Bennington, Vermont, June 2007. *Above right:* Sally with Afghan students Matiullah, 18, and Soraya, 17 (*far right*).

then Afghanistan's deputy minister of interior, now an adviser to the United Nations Assistance Mission in Afghanistan, she chose a site for the school. The Goodrich Foundation has since helped support additional schools and an orphanage in nearby Wardak Province and construct a well and water distribution system in Kunar.

This part of Afghanistan is mostly Pashtun, the country's dominant ethnic group and its most conservative one. The Taliban first came to power in the Pashtun lands and have been gathering strength there, abetted by the local populace's disillusionment with the government of Hamid Karzai and its suspicion of foreign soldiers. A Western woman must be circumspect. When she leaves Kabul, Sally travels under guard, her chador pulled over her light brown hair. She once created a stir in Wardak when her host, a rakish tribal khan named Seraj, tossed her a cigarette in front of onlookers. On another occasion, though, she scandalized Seraj: Negotiating one of the steep village footpaths, half hobbled by her chador, Sally fell flat on her face. The headman was horrified, and extremely angry. Under the code of honor known as *Pashtunwali*, Seraj was completely responsible for his guest's safety. Any injury to her—even one caused by her own clumsiness—meant that he had failed his responsibility. "'Sarrah, Sarrah, this is wery, wery bad,'" she imitates him. "'You cannot come back here. All you ever do is fall.' He'd had a little interpreter right at my elbow watching over me, and this poor kid ended up getting chewed out because I was unsteady. My knees were weak that very first voyage. I remember telling myself after that, *Sally, whatever you do, do not fall.*"

She made amends a year later, when she and Don brought Seraj an American saddle and bridle, precious gifts in a country that prizes horsemanship. After an awkward interval in which Afghans who had never seen a saddle tried to put one on a horse that had never worn one, Seraj leaped onto his mount, did a triumphant dance around the visitors, then took off down the hill.

Ironically, one of the last wars of the 20th century and the first of the 21st have been waged in what is essentially a premodern nation. Some Afghans would dispute that Afghanistan is even a nation, identifying themselves by their ethnic group, tribe, or clan. Many cannot speak their neighbors' language; many more can't read or write. In this kind of society, gestures count for a great deal. When a woman whom Sally is visiting, the mother of her teenage interpreter, starts rummaging through the family's treasures for gifts to give her—prayer beads, bolts of cloth—her generosity brings tears to Sally's eyes. On one occasion, her party stopped in the apple orchard of a nearby village. Rugs were spread in the shade of the trees; the foods served included a coarse, locally grown corn, roasted on the cob. Sally was feeling ill that day and set down her corn after only a few bites. An older man sitting nearby picked it up and began to eat. She understood that it was a gesture of respect. Then she learned that her companion had seen his young son murdered by gunmen. They might have been Taliban or mujahideen; so many young men in Afghanistan belong to militias and will use guns on any pretext. The gunmen pulled up at the family's gas station, the boy filled their tank, and when he asked them for money, they shot him. He was 22.

From the Soviet invasion in 1979 until the present, as many as two million Afghans are believed to have died by violence. Millions more have been displaced. Afghanistan has one of the world's highest rates of infant and maternal mortality. It's one of the most heavily land-mined countries on earth. "Virtually everyone I met in

FOR THE FIRST TIME SINCE HIS DEATH, SALLY FELT SHE WAS DOING WHAT PETER WOULD HAVE WANTED.

Afghanistan has a story of dislocation, suffering, or loss," Sally says. "People there know about 9/11. I don't usually tell the story; usually the Afghan with me tells the story. And I always get this phenomenally sympathetic reaction. They've suffered so much themselves that they understand."

In 2006 the Goodriches arranged for two Afghan boys named Matiullah and Javid and a girl named Soraya to receive educations at schools in New England and Pennsylvania. The young people, whose last names are withheld to protect their families in Afghanistan, live with them during breaks, and their presence is a joy to the Goodriches. Acutely conscious of the lives led by most of their countrymen, the kids work hard. After two semesters as an A student at Peter's alma mater, 18-year-old Matiullah was named a Berkshire scholar. Thin, serious, and just starting to transfer his allegiance from cricket to baseball, he ran for president of his school. Soraya, who has arresting dark eyes and an irrepressible laugh, came to the United States with the goal of quickly finishing high school and heading on to college, but after being offered a scholarship at the prestigious Emma Willard School, she's decided to spend an extra year sharpening her academic skills. She once accompanied Sally to a speaking engagement at the University of Maine at Farmington, where after a few minutes of talking with her, the school's president announced, "I want this girl." Soraya wants to be a doctor, but like Javid and Matiullah, she's intent on returning to Afghanistan. In the end, these children—or the educations they get here—may turn out to be the Goodriches' greatest gift to that country. For now, they are Afghanistan's gift to them. On a recent visit to the house in Bennington, I was served some nan, the fluffy Afghan flatbread, that Don had baked. It was delicious. Mati had taught him how to make it, he said.

It was late March 2007, and Vermont was in the middle of sugaring season. Don, Foster, and Mati kept tromping out through the mud to the nearby sugar shack. Sally was about to leave for another trip to Afghanistan. But she had just learned that she had cancer again; it was too early to say whether she ought to put off her trip. One of her doctors called, and she spoke about her numbers and treatment options with surprising lightness, as if she were talking about allergies, not cancer. Abruptly, she became serious. "I don't have time to be sick," she said. "I don't have time to die. I need another year at least. I don't care what I need to take in the way of treatment, I just need to be around. I need to get as many Afghan kids into the country and support as many Afghans in Afghanistan as I can."

She left two weeks later, having gotten a green light from her doctors. It was a short trip, and the news she brought back wasn't good. Security had deteriorated throughout the Pashtun provinces. In Logar many students' families had received "night letters" threatening them with death. The Taliban and al-Qaeda were said to be offering $10,000 for videotapes showing foreigners being killed and $20,000 for every one captured alive. No one traveled at night anymore.

Yet when Sally came to her school, she found it fully attended.

A high wall was built in deference to the girls' modesty, and a debate was in progress as to whether a van could be purchased for the same purpose to ferry them to and from their homes. This being Afghanistan, the van was voted down. It wouldn't do for the girls to get one before the boys at the neighboring school. A year after its construction, the building is already a little run-down. Many of the classroom chairs are covered with graffiti. To Sally, that's a good sign. It means the children are writing. During a break, a mischievous older girl grabbed Sally's hand and pulled her into a classroom, where she was made to sit at a desk surrounded by a gaggle of laughing girls as one beautiful child dressed in black began painting her hand with henna, a custom at Afghan weddings. As Sally was leaving, the girl who had first waylaid her playfully whipped out a burka and placed it on her head.

Sally Goodrich isn't an optimistic person, or at least not conventionally optimistic. Given all that she's lost, it would be hard for her to be otherwise. "I don't believe in happiness," she once told an interviewer. "I believe in hope." The hope she has for Afghanistan is tempered by what she has learned of its history, and by the warning she once got from an Afghan expert: Anyone who has a relationship with the country, he said, will sooner or later be heartbroken. On hearing this, she thought, *This is interesting: I went into Afghanistan because I'm brokenhearted, and I'm going to come out brokenhearted.* Still, she hopes that if Afghanistan succumbs once more to its darker forces, the people she loves "can do what the terrorists do and hide in good countries until such time as the terrorists fail." She believes that eventually they will.

When you ask Sally how she survived those first bleak years after her son's death, she says, "I borrowed other people's emotions. I'd lost everything. My family, my faith, my hope. And when that happens, you have to borrow from people who have intact emotions till yours begin to return. My life was a void, so I moved into the void and acted the way Peter would have wanted. Afghanistan is as close as I can get to Peter. It's this beautiful ancient culture with these long-lasting tribal customs. And my being there comes as close to answering *Why?* as I can get. But it's answering that *Why?* in a very Peter way."

We think of a legacy as something that passes from parents to children. It's what we leave them, by design or unavoidably. But sometimes a legacy may operate the other way, and a lost child may pass something to his parents. Such a legacy is exceedingly precious. A while ago, Don Goodrich sent me a poem by Rumi:

Who gets up early to discover the moment light begins?
Who finds us here circling, bewildered, like atoms?
Who comes to a spring thirsty
and sees the moon reflected in it?
Who, like Jacob blind with
    grief and age, / smells the shirt of
    his lost son
 and can see again?

No explanation was necessary. ◘

To donate to the Peter M. Goodrich Memorial Foundation, go to goodrichfoundation.org.

> "I'D LOST MY FAMILY, MY FAITH, MY HOPE. AND WHEN THAT HAPPENS, YOU HAVE TO BORROW FROM PEOPLE WHO HAVE INTACT EMOTIONS TILL YOURS BEGIN TO RETURN."

OPRAH TALKS TO RICHARD BRANSON

One of the most extraordinary men—tycoon, visionary, knight, and founder of Virgin Airlines—opens up about the world as he sees it today, his own risk-inspiring parents, the company he started (at 16!), his new dream to fly you and everyone else to the moon, and—a genius idea if there ever was one—the remarkable foundation he's just launched to help give peace a chance.

In 1966 a British 16-year-old who had dyslexia and was nearly flunking out of school put his education on hold to start a youth-culture magazine called *Student,* which he hoped would one day become England's version of *Rolling Stone.* To finance it, he skipped the usual teenage jobs like store clerk and instead sold advertising space in the magazine; from there, he launched a mailorder record business and opened a music shop on London's Oxford Street.

The magazine did well enough, but 41 years later, those side projects have become the multimillion-dollar conglomerate the world knows as Virgin, the company whose business ventures encompass music, air travel, publishing, and retailing. And the ambitious teenager is now Virgin's charismatic leader, 57-year-old*, Sir Richard Branson (he was knighted in 1999).

Branson, the eldest of three children, may have gotten his audacity genetically: His mother, Eve, a former showgirl, was one of the first flight attendants to fly over the Andes, back when unpressurized cabins meant that passengers had to wear oxygen masks; she also snuck into a male-only glider pilot training program by pretending she was a boy. Though Branson's father, Ted, chose a less colorful career in law, both parents encouraged their only son's daring nature; Branson has become as famous for his adventures—crossing two oceans via hot air balloon, and another aboard a powerboat—as for his seemingly limitless entrepreneurial imagination.

His newest, and greatest, idea is a modest humanitarian proposal: to save the world. Branson and his friend Peter Gabriel, the British rock star, have assembled a council of 12 internationally renowned statesmen and women whose goal is to stop wars, promote peace, stamp out diseases, and curb global warming. Called the Elders, the group is privately funded to avoid becoming beholden to any political or special-interest party. It will be chaired by Archbishop Desmond Tutu. (For more information on the members of the Elders, see page 320.)

"Most wars are completely unnecessary," Branson tells me on the afternoon of our conversation. "Intelligent people must come up with alternative ways to disagree." For a man whose optimistic outlook led him to attempt the improbable four decades ago,

All ages from December 2007.

the Elders is a fledgling investment that could bring an extraordinary return: the possibility of long-standing world peace.

OPRAH: *What's the source of your drive to contribute to the world? It feels like an extraordinary force.*

RICHARD: [*Laughs*] If anybody knows about that force, you do! I love creating things, and as an entrepreneur, I've taken on quite a lot of major corporations and done well. Capitalism is the only system that works, but it has its flaws; for one, it brings great wealth to only a few people. That wealth obviously brings extreme responsibility.

OPRAH: *That's not so obvious. You could decide to play all day: fly balloons, race around the world, stretch out on an island and drink tequila.*

RICHARD: True. In part, giving back has to do with the way I was brought up and the fact that I've traveled widely and seen terrible situations in the world. To sleep well at night, those of us who are in a position to help must address these situations. I'd get far greater satisfaction out of, say, walking into a hospital I'd built in South Africa than I would by sitting on a beach. I'm fortunate enough to be in a position to make a difference, and I don't want to waste that. I suspect I was also lucky to have parents who drove me from a young age.

OPRAH: *Did your parents inspire your creativity and courage?*

RICHARD: They certainly encouraged it. They're also good examples of it. My mother has done everything from belly dancing to climbing mountaintops, and in her late 80s, she hasn't slowed down. She spends a lot of time with the Berbers in Morocco, teaching them English. We're still a very close family, and that closeness has given me lots of strength. My parents travel with me wherever I go. They were with me at the first Elders conference in South Africa.

OPRAH: *Where did the idea for the Elders come from?*

RICHARD: In Africa, villagers look up to elders; they are the moral voice of their community. My friend Peter Gabriel and I felt that the world needed a group of wise leaders to look up to—men and women who are beyond ego, who can look past their borders and take on global issues. That's why we created the Elders—a group of 12 respected people who can intervene in the world's conflicts. Before the Iraq war, I was involved in attempting to avert the conflict. I felt that the only way it could be stopped would be for an elder of great stature to persuade Saddam Hussein to step down

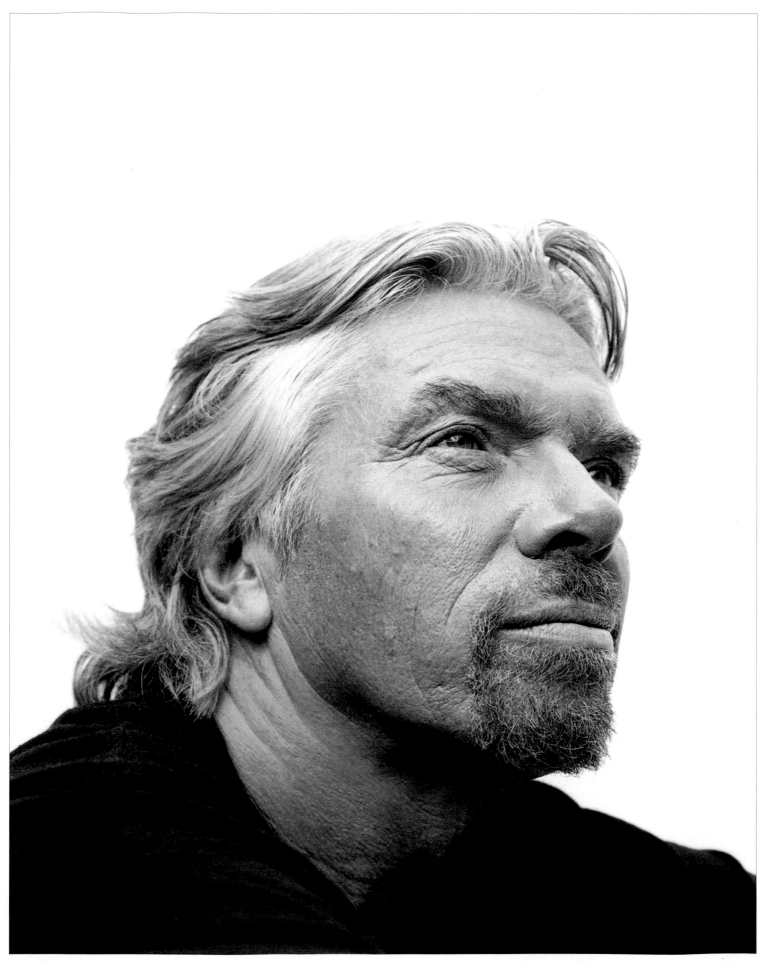

and go live elsewhere, in Libya or Saudi Arabia—the same way Idi Amin [the late Ugandan dictator and president] was persuaded to step down. I had hoped we could avoid maiming and killing thousands of people and all the misery to follow. Nelson Mandela seemed to be the obvious elder to do that, since he'd already spoken out against the war. I talked to him, and he agreed to see Saddam if Kofi Annan [former secretary-general of the United Nations] would go with him and if South African president Thabo Mvuyelwa Mbeki gave his blessing. A week later, both agreed, but that same week, the bombing began. So the conversation between Hussein and Mandela never took place.

OPRAH: *Did you ever wonder what might have happened if the conversation had been initiated just one week sooner?*

RICHARD: I don't live my life thinking about "if only." I just try to think positively about the future. We'll never know for certain what would have happened if we'd gone to Iraq. The important thing is that we've got to do everything we can to prevent other wars. Peter and I created the Elders because we want leaders to arbitrate in conflict situations like the one between the Algeria-supported Polisaro Front and Morocco over the Western Sahara, or the crisis in Darfur. We all know about the big world conflicts: Israel and Palestine, Zimbabwe, and so on. But there are smaller conflicts that aren't even on the world's radar screen; most of the world has no idea that Ethiopia invaded Somalia a year ago. It makes sense for the Elders to sit down with both sides and see whether leaders can come to an understanding. Ten days from now, we're going to the Sudan.

OPRAH: *Which of the Elders are going?*

RICHARD: Archbishop Desmond Tutu, Jimmy Carter, and [former First Lady of South Africa] Graça Machel. [Former United Nations envoy] Lakhdar Brahimi will join them. The group will meet with both the government and the opposition in the capital city of Khartoum. They'll then travel to Darfur and visit local community leaders. They hope to strengthen the framework for assuring permanent peace in Sudan.

OPRAH: *Will you be there?*

RICHARD: Yes—but I'm going so that I can observe and learn. As individuals, each of the Elders has the potential to stop wars; collectively, these 12 men and women are powerful. When someone like Nelson Mandela or Kofi Annan is on the phone, people will take that call.

OPRAH: *What is your ultimate hope and expectation for the Elders?*

RICHARD: I'd love for the Elders to still be around in a thousand years' time. I want to see the group build credibility in the world. I'd also like them to address other major issues, like global warming, dwindling fish stocks, and the horror of unnecessary disease. For instance, AIDS should never have gotten out of control in Africa; it's unforgivable that the world community allowed it to get out of hand.

OPRAH: *If the Elders had existed 20 years ago, what difference do you think they might have made in the spread of AIDS in Africa?*

RICHARD: They would have alerted the world to the issue, and if a particular president was denying that AIDS was related to HIV and that it was becoming a crisis, they would have had a quiet word with him or her. By moving quickly in situations like that, the Elders would be able to caution the world, and then get the resources to deal with a problem in its infancy.

OPRAH: *What happened the first time you gathered the Elders in one room? Were you nervous or intimidated?*

RICHARD: Well, I'd already been spending a lot of time with Archbishop Desmond Tutu. He's one of the best human beings alive.

OPRAH: *There's no better spirit or vibe to be around.*

RICHARD: And he has an absolutely wicked sense of humor!

OPRAH: *Yes! I think the fact that he's funny would surprise people.*

RICHARD: I'm sure he's told you the one about getting to the kingdom of heaven to find two signs at the entrance: One reads FOR HENPECKED MEN ONLY, and the second reads OTHERS. There's a massive queue of men lined up under the HENPECKED sign, and only one man beneath the OTHERS sign. God says to that one man, "You're lucky. How did you make it into this line?" "Well," the man says, "my wife told me to stand here!" And Tutu tells this joke while his wife is sitting right there next to him. Anyway, Peter and I had been working on this idea for five years before we convened the group, so we were exhilarated. Then Nelson Mandela arrived and made a very moving speech. [View this and the other Elders' speeches on theelders.org.] It was the birth of something special. And it's wonderful to have you on the sidelines.

OPRAH: *I'm doing my part! I can tell the world about it. You always look so radiant and joyous in your photos. Is that your natural temperament?*

RICHARD: I have tremendous stability in my life. My wife and I have been together for 32 years, and we're very happy. I've got two wonderful children, my parents, and great friends around me. And then there are the more than 50,000 wonderful people who work for the Virgin companies. I have no excuse not to be happy.

OPRAH: *I love that. What was it like to start Virgin?*

RICHARD: I was young and inexperienced. At first I wasn't even allowed to register the business name because the word *virgin* was thought to be rude. I had to sit down and, in my best 15-year-old penmanship, write a letter to the registry office that began, "Surely the word *virgin* is anything but rude; it's the opposite of rude." They eventually relented.

OPRAH: *That was so enterprising of you. I began my company with four people, and now I have about 750. The staff felt like a little family until we had 40 or 50 people. How do you maintain a sense of connection with 50,000 employees? Can you?*

RICHARD: It's impossible to feel the same connection as when there are only four or five starting off, but the people who work for me are working for what I believe in. The leaders who run our companies do so on the basis of those who came first and who said, "A company is its people." I hope my companies are run on the basis of praising their workers and looking for the best in them, not criticizing them. In the same way that you water a plant and it sprouts leaves, people flourish when you praise them. We have people who would kill for Virgin because they're so proud of it—they believe in what we're creating.

OPRAH: *As a boss, are you a good delegator?*

RICHARD: I've had to learn the art of delegation—we've got more than 200 companies! I have to take the time to find people who are more knowledgeable than I am, and then I have to accept that everything won't go exactly the way it would if I were leading. Sometimes things go a lot better.

OPRAH: *What are you most hopeful about right now?*

RICHARD: People are basically decent. Sadly, they sometimes don't appoint very good leaders, and those leaders create some horrendous messes. Yet I'm hopeful that after Iraq, those in charge will think twice about taking us down that route again. I hope that the 600,000 civilians we've lost—men, women, and children—will not have died in vain.

OPRAH: *How do you feel about the survival of the planet?*

RICHARD: This issue is of paramount importance—global warming could snuff out humankind. It's an invisible war that could ultimately destroy life itself, and we need politicians and businesspeople to

Branson with Archbishop Desmond Tutu at the Elders launch in July 2007.

get together and treat it as a third world war. If we can't get our governments to wake up and do something about it, then I'm not hopeful.

OPRAH: *What do you know for sure?*

RICHARD: I know that I've got to live life to its fullest because I'm going to die one day. I don't want to waste a minute.

OPRAH: *Is that why you're so adventurous?*

RICHARD: I was a risk-taker as a young man, and I don't regret it. I'm not adventurous in quite the same way now, but I still love the challenge of testing myself to the limits, flying around the world, or seeing if I can be the first to fly a balloon across the Atlantic, or trying to take people into space at an affordable price in an environmentally friendly way. I'll be going into space with three generations of my family!

OPRAH: *When are you doing that?*

RICHARD: In July 2009. My mother will be 90 then, and my dad will be 93. My children will be in their early 20s. My wife is the only one who isn't going; she's much too sensible.

OPRAH: *That is the coolest thing!*

RICHARD: By the end of 2008, we will have finished building the spaceship. We'll have extensive tests for another few months, and then we'll build this incredible spaceport in the New Mexico desert.

OPRAH: *Wow! How long will you be in space?*

RICHARD: The initial flight will be quite brief—about three hours. Later we'll develop longer flights. We've got plans to build a hotel that will circle the moon. People will be able to take short rides from the hotel using the moon's gravity. We're dreaming, and the first part of that dream will become real shortly.

OPRAH: *How do you get these ideas? As you're brushing your teeth or showering, do you suddenly think,* I know: I'll create a spaceship, put my whole family on it, and have a hotel that orbits the moon?

RICHARD: When people tell me something is impossible, I try to prove them wrong.

OPRAH: *Do you ever chill?*

RICHARD: I do. I'm fortunate to have Necker Island [Branson owns this 74-acre isle in the British Virgin Islands], and I bring friends and family there. I kite surf, which is very relaxing. I play a lot of tennis and do some sailing. It's important to keep the body fit, and rather than doing that in a gym, I like being active.

OPRAH: *Last question. The Elders have the potential to do powerful work in the world. But what is your hope for ordinary citizens at home?*

RICHARD: Peter Gabriel's desire is to use the Internet to connect leaders and citizens everywhere. In particular, we'd like to use retired people as a resource. There are so many incredible people who have knowledge that is often wasted in their later years; why shouldn't a doctor continue using his or her expertise? We want to create local groups of respected elders who can play a part in their communities. I think every person can make a difference. You don't have to be one of the Elders. You don't have to be well known. You just have to be determined to care about people. That's all it takes. **O**

THE ELDERS

Former presidents and ambassadors. Nobel Peace Prize winners. Humanitarian heroes. Richard Branson's global dream team of conflict mediators is a force to be reckoned with—and grateful for.

1 DESMOND TUTU was the first black general secretary of the South African Council of Churches and, as Archbishop of Cape Town, the first black leader of South Africa's Anglican Church. He won the Nobel Peace Prize in 1984, in recognition of his efforts in the fight against apartheid. In 1995 he was appointed chairman of South Africa's Truth and Reconciliation Commission.

2 NELSON MANDELA's unwavering stand against apartheid led him to a life sentence in prison in 1964. Thirty years later—27 of them spent behind bars—it led him to the presidency of South Africa. Mandela now concentrates on fighting the spread of HIV/AIDS in Africa.

3 GRAÇA MACHEL is an international advocate for women's and children's rights, a former minister of education and culture in Mozambique, and a former First Lady of both Mozambique and South Africa. In 1994 she was appointed by the UN secretary-general to assess the effects of war on children; her groundbreaking report led to the appointment of a special representative on the impact of armed conflict on children. She is married to Nelson Mandela.

4 KOFI ANNAN was secretary-general of the UN from 1997 to 2006. In that post, he led reforms to make the UN more effective and pursued a human rights agenda. He advocated the UN's Millennium Development Goals, helped create the Global Fund to Fight AIDS, Tuberculosis, and Malaria, certified Israel's withdrawal from Lebanon, and contributed to a cease-fire between Israel and Hezbollah. In 2001 he and the UN were jointly awarded a Nobel Peace Prize.

5 ELA BHATT is a champion of women workers in India. A former member of India's Parliament, she helped establish Women's World Banking, an organization that provides financial services to women, and is the founder of the Self-Employed Women's Association, a union with roughly a million members.

6 LAKHDAR BRAHIMI, a former ambassador for his native Algeria, was instrumental in ending conflicts in Lebanon and Yemen, as well as apartheid in South Africa. He presided over the Bonn Conference on Afghanistan in 2001 and facilitated the establishment of an interim government in Iraq in 2004.

7 GRO HARLEM BRUNDTLAND, MD, was the youngest person and first woman to hold the office of prime minister of Norway. She has served as director-general of the World Health Organization and chair of the World Commission of Environment and Development, and is currently a special envoy of the United Nations secretary-general for climate change.

8 FERNANDO HENRIQUE CARDOSO was elected to two terms as president of Brazil (from 1995 to 2003), having been deeply involved in his country's struggle for democracy. A sociologist by training, he is an influential expert on international development, dependency, democratization, and state reform.

9 JIMMY CARTER, the 39th president of the United States, mediated the Camp David agreement between Egypt and Israel, completed negotiation of the SALT II treaty with the former Soviet Union, and established full diplomatic relations between the U.S. and China. He was awarded the Nobel Peace Prize in 2002 for his efforts in the advancement of democracy and human rights.

10 LI ZHAOXING* has served as Chinese foreign minister, ambassador to the United States, and, from 1992 to 1995, ambassador to the United Nations. As a member of the UN Security Council, he was involved in the redemocratization of Haiti.

11 MARY ROBINSON became Ireland's first female president in 1990. A longtime human rights advocate, she was the first head of state to visit Rwanda following the genocide there. As UN High Commissioner for Human Rights from 1997 to 2002, she strengthened UN monitoring in conflict zones such as Kosovo. She is the founder and president of Realizing Rights: The Ethical Globalization Initiative.

12 MUHAMMAD YUNUS, founder of the Grameen Bank, is the most prominent champion of "microcredit"—loans for the poor, granted without collateral. This revolutionary concept, which won Yunus the Nobel Peace Prize in 2006, has helped millions of impoverished people in his native Bangladesh.

13 AUNG SAN SUU KYI was awarded the 1991 Nobel Peace Prize for her fight to bring democracy to her native Burma; the ruling military party has kept her under house arrest for most of her political career. She is an honorary member of the Elders; a chair—vacant until her release—is reserved for her at their meetings.

14 PETER GABRIEL, though best known for his music career, has worked extensively with Amnesty International. He is a co-founder of Witness, a group that provides video cameras and editing equipment to human rights groups, and of the Elders. **◐**

Since the original publication of this article, Li Zhaoxing is no longer serving as an Elder.

THE NEXT GENERATION

The Elders aren't the only ones setting out to change the world. A younger group of peacemakers—the children and grandchildren of global leaders—is mobilizing to stand up for the victims of oppression and war. Suzanne Boyd profiles Gen II.

In a New York photography studio in late September, Kerry Kennedy and Martin Luther King III are standing away from the cameras, heads bent toward each other, deep in conversation. King is the son of Dr. Martin Luther King Jr., Kennedy is the daughter of Robert F. Kennedy, and as they talk, their faces in profile poignantly recall their fathers'. It is impossible not to imagine that 40 years ago, the civil rights leader and the senator who championed social justice might have huddled in just this way.

On a coffee table lies a copy of *The New York Times*. One headline refers to Louisiana's Jena Six, the group of African-American youths seen by many as the victims of a racially biased justice system; other stories are about Iraq. It seems both a fitting tribute and a rueful irony that the children of two men who fought against racism and a divisive war have convened on this day, and at this time, when the world is still bedeviled by strife and afflicted with an at-large malaise.

But they're here as part of their efforts to change their time; the photo shoot is all about Gen II Peacemakers, a group that includes King, Kennedy, and a handful of others who likewise inherited world-changer DNA. Their goal is to bring relief to trouble spots around the globe, by getting all sides in a given conflict to sit down and talk. Their motivation, in the words of member Naomi Tutu: "We're all prisoners of hope."

"I think that after my mom's passing, I wanted to figure out what I was going to do with the rest of my life," says King, referring to Coretta Scott King, who died in January 2006. Before that time, King had served as president of the Southern Christian Leadership Conference, the organization his father helped create, and the King Center, which memorializes his parents' work. But now he wanted to continue that work, and to that end he created the nonprofit organization Realizing the Dream. Gen II is one of the organization's chief initiatives; it was sparked by a trip to Israel in autumn 2006, when King was looking for "constructive ways to be helpful in the peace process."

King envisions a sort of United Nations in microcosm, minus the agendas and special interests, with each member of Gen II bringing his or her own resources and contacts to bear in creating actionable, nonviolent solutions to humanitarian crises while pursuing social, economic, and political justice. The group's logo—a photograph of King III's hand flashing the peace sign—is a visual double entendre, symbolizing not just peace but the number 2, as in "generation next."

Kerry Kennedy, who created the Robert F. Kennedy Memorial Center for Human Rights, wrote the book *Speak Truth to Power,* and has campaigned against the death penalty, says, "We have these big tails that we try not to let wag the dog. But they can be put to good use." When King approached Kennedy about joining Gen II, she says, "I immediately signed up."

Christine Chavez, on the other hand, thought somebody was playing a joke when King introduced himself on the phone. Chavez is the granddaughter of the late farm laborer, activist, and co-founder of the United Farm Workers of America, Cesar Chavez. "When my grandfather was in jail in the '70s, Coretta Scott King came out and visited with him and the farmworkers. And although he never met Dr. King, they communicated by telegram." The family synergies don't stop there, however. "Kerry Kennedy's father put farmworkers on the map by doing a Senate hearing about how they were being treated and by traveling to Delano when my grandfather was on a hunger strike." After working for the United Farm Workers union for years, Chavez is currently the district director for a senator in the California state legislature and is that office's liaison to the labor movement.

Nontombi Naomi Tutu is the daughter of Archbishop Desmond Tutu, who stood strong against apartheid in his native South Africa and whose spiritual leadership paved the way for the transition to democracy. She is the founder and chairperson of the Tutu Foundation for Development and Relief in Southern Africa and focuses on the rights of young women.

Justin Trudeau is the son of the late Canadian prime minister Pierre Trudeau, whose legacy includes the preservation of national unity and the embedding of the Charter of Rights and Freedoms in his country's constitution. He was the first world leader to meet with John Lennon and Yoko Ono on their peace tour. Justin is on the board of Canada's national youth service program and will be running for a parliamentary seat in the next federal election.

As the five peacemakers meet and greet in the photo studio, there's a palpable buzz—the same kind of energy that charged the group's inaugural meeting in London in July, when they started hammering out an agenda and came up with their mission statement, the Declaration of Interdependence. "Most of us didn't know one another before London, but the energy and warmth almost right away was just amazing," says Tutu. "We examined. We debated. We

THE PEACEMAKERS: Martin Luther King III, Christine Chavez, Naomi Tutu, Kerry Kennedy, and Justin Trudeau, photographed for *O* in New York City, September 18, 2007.

were saying to each other, 'Oh my goodness, I'm so glad to meet you, because your grandfather was one of my greatest heroes.' That connection helped us."

The group has identified four target spots: Darfur, the Middle East, Burma, and North Korea. The plan is to start with a fact-finding mission to each area, building relationships with key people and organizations in the process. Press conferences, summits, and reports will focus attention on humanitarian crises. Trudeau says, "We are about shining a light. In many places, human rights abuses take place under cover of night. That is not a metaphor. That is literally true." On the other hand, as Tutu says, "We don't want to be disaster tourists." Gen II members will speak out and use their influence with key leaders and decision makers. They will organize relief efforts and raise financial aid. The members also want to leave behind tangible things: systems for clean drinking water, improvements to hospitals. And they want to expand their circle outward. "We don't want to just be about ourselves," says Chavez. "We want other people to be involved in this process as well. I think the time is right. There's a war going on, there's a sense of despair, and I think people are looking for something."

Three of Gen II's founding members aren't in attendance at the photo shoot, but their presence is

THEIR GOAL: TO BRING RELIEF TO TROUBLE SPOTS AROUND THE GLOBE. THEIR MOTIVATION: "WE'RE ALL PRISONERS OF HOPE."

felt nonetheless. Arun Gandhi, grandson of the late Mahatma Gandhi, cofounded India's Center for Social Unity, whose mission is to alleviate poverty and caste discrimination; he also cofounded the M.K. Gandhi Institute for Nonviolence in Memphis, in 1991. Nadim Gemayel, the son of Bashir Gemayel (the Lebanese military commander who, as president-elect, was assassinated in 1982), is politically active in Lebanon. And Dalia Rabin-Pelossoff, daughter of the late Israeli prime minister Yitzhak Rabin, who was assassinated after signing the Oslo Accords peace agreement with the Palestinians, chairs the Yitzhak Rabin Center for Israel Studies Administrative Committee and is a former member of the Knesset.

In 1968 Dr. King said, "We must all learn to live together as brothers or we will perish together as fools." In 2007 Kerry Kennedy suggests the best way to get there: "The government's not going to do it. The military is not going to do it. The multinationals aren't going to do it. Wal-Mart's not going to do it. Margaret Mead said, 'Never doubt that a small group of thoughtful, committed citizens can change the world; indeed, it's the only thing that ever has.' And this is a small group of determined people. A group of smart, committed, determined people." ⦿

Giving students a tour of the new leadership academy, November 2006.

"I SEE IN THESE GIRLS' FACES THE LIGHT OF MY OWN"

Another year! It's true what they say—getting older makes time fly. And it's also true that you have to work harder to stay healthy. I've been on Bob Greene's "Best Life" plan since the summer of 2006. I eat what I want, when I want, and sometimes have only dessert for dinner. And because my life is completely full, I don't eat emotionally anymore. I know that what makes you healthiest is living your heart's desire. I've been as busy as anybody, but not always working on what was important to me.

I've also known since I became an adult that I'd need to find a way to give back what I have been given. It's the circle of life. A lot of people see my fame and wealth, but they don't realize that what created it all is a value system that operates on the principle of cause and effect: What you put out comes back. Do the emotional and spiritual work required to develop authentic power (using your personality to do your soul's work), and you will always be rewarded. What I know for sure: There is no greater calling than service to others. And there is no better way to have your blessings multiply.

Shortly after I arrived in Chicago, I started a mentorship program for teenage girls living in the Cabrini-Green housing projects. I was able to work with them only once a week, which wasn't enough time to instill values in girls whose upbringing wasn't aligned with my teachings. I had to end the program. Months later I came up with the misguided idea of moving families out of the projects and into new homes. Trying to show people how to build successful lives was overwhelming—I had taken for granted that they understood what it means to go to work, be on time, and make sure their children go to school and do their homework. So I failed with that idea, but I learned something invaluable: In order to make meaningful changes, you have to transform the way people think.

Going to Africa changed me forever. I was sitting in Nelson Mandela's living room when I told him I wanted to commit $10 million to build a school for girls who had no other chance to make it in the world. He was thrilled, and immediately called the minister of education to meet with me. Thus the dream began. Forty million dollars later, the Oprah Winfrey Leadership Academy for Girls–South Africa stands primed to open on January 2, 2006. This is the best investment I have ever made, building a future for girls who more than deserve it.

My cup runneth over as I see in these girls' faces the light of my own. I know now why I never had children: These are the daughters I've been coming to my whole life. I am blessed to be able to feed, clothe, nurture, and inspire them, and provide teachers and counselors who will do the same. I know for sure that this school will change the trajectory of their lives. They will excel and pass their excellence on to their families, their nation, and our world.

The school's fundamental value is to encourage each girl to develop her critical thinking to create the best life possible for her, and then use her life in service to others, no matter her calling. I interviewed every one of the girls as part of the final admission process. When I asked one 11-year-old, "Why do you want to come to my school?" she responded, "It is my tomorrow!"

Indeed it is: hope, possibility, success, the future for generations to come. Through the whole process of choosing the bricks, every piece of tile in the bathrooms, the sheets, the uniforms, I knew I was giving something special to the girls. But what they've given me is a heart whose fullness has no measure.

Oprah

ABOUT THE CONTRIBUTORS

CHRIS ADRIAN's second novel, *The Children's Hospital,* was published by McSweeny's in 2007. He is a pediatrician and divinity student in Boston.

AIMEE LEE BALL is the coauthor of four books, including *Changing the Rules* with Muriel Siebert.

CELIA BARBOUR is a writer, editor, and mother of three who lives in Garrison, New York.

NAOMI BARR is a research editor at *O.*

MARTHA BECK writes a monthly column for *O.* She is a life coach and the author of *The Four Day Win, Leaving the Saints,* and other books.

RACHEL BERTSCHE is an associate producer at Oprah.com.

AMY BLOOM is a novelist, short story writer, and psychotherapist. The award-winning author of five books, including her latest, *Away,* Bloom teaches creative writing at Yale University.

ANTHONY BOURDAIN is a chef, author, and host of *No Reservations* on the Travel Channel.

SUZANNE BOYD was formerly editor in chief of *Flare,* Canada's top fashion magazine, and *Suede,* an urban lifestyle magazine.

POLLY BREWSTER is an assistant editor at *O.*

LIZ BRODY is *O*'s health and news director.

GERALDINE BROOKS's third historical novel is *People of the Book.*

SARAH BROOM is a writer living in New Orleans.

HOLLY BRUBACH has written for *The New Yorker, The New York Times, Vogue,* and *The Atlantic.*

SUSAN CHOI's novel, *American Woman,* was nominated for a Pulitzer Prize. Her latest novel is *A Person of Interest.*

SUZAN COLÓN is a senior editor at *O.*

ELIZABETH CUTHRELL is a screenwriter and producer living in New York City.

SARA DAVIDSON's most recent book, *Leap! What Will We Do with the Rest of Our Lives?,* has been picked up by ABC to be made into a pilot for a dramatic series featuring Goldie Hawn.

HOPE DAVIS is an actress who stars in the film *Charlie Bartlett.*

TRISH DEITCH is a copy editor at *The New Yorker* and a writer living in Brooklyn.

AMY DICKINSON writes the daily "Ask Amy" advice column in the *Chicago Tribune.* Her memoir about her childhood, *The Mighty Queens of Freeville,* will be published in 2009.

BEVERLY DONOFRIO is the author of the memoir *Riding in Cars with Boys,* which was adapted into the 2001 film starring Drew Barrymore.

TISH DURKIN has written for *The Atlantic Monthly, Rolling Stone, The New York Times Magazine,* and *The New York Observer.*

JEFFREY EUGENIDES, the Pulitzer Prize–winning author of *Middlesex* and *The Virgin Suicides,* is the editor of an anthology of love stories, *My Mistress's Sparrow Is Dead.*

JOSHUA FERRIS's novel, *Then We Came to the End,* was published in 2007. He is working on his second novel.

MARY A. FISCHER is the author of the memoir *Stealing Love: Confessions of a Dognapper.* A senior writer at *GQ* for many years, Fischer has also contributed to *Rolling Stone* and *Men's Journal.*

HELEN FISHER is an anthropologist, a research professor at Rutgers University, and the chief scientific adviser to chemistry.com.

CAITLIN FLANAGAN is a frequent contributor to *The Atlantic Monthly* and is the author of *To Hell with All That: Loving and Loathing Our Inner Housewife.*

SCOTT FRAMPTON is a freelance writer based in New York.

WHITNEY FULLER is the events coordinator and Web editor at Pasanella and Son Vintners in New York City.

CHEE GATES is a staff writer at *Fitness.*

NIKKI GIOVANNI is a poet and the author of more than 25 books. *Gemini,* her autobiography, was a National Book Award finalist. Her 2002 spoken-word album, *The Nikki Giovanni Poetry Collection,* was nominated for a Grammy.

NANCY GOTTESMAN is a writer living in Los Angeles.

BARBARA GRAHAM is the author of *Women Who Run with the Poodles: Myths and Tips for Honoring Your Mood Swings.* She is working on a memoir.

JESSE GREEN is a theater writer for *The New York Times* and the author of *The Velveteen Father: An Unexpected Journey to Parenthood.*

AMY HERTZ is a writer who divides her time between New York and San Francisco.

P. HUNTER is a contributor to *O.*

LAUREN IANNOTTI is the articles editor at *Marie Claire.*

WALTER KIRN is a novelist and critic whose books include *Thumbsucker, Up in the Air,* and *Mission to America.* He lives in Livingston, Montana.

DEBORAH COPAKEN KOGAN is the author of the best-selling memoir *Shutterbabe.* A former war reporter, Kogan now lives in Manhattan with her husband and three children.

LISA KOGAN is *O*'s writer at large. Her column appears monthly.

RABBI JENNIFER KRAUSE's first book is *The Answer: Making Sense of Life, One Question at a Time.*

QUEEN LATIFAH is a Grammy-winning singer and Oscar-nominated actress.

ADRIAN NICOLE LeBLANC, a 2006 MacArthur Fellow, is working on a book about stand-up comedians.

GABRIELLE LEBLANC is a neuroscientist, biomedical consultant, and writer living in Washington, D.C. Her work has been published in scientific journals, among them *Nature* and *Stroke.*

ANDREA LEE is the author of the novel *Lost Hearts in Italy.* She has written for *The New Yorker* and *The New York Times Magazine.*

GENINE LENTINE is a poet whose work has appeared in *American Poetry Review.* She collaborated with former U.S. poet laureate Stanley Kunitz on *The Wild Braid: A Poet Reflects on a Century in the Garden.*

BERNIE MAC is a comedian, actor, film writer, and star of *The Bernie Mac Show.*

DENNIS MAHER was exonerated after 19 years of wrongful imprisonment.

KATHRYN MATTHEWS is a frequent contributor to *O*'s Bodywise and Mindwise sections. She also writes for *The New York Times, Town & Country,* and epicurious.com.

PHILLIP C. McGRAW, PhD, hosts the daily television show *Dr. Phil* and is the author of six best-selling books, including *Real Life.* He writes a monthly column for *O.*

CATHLEEN MEDWICK is the author of *Teresa of Avila: The Progress of a Soul* and is a regular contributor to *O.*

MAILE MELOY is an award-winning author of two novels and one book of short stories. She has written for *The New York Times, The New Yorker,* and *Slate.*

CLAIRE MESSUD is the author of the novel *The Emperor's Children.*

VALERIE MONROE, *O*'s beauty director, is the author of *In the Weather of the Heart,* a memoir.

CHRISTINE MONTROSS is a psychiatry resident at Brown University. She is the author of *Body of Work,* a memoir about life in the anatomy lab.

SUSANNA MOORE's latest novel is *The Big Girls.* Her next will center around a woman in 19th-century Japan.

CATHERINE NEWMAN, a columnist for wondertime.com, is the author of the memoir *Waiting for Birdy.*

MELBA NEWSOME is a freelance writer based in Charlotte, North Carolina. Her work has appeared in *National Geographic, Time, Details,* and *The Los Angeles Times Magazine.*

SIGRID NUNEZ's fifth novel is *The Last of Her Kind.*

BARACK OBAMA is a civil rights attorney, a United States Senator from Illinois, and is, at press time, the Democratic candidate for President of the United States.

PEGGY ORENSTEIN is the author of *Waiting for Daisy,* a memoir about her struggle with infertility.

SUZE ORMAN, host of CNBC's *The Suze Orman Show,* is the author of several books on personal finance, including *Women & Money: Owning the Power to Control Your Destiny.* She writes a monthly column for *O.*

GENERAL PETER PACE of the United States Marine Corps was Chairman of the Joint Chiefs of Staff from 2005 to 2007, the first Marine appointed to the United States' highest-ranking military office.

COLIN POWELL is the former Chairman of the Joint Chiefs of Staff and the former Secretary of State.

SARA REISTAD-LONG contributes frequently to *Esquire, Gourmet,* and *Self.* She lives in New York City.

ELAINA RICHARDSON is the president of Yaddo, an artist's community in Saratoga Springs, New York.

FRANCES RICHEY is the author of *The Warrior,* a collection of poems, and is the poetry editor of New York University's *Bellevue Literary Review.*

AMANDA ROBB is an *O* contributing writer. She is working on a book about the abstinence movement.

LISA ROMEO, a New Jersey–based writer, is at work on a memoir. Her writing has appeared in *The New York Times.*

SHARON SALZBERG is cofounder of the Insight Meditation Society in Barre, Massachusetts. Her most recent book is *The Force of Kindness.*

LIESL SCHILLINGER is a writer and editor who worked for more than a decade at *The New Yorker.*

ALICE SEBOLD is the author of *The Lovely Bones.* Her new novel is *The Almost Moon.*

DAVID SEDARIS is the author of the bestsellers *Dress Your Family in Corduroy and Denim* and *Me Talk Pretty One Day.* His latest is *When You Are Engulfed in Flames.*

REBECCA SKLOOT is a contributing editor to *Popular Science.* She also writes for *The New York Times Magazine* and *Discover.*

LAUREN SLATER is a psychologist and writer. She is a contributing editor to *Elle* and was guest editor of *The Best American Essays 2006.*

EVAN SMITH is editor in chief of *Texas Monthly.*

MARY SOUTH is the author of *The Cure for Anything Is Salt Water.*

ELIZABETH SWADOS has written novels, children's books, and nonfiction, including her 2005 memoir, *My Depression.* She has also worked in theater for the past 30 years as a playwright, composer, director, and five-time Tony Award nominee.

RENÉ SYLER's memoir is *Good Enough Mother.* She was formerly an anchor on CBS's *The Early Show.*

PETER TRACHTENBERG is working on his second nonfiction book, *The Book of Calamities: Five Questions About the Meaning of Suffering.*

JUSTINE VAN DER LEUN is a freelance writer based in Sag Harbor, New York.

PATRICIA VOLK's books include *To My Dearest Friends* and *Stuffed: Adventures of a Restaurant Family.* She has written for *The New York Times* and *The New York Times Magazine.*

SUZY WELCH, a contributing editor at *O*, is the coauthor of *Winning.*

JOHN EDGAR WIDEMAN is a Brown University professor and two-time winner of the PEN/Faulkner Award for Fiction. He is the author of the short story collection *God's Gym.*

PENNY WRENN, a former editor at *Esquire* and *Redbook,* is a writer in New York City.

SELENE YEAGER is a health and fitness writer and a certified personal trainer. She is also a contributing editor at *Prevention.*

EMILY YOFFE is a columnist for *Slate* and the author of *What the Dog Did.*

PHOTOGRAPHY AND ART CREDITS

INDEX

BREATHING SPACE

ANTIBES, FRANCE, ON THE MEDITERRANEAN COAST

Photograph by Kevin Galvin

Published by Oxmoor House, Inc.
Book Division of Southern Progress Corporation
P.O. Box 2262, Birmingham, Alabama 35201-2262

ISBN-13: 978-0-8487-3233-2
ISBN-10: 0-8487-3233-2
Library of Congress Control Number: 2007942881

Printed in the United States of America
First printing 2008

To order more books, call 1-800-765-6400.

O, The Oprah Magazine
Founder and Editorial Director: Oprah Winfrey
Editor in Chief: Amy Gross
Editor at Large: Gayle King
Design Director: Carla Frank
Executive Editor: Catherine Kelley
Production Director: Kristen Rayner
Associate Editor: Brooke Kosofsky Glassberg
Assistant Photo Editor: Kathy Nguyen

HEARST BOOKS
VP, Publisher: Jacqueline Deval

OXMOOR HOUSE, INC.
VP, Publisher: Brian Carnahan
Editor in Chief: Nancy Fitzpatrick Wyatt
Art Director: Keith McPherson
Managing Editor: Allison Long Lowery

O's Big Book of Happiness
Editor: Terri Laschober Robertson
Copy Chief: L. Amanda Owens
Director of Production: Laura Lockhart
Senior Production Manager: Greg A. Amason

CONTRIBUTORS
Designer: Erika Oliveira
Compositor: Carol Damsky
Copy Editor: Catherine C. Fowler
Proofreader: Leah Marlett
Indexer: Mary Ann Laurens
Editorial Assistants: Amelia Heying, Kevin Pearsall
Interns: Erin Loudy, Shea Staskowski, Lauren Wiygul

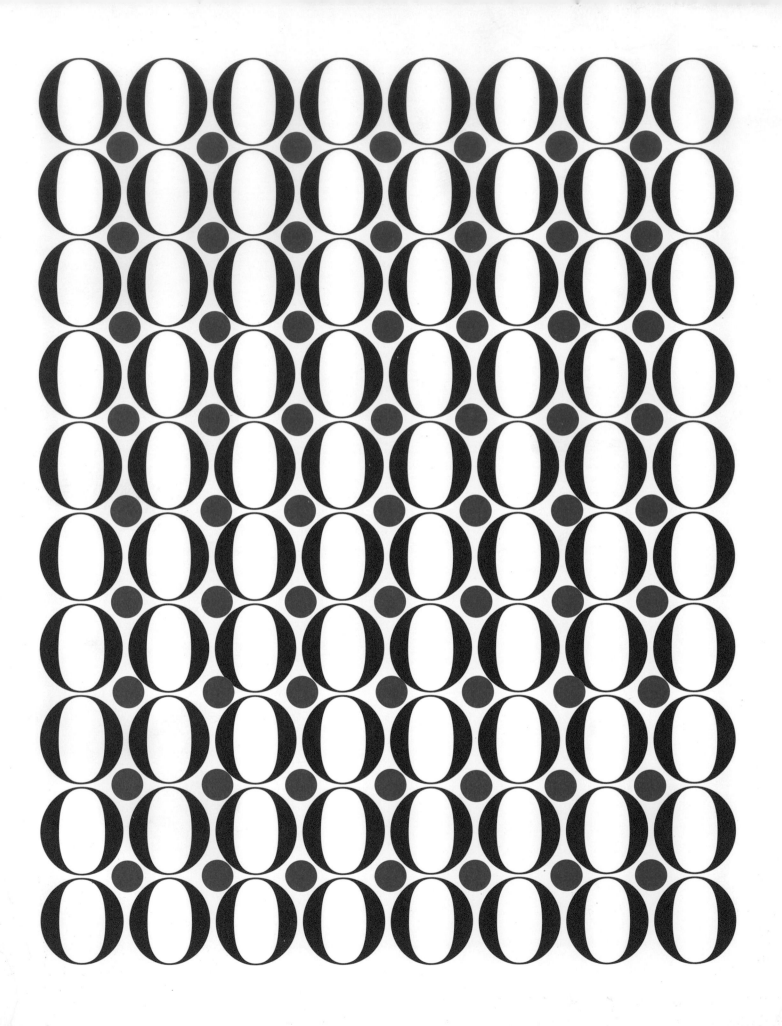